MW01004617

The Ethnography of Vietnam's Central Highlanders

'At the end of this stylish, intricately assembled and insightful book, the author notes that it is time for critical anthropology to break the shackles of introspective textual analysis and look at itself with the conceptual tools developed to analyse other social phenomena. Oscar Salemink has taken up this challenge and produced a monument to the misanthropy, misplaced intelligence and extraordinary ingeniousness with which the Highland people have been treated in anthropological writing and its application. Without ever claiming to speak for the Montagnards, he notes ominously that if they do not represent themselves, others will.'

Andrew Hardy, National University of Singapore

Oscar Salemink skilfully unravels the multiple relations between the ethnographic representation of the indigenous ethnic groups in the Central Highlands of Vietnam (sometimes called 'Montagnards'), and the changing historical context in which, and for which, the ethnographies were produced and consumed for more than a century. Looking at the ethnographic discourses with respect to the indigenous population of Vietnam's Central Highlands through periods of Christianization, colonization, war and socialist transformation, the book analyzes how changing ethnographic representations had a profound but varied impact on the people who formed the objects of such discourse. The author conceptualizes this impact in terms of tribalization, ethnicization, territorialization, governmentalization, marginalization and gender transformation. The book makes a significant contribution to our knowledge of the ethnic minorities in Vietnam who have become the object of development interventions and fierce academic debate.

Oscar Salemink is lecturer in social and cultural anthropology at the Vrije Universiteit, Amsterdam.

Anthropology of Asia series
Series editor: Grant Evans
University of Hong Kong

Asia today is one of the most dynamic regions of the world. The previously predominant image of 'timeless peasants' has given way to the image of fast-paced business people, mass consumerism and high-rise urban conglomerations. Yet much discourse remains entrenched in the polarities of 'East vs. West', 'Tradition vs. Change'. This series hopes to provide a forum for anthropological studies which break with such polarities. It will publish titles dealing with cosmopolitanism, cultural identity, representations, arts and performance. The complexities of urban Asia, its elites, its political rituals, and its families will also be explored.

The Ethnography of Vietnam's Central Highlanders

A historical contextualization, 1850–1990

Oscar Salemink

UNIVERSITY OF HAWAI'I PRESS
HONOLULU

Published in North America by
University of Hawai'i Press
2840 Kolowalu Street
Honolulu, Hawai'i 96822

First published in the United Kingdom
by RoutledgeCurzon
11 New Fetter Lane
London EC4P 4EE
England

Printed in Great Britain

Library of Congress Cataloging in Publication Data
A catalog record for this book has been requested

ISBN 0–8248–2579–9

In memory of my mentor
Professor Peter Kloos
1936–2000

Contents

Maps and charts

Figures

Preface

When I studied anthropology at the University of Nijmegen in the Netherlands, there was a general awareness of the fierce debates that the American involvement in Vietnam sparked within the international anthropological community. This debate was triggered by the advertisement of a position as 'Research Anthropologist for Vietnam' in the *American Anthropologist* 70: 852 (1968), which invited professional anthropologists to apply for a position with the Psychological Operations Directorate Headquarters of the US Military Assistance Command in Vietnam. The resulting, wide-ranging debates reflected on the disciplinary history of anthropology in the context of colonialism, with accusations being leveled against anthropology as the 'handmaiden of colonialism' – a debate epitomized in the volume *Anthropology and the Colonial Encounter* edited by Talal Asad (1973). Others mused about the role and responsibilities of a 'critical anthropology', e.g. in Dell Hymes' *Reinventing Anthropology* (1973). Many anthropologists in the US and elsewhere began to question the ethical principles that should guide anthropological research. By the time I studied anthropology, many of the 'new' ideas about anthropology had become commonplace.

Indeed, many leftist students – including myself – went one step further and embraced the French Marxist anthropology of Godelier, Meillassoux and others. With respect to the body of theory about ethnic groups and minorities – one of the important theoretical debates in anthropology – their analyses did not seem very convincing. Simply put, their argument blamed ethnic discrimination and oppression to the capitalist system via theories of the exploitation of minorities through the double labor market and by the appropriation of their natural resources. The implication of such theories was that the discrimination and oppression on ethnic minorities could only be overcome in a Socialist society. This naturally led me to ask the question: what was the position of ethnic minorities in contemporary Communist countries? Being impressed with the images of Vietnam from high-school days onward – in 1975 I wrote an essay on the 'Vietnam War' partly based on a publication of one later supervisor, Prof. Jan Pluvier – I decided that I wanted to do research in Vietnam on this issue. However, as many pointed out to me then, doing research in Vietnam would not be easy, partly because of the role that anthropology had played during the consecutive Indochina Wars. When I wanted to read up on that issue, it appeared to me that despite the fierce debates in the discipline, there was very little hard evidence and in-depth analysis about the role of anthropology in Vietnam. My provisional conclusion was that any research into the contemporary situation of ethnic minorities in Vietnam which did not take into account this history of anthropological and – more broadly – ethnographic investigations in Vietnam's ethnic minority areas was bound to be seriously flawed.

During the 1980s there were a number of scientific cooperation projects between Vietnamese and Dutch universities (the Vietnam-Holland Projects), which on the Dutch side had their origins in the 'solidarity movement' with Vietnam. The only project in the field of social sciences and humanities was the 'VH 26' project, headed by Prof. Jan Pluvier of the Institute of Modern Asian History (IMAG), University of Amsterdam, and Prof. Phan Huy Lê of the Faculty of History, Hanoi University. Raymond Feddema of IMAG supervised my MA thesis (1987) which dealt with French ethnography of the Central Highlands before 1955. The sources for that thesis were the collections of the CeDRASEMI (Centre de Recherche et de Documentation de l'Asie du Sud-Est et Monde Insuliendien – then in Valbonne); the Institut National des Langues et Civilisations Orientales (INALCO – Paris); the Bibliothèque Nationale; the Ecole Française d'Extrême-Orient (EFEO – Paris); the Missions Etrangères de Paris; the Archives Nationales – Section d'Outre Mer (ANSOM, then in Paris); and the Archives d'Outre-Mer (AOM) in Aix-en-Provence. In 1987 and 1988 I was one of the two first Dutch students to study Vietnamese in Hanoi, hosted by the Faculty of History and the Faculty of Vietnamese Studies of Hanoi University. I used that time to explore the collections of the National Library, the Social Sciences Library (now the Institute for Social Science Information) and the Institute of Social Sciences in Ho Chi Minh City.

With a Ph.D. scholarship from the Netherlands Foundation for the Advancement of Tropical Science (WOTRO), I resumed my research in 1989, jointly supervised by Prof. Jan Pluvier and the late Prof. Peter Kloos. In 1989 and 1993 I came back to Paris for follow-up research at the EFEO and the Service Historique de l'Armée de Terre (SHAT) in Vincennes, as well as for eight in-depth interviews with ethnographers, missionaries, and former military and civilian colonial officers. I also spent time studying the M.A. Jaspan papers in the Archives of the University of Hull.

In 1990 I spent almost half a year in the US for research in the collections of the National Archives (Washington, DC) and the Washington National Records Center (Suitland, MD); the Library of Congress; USAID; the Military History Institute of the Army War College in Carlisle Barracks (PA); the Marquat Memorial Library and the JFK Special Warfare Museum, both at the US Army Special Warfare Center in Fort Bragg (NC); the Smithsonian Institution Archives and the National Anthropological Archives at the Museum of Natural History at the Smithsonian Institution (Washington, DC); the National Security Archive in Washington (DC); the Echolls Collection and the Department of Manuscripts and University Archives at Cornell University (Ithaca, NY); the University

Archives and Historical Collections of Michigan State University (East Lansing, MI). I conducted interviews with many (former) anthropologists, missionaries (of the Summer Institute of Linguistics and the Christian and Missionary Alliance), Special Forces and US Army veterans, State Department, USAID, CIA officials, and the Montagnard refugee community in North Carolina as well as with prominent members of the Dega (Montagnard refugee) community in North Carolina. Interviewees include the late William Colby, former Director of Central Intelligence; Colonel Gilbert Layton of the CIA who designed the Special Forces entry in the Central Highlands; and Dr. Gerald C. Hickey, the most prominent American anthropologist specializing in the Vietnamese Central Highlanders.

In late 1990 I came back to Vietnam for archival research in Hanoi and Ho Chi Minh City (National Archives Center 1 and 2: collections of the French Gouvernement-Général de l'Indochine, the Résidence-Supérieure d'Annam and South-Vietnam's Ministry of Development of Ethnic Minorities and Council of Ethnic Minorities) and the National Library, as well as for field research in the provinces of Gialai-Kontum and Lâm Đồng in the Central Highlands during the first half of 1991. This research was facilitated by the Faculty of History of Hanoi University, especially Prof. Phan Huy Lê, Dr. Nguyên Văn Chính, and Mr. Pham Văn Thành who accompanied me to the Central Highlands and assisted me in my research. Given the sensitive nature of the research and the subject matter, I will not disclose the identity of informants and of localities for reasons of privacy and – especially – protection. In terms of numbers, I recorded eight interviews with officials in Hanoi to find out more about the assumptions guiding policies at the center; and 84 in-depth interviews with officials and local citizens in the Central Highlands.

Given the nature of the research (I did not stay long in any one location) there has been no attempt to do a village study or 'rounded' ethnographic survey. Instead, I have concentrated on oral history, even though well aware of the methodological pitfalls of this method, especially in an area which has known so much conflict, with so many divided loyalties. I have tried to contextualize the stories collected by comparing these narratives with the information that can be found in the written records, which constitute 'partial truths' as well. One example of how this method worked out can be found in Chapter 4, where I offer an interpretation of a millenarian movement which is at odds with the accepted versions based on the colonial records. In general, I hope that the quality of my analysis matches the abundance of sources that I have worked with.

To a major extent, the results of my studies document the changing and often diverging ethnographic discourses about the people of the Central Highlands as an ongoing struggle for hegemony between evolutionist and relativist perspectives. It is fair to state clearly from the outset that in this equation I – both personally and professionally – endorse the latter perspective. This endorsement is not unequivocal, because I am well aware of the political uses to which such perspectives were put. Yet, despite such contextual considerations, and in spite of their internal contradictions, cultural relativist perspectives tend to take better account of the interests, the aspirations, the concerns of the people under study than did evolutionist perspectives. Moreover, relativist perspectives tend to be less scientistic in nature, and make an attempt at representing or incorporating 'emic' viewpoints. Even where this is a largely rhetorical move, it creates more space for auto-ethnographic narratives and other forms of self-representation which contribute to the opening up and democratization of the anthropological discipline. None of this is unproblematic, however, as I shall show in the chapters that follow. Both complicity and naiveté are uncomfortable companions in the ethnographic endeavor.

Acknowledgements

Though one name appears as author of a book like this one, it is always a collective effort to the extent that literally hundreds of different people and institutions contribute to make it possible. I am indebted and grateful to all of them, even though it may not be possible to acknowledge each person by name; I apologize for any omission in this regard.

Financially, the research for this book has been made possible by grant No. W52-456 of WOTRO (the Netherlands Foundation for the Advancement of Tropical Science) as well as by small grants from the Treub-Maatschappij (Society for Scientific Research in the Tropics) and from the NSAV (Netherlands Sociological and Anthropological Society). I have conducted research while I was studying or working at, or affiliated with, the University of Amsterdam (Institute for Modern Asian History, Department of International Relations; Centre for Asian Studies Amsterdam, Amsterdam School for Social Research); the Free University in Amsterdam (Department of Anthropology and Sociology of Non-Western Societies); the Catholic University of Nijmegen (Department of Cultural Anthropology, Centre for Pacific Studies); and Hanoi University (Faculty of History, Faculty of Vietnamese Studies). I gratefully acknowledge the unrelenting support and trust of my two thesis supervisors, Prof. Jan Pluvier and the late Prof. Peter Kloos. I also acknowledge the support of Prof. Phan Huy Lê and Dr. Nguyên Văn Chính of what is now Vietnam National University in Hanoi, who worked hard to facilitate my field research in the Central Highlands, as well as the ethnologist Mr. Pham Văn Thành who accompanied and assisted me in the Central Highlands.

While doing research in France, I was hosted by Prof. Georges Condominas at the Centre de Recherche et de Documentation sur l'Asie du Sud-Est (CeDRASEMI in Valbonne, France); by Cornell University, the University of Hull, Hanoi University, the Institute of Social Sciences in Ho Chi Minh City, and the People's Committees of Gialai-Kontum and Lâm Đông provinces in Vietnam. Apart from my official institutional hosts, many libraries, documentation centers and archives opened their doors for me, and their staff have gone out of their way to provide the best possible service that I could wish for in all the countries where I conducted research. I have had access to many rare collections, like the microfilmed collection of National Liberation Front journals and pamphlets from the 1960s, conserved at the National Library in Hanoi; or the records of the Ministry of Development of Ethnic Minorities of the former South Vietnamese régime which, according to the then director of National Records Center 2 in Ho Chi Minh City Dr. Phan Đình Nham, had never been studied after 1975. In this regard, three experiences stand out. In 1987 and 1988, staff of the Social Sciences Library in Hanoi (now the Institute of Social Science Information under the National Center for Social Sciences and Humanities) made me sing Dutch songs in return for the privilege of borrowing 'restricted access' books. In 1990, Mr. Fred Fuller, reference librarian of the Marquat Memorial Library at the US Army Special Warfare Center in Fort Bragg had prepared a table and a pile of material for me when I arrived there for research. And in 1990 a former high-ranking CIA officer granted me a relevant portion of his personal archive on condition that I would cut out the 'secret' stamped on the pages.

I have enjoyed the hospitality of many persons, groups and communities while conducting research. In the US, many interviewees volunteered to pick me up from the airport when I arrived, spared a day to answer all my questions, accommodated me for the night, and brought me back to the airport the next day. Dr. Gerald Hickey hosted me for three days in Chicago, and answered my many questions, while Prof. George W. Stocking Jr. of the University of Chicago helped me get a fee waiver for Freedom of Information Act (FOIA) requests regarding US Army and CIA records. Special Forces veterans and Montagnard refugees in North Carolina invited me to their functions and celebrations. Some of Vietnam's most knowledgeable and respected ethnologists, including Prof. Đang Nghiêm Van and Mr. Nguyên Huu Thâú, shared their profound knowledge with me. Provincial, district and commune authorities in the Central Highlands received me cordially, and people from local communities around Kontum town, in Ayun Pa district (Gialai province), in Di Linh and Bao Lôc districts (Lam Đông province) eagerly came forward with everything that I wanted to know and that they wished to share.

Intellectually, I am indebted to many more people than I can mention. Dr. Raymond Feddema of the University of Amsterdam introduced me to Vietnamese studies and to Vietnam. Dr. John Kleinen of the University of Amsterdam shared my interest in colonial studies. Dr. Peter Pels of the University of Amsterdam became a 'soul-mate' in many senses of the word, and helped me explore postcolonial theory when we organized the 'Colonial Ethnographies' seminar together in 1993 and proceeded to jointly publish edited volumes on the history of anthropology and colonialism. Three chapters of this book are directly related to publications that I co-edited with Peter Pels. Two major sources of inspiration for this research have been George Stocking and Georges Condominas, whose seminal work has established standards that seem impossible to reach, and that are therefore attractive to try to emulate ...

Parts of this book have been published previously. The introduction is a re-working of 'Introduction: Five theses on ethnography as colonial practice' which I co-authored with Peter Pels (1994). Chapter 4 is an adaptation of my

'The Return of the Python God: Multiple interpretations of a millenarian movement in colonial Vietnam' (1994). Parts of Chapter 5 have been published as 'Primitive Partisans: French Strategy and the Construction of a Montagnard Ethnic Identity in Indochina' (1995) and as 'Ethnography as Martial Art: Ethnicizing Vietnam's Montagnards, 1930–1954' (1999). Different versions of Chapter 8 have been published as 'The King of Fire and Vietnamese Ethnic Policy in the Central Highlands' (1997) and as 'Sedentarization and Selective Preservation among the Montagnards of the Vietnamese Central Highlands' (2000). I am grateful to the publishers for graciously letting me use these previously published texts. I am grateful to Gordon and Breach Publishers, University of Wisconsin Press, University of Michigan Press, and Curzon Press for permission to reproduce this previously published material. Acknowledgements are also due to Presses Universitaires de France and Georges Condominas for permission to reproduce map 1, and to Yale University Press for permission to reproduce maps 2, 4 and 5.

Various people have been helpful in creating the time and the space for me to write up my thesis. Prof. Frans Hüsken and Dr. Toon van Meijl offered me the hospitality of the Department of Cultural Anthropology of the Catholic University of Nijmegen. Dr. John Ambler, Representative of the Ford Foundation for Thailand and Vietnam from 1995 till 1997, gave me two weeks which helped me finish the last chapters. My position as Ford Foundation Program Officer in Vietnam has helped me work more effectively, and simultaneously keep abreast of developments in the field. It may be obvious, though, that the opinions in this book are mine, and not necessarily those of the Ford Foundation. Various other colleagues helped me during the last stages of preparing this manuscript. They include Yves Goudineau, Andrew Hardy, Nguyên Văn Thăng, Christine Hemmet, Père Gérard Moussay and Christopher Goscha. I am also deeply indebted to my thesis supervisor Prof. Peter Kloos, who never tired of encouraging me to continue, but who passed away prematurely in the summer of 2000. All of those mentioned and many others contributed to, or commented on, this book; however, any deficiencies are entirely mine.

The most important people who have had to create time and space to see me through this odyssey are my family. My mother and my late father – whose premature death interrupted my field research – supported me throughout my scientific career; but it is my wife Wilma Doornbosch and my daughters Lisa and Rosalie who have had to suffer most from my long leaves of absence from family life, or from my absent-mindedness when I was around. It is to them that I dedicate this book.

Many names have been left out deliberately, for reasons of protection or privacy. I apologize to all those not acknowledged but who should have been mentioned here.

Oscar Salemink

Abbreviations

AID	US Agency for International Development
Annales	Annales de la Propagation de la Foi
ARPA	Advanced Research Project Agency
ARVN	Army of the Republic of Viet Nam (South Vietnam)
ASEMI	Asie du Sud-Est et Monde Insulindien
BAVH	Bulletin des Amis du Vieux Hué
BEFEO	Bulletin de l'Ecole Française d'Extrême-Orient
BSEI	Bulletin de la Société des Etudes Indochinoises
CA/PSYOP	Civic Action/Psychological Operations
CEFEO	Cahiers de l'Ecole Française d'Extrême-Orient
CIA	Central Intelligence Agency
CIDG	Citizens Irregular Defense Groups
CINFAC	Cultural Information and Analysis Center
CMA	Christian and Missionary Alliance
CORDS	Civilian Operations and Rural Development Support
CRESS	Center for Research in Social Systems
DOD	Department of Defense
DDRE	Director of Defense Research and Engineering
DDRS	Declassified Documents Reference System
DRV	Democratic Republic of Vietnam (North Vietnam)
DSB	Defense Science Board
EFEO	Ecole Française d'Extrême-Orient
EandR	Excursions et Reconnaissances
FULRO	Front Unifié de la Lutte des Races Opprimées
GCMA	(1) Groupes de Commandos Mixtes Aeroportés
	(2) General Cooperative Montagnard Association
GVN	Government of Viet-Nam (South Vietnam)
IIEH	Institut Indochinois pour l'Etude de l'Homme
IVS	International Voluntary Service
MAAG	Military Assistance Advisory Group
MACV	Military Assistance Command – Vietnam
MDEM	Ministry of Development of Ethnic Minorities
MIT	Massachusetts Institute of Technology

MSUG	Michigan State University Vietnam Advisory Group
NCO	Non-commissioned officer
NGO	Non-governmental organization
NLF	National Liberation Front (South Vietnam)
NSC	National Security Council
OSA	Office of the Special Assistant (US Embassy, Saigon)
OSS	Office of Strategic Services
PMS	Pays Montagnard du Sud
PMSI	Pays Montagnard du Sud-Indochinois
RAC	Research Analysis Corporation
RF/PF	Regional Forces/Popular Forces
RI	Revue Indochinoise
RVN	Republic of Viet Nam (South Vietnam)
SEADAG	Southeast Asia Development Agency Group
SEI	Société des Etudes Indochinoises
SF	US Army Special Forces
SIL	Summer Institute of Linguistics
SORO	Special Operations Research Office
TIIEH	Travaux de l'Institut Indochinois pour l'Etude de l'Homme
USAID	US Agency for International Development
USIA	US Information Agency
USIS	US Information Service
USOM	US Operations Mission
WBT	Wycliffe Bible Translators

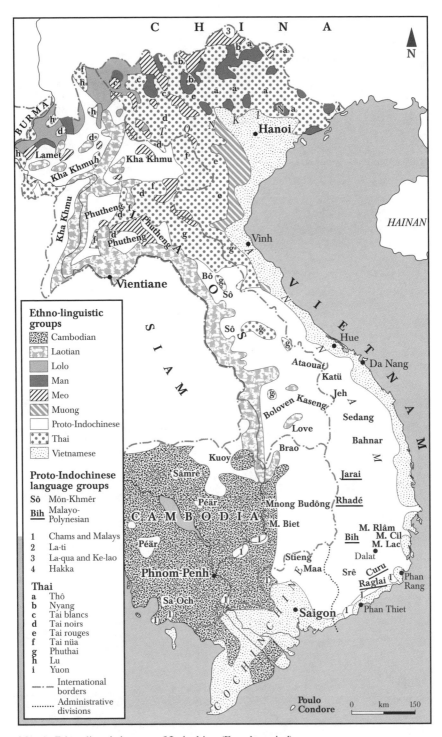

Map 1. Ethno-linguistic map of Indochina (French period).

Source: Leroi-Gourhan and Poirier 1953.

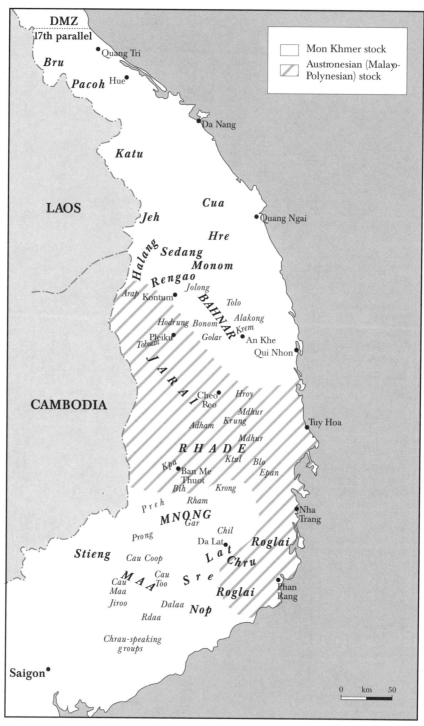

DMZ
17th parallel
● Quang Tri

Bru

Pacoh Hue ●

● Da Nang

Katu

LAOS

Cua

● Jeh ● Quang Ngai

Hre

Halang *Sedang*
Monom
Rengao
Arap Kontum ● *Jolong*
Tolo
Hodrung Bonom *Alakong*
Pleiku ● Golar *Krem*
Tobuan *An Khe* ●
Qui Nhon ●

CAMBODIA

Cheo ● *Hroy*
Reo
Mdhur
Adham *Krung*
Tuy Hoa ●
Mdhur

R H A D E
Ktul *Blo*
Kpa Ban Me *Epan*
Thuot
Bih *Krong*

Preh *Rham*
MNONG Nha ●
Gar Trang
Chil
Prong Da Lat ●
L a t *Roglai*
Stieng *Cau Coop* *Chru*
Cau *S r e*
Cau *Too* *Roglai*
Maa *M A A* Phan ●
Jiroo *Dalaa* *Nop* Rang
Rdaa

Chrau-speaking
groups

Saigon ●

0   km   50

☐ Mon Khmer stock
▨ Austronesian (Malay-
Polynesian) stock

Map 2. Ethno-linguistic groups of the Central Highlands (US period).
Source: Hickey 1982a.

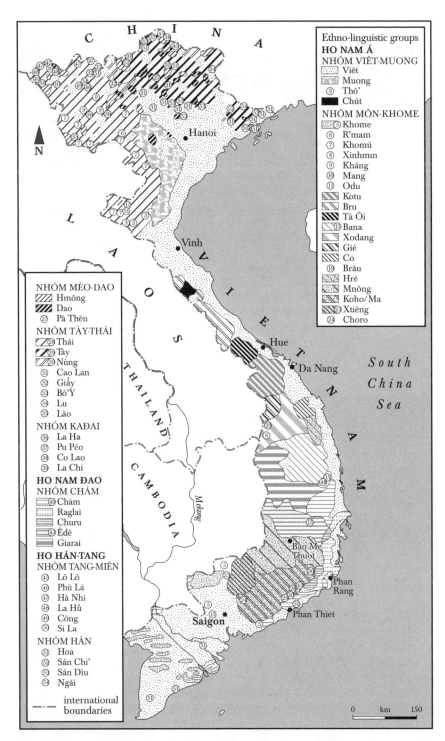

Map 3. Vietnam's official ethnographic map (contemporary period).

Source: Nguyên Van Tài 1984.

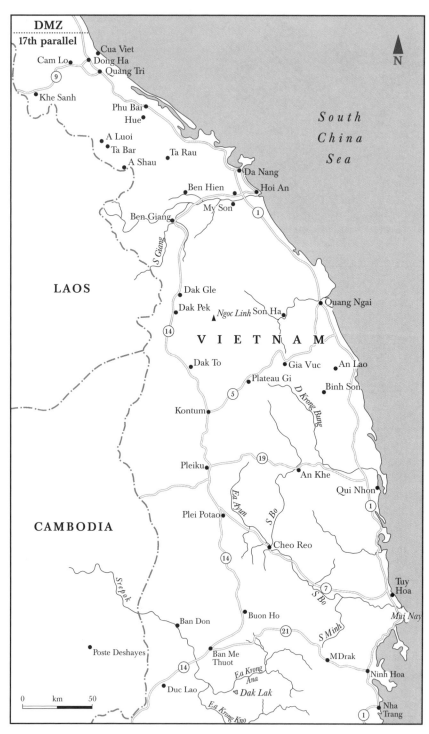

Map 4. Northern portion of the Central Highlands.
Source: Hickey 1982a.

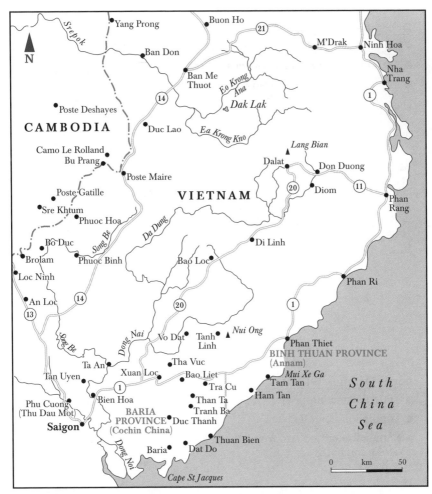

Map 5. Southern portion of the Central Highlands.

Source: Hickey 1982a.

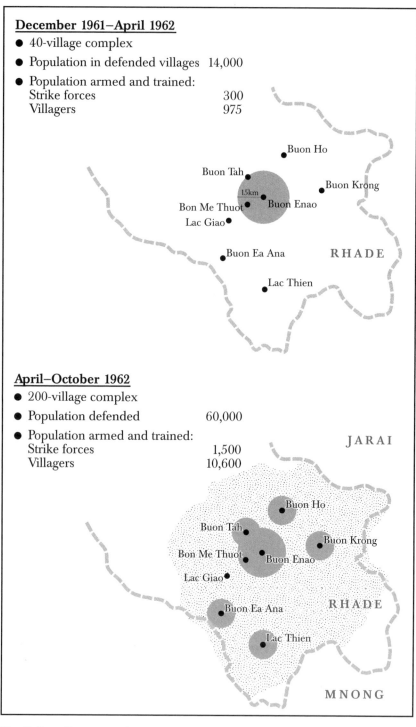

December 1961–April 1962

- 40-village complex
- Population in defended villages   14,000
- Population armed and trained:
  Strike forces   300
  Villagers   975

Buon Ho

Buon Tah

15km

Buon Krong

Bon Me Thuot   Buon Enao

Lac Giao

Buon Ea Ana   R H A D E

Lac Thien

April–October 1962

- 200-village complex
- Population defended   60,000
- Population armed and trained:
  Strike forces   1,500
  Villagers   10,600

J A R A I

Buon Ho

Buon Tah

Bon Me Thuot   Buon Krong

Buon Enao

Lac Giao

Buon Ea Ana   R H A D E

Lac Thien

M N O N G

Map 6. Buon Enao expansion.
Source: Kelly 1973.

1 Introduction

Ethnography, anthropology and colonial discourse[1]

The subject matter of this book is the multiple relations between the ethnographic representations of the 'Montagnard' ethnic groups in the Central Highlands of Vietnam, and the changing historical context in and for which the ethnographies were produced, and in which they were 'consumed'. In what follows I shall develop two major arguments. The first argument holds that economic, political and military interests within a specific historical context condition ethnographic practice. The second argument holds that the ensuing ethnographic discourses in turn influence the historical context by suggesting and facilitating ethnic policies, and by contributing to the formation or change of ethnic identities through processes of classification.

I assume that ethnographic knowledge is not simply a more or less accurate reflection of indigenous society, but is an essentially human endeavor. I take ethnography to be a (textual) representation of a particular society constructed by outsiders, conditioned by their interaction with informants and by differing interests which influence ethnographic practice. Where circumstances are changing, a constant reconstruction of ethnographic knowledge takes place, reflecting the changes in the historical context as well as the changes in indigenous society. For this reason I prefer the concept of *discourse* with its constructivist and processual connotations to the concept of *knowledge*, with its reflective and static connotations. Mainly for stylistic reasons, however, I shall continue to use the word 'knowledge', which I see as not necessarily embodying 'truth', but as a way of approaching, interpreting and especially constructing and asserting truth.

With regard to the ethnographic practices preceding the making of ethnographic texts, Pels and Salemink (1994, 1999) make a useful distinction between *préterrain*, ethnographic occasion and ethnographic tradition (1994, 1999). *Préterrain* is a concept coined by Georges Condominas, the great ethnographer of the Mnong Gar in Vietnam, to denote the local colonial *milieu* from where the ethnographer departs when doing fieldwork, and where s/he returns for comfort (Condominas 1973: 9). But Pels broadens the definition to include 'the power relationships in which an ethnographer ... gets caught upon arrival in the field' both in the colonial and the indigenous societies and in their interaction (Pels 1994, 322). A second moment is the *ethnographic occasion* which is the actual encounter between the ethnographer and those who are represented, and which forms the basis for the writing of the ethnographic text. A third moment is the insertion of the text into a specific *ethnographic tradition* which is directed at specific audiences. This heuristic distinction of the ethnographic process in three distinct moments illustrates the extent to which the ethnographic text is a result of negotiation between ethnographer, the *ethnos* to be represented, and the wider context.

Just as ethnographic knowledge, I consider ethnic identity to be a social construction, mediated by a continuous process of negotiation of cultural difference between various social actors – those within and outside of the 'ethnic group' – with a major part played by the modern state in its efforts to describe and classify its population. In the theoretical discussion regarding ethnicity between 'primordialists' and 'situationalists' (Brown 1994: xi–25), or between 'essentialists' and 'constructivists', I would probably be seen as siding with the latter. I would subscribe to the view of ethnicity which sees it as a sense of community and belonging stemming from an imagined notion of common ancestry (Keyes 1976, 1997). This is not to say that ethnic identity is not 'real', or simply a consequence of political manipulation by political elites. Like other social phenomena they are the consequence of human agency, having their own reality – even if that reality is not immutable. Seen from this perspective it is possible to see the parallels between ethnography and ethnic identity. Indeed, in the chapters that follow I shall argue that changing ethnographic representations have an impact on the self-perceptions of the 'objects' of ethnography – i.e. the people who are described – and hence on their ethnic identities.

Assuming that anthropology and ethnography are not practised in an intellectual and a social void, this historiography of anthropology implies a lack of respect for the disciplinary boundaries of anthropology in two ways. First, contrary to the now common assumption that ethnography is the descriptive (or even the field research) part of anthropology, it is assumed that professional anthropology is a fairly recent manifestation of ethnographic practice, but which receives much attention in the overly evolutionist and idealist historiography of anthropology. Ethnography, then, is taken in a broad sense. Missionaries, military explorers, colonial administrators, plantation owners, development workers, counterinsurgency experts, government officials, politicians, indigenous leaders – male and female – construct ethnographic images of these indigenous groups (often called 'Montagnards') according to their experiences and in order to suit their interests. These ethnographic representations interacted with those by professional anthropologists, who created their representations in dialogue with, sometimes in opposition to, but always against the backdrop of those 'non-professional' ethnographic representations.

The second transgression of the disciplinary boundaries of anthropology is a consequence of the first, as it refers to the historical context in and for which ethnographic knowledge was produced. It is often ignored that ethnographic knowledge is a precondition for the administration of indigenous peoples, be it in pre-colonial, colonial or modern times, and that this knowledge must be systematized in an ethnographic discourse and practice. Eventually, this ethnographic knowledge is institutionalized and professionalized at different points in time. I do not contend that ethnography is a mere reflection of the prevailing interests. Ethnography is an often highly individual achievement, as the example of the colonial administrator Léopold Sabatier will show (Chapter 3). Nevertheless, the reception of the ideas of outstanding ethnographers is contingent upon the balance of power within a specific, but changing historical context. That balance of power is both localized and affected by regional and global developments.

To a major extent, this study takes up the discussion of the 1960s and 1970s about the (political) uses of anthropology (e.g. Horowitz 1967, 1971; Asad 1973), but tries to raise the level of understanding through a meticulous historical contextualization of the ethnographic representations of the indigenous population of a limited geographic area (the Vietnamese Central Highlands) over a relatively long period of time (1850–1990). The debates on the politics of anthropology took place against the backdrop of what some call the Vietnam War and others the American War – according to their perspective – but what I prefer to call the Second Indochina War (1954–75, but the starting date varies from 1954 *via* 1960 to 1965). This war prompted many social scientists to take sides against the use of anthropology for suppression and counterinsurgency. Perhaps the long period of war and conflict in Vietnam, and especially in the Central Highlands (from the early 1940s through the early 1980s), does not make the context of ethnographic production, reproduction and consumption representative for the context of anthropology as such. The aim of this study, however, is not to write a general history of anthropology, but a *contextual analysis* of discursive changes in the ethnography of the population of a geographically limited area over a relatively long period of time. A contextual analysis is necessarily localized and time-bound, and highlights relations linking ethnographic practice and discourse with the context of their production and use. Such relations are arguably more clearly visible in situations of open conflict, when ethnography can be seen to play a controversial role amidst opposing interests.

Three examples of the abuse of ethnography in the area of study will illustrate this point. The French anthropologist Georges Condominas conducted his fieldwork among the Mnong Gar during the early years of the First Indochina War (1945–54, but some say 1946–54), intended as a colonial study of 'culture contact'. Developing into a critic of colonialism, he published his eminent ethnography in diary format, *Nous avons mangé la forêt* (We have eaten the forest), well after the conclusion of that war, in 1957. When he returned to Vietnam and to his research site, first in 1958, then 1962, he found himself witness to the destruction of the Mnong way of life, of their communities and villages which made way for 'strategic hamlets' designed by American military advisors to combat the 'Vietcong'. Recounting his experiences and anxieties in his beautiful book *L'exotique est quotidien*, he coined the concept of 'ethnocide' to describe the processes at work (1965: 469). In his 'Distinguished Lecture' for the American Anthropological Association in 1972, he noted the irony of the fact that he was invited to deliver that lecture in the absence of any sizeable English translations of his work. The only exception to this was an illegal translation, *We Have Eaten the Forest* in the Joint Publications Research Service series printed by the US Department of Commerce (1962) which had marked on each page 'Government Use Only'. Condominas remarked that this translation was distributed to the 'Green Berets', a nickname for the US Special Forces whom he calls 'the technicians of death, of their death':

> But you will understand my outrage when you know that I had learned the news of this 'piracy' some years after having seen the evidence that Srae, whose marriage I describe in *Nous avons mangé la forêt*, was tortured by a sergeant of the Special Forces in the camp of Phii Ko'.
>
> (Condominas 1980: 103)

A second case of abuse of ethnographic information involves Gerald Cannon Hickey, the well-known American ethnographer and historiographer of the 'Highlanders' – as he prefers to call them. Trained in Chicago as an anthropologist in Sol Tax' 'action anthropology' tradition, Hickey developed a scholarly interest in Vietnam. He associated himself with the Michigan State University Vietnam Advisory Group in the 1950s, and came to work from 1964 till 1973 in Vietnam with the RAND Corporation, a US Navy think tank. Over the years Hickey developed a deep affection for the Highlanders in general, and for their aspirations toward autonomy. In the second volume of his *Ethnohistory of the Vietnamese Central Highlands*, entitled *Free in the Forest*, he describes the emergence of an ethnonationalist movement and of a 'pan-Highlander' political leadership, arrived at through intermarriage of elite families from various ethnic groups – illustrated by genealogical charts (1982b: 327–331). Hickey described in great detail a political movement with the acronym of FULRO, which emerged in Special Forces camps in opposition to the policies of the (South Vietnamese) Republic of Vietnam and continued to fight after 1975 against the reunified (July 1976) Socialist Republic of Vietnam. He added a list of 'One Hundred Highlander Leaders: Ethnic affiliation, approximate birth date, and religion' (1982b: 304–07). After his books were published and arrived in Vietnam, Vietnamese security officials who were still fighting FULRO started to arrest every person mentioned in the book. Thanks to the courageous intervention of a Vietnamese ethnologist these persons were gradually released.[2] Like Condominas, Hickey obviously did not intend this to happen, and was very upset when I wrote to him about it.

A third near-incident took place in 1991, after I had concluded my field research in the Central Highlands. During those days, this area was still off-limits for most foreigners, and the province of Dak Lak, the epicenter of the Montagnard political opposition, was still off-limits for me. My field research was almost constantly monitored by officials from various State levels. Yet, in the fall of 1991 I learned that various Vietnamese scholars who had facilitated my research project in Vietnam, had been interrogated by security officials because twelve Montagnards had been able to send a letter to the Human Rights Council of the United Nations in Geneva, complaining about the treatment of

Montagnards by the Vietnamese authorities. The most immediate response on the part of Vietnamese authorities was to find out the identity of the signatories and the identity of the person who had taken the letter out of the country. The suspicion was that I had smuggled that letter out of the country (which I had not), but I was apparently 'exonerated' after the interrogations of my hosts. Learning from friends about this event made me wary about publishing ethnography, and especially about disclosing sources, because I have no intention of endangering informants or others out of ethnographic 'naiveté'. These three examples illustrate that war and conflict give rise to specific *préterrains*, ethnographic occasions and ethnographic traditions, which can bring out the contextual relations of ethnographic practice and discourse more clearly.

Since this is a localized and time-bound contextual analysis of the ethnography dealing with the indigenous population of the Central Highlands in Vietnam, this study can easily be mistaken for an ethno-history of the 'Montagnards', or for a historical ethnography. Though it has not been my intention to write an ethnohistory or an ethnographic monograph, this book can be read as such. The various chapters are ordered more or less chronologically, and contain ethnographic detail – or else comments on ethnographies written by others. To some degree, it mirrors Gerald Hickey's *Ethnohistory of the Vietnamese Central Highlands* (1982a, b), but it is also a running critique of those two volumes. To put it succinctly, Hickey's treatment of historical sources in Volume I, *Sons of the Mountains*, is uncritical, while in Volume II, *Free in the Forest*, he identifies uncritically with certain ethno-nationalist leaders and their ideas.

Ironically, this introduction will contain some basic and general historical, geographic and ethnographic information, gleaned from existing ethnographies and presented here as ethnographic 'facts'. This information is intended to make the subsequent analyses of ethnographic discourse intelligible. But before turning to a description of the local setting, I would like to spell out some of the assumptions situating this study theoretically. The following six sections contain five theoretical hypotheses that have been developed jointly by Peter Pels and myself, resulting in a preliminary set of questions guiding this study. After these sections follow sections about the local geographic, historical and ethnographic contexts and about the structure of this book.

Beyond a history of anthropological 'big men'

Despite the influence of Thomas Kuhn on critical assessments of anthropology, disciplinary histories written by anthropologists still tend to be self-serving. To this day, it seems obvious to look upon the great thinkers of anthropology, those who revolutionized its theories and methods, as the main carriers of the history of anthropology. It is, however, possible and indeed necessary to consider the history of anthropology from another angle. The emphasis on the 'big men' (and to a lesser extent 'big women') of anthropology in disciplinary histories obscures the way in which ethnography was linked to the construction of colonial and neocolonial societies. In the following text some assumptions are elaborated with regard to the historical relevance of ethnographic practice, understood in relation to the anthropological discipline and to its respective local and historical contexts. These assumptions, developed jointly with Peter Pels in the context of our 'Colonial Ethnographies' project, are not definitive outcomes of a rewriting of anthropology's history, but first steps toward a critical reflection on the relations between ethnography and anthropology within their respective local and historical contexts. This book hopes to elucidate the emergence and development of ethnographic and anthropological discourses and practices in the context of colonial, neocolonial and post-colonial Vietnam.

A first assumption underlying this dissertation is *that disciplinary histories tend to obscure the way in which academic anthropology was linked to the construction of colonial and neocolonial societies through ethnographic practice.* When the collection of essays on *Anthropology and the Colonial Encounter* (Asad 1973) was published, its message was drowned in heated arguments. Despite Asad's statement that 'it is a mistake to view social anthropology in the colonial era as primarily an aid to colonial administration, or as the simple reflection of colonial ideology', a contemporary effort of critical anthropologists (Hymes 1974) resulted in debate about the way in which British anthropologists had been engaged in 'aiding and abetting British colonial policy in Africa' (Scholte 1975: 45).[3] Indeed, in that context, the volume edited by Asad was understood as making precisely that point (cf. Loizos 1977: 137; Ortner 1984: 138). Similarly, the claims that anthropology provided an ideology legitimating European feelings of superiority (cf. Lewis 1973) was countered by professions of left-wing sympathies (Gluckman 1974; but see Brown 1979) or the ahistorical statement that 'the only inferiority which most social anthropologists have ever stressed has been a technical one' (Firth 1977: 152).

The issue of the practical or ideological complicity of anthropologists in the construction of colonial (or neocolonial – Horowitz 1967; Wolf and Jorgensen 1970) power was crucial for debates accompanying a radical shift of claims to anthropological authority from classical anthropology to the more politicized perspectives of the 1970s (Pels and Nencel 1991). It was often accompanied by denunciations of the opponent's lack of historical consciousness made by both parties.[4] Yet, history was a remote concern for most participants in the debate. Forster's balanced overview of the New Left critique shows that the critics focused on the theoretical limitations, or the lack of social responsibility, of classical anthropology (Forster 1973: 24), not on its history. Similarly, neither were defenders of classical claims inclined to study history very closely: Leach presumed the existence of a 'sociology of *colonialism*' in functionalism (Leach 1974: 34; our emphasis), ignoring the fact that it was usually called 'culture contact' (Leclerc 1972: 55). Gluckman's formal denial that as an anthropologist he was ever a member of His Majesty's Government (1974: 43) of course does not imply that he abstained from doing the work of government (see Scholte 1975; also Brown 1979). In contrast, many contributions to *Anthropology and the Colonial Encounter* provided some of the first studies of anthropology in its historical, colonial context.[5]

More recent assessments of the impact of the critique to which Asad's volume was a contribution show a similar lack of historical consciousness. *Anthropology and the Colonial Encounter*, despite occasional praise (Clifford 1986: 9), is usually included in disparaging assessments of the critique of the 1960s and 1970s. The critical anthropologists' negative portrait of the anthropologist has, for the new generation, 'hardened into caricature' (Clifford 1986: 9); the critique 'merely scratched the surface' (Ortner 1984: 138) and its overall effort 'was too immoderate and ungrounded in practice to have much effect' (Marcus and Fischer 1986: 35). Yet, the critique went sufficiently deep as to have the effect of inverting and unsettling anthropologists' claims to academic authority (Pels and Nencel 1991). It will remain relevant for as long as much of postcolonial anthropology is still based on raw materials delivered by 'informants' which are processed into 'cultural' identities that can be sold on Western academic markets (Galtung 1967; also Lewis 1973).

Such attempts to 'write off' academic debates usually go together with attempts to inscribe oneself in the discipline (Pels and Nencel 1991: 17), for instance, by claiming the American culturalist experience as the rationale of all anthropology (Marcus and Fischer 1986: 22), or by setting up one's own standard by calling others 'provincial' (Leach 1974: 33; cf. Diamond 1974: 37–8). It is a rhetorical absolutism which hides a 'parochialism of the present' (Levenson, quoted in Stocking 1982: 5) by formulating its own claim to authority in terms of the rationality of the discipline as a whole. This can only lead to what George Stocking called a 'presentist' attitude towards history (1968: 1–12), evident from a large number of efforts by anthropologists to write the history of their discipline.[6] However, despite the influence of Thomas Kuhn's call for a historicizing disciplinary history (1970) on critical debates within anthropology (cf. Scholte 1966, 1978, 1983), its use was mostly restricted to a strategic use of the paradigm concept, amounting to a proliferation of 'Whiggish histories'. As Regna Darnell noted:

> A great deal of purported history of anthropology . . . is far from contextually accurate or historically sophisticated. Practitioners as quasi-historians frequently use history to argue for present theoretical concerns (1982: 268).

In spite of attempts both before and after the publication of *Anthropology and the Colonial Encounter* (Asad 1973), is doubtful that the call for a historical contextualization of anthropology has been sufficiently 'historicist', taken as the ideal to 'understand the past for the sake of the past' (Stocking 1968: 9).[7] It is remarkable that the relevance of anthropology for the colonial encounter has hardly been a subject for historical study (but see Brown 1979; Johnson 1982; Cell 1989) until Volume 7 in the *History of Anthropology* series (Stocking 1991a) – although this relevance has by now been accepted by the majority of anthropologists as a 'commonplace' (Stocking 1991b: 4). This is – at least partly – due to the fact that the status of anthropology as an academic discipline is too much taken for granted, even in much scholarship of professed 'historicist' character. Therefore, an essential methodological move in the study of the history of anthropology needs to be made: the dialectical move of accounting for the extra-academic and extra-disciplinary influences on the constitution of the discipline.

In 1953, Meyer Fortes wrote that '[i]t is characteristic and important that anthropological studies owe a great deal to enthusiasts from outside the academic world, to officers of the Crown, to missionaries, traders and travellers' (Fortes 1974: 420). In France, Maurice Leenhardt was an important missionary presence among anthropologists (Clifford 1982), while in Germany, Father Wilhelm Schmidt and his journal *Anthropos* made a decisive impact on behalf of his congregation, the missionary Society of the Divine Word (Brandewie 1990). Yet, histories of anthropology do not usually consider missionary anthropologists and when they do, their missionary background is thought to be of no importance.[8] Dutch ethnology and anthropology trace their roots to 'Indology', the body of knowledge concerning colonial Indonesia, which was taught in Delft from 1848, and later Leiden and Utrecht, for aspiring colonial civil servants for the Dutch East Indies (Fasseur 1993; Kloos 1989). The importance of the administrative background is illustrated by the facts that in Britain, Cambridge anthropology owed a lot to the Orientalist and administrator Sir Richard Temple, and that as late as 1953 Meyer Fortes succeeded to a Cambridge professorship which was handed down by two former members of the Indian Colonial Service, T.C. Hodson and J.H. Hutton (Fortes 1974: 427). Malinowskian functionalism could not have established itself without the support of missionaries like J.H. Oldham or administrators like Lord Lugard (see Cell 1989; Stocking 1985, 1991a). Events like the Protestant missionary conferences at High Leigh (1924) and Le Zoute (1926) tied up extra-academic missionary anthropology with the network of Oldham and Lugard (Forster 1989: 27). These cases indicate the importance of non-academic influences on the establishment of academic anthropology.

In a sense, there is a seductive logic to the focus on disciplinary histories, for it seems obvious to look upon those who revolutionized its theories and methods as the main carriers of anthropological history. Yet, we should take account of the fact that 'disciplinary history does not exist until its view of the past is ratified by members of the discipline' (Darnell 1971: 87). Disciplinary history holds on, for example, to the legend that Malinowski 'invented' modern fieldwork methods (Kuper 1983: 13). In fact, Malinowski managed to produce this impression by consistent 'self-fashioning' (Clifford 1985), a propaganda which concealed the fact that he drew upon earlier examples (Stocking 1983a). To a large extent, the professionalization of fieldwork in British anthropology depended on the tactical denigration of both missionary and administrative ethnographies (Pels 1990; Thomas 1989: 69 ff.). One has to study, not accept, the way in which *Argonauts of the Western Pacific* set up the boundaries between the academic 'Ethnographer' and his rivals (cf. Malinowski 1922: 1–25). Moreover, the emphasis on the intellectual giants of the discipline obscures the links between anthropology and colonial work, for the simple reason that the giants dedicated themselves to a purely academic career, while lesser figures often operated outside the academy. Lastly, the discussion about anthropology and colonialism almost completely ignores the pre-professional fieldwork phase, and consequently, the impact of Indian civil servants like Herbert Risley and Richard Temple on academic anthropology.

Foucault argued that one can only understand a discipline through the ways in which it fixes its limits (1972: 224). This implies that one has to move beyond academic anthropology to understand its emergence and reproduction. *Anthropology and the Colonial Encounter* embodied that realization, through, among other things, a number of papers on administrative ethnographic practices (Lackner 1973; Clammer 1973; Owen 1973), and through Asad's argument that it was not the complicity of anthropologists with colonialism, but the location of anthropology in the colonial context, that was the crucial issue (1973: 18–19).

Anthropology as professionalized ethnography

A second assumption underlying this work holds that *in order to understand the historical relationship between anthropology and colonialism, it is better to regard academic anthropology as a specific instance of ethnographic practice than the other way around.* Although the recent studies of ethnography from a literary perspective have brought to light previously unacknowledged relations between text and (colonial) context (Clifford and Marcus 1986), these tend not to broaden their scope beyond the confines of the discipline (but see Fabian 1983; Pratt 1985). They usually rewrite anthropological history to suit their present demands (but see Fabian 1983; Pratt 1985). The call for experimentation with ethnography is in itself a new claim to academic authority, and a weak one at that, because the problems it identifies (power inequalities in ethnographic representation) are not solved by the solution it proposes (new representations – Fabian 1991: 193). 'Dialogic' experiments make much of a seemingly democratic encounter with the interlocutor, but tend to ignore, as Said puts it, that 'this kind of scrubbed, disinfected interlocutor is a laboratory creation with suppressed, and therefore falsified, connections to the urgent situation of crisis and conflict that brought him or her to attention in the first place' (1989a: 210). Moreover, these approaches tend to reify the ethnographic genre, and consequently, its exoticism and its 'subsumption' of theory (Thomas 1991a). Thus, the literary turn in anthropology can be interpreted as part of a 'process of domestication' of the crises of the 1970s in which the attempts to change power relationships are substituted by the reading of hegemonic texts (Stocking 1991b: 4).

However, if one resists the temptation to read from the text outwards – the 'reading-back' into history (cf. Boon 1989) in an attempt to understand history from the vantage point of the ethnographic text – and instead, reads the history of its production *into* the text through a contextual analysis of its production, the literary means of producing ethnography are important. Marie Louise Pratt has pointed out the continuities between academic ethnography and the 'manners and customs' genres that preceded it (1985). She argues that the ethnographic authority claimed in the academic sphere (Pratt 1986; see also Clifford 1983a; Rosaldo 1986) is continuous with its non-academic predecessors. Johannes

Fabian (1983) has come to similar conclusions, demonstrating the importance of the manipulation of temporal dimensions for the construction of the objects of anthropology, both theoretically and ethnographically. In particular, he argued that ethnography, by rhetorically denying the contact between anthropologists and informants (their 'coevalness'), has an in-built tendency to ignore its historical context – a conclusion confirmed by Pratt (1985: 121; see also Thomas 1991a, 1991b: 3). Most important for the present purpose is that he located the emergence of the ethnographic genre in the premodern shift from sacred to secular time and the transformation of the practice of *travel* (1983: 2–11).

In a series of studies crucial for understanding the history of anthropology, Justin Stagl (1974, 1980, 1990, 1995) has shown that from the sixteenth century onwards, a discourse on travel took shape in Europe. It drew upon earlier genres, directions for pilgrims in particular (1990: 317), but adapted these to changing conceptions of time and space. The 'incorporating' cosmology characteristic of crusade, pilgrimage and mission, which was essentially directed inwards at a centre (Rome, Jerusalem), gave way to a 'distancing' cosmology of exploration which started out from the now and here to discover the then and there (Fabian 1983: 27). It is impossible here to do justice to the full range of historical possibilities suggested by Stagl, but two elements of the history of anthropology are crucial for the present argument: the importance of the technology of writing, and the close link to European state-formation.

Stagl shows how the *ars apodemica*, the art of travel, transformed 'implicit cultural patterns of travelling' presented orally or in handwriting into a 'formally codified' manual disseminated in print to the reading public (1990: 319). Under the influence of the philosopher Petrus Ramus (1515–72) and his 'natural method' of the organization of all knowledge, the *ars apodemica* developed an encyclopedic manual of travel (1990: 303), a paradigm for later, more strictly anthropological manuals such as Degérando's *Considérations sur les méthodes à suivre dans l'observation des peuples sauvages* (1800; in Moore 1969) and the Royal Anthropological Institute's *Notes and Queries on Anthropology* (1874). As Fabian argues, the Ramist method of storing, reproducing and disseminating knowledge acquired, through the technology of printing, general acceptance of a conception of knowledge in visual terms, a 'diagrammatic reduction of the contents of thought' (1983: 116). These manuals were characteristic of a period in European history when knowledge of others was acquired 'on the road', during travel, and provided a classification of knowledge that made it transferable and exchangeable from one context to the other, just as commodities are made exchangeable on the market. Interestingly, Stagl remarks upon the fact that the manuals tended to enumerate the 'singular phenomena' to be observed, creating reports 'far removed from the original experience of the traveller' (1990: 322) – a 'denial of coevalness' which was carried over into ethnography (Fabian 1983). As shall be explained later, the term 'ethnography' emerged in the context of this organization of knowledge.

The *ars apodemica* was also intimately linked to processes of state-formation in early modern Europe. Each manual included descriptions of the main nations of Europe, indicating 'the close link between the *ars apodemica* cosmographies and the descriptions of polities' (Stagl 1990: 319). In the seventeenth century, the *ars apodemica* lost much of its former goal of improving the traveler's personality (institutionalized in the 'Grand Tour' of young European noblemen) and concentrated more exclusively on the gathering of knowledge – 'a transition to the methodology of expeditions' (1990: 324). This shift 'from the centre to the periphery' resulted in a number of specializations: the instructions for copying inscriptions and using libraries and collections developed into an auxiliary discipline of history; the collection and conservation of minerals, fossils, plants and animals became important for 'natural history', one of Linnaeus' students drawing up an *Instructio Peregrinatoris* (1759); and the questionnaires, basic to the art of travel from its beginning, were systematically applied by academicians like Robert Boyle to guide the collection and verification of knowledge by travellers (Stagl 1990: 324).

Specialization also resulted in the giving of very specific political instructions: the prince who financed a traveller often added a secret set of instructions, connected with the commercial and political aims of the voyage, to the official ones (Stagl 1990: 325). The relationship with the state is also evident from the resurgence, in Göttingen, of the by then largely obsolete *ars apodemica* in the second half of the eighteenth century, in a school which gained a European reputation under the leadership of August Ludwig Schlözer and Johann Christoph Gatterer (Stagl 1974: 73–91). The art of travel became associated with the discipline of *Statistik*, destined to educate capable servants of the state – a concept later appropriated by those who only wanted to gather quantitative knowledge (1980: 375). It is in this context that the concept of *Ethnographie* was first mentioned as early as 1771, even 1767 (Vermeulen 1992: 6, 1996: 11). In the 1780s it acquired common usage among German scholars (Stagl 1974: 79–80; see also Fischer 1970).

The *Oxford English Dictionary* puts the date of the first mention of the term 'ethnography' in the English language at 1834, in a source which states that 'the term ethnography (nation-description) is sometimes used by German writers in the sense which we have given to anthropography'.[9] According to the *Grand Robert*, the French term *ethnographie* was first used in 1819, when the Napoleonic wars, which prevented the further development of the expeditions and methodologies of Bougainville, Lapérouse and Dégerando, had come to an end (Stagl 1990: 326).[10] If we restrict ourselves to the use of the term in the English language, we see that according to the *Oxford English Dictionary*, the complex of terms (ethnography, ethnographic(al), ethnology) appears rather late, in the 1830s and early 1840s. Its meanings are negotiated until the terms are defined by the *Encyclopedia Brittanica* in 1878 as follows: 'Ethnography embraces the descriptive details, and ethnology the rational exposition of the human aggregates and organizations'.

In Britain, too, the words crop up in a context which ties 'ethnography' firmly to the practice of travel – expeditions in particular – and the taxonomic organization of knowledge derived from Ramism and summarized by the term 'natural history' (cf. Fabian 1983: 8; Foucault 1970: 125 ff.). A number of expeditions had already been sent into West Africa since the late eighteenth century but the initiative was lost and merged with the Royal Geographical Association in 1831 (Curtin 1964: 17, 151; Voget 1975: 105). Shortly afterwards, T.F. Buxton formed a House Committee for the Protection of the Aborigenes, for which a professor of anatomy, Thomas Hodgkin, acted as informal advisor. Hodgkin and his friend and colleague J.C. Prichard founded the Aborigenes Protection Society in 1837, to save indigenous peoples from possible extinction and study them at the same time. Meanwhile, Buxton had given the impetus towards the Niger Expedition, which combined the fight against the slave-trade, the promotion of African commerce and industry, and missionizing with observation and exploration (Curtin 1964: 298–303).

From this context of merged humanitarian, commercial and scientific concerns, the first ethnological association began to emerge. On the suggestion of Hodgkin, William Edwards founded the *Société Ethnologique* in Paris in 1838. A lecture by Prichard led the British Association for the Advancement of Science to commission three medical doctors (Hodgkin, Prichard, and Richard Owen) to draw up a questionnaire for the study of native races threatened by extinction, which they did on the basis of a model provided by Edwards (Curtin 1964: 330–2). This questionnaire became the basis of the 1874 *Notes and Queries* (Voget 1975: 105). In 1842, Prichard published his *Natural History of Man*, which he called an 'ethnographic outline', and in which he defined ethnology as 'the history of nations'. In 1843, Hodgkin and Prichard decided, for organizational reasons, to meet separately from the Aborigenes Protection Society as the Ethnological Society of London, which in 1871 became, after a troubled history of debates, separations and a merger between monogenists and polygenists, the Anthropological Institute (Curtin 1964: 331; Reining 1962; Stocking 1971, 1987).[11] The connection with the state is again evident from the fact that Prichard drew up the 'ethnology' section of the Admiralty's questionnaire in 1849 (Curtin 1964: 334).

During the second half of the nineteenth century, scientific racism and the debates between monogenists and polygenists had changed the intellectual orientation of ethnologists and anthropologists to such an extent that taxonomic 'history' was now replaced by a 'naturalization of time' in terms of evolution (Fabian 1983: 11ff.). It should be pointed out, however, that Victorian anthropology was still characterized by a method of gathering knowledge 'on the road', by the *travelers* that provided Tylor and Frazer, among others, with their data (Stocking 1987: 78–102). Ethnography continued to be understood as the collection of 'manners and customs', an activity for which the current questionnaires provided the model, even if the taxonomy of the questionnaire had now been transposed to an evolutionary taxonomy of 'stages' in the development of mankind. Still, ethnographic knowledge took the form of bits and pieces of knowledge that, by being classified in a questionnaire, could be transferred to another realm of thought.

This situation changed when imperial domination reached the stage where administrators, missionaries and others could start to 'settle in'. Two important aspects, however, should be noted in the context of this section. In the first place, the colonial situation may partly account for differences in the process of professionalization of ethnography. One ought to consider, for instance, the influence on Malinowski's 'invention' of modern fieldwork of the fact that he, because of the lack of cooperation from the missionary Savile and the suspicion of local authorities during World War I, was forced to rely much more on his own devices than was common at the time. The introduction to *Argonauts* can be read as a charter for a certain form of fieldwork – participant observation – which could be executed by the professional anthropologist on her or his own. With the Malinowskian 'revolution' in ethnography, the ethnographic questionnaire became obsolete. Not only did *Argonauts* successfully propagate a change in the ethnographic genre, it was also a culmination of a change in the conceptions of research – initiated, among other, by Haddon and Rivers. Research was now conceived of as a scientific methodology that, in contrast with the questionnaire, could not be easily mastered by laymen (see Pels 1991). Within Anglo-Saxon anthropology, questionnaires were gradually replaced by courses in methodology; the last edition of the *Notes and Queries* (1951), composed by professional British anthropologists, already had the format of an introduction to anthropology rather than a questionnaire. As is often the case in professionalizing strategies, the professionalization of ethnographic practice was achieved by the exclusion of other ethnographic methods and genres (like the questionnaire or the glossary), and of possible rival ethnographers like missionaries and administrators (Pels 1990; Thomas 1989: 69 ff.). Thus, ethnographic knowledge, constructed on the basis of an extended period of fieldwork by a trained anthropologist, constituted a claim to authority that enhanced the anthropologists' monopoly of this kind of knowledge. Fieldwork became the hegemonic form of ethnography for most anthropologists.

Yet, trajectories of professionalization were not always the same: in France, for instance, the influence of administrators like Delafosse, missionaries like Leenhardt and the development of Griaule's work from expeditionary to initiatory fieldwork suggest extra-academic sources for the French emphasis on a 'documentary' ethnography (Clifford 1982: 138–41, 1983b). Ethnographic questionnaires were common in France until well after World War II (e.g. Mauss 1967). To this day there is, comparatively speaking, more room in France for lay ethnographers in scientific journals and fora. Boas introduced a similar emphasis on the collection of documents by laymen – in his case, native American informants – to American anthropology, which was clearly related to his historical orientation brought from Germany (see Stocking 1974: 85–6), even though Boas' pupils later tended to embrace British-style fieldwork. European 'continental' traditions of scholarship – including those brought to the US – were largely overwhelmed by the British domination of ethnographic discourse.

Such an emphasis on ethnographic traditions may well counter the overemphasis on the present 'experimental moment' in anthropology (Marcus and Fischer 1986). It should not come as a surprise that some recent attempts at ethnographic experimentation take their cue from national traditions that resisted British hegemony in anthropology. James Clifford's essay on Marcel Griaule is revealing in this sense, because Griaule's example shows how anthropology could be characterized by a continuous process of experimentation with ethnographic forms (1983b). Moreover, Malinowski's *Argonauts* was clearly a literary experiment (Thornton 1985); other examples should include Evans-Pritchard's *The Nuer* and Bateson's *Naven* (cf. Kuper 1983: 74; Marcus 1985), Bateson and Mead's *Balinese Character* (1942: xi) or Condominas' ethnography of the Mnong Gar in diary form (1957). This does not exclude the existence of a hegemonic form of ethnographic authority; on the contrary, this hegemony may account for the fact that certain ethnographic experiments, such as Audrey Richards' *Chisungu* (1954) or Zora Neale Hurston's work (Gordon 1990) were largely ignored in established, academic anthropology.[12]

Thus, the reversal of priority from academic anthropology to ethnographic practice not only shows the relationship of anthropology to colonial situations more clearly, it also questions the common assumption that academic anthropology, and canonized fieldwork methodology in particular, is the *telos* to which all ethnography strives. The rest of the argument of this study, therefore, concentrates more exclusively on the way in which a study of the colonial context of ethnography frees it from academic prejudices.

Anthropological theory and colonial practice

A third assumption underlying this work is that *ethnographic holism, cultural relativism and functionalism are as much products of colonial practice as they are theoretical innovations of academic anthropology*. When colonial domination necessitated the 'settling in' by administrators and missionaries, the attitudes characteristic of ethnography 'on the road' (cf. Fabian 1983) changed and eventually led to the trajectories of professionalization sketched above. The relevance of ethnography for the development of both colonial society and academic anthropology during this stage of 'settling in' is brought out by the fact that the attitude of ethnographic holism developed from this situation. Moreover, recent studies suggest that there were local 'ethnographic traditions' in which the academic anthropologist participated on arrival in the field.

In this context, the historical validity of literary approaches again becomes evident. James Clifford has argued that all fieldworkers have worked on the assumption that social wholes can be understood and described by concentrating on certain significant elements of society: key institutions like the Kula, Azande witchcraft, or initiation, or methodological constructs like genealogy or social structure. Such synecdoches are necessary for the representation of 'relatively short-term professional fieldwork' (Clifford 1983b: 129–30); without the idea that a specific part of society can stand for the whole, fieldwork would be questionable because 'social wholes cannot be directly perceived by a single human observer' (Thornton 1988: 288). Clifford argues that this emphasis on social wholes is a reflection of a nihilistic world in which, from Yeats to Achebe, 'things fall apart' (1983b: 130).

However, there is reason to suppose that ethnographic holism was not merely fostered by the European's yearning for an integrated society, but by the practical demands of the colonial situation. In the next chapter, the work by Father Jean Guerlach will illustrate how French missionaries in pre-colonial Indochina, early on professed a proto-holism in their ethnographic writing. Forced by a precarious existence among the Bahnar 'savages' to accommodate to their way of life, a situation reminiscent of fieldwork, Father Jean Guerlach realized as early as 1887 that the different spheres of life were intimately tied together. This ethnographic holism *avant la lettre* was not formalized in a theoretical statement on the organization of society, perhaps because his goal was religious conversion, and understanding religious beliefs was a means to that end. For this practical reason, his description focused on religion, and on the role of the sorcerers in particular, who were seen as the main obstacles to conversion. But Guerlach did not take religion as a synecdoche for understanding the whole of Bahnar society. Some of his successors, however, with more theoretical feedback and in a changed colonial situation, tended to use 'religion' as the key to all social affairs. The synecdoche 'religion' was common to many missionaries, especially in the latter half of this century, but in some cases missionary practice tended towards a less holist, 'selective' ethnography (Pels 1994).

In *Victorian Anthropology*, George Stocking pointed out that the ethnographies by early missionaries and administrators foreshadowed 'a more intensive ethnographic style whose data would in fact sustain a more holistic interpretation' (1987: 104). The synecdoche that was most probably dominant in understanding social wholes in the political field was what Europeans perceived as 'customary law'. From 1843 onwards, Dutch curricula for colonial administrators for the Netherlands East Indies in Delft and Leiden taught – besides the ethnography, languages and literature of Indonesian peoples – *adatrecht* or customary law; a body of theory which in the early twentieth century was synthesized by the Leiden scholar C. van Vollenhoven (Kloos 1989: 41–2). In Africa, the development of Indirect Rule shows that Frederick Lugard, whose primary worries were the conquest and control of Northern Nigeria, did not formulate a theory of local political institutions. When instituting Indirect Rule after 1898, he was mainly interested in delegating his own authority to the Fulani chiefs, not in incorporating theirs (Pels 1996). His former Chief Secretary, Donald Cameron, held a different view when he was Governor of Nigeria in 1934:

> [Indirect Administration], based on several principles, is designed to adapt for the purposes of local government the *tribal institutions* which the native peoples have evolved for themselves, so that the latter may develop in a *constitutional* manner from their own past, guided and restrained by the sanctions and traditions which they have inherited...
>
> (Cameron, in Kirk-Greene 1965: 193; our emphases)

This conception of Indirect Rule was developed during Cameron's tour in Tanganyika, where he promoted rule through 'hereditary tribal chiefs'. 'Tribal institutions' were the customs of a tribe, and the customs of a tribe were the laws of hereditary succession. Thus, Cameron and his officers could shift conceptually from 'institution' to 'constitution', a practice reflecting the legalist interests of administration. For administrative ethnography in Tanganyika between 1925 and 1931, research implied looking for customary laws (Pels 1993: 34–40, 1996). The customary law of hereditary succession was, for Cameron, needed to guarantee controlled political evolution in Tanganyika; if the African was not kept in touch with his own customary ways, he would become a 'detribalized', 'leaderless and uncontrolled', in short, a 'bad imitation' of the European.

It is important to realize that the ethnographic holism of colonial discourse – whether of a legalist or any other kind – is often characterized by both proto-relativism and proto-functionalism, even if it sometimes was a 'functionalism of the abhorrent' (Stocking 1987: 104). By 'proto' is meant that such notions already existed in an embryonic, often implicit form. Ethnographic holism was proto-relativist, in the sense that it called for a recognition of 'the values set up by every society to guide its own life' (cf. Herskovits 1973: 76–7), even though it did not, as in Cameron's case, deny a complementary idea of political evolution. It was proto-functionalist to the extent that it premised the good functioning of social wholes under colonial rule on the integrity of a collective system of embodied legal strictures, often caught in the term 'tribe' (or, in India, 'caste'; Dirks 1992). This point was, indeed, made by Malinowski, when he said that Lugard's Indirect Rule (at a time when the latter had moved more closely to Cameron's perspectives) was 'a complete Surrender to the Functional Point of View' (quoted in Cell 1989: 483). The so-called 'legalist' character of functionalist anthropology, as noted by David Goddard (1972), and the influence of the Sudan Administration's legalist perspective on Evans-Pritchard's *The Nuer*, traced by Douglas Johnson (1982), suggest that there were even tighter relationships between colonial ethnographies and academic anthropology than just the general necessity of a holistic perspective. In Chapter 3 I shall show how this proto-relativism and proto-functionalism was brought out well in the career of the French ethnographer Léopold Sabatier, from 1913 till 1926 administrator of Darlac province in Vietnam. His example will show that administrative ethnography could create fertile ground for the relativist and functionalist theories of academic discourse.

This homology of colonial and academic discursive patterns is reinforced by the fact that an increasing number of studies show that there were local ethnographic traditions into which academic anthropologists fitted quite easily after arrival in the field. Fardon and others have pointed out that the 'literary turn' in anthropology adopts an idea of ethnography as an encounter between a fieldworker and the 'Other', and thereby ignores that most anthropologists work within 'conventionalized regions of enquiry' and that 'ethnographies are also reworked versions, inversions and revisions of previous accounts' (Fardon 1990: 22, 25). Yet, in the same volume David Parkin tries to account for a specific 'East African' ethnography by focusing on academic institutions only, and in particular on the division of labor between the East African Institute of Social Research headed by Audrey Richards and the Rhodes-Livingstone Institute under Wilson, Gluckman and others (Parkin 1990: 187–90). He ignores the fact that the title of Richards' collection on *East African Chiefs* (1959) cannot easily be understood without taking account of the history of Indirect Rule in Eastern Africa, with its predominant emphasis on 'chiefs' ruling 'tribes'. Work in Uganda and Tanzania was very much determined by ethnographic insights shared by administrators and anthropologists and embodied by people like Philip Gulliver, John Beattie and Henry Fosbrooke, who became academic anthropologists after having served in the Tanganyikan administration. Fardon, too, seems to dismiss missionaries, administrators and explorers from the history of local ethnographic strategies (1990: 3).

In other words, even when a history of ethnographic traditions is considered, it tends to ignore what Georges Condominas – speaking from experience – called the *préterrain*, the local colonial milieu from which the academic ethnographer departed and to which he returned in times of 'surfeit of native', as Malinowski called it (Malinowski 1922: 6; Condominas 1973: 9–10). The *préterrain* influenced many an academic's ethnography. Raymond Firth pointed out that the 'informal, often covert, constraints' of colonial society on anthropology were, paradoxically, 'largely a function of the positive assistance that the anthropologist receives'.

> To hold that cooperation and constraint may go hand in hand cannot be novel … to anthropologists familiar with the theory of reciprocity. When an anthropologist has had help in the field from a local administrator, an agricultural officer, a storekeeper, a plantation manager, a missionary, who has not only lent him equipment and given him hospitality but also discussed with him pressing problems frankly, with a mixture of hope and despair, the anthropologist may feel constrained to reply in kind. … [T]hough the anthropologists tends not to share some of his host's major assumptions about the colonial situation, he is often led to examine these assumptions more carefully than otherwise he would.
>
> (Firth 1977: 146–7)

Acknowledging the often subconscious influence of the colonial *préterrain* is more important for the study of anthropology's relation to colonial society than accusations of collaboration or complicity on the part of the anthropologist. Firth exaggerates the extent to which anthropologists could 'examine' colonial assumptions, but brings out well that their contact with colonizers necessarily led to the sharing of discursive patterns. From this perspective it is significant that the subjects and viewpoints of Evans-Pritchard or the Rhodes-Livingstone scholars were often taken from their respective colonial administrations, as were the classifications of tribes and states in Northern Nigeria of present-day scholars (Sharpe 1986), the images of Bali of Bateson and Mead (Schulte Nordholt 1994), and academic views of the lineage systems of the Uluguru mountains in Tanganyika (Pels 1993: 40). The missionary Thomas Cullen Young's support for the Reverend Yesaya Chibambo's history of the Ngoni of Nyasaland, who in turn exerted, as expert guide, a major influence on the research by the anthropologist Margaret Read, suggests the importance of the missionary *préterrain* for academic ethnography (Forster 1991; 1994). It shows the crucial influence of the mission school's spread of literacy, a practice which not only produced many an anthropologist's fieldwork assistant, but also taught Africans to represent themselves in ethnographic form (as was noted early by Balandier, 1962: 91). It can also be argued, however, that the missionary *préterrain* was sometimes less conducive for academic and administrative ethnographic concerns (Pels 1994).

Ethnographic production and consumption is materially mediated

A fourth assumption underlying this study holds *that a historical study of the production and consumption of ethnography necessarily implies an analysis of the ways in which these were materially mediated.* It has been remarked above that ethnography obscures the historical mediations on which its production is based: the contact or 'coevalness' of ethnographer and informants (Fabian 1983; Pratt 1985; Thomas 1991b: 3). This situation is reflected in the way in which the concept of 'ethnography' frequently subsumes fieldwork practice, and is often equated with 'participant observation'. From Tylor to Malinowski, ethnography was taken to be a 'classificatory science' (Tylor 1993 [1871], I: 7; Malinowski 1922: 25). Therefore, if 'ethnography' is taken literally – as the classification in writing of 'cultures', 'races' or 'nations' – one should be careful to distinguish it from fieldwork as research practice (cf. Thomas 1991a: note 3). Malinowski distinguished 'ethnographic fieldwork' from other forms of research such as 'archaeological' or 'zoological (1922: 24). Nowadays, however, ethnography is often called a 'method', which includes dealing with problems of access to the field, field relations and interviewing techniques (e.g. Hammersley and Atkinson 1983: ix and *passim*), activities which are not specific to ethnography. Terms like 'ethnographic collections' or 'ethnographic observation' obscure that neither collecting artifacts nor observing acts necessarily lead to the classification of an *ethnos*. Conversely, the common use of the pleonasm 'ethnographic writing' (e.g. by Clifford, 1986: 14, Pratt, 1986: 35) raises the question: what else ethnography can be but writing (cf. Fabian 1990: 757). There is a peculiar see-saw historical movement here: whereas Malinowski tried to subsume ethnography to the professional's claim to intensive fieldwork as a scientific method, now fieldwork seems to be subsumed under the practice of writing culture. If one wishes to understand the processes of production and consumption of ethnography, this subsumption needs to be resisted.

Put in another way: it is necessary to shift attention from the nature of ethnographic representations to the work of representing (cf. Fabian 1990). Recent studies of ethnography still partake of a discourse of representation that moves within the boundaries of the 'truth' and 'falsity' of its representations and the way they reflect reality: Marcus and Fischer aim at a more 'accurate view and confident knowledge of the world' (1986: 14–15), and James Clifford at 'partial', 'dialogical' truths which represent 'negotiated realities' (Clifford 1986: 15). These 'aesthetic responses' to a situation of imperial contest that can, according to Said, better be classified as 'anesthetics' (1989: 211), because they tend to ignore the historical transformations of knowledge that were necessary to create the impression that others' realities *can be* represented by ethnography (cf. Fabian 1983, 1990). In other words, the content of an ethnographic text needs to be understood through an analysis of the historical context of its production: the fieldwork process, which is itself a symptom of the accessibility of others created by European colonialism.

However, before assuming that the content of the ethnographic text is an example of intellectual colonization of 'others', one first has to analyse the ways in which it was consumed by different audiences, both within and outside the colonial situation. This argument is not meant to deny the importance of the kind of analysis pioneered by Said (1978), but to argue for an elaboration of it. Said insisted on the blurring of the distinction between pure and political knowledge (1978: 9; 15–16), which is a methodological precondition of this study. Said is concerned with demonstrating that Orientalism's representations can be analysed '*as representations*, not as "natural" depictions of the Orient' (1978: 21). But here an intermediary instance can be added, namely the fact that any representation of 'others' is a historical depiction. Neither its 'naturalness' – that is, its pretense to reflect 'the Orient as such' – nor its character as representation – which excludes 'any such real thing as "the Orient"' (1978: 21) – sufficiently characterize the historical processes in which these representations were put to use. Said's claim that anthropology and empire were never separated (cf. Said 1989a: 214), connects them too crudely by not operationalizing 'anthropology' in terms of ethnographies and 'empire' in terms of local colonial situations – which may be understood as including neocolonialism and internal colonialism.

Although Said is at pains to relate discursive patterns back to the imperial contest from which they derive (1989a: 211), the approach toward representations of the colonized through textual analysis only, often fails to capture the historical mediations through which these representations were produced. A number of recent studies, for example, seem to be based on the assumption that the study of hegemonic imagery is identical to the study of the production of hegemony (cf. Rabinow 1986; Mitchell 1988, Mudimbe 1988). Studies of the colonial 'invention of tradition' seem to take the 'ideological' function of invented traditions for granted (cf. Ranger 1983: 229, 236). They fail to ask whether and how, if 'invention' only means 'made up by the colonizer', the colonized shared this invention; or conversely, when the 'tradition' was an invention co-authored by colonizers and colonized, for whom it was an invention (a new idea) and for whom a tradition (an existing practice), and again, why it was adopted (Thomas 1992: 213). The notion of the 'microphysics' of colonial power (Pels 1999; cf. Foucault 1979a: 26) is necessary to adequately capture the material mediations through which representations of others were made to mold or modify colonial relationships.

Two examples from the construction of colonial power through ethnography will show how a microphysics of power mediated the impact of ethnography: the influence of writing (as technology); and second, the importance of the construction of ethnographic occasions. Writing as technology mediates writing as text. It has already been argued that writing, and printing in particular, necessitated a visual conception of knowledge. This 'diagrammatic reduction of the contents of thought' (Fabian 1983: 116) contributed to the creation of the tabulated lists of the traveller's manuals and the absence of the observer from the information stored. The argument can be generalized beyond the historical impact of printing technology, to writing as such. Information gathered in writing divorces content from its context of utterance and therefore emphasizes the referential aspect of language and ignores the performative (proxemic, kinesic and gestural) aspects (Washabaugh 1979: 32). This could have the result, for example, that a Tanganyikan administrator, in his urge to find out who was the 'true' representative of a local group in terms of hereditary right to office, ignored the fact that Waluguru rarely contradict a superior in his presence and that they often show their disagreement by staying away or not answering. By limiting his questions to the truth and falsity of claims to office (the referential aspect), the administrator could hardly be expected to find out that there were no chiefs at all before the government appointed them. In colonial Tanganyika, this led to the replacement of transitory 'big man' positions by rigid bureaucratic hierarchies (Pels 1994, 1996, 1999). Similar processes accompanied the codification of 'customary law' and suggest parallels with, for instance, the *adatrecht* studies in the Netherlands East Indies (Schulte Nordholt 1994) and the *droit coutumier* in the Central Highlands of colonial Indochina (see Chapters 3 and 5).

Another important material mediation of ethnography was the (gendered) construction of the ethnographic occasion. Johannes Fabian (personal communication) has suggested that some of the best colonial ethnography was produced 'on the pillow', between European travelers and their native concubines. But the issue of male–female relationships and gender constructions in colonial ethnography is far broader than this. The *baraza* (council meeting) of the administrator in colonial Tanganyika, normally used as the occasion on which he outlined his desires and directives to the Native Authorities appointed by government, was also used as an instrument for gathering ethnographic knowledge. The *baraza* consisted of those native leaders already appointed, ignoring the big men who lacked a government position, but more importantly, the leading women who wielded a considerable amount of power within traditional society (Pels 1993: 52–3, 145–7). As similar processes have taken place in Sri Lanka (Risseeuw 1988), we may suggest that this misconstruing of – especially matrilineal – discourses on gender and politics was widespread under colonial rule. Administrators are hardly expected to reflect consciously on the construction of these ethnographic occasions, thus creating 'ethnographic evidence' that women were politically insignificant. Many academic ethnographers, however, can be said to suffer from a similar blind spot. In her seminal re-study of the Trobrianders, Annette Weiner (1976) critiqued Malinowski not for his sexist fantasies as posthumously published in his diary, but for his incapacity to describe women's role in important ritual exchanges. Such distortions of local political process were not simply the result of consciously held sexist beliefs, but of the material practices – the ethnographic occasions – in which these ideas were embodied. In Chapter 5, I shall argue how war as a gendered ethnographic occasion not only produced biased ethnographies that excluded women, but indeed proved to be fertile ground for a process of gender transformation.

In fact, it is important to realize that the two material mediations – writing and the construction of ethnographic occasions – often worked to reinforce one another. Bureaucracy is predicated upon the transmission of knowledge in writing. In the colonial situation, this often resulted in the uncritical reproduction of knowledge available in writing by subsequent administrators. This lent an inordinate weight to the original ethnographic occasion in which the knowledge thus passed on had been formulated (for an example from Balinese administration, see Schulte Nordholt 1994). Needless to say, the validity of the synecdoche of 'customary law' was, in that context, never questioned.

The act of representing is as relevant as its 'truth'

A fifth hypothesis for this study is that *ethnography was mostly relevant for colonial society, not in terms of the truth or falsity of its representations, but because it instituted representation as such* (both in the literary and political sense). A common assumption of discourses on ethnography is that better knowledge of others leads to more legitimate control over them, an argument common to those who discussed the relevance of anthropology for colonial government (cf. Fortes and Evans-Pritchard 1940, Leroi-Gourhan and Poirier 1953, Malinowski 1929), or – in the present day and age – for development interventions. This can be contrasted with the view that representations of others produced from a position of power are inevitably ideological inventions of tradition (Ranger 1983). The two positions show opposed attitudes towards the relationship between power and knowledge: the first argues that true knowledge of others' routines may ensure their participation in the colonial process on their own terms and thus lead to a decrease of power inequalities; the second, that visions of others constructed from a position of power are inevitably false and thus ensure the continuation of power inequalities.

But the focus on the truth and falsity of colonial representations obscures the importance of the institution of political representation as such, and this institution of political representation in former colonies was often achieved through ethnography. As argued in the previous section, the material mediations of the process of representation were often more important than the contents of the representations themselves. It is worthwhile to refer to Marie Louise Pratt's view that 'ethnographic texts are means by which Europeans represent to themselves their (usually subjugated) others' (Pratt 1992: 7). The catch lies in the clause 'usually subjugated', because Pratt also shows that there are 'auto-ethnographies': 'instances in which colonized subjects undertake to represent themselves in ways that *engage with* the colonizer's own terms' (Pratt 1992: 7). While 'auto-ethnography' implies a kind of self-determination through representation, it also presupposes a major degree of adaptation to the practices of colonial power.

In this context, it is crucial to acknowledge the administrative and military interest in the management of territory. In 1741, the *Vereenigde Oost-Indische Compagnie* (VOC: United East Indian Company) Representative in the East Indies and Governor of Batavia, Gustaaf van Imhoff, had already underlined the importance of local knowledge in a letter to the VOC Board in Amsterdam:

> ... servants of the Company upon arrival in the Indies should be committed to learn native languages and customs, and ... excellence in this respect should play an important role in their careers.
>
> (Kloos 1989: 41)

After the dissolution of the VOC in 1798 and the British 'interregnum' in Indonesia during the Napoleonic Wars, the new Dutch colonial administration of Java initiated in 1818, a course in Javanese language and ethnography at the Military Academy in Semarang. In 1843 this 'Indology' curriculum was transferred to Delft, and later on (1904) to the University of Leiden (with a second, privately-funded program opening at the State University of Utrecht in 1925) to form the core of the training for the Dutch colonial civil service in the Orient. This established academic ethnology and customary law studies in Holland, where the disciplines of anthropology and 'sociology of non-Western societies' directly trace their origins to the 'Indology' program (Kloos 1989).

The importance of ethnographic mapping in military rule and administrative control is exemplified by the classical statement by Colonel (later Marshall) Galliéni about the connection between military control and an explicit ethnic policy:

> It is the study of the races that inhabit a region which determines the political organization to be imposed and the means to be employed for its pacification. An officer who succeeds in drawing a sufficiently exact, ethnographic map of the territory he commands, has almost reached its complete pacification, soon followed by the organization which suits him best. ... Every agglomeration of individuals – a race, a people, a tribe or a family – represents a sum of shared or opposed interests. If there are habits and customs to respect, there are also rivalries which we have to untangle and utilize to our profit, by opposing the ones to the others, and by basing ourselves on the ones in order to defeat the others.
>
> (Galliéni 1941: 217; see Chapter 2)

This shows that one of the initial moves in colonial discourse is the ethnographic one: the fixing of an ethnic identity to a specific territory – called the 'geographical disposition' of ethnography by Edward Said (1989a: 218).

Definitions of ethnic identities and their corresponding territories have been carried over from the colonial situation in which they were formulated into academic spheres (Pinney 1990; Sharpe 1986). The emphasis on territory of functionalist anthropologists (Fortes and Evans-Pritchard 1940: 6, 10) may well be related to discourses informed by administrative interests. In any case, it is clear that management of spatial categories was an important tactic of colonial discourse (Noyes 1994; Byrnes 1994).

This may be seen in terms of what Condominas called *tribalization* (1966: 168): a process by which fluid entities, with no fixed boundaries distinguishing them, became ethnic groups. The French colonial administration created 'tribes' on the basis of an 'ethno-linguistic' classification, despite the common opinion in early ethnographic sources that hardly any supra-village organizations existed in the Vietnamese Central Highlands at the time of French 'penetration' (see Chapters 3, 4 and 5). This process of tribalization has also been documented for colonial Tanganyika (Iliffe 1979: 318–41). Nowadays, the 'tribes' are not just ethnic minorities in a nation-state, but take colonial classifications for granted in their own political organizations and in their own 'ethno-histories'; they adopt the discursive language of the state in order to make themselves heard.

Such uses of ethnographic classifications show the extent to which they were limiting devices in a double sense. Contrary to what those who defended the application of anthropology in the colonies expected, ethnographic classifications functioned initially as a way to immobilize groups of people by drawing boundaries around 'their territory' – a process against which some groups like the Nuer rebelled (Johnson 1979). Moreover, it has already been shown that the selection of a 'chief' in colonial Tanganyika under Donald Cameron depended on a theory about 'tribes' which declared the chief to be the 'representative' of 'his' people. Pels describes how in colonial Tanganyika, the ethnographic occasions on which this kind of knowledge was gathered, reduced the normally fairly democratic meetings of big men and women to rituals of bureaucratic command in which only the administrator and so-called 'representative' chiefs, subchiefs and headmen, appointed by the British, took part. Thus, the primary effect of ethnographic representation was to immobilize the Waluguru people and reduce their participation in colonial politics (Pels 1994). In Chapter 2 I shall describe a similar *Politique des chefs* for the Central Highlands by which French colonial officers tried to incorporate Highland villages into their colonial order by creating a Montagnard village leadership accountable to the French rule.

Several other staple concepts of ethnography show this interest in control through representation. The ubiquity of the synecdoche of 'customary law' and the way in which it reflected the legalist interests of administration has already been noted. Jan Breman (1987) and Jeremy Kemp (1987) have argued that the notion of the village community was an administrative construction of colonial rule in Asia. The 1970s debates on rural ('moral' or 'rational') economy and peasant revolt involving the theories of James Scott and Samuel Popkin had their roots in political practices for which the concept of 'village' was also crucial (Scott 1976; Popkin 1979; Salemink 1998, n.p.). Feminist anthropology, in particular, has shown how problematic these holistic notions are by arguing that every group or collectivity is split in at least two genders, with differing interests. Ethnographic holism is not only to be criticized on rhetorical and methodological grounds (Thornton 1988), but also politically.

Therefore, auto-ethnographic expressions can be problematic insofar as they claim ethnographic authority by excluding other voices. Tempting as it may seem to view auto-ethnographic expressions as approaching the ideal of a truly 'democratic' representation, the fact that it is an ethnographic representation makes it as politically problematic as the 'dialogic' ethnography championed by anthropologists of the literary turn. 'Auto-ethnographers' have tended to objectify the self in terms borrowed from colonial ethnographic imagination, reinventing tradition or exoticizing their culture on the way. Allan Hanson (1989) and Toon van Meijl (1990) claim that auto-ethnographic practices by Maori anthropologists tend to convey the view and express the interests of local elites, just as the Reverend Yesaya Chibambo's history of the Ngoni legitimated the rule of the Ngoni over other ethnic groups in Nyasaland by arguing that theirs was a form of 'Indirect Rule' akin to that of the British colonizers (Forster 1991). In the chapters that follow I shall show how in the Central Highlands, Montagnard auto-ethnographies have been subjected to either (neo)colonial or nationalist narratives in an effort to claim ethnographic authority for political causes that were not just ulterior to their lives, but that effectively excluded and marginalized them. On the other hand, in a situation where Central Highlanders have been increasingly incorporated into the purview of the state, their representation has progressively come to influence their daily lives. It is important that their voices – in the plural – be heard even if this implies an adoption of a discursive language that may have been alien not so long ago; if they do not represent themselves, others will.

Who needs ethnography?

In colonial and neocolonial situations, ethnography is both a product *of* and a product *for* colonial rule, mediating between colonialism and anthropology. For a historian of anthropology an inductive and historicizing approach is needed, guided by the question 'Who needs ethnography?' because ethnography is located in widely diverging patterns of interest. In the previous sections, ethnography was largely located in the administrator's desire to produce static, localized ethnic identities and to identify the central institutions or persons (like 'chiefs') on which to apply the State's measures. This seems plausible, because of the long-standing historical link of ethnographic practice with state-formation. This link emerged in a process of transformation of travel, a shift from the incorporating cosmologies of crusade, pilgrimage and mission to the outgoing orientations of explorers and *Statistiker*. Therefore, missionary ethnography takes up a different position, because mission is a different kind of travel: a practice of incorporation of 'pagans' into the church. Before falling back upon anthropological stereotypes of missionaries who only come to 'teach' (while anthropologists come to 'learn'), the different tensions within missionary ethnography should be studied (see Chapter 2).

But not all colonizers were equally interested in ethnography. Ethnography seemed to belong more to the political and religious or intellectual sectors of (neo)colonial society: missionary, administrator and anthropologist engaged in it while settlers did not produce much of the kind. One may ask the question why strictly economic enterprise was not fertile ground for ethnography while politics and religion were. In many colonial situations there were considerable tensions between missionaries, settlers and administrators. Usually, settlers were not interested – or better: had no interest – in producing images of collective otherness. The dispute between Donald Cameron's administration and the settler-dominated polity of Kenya showed the lack of interest in tribal identities on the part of the settlers – after all, labor power does not come in tribal groups. Likewise, it is irrational for colonial settlers who appropriate lands that was already used or claimed by others to create a record of such populations and – hence – claims to those lands (Wolfe 1994). For the Central Highlands this conflict between an economic interest in the agricultural potential of the land and a political interest in its population was played out as a rivalry between evolutionist and cultural relativist representations of Montagnards (see Chapters 3 and 5).

Nowadays, similar non-debates take place over the issue of logging and the disruption of indigenous groups in Amazonia and Southeast Asia, with conservationists extolling the environmental wisdom of traditional cultures, and loggers and states blaming the 'backward' shifting cultivators for destroying the forests. It is obvious that the first group would be inclined to engage in ethnography, and the latter group not, for the simple reason that the sheer fact of ethnography is contrary to the interests represented by loggers. In recent times, we can see how classical ethnographic descriptions are integrated in the 'tourist gaze'.[13] They serve as base material for new travelogues, and, more banal, for the promises of 'exotic cultures', dotting the tourist guides that promote visits to 'exotic cultures' and promise 'participant observation' in 'traditional' ceremonies in 'unspoilt' locations (see Volkman 1990). While ethnographic images are appropriated by the tourist industry, (auto-)ethnographic descriptions play a role in the resistance of minorities to state power, whether they be native North or Latin Americans, Kikuyu or Luo against the Kenyan state, or 'tribals' in India.

For the historian of anthropology who attempts to go beyond a history of anthropological 'big men' and wishes to link the politics of ethnographic representation with historical developments in a particular area, the question 'Who needs ethnography?' is a central leitmotif for historical analysis. As implied above, it makes a difference whether the ethnographer is a man or a woman (actually there were only few women ethnographers in the Central Highlands), a settler, a missionary, a military officer, an administrator, or a professional ethnologist-anthropologist – to name just a few categories. The colonial *préterrains* and the ethnographic occasions for these categories of ethnographers tended to differ because they represented divergent interests, even though these interests themselves changed along with the historical context. They would engage in ethnography for different reasons, and constructed – or inserted themselves into – different ethnographic traditions (for an elaboration of this argument, see Pels and Salemink 1999).

The question 'who needs ethnography?' can be subdivided in additional questions like 'who engages in ethnography?'; 'what is the purpose of the ethnography?'; 'what is the intended audience of the ethnography?'; 'what is the actual audience of the ethnography?'; and 'what is the institutional context of ethnographic practice?' Even when absolute answers may be elusive, such questions help clarify both the context and the effects of ethnographic discourse. The substance and focus of ethnographic endeavors changed over time, according to the primary interests of the ethnographers. It is not coincidental that missionaries were often interested in religious phenomena (often branded 'superstition'); that military explorers were mostly interested in identifying political leadership; that many administrators produced tribal customary law codes. It is not by accident that tribal/ethnic classifications changed over time, and that indigenous populations increasingly adopted the labels that had been imposed on them, thereby hardening ethnic boundaries. It fits the usual pattern that male ethnographers were interested in matrilineal societies, often dubbed 'matriarchal' and hence considered primitive, and wrote about starting a process of 'male emancipation' through the imposition of colonial rule, resulting in the disenfranchisement and marginalization of women in indigenous society and changing gender identities. Also the institutional context of ethnographic practice changed over time, creating different publication channels and support systems for ethnographic endeavors. Processes of institutionalization and professionalization of ethnographic practice would be attended by attempts to either make 'amateur' ethnographies conform to more professional formats, or alternatively to co-opt professional anthropologists for practical purposes.

This does not mean that ethnography can simply be reduced to a function of the ethnographer's background and social position. The writing of ethnography is a creative process, and as such a highly individual achievement. Moreover, ethnography is the outcome of an interaction between the ethnographer with representatives of the *ethnos* to be described. Ethnographies were intended to reach different audiences, but did not always accomplish their purpose; some were ignored or forgotten. On the other hand, some ethnographies reached a wider, more diverse audience than expected, and became ethnographic canons that were seized upon by later generations of ethnographers, policy makers and ethnic communities. Yet, there are patterns to discover, not just in the production of ethnography, but also in its consumption: its reception and its uses. A positive reception among the intended audience forms the reward and may be an incentive for the (continued) production of ethnography. The reception of the work by Léopold Sabatier, described in detail in Chapters 4 and 6, is a case in point. His work was initially applauded, then brushed aside as irrelevant when it did not fit the policy priorities of the times. In the late 1930s, in changed historical circumstances, his work was 'rediscovered' and held up as a model for ethnographic research and administrative practice alike. In other words, the 'career' of his highly individual ethnographic oeuvre can be analysed sociologically and historically.

In recent decades the intended audience of professional anthropological ethnographies may have become peers and colleagues within the discipline, rather than a wider community of professional and amateur ethnographers, administrators, missionaries, military officers, journalists, etc. One result of this process of professionalization of the anthropological discipline is a disjunction between the criteria for individual careers and those for the appreciation of the discipline as such in the wider scientific community and society. This may partly explain why many ethnographic insights acquired through a long exposure to indigenous society have made so made so little impact on the ethnographic imagination about Central Highlanders. More specifically, professional anthropology has made very few inroads into a number of commonly held views of Montagnard society that have guided colonial, neocolonial, internal colonial and post-colonial policies to date. Such ethnographic assumptions have proven to be extremely resilient and hard to debunk, and continue to dominate the public debate. Such assumptions, whatever the contents, are a necessary element of any policy, any assessment, any analysis, any statement *vis-à-vis* Central Highlanders, including mine. In the following section I shall describe some of these commonly held assumptions, and set my own ethnographic assumptions against that backdrop.

Ethnographic assumptions

This attempt at ethnographic contextualization cannot do without some minimal geographic, ethnographic and historical description of the Central Highlands. That region is an upland area located between the 17th Parallel to the North, the Annam Cordillera (Chaîne Annamitique, Truòng Son) running along the South China Sea to the East, the Mekong Delta to the South and the Valley of the Mekong River to the West. The area is characterized by rugged mountainous terrain crossed by deep river valleys, and a number of fertile high plateaux made up of red basaltic soils, which include the Plateaux of Kontum and Pleiku; the Plateau of Darlac/Dak Lak; and the Plateaux of Djiring and Blao (or Di Linh and Bao Lôc). The Annam Cordillera rises up steeply from the coastal strip of Trung Bô, Annam, or Central Vietnam, with peaks of up to 2598 meters. To the West the topography becomes more undulating, gradually sloping down to the Mekong Valley. Most of the area drains waters into the Mekong River, major exceptions being the Song Ba and the Đông Nai rivers and tributaries which empty themselves into the South China Sea.

This area is divided by the national borders separating Vietnam, Laos and Cambodia. Those lowland states have their roots in civilizations based on wet rice agriculture, characteristic of tropical monsoon Asia, with most of the annual rain falling between April and November. George Coedès (1948) has made a distinction between the 'Indianized' civilizations of Cambodia and Laos, which have adopted *Theravada* Buddhism and have been influenced by Indian cultural, religious and political notions, and the 'Sinicized' Vietnamese civilization with strong Chinese influences expressed in Mahayana Buddhism, Confucianism and Daoism, and in political, cultural and aesthetic preferences. The cradle of the Vietnamese state and civilization was located in the Red River Delta, but after gaining independence from China in AD 938, the 'new' Vietnamese state gradually expanded its territory to the South (*Nam Tiến*), absorbing another 'Indianized' state located on the coast of what is now Trung Bô, Champa, and a part of the Khmer kingdom, the Mekong Delta. Surrounded by 'Indianized' and 'Sinicized' states on all sides, many authors insist that the Central Highlands constitute one 'culture area' which has kept outside cultural influences at bay for a long time – hence my use of the term 'indigenous population'. In this study I focus on the upland area within present-day Vietnamese territory, even though the borders between Vietnam, Laos and Cambodia are of relatively recent making, and were until recently not undisputed.

The Central Highlands region has undergone some name changes in recent history. In pre-colonial times, the area was known in the Vietnamese Lowlands as *Rung Moi* (or the Forests of the Savages). In early colonial times when the area had not yet been explored, French documents referred to the *Hinterland Moï*, then later *Pays Moï*, or simply the *Hauts-Plateaux*. During World War II, the label *Montagnard* became fashionable to denote the indigenous population, and the French delineated a '*Pays Montagnard du Sud-Indochinois*' (PMSI) which was meant to counter Vietnamese nationalist claims to the area as part of a sovereign Vietnam – and a name that remained popular among a number of indigenous leaders. During the brief (but perhaps too long for a war: 1955–75) existence of the Republic of Viet Nam (South Vietnam, below the 17th Parallel), the area was known in Vietnamese as *Cao Nguyên* (High Plateau), while Americans referred to it as Central Highlands. After 1975, the area was rebaptized *Tây Nguyên*, or 'Western Highlands'. Currently, *Tây Nguyên* officially consists of the four provinces of Kontum, Gia Lai (Pleiku), Dak Lak (Buon Ma Thuot) and Lam Dong (Da Lat), but many of the *Truòng Son* or Annam Cordillera upland areas and their indigenous populations are located in other provinces bordering these four. In the English language, the area is most commonly known as Central Highlands, which is the name that I prefer to use.

Likewise, the indigenous population has undergone many name changes, both in terms of distinct 'tribal' or 'ethnic' identities and as a generic category. In pre-colonial times, they were called *Moi* by lowland Vietnamese, *Kha* by the Lao and *Phnong* by the Khmer. All these three words can be glossed as 'savage', but with servile connotations added by the slave trade that was concentrated in the Highlands. In early colonial times, the French would simply adopt those pejorative labels or would call them *Sauvages* ('savages'), until more respectful ethnic labels became politically expedient in the 1940s. They tried and rejected political labels like *Pémsiens* (from the acronym PMSI – a political construct) and scientific labels like *Proto-Indochinois* (conveying the notion that this was the indigenous population of Indochina), and finally stuck with the term *Montagnards* (literally 'mountain dwellers'). The word 'Montagnard' was adopted by most Americans after 1955, shortened to 'Yard' by many US Special Forces. Other Americans translated 'Montagnard' into 'Highlander', the term preferred by Gerald Hickey. The South-Vietnamese regime coined the official label *đồng bào thuong* (highland compatriot) but the compatriots quickly became *người sác tộc*, or 'colored people'. Communist scholars and politicians rejected the latter label as racist, and prefer to use *dân tộc thiểu số*, or 'ethnic minorities'. In line with Stalinist national theory, there is no distinction between 'nation' and 'ethnic group' in current Vietnamese idiom. Contrary to previous regimes, the current regime has no generic label for the indigenous population of the Central Highlands; instead, it distinguishes between the 'Kinh' or 'Việt' ethnic majority and the 53 officially classified ethnic minorities – three less than in China. Political dissidents in the US striving for autonomy for the Central Highlands have started to adopt the ethnic label of *Dega*, but its use is not widespread. In this study I will mostly use the term 'Montagnard', simply because it is the ethnic label that internationally has the most currency despite its political connotations.

Using such labels, however, glosses over the great cultural diversity that one encounters in the Central Highlands. According to the official ethnic classification of Vietnam, of the 54 ethnic groups in Vietnam, 19 belong to the indigenous population of the Central Highlands and Annam Cordillera south of the 17th Parallel (but in recent decades the ethnic composition of the area has been compounded by the massive in-migration of lowlander Kinh and northern upland minorities into the Central Highlands). Given this diversity, it is very difficult to generalize because it is always possible to find exceptions. This classification into distinct ethnic groups assumes the existence of bounded groups, held together by a common language, culture, polity and territory. But the present classification is just the last one in a series of ethnic classifications, undertaken by successive political regimes and affiliated scientists. In most cases, these classifications were not based on ethnic self-identification, but on linguistic differences observed by outsiders. A common assumption in the nineteenth and twentieth centuries was that linguistic difference must coincide with cultural and political difference, making it possible to distinguish ethnic groups (or 'tribes') whose territories could be projected onto a map. In his *Political Systems of Highland Burma*, Sir Edmund Leach (1954: 291) critiqued this tendency among ethnographers of his generation:

> My own view is that the ethnographer has often only managed to discern the existence of '*a* tribe' because he took it as axiomatic that this kind of cultural entity must exist. Many such tribes are, in a sense, ethnographic fictions.

In this ethnographic classic, Leach showed that the adoption and construction of one's ethnic identity was a dynamic process, motivated by the human desire for political power and prestige. In a seminal paper entitled *Feasting and Social Oscillation: Religion and Society in Upland Southeast Asia* (1973), Thomas Kirsch expanded Leach's theoretical argument to include not just the political domain, but also culture and religion, and to cover not just Kachin society in Highland Burma, but all of what he calls 'hill tribes society' in mainland Southeast Asia. In this paper, Kirsch claims that people rose to political prominence within their community and beyond through feasting, which had a religious significance, but that the position of such elites was not stable or hereditary. The 'waxing and waning' of what I would call 'big men' seizing upon economic, political and/or military opportunities led to a 'social oscillation' of hill tribe societies between 'autocratic' and 'democratic' poles. In the following chapters I shall describe similar processes for the Central Highlands of Vietnam. One implication of this is that in the Central Highlands one did not normally find bounded 'tribes', neatly distinguished and distinguishable.

Hickey (1982a: 4) observed that often 'the ethnic label commonly used in the literature is not the name by which the members of the group refer to themselves, although in many cases they recognize and accept the designation used by others.' In his essay 'Ethnic Identification in Vietnam: Principles and Processes', the Vietnamese ethnologist Đang Nghiêm Van recognizes that while language, costume and other cultural traditions are important markers for ethnic identification, they yield in importance to people's self-consciousness of their ethnic identity (1998: 19). But let us take a closer look at two official ethnic categories in Vietnam: the Hrê and the Kotu (alias Cotu/Katu). Hickey reports that the label 'Hrê' was initially used by the French to denote the indigenous population living along the Sông Rê; other communities were also known by the name of the river along which they lived (Hickey 1982a: 16). But in time, 'Hrê' became an ethnonym for the population in that area, and is now one of the official ethnic categories in Vietnam. A similarly arbitrary process of labeling gave rise to the insulting ethnonym 'Katu', which was the name that a French colonial officer gave in 1913 to a refractory upland population that caused trouble for the colonial order. According to another French officer, Le Pichon, who retraced the footsteps of that officer in the late 1930s, Katu means 'savage' in the local dialect, and that label was invariably reserved for 'others' living deeper into the forest, up the mountain (1938: 363):

> In the course of my tours I asked the Moï that I encountered: 'From where are you?' – 'We are people from that village.' – 'Do you know the Katu?' – 'Yes, they are the people who live up there in the mountains.' And up there in the mountain one would indicate other mountains on the Lao side. I did not conclude from this, however, that the savages did not exist in the region!

Katu – the 'savage' people who lived higher up the mountain – became the 'official' ethnic label which appeared on maps and in administrative and ethnographic documents (Hickey 1982a: 11). During the 1970s, evangelical linguists from the Summer Institute of Linguistics would classify 'Katuic' as one of the subgroupings of the Mon-Khmer, or Austroasiatic, language family (Thomas 1973). The 'Cotu' are now one of the 54 official ethnic groups of

Vietnam – rather than Katu, 'which designates something not very noble,' as Đang Nghiêm Van acknowledges (1998: 36).

This implies that the already great diversity of official labels is compounded by confusion about the cultural substance classified by these labels. The languages spoken in the Central Highlands are commonly divided into two major language families: Austroasiatic (or Mon-Khmer, of which Vietnamese is considered a branch as well) and Austronesian (or Malayo-Polynesian, related to the various Malay languages). But what if local sub-groups of the Churu ethnic group speak dialects that belong to two different language families? What if many, if not most, minority people are effectively bi- or multilingual, when they communicate with outsiders? Linguistic difference, which was the basis for ethnic classification, was not neatly organized along boundaries; the differences were gradual, flexible, and fluid. The linguistic 'boundaries' drawn on the map did not necessarily converge with cultural or political realities, as I shall describe in the following chapters. Though there have been village communities or groups of villages with bounded territories, there were no 'tribes' inhabiting distinct tribal territories. This does not mean that the ethnic labels are fictional. The ethnonyms have a history, and have now become accepted as a way of identifying oneself in the Vietnamese nation-state; it is indicated on one's identity card, and is a condition for certain (educational) benefits. So today most local people are able to identify themselves as Jarai, Ede, Churu or Raglai; as Bana (Bahnar), Sedang, Koho, Mnong, Ma, Hre, Cotu, Gie-Trieng, etc. (see maps and charts for ethno-linguistic maps of the Central Highlands and Vietnam as well as for the list of the 54 'official' ethnic groups in Vietnam).

The challenge now is how to characterize Montagnard society and culture in the face of such historical diversity. Perhaps it is useful here to return to Kirsch' notion of 'hill tribes society' – even though the concept of tribe is questionable. Perhaps the most common trait is their difference from lowland societies – the Vietnamese, Cham, Khmer and Lao polities and 'hydraulic' civilizations based on irrigated rice cultivation. In pre-colonial times this difference was obvious in the absence of durable political entities, of towns, of areas with high population density, of any of the major Southeast Asian religions in the Highlands. Given the cultural diversity among Central Highlanders themselves, the most that I can aim for in this limited context is to give a few topical vignettes. For the sake of clarity and brevity I shall dwell on some of the most common notions about Highlanders in Vietnam and make some comments about these assumptions. I shall do that in a few paragraphs on Montagnard residential patterns, their economy and agriculture, kinship, religion, and their political organization.

A common assumption about Montagnard residential patterns is that they are nomads – or at least semi-nomads – who roam around, burning down the forest to clear and cultivate upland rice fields for a few years, and move on when the soil is exhausted. In the Vietnamese press, some scientific and many political documents, Central Highlanders are still labeled 'semi-nomads'. Successive ethnic policies like the current 'Fixed Cultivation and Settlement' program are predicated on the assumption that Central Highlanders have to be (re)settled in order to achieve a 'stable' lifestyle. Contrary to such assumptions, many groups used to have fixed, bounded territories that they called their own, with elaborate systems for delineating clan or community land. In the past, many Bahnar or Edê communities ritually reaffirmed their land use rights, but they have stopped doing so as land is now allocated through a bureaucratic process which usually does not take local land-use patterns into account. The archetype Montagnard village is a village with a series of elevated longhouses, inhabited by several households belonging to the same clan. In the middle of the village would be a high-roofed communal house, with a decorated pole in front for the ritual buffalo sacrifice. On the side of the village would be a gravesite with burial statues. This archetype is in fact an amalgam of various architectural patterns. The stilted longhouse was common among Edê and Jarai, but not the Bahnar who used to build for nuclear families. Mnong and other groups would build their houses on the ground. The communal house can still be found in some Jarai, Bahnar and Sedang villages, but not in Edê villages.

With regard to their economic activities, a common assumption is that Montagnards are 'slash-and-burn' agriculturalists who 'wantonly' destroy the forest to clear fields for cultivation of upland rice and some vegetables – never sufficient to meet their needs, though. After the soil is exhausted, they are believed to pack their belongings and try their luck elsewhere. They are believed to be the main culprits of the heavy deforestation of Vietnam's highland areas – an assumption shared by the various colonial, neo- and post-colonial regimes which tried to curb the *rây*, or shifting cultivation system by introducing more 'modern', sedentary farming methods. However, with subsistence crops in particular, these interventions have often failed because they did not take sufficient account of the ecology of tropical mountain areas. In most places, soil fertility and the terrain would not allow permanent farming, while ploughing often sloping plots of land would lead to erosion and degradation. Central Highlanders cleared plots with controlled use of fire, using a hoe to clear and weed the field and a dibble stick to sow multiple crops on one field. After two to three years the soil would be exhausted and left to regenerate by the forest. In fact, they would expect to come back and clear that plot of land in ten to twenty years, making for a long-fallow system of rotational farming. The fallows would typically be used for grazing cattle, or growing low-intensity crops like grasses (used for thatching) or 'green manure' (nitrogen-fixing weeds that quickly regenerate soil fertility and can often be used as fodder).

Most communities engaging in shifting cultivation had a delineated territory and an elaborate local knowledge and regulatory institutions (later translated into 'customary law') by which suitable, sufficiently regenerated plots of land were periodically reallocated to households to clear and work. Many communities were (and are) shifting cultivators, but wherever ecological conditions permitted groups developed permanent rain-fed fields, or irrigated rice fields on flat terrain with abundant water. Now, many groups grow cash crops like coffee, rubber, tea, pepper, cinnamon on a permanent basis. Admittedly, shifting cultivation is only sustainable with low population densities; the continuous in-migration into the

Central Highlands since the 1950s has radically altered the demographic composition and the size of the population, increasingly rendering traditional shifting cultivation systems ecologically increasingly unsustainable given the scarcity of land and resources. Agriculture was usually combined with animal husbandry, hunting, fishing and gathering of timber and non-timber forest products. Many of the thus collected products (like buffaloes, tamed elephants, elephant tusk, rhinoceros horns, beeswax, special woods like eagle, aloe, cinnamon, medicinal plants and so on) were used in the long-distance trade with lowland areas, allowing Montagnards to acquire necessities like salt, iron or prized prestige items like colorful silk fabrics, bronze gongs from Burma, or ceramic jars from China.

Popular descriptions of Montagnard kinship often refer to an amalgam of matrilineal descent and inheritance, clan-based residence and pre-marital sexual promiscuity. French ethnographers used the concept of *matriarcat* [matriarchy] to denote kinship systems in certain Montagnard societies. Contrary to 'matrilineal', 'matriarchal' carries the connotation of a sexual balance of power tilted towards women. Following ethnologists of the 19th century, including Bachofen, Tylor, Frazer, Morgan and Engels, matriarchy was opposed to the notion of patriarchy, taken to be the normal state of affairs in civilized society. Friedrich Engels and many of his Marxist followers even considered the historical victory of men over women a condition for social progress. Hence, matrilineal societies that by extension are consistently labeled 'matriarchal' are considered 'primitive' and 'backward', two notions that are often used in relation to Montagnard societies. While Vietnamese ethnographic discourse makes a distinction between *mâu hê* [matrineal] and *mâu quyên* [matriarchal], the two concepts are often lumped together – both in scholarly writing and in the press. Similarly, the practice of several nuclear families belonging to the same clan or extended family living together in one long-house struck outsiders as an obstacle to progress because of the force of 'tradition' reigning in such circumstances. This has led to interventions – in the name of progress – by outsiders in Montagnard residential practices and kinship which have been mostly successful. Vietnamese sources cry victory when the longhouses are 'broken up' and when Central Highlanders, forced by Vietnamese law, adopt patrilineal ('patriarchal') descent. In fact, many groups traditionally had patrilineal or cognatic kinship, which did not make them more 'civilized' than other groups, but maybe that is not the issue; the issue is the construction of cultural difference with the majority through imaginations of Montagnard primitiveness. Alleged sexual promiscuity of Montagnard youngsters – especially girls – and the fact that girls take the initiative in courting in matrilineal societies have sparked many erotic fantasies on the part of outsiders, fueled by images of bare-breasted girls and burial statues explicitly depicting sexual organs, pregnancy and intercourse. Read any fiction story about Montagnards, and read how the male 'Hero' takes one or more Montagnard girls for wife or concubine, who eventually will be left behind because she cannot be civilized.

Central Highlanders stayed aloof from the major religious traditions in Southeast Asia like Buddhism and Islam. Even though their traditional religion, often labeled 'animism', has many beliefs and practices in common with lowland folk religions (especially ancestor worship and spirit cults), their beliefs, practices, rituals, ordeals and divinations are often portrayed as utterly backward and primitive by outside agents. Many practices – like burials and re-burials of the deceased – are considered 'unhygienic', and many rituals – like the iconic buffalo sacrifice – are considered 'wasteful' – even though they constitute a redistribution of wealth and foodstuff (protein) by slaughtering and cooking an animal that was not used as draught animal in most places. As most groups did not have their own script to create a written record, their religion, their knowledge and their customary laws were considered invalid, lacking the rigor and consistency to be called 'modern'. Many groups had a number of gods in common, which facilitated religious exchange and the periodic emergence of millenarian movements which scared outside political authorities because they transgressed 'tribal' boundaries (see Chapter 4). Apart from the 'gods' – often associated with a mythical 'golden age' – there were many different kinds of spirits: spirits of the dead, spirits embodied in specific animals, spirits associated with specific places. Their religious beliefs commanded respect for the ubiquitous spirits present in so many natural phenomena, instilling a respect for nature that allowed Central Highlanders by and large to maintain a sustainable equilibrium with (local) nature – for as long they made the decisions within their territories. Even though there is now an emerging interest in sustainable natural resource management practices, only few observers have emphasized the religious aspects of the indigenous natural resource management practices. Subjected to many attempts under various successive regimes to induce Montagnards to abandon 'super-stition', and with fewer resources left (or with little control over these resources), Central Highlanders have increasingly adopted 'new' religions (Catholicism, Protestantism, Communism) that seem to make more sense in the present-day world (see Chapter 8).

In terms of political organization, a common assumption on the part of outsiders is that the indigenous population of the Central Highlands is made up of clearly distinct tribes, distinguishable by their language, their traditional costume, architecture, and – more in general – their 'manners and customs' (*moeurs et coutumes, phong tuc tap quán*). It is often assumed that daily life among Central Highlanders is ruled almost absolutely by old men, be it in the guise of village chiefs, shamans or village elders. In fact, political life in the Central Highlands was much more 'decentralized', if not fragmented. At the time of the early French explorations, explorers often complained about the absence of supra-village political organizations that could give them a key to this politically fragmented society. In fact, there were supra-village institutions which did not have a political character. Some villages shared a common territory for shifting cultivation. Some religious institutions commanded respect in a wide area, such as the three Jarai *p'tao*, shamans who held a privileged position with regard to the elements fire, water and wind (see next section and Chapter 8). The word *p'tau* (*patau* or *pötau*) is of Cham origin, employed to designate politically and/or religiously superior persons, like kings, princes, local leaders, but also influential priests or *shamans*. Commonly, the word was translated as 'king', hence the confusion among Western observers, who search for kings with the habitual pomp and regalia, but find minor chiefs or religious leaders instead. Most important, however, were the 'big men' who rose to a position of prominence because of their descent, their military prowess, their economic success, their religious prestige, which was associated with their (economic) capacity for feasting. Such 'big men' often had many slaves, either captured or from households that were indebted. Captured slaves were mostly sold to the slave traders from Laos, Cambodia and as far as Thailand, while indebted slaves were added to their household and practically indistinguishable from other household members. Such 'big men' usually were cunning in their dealings with outsiders, which gave them a leverage over their fellow villagers, but they were never absolute masters – not even within their own village or family. During their early explorations, the French often dealt with such 'big men', either making allies or enemies out of them (Chapter 2).

Relations between Montagnards and outsiders

Emphasizing cultural differences between Lowlanders and Highlanders and ensuing misperceptions of Highlander culture does not mean that this difference was absolute, nor that Lowlanders and Highlanders were naturally antagonistic, as was and is often assumed by outsiders. It does not mean that there was no contact or commerce. Indeed, there have been more or less successful attempts by Lowland states to impose some political order in the Highlands, and Highlanders played a role in lowland court rituals. More important, trade has linked Highlands and Lowlands alike with international trade networks. This is evident from the lists of forest products like elephant tusks, rhinoceros horns, beeswax, aloe and eagle wood and cinnamon, exported by lowland states – as recorded, for instance, in old reports of the Dutch East-India Company about mainland Southeast Asia. It is equally evident from the range of 'imported' prestige items like bronze gongs from Burma and jars from China, but especially (sea)salt, a necessity for survival in the Highlands.

Despite the perception of perennial antagonism between Lowlanders who were organized in states, and Highlanders who retained real autonomy, there has been a rich history of political contacts. Until their defeat by the Vietnamese in 1471, Champa was a powerful 'Indonesian' Hindu state on the coast of Central Vietnam, and maintained a reduced presence in the principalities of Panduranga (Phan Rang) and Kauthara, located in the present-day provinces of Ninh Thuân/Bình Thuân and Khanh Hóa into the eighteenth century. However, for centuries Champa consisted not only of the coastal lowlands, but of parts of the Central Highland area as well – what Jacques Dournes has called *'Haut-Champa'* (1970). Around the turn of the century many ruins, statues and other vestiges of this Cham presence still existed in sites like Kon Klor and Kodo/Bomong Yang (near Kontum); Yang Mum (near Ayun Pa in present-day Gialai province); Yang Prong north of Ban Don in Dak Lak, close to the Cambodian border; and in the form of 'treasures' of Cham princes among Churu and Roglai groups in present-day Lâm Đông (Dournes 1970; Hickey 1982a: 91–107). Aymonier (1890a), Leclère (1904), Maitre (1912a), Bourotte (1955), Boulbet (1967) and Hickey (1982a) all recorded legends among Montagnards on the Cham and their overlordship.

When the Vietnamese replaced the Cham as overlords in the Lowlands, they soon became the dominant population through a process of systematic colonization by the establishment of military colonies, *đồn điền*. However, they did not venture as deep into the Central Highlands as the Cham, and did not attempt to colonize the Highlands. But with the reunification of Vietnam in 1802 by Emperor Gia Long of the Nguyên dynasty, attempts were made to 'pacify' the Highlands. One example was the so-called *Son Phòng* or 'mountain defense' program in Quang Ngãi and Bình Đinh provinces, which was started in 1863 under Emperor Tu Đúc by mandarin Nguyên Tân, who recorded his strategy in 1871 under the title *Lê Tiêu Phu Su'* (published in French in 1904). The *Son Phòng* – which continued an eighteenth century Vietnamese mountain pacification scheme – combined the establishment of a strong military presence in strategic locations with the political incorporation of local chiefs in the Vietnamese administration, with establishing trade monopolies and with tax collection. Local chiefs were respected, something which was facilitated by the collection of geographic and ethnographic information. Trade was supervised, monopolized and taxed by the state, including items that Highland populations needed (salt) as well as highly lucrative highland forest products, like cinnamon (*Lê Tiêu Phu Su'* 1904; Hickey 1982a: 182–4). But according to French sources, in the latter part of the nineteenth century the *Son Phòng* degenerated into a system of corruption and legalized swindle, creating unrest among Highland populations. In 1898 the French started to dismantle the *Son Phòng* in their 'protectorate' of Annam (Aymonier 1885; Brière 1890; Durand 1907).

The tributary relations that the Jarai *P'tau Apui* ('King of Fire') and *P'tau Ia* ('King of Water') maintained with the courts of Phnom Penh and Huê are another example. These two 'kings' were powerful shamans with a religious and ritual status that was recognized by surrounding populations, including the Lowland courts, thus assuming a political importance there which they did not possess in their own societies (see Chapter 8). The two 'kings' were mentioned in various Vietnamese annals and manuscripts as the *Hoa Xá* and *Thuy Xá*, princes of the small 'kingdom of fire' and 'kingdom of water', who exchanged gifts with the Nguyên lords of southern Vietnam before the Tây Son Rebellion (1771–1802) which occasioned the reunification of the country. For our purpose it is interesting to note that in 1820, under the second Nguyên emperor Minh Mang or Minh Mênh, 'diplomatic relations' between the 'King of Water' and the court of Vietnam were re-established with a tribute and gifts of elephant tusks, perfumed wood, and other forest products. In 1831, a triennial tribute by the two Jarai 'vassal kings' was institutionalized, which took place in Phu Yên province, with the Emperor returning gifts of cloth and other valuable or ceremonial items. The exchange of gifts continued through the reigns of Thiêu Tri and Tu Đúc, until the French took over the management of the relations with the Highlanders from the Court of Huê (Nghiêm Thâm and Voth 1972; Dournes 1977: 109–22; Hickey 1982a: 121–89).

These two examples (there are many more) tell us that there were extensive economic, political and cultural contacts between Montagnards and the Vietnamese state in precolonial times. When Annam (Trung Bô) and Tonkin (Bác Bô) were turned into French protectorates in 1883, the Vietnamese administrative system had already crumbled and collapsed in many areas, first of all in those Highland areas where they only had a tenuous hold. A French naval officer, Amédée Gautier, who explored the area north of Conchinchina (Nam Bô) in 1882, interacted with local leaders of Lao, Vietnamese, Chinese and mixed descent living with Montagnards, still maintaining a rudimentary Vietnamese administrative infrastructure that had been more elaborate in the past (Gautier 1882, 1884, 1935; Maitre 1912a: 463–4; Dubourg 1950). When the French gradually took over the administration of Indochina and attempted to separate Lowlanders and Highlanders in later years, they would never be completely successful. On many occasions, Vietnamese rebels would seek refuge among and support from Highlanders, starting with the Tây Son Rebellion, through the *Cân Vuong* movement in the early years of the French colonization, to the Viêt Minh and National Liberation Front guerrilla movements against the French and the Americans. These records of contact through trade, exchange and support between Lowlanders and Highlanders in (pre)colonial times debunk the still common notion that Highland groups are located in 'remote' areas and have always been 'isolated' from mainstream civilization.

The composition of the book

This book is both chronologically and thematically structured, because it seems to me that such an approach is inherently comparative. What I mean is that the chapters are laid out chronologically, so that one can read the book more or less as a historical sequence. Yet, each chapter also discusses a certain theme, meaning the emergence and the impact of a certain ethnographic discourse. This will result in some chronological overlap, as various discourses often co-existed (and co-exist) simultaneously – next to and in opposition to each other. Some chapters, including this Introduction and Chapters 4, 5 and 8, are modified versions of – or loosely based on – previously published articles; the original publications are mentioned in the notes.

Chapter 2 discusses the early contacts between Montagnards and Europeans during the latter's attempts to bring Indochina under colonial rule. Ethnographic discourse about Montagnards was dominated by two categories of ethnographers – Catholic missionaries and military explorers – whose accounts can be characterized as evolutionist. The main emphasis of these ethnographic accounts is on religious beliefs and practices, mapping and ethnographic classification. Though this chapter ends with the death in 1914 of the military explorer and canonical ethnographer Henri Maitre, whose work forms the apotheosis of this evolutionist discourse, the evolutionist perspective would resurface in many different guises until 1990. However, as an explanatory ethnographic theory, evolutionism was gradually taken over by a relativist ethnographic discourse initiated by colonial administrators like Léopold Sabatier whose work is discussed in Chapter 3.[14] With the unfolding of the *Dieu Python* millenarian movement in the Central Highlands and the Annam Cordillera (including the Laotian and Cambodian parts), analysed in Chapter 4,[15] relativism takes hold in the face of increasing internal and external political threats to French colonial rule through World War II. This period is characterized by a process of tribalization, coupled with the institutionalization of ethnographic practice. Chapter 5[16] discusses the First Indochina War as an ethnographic occasion, which combined the need for political co-optation of Montagnards with a professionalization of ethnographic practice that propelled the eminent French anthropologist Georges Condominas into prominence. This led to the ethnicization and territorialization of the Montagnards in a separate area, the *Pays Montagnard du Sud-Indochinois* (PMSI), with a Special Status (*Statut particulier*). War also accelerated a gender transformation that disenfranchised women who had traditionally enjoyed important rights, especially in matrilineal societies.

Although Chapter 6 takes up the American presence in Vietnam, it starts with an aborted American plan for starting a guerrilla campaign in the Central Highlands during World War II, against the French. The ideas that lay at the basis of this plan would be revived during the early 1960s when the counterinsurgency paradigm took hold among top US policy makers. Before the full-fledged American invasion of Vietnam in 1965 the American counter-insurgency programs in Vietnam were devised and implemented by the CIA and the US Army Special Forces ('Green Berets'), who developed a relativist ethnographic discourse concerning the Montagnards, initially almost independent of previous French discursive practices. Chapter 7 looks at the uses of anthropology by and the ethnographic discourses of, various categories of stakeholders – missionaries, CIA, Special Forces, US Army, Navy and Air Force – at the time that the US maintained a very important military and other presence in Vietnam. American ethnography of the Montagnards culminated in the person of Gerald Hickey, who played a role in two of the major controversies surrounding the Montagnards: their autonomy aspirations, and the resettlement policies. Chapter 8[17] takes a closer look at the post-1975 ethnographic discourse and ethnic policies on the part of the reunified Vietnam under the Communist regime, based on fieldwork in the Central Highlands in 1991. Elaborating on a case of non-succession of the *p'tau apui*, or 'King of Fire', I discuss two critical ethnic policies of the Socialist Republic, namely the 'Fixed Cultivation and Settlement' program, and the 'Selective Cultural Preservation' policy.

In Chapter 9, I compare by way of conclusion the French, American and Vietnamese ethnographic perspectives with respect to the Central Highlanders. Even when ethnographic practice became progressively institutionalized and professionalized, and the Montagnard population was subjected to processes of tribalization, ethnicization, territorialization and gender transformation, there were discursive continuities throughout the 140-year period covered in this book in two rival paradigms: evolutionism and cultural relativism. From the outset I would like to make it clear that the labeling as 'evolutionist' and 'relativist' is the author's construct, in an attempt at creating order in a very diverse discourse. My argument is that during different historical periods, changing *préterrains* and ethnographic occasions gave rise to the dominance of one of either perspectives on the Montagnards. A contextual historical analysis of ethnography that does not respect the disciplinary boundaries will be a source of support for an anthropology that likes to see itself as a source of social and cultural critique.

2 Missionaries, explorers, and savages

The construction of an evolutionist discourse

[We must] encourage missions and other enterprises which are likely to be of service in spreading useful knowledge.

(Bismarck at the Conference on Colonial Questions, Berlin, 1884.
In: Neill 1986[2]: 359)

Introduction

When the first Europeans arrived in Asia, they were not very much interested in the peoples living in the mountainous areas of mainland Southeast Asia. Commerce and conversion being the main motivations for their ventures, the Europeans contacted the more accessible lowland states, where the political forms of principalities and kingdoms and the civilizations based on wet rice cultivation in a way mirrored the European state of affairs. If the populations living in the mountainous areas bordering Laos, Cambodia, Vietnam (Cochinchina) and, still, Champa, were mentioned at all, it was only in passing.[1] When, for instance, the Portuguese Jesuit missionary Christoforo Borri in his 'Account of Cochin-China' (or. 1631) spoke of 'a ridge of mountains inhabited by the *Kemois*', it was only in order to describe the borders of Cochinchina (Borri 1811[3]: 773).

Similarly, when the Dutch East-Indies Company merchant Gerard van Wuysthoff relates of his voyage in 1641/42 to the kingdom of *Lauwen* (Laos), he mentions a place called *Phonongh*, to the east of Sambor and Sambock on the Mekong river in Cambodia. Chinese merchants would venture there in order to acquire gold, elephant tusks and rhinoceros horns (Muller 1917: 157).[2] Borri describes the highlanders as a 'savage people, for though they are Cochin-Chinese, yet they no way acknowledge or submit to the King, keeping in the fastnesses of the uncouth mountains, bordering on the kingdom of Lais [Laos]' (1811[3]: 773). Van Wuysthoff, on the other hand, maintains that the *Phonong* are dominated by the Cambodians and the Cham (Muller 1917: 157). This difference of opinion may reflect the divergent goals of missionaries and traders: while the former tended to emphasize the Montagnards' political autonomy from the courts, the latter would simply observe that they are part and parcel of the trade networks which connect the interior with the coastal ports.

Nevertheless, European observers were hardly interested in the mountain peoples of Indochina, for although they produced many of the trade items for the Asian commercial networks at the time, their produce was collected by the several courts and peddlers in the region, and shipped from ports in the lowlands.

Once Europeans came to be firmly established in the different countries grouped together as 'Indochina', interest in the highlands and their inhabitants grew as a concomitant of the political and military vicissitudes attending the process of European expansion. Not surprisingly, then, it would be French missionaries who entered into durable contact with Montagnards, as their position in Vietnam gradually strengthened in the face of intermittent persecution by the Vietnamese authorities. Following in the footsteps of the missionaries came French military explorers, who tried to find trade routes into southern China, or sought to establish the borders of their possessions once the colony of Cochinchina and the later French protectorates in Indochina had been established. For almost a century, their descriptions of the Central Highlanders were the only ones available, and the ethnographic discourse they initiated, firmly entrenched in nineteenth century evolutionism, has never since ceased to influence the perception of the Central Highlanders.

This chapter will describe the establishment of the mission station at Kontum, and the role which ethnography played in early missionary activities. A further section will deal with the establishment of (nominal) European rule in the Central Highlands by military explorers. A final section will compare the ethnographic discourses of the missionaries and the military explorers, and trace the construction of an evolutionist discourse in ethnographic writing concerning the Central Highlanders. I shall argue that the evolutionist perspective on the Central Highlanders is fundamentally ahistorical, in particular when informed by Social-Darwinist theories. Even when it eventually was contested by other, rival discourses, this evolutionist discourse has reemerged in various historical contexts throughout the modern history of the Central Highlands.

Missionary ethnography and the crusade against pagans

It would be the French missionaries of the *Missions Étrangères de Paris*, who first got into sustained contact with the 'savages', as they would call them. Since its foundation in 1663, simultaneously with the French *Compagnie des Indes Orientales*, the *Société des Missions Étrangères* has coupled religious activities with patriotism and trade. Commissioned by the Pope to convert Vietnam, French missionaries gradually replaced Portuguese and Spanish missionaries in Vietnam in the eighteenth and nineteenth centuries, until they had a virtual monopoly on Christianization toward the end of the last century. The spread of Christianity undermined not only Buddhism as a folk religion, but also Confucianism, which was the dominant state ideology in pre-colonial Vietnam. The interest of the Vietnamese elite in upholding Confucianism as state religion, and the interest of the missionaries in undermining the authority of the Emperor and mandarins as

Figure 2.1 The five French missionaries proselytizing among the Bahnar in 1892 before
the carved wooden window of the old church in Kontum (from left to right:
Guerlach, Jannin, Poyet, Irigoyen, Vialleton).

Source: Archives des Missions Étrangères de Paris.

protectors of Confucianism, inevitably led to religious and political conflicts. In
the nineteenth century, there were several waves of repression of Catholics in
Vietnam. Many missionaries, on the other hand, campaigned actively for
military intervention by France. The repression of Catholics often did occasion
French military intervention in and partial occupation of Vietnam, which
became the target of a proactive colonial lobby in France. Vietnam was perceived
as the gateway to southern China, and thus as an opening to that huge market.
In such circumstances, the missionaries and their local followers often acted as a
fifth column for France (Lê 1975: passim; Lê Thanh Khôi 1981: 287–91,
368–70; Tuck 1987: passim).[3]

Until the middle of the nineteenth century, there were no firsthand accounts
by Europeans of the people inhabiting the mountainous parts of mainland
Southeast Asia. Thus Richard, in his *History of Tonquin*, could write in 1778 that
'travellers have never penetrated into the interior of the country [of Champa]'
(Richard 1811[2]: 768); and Crawfurd, relating of his embassy to the courts of Siam
and Cochinchina in 1823, would mention the *Moi* in Cochinchina, 'of whom
little is known but their name, and that they are an uncivilized but inoffensive
people' (Crawfurd 1967[2]: 468). To my knowledge, it was the missionary Père

Gagelin who in 1830 first sought direct contact with the '*sauvages*' inhabiting the mountains of Cochinchina. Since in Cochinchina no one would venture into those 'inaccessible' mountains for fear of those 'savages', P. Gagelin had to turn to the Sen-Fi, the Cambodian mandarin charged with the control of the Montagnards. The Sen-Fi then sent for a Montagnard, whereupon the following conversation developed, as reported by P. Gagelin:

> [Question] 'How is it that you like to stay in the forest, and that you don't come to live with the Cambodians? You are born for society, and your state is against the normal laws of nature.' [Reply] 'When we appear in open landscape, we become afraid; but when we are in the bush, in the midst of tigers and other wild beasts, we are in safety.' [Q.] 'It would be very advantageous for you to become acquainted with the Cambodians in order to learn some skills, at least to make a bit of cloth.' [R.] 'We don't believe that we have to lead a life different from our ancestors.'
>
> (Gagelin 1832: 378)

Even if distorted, this conversation shows in a nutshell the problematic of 'development', in the guise of conversion or otherwise. The priest is trying to open up the indigenous society by imposing his definition of both the current and the desired situation; the Montagnard can only defend himself either by adopting the ways of expression of the foreigner, or by joking or feigning ignorance. In the subsequent conversation, the priest ascertains for himself that foreigners would enjoy the hospitality of the group, contrary to what he was told by both Kinh (lowland 'ethnic' Vietnamese) and Khmer; he is looking for a crack in the wall – a starting point for conversion:

> One would have to begin by gradually acquainting with them, while remaining at a certain distance from them, and studying their inclinations in a more special way in order to win their trust. One would have to make men of them first, in order to make Christians of them.
>
> (Gagelin 1832: 382)

Father Gagelin could not undertake this task himself, being the first Catholic missionary to fall victim of the anti-Christian edict issued by the Vietnamese Emperor Minh Mang in 1833 (Launay 1894-II: 543–55). But once the possibility of a mission station in Montagnard country was contemplated, it was only a matter of time before the first attempt at penetration would be made in an area where the power of the Emperor and the mandarins was not felt.

In 1825 Emperor Minh Mang banned the Christian religion, and after that ordered the active repression of Christians because of their share in rebellions during the 1830s. This prompted the bishop of Qui-Nhon in Annam, Mgr. Cuénot to study the possibilities for a mission station in the Central Highlands, out of reach of the mandarins. In 1839 he reported on an attempt at conversion in Laos. In 1841, he gave a short description of the Cham, the Rhadé and the

Jarai, which focused on the *p'tau apui* (Master of Fire), who apparently enjoyed unlimited prestige among the Jarai, and entertained tributary and commercial relations with the Court of Annam in Hue. The Vietnamese traders, whose rights were acknowledged both by the Jarai *p'tau* and the Court, were thought to be the main obstacle for missionary activity among highlanders (Cuénot 1841: 139–45). Cuénot's analysis turned out to be correct, as the first attempt in 1842 to establish a mission station in Jarai territory failed when Vietnamese traders arrested the priests Duclos and Miche while their host, the *p'tau apui*, did not intervene. Those Highlanders who had let them pass, reportedly Rhadé, were rebuked by the Vietnamese authorities. The missionaries were brought to Hue, where they were held in prison, accused of rebellion with the help of Laotian soldiers. Sentenced to death, along with three other French priests, they were released in 1843 because of the military action by the French Navy. Their report reached Mgr. Cuénot, who arranged to have it published in the *Annales de la Propagation de la Foi* (Duclos and Miche 1844: 89–105).

After this failure in 1842, there were at least two other attempts at penetration of the Highlands in Quang-Ngai and Quang-Nam, but to no avail. In 1848, a Vietnamese priest, Father Dô, was sent out to study languages and cultures of the Montagnards, and to find the safest way to get out of reach of the Vietnamese mandarins. He did so by working for an authorized Vietnamese trader in An-Son (Tây Son), Bình Dinh province. In 1850 he guided the two French missionaries Combes and Fontaine into Bahnar territory, where they managed to maintain themselves in the face of many difficulties, thanks to the support of an influential Bahnar leader, Kiêm, who monopolized the trade with the Vietnamese in a considerable area. Father Dô became Kiêm's brother by performing a 'pagan' ritual, consisting of the sacrifice of a chicken and the drinking of a jar of wine, mixed with some drops of blood of both parties. Although the alliance with Kiêm was to be highly profitable for the missionaries, they would condemn and forbid such 'pagan' rituals and the use of rice for making wine when they had the power to do so. Kiêm used his influence with other Montagnards to allow the missionaries to settle down on the banks of the river Bla, where they would be joined by the priests Desgouts and Dourisboure, and eventually founded the mission station of Kontum (Dourisboure 1929: 1–29).

The first ethnographic accounts of the Montagnards, based on an actual presence in Montagnard territory, were written in 1853 by P. Combes and in 1870 by P. Dourisboure. To facilitate conversion, they carried on ethnographic studies, based on personal experience and observation. The first extensive description by P. Combes of the *moeurs et coutumes* [manners and customs] of the Bahnar appeared in the *Annales de la Propagation de la Foi* (1855: 405–37) under the title 'Missions du Laos'. The same text was added as an appendix to P. Dourisboure's account of the history the mission of Kontum, *Les sauvages Ba-Hnars (Cochinchine orientale): Souvenirs d'un missionnaire* (1873).[4] From a political point of view, it is significant that in 1855 Bahnar territory was considered to be part of Laos, while in 1873 it was claimed to be part of Cochinchina. Of course, the mission station was meant as a refuge for Catholics (French priests and

Vietnamese converts) from 'Annam', where Christians were occasionally persecuted. But for the missionaries to be formally out of reach of the mandarins, the Highlands could not belong to Annam – as the French used to call the country then. Hence the reference to Laos, whereof little was known at the time. France spent the years 1858 to 1862 conquering the southern part of Vietnam, consisting of Saigon and the Mekong Delta, and called it their colony of Cochinchina, whereupon the missionaries did not hesitate to see their mission as part of Cochinchina, despite the great distance. In later stages, the region would again be added to Laos, then to Annam when all of Indochina was 'pacified', and declared autonomous under direct French rule after 1945.

Despite the claim to belong to Cochinchina, the Kontum mission was not secure until the effective occupation of all Vietnam by the French in the latter half of the 1880s. The missionaries were threatened by malaria, by nearby groups like the Sedang and Jarai, and by Vietnamese mandarins, who occasionally tried to subdue the Catholic refuge in their 'hinterland'. This culminated during the 'Save the King'-movement (*Cân Vuong*) and the 'Revolt of the Literati', which followed upon the imposition of the French protectorate on Vietnam in 1884, and the subsequent appeal for resistance by the young emperor Hàm Nghi. The persecution of Christians by the Literati only helped to harden the missionaries' attitude *vis-à-vis* the Vietnamese authorities (Guerlach 1887b: 514–16; Guilleminet 1952b: 448–56; Simonnet 1977: 34–5). At that time, P. Guerlach turned out to be the strong man of the mission who successfully organized the Bahnar and Rengao (also known as Reungao or Rongao) against more aggressive groups like the Sedang and the Jarai as well as against the Literati. Not only was he militarily successful, but he would also be the major spokesman for the mission, in matters political and ethnographic.

Father Guerlach was quite clear about the role of ethnography in the proselytizing process. The missionaries carried on ethnographic studies to facilitate conversion:

> Since I am in the midst of the savage peoples, I devote myself to the study of their habits and superstitions ... My only goal was to know the religious beliefs well, in order to better demonstrate the absurdity of the superstitions, when necessary.
>
> (Guerlach 1887a: 441–2)

Guerlach and the other missionaries turned their attention not only to religion (regarded as 'superstitions'), because they realized that in 'primitive' society 'everything is connected with everything':

> Among all the primitive peoples, the religious and political systems, the rituals and the domestic habits are so intimately intertwined, that in order to understand their history and national organization well, the knowledge of traditions and religious doctrines is indispensable.
>
> (Guerlach 1887a: 441)

This could be taken for a statement of ethnographic holism, i.e. the realization that different spheres of life are mutually dependent.

The Dutch anthropologist Anton Blok viewed ethnographic holism as a consequence of the anthropological method of participant observation, which came to be the hallmark of professional Anglo-Saxon anthropology from the 1920s (Blok 1977: 49). The method necessitated an extended stay of the researcher among the group under study, whereby the participation in daily affairs would allow for the intensive contact necessary for an intimate knowledge of indigenous culture. Blok is correct insofar as he situates ethnographic holism as a consequence of ethnographic fieldwork, but, as the above quotation of Guerlach shows, this is by no means confined to professional anthropology beginning in the 1920s. In his book on the absence of history in anthropology, Nicholas Thomas criticizes the propensity of professional anthropologists since Malinowski to reject non-anthropological ethnographies as prejudiced and of limited value. Although their aim was interventionist, early missionaries often developed an extensive knowledge of indigenous cultures by virtue of their long residence 'in the field' and their intimate knowledge of the language. Missionary reports, however, hardly fit into the ethnographic format which modern anthropologists require (Thomas 1989: 69–79). Relevant ethnographic observations are often hidden in missionary narratives, as is the case with the account of the history of the Kontum mission by Père Dourisboure. Such missionary narratives were targeted at a metropolitan audience with the intention to foster financial and political support for the missionary activities. The missionary narrative can be distinguished from the ethnographic format employed in Père Combes' appendix to *Les sauvages Ba-Hnars*, which represents the *moeurs et coutumes* [manners and customs] of the Bahnar in a more systematic way, detached from the missionary presence.

The ethnographic knowledge of early missionaries more often than not was the consequence of a purposeful research strategy, as Thomas aptly notes (1989: 69–79). This goes for the missionaries of Kontum, too, who were dependent on an intimate ethnographic knowledge of the local cultures, not only for effective conversion, but also for their sheer survival. The only 'research method' available to them was 'participant observation' in the community where they lived for years at a stretch. Again, it was Guerlach who formulated this missionary research strategy:

> As I did not want to say anything which was not the exact expression of savages' beliefs, I have consulted all the natives who could inform me. I have tried to see for myself everything that a missionary could decently look at.
>
> (Guerlach 1887a: 442)

The condition of the missionaries in the Central Highlands was rather similar to the condition of ethnographic fieldwork by the early professional anthropologists in the 1920s. In both situations the locality of action was very limited, and the success of both missionary and anthropological ventures was contingent upon the quality of knowledge of the local culture based on direct contacts with the host population. It is hardly surprising, then, that such a similar position within the host society would, both in early missionary writing and in early professional ethnographies based on anthropological fieldwork, favor an awareness of the 'wholeness' of the host culture. This holistic approach *avant la lettre*, based upon *participant observation*, produced descriptions of the manners, customs and religious beliefs and practices of the local populations, often subdivided in chapters, meant to reflect the different aspects of society in 'reality'.

But ethnographic holism is not simply a reflection of the local situation. Rather, as Robert Thornton argued in 'The Rhetoric of Ethnographic Holism' (1988), it is a rhetorical construct, implying not only the unity of the society (tribe, ethnic group, nation), but also its compartmentalization in 'social parts' which together form a 'social/cultural whole'. This classification of social life, which then is closed into an ethnographic whole, functions as a rhetorical trope: it is implied that together the parts/chapters in the narrative form an ethnographic whole as a reflection of the 'social whole' in the 'real world', thus legitimizing the ethnographic genre. The actual ethnographic descriptions of the missionaries did not, however, relate the several cultural spheres to each other for lack of an adequate theoretical model, like later anthropologists would have in functionalism and other theoretical paradigms. Of course, the aim of the missionaries was not theoretical but practical, for they wanted to use their knowledge to convert the local population.

Naturally, the missionaries focused on Montagnard religion, which was to be replaced by Christianity. Their religion was seen as based on fear and terror, inspired by the *beidjaou* or sorcerers, whose position had to be undermined since they were the main obstacles to conversion to Christianity. In the writings of Dourisboure, Combes and Guerlach every setback was ascribed to the nefarious work of the devil. Père Guerlach even claimed that the *beidjaou* were accomplices of the devil, and repeatedly confessed his hatred for them:

> I have learnt details which prove that the devil intervenes in the initiation of sorcerers.
>
> (Guerlach 1887a: 514–16)

If one accepts that it is the devil who controls Montagnard society through the sorcerers and their pagan practices, then the realization of the 'wholeness' of the local culture needs no further explanation by way of a social or cultural analysis. The implicit message is that such an intellectual exercise is superfluous since we are dealing with pagans and savages, in need of salvation through the Gospel. However savage they may be, the effort is still worthwhile for they belong to the human race:

> I conclude ... that all the savages who live in the vast country situated between Cochinchina, Cambodia and Laos belong to the same branch of the great human family.
>
> (Combes in Dourisboure, 1929: 312)

It is interesting to note how Christianized Montagnards by the process of conversion not only cease to be pagan but to be savage, too.

The missionary ethnographic writings were not simply intellectual exercises, but were intended to gain support for their activities from the metropolitan public in France through such missionary journals as *Les missions catholiques* and the *Annales de la propagation de la foi*. The aim was twofold: political support for military protection of the missions from the general public; and financial support for their activities from the Catholic public. A variety of rhetorical means were used to that end. Political support was sought for the imposition of French rule in Vietnam and the Central Highlands, which would render the missionary activities certainly less hazardous. Throughout the nineteenth century, the French Catholics had been an important part of the colonial party (cf. Cady 1954: passim). A usual rhetorical trope consisted of depicting the missionaries and their Catholic converts as martyrs, victims of persecution by the Vietnamese mandarins. The only way to effectively protect the missionary effort, then, would be the occupation of Cochinchina, Annam and Tonkin, the three parts which the French distinguished in Vietnam. Simultaneously, financial support was sought for the mission in the Highlands. This was done by depicting the missionary effort as a *crusade*, not simply against paganism, but against the work of the devil himself, who putatively controlled the lives of the Montagnards through the actions of the local sorcerers. Their reliance on the devil made them into real 'savages', as the Montagnards invariably were called in early missionary writings.

Apart from staying alive and establish themselves permanently, the main effort of the missionaries was directed against the indigenous sorcerers. Father Guerlach, the most militant priest in the early years of the Kontum mission, tried to limit the influence of the sorcerers by presenting Western technology as magic, and pose himself as a still mightier sorcerer, the 'great *beidjaou* of the Christians'. And he did so consciously:

> I am quite ready to fight the pagan impostor with his own arms.
>
> (Guerlach 1887a: 455)

Father Combes, who wrote the first ethnographic account in 1853, told of the way in which the act and the effects of writing were considered to be magical actions in themselves. In his words, the missionaries (and to a lesser extent Vietnamese) were respected for their power over 'the paper that speaks' (Combes in Dourisboure 1929: 312–13). In the last decade, a number of post-modern anthropologists have commented upon the social effects of writing as a technology, hinting at processes of classification, ethnic identification, and the construction and transfer of knowledge on indigenous societies. In the next chapters, I shall try to make clear how European and Vietnamese writing affected Montagnard society. But also the act of writing itself directly affected Bahnar society as it was considered to be a magical act. The status this conferred upon the missionaries helped to enhance their position within Montagnard society at a time when they still lacked the force to impose themselves on the Montagnards by virtue of the absence of a military colonial presence.

In so far as the missionaries posed as mighty sorcerers by presenting Western technology as magic, they had to some degree adapt to local custom, which was one of the methods of conversion. Such adaptations were simply necessary in order to establish and maintain themselves in the host society. This was most evident in the alliances such as the one contracted between the Bahnar 'chief' Kiêm and Father Dô, performed in the traditional way, requiring animal sacrifices and the shedding and drinking of each other's blood, among other 'pagan' rituals. Such alliances were necessary to maintain and enhance their status *vis-à-vis* the Bahnar and neighboring groups in the years before the French occupation of Annam. As soon as the Christian community had been firmly established in the Kontum area in the 1880s, the missionaries could work the other way around: Conversion was facilitated by the adaptation of local customs, beliefs and rituals to Christian dogma and ritual by modifying them.

But maybe the most important cause of the success of the Kontum mission among the Bahnar was the military force which the Bahnar derived from the weapons and the political organization provided by the missionaries. In particular, the militant Father Guerlach was very capable in this respect. In 1883, right after the imposition of the French protectorate on Annam, Mgr. Van Camelbeke, bishop of Qui-Nhon, sent Guerlach to Kontum, along with Father Irigoyen, in order to replace the old Dourisboure, and to support Father Vialleton who had come to Kontum in 1875. Guerlach immediately set out to organize both the Bahnar and Rengao around Kontum in order to better resist more aggressive neighboring groups, like the Sedang and the Jarai. At the time, the Highlands were subject to slaving raids that supplied the flourishing slave markets in Cambodia, Laos and Siam. This situation incited many Montagnard villages and groups of warriors to engage in raids against other villages or groups, leading to excessive intervillage warfare and causing great insecurity and instability in the entire Highlands region. The Bahnar and Rengao in particular were subject to raids by Sedang and Jarai groups, until Father Guerlach, using his guns, managed to gather some 1200 Bahnar warriors in a successful attempt to counter Jarai encroachment upon Bahnar territory. Of course, this event greatly enhanced the prestige of the missionaries among the Montagnards, but the obvious alliance of the missionaries with some Bahnar and Rengao groups in the vicinity of Kontum restricted their success to those groups only.

Missionaries and colonial rule

In the 1880s, the missionaries began to be more directly involved in the military activities and the politics of French colonial expansion. French military explorers began to penetrate the Highlands from Cochinchina, the southern portion of Vietnam, which had been turned into a French colony between 1862 and 1867. This penetration by military explorers from Cochinchina preceded the attempts at pacification, which would be pursued after the establishment of the French protectorate over Annam and Tonkin (1882–85). During the first years of colonial administration in Annam,[5] the Mission supported attempts at penetration, passing on their knowledge to French officials and actively supporting military penetration. The mission station of Kontum was regarded, and actually functioned, as an outpost of the French penetration of the Highlands. Virtually monopolizing ethnographic knowledge on the Montagnards, the Mission aided the colonial penetration by means of a conscious transfer of ethnographic insights (especially into contacts and networks), as well as an unconscious transfer of knowledge insofar as military and civil colonial officials drew upon ethnographic notes of missionaries in their dealings with the local populations. Thus, early French perception of the Montagnards was greatly influenced by missionary representations.

The involvement of the missionaries was evident in all three major events taking place in the Highlands during the last two decades of the century. During the 'Revolt of the Literati' (1885–88), an early expression of Vietnamese resistance against the French occupation of Tonkin and Annam, Catholics were targets of the movement, because they often acted as a fifth column for the French. During the Mayréna Affair (1888–90), the Belgian adventurer Mayréna, charged with an official mission to counter Siamese (British, German) influence in the Highlands, relied on support from the missionaries of Kontum to found a 'Sedang Kingdom', expecting the auriferous rivers in Sedang country to be highly profitable. After official disavowal by the colonial authorities, Mayréna was denied further access to 'French' Indochina. Guerlach then brought his 'Bahnar-Rengao Confederation' under nominal Vietnamese authority, even when Siamese military columns tried to enforce Siamese claims to Laos and the Highlands. During the expedition of the 'Mission Pavie' (1890–93), installed to secure Laos and the left bank of the Mekong river for France, Kontum functioned as the base area for military expeditions by the captains Cupet and De Malglaive.[6] All three events were related to the claims that France developed to the territory east of the Mekong. These claims were upheld in the face of the Vietnamese struggle to remain independent, and of Siamese efforts to extend their influence eastward towards the South China Sea, by and large following the Annam Cordillera (*Chaîne Annamitique* or *Truòng Son*) in the eastern part of the Highlands. The French considered the Mekong River to be a secure border against any British or German schemes rather than a viable transport route. Already in the 1860s, the great 'Mekong Expedition' of Doudart de Lagrée and Francis Garnier proved that the Mekong was not a viable route to southern China, which shifted French colonial interest to the Red River in Tonkin as a possible commercial artery. Although there is much talk of ethnographic study in the reports, not much more is done than noting the existence of indigenous populations (Garnier 1873: passim; Taboulet 1970: 5–88; Valette 1969: 7–12; Villemereuil 1883: passim).

During the heyday of the royalist *Cân Vuong*-movement (1885–88), the Kontum Mission functioned as a stronghold for the French.[7] In 1885, the young emperor Hàm Nghi fled the court with the influential regent Tôn Thât Thuyêt to the mountains in Quang-Nam. There he appealed to the people of Vietnam and to the mandarins to revolt against the protectorate that France had imposed upon 'Annam' and 'Tonkin' in 1884. The French tried to crush the movement with military force, but did not have the power to protect the Catholic minority. The royalists assumed that the Catholics acted as a fifth column for the French – an assumption which was affirmed by events. An-Khê, a Vietnamese settlement on the road from Qui-Nhon on the coast to Kontum, was one of the bulwarks of the *Cân Vuong*. The An-Khê stronghold was led by Mai Xuân Thuong, who claimed to be a descendant of the famous Tây Son rebels of the eighteenth century. With the help of Jarai allies, the royalists tried to attack Kontum, but found the two main routes leading to Kontum blocked by father Guerlach with an armed Bahnar band, and by Pim, the son of the Bahnar chief Kiêm. To the north, Guerlach had secured the alliance of the Sedang. Kontum was then blockaded for almost three years, until the French Navy and its Vietnamese allies captured An Khê in 1887. Guerlach used the occasion to forge new alliances against the Jarai, and managed to oust the Jarai from former Bahnar territory with a considerable army, much to the surprise of the Bahnar themselves (Guerlach 1887b: 538–89; Maitre 1912a: 519–32; Simonnet 1977: 237–41).

The movement was repressed and Hàm Nghi captured by the French, but a new problem surfaced in the Highlands. In 1888, Hàm Nghi had sent a request for help to the King of Siam. Although the message had been intercepted by the French Resident of Bình Đinh province, there was an increase of Siamese activities east of the Mekong, which led to great concern among the French. In the same year, 1888, the Governor of Cochinchina, Le Myre de Vilers, charged the Belgian adventurer Charles David de Mayréna with a mission to penetrate the Highlands, in particular the Kontum area. Mayréna was supposed to take control of Kontum and the surrounding territory in the name of France, as long as the status of both Laos and the Highlands were still insecure pending research in the Vietnamese archives.[8] Carrying letters of recommendation of the *Gouverneur de Cochinchine* and of the bishop of Qui-Nhon, Mayréna presented himself in Kontum, where he acquired the support of Father Guerlach for a Sedang Federation. Helped by his impressive appearance, Mayréna managed to conclude ritual alliances with some Sedang leaders, which he interpreted as their 'submission'. He then acclaimed himself as *Marie 1er*, *Roi des Sédang*, and devised a constitution for his 'kingdom'. With the Catholic religion branded as state religion, the Sedang constitution was co-signed by Guerlach and Father Vialleton, head of the Kontum mission station. Vialleton brought the 'Bahnar-Rengao confederation' into the Sedang Kingdom. This alliance was initially recognized by the Résident-supérieur of Annam, Rheinart, who was not yet aware of Mayréna's separatist ambitions with his kingdom.

In September Mayréna left the Highlands in order to negotiate in Qui-Nhon and Haiphong on the status of his kingdom. He tried to capitalize on the strategic location and the uncertain political situation of the Highlands, as well as on rumors concerning gold deposits in the Sedang area. He gained no results with the French administration, despite – or because of – threats to seek British and German protection. He went back to Europe and became a living legend in the cafés of Paris, but he did not succeed in attracting the interest of major European powers for his kingdom. He was more successful economically, and made a comfortable living by selling state obligations and aristocratic titles of his Sedang Kingdom. In Brussels, he found Belgian investors willing to finance a major expedition to take possession of the Sedang kingdom. On the way to Indochina, the expedition fell apart due to internal conflicts and in the face of opposition by the French, British and Dutch colonial authorities. Mayréna was abandoned by his companions, was denied passage to Indochina by the Singapore authorities, and went to the small island of Tioman near Singapore, where he died in obscure circumstances in 1890.

The abortive attempt to establish a separate kingdom created a scandal in colonial circles, where the missionaries were blamed for their support to Mayréna. In a letter to Émile Jamais, Undersecretary for the Colonies, Governor-General Richaud of French Indochina complained about the disloyal behavior of the missionaries:

> M. de Mayréna's efforts to have himself acknowledged as king of these territories would not in itself be a serious matter. What is gravely important is the fact that the Mission should have chosen sides with a person who is claiming to detach from a country placed under our protectorate a region which is dependent on it.[9]

Résident-Supérieur Rheinart of Annam made it clear in a letter of 27 November 1888 to Mgr. Van Camelbeke, bishop of Qui-Nhon, that the 'tribes' could not be considered independent:

> The political map of Indochina contains no 'blanks', any more than the religious map drawn up by the *Société des Missions Étrangères*. The country is divided into states which are regularly constituted and recognized, leaving no room for independent tribes.[10]

Rheinart hushed the affair and sent Resident Guiomar of Qui-Nhon to Kontum in order to liquidate the kingdom (which had been a legal fiction anyway, as the Montagnards themselves were hardly involved). Guiomar, however, was far from convinced of the patriotism which allegedly motivated the missionaries' actions:

> The missionaries consider the country which they occupy as their property and they never willingly encourage any European at all to settle there. ... After first dreaming of founding a free state like that of the Jesuits in Paraguay and thinking that they found in Mayréna a pliable instrument who would be entirely at their disposal, they soon discovered their mistake and found that he had an appetite for independence. So they preferred to abandon their projects rather than find themselves subordinated to a master. This business has nothing to do with Patriotism.[11]

The missionaries made up for their mistake by putting their 'Bahnar-Rengao Confederation' formally under French authority.

Guiomar found it expedient to invest the missionaries with administrative authority for pragmatic reasons:

> Will one still find them so helpful when they see that we are slowly but progressively extending our control over territories which they regard as theirs, and where we will be bound in the nature of things to exercise a certain amount of restraint over their activities? I am afraid we will not, and I fear we will soon be confronted by a latent hostility which will be all the more dangerous because we cannot combat it openly.
>
> (ibid.)

Fearing conflicts between the missionaries and colonial officials once a secular administration would be established, Guiomar advised that the administration should keep out and let the missionaries continue to administrate the area themselves.

This is not only a confirmation of the *de facto* situation, but also a recognition of the monopoly on ethnographic knowledge by the missionaries. This is also evident from Guiomar's realization that ... 'until today the Fathers have had complete freedom of action in these regions, together with a certain authority which they owe to their European origin and above all to their knowledge of the language.' (ibid.) Thus, their political authority derived from their ethnographic authority regarding Montagnards *vis-à-vis* other Europeans. Guiomar's thinking is impregnated with the discourse as it was pronounced by the missionaries for consumption by European Catholics, viz. that the Montagnards were violent savages, lacking everything, inhabiting the most unpromising and unhealthy lands, and having no intrinsic value. In this context, Guiomar finds that 'it would be burdensome and even useless to proceed with [our occupation of the Bahnar and Sedang country]', and he would be happy to leave it to the missionaries, 'who will be all the more helpful to us for being given more independence' (ibid.).

The 'Mayréna Affair', as it became known, gave rise to a voluminous literature, some with serious pretensions, others with romantic motives. An unpublished manuscript by the Belgian Jacques Maran (1892; EFEO Mss. Europ.) was followed by an article by Jean Marquet, 'Un aventurier du XIXe siècle: Marie Ier, Roi des Sédangs (1888–1890)' in the *BAVH* (1927) and a book by Marcel Soulié, *Marie Ier, Roi des Sédangs (1888–1890)* (1927). These accounts were discussed extensively by Marcel Ner in the *BEFEO* (1927). The famous French novelist and politician André Malraux based his book *La voie royale* (1930) on the adventures of Mayréna and on a vague notion of the historical tributes which the Jarai *p'tau* and the Khmer Kings sent each other triennially. In his *Antimémoires* (1947), too, Malraux made occasional, veiled reference to the Affair. As late as 1978, a French missionary found it opportune to defend the missionaries of Kontum against 'infamous attacks' and slander in a serious French anthropological journal (Léger 1978: 231–247). Outside of France, the

Mayréna Affair was covered by Sir Hugh Clifford (1926), a senior colonial official in Asia and British Africa. More recently, the 'Mayréna Affair' was dealt with extensively by the American anthropologist Gerald C. Hickey in his book *Kingdom in the Morning Mist* (1988). Hickey did not use the voluminous archival material on the 'Affair' in several French archives as it was intended as a 'commercial' book (personal communication). Through this body of literature, not to mention the numerous occasions when the 'Mayréna Affair' was referred to in passing, the event acquired mythical proportions, even enhanced by his mysterious death.[12]

Even with the end of the 'Mayréna Affair', the status of the Highlands was not yet clarified. Between 1890 and 1893, the Mission actively supported the members of the 'Mission Pavie' and other French agents, who tried to secure the left bank of the Mekong, including Laos and the Central Highlands (which were not yet an integral part of Annam), from Siamese territorial claims. (The 'Mission Pavie' will be dealt with more extensively in the next section on military explorations.) The missionaries were allowed to administer the Kontum area from 1898 to 1907 in the name of the French protectorate, in the format of the *Délégation de Kontum, sous le contrôle du commissaire d'Attopeu*; Kontum thus became temporarily part of *Bas-Laos* (southern Laos), in spite of the Vietnamese claims to the Highlands which legitimized the French claims versus Siam (Guerlach 1906: 110).

Not every French colonist and administrator was charmed by the concept of missionary rule in parts of Indochina. Guided by anticlerical and freemasonic currents in French culture around the turn of the century, colonists (*colons*) and journalists every now and then attacked the missionaries in colonial newspapers. When Camille Pâris and A. Barsanti published a pamphlet (*Missionnaires d'Asie. Oeuvre néfaste des Congrégations. Protectorat des Chrétiens*, 1905) against the 'nefarious works' of the missionaries, Father Guerlach felt obliged to retort in a booklet with the ironical title *L'oeuvre néfaste* (1906). Echoing Resident Guiomar, Pâris and Barsanti accused the missionaries of Kontum of having attempted to establish a theocratic state, similar to the Jesuit State of Paraguay, with the help of Mayréna. They remarked that the net result was that the missionaries were allowed to rule the Kontum area relatively undisturbed. Guerlach replied that he had acted out of patriotism, as Mayréna did carry an official order in the name of France and letters of recommendation of high-ranking French officials. In his words, the missionaries had just wanted to spread French authority, but they were duped by Mayréna who had misused the support of the missionaries for his own profit. Also underscoring the patriotic attitude of the missionaries when members of the 'Mission Pavie' faced Siamese incursions into the Highlands, Guerlach proudly declared his loyalty and usefulness to the colonial régime:

> When I came to the Bahnar for the first time, the land was in the most complete state of anarchy and commotion ... When the French Administration will establish itself in the land, it will find it calm and pacified.

> (Guerlach 1906: 108)

With the establishment of a regular colonial administration by the appointment in 1907 of Jules Guénot as *Délégué* of Kontum, relations between the mission and the administration deteriorated, as Guiomar had predicted in 1889. This was due to a certain competition over the spheres of influence and competence. After all, the success of the mission among the Montagnards had to a large extent depended upon the military organization they provided to some groups, and upon their monopoly of Western goods, often presented as magic. These assets naturally decreased in value with the establishment of a regular colonial administration in Kontum, which caused a series of conflicts between the Mission and the colonial administration on their respective spheres of influence with respect to the Montagnards. Missionaries were accused of using not only persuasive means of conversion: expulsion of non-Catholic Montagnards from Catholic villages, holding slaves, appropriation of village lands, insulting officials, attacks on people, and murder, to name a few items on the list.[13] Official chroniclers of the Mission would 'accuse' individual colonial administrators of freemasonry, of hindering the mission and of promoting apostasy (Simonnet 1977: 258–60). This conflict reached a high point in the 1930s when colonial officials openly promoted the spread of Buddhism among the Montagnards.[14]

Since the success of the mission remained restricted to some Bahnar and Rengao groups in the vicinity of Kontum, the missionary attention shifted from the Montagnards to the ethnic Vietnamese again. The mission station at Kontum was originally meant to serve as refuge for Catholic Vietnamese from the lowlands, so there was a continuity of policy here. After the turn of the century, when the region around Kontum was sufficiently 'pacified', the missionaries promoted the immigration of Christian Vietnamese people to Kontum. Thus, Kontum increasingly became an enclave of ethnic Vietnamese (Viêt or Kinh) in Montagnard country. These developments led the missionaries to base their policy on the presence of ethnic Vietnamese in the area around Kontum. When compared with the Catholic Vietnamese, who were very loyal to the French and considered to be 'trustworthy', the Montagnards, who tended to remain somewhat aloof and keep some degree of autonomy – if they did not reject the missionaries completely – seemed unreliable and unpredictable, prone to apostasy and 'superstition'. In the mind of leading missionaries, for the Montagnards to become true Christians they had to change culturally, which could only be forced upon them by the presence of an ethnic Vietnamese community (Durand 1907: 1158–71; Kemlin 1922: passim; Simonnet 1977: 259–61).

In the ethnographic discourse by the missionaries the Montagnards were depicted as good-for-nothing savages, who were childlike, evil, violent, and not to be trusted. The early missionaries, who called their mission post the *Mission des Sauvages*, believed that the Montagnards were terrorized by the sorcerers, who were thought to be the personification of the devil. The Montagnards constituted an inferior race compared to the ethnic Vietnamese, and were considered hardly capable of development and civilization. Nevertheless, Christianization could only succeed if it was accompanied – even preceded – by 'civilization' (cf. Launay

1894-III: 286). Montagnard culture had to disappear if Christianity was to succeed. But the employment of Viêt collaborators in the Kontum Mission tended to preclude missionary success among the Montagnards, instead of helping them develop through change. In 1908, therefore, Father Jannin took up the idea, initially scorned by everybody, to establish a Montagnard school for the formation of Bahnar catechists. The school was moderately successful in so far as it adapted the curriculum to Bahnar culture. But Christian Simonnet, chronicler of the Mission of *les Grands Plateaux*, saw an insurmountable problem in the gap between the 'evolutionary level of the Bahnar and the study and lifestyle required from priests', risking either '*déracination*' or a 'too perfect readaptation' (Simonnet 1977: 261–5).

Père Kemlin, missionary and ethnographer

The increased independence of the missionaries from the indigenous communities allowed missionary ethnography to culminate in the work of Father Kemlin, published in the *Bulletin de l'École Française d'Extrême-Orient* (*BEFEO*), the journal of France's prestigious bulwark of Orientalism in Hanoi. In a series of three essays in the *BEFEO*, 'Rites agraires des Reungao' (1909–10), 'Les songes et leur interprétation chez les Reungao' (1910), and 'Alliances chez les Reungao' (1917), Kemlin ventured deep into the vernacular belief systems, religion included. The later French anthropologist Condominas would call Kemlin's work 'a model of the *genre*; nobody has penetrated so deeply and with such richness into the mentality of the Montagnards' (Condominas 1966: 140).

Above, we have mentioned the distinction between the missionary narrative and the ethnographic format. Former accounts by missionaries would conform to the rules of the missionary narrative rather than those of the ethnographic description, which is inevitable for reports destined for and published in French missionary journals with the aim to attract the attention and sympathy of the metropolitan Catholic public for the missionary effort. In a publication of 1909 on the Jarai in *Les Missions Catholiques*, Kemlin adopts the 'missionary narrative style' reminiscent of earlier accounts by Père Guerlach, expressing his contempt for this 'country putrefied by superstitions and vain observances' (1909a: 248) and summoning his public to pray for the Jarai. Kemlin's ethnographic articles in the *BEFEO*, on the other hand, betray a genuine interest in Rengao culture, and abide by the rules of the ethnographic format, as could be expected in a journal with explicit scholarly pretensions. The choice of a systematic ethnographic format, excluding the missionary narrative and moral judgement in favor of ethnographic precision, is not only dependent on individual interest and preferences and on publishing opportunities (cf. Thomas 1989: 69–79), but reflects the changing context of the missionary enterprise. The missionaries grew less and less dependent on the Montagnards for their missionary success, for their physical survival even, as the setting became more secure with the penetration of a regular colonial administration. Together with the exemption from formal political responsibility this rendered a more detached view possible.

Kemlin's last essay, 'Alliances chez les Reungao', was particularly illuminating on Rengao religion, as it showed that the Rengao not only contracted alliances with other humans, but also with the spirits of plants, animals, or geographic objects. Kemlin considered the religious worldview at the base of the alliances as animism, sometimes resulting in fetishism:

> Perhaps I have dwelt a bit long on this subject, passing in review all of the categories of beings which may be useful to us. But this detailed study seemed necessary to me in order to make understand not only the nature of the different alliances which the Rengao may bind to the world above, but also of the cult which they render to the spirits, as well as the foundation of *Moï* fetishism.
>
> (Kemlin 1917: 111)

Kemlin's study of Rengao religious practices served not only scientific but also practical ends, in so far as the work showed clearly that Rengao religion was primarily an individual affair, with hardly any formalized leadership (Kemlin 1917: 113).

This insight nuanced the view that Montagnard religion was imposed by sorcerers, who invoked the devil with their machinations. It also made it clear for Kemlin that the missionary ideal of a universal religion common to all ethnic groups must seem nonsense to them, and that the missionaries must appear as singularly eccentric men, who had no idea what was going on in this world. But Kemlin was well aware that the attraction of the Catholic religion did not lie in its theological qualities, but rather in the practical advantages offered to new converts in economic and political fields. Already the former Governor-General De Lanessan noted in his *Les missions et leur protectorat* (1907: 42–3) that conversions were more often than not economically motivated, and tended to disjoin individuals from their family and community, resulting in great social tensions. This was not unknown to the first missionaries of Kontum, like Père Dourisboure, who commented on the absence of authority among the Bahnar where 'no authority, civil or domestic, is recognized. Each individual is a private person and nothing else' (cf. Launay 1894-III: 283). That is why the Christianized Montagnards were grouped together in separate villages, where 'he civilized them while christianizing them more and more' (Launay 1894-III: 286). The ethnographic work of Kemlin was thus a cultural explanation of the difficulties the missionaries encountered with respect to the conversion of the 'savages', and served as legitimation of the shift of missionary attention to the Kinh Catholics, who migrated in steady numbers to Kontum.

The work of Kemlin would be the last missionary ethnographic statement with scientific authority on the Montagnards until Jacques Dournes arrived after World War II to work among the Koho of Haut-Donnaï, and later among the Jarai of Cheo-Reo. This relative absence of missionary ethnographic writing between the two world wars reflects not only a shift of attention of the missionaries of Kontum to the Kinh community in Kontum, but also to the Catholic Montagnard community which was already more or less domesticated. The latter were to be 'civilized', which means that they adapted to the culture introduced by the French missionaries, and to a lesser extent to the culture of the Kinh Catholics. In this context of consolidation of conversions in the face of rivalry between mission and administration, too much missionary attention for the indigenous cultures seemed counterproductive in terms of conversion and Christianization. Instead, it would be the colonial administrators who eventually turned to ethnography as an instrument of colonial rule.

Only when the existence of the Kontum mission was threatened once again, did a missionary evolutionist discourse reemerge, in the 1970s. The threat of the pagans had given way to the threat of atheist Communists, the new barbarians – as many missionaries saw it. The narrative of the Mission, once presented as a formidable crusade against the pagan savages, was now turned into a crusade against the Communists. This was clear from the work by Mgr. Paul Seitz, bishop of Kontum until 1975, and by Christian Simonnet, chronicler of the *Mission des Sauvages* turned *Mission des Grands Plateaux*. Seitz speaks of a Montagnard culture, ruled by tradition, untouched by history, which suddenly is turned upside down by 'red hordes', who destroy the missionary action among the Montagnards, and thus destroy the Montagnards and their souls. Using terms like 'future shock', acculturation, and transformation, and referring to eminent anthropologists like Condominas, Margaret Mead, and Lévi-Strauss, Seitz saw the 'traditional' culture, reduced to folklore items, ripped apart by intolerant Vietnamese policies, ignoring the history of Western penetration and colonial rule altogether. The *Men of Dignity* (*Les hommes debout*, 1977), so eager to preserve their liberty and independence, now supposedly bend down under the Communist yoke. Simonnet, still impressed by the narrative of Dourisboure, describes the history of the 'savages' turned Montagnards as a result of a *politique d'égards*. After the chapters in which the Montagnards are depicted as true savages, threatening their Christian benefactors with their violent, childlike and unpredictable behavior, other chapters follow where they play the role of innocent victims, sacrificed by lowland Vietnamese political interests in which they have no part. Thus, Montagnards were depicted as noble savages destroyed by the new 'barbarians', the ethnic Vietnamese.

Military explorations and ethnographic models

After the great expedition of the *Commission d'Exploration du Mekong* of 1866–68, headed by Doudart de Lagrée and by Francis Garnier (cf. above), a series of explorations of the Central Highlands were undertaken from Cochinchina, which had been wrested from Vietnam and turned into a French colony. The unsuccessful attempt by Francis Garnier and the merchant Dupuis to take control of the Red River in Tonkin served to underscore the colonial aspirations of France. After licking its wounds, France was eager to compensate for its humiliation by the German armies in the war of 1870, and for being deprived of its provinces on the left bank of the Rhine, Alsace and Lorraine. With a vociferous colonial party at home, intent upon the acquisition of territories outside Europe, the occupation of Annam and Tonkin, as the remaining parts of Vietnam were dubbed, could only be a matter of time. The juridical instrument with which France hoped to impose its will on a refractory court in Hue was the establishment of a protectorate (Cady 1954: 267–96; Laffey 1969: 282–99).[15] In anticipation of the inevitable conflict, the Governor of Cochinchina would send expeditions northward in order to explore the *hinterland* of Cochinchina, bordering on Annam, Cambodia and Laos. In a letter to the explorer Gautier, Governor Le Myre de Vilers would express his interest in the Montagnards as future subjects:

> The Colonial Government has a great interest in entertaining relations with the savage populations that one day we must group under our protectorate from the Red River in Tonkin to the Sông Be and Dong Naï in Cochinchina.
>
> (Le Myre de Vilers in Dubourg 1950: 123)

The first explorations were executed by the naval doctor Jules Harmand in 1877, who was charged by the French Department of Public Education with a scientific mission in the northern part of the Highlands, in order to find a route between Hue and Bassac in southern Laos. The importance if his work lay in his denunciation of the slave trade which was taking place along the Mekong and which disrupted the entire region on the east bank of the Mekong. The image of continuous raids against villages and the capture of Montagnard and Kinh people to be sold in the great slave markets of Phnom Penh and Bangkok shocked both Harmand and his contemporary audience. His plea for suppression of the slave trade was heard by the Governor of Cochinchina, who commissioned M. Sylvestre, chief of indigenous justice, to investigate the issue of slavery in Cochinchina. Eventually, the French authorities did take measures to suppress the slave trade once they gained control of the region (Harmand 1877a, b, 1879a, b, c; Sylvestre 1880: 95–114).[16] Before Harmand's journey to Laos, he briefly visited the *Moïs* of the upper reaches of the Don-nai river (Đông Nai), where he found that 'these people, however close to nature they be, have a hundred times better character than the *Annamese*' (Harmand 1877a: 530). At a time when a conflict with Vietnam drew inevitably near, such promising contacts in a region at the back of 'Annam' were not to be ignored.

The first civilian Governor of Cochinchina, Le Myre de Vilers, was appointed in 1879, after an era during which the colony was ruled as a French Navy possession by the 'Admirals'. Le Myre de Vilers took a special interest in the unexplored territories to the North, and sponsored several expeditions, big and small, to find the sources of the Donnai river. The first exploration in 1880, by the naval doctor Paul Néis and Lt. Septans, would never reach those sources. Instead, they stayed with a group of Montagnards near Baria, probably the Cau Maa, who used to pay tribute to the emperor in Hue but now did so to the colonial administration. Their description of the Montagnards focused on their physical appearance only. At the request of the Governor, they contacted a person known as *Patao*, whose fame as 'king of the Cau Maa' had reached Saigon by way of Kinh peddlers, the *thuôc lái* or *các lái*.[17] Patao turned out to be a trader of Lao descent, who had settled down and gained influence in the area, and who was interested in trade with the French (Néis 1880: 22, 28).

In 1882 three more expeditions took place under the auspices of Le Myre de Vilers. Lt. Septans and Lt. Gauroy explored the area around Brelam, where Père Azémar had had his mission station among the Stieng (cf. Azémar 1935). The contacts with *Patao* were followed up by L. Nouet, a civil servant, who was expected to investigate the border area between Annam and Cochinchina. That area was dominated by *Patao* who sought French protection against villages under 'Annamese' rule. Nouet's observations situated the Montagnards at the bottom of the evolutionary ladder:

> These human beings, superior to the animals by their use of fire, wander like these in the wilderness, in search of an insufficient subsistence, for the *Moi* are always hungry.
>
> (Nouet 1935: 89)

Surprised that the Montagnards did not obey a French decree from 1875, forbidding the practice of *rây* (shifting cultivation), Nouet mused on the consequences of a strict enforcement of the policy, speculating about their extinction. Colonization of the area by Viêt lowlanders would be a better solution than isolation, which would only perpetuate the present condition:

> If this population is destined to succumb, it would be better if it dies in struggle, even with unequal weapons ... Maybe the struggle for existence will develop among the savages a resisting force which is unknown today and only waits for an occasion to reveal itself.
>
> (ibid.: 100)

The Social-Darwinist fascination with the 'survival of the fittest' would be a recurring theme in French evolutionist texts on the Montagnards, who were considered as regressing, and headed for extinction.

By far the most interesting expeditions were led by Lt. Amédée Gautier, who conducted two successive explorations into the area of Brelam and of the upper Donnai River. He had to contact *Patao* again, in order to find out if he could be of use for the colonial administration, and if it was opportune to support his claims of being 'king of the *moi*'. Gautier described *Patao* as cunning and intelligent, but also as crooked, and not useful for the administration because of his propensity toward robbery. Gautier was then commissioned to contact the local population directly, in order to study them and gain their submission to France. Contrary to his predecessors, he took account of the ethnographic methods he used, valuing direct observation and the study of the vernacular language. Thus, he arrived at quite different conclusions than Nouet as to their 'character':

Until now, in order to judge the *moïs* one limited oneself to the observation of those who inhabit our colony. Due to this system one has formed the most false idea about these savages as one can possibly imagine.

(Gautier 1882: 48)

He contrasted the submitted Montagnards with the independent Montagnards, who were not degraded and corrupted like the first. Gautier stressed the latter's virtues: honesty, courage, industriousness, love for the family, and respect for others' rights (Gautier 1884: 139–49).

Gautier illustrated his image of the 'noble savage' with sometimes convincing examples. He contrasted, for example, the slave trade from which the domesticated Montagnards suffered to the indigenous form of slavery, which in his view was a wrong term, as the slaves were treated as additional, but otherwise ordinary members of the household (Gautier 1882: 48–50; see also note 16). In due course, Gautier obtained the formal submission of many villages, and levied taxes in the name of France. After Le Myre de Vilers had been replaced as Governor of Cochinchina by Thomson, who was not at all interested in the Montagnards or in the continuity of the policies of Le Myre de Vilers, Gautier fell out of grace. He was seen as way out of line and out of control and his approach was seen as fruitless. When *Patao* was informed about Gautier's fall from grace and made an attempt to kill him, Gautier was recalled to Saigon, and immediately sent back to France. His – for those days – extraordinary judgement based on sympathy, meant that his ethnographic work made no impact because it fell on deaf ears: the intended audience wanted to read different lines. His singularity even compromised his military career (Dubourg 1950: 129–38).

The Harmand Convention of 1882, negotiated by Jules Harmand between France and the court of Hue, prepared the imposition of the French protectorate on Vietnam. Although from 1884 onward the French forces occupied the Annamese and Tonkinese plains, the Central Highlands remained relatively unexplored territory for the time being. Yet, following the Mayréna Affair, the French claimed this area in order to cope with Vietnamese guerrillas who found shelter in the mountains. They resisted claims to this area by the Siamese government by allegedly protecting the nominal Annamese sovereignty over the Highlands, stretching it to the Mekong River in present-day Cambodia and Laos. In the wake of the Mayréna Affair, Captain Luce was commissioned to find evidence in the Imperial Archives of Hue regarding such Vietnamese claims over the left bank of the Mekong. In May 1889, Luce produced his 'evidence', being the mention made in the annals of the Ministry of Rites of tributes sent by *Thuy Xá* and *Hoa Xá*, the 'kingdoms' of the Jarai *p'tau apui* (Master of Fire) and *p'tau ia* (Master of Water) (Luce in De Reinach 1901: 30–2).

The French underscored their claims to the Highlands with military expeditions, penetrating the difficult area in order to contact the population and to explore the country. The explorers were commissioned to gather ethnographic data, with special reference to the political systems of the various ethnic groups. The most important expeditions from a political point of view were the ones headed by the captains Cupet and De Malglaive. Both captains took part in the famous 'Mission Pavie' which succeeded in winning Laos over to the French and ousting the Siamese from the Central Highlands in 1890. The conflicts between France and Siam resulted in 1893 in a short border war and a naval blockade of Bangkok. In the subsequent treaty, Siam abandoned all claims to the lands east of the Mekong River. In their reports, members of the Pavie Mission pleaded for an immediate occupation of the Central Highlands which by 1893, after the 'Franco-Siamese Treaty', were formally, if nominally, under French authority. Captain Cupet in particular argued that the only way to avoid future insurgencies in the plains of Annam would be a firm French hold on the mountainous hinterland (Cupet 1893: 177–247; Cupet in Pavie 1900: 407–24; Maitre 1912a: 526–34; Matgioi 1897: passim). Both captains Cupet and De Malglaive envisaged a 'peaceful conquest' of the area through a military and political organization which either would use the existing leaders or would have to create 'chiefs'. This *politique des chefs* would have to be coupled to the promotion of trade through French-controlled markets, and to a temporary avoidance of taxes and corvée labor (Cupet 1893: 248–56; De Malglaive in Pavie 1902: XXVI).

Contrary to missionary ethnographers, military explorers like Cupet saw the Montagnards as *barbarians* rather than *savages*, following the early evolutionary division of the history of humankind by Enlightenment philosophers in three stages, *l'état sauvage*, *l'état barbare* and *l'état civilisé*. As 'barbarians', the Montagnards were credited to have a rudimentary political system, to practice agriculture, to have a language, a religion, in short, to have culture. This implied that the Montagnards had leaders whom the explorers could contact and use through the *politique des chefs* – similar to British indirect rule developed later. However, the Montagnards were contrasted with the Vietnamese, Khmer and Lao civilizations in the plains, in that they resisted French domination, were not submissive like the Vietnamese, and were not to be trusted as was shown by the killing of military officers and explorers like Robert (1901), Grosgurin (1903), Odend'hal (1904) and Maitre (1914). After all, they remained barbarians. In general, they were seen as having harmful habits, like shifting cultivation, slavery and superstitions, which had to be eliminated under French rule. The participants of the *Mission Pavie* attributed the Montagnards' spirit of independence to two basic sentiments which putatively dominated their behavior: self-interest and fear. The French, then, should base their policy of using or creating local chiefs on these two sentiments (Cupet, 1893; Cupet in Pavie, 1900; De Malglaive in Pavie: 1902).

We may contrast the context of the missionary ethnographic practice with the military penetration. The missionaries initially led an awkward existence among the indigenous population that they wanted to convert. They did not have enough power to enforce changes, so they had to persuade by showing that their religion and their knowledge was superior. Therefore they had to study the culture and first and foremost, the religion of the local population. They considered this population as savages who were in need of a real religion. The word 'savages' not only legitimized their efforts at conversion, but also had to convince their Catholic, European audience of the hardships they suffered, thus evoking compassion and much-needed financial support. The context of the missionary ethnographic practice changed with the military penetration of the Central Highlands, which the French wished to control for strategic reasons.

While members of the Mission Pavie pleaded for a peaceful conquest of the Central Highlands, De Lanessan, Governor-general of French Indochina from 1891 to 1895, was more concerned with the pacification of the mountain areas of Tonkin, surrounding the Red River delta. These areas were divided in four military zones, where the military had a free hand in the military and civil administration of the area. The colonels Galliéni, Servière and Pennequin were considered to be rather successful in obtaining the submission of the rebel groups. Nevertheless, De Lanessan came into conflict with them because they tended to ignore the civil authorities and to alienate the local population unnecessarily with their brutal conduct. The Governor-General wanted to rule *via* the Vietnamese mandarins, using the existing political infrastructure, in order to reduce the expenses for government and to divert funds to the building of an economic infrastructure. This policy of so-called *association* between France and its colonies, first expounded by the explorer Jules Harmand in 1887, met with strong criticism from the French *colons* and other protagonists of *assimilation*. The latter reproached De Lanessan for being an *annamitophile*, as the famous explorer and physician Yersin, among others, phrased it. In this climate, De Lanessan did not favor more expeditions to the Central Highlands, let alone a military occupation of the area (De Lanessan 1895: 56–112; Yersin 1893: 42–51; Aubert 1931: 9–10; Lewis 1962: 129–53; Hickey 1982a: 245–58).

It is useful to take a closer look at the policy which Galliéni and Pennequin developed in the *territoires militaires* of Tonkin, a very heterogeneous area from an ethnic point of view. Their 'oilspot-method' (*tâche d'huile*) combined military repression of the rebellion with the political and social organization of the region. First a fort would be constructed in a strategic site in the fractious region, from which the surrounding population(s) would be militarily pacified. Then the infrastructure would be developed – roads, military posts and supervised markets constructed. When this area would be entirely controlled, a neighboring area would be pacified. Thus, this 'structural pacification' would spread like an oil spot. The political leadership in the area would be more or less respected, if the local leaders would formally submit to French authority. Local potentates, like Đê Tham and Đeo Van Tri, would be left in power, if they agreed to submit nominally and not to bother the French. Colonel Pennequin defined the role of the French authorities as a restricted one, granting each race its autonomy and keeping a balance between the different interests of each race (De Lanessan 1895: 56–112; Galliéni 1941: passim; Boudarel 1976: 137–40).

It would be Galliéni, famous as the cold-blooded defender of Paris during World War I, who formulated an explicit ethnic policy, connecting political control with the ethnography of a region during the 'pacification' of the northern mountain regions during the 1880s and 1890s:

It is the study of the races that inhabit a region which determines the political organization to be imposed and the means to be employed for its pacification. An officer who succeeds in drawing a sufficiently exact ethnographic map of the territory he commands, has almost reached its complete pacification, soon followed by the organization which suits him best. ... Every agglomeration of individuals – a race, a people, a tribe or a family – represents a sum of shared or opposed interests. If there are habits and customs to respect, there are also rivalries which we have to untangle and utilize to our profit, by opposing the ones to the others, and by basing ourselves on the ones in order to defeat the others.

(Galliéni 1941, or. 1913: 217)

This argument for a divide-and-rule policy on the basis of ethnographic knowledge would be very influential in the years to come. Around the turn of the century several ethnographic monographs and handbooks would be published by officers of the *territoires militaires*, like Lunet de la Jonquière, Bonifacy, and Diguet, focusing on the ethnic delimitation and the customs and habits of each group in northern Vietnam. McAlister (1967) describes how the resulting ethnic policy eventually affected the outcome of the Battle of Điên Biên Phu in 1954 (See Chapter 5).

The above statement by Galliéni not only posited the 'ideal' relationship between ethnographic knowledge and submission through a 'divide-and-rule policy', but did this by highlighting the distinctions between – often fluid – ethnic groups. In other words, it called for an effort toward ethnic identification, ethnic delimitation, and ethnographic mapping, arriving at an ethnographic classification with more or less scientific pretensions. In his book *Out of Time* (1989), Nicholas Thomas observes that '"pre-anthropological" descriptions of native people notably construct types and systematic differences ... in every colonized region such differences were created or encoded' (Thomas 1989: 38). This ethnographic practice is not simply a byproduct of the evolutionist perspective permeating ethnographic observations at the time, but also a strategic prerequisite for 'pacification' and administration. Thus, classification becomes very much a political act, since the construction of ethnic identities and boundaries reflect current power balances and political alliances in an overall fluid situation. In the following chapters, I shall show how successive attempts at pacification and administration of the Montagnards were attended by new attempts at more or less 'official' ethnic identification and delimitation through a process of ethnographic classification. This process could be initiated either by successive political regimes or by one and the same regime adopting a new perspective. The last time this happened in Vietnam was after 1975 by the current Communist regime. As bureaucratic regimes tend to ground their administration on the divisions at hand, such identities and boundaries are consolidated through a process which Condominas has termed 'tribalization' (Condominas 1966: 168). I shall return to this concept in the following chapters.

The divide-and-rule policy, as developed by Galliéni, would only be implemented with a considerable delay in the Central Highlands, as a result of the position taken by De Lanessan in the colonial debate, and – one might add – due to the lack of political and economical incentives to penetrate the area. However, Galliéni's approach would be considered as a model to follow or to reject, hence it was often referred to in the debates concerning the penetration. The first wave of expeditions took place in the 1880s and 1890s, when the Central Highlands were still contested area. Therefore, it is not surprising that the expeditions by Harmand (1877), Pavie (1890–93), Yersin (1892–93) and Debay (1894), were intended as exploration and penetration of the area, rather than as pacification, as was the case in Tonkin. The main problem then, was the delimitation of the border between French Indochina and Siam. More precisely, France tried to secure the east bank (*rive gauche*) of the Mekong River, which in actual practice meant that the Siamese military penetration, which had started with the Vietnamese collapse in the face of French pressure, had to be stopped and pushed back. As yet, pacification could wait.

Henri Maitre, explorer and pacificator

Following the De Lanessan era in French Indochina, the process of French *pénétration* was not very continuous, since the attempts depended on the *ad hoc* policies of the successive Governor-Generals in Indochina. The visionary Governor-General Paul Doumer, in office from 1897 to 1902 (who would die in 1932 as President of France), tried to equip French Indochina with institutions, infrastructure and an administrative apparatus, turning it into a more profitable colony. Averse to the idea of *populations insoumises* [populations not yet subjected to French rule] Doumer was pushing the process of penetration through the building of roads and – in the Highlands – the high altitude station of Dalat. However, rule of the Highlands from the protectorate of Laos proved less effective, as evidenced by the death of some of the explorers, like Robert (1901), Grosgurin (1903), and Odend'hal (1904). These setbacks to 'penetration' prompted Doumer's successor Paul Beau to reassess the decision of 1895 to govern the present territories of Darlac, Gialai (Pleiku) and Kontum from the protectorate of Laos. A decree of 22 November 1904 realigned Darlac with Annam. This was followed by a decree in July 1905 which established the province of Pleiku-Der, which after another incident in 1907 was split in the *délégations* of Kontum and Cheo Reo (Ayun Pa), as part of the Annamese provinces of Bình Đinh and Phu Yên. In 1913, Kontum became a province of Annam, with a *délégation* in Darlac. The rationale for these seemingly arbitrary territorial decisions was the need for a stronger back-up force for the pacification process by creating stronger links with the stronger French administrative and military position in Annam, compared with both Cambodia and Laos.

The process of military penetration stopped altogether after the killing in 1914 of Henri Maitre, the famous 'explorer and pacificator' of the Central Highlands. Maitre left behind an impressive ethnographic oeuvre. His books *Les régions Moï du Sud-Indochinois: Le Plateau du Darlac* (1909) and especially his *Les Jungles Moï* (1912a) benefitted from the surge of philological and Orientalist publications

Figure 2.2 Mission Henri Maitre, stop near a stream in the open canopy forest.

Source: Henri Maitre (1912), *Les Jungles Moï: Mission Henri Maitre (1909–1911), Indochine Sud-Centrale.* Paris: Larose, p. 292.

around the turn of the century, as well as from the increased accessibility of such sources through the collection of the *École Française d'Extrême-Orient* and its publications. It is certainly not accidental that Maitre posited the relation between ethnography and policy in much the same way as Galliéni, while pleading for the penetration and organization of the Central Highlands:

> Their penetration should not wait. The new Governor-General, Mr. A. Sarraut, has actually decided to reduce these last strongholds, the refuge of troubling and plundering tribes which I shall, perhaps soon, have the honor of studying and subjecting to our yoke, just like I have subjected the Mnong of Cambodia, the Cop and the Dip of Donnai, for the glory of a greater France.
>
> (Maitre 1912a: 558)

Maitre must have been aware of the work of Galliéni and Pennequin which constituted a model for what he did himself. After his death, Maitre himself, silent but still enjoying the prestige of his ethnographic authority, would invariably be invoked in order to legitimize any policy option in the Central Highlands.

In the light of his desire to pacify the populations under study, it is significant that Maitre was obsessed with the classification of the Montagnards on the basis of geographic and linguistic differences. He discarded cultural traits as a basis for comparison for they were contaminated by a heavy Lao and Kinh influence. Both his books combine a narrative of the expeditions with an ethnographic and historical part, reflecting its ambiguous status as report of the military exploration and pacification, and an ethnographic text with scientific claims. In this respect, the last book, *Les Jungles Moï*, is much more systematic than his first book, guided by the philological concepts used by A. Cabaton (1905):[18]

> I am happy to be able to say that my research, guided by the work of Mr. Cabaton, has confirmed it entirely, showing that [his] classification, obtained by comparison of dialects, corresponds furthermore to geographical zones and may be explained by [their] natural conditions.
>
> (Maitre 1912a: 397)

His classification is certainly impressive, and is often more precise and detailed than more recent attempts at classification. Simultaneously, this is a weak point, since the excessive divisions and subdivisions in major, minor and subgroups simply ignore the fluidity of the ethnic boundaries, both in the political and in the linguistic fields.

Politically, the Central Highlands were in a constant flux, certainly during the first years of French penetration. 'Big Men', often in-migrants, acquired high status by virtue of their economic success in the long-distance trade, and of their – related – military prowess, especially in the capture and trade of slaves and elephants. Such 'big men', like Kiêm and Pim who helped the missionaries; like

Figure 2.3 Montagnard ethnic 'types', posing in the ethnographic fashion of the times
before a French colonial building.

Source: Henri Maitre (1912), *Les Jungles Moï: Mission Henri Maitre (1909–1911), Indochine Sud-Centrale*.
Paris: Larose, p. 236.

the *Patao* described by Gautier; like *Mesao* described by Cupet, Yersin and Maitre
(1909: 56–61); and like the *Khun Jonob*, who will be mentioned in the next chapter;
formed alliances and dominated a cluster of villages. Such a cluster would then
be a focus of 'ethnic' identification by the inhabitants. An ethnic classification by
an outsider, even if correctly representing indigenous views, would necessarily be
a snap shot of the current political situation (see also De Hautecloque 1987:
15–25). Linguistically, a similar story can be told. Not only is the linguistic
division of the Highlands highly complex and fluid, as Maitre himself
acknowledges and demonstrates by the number of subgroups and intermediate
groups, but it is also very susceptible to other influences. Both early (Gautier
1884) and later observers (Jonsson 1990, and myself) testified to the multilingual
capacities of the highland people, which renders their move from one group/
village to another for political, economic or other reasons very easy. An ethnic
classification on linguistic criteria would then be on shaky criteria indeed.

Yet, the linguistic division of the Central Highlands would be taken as an
ethnic division, a division into 'tribes'. Despite the fact that virtually all the early
observers of Montagnard society noted that its political organizations hardly ever
exceeded the village boundaries – hence there could be no tribal organizations –
the existence of tribes was taken for granted. A language community thus
became synonymous with a 'tribe'. In a later stage, when the word 'tribe' was no
longer *en vogue*, the concept of 'ethno-linguistic group' came in use. Yet, at that

time the ethnic classification had become more or less a reality by virtue of administrative processes, and the use of the word 'tribe' would be more justified. Tribe is the term that Maitre, too, employs in his classification, which has become classical in its twofold division in linguistic families: the Malayo-Polynesian dialects and the dialects which are more (Western) or less (Eastern) affiliated with Khmer (Maitre 1912a: 397–415).[19] Yet, when delivering the 1912 *Conférence Broca* lecture for the Paris-based *Société d'Anthropologie*, Maitre would implicitly undermine his own ethnographic classifications, by claiming that Montagnard society did not have any social organization above the village level, thus denying the existence of tribes. Commenting on the 'state of anarchy which desolates all the hinterland', Maitre said that 'the Moi nation does not exist and has never existed. The social unit is the village' (Maitre 1912b: 110).

The nevertheless inevitable linguistic and tribal classification of the Montagnards was simultaneously a temporal classification, conforming to evolutionist notions prevailing at the time (cf. Thomas 1989: 36–41). Evolutionism as the guiding principle of ethnology characterized the general discourse legitimizing European domination of the world, a theme which is sufficiently well-known not to be repeated here (Maquet 1962; Harris 1968; Lemaire 1976). In Indochina the words 'savage' and 'barbarian' had a specific meaning for those directly involved with the Montagnards. The French noticed the difference between the civilizations of the plains and the 'tribes' of the mountainous areas. In general, the French felt more comfortable in the presence of the more 'civilized' Vietnamese, and used the qualification of *Moi* or *Moï* (barbarian) or *sauvage* to designate the Montagnards. But a temporal classification is also imposed upon the tribal classification along linguistic lines, for the major Austronesian groups are assigned a higher position on the evolutionary scale than some of the Austro-Asiatic groups:

> The Mnong tribes ... occupy on the social ladder a position clearly inferior to the place held by the Rhadé and the Jarai, for the latter, gifted with a rudimentary civilization, have been able to ameliorate to a certain degree the conditions of their primitive existence.
>
> (Maitre 1909: 52)

The most remarkable part of Maitre's *Les Jungles Moïs* is his 140-page 'Essai d'Histoire' on the Montagnards. This history is impressive, unsurpassed in its richness of detail and use of sources. Yet, it is not a history of the Montagnards, just as this book is not a history of the Montagnards; it is a history of outsiders relating to Montagnards, the sources being those foreigners' accounts of such contacts. Therefore, it is not an account of how the Montagnards became what they are now, for they are represented as an unchanging entity, subject to penetration by more aggressive, more civilized nations. It is certainly an evolutionist account of the Montagnards, but not an account of the evolution of the Montagnards, for their history is a history of regression before more aggressive neighboring nations:

Upon contact with these superior elements, the *Moï* withers and degrades and, in a not too distant future, he will only exist in a hybrid state of half-breed, bound for extinction.

(Maitre 1912a: 415)

This Social-Darwinist version of evolutionism denies the Montagnards the capacity to evolve toward civilization. Contact with civilization is equated with degradation for the Montagnards, who 'will within a few years, be *civilized*, thus consequently lost, morally and physically corrupted and undermined' (ibid.: 416). Despite its preoccupation with temporal classification of geographically dispersed groups, evolutionism is fundamentally ahistorical. While Montagnard culture is perceived as unchanging, their history is construed as a history of regression and degradation.

Maitre's last book, *Les Jungles Moï*, is no doubt the culmination of French evolutionist ethnography concerning the Montagnards. With its detailed ethnic classification of the Montagnards and its 'historical essay', and with its scientific pretensions, *Les Jungles Moï* would remain unsurpassed, and would for a while be seen as *the* standard text on the Montagnards. Maitre foresaw the rapid disappearance of the Montagnards as a consequence of their subjection to France. His own ambition was clear in this process, as he envisaged himself both as the great pacifier of the tribes, and as the great ethnographer. Ethnography was both necessary for pacification, and urgent *because of* the pacification, hence extinction, of the tribes. He did not live to fulfill his ambitions, however, for in 1914 he fell at the hands of a Mnong leader, N'Trang Lung, who obviously did not like what Maitre had in store for the Mnong, despised by Maitre as a lowly, regressive tribe (see above). World War I precluded any French efforts at continuation of the pacification effort, which would leave large tracts of the Highlands as *région insoumise* until the end of the 1930s. But although it was Maitre who pleaded for an effective organization of the Highlands – much like the members of the Pavie Mission had done before him – his ethnographic perspective was in a sense contrary to his ideal of pacification. The submission of the Highlands, which inevitably entailed the administration of their populations, was intended to occupy the geographic space for strategic reasons only, since the Montagnards were generally thought to disappear upon contact with French Civilization.

An ahistorical, evolutionist discourse

In the context of missionary and military penetration of the Central Highlands, an ethnographic practice developed which was characterized by evolutionism, and eventually Social-Darwinism. Following prevailing designations by more civilized, neighboring nations, the Montagnards were considered to be savages or barbarians respectively, possessing only a rudimentary political and cultural organization. The missionaries of Kontum largely depended on adequate ethnographic knowledge, not only for success at conversion, but even for their sheer physical survival. In the course of time, they developed a virtual monopoly on ethnographic knowledge, which they turned to their advantage, not only in their dealings with Montagnards and Vietnamese, but also with the French authorities. Their missionary narratives and ethnographic descriptions, destined for public consumption in metropolitan France, depicted the Montagnards as savages with pagan, even diabolical habits, who were in need of a true religion. This contrasted with the perspectives of the military explorers who tended to credit the Montagnards with a rudimentary political organization which earned them the designation 'barbarian' by some of the explorers. The explorers tried to build upon the political organization they found in order to subdue the various ethnic groups.

According to the Social-Darwinist version of evolutionist thinking, the more 'primitive' tribes of Indochina would eventually disappear due to the nefarious contacts with more civilized nations, notably Vietnam, Laos, Cambodia, and certainly France. The Montagnards, who were generally thought to be the aboriginal population of Indochina, supposedly had been forced to retreat before the more civilized *races*. Theirs was a *vanishing race*, incapable of evolution, and would in due time be replaced by the *more prolific Vietnamese race* and the more enterprising Lao. They were considered to be an obstacle for the development which would inevitably take place under French domination. Therefore, the French administration only had to make sure that they controlled the Montagnards in the beginning. Later on these would simply disappear, according to the Social-Darwinist formula of the survival of the fittest. This opinion was best summarized by Lavallée in the first issue of the *BEFEO*:

> It seems that the moï race will remain a useless force for the civilizing action, to which it will only create obstacles. Its poor vitality will not allow it to maintain its position at the level of the more active races of Annam and Laos. It will be a good thing for the colony that the savage race will merge with the neighboring peoples.
>
> (Lavallée 1901: 291)

Thus, the spread of civilization and the development of the region was presumed to rely on an influx of Kinh (ethnic Vietnamese) and Lao people into the Central Highlands.

Although the *Moï* were assigned a low status – either savagery or barbarity – in the evolutionist classification of mankind, they were paradoxically held incapable of evolution themselves. In this respect, evolutionist theory was fundamentally ahistorical, as is shown by the 'Essai d'Histoire' of Henri Maitre. The spread of civilization inevitably would entail the arrival of ethnic Vietnamese to the Highlands, both from the perspective of the Catholic missionaries and of the military explorers. It would be Léopold Sabatier, who was appointed as *Délégué* of Darlac in 1913, one year before the death of Henri Maitre, who broke out of this paradox and showed that the Montagnards and their culture were valuable in themselves, and were perfectly capable of development. Sabatier was the one to provide for both an effective administrative and ethnographic model, which could only be developed in a comparatively stable, administrative context. In the course of the 1930s, Sabatier's ethnographic model (much more so than his administrative model) was emulated and became dominant, to the extent that by 1943 a prominent administrator/ethnographer could state that nobody would then repeat the ominous words by Lavallée, cited above (Guilleminet 1943a: 26).

Yet, the rise of a competing, relativist perspective on the Montagnards did not eliminate the evolutionist perspective, which at later times, in different contexts, would surface again in order to attend various claims on the Central Highlands. The first instance would arise in the 1920s, when their fertile soils were claimed for the establishment of rubber plantations. The military campaigns from 1933 to 1935 to subdue N'Trang Lung, the Mnong chief who had killed Maitre in an ambush in 1914, would yield military ethnographies with certain evolutionist tinges, but eventually gave way to the cultural relativist mood of the times. After the formal independence of the two Vietnams in 1954, the evolutionist discourse reemerged as an important ingredient of South Vietnamese attempts at 'nation-building' and modernization, accompanied by forced integration of minorities. In North Vietnam, which never abandoned its claims to the southern half of the country, evolutionism was a constituent element of the Marxist state-ideology. During the American intervention in Vietnam, an evolutionist discourse concerning the Montagnards in Vietnam would be adhered to by those factions within the US civil and military bureaucracy, which favored the use of conventional warfare tactics and the forced 'modernization' of Vietnam. Thus, the protagonists of warfare through defoliation, depletion of the countryside, population resettlement in strategic hamlets, and forced urbanization, came to face more relativist factions favoring counterinsurgency strategy and tactics. But the role and different forms of the evolutionist discourse will form the substance of subsequent chapters.

3 Léopold Sabatier

Colonial administration and cultural relativism[1]

Introduction

The concept of cultural relativism has been closely associated with a professionalizing anthropological discipline, as is brought out in the academic careers of Franz Boas and Bronislaw Malinowski (see Asad 1973; Lemaire 1976; Stocking 1991; Alvarez Roldán 1995). Cultural relativism seems more intimately entangled with the anthropological discipline than evolutionism, which in the nineteenth century was a social discourse pervading many spheres of life. In Chapter 2, I argued that evolutionist concepts were employed by ethnographers who may or may not have been conscious that they participated in an evolutionist discourse with often Darwinist overtones, for although the word 'evolution' was frequently used, the concept of evolutionism was not. Similarly, in the 1920s, a relativist discourse regarding the Montagnards developed within colonial administrative practice, even though the main initiator, Léopold Sabatier, may not have been aware of the concept of cultural relativism within ethnography. The label 'relativist' for the discourse as initially pronounced by Sabatier is mine and not his. Until after World War II it was hardly used by French ethnographers and ethnologists. Yet, the fact that the discourse initiated by Sabatier differed from prevailing evolutionist thinking was clearly recognized by his contemporaries, and the contradicting political implications of both discourses triggered a sharp conflict within colonial Indochina, with repercussions in metropolitan France.[2]

Although a discussion of the relativist discourse proper should start with Sabatier, his work could only be realized in a more or less stable administrative context. The tracing of this discourse through the colonial era in Vietnam clearly shows its strong association with administrative interests as well as with military interests. Admitting that the oeuvre by Sabatier is a highly individual accomplishment, I argue, first, that the reception of his ideas was mediated by the historical context of economic, political, administrative, strategic and other interests. Second, I argue that the inception of this discourse was contingent upon the specific administrative context in the Central Highlands, and upon the ethnographic groundwork done in the framework of the *Ecole Française d'Extrême-Orient*, not in the least by the famous metropolitan anthropologist Marcel Mauss.

In this chapter, I propose to develop this argument by looking at the ethnography proposed by and practised in the context of the newly established *Ecole Française* during the first decades of this century. A second section will deal in some detail with the ethnographic and administrative oeuvre by Léopold Sabatier, and his representation of Rhadé culture and tradition. A third section will deal with the fierce debate triggered by Sabatier's controversial policies in the context of the Rubber Boom of the 1920s and the consequent land rush in the Central Highlands. A last section deals with the contradicting economic and political interests governing the Central Highlands, and their sublimation into a policy of isolation with respect to the Montagnards.

Government ethnography and the Ecole Française d'Extrême-Orient

In 1898 the *Ecole Française d'Extrême-Orient* (EFEO) was established in Hanoi, its 'principal object [being] the scientific study of the history, the races, the languages and the religions of Indochina' (Cf. Mauss 1900: 3). In the course of its existence, it brought forth a number of renowned Orientalist scholars, like its first director Louis Finot, Henri Parmentier, Georges Coedès, Paul Lévy, Paul Mus, etc. In its seat in Hanoi, the capital of French Indochina, it had a great collection of manuscripts and published material on the history, archaeology and philology of Southeast Asia. Although ethnography was among its tasks, no full-time, professional ethnologist was recruited until 1937. In line with the then prevailing distinction between professional ethnologists practising 'armchair science', and amateur ethnographers who provided the data, the *École* relied on missionaries, military explorers and administrators for the collection of ethnographic data. It did, however, have trained and well-respected collaborators, the 'correspondents', like the missionary Kemlin and Prosper Odend'hal who in 1904 was killed in the village of the *P'tau Ia*, the 'Master of Water'.

In the first volume of the *Bulletin de l'Ecole Française d'Extrême-Orient (BEFEO)*, an article on the ethnography of the Montagnards was published by A. Lavallée (1901). The *EFEO* had commissioned the author to do research in the Central Highlands, which was still a part of Laos then. Evidently not trained in ethnographic methods, Lavallée held crude views on the Montagnards, stating, for instance, that the Rhadé spoke a 'Malayo-savage language' (Lavallée 1901). It was obvious that more rigorous research methods had to be developed in order for ethnography to attain a more scientific status, in line with the (aspired) reputation of the EFEO. Already in 1900, a *Carnet d'instruction pour les collaborateurs de l'École Française d'Extrême-Orient* had been printed, with guidelines for archaeological, linguistic and ethnographic research for aspiring scientists. This booklet (*carnet*, as it was colloquially referred to) was composed by Marcel Mauss with help from Captain Bonifacy, who had acquired a certain fame in the discipline through his ethnographic work in the refractory *territoires militaires* in the mountains of Tonkin. Contradicting the widespread assumption that the 'non-civilized tribes' of Indochina would have 'no common ties, no language nor customs' (Mauss 1900: 6), it proposed to establish a linguistic classification for the tribes by way of standard vocabularies with standard transcriptions. This would help the researcher to 'presume the identity of the race' (ibid.: 6). The ethnographic description proper should be divided under thirteen different headings: Generalities, habitation, clothing, nutrition, hunting and fishing, means of transport, agriculture, commerce, industry, war, society, art, and religion.

In the previous chapter we have established the sequence Odend'hal – Cabaton – Maitre; it is clear that Odend'hal used the *carnet d'instruction* for the collection of vocabularies, before he was killed by the *p'tau apui*. Apparently he took the instructions in the archaeological section of the *carnet* too serious when insisting on seeing the *p'tau*'s sacred saber. On the basis of Cabaton's analysis of the linguistic data collected by Odend'hal (Cabaton 1905), Maitre arrived at a first 'ethno-linguistic' classification with scientific pretensions of the Highland 'tribes'. Odend'hal, however, was certainly not the only one to use the EFEO's *carnet d'instruction* for collecting data, for the *carnet* was distributed among all the local colonial administrators with *Moi* populations within their jurisdiction. With his *Circulaire no. 29* of 27 June 1903, the Governor-General of French Indochina instructed all provincial Residents to make a 'first attempt at ethnological statistics' in their province, in accordance with the *carnet d'instruction* composed by the *Ecole Française*. Between 1903 and 1905, all Indochinese provinces sent in their ethnographic reports, which varied considerably in format and quality. The reports and vocabularies, some of them compiled by missionaries like Guerlach and Kemlin, were preserved at the *Ecole Française* (and still are: EFEO, Collection Mss. Europ.). A few of the more serious ethnographic descriptions were subsequently published in colonial, geographical or ethnographic journals (An., 1903; Baudenne 1913; De Belakowicz 1906; Besnard 1907; Brière 1904; Céloron de Blainville 1903; Cottès 1905; Guignard 1911; Haguet 1905; Macey 1907; Trinquet 1906). The publication of the reports must have been a self-selecting process, depending on the interest and initiative of the respective author.

This joint effort toward ethnographic and linguistic mapping by the *Ecole Française d'Extrême-Orient* and the colonial administration was a first step in a remarkable and enduring collaboration in the linguistic and ethnographic fields. It is hardly conceivable that the colonial administration would devote so much time and energy at ethnographic description for scientific purposes only, but records on the practical use of the ethnographic reports, and their impact on the perception of the Montagnards, are lacking. It is possible, however, to situate the issuance of *Circulaire no. 29* in a context of increasing administrative intervention in the Montagnard areas directly adjacent to and administratively dependent on the coastal provinces of Annam.[3] Until 1898, the Vietnamese administrative structure in the provinces of Annam had been kept more or less intact, with French Residents ruling through mandarins, and the Vietnamese administrative organization of the mountains, the *Son Phòng*, still in operation. Originally, the *Son Phòng* was a Vietnamese military pacification program of the *hinterland* of the provinces of Quang Ngãi, Quang Nam and Bình Đinh, as it had been initiated in

1863 under the reign of emperor Tu Đúc (see Chapter 1). In the course of time, the *Son Phòng* had turned into a system of lucrative monopolies of both tax collection and trade in precious forest products and in slaves in the entire *hinterland* of southern Annam.[4] According to French contemporary sources, the *Son Phòng* was rife with corruption and abuse by the *các lái* or *thuôc lái,* the concessionaries who acted as intermediary between the Highlanders and the Vietnamese court and markets. Their alleged exactions created a notoriously unstable situation, characterized by rebellions and raids by Montagnards on Viêt villages. Daufès, chronicler of the *Garde Indigène d'Annam* (founded in 1886), related that in the 1890s this indigenous colonial militia was almost exclusively occupied with the defense of Vietnamese villages against Montagnard incursions (Daufès 1934: 113–37).

When Paul Doumer came to the colony as incoming Governor-General (1898), he envisaged both the reinforcement of French control in the indirectly ruled territories of Indochina, and the penetration of the unsettled *hinterlands*. One of Doumer's acts was the reorganization of the *Son Phòng,* for which he received the token approval of the Emperor's Secret Council (*Co Mât*) in October 1898, through the services of *Résident-supérieur* Boulloche of Annam. This reorganization entailed the suppression of the *các lái* as intermediaries between Montagnards and others; the establishment of supervised markets; the collection of monetary taxes; the right to request corvée labor; the interdiction to use fire or sound signals; and the possibility for Frenchmen to acquire land concessions for plantations (Trinquet 1908: 346–8; Hickey 1982a: 273–5). Unexpectedly, the reorganization of the *Son Phòng* led to a marked increase of violent incidents between Montagnards and Kinh people, to which I shall return in a moment. This increase resulted in a renewed interest in the exact process of the *Son Phòng,* as expressed in the publication of a translation of a 1871 report by Lê-Tiêu-Phu-Su, *Phu Mán Tap Luc, la pacification de la région des Moï* (1905), and the partial publication of Durand's manuscript of 1899 on the *Son Phòng* in *La Revue Indochinoise* (1907).

The reorganization of the *Son Phòng,* practically amounting to its abolition, deprived the *các lái* and the colluding mandarins of their monopolies and of rich sources of revenues. So when the raids by Montagnards on lowland Vietnamese villages increased after the reorganization, the French blamed these erstwhile *các lái* and mandarins as fomenters of the unrest (Trinquet 1908: 349, 381–2; Bourotte 1955: 93). There are, however, dissenting opinions on the real causes of Montagnard resistance. Daufès, for example, maintained that the power vacuum resulting from the reorganization of the *Son Phòng* led to virtual independence of the Montagnards, who took the opportunity to settle old accounts (Daufès 1934: 113). The *Résident* of Phan Rang, Le Goy, put the blame for the violence entirely on the Montagnards, who 'are dissatisfied with the proximity of the French, because they fear that they can, less easily than before, terrorize the Annamese, who really are on our side.'[5]

Whatever the real cause of the volatility in the mountain areas adjacent to the coastal plains, among the French a common opinion began to emerge that they had to move in and rule the Montagnards themselves, without interference by mandarins, *các lái*, or other lowlanders. This opinion was strengthened by the violent death in the first years of the century of a number military officers and explorers in the Central Highlands, like Robert, Grosgurin and Odend'hal. In the first years of this century, the French took over a number of Vietnamese forts controlling Montagnard territory in the mountains bordering the plains of Annam. Simultaneously, they established a number of military posts within Montagnard territory itself, both in the Annam Cordillera and in the Central Highlands proper, thus gradually extending their influence. In the Doumer era, new provinces were established (Pleiku, Darlac, Haut-Donnaï) which between 1904 and 1907, under Governor-General Paul Beau, were detached from Laos and officially assigned to Annam.[6] The first head of the new province of Haut-Donnaï, Ernest Outrey (who would later represent colonial interests in the French parliament on behalf of the colony of Cochinchina), found upon his arrival in 1900 a Vietnamese administrative infrastructure of *cantons* and *communes*. Apparently, the Vietnamese administration had penetrated further into the Highlands than the French ever before or after were ready to admit. Outrey simply took over this administration, realizing that he transgressed the limits of the protectorate:

> This organization is evidently closer to the system of Direct Rule than to the system of the Protectorate. I will not hide for you that this seems more practical to me among a people as primitive as the *Moï*.[7]

This is an important assertion, because it shows that already in an early stage of colonization French officials were well aware of the orientation of the administrative system they deemed suitable for the Central Highlands, i.e. direct rule. At least Outrey was aware of the paradox involved, viz. the creation of an enclave of direct colonial rule in a protectorate. Others may argue that the status of protectorate for Annam and the other states of the *Fédération Indochinoise* was only hiding the reality of French colonial control in Indochina, and they may be right. Yet, the Highlands had a special status within Annam from the moment they were made part thereof. Nothing serves better to demonstrate this than the later French attempts to keep ethnic Vietnamese out of the Highlands altogether, and the continuous discussions on separating the Highlands from Annam again for political reasons. The foundation for this policy in the Highlands was laid down around the turn of the century, with the reorganization of the *Son Phòng* and with the subsequent absorption of the Vietnamese administrative system in the Highlands by the French. With the official suppression of the *Son Phòng* in 1905, and the adoption of a policy to exclude the *các lái* not only as intermediaries, but altogether from the Highlands (Trinquet 1908: 346), the road toward direct rule in the Central Highlands was open.

In this context of suppression of the Vietnamese administrative system and the gradual adoption of a system of direct French rule in the Central Highlands and the Annam Cordillera, the French Governor-General required more or less standardized ethnographic and linguistic descriptions for those areas where French colonial officials were trying to set up a colonial administration. The violence surrounding the suppression of the *Son Phòng* and the military character of the French penetration in those areas were reflected in the reports. The violence and aggressiveness of the Montagnards were emphasized, as well as their primitiveness and lack of foresight, especially in the economic realm of agriculture, industry and commerce. Yet, the descriptions were sufficiently detailed to show that the Montagnards were organized culturally, socially, politically, economically, and religiously, however primitive this may have appeared in French eyes. For administrative purposes, this insight would suffice for the time being, as the administrative organization imposed on them was generally derived from the Vietnamese political system.[8]

For the *Ecole Française*, the results of the '*statistique ethnologique*' were apparently less satisfying, for already in 1902 a new '*Essai d'une instruction pour l'étude sociologique des sociétés indo-chinoises*' was announced during the 'First International Congress of Far Eastern Studies', held in Hanoi. The drafting of the '*essai d'instruction*' was prepared by the eminent French sociologist and ethnologist Marcel Mauss, who signaled a double interest in the sociological study of Indochinese societies:

> A practical interest, for only [sociological research] can make available for administrators and colonists a repertory of facts, the knowledge whereof is indispensable for understanding and directing the indigenous societies; and a scientific interest, for it is certain that this research would yield a considerable number of typical facts to sociology.
>
> (Mauss 1902: 115)

In this announcement for a new questionnaire, Mauss distinguished four methodological principles: objectivity, precision, abundant proof, and analysis. The instruction would be divided in three distinct parts. The first part concerns the acquisition and classification of material objects for museums. The second part concerns the 'total study of social facts' by ethnographers among 'savage' groups. The third part, then, concerns the study of folklore within the civilized societies of Indochina (ibid.: 116).

In collaboration with (now) Colonel Bonifacy, Mauss composed a *Questionnaire de l'Ecole Française d'Extrême-Orient* (1903), which predated for some forty years his posthumously published *Manuel d'Ethnographie* (or. 1947), meant for use by 'travelers, administrators and missionaries' (Mauss 1967: III). The instructions were meant for the observation of 'social facts' when studying 'societies called *primitive*' – like the 'Moi of Annam [who] are archaic and proto-historical' (ibid: 7). Mauss' instructions were greatly influenced by the *Notes and Queries on Anthropology* (or. 1874) of the Royal Anthropological Institute, but there was no reference to Degérando's ethnographic questionnaire which was only saved from oblivion in the 1960s by George Stocking and F.T.C. Moore. However, being an original thinker, Mauss left his own imprint on the desirable organization of data.

As the main proponent of ethnographic holism in France, with his insistence on the 'total social fact', he still had to compartmentalize society in distinct spheres. The 'observable facts' were arranged under the headings 'social morphology', by which he meant the geography, organization and utilization of the space occupied by a social group; 'technology', and 'aesthetics'. The 'social facts', then, were arranged as 'economical phenomena', 'juridical phenomena', 'moral phenomena', and 'religious phenomena', among which he clearly preferred the juridical and religious realms as fields for research (Mauss 1967: passim).

Later ethnographers left no records whether they used or were aware of Mauss' Questionnaire.[9] The only work which obviously borrowed from the *Questionnaire*, was the semi-official *Cours d'ethnographie indochinoise* (1919) by Colonel Bonifacy, who was both a member of the *Société d'Anthropologie de Paris* and a correspondent of the *Ecole Française d'Extrême-Orient* (and involved in the drafting of the Questionnaire, cf. Mauss 1967: 11). This work, published by the *Gouvernement-général de l'Indochine*, explained the most common ethnographic concepts for students of the Agriculture and Forestry College in Hanoi, and contained a rudimentary ethnographic classification of the major populations in Indochina. Although the eventual utilization of the teachings of Mauss by later ethnographer cannot be ascertained, a predilection for the same juridical and religious domains may be discerned there.

In the previous chapter we noted the missionary preference for studying religious phenomena. For instance, the agrarian rites, the interpretation of dreams and the concept of alliance among the Rengao, as analysed by Père Kemlin, would be classified as religious phenomena by Mauss. Kemlin's interest in religious phenomena would later be emulated by many other ethnographers (like Guilleminet, Huard, Maurice, Jouin, and Dournes). More important in this context, however, is Mauss' insistence on juridical phenomena, which in the context of colonial Indochina would take the shape of the *droit coutumier*, the customary law code as noted down for several ethnic groups in the Highlands – but which also has relevance for the lowlands as written-down village rules (*huong uóc*, cf. Grossheim 1995; 1997). The interest of the colonial administration and the *Ecole Française d'Extrême-Orient* alike in the codification of the '*coutumiers*', was aroused by the oeuvre of Léopold Sabatier, administrator of Darlac from 1913 to 1926. Sabatier would create both an administrative and an ethnographic model with respect to the Montagnards, combining direct colonial rule in Darlac with a relativist ethnographic discourse on their culture, in particular Rhadé culture.

Léopold Sabatier and the invention of Montagnard tradition

Like many other French colonists, Léopold Sabatier came from a marginal region in France, before he arrived in Indochina.[10] Born in a lower middle class family on the first of April, 1877, in Grignan in the mountainous Drôme region in the south of France, he did not receive a particularly good education. As he did not find a job easily after military service, he decided to look for adventure in French Indochina, where he was appointed to a low-ranking job as civil servant in 1903. Having a difficult, suspicious character, he found it hard to adapt to the routine of an administrative job supervised by others. Coming from a mountainous region himself (he would later retire in the Pyrénées region), he applied for a job in the still unruly Central Highlands (Boudet 1942; Dubois [ms]1950: 3–5).

Sabatier served for three years as assistant of Jules Guénot, who as head of the *délégation* of Kontum had succeeded Père Vialleton as French representative, and chose Guénot's side in the latter's – sometimes violent – conflicts with the Catholic missionaries, who still considered the area their fiefdom. Guided by Guénot, who in 1917 would be killed in Kontum, Sabatier observed the detrimental consequences of the deculturation imposed upon the Montagnards by the missionaries, and shared Guénot's view that only a special policy could save the Montagnards. Yet, in Kontum province the Residents Guénot and Fournier were forced to follow the lines set by the missionaries, who until 1907 had administered the region, basing themselves primarily on the Christian community of ethnic Vietnamese in Kontum (Dubois 1950: 12–56; Guénot 1917: 95–132; Lechesne 1924: 9–13).

After countless conflicts with the missionaries, who created many difficulties for him by press campaigns and other means, Sabatier's position in Kontum became untenable after a he made a request for an official investigation concerning certain allegations, which was turned down by the *Gouvernement général* (RSA 4048). In 1913 he was appointed *Délégué* of Darlac, an autonomous district of the new province of Kontum. In Darlac, two hundred kilometers to the south and shunned by most colonial officials, the new *Délégué*, enjoying a considerable autonomy of action, could 'live his dream' (Bourotte 1955: 94) and 'save the *moï* race in Darlac, which became his field of experimentation' (Dorgelès 1944: 17–18). Eventually, he became known as the 'apostle of the Rhadé', as French Indochina's official archivist Paul Boudet described him in an article in the wartime colonial weekly *Indochine* (Boudet 1942). According to Roland Dorgelès, a prose writer who in 1923 visited Ban Me Thuot, the new capital of Darlac, Sabatier had sworn to 'liberate' the Moïs from 'barbary' and to make human beings out of them rather than coolies (Dorgelès 1944: 18). His approach was certainly unconventional and also controversial within French Indochina at that time, as was obvious from Bonifacy's scathing critique of Dorgelès sympathetic portrayal of Sabatier (Bonifacy 1925: 15–21).

Sabatier kept out the Vietnamese and Chinese traders but also French missionaries and businessmen, in an effort to create a 'human reserve' to protect the Montagnards. He tried to work as much as possible with the Rhadé ethnic group, which populated the plateau of Darlac. A small man with a big moustache and piercing eyes, who made a severe impression, Sabatier viewed the Rhadé as big children ('*grands enfants*') whom he, as a stern father, must bring up by guiding and chiding them ('*guider et gronder*', cf. Dorgelès 1930: 26). In 1915 he founded the 'Franco-Rhadé School' where children from the colonial center of Ban Me Thuot and the surrounding villages received instruction in French language, history and geography, as well as in Rhadé culture. During the first years' instruction was given by a Cambodian and a Kinh teacher, but they were soon succeeded by Rhadé teachers under a French headmaster, Dominique Antomarchi. Despite the fact that Darlac officially belonged to the protectorate of Annam, no Vietnamese was taught. Antomarchi developed a Rhadé script to be used in the curriculum instead of *Quôc Ngũ*, the romanized Vietnamese script (Monfleur 1931: 18, 25; Antomarchi 1946; Bourotte 1955: 94–5).

After a few years in Darlac Sabatier became fascinated with the poetic oral tradition of the Rhadé, which prescribed rituals and regulated relations between individuals, social groups and the spirits. Already by 1913, when an indigenous law court had been established in Kontum, he must have been aware of the existence of a Montagnard oral 'law'. Also in the *Délégation* of Haut-Donnaï, initial attempts at understanding the customary law were hesitantly made by Canivey (1913) and by Cunhac (1921, cf. Dournes 1988: 10). The court was presided over by a judge, usually a powerful 'big man' who knew the traditional customs well. Having heard the parties involved, the judge would chant the verses that he deemed relevant for the case. Sabatier started to note down the verses, and composed a *coutumier*, after the model of the written local law code that many Vietnamese villages possessed. In 1923, when the delegation of Darlac was raised to the status of a separate province with Sabatier as Resident, an indigenous law court (*tribunal coutumier*) was formally established. The indigenous 'laws' which had been collected and translated by 1919, were posthumously published in 1940, together with the jurisprudence that developed within the law court.

Sabatier's presentation of the *coutumier* touched upon a number of issues of ideology and policy. The key issue, he suggested, was to protect the Rhadé against both the lowlanders and Europeans who would be after their land: '[The foreigners] think that you don't have laws, but that is not true, for you have them like your ancestors had before; they had designed them to protect the land, the soil and the populations of Darlac.' (Sabatier and Antomarchi, 1940: preface). But the laws had been forgotten and misused by their own chiefs: 'But you have forgotten them, and the few – if any – among you who know them, use them to confuse and repress the inhabitants.' (ibid.) This failure of collective memory in fact accounted for the current sorry state of the Rhadé: 'For this reason you have become cowardly and fearful; your villages are depopulated, your race is vanishing.' (ibid.) And it was only through the codification of the *coutumier* that their future could be guaranteed:

> Tomorrow or after tomorrow the foreigners will come to plunder your homesteads, grab your lands, and you, you will become their slaves. In order to prevent that from happening, I decided with all the Chiefs of Darlac to write down your laws in order to preserve them forever. ... So if you don't want to be deprived of your lands, if you don't want to be the slaves of strangers, if you want your villages to become large and populated as in the past, then learn your laws, obey them always.
>
> (ibid.)

The foreigners Sabatier referred to were the Kinh, who were depicted as the main threat to Rhadé society. The French posed as the protectors of the Rhadé and their putative tradition. Sabatier's *coutumier* may have been expressed in a traditional idiom, but like many such efforts of codification of native law, it was not always traditional in content. The poetic language of Rhadé oral tradition was very fluid and ambiguous. It described the proper behavior of kinship groups toward the spirits and toward each other, and it was used to mediate in case of conflicts between groups by means of reconciliation and compensation rather than punishment, as would be the case in Western law (Dournes 1988: 10–13). Verses that were chanted by a village elder in case of conflict between two parties to achieve reconciliation and arrive at compensation for damage done, were now transformed into legal articles pronounced by a judge in a French-backed courthouse. Like other such codifications of customary law – notably the *Adat* in the Netherlands East Indies – Sabatier's efforts both changed and ossified social relations, which often bore the mark of French colonial rule, despite the fact that they were presented as 'traditional'.[11]

The selections, formulations and translations not only reflected French legal concepts, but many 'laws' were even consciously modified or invented in a way which benefited French colonial rule. Before Sabatier, Rhadé customary law did not resemble modern statutory law as we know it, representing a central authority of king or state. It certainly did not define any rules of obedience toward official village heads. However, Sabatier claimed that the village heads, now appointed by the French, had existed in the past, but had lost their authority, which the French had simply restored. The institution of village heads, by and large a French invention, was now sanctioned by the *coutumier*. Instead, there had been 'big men' in the Central Highlands, who had been very influential in one or even several villages by virtue of their position in the trade networks trade that linked uplands with lowlands and Montagnards with Vietnamese, Laotians, Siamese and Chinese traders and polities. Contrary to the French view of the Montagnards, they had not been 'isolated' before European contact. Rather, it was the French themselves who had isolated the Central Highlands in order to establish their own influence in the area. In this respect, it is significant that the French forbade the – very rapid – transmission of messages through fire or sound signals (drums), with the suppression of the *Son Phòng*, thus effectively cutting off communication. Since a number of these 'big men' had been the most outspoken opponents of French penetration, their political power had been destroyed by the French. The same happened with their economic power, by French efforts at preventing the long distance trade in the region (Maitre 1909: 161–2). Other law articles concerned the relations with groups and villages that did not acknowledge French authority or pay taxes – the '*insoumis*' ('unsubmitted' people – who were not yet 'pacified') and the '*pirates*' (rebels against French rule). Such laws were formulated in the traditional idiom of the Rhadé (Sabatier n.d. [EFEO, MSS Europ. 138]; Sabatier and Antomarchi 1940: passim).

Another effect of the codification of customary law in matrilineal Rhadé society was a process of gender transformation. In her analysis of historical changes affecting women in Sri Lanka, Carla Risseeuw describes gender transformation as a process of social change by which 'women and men find themselves in changed positions vis-à-vis each other, both in society at large and on the micro-level of family and interpersonal relationships.' Simultaneously, 'their conception of themselves and their sex is similarly subject to change' (Risseeuw 1988: 14). While matrilineal Rhadé and Jarai societies were considered 'matriarchal' and hence 'archaic' societies by the French (cf. Condominas 1955: 555), colonial administrators like Sabatier tended to listen exclusively to male informants, because elderly males assumed the authority of representing the clan or community to outside visitors. In the following chapters I shall show that this gendered construction of ethnographic occasions not only influenced ethnographic discourse, but made a real impact on the gender relations within Montagnard societies. Often, however, the male domination of ethnographic occasions did not preclude many male ethnographers from practising 'ethnography on the pillow' by taking local concubines. Sabatier is a case in point, as will be explained in the next paragraph.

While Sabatier and other administrators relied on male interlocutors, he tended to suppress local 'big men' as rival contenders for power. In this context, the one highland leader who benefited from the imposition of colonial rule was Ma Krong (alias Ma Ngay), better known by his Lao-Siamese title Khun Jonob. Of mixed Lao-Mnong descent, Ma Krong controlled the capture and trade of elephants in the region surrounding the local center of Ban Don. He had initially opposed French penetration, because of his Siamese connections. Sabatier, however, was able to ally himself with Ma Krong, eventually becoming his son-in-law when Ma Krong's daughter gave birth to their daughter H'Ni (Annie) in 1923. Sabatier used Ma Krong's influence over the Mnong and Rhadé to improve the collection of the head tax. This tax, together with the considerable tax levied on the international elephant trade, enabled Sabatier to establish an administrative infrastructure in Darlac, financially independent from the colonial center. In addition to education and medical assistance, he was able to fund the construction of a network of roads built by the corvée labor of Montagnards and forced labor of convicts. He even had a telephone line established between the new administrative center of Ban Me Thuot and Ma Krong's residence at Ban Don. On his part, Ma Krong saw his economical power enhanced by the formal political power which French authority bestowed upon him. For decades, he would serve as judge in the Ban Me Thuot customary law court from its inception in 1923 until after World War II (Monfleur 1931: 15–19; Dubois 1950: 57–152; Bourotte 1955: 94; Hickey 1982a: 297–308).

Sabatier's most celebrated co-optation of 'traditional' Montagnard culture was the *palabre du serment* ['palaver of the oath'], a ceremony in which village chiefs and other influential men from the province of Darlac sweared an oath of allegiance to the French. The *palabre* was actually a transformation of an older ritual at the beginning of the new year, the *mnam thun*, when the rich and powerful feasted to reinforce their alliances and relations of supremacy and dependency. There is disagreement in the sources about when the *palabre du*

Figure 3.1 Khun Jonob, the elephant hunter from Ban Don who became Sabatier's close collaborator and judge in the customary law court of Ban Me Thuot, and his wife.

Source: 'Le Koun-Iounop et sa femme', from: Auguste Pavie (1900), *Mission Pavie, Géographie et Voyages, t. 3: Voyages au Laos et chez les sauvages du Sud-Est de l'Indochine par le Cap. Cupet,* Paris: Ernest Leroux, page 292.

serment was held for the first time, but it became famous with the well-described celebration of 1 January 1926, in the presence of Louis Finot, director of the *Ecole Française d'Extrême-Orient* (EFEO), and of Pierre Pasquier, the senior French official (*Résident-supérieur*) of Annam. Sabatier made a speech exhorting the chiefs and others present to obey the traditional law (as interpreted by himself) and the village heads (selected by him); to stop the slave trade; to avoid and isolate the rebels; to heed the prescriptions of French medical care; to contribute corvée labor for road construction; to send the young men to the militia; to send the children to school; and to take good care of the land in respect of the *pô lan*, the ritual female guardian of the land. Each time, the chiefs had to touch a bracelet in token of their obedience (Sabatier 1930).

The ceremony was concluded by the ritual sacrifice of a buffalo, donated by the wealthiest and most prestigious participant (now Sabatier himself, as the French Resident of Darlac), which created obligations for the others present. Claiming to be the pre-eminent expert of Rhadé (and Mnong) history, and the protector of their culture, Sabatier, referred to as *Ay Prong* (grandfather), put himself in a direct line with the ancestors whose will he pretended to know:

> You must obey me because I know the past, yesterday, today and tomorrow. You must obey me because then you do what the spirits want, who are all with me for the prosperity, the health, the freedom of you all, for the peace of the great land of Darlac. You have to obey me because if you don't, I shall leave you and with me all the spirits of Darlac and of your ancestors whom you follow. You will always be wild dogs and you will become the slaves of foreigners. Do you understand? ... The foreigner robs you, exploits you, subdues you, despises you, and you say nothing. Some help him for their private profit against the common interest. I protect you, and this does not please many.
>
> (Sabatier 1930: 33, 41)

The *coutumier* and the *palabre du serment*, being purposeful modifications of traditions, may be considered as inventions of tradition for political goals. Hobsbawm and Ranger have pointed out that tradition should not be regarded as a static reality. It can be more fruitfully defined as a social construction on the part of the colonial powerholders to legitimize their power to the dominated population (Hobsbawm and Ranger 1983: passim). In order to be able to govern the disparate and diverse Montagnard populations, the colonial administration had appointed village headmen early on, and invested these headmen with a degree of authority that village elders had never had before. In a 1937 report to the Minister of Colonies, the then Governor-General Brévié linked the question of village headmen to the administrative circumscription of ethnic groups and the codification of customary law:

> It will be essential to determine the groupings that could be constituted, and that will be encompassed in distinct administrative circumscriptions. We

shall re-create the ancient tribes, and we shall give each village a chief whom we will support with all our authority. We shall create chiefs where we need. ... It will therefore be all-important to codify these oral arrangements [*coutumiers* – OS] while making, with caution, the necessary modifications.[12]

As Brévié noted in 1937, it was deliberate French policy to modify the *coutumiers* in a way suitable for the administration. This issue was specifically addressed some years later, when the *Ecole Française d'Extrême-Orient* announced that Marcel Ner, one of its ethnographic correspondents, would separate the 'really traditional' Rhadé laws from Sabatier's political wishes in the *Biduê, coutumier rhadé* (Ner 1940b: 3). On the basis of the testimony of 'the elderly who dictated the outumier rhadé, and the teachers who transcribed it', Ner concluded that Sabatier had 'requested that it would be adapted to the demands of the Administration and to the rule of hygiene; but [that] its expression remains archaic' (Ner 1952: 49). More recently, Jacques Dournes, who served as a missionary in the area until the 1960s, made it clear that the *coutumier rhadé* deprived women in the matrilineal Rhadé society of many rights by ignoring their role in practical and ritual affairs (Dournes 1978b: 188).

Sabatier's efforts were not only oriented toward the 'regeneration' of the past through the adaptation and invention of traditions. He was equally successful in bringing the fruits of 'progress' to the Rhadé. The establishment of the Franco-Rhadé school and the construction of a road infrastructure have been mentioned above. Financed from the provincial sources, without financial support from the center, Sabatier, with the help of French doctors and Rhadé nurses, endowed Darlac with a relatively efficient medical organization, geared toward the struggle against malaria, leprosy and syphilis, which were the most dangerous diseases in the Highlands. He introduced coffee seedlings in Darlac, and distributed these among the Rhadé, in an effort to make them economically competitive in a future market. A middle range category of indigenous supra-village officials was created, the *chefs du canton*. Elected by the village headmen and assisted by graduates from the Franco-Rhadé school, they saw to the execution of his commands and reported any irregularities to him as the Resident of Darlac province (Dubois 1950: 109–52). After he had started recruiting Rhadé warriors in 1915, he was also able to rely on a *Garde Indigène*, which in Darlac consisted primarily of Montagnards. It was remarked that the recruits for these *Bataillons de Tirailleurs montagnards du Sud-Annam*, or simply *Tirailleurs mois*, were often marginal young men who had been evicted from their village because of some moral or physical defect. Still, their remarkable fighting qualities fitted well in the French efforts to control the Highlands and to have a loyal, non-Viêt force at its disposal, by pitting one ethnic group against the other (Daufès 1932: 190; Maurice 1941b: 226).

From a pragmatic point of view Sabatier's efforts were quite successful. He was able to create an administrative and geographical infrastructure for Darlac which in those days was unique for the Central Highlands (Monfleur 1931). His achievement depended on an intimate knowledge of Montagnard culture, which if properly handled would make the Montagnards not only amenable to French colonial rule, but also politically and militarily useful. Sabatier created an ethnographic image of the Montagnards quite different from that created by the early missionary and military ethnographers. This cultural representation might be called 'relativist' in the specific local sense that the ethnic groups of the Central Highlands, and especially the Rhadé, were regarded as equally valuable as the ethnic Vietnamese. Sabatier broke away from the evolutionary discourse that described the Montagnards for what they lacked – like a state or political organizations, a law, a script, industry and commerce, or even religion. Instead, Sabatier showed they had a law code, a script, a political system, were good (colonial) soldiers, were amenable to colonial government and to education. Far from being irredeemably 'savage' or 'barbarian', the Montagnards themselves were capable of Western-style development – or *évolution*. In other words, they were deemed '*perfectible*', as the French called it, without the need for engagement with or emulation of ethnic Vietnamese in the process. Their 'race' would not vanish and their cultural identity would be preserved, provided that it was protected by direct French rule, and that ethnic Vietnamese were denied free access to the Highlands.

Sabatier's ethnographic oeuvre not only legitimized French rule in the Highlands; it also made a special policy with regard to the Montagnards possible. Although practised as a concomitant of direct colonial rule, it was also a highly individual accomplishment. Already in 1918 Sabatier's policy was noticed favorably by the central colonial authorities in Hanoi as an example to follow, and again in 1923 influenced Pasquier, then *Résident-supérieur* of Annam, in formulating a policy regarding the Central Highlands (Pasquier 1923: passim).[13] However, when interest in the fertile lands of Darlac grew with the Rubber Boom of the 1920s, his 'policy of attraction and peace' became hotly disputed. The implementation of this policy was to be delayed by Sabatier's forced resignation from office in April 1926, in the face of accusations that he resisted the opening of Darlac province for European colonization. For the next decade an evolutionary view dismissive of the Montagnards and neglectful of their interests would attend the efforts at economic exploitation of the Central Highlands.

The rubber boom and the conflict of economic and political interests

Around the turn of the century, tests in the Highlands of eastern Cochinchina, the French colony in the southern part of Vietnam, demonstrated the suitability of the red and gray soils of its basaltic plateaus for the cultivation of rubber. In the next few years rubber was to command record prices on the world market. During this first of two early twentieth century rubber booms, large areas already 'pacified' were confiscated for the benefit of large European enterprises like Michelin, as well as for private colonists, who established rubber plantations. In Cochinchina the power balance was such that the indigenous Montagnard population was simply evicted from their lands and employed on the new rubber estates, without much effective protest. The relative absence of an ethnographic practice and record concerning the Montagnards of Cochinchina in the beginning of this century reflected the lack of interest for the fate of the relatively powerless Montagnards (De Montaigut 1929: 65 ff.; Thompson 1937: 130–63; Murray 1980: 255–313).

A second rubber boom followed the implementation of the Stevenson Plan of 1922. The Stevenson Plan was a decision of the major rubber producing states to limit rubber production in order to keep the price artificially high after a drop in demand since the end of World War I. The rise of the price of rubber aroused the interest of French financial circles in the soils of the Central Highlands of Annam, which were not yet entirely 'pacified' and where a colonial administration was just developing. The resulting land rush led to a conflict between the protagonists of economic colonization and those of political and strategic colonization. Those associated with major rubber companies and financial circles in the metropole and in Saigon wanted a 'rational' exploitation of the land, regardless of the consequences for indigenous populations who lived off it. According to still prevailing evolutionist opinion, economic colonization of the Highlands would be in the best interest of the Montagnards, who would simply 'vanish' as a race if they did not give up their 'backward and harmful' agricultural practice of shifting cultivation, and start working at the rubber plantations. The eventual successor of Sabatier, Giran, who in 1926 would open Darlac for colonization, put the matter succinctly when he suggested that 'a handful of Frenchmen living in the midst of the population would do more for their evolution than all the most eloquent official palavers' – by which he clearly referred to Sabatier's *palabre du serment* (Monfleur 1931: 20 – translation in Hickey 1982a: 308).

Opposing this *mise en valeur* (economic exploitation) option was that of the *mission civilisatrice* favored by the military and some officials within the colonial bureaucracy. Typified by Sabatier, they sought to develop an effective ethnic policy, informed by ethnographic knowledge and based on direct contacts between the French and the Montagnards and on the exclusion of ethnic Vietnamese from the Highlands. To strengthen the hold of the French on Indochina, the strategic Central Highlands were to be made into a 'friendly' military base in possibly hostile territory, in case of a Vietnamese insurrection in the plains, or of an attack from abroad. In the process, France would pride itself in fulfilling its civilizing mission by protecting the indigenous populations, respecting their cultures and encouraging their gradual development.

The conflict between the various interests came to the surface around 1923, when the French *Résident-supérieur* of Annam, Pierre Pasquier, had to formulate a policy regarding colonization of the Central Highlands and the in-migration of ethnic Vietnamese. Although his initial plan was based on an enquiry among local officials, among whom Sabatier was most prominent, others also tried to influence Pasquier with reports or publications. These reports neatly reflected the interests that were at stake, and often contradicted each other. The colonial administration would argue from the perspective of political control; the Catholic Mission from the perspective of conversion; the Army from a military point of view; and the colonists and businessmen from an economic point of view.

In 1922, Monseigneur Kemlin of the Catholic Mission of Kontum, who enjoyed a reputation as ethnographer and correspondent of the prestigious EFEO, published a pamphlet on the issue of Vietnamese in-migration in the Highlands, and had it distributed in Darlac, too, much too the dismay of Sabatier. Accepting the inevitability of European colonization, with its attendant appropriation of Montagnard lands and exploitation of their labor, Kemlin insisted that the real issue was the in-migration of ethnic Vietnamese. The experience of the Vietnamese Christians in Kontum would show that the Montagnards could learn from the Vietnamese community in the fields of agriculture (abandoning shifting cultivation), commerce (introduction of money), industry (introduction of a work ethic), hygiene, education and religion (elimination of superstition). Furthermore, the Vietnamese presence would enhance the political security of the area, insofar as the Montagnards could take Kinh ('*annamite*') deference toward European authority as an example, while the Kinh could provide the Administration with information in case of Montagnard rebellion. Kemlin predicted that ethnic Vietnamese would be brought in anyhow since the plantations would need a regular labor force (Kemlin 1922). The Catholic Mission was very much opposed to Sabatier's policy of isolating the Montagnards from the outside world, notably from the Mission itself. A later chronicler of the Kontum Mission would attack Sabatier for being a freemason, 'a Mayréna without glamour', who wanted to create his own exclusive fiefdom (Simonnet 1977: 258–62) – mirroring earlier accusations against the missionaries that they wanted to establish a theocratic state during the Mayréna Affair.

That same year an anonymous article in a French journal representing business interests in the colonies argued in favor of Galliéni's 'oil-spot method'. Invoking Galliéni's suggestion that a sufficiently accurate ethnographic map was almost the equivalent of pacification, the anonymous author sought to combine an ethnic policy in the political sphere with a liberal policy in the economic sphere. Administrative divisions should follow ethnic and linguistic lines. French influence would spread by political means and through the provision of services, like using the supply of scarce salt as an economic tool to curb rebelliousness. Thus, Montagnards would have to give up shifting cultivation, and the area could be opened for European colonization and the establishment of plantations, following the example previously set in the highlands of Cochinchina. Although Vietnamese, Khmer and Lao merchants, whom the author invariably saw as cheaters, would be evicted, a number of Kinh would be admitted as coolies for the European plantations.[14] Through the combination of political measures and economic 'freedom', France's *mission civilisatrice* would complement the *mise en valeur* by European colonization in the economical sphere (M.C. 1923: 548–64). In general, the French press in Indochina, for the most part in the hands of diehard *colons*, clamored for the opening of Darlac province for colonization. That would entail the appropriation of Montagnard lands for the establishment of French plantations, and the migration of Vietnamese coolies to the concessions (Dubois 1950: passim).

In contrast to the missionary and business interests, a classified study by Lieutenant-Colonel Ardant du Picq emphasized the strategic value of the Highlands in case of a foreign attack or a revolt in the Vietnamese lowlands. In his voluminous report (over 100 pages), largely based on existing ethnographic literature by missionaries and military explorers, notably Henri Maitre, and the experiences of the colonial officials in the area, Ardant du Picq even foresaw the possibility of a guerrilla war in which the Montagnards might act as partisans. Drawing largely on Sabatier, he was very optimistic about the possibility of using the military capacities of the Montagnard warriors if the colonial administration could gain their confidence through a special policy:

> We have to save this race, to eliminate all harmful foreign influences through direct rule, we have to tie these tribes to us through the implementation of the principles which the *Résident-superieur* of Annam has superbly put to light ... These proud peoples with their spirit of independence will provide us with elite troupes, as safety valves in case of internal insurgency, and as powerful combat units in case of external war.[15]

An intermediary position was taken by Paul Lechesne in a booklet published early in 1924. Although apparently an outsider from the coast of Annam (i.e. not a colonist, a civil servant, a military man nor a missionary), Lechesne's presence at the *Palabre du serment* of 1924 testifies to a lively interest in the Highlands. Insisting on the importance of considering the varying mentalities and special circumstances of each province, he acknowledged the political and military value of Sabatier's policy in Darlac, comparing the utilization of Rhadé warriors with the British use of Ghurkas and Sikhs in India. But he also insisted on the economic value of opening the land for colonization and immigration, as *Résident* Fournier had done in Kontum, where the presence of the Catholic Mission had prepared the way for the colonial administration. A flexible policy would leave room for both perspectives, while realizing that the development which Sabatier brought to the Rhadé inevitably would lead to the opening of Darlac in the future (Lechesne 1924).

Faced with such opposing interests and viewpoints, sustained by different images of the Montagnards as either backward savages or as useful *protégés*, Pasquier's circular of July 30, 1923 attempted a synthesis along lines previously suggested by former Governor-General Albert Sarraut. In *Mise en valeur des colonies françaises*, Sarraut (1923) envisaged a combination of political paternalism, which adapted indigenous policies to the perceived needs of every 'race' according to its degree of evolution, with economic liberalism, leading 'automatically' to the economic development of the colony and its populations. The combination of 'rational' economic exploitation of the colonies with a differentiated 'racial' policy – separating a Western from an indigenous economic sphere – amounts to what the Dutch colonial economist Boeke has called a dual economy (Boeke 1955; see also Brown 1973: 175). Pasquier followed Sabatier in seeking to protect the Montagnards against their more developed and powerful

Figure 3.2 The *Palabre du Serment* (Oath swearing ceremony) in Ban Me Thuot, visitor's camp (1946).

Source: Musée de l'Homme, 49-2322-598. Photo: Mouzon.

neighbors. In line with his slogan 'to all their own chiefs – to all their own judges – to all their own laws', Pasquier proposed that a *coutumier* should be established for every ethnic group. Moreover, every year the chiefs should swear a ritual oath of loyalty to the French Resident, the *palabre du serment.* The Highlands would be divided in three zones in which policy would be adapted according to the degree of pacification and evolution of the local population, and Vietnamese traders should be eliminated as much as possible by the establishment of supervised markets. This 'well-oriented racial policy' would allow for a gradual evolution while avoiding the stagnation that allegedly characterized the Indian reservations in the US (Pasquier 1923; Variétés 1935: 220–64).

Though prescribing the composition of *coutumiers* for administrative purposes, Pasquier took a different line from Sabatier with regard to colonization. Acknowledging that in the Highlands all land was claimed by the Montagnards, Pasquier nevertheless felt the need to 'intervene in their conventions in order to find formulas reconciling the interest of the colonists with the customs of our protégés' (Pasquier 1923: Préliminaire de l'arrêté no. 1085-D). Europeans were to be allowed to obtain 'temporary' concessions from the colonial administration in the 'free' zones. This implied that although the concessions had a maximum term of 99 years, the customary rights of the indigenous population to the land were drastically limited, because allocation of the concessions was left to the provincial Residents (who would also determine policy on the issue of Vietnamese in-migration for the plantations). Simultaneously, this procedure would guarantee that no concessions would be granted during Sabatier's rule in Darlac, for he fiercely opposed European colonization. The intention was that the Montagnards would gradually give up shifting cultivation by adapting to a situation of restricted availability of land.

The conflict, however, was not settled by Pasquier's *circulaire*. In 1925, Sabatier objected to the projected colonization in a report insisting that no concession be granted without asking the permission of the native group claiming the land. He supported his plea with a study of traditional Rhadé land tenure systems, symbolized by ritual land ownership of the *pô lan* – the female guardian of the land on behalf of the clans. A second report urged the restriction of concessions and the recruitment of only Montagnard laborers on the plantations, in order to forestall Vietnamese in-migration (Sabatier in EFEO [MSS Europ. 138]; Hickey 1982a: 305–06). Even after the division of Darlac into zones, when European companies made requests for concessions, totaling 167,845 hectares, Sabatier continued to stubbornly resist the colonization of Darlac, refusing to lease out the concessions. His position and attitude created a scandal in circles of French colonists, with repercussions even in the metropole. He was severely attacked in the colonial newspapers like *L'Opinion*, *L'Avenir du Tonkin*, *L'Impartial*, and *Le Monde Colonial illustré*, and rumors were spread that he even tried to keep out land prospectors by blowing up a bridge.[16]

Sabatier did not stand quite alone in his resistance against the colonization of Darlac. He enjoyed the friendly support of Pierre Pasquier, *Résident-supérieur* of Annam, but also of intellectuals who viewed with pleasure his attempt to create a virtual human reserve, where a primitive tribe would be preserved in its 'savage' state. One of these was Jean Brunhès, professor of human geography at the *Collège de France*, who had visited Darlac during a mission in Indochina in 1923, and had reported favorably on Sabatier's oeuvre (Brunhès 1923). The same goes for the then famous novelist Roland Dorgelès, who depicted an exotic image of Sabatier's Darlac in *Sur la route mandarine* (1925), borrowing extensively from the *coutumier* Rhadé. Less well-known are the contacts that Sabatier maintained with well-known ethnologists, like Jeanne Cuisinier and Lucien Lévy-Bruhl. Cuisinier, who would become famous as ethnographer of the Muong ethnic group in Tonkin, visited Darlac in 1925. In a Paris lecture of March 1927, she praised Sabatier for his ethnographic work, notably contained in the *coutumier*, and discusses the matrilineal descent (*'matriarcat'*) and the role of the *pô lan* in Rhadé society with reference to concepts of Lévy-Bruhl as developed in *La mentalité primitive* (Cuisinier 1927). Lucien Lévy-Bruhl himself, with Marcel Mauss one of the co-founders of the *Institut d'Ethnologie* in Paris, was very much interested in Sabatier's Darlac, which he would like to preserve as a living laboratory of the 'primitive mentality' in which he was interested. The two entertained a lively correspondence, from which Sabatier derived his scientific arguments to preserve his Darlac as a human reserve:

> The reading of Mr. Lévy's study [La mentalité primitive] reveals to me that [my studies of dialects and customs] can have a certain scientific value. We shall use them for it is the scientific thesis which will save the tribes of Darlac.
>
> (Sabatier in letter to Pasquier, n.d., in Dubois 1950: 150–1)

The opposition against Sabatier gained in strength, however, when Colonel Sée, a planter in Kontum and owner of *L'Opinion*, charged Sabatier with having destroyed roads to keep him out of the province, and published accusations of abuse of power by Sabatier.[17] When the public prosecutor in Saigon, Collonna, received a series of seventeen charges against Sabatier, brought by a number of subaltern Rhadé employees, *Résident-supérieur* Pasquier sent his secretary D'Esloy to Ban Me Thuot, in order to investigate the matter. Although Sabatier was easily acquitted of the charges, D'Esloy found the atmosphere depressing and Sabatier tense and nervous. Moreover, a number of Rhadé, including his erstwhile ally Ma Krong, complained of the amount of corvée labor he demanded for his projects, of the school that 'swallowed' their children, of his habit of sleeping with Rhadé girls, and of his authoritarian manner in general. In this climate, only four months after his apotheosis, the *palabre du serment* of 1926, Sabatier was requested to submit his resignation, probably upon the instigation of the new Governor-General Alexandre Varenne, who was inclined to promote the colonization of the Highlands for budgetary reasons. Sabatier immediately left Darlac with his daughter H'Ni, and was denied henceforth access to Darlac. The interests of the *colons* had taken precedence over the politico-military interest in appeasing the Rhadé (Monfleur 1931; Boudet 1942; Dorgelès 1944: 28–32; Dubois 1950: 167–89; Hickey 1982a: 307–09).

In 1927, Sabatier left Indochina for France, but again found himself the target of accusations by colonial pressure groups, notably by Ernest Outrey, former administrator of Haut-Donnai and now *député* for Cochinchina in French parliament, and by Colonel Sée, who had come to France for the occasion. His case appeared to be closely intertwined with the position of Alexandre Varenne, who had reserved the limited issuance of concessions for the *Compagnie Agricole d'Annam*, owned by his close friend Mailhot. Other capital groups, represented by Outrey and Sée, saw in the attack on Sabatier a means of undermining the position of Social-Democrat Varenne, and of opening Darlac for further colonization. Supported by Lévy-Bruhl and Brunhès, and successfully defended in French parliament by the novelist Roland Dorgelès, Sabatier was finally rehabilitated by Doumergue, President of the French Republic, and awarded the *Légion d'Honneur*. His publication in 1927 in Paris of *La chanson de Damsan*, a stunning Rhadé epic, might have played a role in enlisting support from French intellectuals. Showing that Rhadé oral literature was beautiful and therefore valuable, the epic may have convinced many that Rhadé culture was special and worthy of protection. Sabatier returned to Indochina in 1928 to take up office as Inspector of Administrative Affairs in the Central Highlands – only to resign disappointed in 1929, when he was again denied access to Darlac and Kontum. His appearance had caused great unrest among the Montagnards who saw their lands appropriated at a rapid rate (Dubois 1950: 193–224). Returning disappointedly to France with his daughter H'ni [Annie], Sabatier retired in Montsaunès in the French Pyrénées, where he died in 1936 (Boudet 1942; Dorgelès 1944: 28–32; Dubois 1950: 225–6).

The political value of Sabatier's ethnographic work is brought out in a decision by the *Deuxième Bureau* (the Political Section) of the Protectorate of Annam to buy all the available copies of the *Bidué, Code des tribus du Darlac* (in Rhadé) that Sabatier had commissioned from the *Imprimerie d'Extrême-Orient* in Hanoi. Although this decision was allegedly made with the consent of Sabatier, he himself complained in a letter to a friend that he had heard nothing from the printing office.[18] By this act of practical confiscation, the publication could not be used and was therefore rendered harmless *vis-à-vis* the dominant colonial interests in 1927 (before Sabatier's eventual rehabilitation). After his rehabilitation in France, Sabatier was repeatedly requested by Lévy-Bruhl to finish his ethnographic oeuvre. Exclusively for this purpose Lévy-Bruhl even obtained a prolongation of Sabatier's leave of absence for almost an entire year, but – apart from his health situation, which had deteriorated proportionally to his demoralization – he simply had no pleasure in devoting himself to ethnography for the sake of science alone (Dubois 1950: 219–20).

In 1930, at the request of his friend Pasquier, now Governor-General in Hanoi, he published an official account of the *Palabre du Serment* (1930), which he must have considered 'a souvenir of this Darlac of the past which you have known and is no more'.[19] Again, in a letter dated 11 June 1930, Pasquier asked him to write an ethnographic report which would serve as the basis for a special policy in Darlac and Kontum:

> The program would consist of the study, on the basis of your actual documentation, of the linguistic and ethnographic characteristics (traditions, legends) which would set the *Moïs* of Darlac and Kontum apart from the other aboriginal populations of the Annam Cordillera.[20]

This time, Sabatier did not comply with Pasquier's request, regarding the proposed study as inconsequential and useless.

The 'coolie question'

Sabatier's successor Giran opened Darlac province for colonization, and soon the entire area of the province was claimed by various investment groups and by individual colonists. The irony was that Sabatier's effective indigenous policy and his impressive infrastructural achievements had made Darlac accessible for both French and Vietnamese, and thus made it ripe for colonization, as a later Resident of Darlac noted (Monfleur 1931: 19). It was expected that with Sabatier, his achievements would vanish, especially when it soon became clear that the regulations concerning the concessions were not implemented, and that the land rights of the Rhadé people were violated. Soon, however, the colonists' dream would end. Resisting the expropriation of their lands, most Rhadé were unwilling to work at the plantations. The conflicts between Montagnards and the newly arrived colonists, and the lack of an adequate labor force made most aspiring concessionaries abandon their claims. The eight concessions that remained, owned by three major investment groups, covered only a limited surface area. Moreover, when the economic crisis of 1929 prompted a decline of the rubber price, the clearing and cultivation process was slowed down considerably. This prompted the plantations to spread their risks through crop diversification, planting coffee and tea next to rubber. The colonization process deteriorated relations between French and Montagnards, who stopped sending their children to the Franco-Rhadé school. In 1929 there were even a few armed attacks by Montagnards on rubber plantations and trucks – to which the colonial army responded by air assaults on insurgent villages.[21]

To remedy a situation characterized by conflicts over land, Marcel Ner, considered to be an ethnographic expert as correspondent of the EFEO, was commissioned to inquire anew into the traditional land rights of the Rhadé, probably in 1928 or 1929. In a voluminous report of 160 pages, 'Rôle des Pô lan. Régime foncier des habitants du Darlac' (n.d), Ner denied that the *pô lan* were the owners of the land, as Sabatier had represented it.[22] Their function was merely ritual, as mediators between men and spirits. Sabatier, however, had grossly exaggerated their role, as he was interested in a strong territorial organization of the Rhadé for administrative and political purposes. By representing the *pô lan* as proprietors of the soil, he could argue that all the land in Darlac was effectively claimed, owned and used, and therefore could not be leased out by the state as domanial concessions. Yet, Ner criticized the carelessness of the authorities, which had acted without giving proper thought to the possible consequences of their policy. His analysis put the blame for the 'actual crisis' on the unchecked land rush taking place after Sabatier's resignation, resulting in a scarcity of land for the Rhadé, and a scarcity of labor for the plantations (Ner n.d.: passim).

It is interesting to note that Sabatier, despite the gendered construction of his ethnographic occasions and despite his attempts to restore the authority of (male) chiefs, would not only respect but actually inflate the role of the *pô lan*, the female guardian of the clan land who periodically performs the rituals that reaffirm the boundaries of the clan territory (De Hautecloque-Howe 1987: 63–74). In that sense he was an exception to a pattern that would emerge in time, starting with Ner's politically expedient refutation of Sabatier's findings. Missionaries, administrators, military officers, teachers and medical personnel would condemn and combat precisely those practices as 'savage' or 'backward' which provided support for women's access to assets and resources within this agricultural and kinship system. Shifting cultivation was seen as a waste of forest resources, and communal land rights, periodically affirmed ritually by the *pô lan* in Rhadé society, were not recognized by the colonial administration. 'Slavery' and domestic service – often confused and misunderstood – were actively combated, depriving poor or indebted people from a secure livelihood by becoming part of their creditor's household. Also, colonial administrators discouraged the custom of substituting deceased husbands by their younger brothers as 'tyrannical', thereby not simply reflecting their male bias, but in the process eroding the livelihoods of widows and their offspring.

As Ner noted, European colonization threatened the *pax gallica* – indeed the colonial order itself – thereby jeopardizing the administrative structure of the Central Highlands. For convenience's sake, any trouble occurring in the Highlands was attributed to the presence of ethnic Vietnamese, generally depicted as 'pirates' (nationalists or Communists), cheaters and land grabbers. To avoid an unfettered Kinh in-migration in the Highlands, the colonial administration would have preferred alternative sources of labor at the plantations, preferably local. In a significant variation to Sabatier's discourse pronounced at the *Palabre du serment*, Rhadé chiefs were exhorted to provide the plantations with labor in order to avoid Kinh in-migration:

> With respect to the Rhadé labor force, they come to work freely at the same prices but are more inconsistent [than Kinh labor – OS] and change often. This year, however, after the advice given by the Resident, the Rhadé have understood the necessity of work in order to avoid the invasion of their country by the Annamese [Vietnamese] whom they hardly like and who could supplant them.
>
> (Monfleur 1931: 47)

The threat of a new wave of in-migrants taking over their lands – after the French plantations – was used as an argument for plantation work.

Whereas the indigenous population was widely used for clearing land for plantations, the plantation owners found Rhadé labor not very reliable as plantation workers, and resorted to the practice of bringing in labor from elsewhere. The use of Javanese coolies, considered politically harmless and closer to the Montagnards ethnically and linguistically, was contemplated as a possible solution. Earlier in the century, a similar desire for Javanese plantation labor for the rubber plantations in eastern Conchinchina had surfaced. In 1906 the Netherlands East-Indies colonial authorities permitted the Indochinese plantations to recruit labor on Java. This experiment became a success for the plantations because the Javanese coolies turned out to be skilled and reliable workers, and most of them renewed their contracts after three years. World War I lessened the willingness of the Dutch colonial authorities to part with 'their' Javanese labor, and stricter conditions on their emigration made Javanese labor too expensive in comparison with coolies recruited in impoverished Tonkin. While a population count in 1928 demonstrated the continued presence of Javanese workers in Indochina, the Netherlands East-Indies colonial government put too many obstacles in the way of a renewed labor migration during the late 1920s. And since Chinese labor was by comparison too expensive, the plantations had to employ Vietnamese labor, albeit under a strictly regulated residential regime in the Highlands. According to an ordinance (*arrêté*) of 15 November 1930, Vietnamese coolies were not allowed to leave the plantations during their contractual term, and had to return to the plains immediately thereafter. Every area not supervised by a European was forbidden for Vietnamese lowlanders; contact with Montagnards could only take place in the supervised markets and the areas with an existing Vietnamese settlement. By restricting contacts between the ethnic Vietnamese coolies and Montagnards, the colonial administration tried to reconcile the economic interest of a mainly Kinh labor force required by the plantations with the political interest of isolation of the Central Highlands.[23]

Tribes and tribalization

In the early days of the French colonial presence in Indochina, military explorers led expeditions into the Highlands, combining geographic and ethnographic research with pacification. In Chapter 2 we saw that an important result of the military penetration was the identification of ethno-linguistic groups and their classification as 'tribes'. This tribal classification effectively set in motion a process of *tribalization* in the Highlands, in that ethnic identities and ethnic boundaries were constantly (re)constructed through French ethnographic and administrative practices – a process termed 'bureaucratic reproduction' by Henk Schulte Nordholt (1994). It was only after the French used the language groups as the basis for administrative divisions – a process started by Léopold Sabatier – that these groups developed a sense of tribal identity. Through his ethnographic and administrative work regarding one such 'tribe' – the Rhadé of Darlac – Léopold Sabatier set a new model with his work. Parting with the notion that Montagnards were no partner in France's 'civilizing mission', he devised an administrative model that attempted to achieve development on the basis of the local population and their culture (or at least his version thereof). To this end he combined innovative, low-budget administrative work with ethnography which constituted ('re-created') the Rhadé *tribe* as the constitutive population of Darlac province, and their culture and customary law as the basis for administration and adjudication in the province.

Sabatier's unconventional administrative model based on hybrid notions of Rhadé culture attracted much attention in the colonial bureaucracy. In a decree of 1923, the *Résident-supérieur* of Annam Pierre Pasquier by and large followed Sabatier's administrative model, albeit only in part. He recognized the *coutumier* as basis for adjudication and administration in the *Pays Moï*, and decreed that *coutumiers* would have to be drawn up for all the major ethnic groups. He partially protected indigenous land rights by making concessions temporary (99-year) leases depending on consent and recompensation of the traditional land owners. He instituted a zoning policy designed to keep both European and lowlander colonizers out of the most sensitive areas. He ordered that vernacular scripts had to be devised (along the lines of Sabatier's Rhadé script, cf. Sabatier 1921) and used in primary education (Pasquier 1923, in *Variétés* 1935). The composition of a *coutumier* after the model set by Sabatier became both a standard administrative and a standard ethnographic practice since its composition and utilization in tribal law courts had been prescribed by *Résident-supérieur* Pierre Pasquier in 1923.

The colonial administrators and ethnographers who engaged in the composition of a tribal *coutumier* considered it to be – in the words of Lafont (1963: 257) – 'the reflection of society', at least for the tribe involved. Thus, the *coutumier* became the synecdoche by which Highland 'tribes' could be known and understood. In the French ethnographic tradition within Indochina its composition acquired a status similar to the ethnographic monograph based on fieldwork in the Anglo-Saxon world. Its administrative usage greatly enhanced the process of tribalization, although Théophile Gerber, one composer of a *coutumier*, realized that 'the term 'tribe' applied to the Stieng is improper' (Gerber 1951: 227), as no tribal authority structure existed. Among the Stieng there did not exist 'oral traditions, condensed in chants which are transmitted from generation to generation and which constitute their coutumier'. Small wonder that Gerber was forced to borrow from Sabatier's *coutumier*, in the absence of any discernible customary law among the Stieng to enforce administrative authority (ibid: 243). Though interrupted by the demise of Sabatier's policies during the Rubber Boom of the 1920s, Sabatier's and Pasquier's policies were embraced again in the second half of the 1930s – both in Annam and in upland Cochinchina (Pagès 1935). The convergence of ethnography and administration – most noticeable in the collusion of customary law and policing (*coutumiers* and tribal courts); and of linguistics (glossaries and dictionaries) and education (school primers) – resulted in a process of tribalization. Thus, previously non-existent or fluid ethnic identities were constructed or hardened through the combination of ethnographic and administrative practice, resulting in the formation of fixed tribal identities (Condominas 1966: 168; Salemink 1991: 244).

Sabatier's ethnography was primarily intended for two audiences. The first audience were the Rhadé themselves, whom he tried to convince to follow him if they wanted to survive as a tribe and a separate culture. The second audience was French colonial officers and intellectuals, whom he tried to convince of the beauty and the viability of Rhadé culture. In both cases, he assumed an exclusive ethnographic authority that legitimized his discourse about the essential equivalence of Kinh and Rhadé cultures in the colonial context. His publications, imbued with cultural relativism (without ever using the term), naturally attracted the attention of ethnologists in Indochina and France. This relativism was juxtaposed to the evolutionism of an earlier era, but also to the evolutionist discourse which attended the attempts to establish plantations on Rhadé lands by denying their cultural value and their chance of survival along with their customary land rights vested in women. Thus, the fault line between evolutionists and relativists converged with the fault line between the economic interests of the *mise en valeur* through plantations, and the political interest of appeasing the indigenous population through the *action civilisatrice*. Given the relative absence of strategic considerations in policy formulation in French Indochina, the economic interests had the upper hand through most of the 1920s and until the second half of the 1930s.

Sabatier had to make way for the plantations, but his ethnographic-*cum*-administrative model was rediscovered and reapplied in the late 1930s and

1940s. In the following chapters we shall see this conflict between economic and political interests with respect to the Central Highlands and between evolutionist and relativist perspectives with respect to the Montagnards recurring in varying guises. The next chapter deals with a millenarian movement that in the context of rising political and military tensions in the region provoked a renewed interest in the model of Sabatier, leading to administrative reform in combination with discursive changes in Montagnard ethnography.

4   The return of the Python God

Multiple interpretations of a
millenarian movement[1]

Introduction

In 1937 an indigenous millenarian movement swept the Central Highlands in
the southern half of colonial Vietnam, inspiring most of the indigenous
population in various ways and at different points of time, and even reaching as
far north as Laos and as far west as Cambodia. According to French archival
records, the people known as *Moï*, or Montagnards, believed that the mythical
Dien Python, or Python God, common to all the 'tribes' in the Highlands, had
returned to this earth to announce the Golden Age. This Golden Age would be
preceded by a cataclysm in which only those Montagnards would be spared who
complied with certain prescriptions, notably the possession of magic water,
distributed by Sam Bram, the prophet and incarnation of the Python God. All
others, including foreigners, would be destroyed. Many Central Highlanders
reportedly did not bother to obey the French anymore, and some groups even saw
the time fit to attack French posts. The French colonial administration repressed
the millenarian activities, which they considered to be a threat to the colonial
order. Later, a more expedient interpretation was adopted, representing the events
as a rebellion fomented by Vietnamese Communists. The interpretations varied
widely, reflecting different discourses on the Montagnards, but were consistent in
describing the commotion as an essentially political, anti-colonial movement.
Called 'Python-God Movement' by Gerald Hickey in his authoritative
ethnohistory of the Vietnamese Central Highlands (1982a), it was considered a
major affair by colonial administrators and by presentday anthropologists alike.

When conducting fieldwork in the Central Highlands in 1991, I tried to find
out what had been the impact of the movement in Montagnard collective
memory and on their ethnic identity, as had been described in French archival
sources. In all the localities visited during my fieldwork, I had interviews with
elder people, enquiring after the Python God movement. To my surprise, the
movement appeared to be entirely forgotten in a number of locations that
I visited, and where – according to French documentary sources – people had
engaged in millenarian activities. One place where my elder interlocutors
remembered about the movement were the villages of Bôn Tong Xe and Bôn
Chu Ma in Ayun Pa district, Gialai province – the Jarai heartland close to the

area where the movement started. And contrary to most contemporary and later, politicized interpretations, my Jarai interlocutors claimed that it was a religious affair only, with no political intentions at all, implying that there had been no question of a movement directed against the French presence in the Highlands.[2] This contradiction of recent scholarly interpretation provokes the question whether the importance of the 'affair' had been exaggerated in French documentary sources, and consequently by later analysts. Or had my Jarai informants just 'forgotten' the political aspects of the affair in the light of subsequent violence during three consecutive wars, which might have resulted in nostalgia for the colonial era? These questions forced me to go back to the source material with more penetrating questions about its quality, and about the divergence of later interpretations of the 'movement'.

In this chapter I shall not try to establish the historical 'truth' about the *Dieu Python* movement, for this would imply a hierarchy of texts which is impossible to establish. Instead, I shall analyse the different interpretations of the movement, and the way these were conditioned by the historical context in which they were constructed and in turn affected perception and policy. The source material for this chapter consists of colonial records held in Vietnam, France and the United States, newspaper articles, oral history, and ethnographic and historical interpretations by contemporary ethnographers and later anthropologists. Although I cannot avoid creating my own ethnographic narrative, it is not my aim to add another ethnographic account of the movement, for my aim here is historical rather than ethnographic. Ethnography is the object of this study. This does not imply that I am substituting a historical for an ethnographic account, but rather that I am historicizing ethnography/anthropology. In this instance, however, ethnography and history converge, as millenarian movements and cargo cults are privileged anthropological topics, which have been approached with historical methods since few anthropologists have actually witnessed such movements. Therefore, both anthropologists and historians are forced to rely on the same sources when describing and analysing millenarian movements. This implies that the reconstruction that follows necessarily competes with other narratives. Since other anthropological reinterpretations tended to reinscribe colonial discourse, based on the colonial archive and canonized by summary comparisons with other such movements in other places and other times, I shall refrain from any comparative effort until the conclusion.

In brief, my argument is that colonial interests shaped and privileged a certain representation of the 'Python God Movement' for political reasons. In the next section, I describe two Montagnard resistance movements against colonial rule as a context for the interpretation of later millenarian context of the events. A third section traces French perceptions and policies regarding Sam Bram. In a fourth section, I discuss how these initial interpretations were constructed and reinterpreted in the light of political developments in colonial French Indochina. A fifth section, then, discusses the interpretations by presentday anthropologists, who have their own reasons for uncritically adopting a biased, colonial representation of a millenarian movement. Finally, I shall discuss some of the theoretical implications for the study of a topic – millenarianism – that combines ethnographic and historical method.

The suppression of the Kommadam and N'Trang Lung revolts

During the 1930s, a series of events inside and outside Indochina seemed to constitute a threat to French domination of the colony and the protectorates. The growing concern with security and strategic affairs naturally channeled official attention to the Central Highlands, which were of strategic importance in any scheme for the defense of the colony. Outside the Highlands, this period witnessed the rise of Vietnamese nationalism. In 1930, two uprisings challenged the French hold on the Vietnamese plains. In Yên Bái, the Vietnamese Nationalist Party (VNQDĐ) organized a mutiny among indigenous troops within the colonial army and tried to poison the French garrison, but the movement was severely repressed. In the provinces of Nghê An and Hà Tĩnh, peasants revolted against the mandarins and the French, forming the so-called Nghê Tĩnh Soviets, which came to be supported by the newly founded Indochina Communist Party. When this movement was also repressed, the Communist Party had to go underground. Throughout the 1930s, the French secret police, the *Sûreté*, held such movements in check, arresting and sending nationalists to detention camps. Internationally, French Indochina was threatened from abroad by Japan, which sought to expand its empire in East Asia. After occupying the north of China from 1931 onwards, the Japanese turned their attention to the south, coming closer to the border of Indochina. In the west, the military government of Japan's ally Siam had expansionist ambitions, aspiring to incorporate all Tai-speaking nations, like Laos, and to reconquer territories which it had been forced to cede to France around the turn of the century. With the rise of nationalism, Fascism and Communism in Asia, the tension mounted, and the French colonial government had to take measures to defend the colony. Since the densely populated areas (the deltas, the coastal strip and the Mekong Valley) were narrow and vulnerable in case of attack or uprising, the colonial government and army turned their attention to the strategic Central Highlands, from which most of Indochina could be controlled.

Against this backdrop, the ethnic policy pattern set by Sabatier would resurface again for political reasons, when the military pacification of the Highlands seemed to be more or less completed but the establishment of new plantations was effectively hampered by the world economic crisis. Chapter 3 described the process of tribalization that was initiated through the work of Sabatier. During the 1930s, the tribal classification realized in ethnographic and administrative practice was reflected in a classificatory grid distinguishing tribal groups, rather than in 'real' ethnic boundaries. This classificatory grid, shared by French officials, precluded the consideration of the possibility of a 'pan-tribal' movement emerging in the Highlands, although this had been predicted by two authoritative early ethnographers, Maitre (1912) and Kemlin (1917), who both referred to common religious practices among the Central Highlanders. Their predictive statements will be discussed in another section. This section deals with the anti-French movements led by Kommadam and N'Trang Lung during the first half of the 1930s, as a prelude to later millenarian events. The campaigns against Kommadam and N'Trang Lung and the Python God movement took place against the backdrop of mounting political and military tensions threatening the French hold on Indochina.

The tribal divisions seemed to be confirmed by French experiences with these two Montagnard movements of anti-colonial resistance in the Highlands, which were suppressed by a series of military campaigns in the 1930s, just before the 'Python God' movement. The campaigns started with a decision by Governor-General Pierre Pasquier to reduce the 'blank spots' on the map of French Indochina, i.e. those sectors of the Central Highlands which by 1930 were still not 'pacified' or formally subjected to French authority. More specifically, populations in the border areas both in the southern part and the northern part of the Highlands had been resisting French penetration since the establishment of the protectorates of Cambodia, Annam, and Laos. Pasquier's decision to end the 'state of anarchy' within the boundaries of French Indochina led in 1931 to a resumption of the pacification campaigns against those Highland groups that had resisted colonial rule since the turn of the century. The Boloven in the Laos–Annam border area in the northern part of the Highlands, and the Mnong and Stieng along the Cambodia–Cochinchina–Annam border in the south had been resisting French penetration since the turn of the century. The two 'revolts', led by Kommadam and N'Trang Lung respectively, were quelled in the course of long and arduous 'pacification campaigns' which ended with the killing of the leaders in 1935 (N'Trang Lung) and 1936 (Kommadam).

Most contemporary and later observers have interpreted the Boloven Revolt and the rebellion of N'Trang Lung as primarily political movements, because they resisted the establishment of French colonial rule over their territories with firmness. These accounts stressed the political, anti-colonial character of both movements, thus providing a model for a politicized interpretation of the Python God movement, which began shortly after the suppression of these movements.[3] In this section, I shall argue that these movements also included certain millenarian practices and expectations. It is not necessary to try to analyse both movements at great length here, the only purpose being to note these millenarian aspects. In a brief digression, these movements are discussed insofar as they shed light on French perceptions of Montagnard political and religious activities, which were glossed as 'sorcery' (*sorcellerie*). In this section, it is argued that the French interpretations of both movements provided a model for the interpretation of the 'Python God' affair, starting shortly after the suppression of these movements.

The movement headed by Kommadam was a direct heir to the better known 'Holy Men's Rebellion' in the northeast of Siam and the south of Laos around the turn of the century. This latter movement has been described as a 'Buddhist millenarian revolt', directed against both the Siamese central government and the French colonial administration, because it derived its religious content from

Theravada Buddhism which is dominant in Laos and Thailand. There is a millenarian tendency within Thai (and Lao) Buddhism which is linked up with the popular belief in *Phu Mi Bun* ('Men of Merit' or 'Holy Men') who announce the arrival of the second *Bodhisattva*, the *Maitreya*, who is the future Buddha on earth. The *Phu Mi Bun* are prophets and 'miracle men' who distribute sacred water in expectation of an imminent catastrophe (Yoneo Ishii 1975; Keyes 1977: 288–98).[4] In general, the scholars dealing with the events on the Lao side of the border tend to stress the political aspects of the revolt as an anti-colonial movement, while the 'Siamese' scholars stress the religious aspects, connected with Buddhist millenarianism. John Murdock is the only author who consistently treats the rebellion in Laos and Siam as a single movement. According to him, the movement was caused by changes forced by the French and Siamese polities upon the 'economic patterns and traditional leadership structures of the Lower Mekong Region' (1974: 65) and by the power vacuum resulting from the French-imposed demilitarization of the Siamese side of the border.

Kommadam was the one adjutant of 'Holy Man' and prophet Ong Keo who survived a French ambush and managed to resist further French penetration among the Loven and Alak populations on the Boloven Plateau for three decades, eventually reaching a silent agreement with the French authorities. Adjacent territories in Annam, to the north of Kontum, Dak To and An Khê, had hardly been penetrated by the French. This implied that the whole northern portion of the Central Highlands between Saravane and Attopeu in Laos and Hue and Quang Ngãi in Annam, was still not subjugated. Therefore, the construction of *Colonial route* no. 14, which was planned to connect Saigon with Huê via Ban Mê Thuôt, Pleiku and Kontum, could not be completed. For the French, the silent agreement with Kommadam was violated when, in the words of Geoffrey Gunn (1990: 123), 'commencing in 1933 Kommadan's revolt took on a decidedly religious coloration'. Kommadam spread propaganda throughout Laos, announcing the arrival of the new *Maitreya*, thereby stirring the French into action. The pacification campaign against Kommadam was resumed in a concerted effort from Laos to subdue the Boloven and affiliated groups and from Annam to subdue the Sedang, Katu and affiliated groups north of Kontum and west of Quang Nam. In 1935, after the successful 'pacification' of the southern Highlands, commandant Nyo received full powers to pursue Kommadam and his adherents in the northern Highlands, employing *Bataillons montagnards*, consisting of *tirailleurs Rhadé* and *Jarai*. Kommadam was killed in 1936.[5]

The Boloven Revolt under Kommadam's leadership has generally been interpreted as a political movement, in that his explicit aim was to resist French colonial rule. While acknowledging the deeply religious inspiration of Kommadam, Gunn, in a critique of Stanley Tambiah's analysis of millennial Buddhism (1976), considered religion to be the ideological form hiding deeper structural causes for the movement, in this case colonial taxation and exploitation (Gunn 1990: 124–5). In fact, the religious content and context were hardly taken seriously by most of the analysts who focused on the political aspects. Both contemporary and later commentators interpreted the Boloven Revolt as an early anti-colonial movement, fueled by heavy tax and corvée burdens, and by the suppression of shifting cultivation, of the slave trade and of local leadership by the colonial administration. Following the Communist journalist Wilfred Burchett (1957: 245), both François Moppert (1981: 58–61) and Geoffrey Gunn (1988: 241; 1990: 126) traced a genealogy of revolt via Ong Keo through Kommadam to his son Sithon, who was to be a famous leader of the Pathet Lao, the Communist 'liberation movement' of Laos. According to Moppert, this genealogy corresponds with three stages of national liberation: Messianic, national and revolutionary (Moppert 1981: 60).

The revolt of N'Trang Lung (1913–35) took place among the Mnong and Stieng populations in the southern part of the Highlands, more precisely the region of the upper Chhlong River in the tri-border area connecting Cambodia, Cochinchina and Annam. This area was considered traditionally rebellious and therefore politically significant, because it had been the stronghold for two successive movements of pretenders to the Cambodian throne in the second half of the nineteenth century. The area also had a special religious significance, for the governor of the Cambodian garrison town of Srektum on the Chhlong River had the special mission of tracing a footprint of the Buddha that was supposed to be located on the mountain of Núi Bara (Maitre 1912: 489–94). The German ethnologist Adolf Bastian reported on the mythical footprint, located in the Mnong area, which could only be made visible with special ceremonies and sacrifices, and which produced magic water with healing powers (Bastian 1873: 119). Such beliefs, very familiar in popular Buddhism (cf. Marlière 1978), must have fueled the many 'short-lived millenarian movements that emerged' in the Cambodian countryside before World War I, which were attributed to the changes brought about by French colonial rule (Osborne 1978: 227–8). Thus, a political and religious foundation for rebellion was in place well before the Mnong Biat warrior N'Trang Lung led his men in the attack on Henri Maitre.

For a long time, the Stieng and Mnong Biat populations at the upper reaches of the Chhlong River remained out of reach of both French and Cambodian authorities. After two earlier French attempts at penetration around the turn of the century, Henri Maitre was the first explorer to report some results during an official pacification mission ordered by the *Résident-supérieur* of Cambodia. During his second expedition in 1909–10, which produced the material for the exploration narrative of *Les jungles moï* (1912), Maitre claimed to have subdued a number of villages, and to have founded a military post surveying the area. During the leave in France when Maitre composed his book, the new post was attacked and destroyed, leaving the whole region in state of volatility. The *Délégué* of Kratie, Truffot, led a military column into the area to suppress the revolt, but was not successful. In 1913, it was Maitre's turn again to try to effectively occupy the region, with the foundation of the new post of Mera. In 1914 he was killed at the hands of N'Trang Lung, who led a group of 400 Mnong warriors feigning to formally surrender to the French (Nyo 1937: 60–1). After the initial successes of annihilating Maitre's party and a couple of military posts including Mera, the revolt spread rapidly. Truffot was assassinated when leading a military campaign in the area in 1915. After the killing of Maitre and Truffot, the subsequent revolt was merely contained within a limited area, but not really countered by the French administration, which lacked the military means for effective pacification during World War I. Furthermore, the administration was forced to devote all its attention to peasant manifestations and uprisings in Cambodia, which came to be known as the '1916 Affair', a protest movement of Khmer peasants against taxes and corvée labor (Forest 1980; Forest 1981; Osborne 1978).

The Governor-General's decision to reduce the 'blank spots' on the map of French Indochina led in 1931 to a resumption of the pacification campaigns against refractory groups in the southern Highlands. The colonial drive for pacification was fueled by the violent deaths of *Délégué* Gatille of Thudaumot in 1931 and of the engineer Morère who was involved in the construction of Route No. 14.[6] In the 'tri-border area', the military under Commandant Nyo had a free hand in managing the campaign, which was a concerted effort from the three 'countries' involved, i.e. Cochinchina, Annam and Cambodia. French military action, consisting of the destruction of suspect villages and their rice fields, sometimes by aerial bombardments, provoked a violent reaction on the part of the Central Highlanders, who started to attack French military posts in large numbers. Yet they were no match for the superior French forces, which included a Rhadé batallion that was held in high esteem because of their knowledge of the terrain and of the culture (An. 1934: 613; Huard 1937: 867). While fleeing from the French troops closing in on his strongholds, N'Trang Lung was delivered to the French by his own men, and was killed in 1935.[7]

French officers involved in the pacification campaigns against N'Trang Lung (1931–35) reported on the role of 'sorcerers' in the movement.[8] In a report on the results of French penetration from 1931 to 1935, Governor Maurice Pagès of Cochinchina speculated on the role of sorcerers in the N'Trang Lung rebellion:

It is probable that sorcerers, whose influence on these primitives is so tyrannical, have profited from a fortuitous event to provoke the hostility of these villages and declare that the moment had come to let the person disappear who persisted in violating their autonomy.

(Pagès 1935: 213)

Pagès' speculation found support in an ethnographic essay on the religious beliefs of the Mnong, published by Captain Paul Huard in the *Revue des Troupes Coloniales* (1937). In this 'first and modest contribution to the knowledge of the psychology of the Mnong', based on experience acquired during the pacification campaign, Captain Huard mentioned that Mnong warriors were provided with a potion rendering them invulnerable before an attack in January 1933. He came to the conclusion that the Mnong considered many chiefs to be 'good sorcerers', whose offices were indispensable in forging alliances for war purposes (Huard 1937: 878). The French military unwittingly 'facilitated the birth of coalitions between clans that are generally divided' (ibid.: 881) when they established military outpost on a plateau considered sacred by the Mnong. Huard admonished his military audience to observe Montagnard religious beliefs scrupulously, not for fear, but in order to utilize them. Later reports, written during and after the Python God affair, confirmed the participation, in the movement of N'Trang Lung, of 'sorcerers' who engaged in classical millenarian practices. These include the prophecy of an imminent cataclysm, the distribution of 'magic water', and the reassurance that Mnong warriors would be invulnerable to French bullets.[9]

Both the Boloven Revolt and the rebellion of N'Trang Lung were interpreted as primarily political movements, because they resisted the establishment by force, of French colonial rule over their territories. Although the political, anti-colonial character of the movements of Kommadam and N'Trang Lung is usually stressed, both movements were also characterized by religious and millenarian practices and expectations. Contemporary French observers noted the collusion of religion and politics in both movements, glossing religious practice as 'sorcery' (*sorcellerie*). The activities of sorcerers supporting – or acting themselves as – political and military leaders were thought to be dangerous for French rule. On the eve of the Sam Bram affair, sorcerers were blamed for the 'social troubles' occurring in the *pays Moï*, facilitating a politicized view of Montagnard religious practice. Furthermore, both movements were localized affairs, in that they – at least in their later stages in the 1930s – did not spread across putative tribal boundaries, and thus seemed to sanction the geographic aspect of tribal classification, symbolized in the official ethnographic map of Indochina (Malleret and Taboulet 1937). In other words, the perception of both movements neatly fitted into the French classificatory grid which was connected with the process of tribalization, in that revolts were conceptualized as movements geographically restricted by tribal boundaries. Thus, French experience with and perception of both movements provided a model for a politicized interpretation of Montagnard millenarian beliefs and related – religious and political – practice. This model figured in press accounts, military penetration reports and ethnographic studies related to the pacification campaigns. In the next section, we shall see that these movements, ending just before the return of the Python God with the killing of N'Trang Lung (1935) and Kommadam (1936), carried over in localized political and religious activities connected with local variations of the *Dieu Python* cult.

Sam Bram: The making of a movement

In June 1937, some Viêt (ethnic Vietnamese) district chiefs informed the *Résident* of Pleiku about bizarre behavior of the population in the vicinity of Cheo Reo, the Jarai heartland. The Highlanders there reportedly closed the entrance to their villages, sacrificed their buffaloes, stopped working their land, and tried to obtain coins of one *sou* (*centime*) at all cost. The one *sou* pieces became so scarce that Viêt merchants traded them for 20 *sou* coins apiece. Moreover, a number of Montagnard villages refused to perform corvée labor. In July, the same *Résident* reported that the '*agitation*' was the work of Sam Bram, who was said to be wanted in Ban Me Thuot for fraud. The *Résident* of Darlac thereupon produced the information that Sam Bram was living in the village of Ea Luy in Phu Yên province, dressed in Vietnamese fashion, and had himself built a Vietnamese-style house. Predicting a 'bad fate', he forced the population within a 100-kilometer radius to furnish him with money, cattle and alcohol in exchange for holy chants and magic water. The Resident saw great danger in this magic water, as the administration was believed to be impotent against its possessors if they refused to do their corvée. The *Résident-supérieur* of Annam ordered the arrest of Sam Bram, and convened the Residents of the three provinces involved in Ban Me Thuot, under the presidency of M. Jardin, Inspector of Administrative Affairs of Annam.[10]

Inspecteur Jardin and *Garde principal* Padovani had already interrogated Ma Cham (an alias for Sam Bram, who was also variously known as Ma Wih, Mang Cham, Mang Lo, Sam Bam and Dam Bam). In a report of 15 June 1937, Jardin stated that Sam Bram was very influential in his region, and was a well-known collaborator with the colonial administration:

> Ma Cham is very well-known by the Administration of Phu-Yen; not only doesn't he hide himself, but the *Gardes principaux* and district chiefs have even resorted to his influence in order to have the decrees of the Administration implemented in his region.[11]

Like the resident of Darlac, Jardin saw the building of a new house, fitting Sam Bram's status as 'great chief', as the cause of the 'troubles' (*agitation*), as the affair was referred to. In order to pay for the construction, Sam Bram had allegedly resorted to sorcery. He had urged his followers to contribute one *sou*, one piglet and a jar of ricewine, in exchange for a bottle of magic water (Jarai: *Ia Iun*; Bahnar: *Dak Ion*; French: *eau lustrale* or *eau influxe*), and a few grains of rice which would produce a magnificent harvest after planting in the four corners of a fallow field. Jardin supposed that the construction costs had induced Sam Bram to expand his field of action by sending out emissaries. Although conceding that no trace of such emissaries had been found, the Inspector did not doubt that the personal interests of the emissaries had contributed to Ma Cham's authority and had multiplied the revenue in terms of one-*sou* coins. Relegating the activities to the realm of sorcery, Jardin decided not to prosecute Ma Cham because of his past behavior and because he continued to acknowledge the superiority of French power. He was taken to a village outside of the Highlands, where he remained under custody, barred from further contact with the Montagnard population.

Despite Sam Bram's banishment and frequent police tours in the area, the 'agitation' spread out to the provinces of Kontum, Quang Ngãi, Quang Nam, and even affected the Rhadé colonial militia in Ban Me Thuot. Sam Bram's family continued to 'sell' the magic water. In some places, even as far as Cambodia, people tried to emulate Sam Bram, claiming to be related to him. In the vicinity of Ban Don the 'sorcerer' Me Deng reportedly claimed to be Sam Bram's younger brother (in fact Me Deng was a woman – see below), and developed a following in many villages with the promise to destroy colonial rule in the future, as reported in a sort of Pidgin French by the Resident of Darlac:

Continue to obey the Administration, pay tax, go to work when you are summoned, I will have nothing to say. However, if one day I would want to do something against the Administration, it will be clean and swift.[12]

The initial interpretation of the movement as a swindle based on sorcery was replaced by a more politicized interpretation which emphasized the old theme of external Vietnamese involvement. This politicized interpretation was offered by the Catholic Bishop of Kontum, Mgr. Martial Jannin, who filed a highly suggestive report on the religious and political content of the movement. This report was distributed both by Jannin himself and by the colonial administration of Annam, as an annex to its political report to the Governor-General of September 1937. Although the Bishop was the first to pay attention to the religious context of the movement, it was only to ridicule it, as is obvious from the first words of the six-page report ('Don't laugh too much, yes, a new god is born there, among the Moys Jorays!'). He related how a Jarai woman gave birth to a python that could talk and turned out to be *Dam Klan*, the omnipotent Python God. Dam Klan issued six 'commandments', the first of which applied to the dealings with the colonial authorities ('At the moment, all must obey well, but as a matter of form, to the French and Annamese authorities. However, all must remain assured that on the chosen day Dieu-Python will take care of the rest'). Other alleged commandments concerned moral behavior ('no fornications'); a prescription to sacrifice in the usual manner; a prohibition to eat rotting meat, as well as meat of aquatic birds, snakes, crustaceans and some sorts of fish; a prohibition on keeping white animals; and the order to observe each seventh day as a day of rest.[13]

In a section on *les dirigeants*, Bishop Jannin identifies *Dam Bam* as the representative of *Dieu Python*, who is performing miracles, and who is beyond French authority. However, Jannin suggests that the true wire-pullers must be a 'secret committee', aiming at a 'general revolt of the Moïs for the liberation of the country'. A supposed indication for this is the sacrifice of white animals, which by extension came to signify the sacrifice of white people. In fact, the reference to the sacrifice of white animals, presumed incarnations of Europeans, may have been derived from J.-J. Dauplay, who reported this practice in the context of his dealing with the Boloven Revolt (Dauplay 1929: 60). Another such indication is that each village seeking the magic water must establish a shadow administration. The magic water contains the spirit of *Dieu Python*, hence its magical qualities. The traffic in *sous* is presented as a major swindle for the profit of 'Dam Bam et Cie'. If the commandments are not strictly followed, the water contained in the bottle diminishes, but the level will be restored after reconciliation rituals performed by the new village notables. This water will do until the cataclysm, starting one morning when three suns rise, followed by a terrible typhoon that destroys everything and everybody except those villages possessing the magic water. After the cataclysm, the villagers can appropriate the goods of the vanished foreigners, and labor will not be necessary anymore, because of magic rice grains. Jannin stresses the destruction of Europeans as the main goal of the movement, which had so much success among the Central Highlanders – he even speaks of 'thousands of villages', which is a willful demographic error. The real cause of this success, according to Jannin, is the dissatisfaction of the Montagnards with the colonial regime, symbolized by taxes, corvée labor and appointed chiefs. But there is a well-hidden secret committee behind the movement which 'is not far from Annam where there are so many bandits with close or loose bonds with the communists, who have anti-French sentiments'. Referring to violent Montagnard revolts in the past, Jannin admonishes his audience with the wise words '*Prévoir, c'est Gouverner*' [To govern is to foresee].

The political report of Annam of September 1937, to which the missionary report was attached, was presented as a report which 'situates the facts on a more spiritual level – facts which, as much as the observations of a material order, must be close to the truth'.[14] However, this political report still attributed the affair to fraud by Sam Bram, who was constructing a new house. The administration resorted to more severe measures, like the arrest of all 'collaborators and emulators' of Sam Bram. The coins of one *sou* were taken out of circulation and replaced by pieces of half the value. Moreover, the *Sûreté*, the notorious political police, was ordered to find out if there was any support for the movement from *Annamites* (ethnic Vietnamese) from the lowlands for political reasons. In September 1937, the head of the police in Annam, Sogny, filed his report on the movement, which blamed Sam Bram as an agitator against the colonial administration. Sogny speculated that there might be an 'Annamese' connection, motivated by political or economic gains.[15] The political interpretation seemed to be confirmed by events in the border area of Kontum and Quang Ngãi, which had been turbulent after French efforts at penetration after the killing of Kommadam in southern Laos. In October, groups of 'fanaticized Moïs' attacked French patrols, one of which was never heard of again. Again, a link was made with 'revolutionary Annamese' and with Sam Bram, as the attackers thought themselves invulnerable due to the possession of magic water.[16]

When Bishop Jannin proceeded to publish an abstract of his report in the weekly *L'Union* in October of that year, even suggesting foreign interference, the themes brought up by him began to be constantly repeated in subsequent reports by various colonial officials, and resulted in a standard interpretation of the movement. Thus, the commander of the colonial Army in Annam, General Deslaurens, noted in a secret report that the movements (note the plural), so similar in distant areas and among various populations, must 'be instigated by foreign agents in the Moï Country who would have been charged with the mission to create difficulties for the French Authorities'.[17] In the political report of Annam of November, the missionary viewpoint was largely endorsed by *Inspecteur* Jardin, who was responsible for dealing with the movement in Annam:

> Everything leads to believe that it is the associates of Sam-Bram – most probably Annamese – who one fine day had the idea to use the immense credulity of the moïs in order to organize a vast swindle. ... [T]he agents of

this machination are busy consolidating the magical power of Sam Bram in the mind of the moïs of his region.[18]

In the same report the 'ordinary' Montagnards were exculpated because the '*Dieu Python* mystique' was 'a chapter ... in the traditional exploitation of the naive and superstitious moï by cunning Annamese, devoid of scruples'. In this metamorphosis, the Montagnards even acquired traits of noble (if credulous) savages:

> The brain of the Moïs is cloudy, its reactions defy any logic. This is one more reason to keep ourselves in check, also in the neighboring countries, and thus to try to avoid actions which necessitate repressive measures toward populations that – despite everything – remain sympathetic in their savagery.
>
> (Jardin, December 1937)

This became the standard interpretation of the movement in circles of military and civilian colonial officials. In a note by Inspector Jardin on Sam Bram, dated 16 December 1937, this version was sanctioned while the 'swindle thesis' was abandoned. Here, Sam Bram is described as 'a fanatic, a half-wit who is more or less sorcerer', who hardly profited from the traffic in *sous*. The 'economic argument' was even turned upside down, in that any evidence of fraud effectively pointed to outsider involvement. Jardin wrote that 'according to those who know the Moïs for having lived with them and studied them, this idea of swindle through exchange is not a Moï idea'.[19] Put into practice, this interpretation resulted in the persecution of three categories of people in the Highlands, notably 'foreigners' (in particular ethnic Vietnamese), 'sorcerers', and 'chiefs' (appointed or otherwise) who had followed the movement. As far as sorcerers were concerned, the Catholic Mission could be satisfied with the witch hunt unleashed against the 'diabolic' agents of indigenous religion.

In the northern part of the Highlands, the movement did not subside by the end of 1937, and even took on a more violent tinge with attacks by Montagnard warriors on French military forces sent to repress the movements. Yet, the Residents of the provinces of Quang Ngãi and Kontum excused the Montagnards, and pleaded for '... a certain indulgence regarding the mistakes made by these big children that are the Moïs, whose extraordinary credulity in their sorcerers and in their soothsayers is at the root of all their actions'.[20] So when the rebellion continued, a few Montagnards and twelve Viêts were arrested, the latter suspected of fraud connected with the rebellion. The exact role of the Viêts was not reported. [21] However, some Highland groups in the northern part of the Highlands adjacent to Laos, as well as some groups on the Boloven Plateau in southern Laos remained 'unruly', and continued to resist French attempts at 'pacification' through World War II. Eventually, the 'tribal' resistance in the mountain districts of Quang Ngãi, Quang Nam and Quang Tri connected up with the activities of Vietnamese Communists from 1940 onward.[22]

In the southern part of the Highlands, a renewed agitation was reported in the province of Haut-Donnaï and in the border area of Cochinchina and Cambodia (Haut-Chhlong). In May 1938, four sorcerers were arrested in Haut-Donnaï, for agitation. In Haut-Chhlong, the erstwhile stronghold of N'Trang Lung, the involvement of 'sorcerers' in the rebellion of N'Trang Lung became better known with the suppression of sorcerers in the course of the Python God affair, resulting in the killing of three of them, and the arrest of another one in January 1938. According to a confidential report of 3 February 1938 by General Martin, military commander of the 'Division Cochinchine-Cambodge', two of them had escaped from prison in 1937. They had been held there for their participation in an attack on a French post in 1935, on which occasion they had possessed 'magic water'. In the same report, a Cambodian is mentioned who since 1930 had distributed magic water and announced the end of the world in a long cataclysmic night.[23] In a later (1939) study of Mnong Biat spiritual life, the administrator of Haut-Chhlong, Captain Jean Boucher de Crèvecoeur, traced a direct line between the revolt of N'Trang Lung and the millenarian activities of 1937 and 1938 in Haut-Chhlong, which occurred in relation to the cult of the Python God.[24]

A clear pattern established itself, in that those populations which had just been 'pacified' with the killing of anti-colonial leaders like N'Trang Lung in Haut-Chhlong (1935) and Kommadam on the Boloven Plateau (1936), again resorted to violent rebellion against French rule. They were encouraged by millenarian expectations connected with the *Dieu Python* mystique, and protected by the healing qualities of the magic water, distributed by Sam Bram or his local emulators. In most of the Highlands, however, colonial peace seemed to return in the course of 1938, with the arrest of several 'sorcerers'. The success was attributed to a policy of restraint (*'politique de réserve'*) on the part of the French Residents in the Highlands. They preferred a peaceful return of the *'dissidents'* to their villages by themselves, to a bloody repression of the movement. Sanctions were applied according to customary law. Such a policy of restraint was recommended by Inspector Jardin, who had concluded that time would do its work.[25] However, the actions and movements of Viêt people in the Highlands were severely restricted and controlled, because their involvement was now taken for granted – although no trace of evidence was produced. For the French, then, most of the Highlands seemed pacified again on the eve of World War II, apart from the region north of Kontum, inland of Quang Ngãi and the area bordering on Laos.

Restraint was not applied with respect to the conviction of the sorcerers involved in the Python God mystique. On 2 September 1938, Sam Bram was sentenced to ten years in prison and a fine of 500 piastres by the Indigenous Law Court of Darlac, for 'sorcery with the aim of fraud by abuse of influence'. Both sentences were halved by the Resident of Darlac. On the same charge, Me Deng and her husband Y Hlao were sentence to three years in prison by the same tribunal, on 5 November 1938; this sentence was also halved. The *Tribunal moï* of Haut-Donnaï province convicted 14 persons, charged for 'sorcery, secret meetings and conspiracy against the security of the state', to sentences from 8 to 20 years in prison, on 13 December 1938.[26] There are several versions of what happened to Sam Bram. According to some, the Japanese released Sam Bram from jail in 1945 (Hickey 1982a: 357; Đang Nghiêm Van 1988, personal communication). A semi-official French history of the Montagnards would have it that Sam Bram was acquitted (Bourotte 1955: 100–1). But Jacques Dournes' Jarai informants told him that Sam Bram died after having been tortured by the French (Dournes 1977: 95).

Interpretations and reinterpretations

The French administrative reaction to the Python God movement seemed to be dictated by *ad hoc* decisions. The only coherent contemporary analysis of the mystique was the report by Bishop Jannin of Kontum, which had an obvious politico-religious aim. In this section, it will be argued that both the missionaries and the colonial authorities deliberately ignored available ethnographic knowledge on previous Montagnard millenarian movements. Such knowledge was contained in the ethnographic work by the explorer Henri Maitre and the missionary Jean Kemlin, who had both predicted, in the early decades of the century, the occurrence of such movements. This neglect is connected with the tribalizing classificatory grid, which tended to conceptually rigidify ethnic boundaries, and with the convenient analogy with earlier tribal revolts. On the basis of extremely thin evidence, missionaries and colonial officials construed an image of a politicized, multi-ethnic movement, which in due course made the conceptualization of a distinct Montagnard ethnic identity possible, with all its cultural, political, territorial and military implications.

The work of Henri Maitre constituted the culmination of an expeditionary ethnographic genre practiced by military explorers in the early days of the French colonial presence in the Central Highlands. In *Les jungles moï* (1912a) Maitre arrived at an elaborate ethnic classification, based on observed linguistic differences, and influenced by philological and diffusionist thinking which permeated ethnology (see Chapter 2). Maitre's authoritative classification influenced both ethnographic and administrative practice after World War I, and thus sanctioned the process of tribalization. In his historical essay in *Les jungles moï*, Maitre cited a great number of revolts and movements that shook the Highlands well before the establishment of French colonial rule, even before any French presence. Some of those movements were religiously inspired, such as the movement of Ia Pu. Ia Pu was a Buddhist monk from Laos who around 1820 wielded strong influence in the southern part of Laos, in particular among the *Kha* (a Lao word for *Moï*), and who distributed water which was considered a powerful talisman against disease. The movement was reportedly suppressed when Lao princes killed Ia Pu.[27] According to Maitre, there was a common religious underpinning for these movements, which we would now call millenarian:

> In order to understand well this blind trust put by the Moï of central Annam in various rebels and imposters who every now and then cause rebellion in

the region, one needs to know that these tribes wait for a Messiah who, according to their traditions, will restore the Golden Age for them and will deliver them from all their oppressors. This explains their ardor to welcome all those who claim to be sent from heaven; each time, indeed, these naive populations believe in the arrival of the desired Messiah.

(Maitre 1912a: 477)

In retrospect, this appears to be a predictive statement which applies perfectly to *Dieu Python*, as the French would call the impersonation of the Python God – Sam Bram.

Five years after Maitre, Father Jean Kemlin published his essay 'Alliances chez les Reungao' (also known as Rengao or Rongao) in the prestigious *Bulletin de l'Ecole française d'Extrême-Orient* (*BEFEO*). French missionaries had engaged in ethnography ever since the establishment of their mission station in Kontum in 1850. Their ethnographic practice focused on Montagnard religion which was interpreted as based on fear and terror inspired by sorcerers, who were regarded as accomplices of the devil. Ethnography, then, was to help the missionaries combat the sorcerers. Missionary ethnography culminated in the work by Father Kemlin who explored Rengao religious practice in a series of detailed essays in the *BEFEO*. Kemlin did not restrict himself to the Rongao, but gave many Bahnar, Sedang and Jarai equivalents of the practices and spirits he identified, which were presented as variations on a common theme. Although Maitre and Kemlin referred to each other's work, Kemlin was – contrary to Maitre – not preoccupied with ethnic classification and the identification of political and territorial boundaries. From his use of 'tribal' designations and of the term Moï, it is evident that he conceived of the Central Highlanders as not only sharing the same territory, but also fundamentally the same 'cultural' practices, or at least religious practices. This non-tribal quality may be characteristic of missionary ethnography, as opposed to administrative ethnography, as is also noted by Peter Pels (1994). For a missionary like Kemlin, who was eager to extend his efforts at conversion beyond some Rengao and Bahnar villages among neighboring groups with only slightly different religious practices, this is a rational option.

Kemlin presented the Rengao world as animated by spirits (*iang*), the most important of which is Bô Brôk (or Bok Glaih in Bahnar), the 'God of Thunder', who is a special source of power among the various highland groups. It is possible for humans to have several kinds of alliances with other humans, but also with a wide variety of localized or more powerful spirits. Those with privileged alliances with powerful spirits are the *bojâu*, the sorcerers who were so detested by Kemlin's predecessors (and by himself, as is evident from his conflicts with the colonial administration over the treatment of non-Catholic Bahnar – see Kemlin 1917: 34–43). The most popular spirit is a female goddess, known as *Ia Pom*, who is associated with the times of the mythical heroes (*dam*):

Still now, [the Rongao] hope for her coming on earth like the coming of a Messiah who must bring back the Golden Age. This general anticipation causes all the moï populations to immediately believe the first imposter who pretends to be *Ia*. The title of *Ia* ... is now almost indistinctly conferred to all creatures regarded as the incarnation of a *iang*.

(Kemlin 1917: 58)

In the subsequent pages, Kemlin narrated a number of legends and historical cases involving both *dam* and *Ia*, including the *Pho Mi Boun* ('Holy Man') movement that started on the Boloven plateau (ibid.: 62).[28] Like Maitre, Father Kemlin noted a readiness on the part of the Highlanders, irrespective of their 'tribal identity', to engage in millenarian activities surrounding the claims of *Ia* – reincarnations of *iang* (spirits).

When confronted with *Dieu Python*, Kemlin's successors in Kontum obviously considered the cult as a religious rival, as it even affected the Catholic Bahnar of Kontum. Although claiming that the 'diabolical excesses' of Sam Bram caused no great alarm from a religious point of view, the report by Bishop Jannin was an attempt to get rid of Sam Bram. The rhetorical means that he used to achieve this were first, blaming the sorcerers who supposedly had stirred it up, and second, suggesting the involvement of Vietnamese Communists in the agitation. The missionary report was the first and for the duration of the movement and its repression, the only interpretation which made an effort to delve more deeply into the religious content of the movement. Jacques Dournes, a later ethnographer, however, claimed that many suggestions of Jannin were gross misrepresentations, intended to stir the colonial authorities into action, as was evident from the internal contradictions in the Jannin's text (1978a: 96–9). One example given by Dournes is the sacrifice of white animals, which Jannin interpreted as signifying the massacre of Europeans. Dournes claimed that whereas white animals are held in high esteem, Europeans are not considered to be white. Their complexion is pale, like that of corpses, while missionaries, with their black beards and cowls, are considered 'evil black spirits' by Jarai and Mnong informants (Dournes 1978a: 91). But despite these ethnographic misrepresentations, at the time of dissemination the missionary report constituted a virtually unchallenged claim to ethnographic authority, rendering its political message more convincing for the audience of colonial administrators for which it was intended.

Jannin's claim to ethnographic authority was enhanced by the prestige enjoyed by his predecessor as head of the Kontum mission, Kemlin, who had been an official ethnographic correspondent for the *Ecole Française d'Extrême-Orient*. The oeuvre by Kemlin was the culmination of missionary ethnographic practice, just as the work by Maitre was the culmination of explorative ethnography. In the *interbellum* decades, French action in the Highlands was invariably legitimized with reference to the work of Maitre and Kemlin, who both in a sense predicted the future occurrence of millenarian movements among the Montagnards. It is simply inconceivable that Mgr. Jannin would have been ignorant of the historical occurrence of millenarianism and of the religious propensity toward millenarianism among the Montagnards. For Jannin, who succeeded Kemlin as head of the Kontum Mission, had already been in Kontum at the time that Kemlin published his ethnographic work. On the basis of Kemlin's essay it was possible to pinpoint specifically which type of sorcerer/ess (*bojâu*) was associated with the reincarnation of an *Ia*, and as such could possible challenge colonial rule; but this was not even attempted. Jannin's report on *Dieu Python* must be seen as a deliberate attempt to influence policy by ignoring such relevant knowledge. Simultaneously, he rendered Montagnard religious practice suspect by classifying it indiscriminately as 'sorcery'. Jannin rhetorically associated the concept of sorcery with economic gain ('fraud'), and more importantly with political subversion. This deliberately politicized part of the missionary interpretation was accepted by the colonial administration, which issued orders to arrest any sorcerers engaging in 'bizarre behavior'.

One may equally wonder why colonial officials, who routinely referred to the ethnographic oeuvre by Henri Maitre in order to legitimize ethnic policy in the Highlands, were seemingly unaware of his predictions in the matter, and accepted the missionary account without more ado. Moreover, French colonial officials ignored contemporary ethnographic and administrative dealings with sorcery, which were characterized by ambivalence. Administrators indiscriminately used the word *sorcier* to denote any Montagnard associated with religion, or having mystical or healing power. In this context, it should be noted that the French word *sorcier/sorcière* may be translated into English either as sorcerer/ess, or as witch. A lot of confusion stems from the fact that the same word was used to denote 'witches', 'chief-sorcerers', 'good sorcerers' and 'healers', as Huard distinguished in a report on Mnong religious beliefs in the context of the N'Trang Lung rebellion (Huard 1937; see also Hickey 1982a: 23–27). Montagnards who were accused of being witches (*sorciers/sorcières*), were often subjected to an ordeal, and massacred or sold as slaves, along with their families, if found guilty. Even in 1937, the French administration still tolerated such practices because they conformed to customary law.[29]

This conceptual confusion, by which various indigenous categories were pejoratively labeled *sorciers* by the French, affected French policy during the Sam Bram affair. Only in 1941, well after the suppression of *Dieu Python*, the administrator and ethnographer Paul Guilleminet tried to put an end to this confusion in a study of the religious and political role of sorcerers in the Highlands. In 1937 Guilleminet had already been *Résident* of Kontum, the seat of Bishop Jannin, and in this capacity had been responsible for administrative dealing with *Dieu Python* in that province. In the article, Guilleminet aimed to 'classify the sorcerers and the information we have on them', and study 'the reactions of a political order that they provoke in the Highlands', because 'diverse incidents, more or less localized revolts, even murders ... have been attributed to ritual reasons and more specifically to the action or bad influence of sorcerers' (Guilleminet 1941a: 9–10). Basing his analysis on Maitre and more specifically on Kemlin, he noted the existence of *Iang* (spirits) and *Ya* (incarnations), and the role of the latter in revolts (ibid.: 26–30). Concerning Sam Bram, Guilleminet observed how 'tribes which today have almost no common bond, which don't

know each other, celebrate the birth of an *Ya* and procure an object coming from
him: the sacred water' (ibid.: 32). While the legends were common among the
Highland people, the responses were very different and localized, giving some
groups occasion to attack the French, while other groups just waited for the
cataclysm to come or did not sow their lands. In the case of Sam Bram,
Guilleminet exculpates the sorcerers (*magiciens*) for the 'serious revolt' which they
did not foresee, since they were 'only modest executing people of the powers'.
On the other hand, 'the *Ya* are dangerous, the ones who are almighty; and the
men in whom they incarnate or who announce their birth are the ones who must
be discredited as soon as possible' (ibid.: 33).

In fact, Guilleminet does nothing else here than analyze *ex post facto* the
movement with the tools provided by Maitre and Kemlin. Indeed, as a reputed
ethnographer affiliated with the *Ecole Française d'Extrême-Orient*, he must already
have been aware of the work of Maitre and Kemlin in 1937, when he was
responsible for administrative dealing with *Dieu Python*.[30] Like Bishop Jannin,
Résident Guilleminet chose to ignore available ethnographic knowledge which
apparently did not suit the interests of the colonial administration. In this
context, it is telling that the missionary interpretation by Bishop Jannin was not
endorsed entirely, but deprived of its one critical element, namely that the
movement was fueled by local dissatisfaction with colonial rule. The more
convenient interpretation of outsider involvement was officially adopted. This
interpretation did not question the French role in terms of policy in the
Highlands, thus ignoring the possible effects of taxation, corvée labor and the
establishment of plantations on land claimed by Highlanders. In areas where
anti-French violence could not be denied, notably the traditionally fractious
areas, this was attributed to the exploitation of the local Highland populations by
Vietnamese peddlers doubling as tax collectors, the *các lái*. In this way French
efforts at creating a directly-ruled Montagnard territory, more or less detached
from the 'states' of Indochina, were underscored.

For French administrators like Resident Guilleminet and Inspector Jardin, the
most puzzling aspect of the 'movement' was the ease with which so many
different 'tribes' were affected so quickly over such a vast territory. During a
conference on administrative reorganization of the Highlands, the multi-ethnic
character of the Python God affair was noted:

> From a political point of view, one generally observes a latent or outspoken
> antagonism between the tribes, an antagonism which the instigators of the
> recent troubles have tried – in vain – to let disappear, at least momentarily.[31]

The transgression of ethnic boundaries was seen as a violation of tribal tradition,
allegedly characterized by mutual antagonism. As we have seen above, this tribal
classification was closely linked with the classificatory grid that framed French
perception in accordance with the tribalization process. The French administrators
were caught in their own web of bureaucratically reproduced ethnographic
classifications. In this context, it is revealing that Sam Bram, his emulators and

his 'followers' were convicted for violating the *coutumier*, this culmination of tribalized identity as prescribed by the French. In his published *coutumier* 'of the Bahnar, Jarai and Sedang tribes of Kontum province', Paul Guilleminet (1952a: 197) cites the conviction of the participants by the customary law court of Kontum.[32] Thus, the Montagnards involved were found guilty for infringing tribal custom rather than revolting against colonial rule.

Although the analyses by Maitre, Kemlin and Guilleminet have shown that in 1937 Central Highlanders held many religious beliefs in common, the responses to the *Dieu Python* mystique were highly localized, almost on a village-to-village basis. The fact that Montagnard religious practices did not stop at presumed or imposed tribal boundaries suggests that the tribalization was 'incomplete' as far as the Montagnards' self-identification was concerned, thereby showing the largely imagined character of such boundaries. French officials noted the regional variation, but did not engage in any serious analysis of this variation, although there was ample room for justified speculation. It is easy to note that the Montagnard actions were most violent in those parts of the Highlands which were recently pacified by military methods, where Theravada Buddhist influence was strongest, among groups and coalitions that once enjoyed power and a fierce reputation as slavers. In fact, French reports made clear that the activities of individual 'sorcerers' engaged in the movements of Kommadam and N'Trang Lung were continued with reference to the Python God. In the absence of an analysis of regional variation, however, the geographic and ethnographic extent of the agitation was taken as proof that there was a movement organized by foreigners – probably Communists. In order not to undermine tribal classification and its political corollary of direct French rule in the Highlands, the image of a unified movement was created, organized by a secret committee sending 'emissaries' across ethnic boundaries. The emphasis on political aspects was consistent with French experience with the localized 'anti-colonial movements' of Kommadam and N'Trang Lung. Thus, an image of a movement of an essentially political character was constructed – or as Maurice Graffeuil, *Résident-supérieur* of Annam, put it, 'this pseudo-religious movement of a political character'.[33]

For Maurice Graffeuil the *Dieu Python* affair provided a stimulus for a special ethnic policy, characterized by the definitive submission of the Montagnards and the exclusion of Viêt influence:

> It is not the first time that the mystique and practice of sorcery have caused trouble among the Moï populations, but the character of the present movement is no doubt more serious because of the intrusion by Annamese who utilize the unbounded credulity of the Moïs. We shall only be sheltered against the return of similar events when the French peaceful penetration of the hinterland of the Annam Cordillera will be completed and when these regions will be definitively organized by us.[34]

Thus, the *Dieu Python* movement, which could hardly be a more authentic cultural expression of the Montagnards if we may believe Kemlin and Maitre, was conveniently interpreted as organized by Vietnamese Communists, and thus classified as an extra-tribal affair which did not really call into question French ethnographic categories and ethnic policies. Yet, it was also invoked in pleas for the detachment of the Highlands from Annam. In the next chapter we shall see how the Python God movement was the immediate occasion for a change in the colonial perception of Montagnards from a bunch of disparate tribes to a single (albeit diverse) ethnic group which was fundamentally different from the surrounding nations. In the context of mounting political tensions, eventually resulting in armed conflict in French Indochina, Central Highlanders underwent the intertwined processes of *ethnicization* and *territorialization* as a result of changing French ethnic representations and policies. Thus, in the course of successive conflicts in Vietnam, the varied population groups known as Montagnards not only came to be seen as a minority group within the nation-state of Vietnam, but increasingly identified themselves as a separate ethnic group.[35]

Sam Bram, a national hero

Few French colonial ethnographers – apart from Guilleminet – made an attempt to analyse what had happened; but if they did, it was an elaboration of the missionary account which was considered a sufficient analysis (Claeys 1939; Maurice 1947; Bourotte 1955). Also a number of later – neo- and post-colonial – anthropologists took this representation as a pan-tribal movement for granted, with some kind of 'foreign' organization and with definite political overtones. This image of the 'Python God movement' neatly fitted in the classical descriptions of multi-ethnic millenarian movements and cargo cults of Norman Cohn, I.C. Jarvie, Peter Worsley, etc. Vietnamese historians and anthropologists like Đang Nghiêm Van, Western anthropologists like Jacques Dournes and Gerald Hickey, and the neo-Marxist historian Geoffrey Gunn all had their reasons for adopting the image of a political movement construed on the basis of colonial records.

In 'Sam Bam, le mage et le blanc dans l'Indochine centrale des années trente' [Sam Bam, the sage and the white man in Central Indochina of the 1930s] (1978a), the late Jacques Dournes spoke of a 'prophetic movement', basing himself on Jarai and missionary sources. During his long-time residence as a Catholic missionary in the Highlands who was not very adept at conversion, Jacques Dournes developed from a staunch supporter of direct French rule during the First Indochina War to an ethnographer sympathetic toward Montagnard – especially Jarai – culture (Lerat 1987). In the 1960s he witnessed the destruction wrought by the war, which he attributed to outside interference into Montagnard lives. When he was forced to leave the Catholic mission in Vietnam in 1970 because of differences over modes of conversion, he also left the Church to become a professional anthropologist at the *Centre National de la Recherche Scientifique* in Paris. Without opportunity to return to Vietnam, his appreciation for Jarai culture turned into near idolatry of his version thereof. Concerning *Dieu Python*, he went at lengths to discredit the account by Bishop

Jannin, by contrasting it with his own knowledge of Jarai mythology and ethnography. In the five accounts by Jarai informants reproduced by Dournes, the emphasis is on the healing power of the magic water and on the ritual requirements for the possessors, notably the food restrictions. Although stressing that many people came from far away to fetch the water, these accounts make no reference whatsoever to any political objective, or even to anything faintly resembling a movement. The French are only mentioned insofar as they arrested Sam Bram. Yet, from the missionary account and the analysis by Guilleminet, Dournes infers that there was a movement, with Sam Bram as its prophet. Comparing the movement with an African prophetic movement and a cargo cult in Papua New Guinea, Dournes claims that the 'movement of Sam Bam, Kimbangu and Yali ... have in common, among other elements, a political tone expressed in the terms 'nationalist', 'conservative'" (Dournes 1978a: 105). In contrast with the later autonomy movement FULRO,[36] which is seen as a 'strictly political and military' nationalism, 'inspired and manipulated by foreigners, from whom it derives the concepts' (Dournes 1978a: 106), he argues that 'at a time that these minority populations were very much threatened, Sam Bram represents the collective, but originally and intentionally non-bellicose (although historically linked to real rebellions) affirmation of their cultural and interethnic identity' (ibid.: 107). Thus, for Dournes the image of Sam Bram as a political movement is used to reconstruct his version of an original, allegedly non-violent Montagnard nationalism under Jarai leadership against colonial rule.

In his *Sons of the Mountains: Ethnohistory of the Vietnamese Central Highlands to 1954* (1982a) the Chicago anthropologist Gerald C. Hickey makes an analysis of the 'Python God Movement' which equally reflects his French sources and his own research situation. Hickey is a Chicago-trained anthropologist who was employed in the 1960s by the Rand Corporation, a major military think-tank linked to the US Navy, to investigate Highlander leadership (see Chapters 6 and 7). In this capacity, he developed into a major expert on the Montagnards, and into their spokesman *vis-à-vis* American and South Vietnamese agencies in the Highlands. Being a part of the American intervention in Vietnam, Hickey noted a resemblance with the French position in the Highlands during colonial times, insofar as both the French and American intervention were intended to counter Vietnamese influence and seek allies in the strategically important Highlands. The basic argument of his *Ethnohistory* is that the Montagnards evolved a common ethnic identity in reaction to French colonial rule and the Vietnamese and American presence in the following period. This common identity was emphasized by an emerging inter-ethnic leadership, and expressed in organizations like FULRO. Insufficiently critical of French sources on *Dieu Python*, he presented the sequence of French reports as the history of the movement. He confused the persons of Bishop Jannin and Inspector Jardin, even introducing a third person in Mgr. Jeannin who had the power to command senior French officials; this person is not mentioned in the original sources (Hickey 1982a: 344–8). At a loss 'whether the movement was purely of highlander origin ... or due to outside agitation', Hickey decides that it must have spread in part because of 'discontent with French rule in the highlands – as was suggested in the previously mentioned Kontum Mission report' (Ibid.: 356–7). Characterizing the Python God affair in Ralph Linton's terms as a 'magical nativistic movement', Hickey proceeds to compare it summarily with the Ghost Dance of American Indians in the end of the last century. Both Montagnards and American Indians were being 'encroached upon by dominant whites and envisaged a better time in the future for not just one group but a whole people' (p. 358). Stressing its multi-ethnic and nonviolent character, Hickey arrives at the conclusion that 'it was the first movement in their history that made its appeal to the highlanders in general and expressed their common identity' (p. 358). Thus, for Hickey the Python God Movement became a first step in the development of a common Highlander identity, and as such formed a prelude to the FULRO autonomy movement that he sought to understand in the 1960s and 1970s.

In an article on 'Sambran (The White Python): The Kha (Lao Theung) Revolt of 1936–39' (1988), Geoffrey Gunn traces the influence of the 'sorcerer Sambran' (he does not indicate how he arrives at the translation 'white python') in southern Laos, on the basis of French colonial records. In this area which for many decades had been the scene of the Boloven Revolt, the activities of one or more emulators of Sam Bram led to a revolt in the province of Saravane in 1938, centering on the Kha refusal to pay taxes and perform corvée labor. Connecting this with James Scott's 'moral economy' explanation of peasant resistance 'in the context of proto-nationalist responses to the intervention of outside powers', Gunn argues 'that despite their apparent millenarian character and abject failure, such movements are important reminders of the political nature of the native resistance against colonial powers' (Gunn 1988: 207; see also Mogenet 1980). Comparing his data with the account by Hickey, Gunn finds that the 'revolt' was much more violent in southern Laos than in the Vietnamese Highlands. Ignoring regional variation in the degree of violence and its causation, Gunn extrapolates his analysis to the Vietnamese Highlands as well. He found it 'difficult to agree with Hickey ... that in spite of the arrest of rebel leaders by the French, the former's roles appear not to have taken on political tones' (Gunn 1988: 214). Further reducing religion to ideology in a vulgar Marxist sense, in his book *Rebellion in Laos: Peasant and Politics in a Colonial Backwater* (1990), Gunn claims that 'Messianism provided the irrational device to rally support around a charismatic figure' (Gunn 1990: 139). Casting his net of economic deprivation all over the Highlands, Gunn cannot fail to see a pervasive movement directed against the colonial order, and motivated by heavy taxation and corvée requirements. By stripping away the religious contents, the events of 1937–38 in southern Laos are interpreted as a proto-nationalist peasant rising, a prelude to later Lao Issara and Pathet Lao liberation movements. Gunn's professed aim is to accord Sam Bram his due place in Lao historiography, namely as 'heroic and patriotic' (Ibid.: 129).

In Vietnamese historiography, Sam Bram was depicted as the leader of an anti-colonial movement, and thus incorporated in the genealogy of later resistance movements. In early 1938, accounts of the events in the conservative Vietnamese press endorsed the official French version, while the left-wing press criticized French policy by sketching a justified rising by exploited Montagnards which was quelled in blood by the French.[37] In a South-Vietnamese publication of 1974, this was made into a 'revolt in order to drive the French out of the Highlands' which failed because the leaders were not yet prepared (Cuu-Long-Giang and Toàn Ánh 1974: 123). According to Communist Vietnamese historiography, the 'patriotic movement headed by Sam Bram ... linked economic demands with aspirations for national independence' (Cao Van Luong 1966: 182), with 'Sam Bram summoning Viêt and Highlanders to unite together against French colonialism' (Ban nghiên cuu lich su Đang 1983: 39). For the northern part of the Highlands, a direct line is traced from the 'Red Sou Water' movement led by Sam Bram to the 'Revolt of Ba-To' in upland Quang Ngãi (1945). This revolt, related to the Viêt Minh movement, continuated a rebel tradition which carried over into the Trà Bông rising by the Cor and Hrê minorities (1959–60) – one of the events which led to the formation of the National Liberation Front, alternatively known as Viêt Công.[38] The Vietnamese anthropologists Đang Nghiêm Van and Nguyên Húu Thâu claim that the predicted cataclysm would only affect the French, not the Viêt. According to both, Sam Bram joined the Viêt Minh against the French after his release from prison in 1945 by the Japanese, which would make him into a Vietnamese patriot (Nguyên Húu Thâu 1964; personal communications, 1988).[39]

   While all of the recent interpretations discussed in this section differ considerably, due to differences concerning regional focus, source materials, research context, and political outlook, there is a certain overlap in the common conception of an essentially political movement of various tribal groups jointly revolting against the colonial order. Above, I have argued that contemporary missionaries and colonial officials construed the Python God affair as a political movement on the basis of extremely thin evidence because it suited their interests. This interpretation, which figured prominently in colonial records and in colonial ethnography, carried over into the analyses made by presentday anthropologists of different nationalities, who based themselves at least in part on these very records. However, it is not simply a legacy of colonial bias. Indeed, there is a certain eagerness on the part of the anthropologists discussed above to conceive of the events as not only an anti-colonial movement, but as a proto-nationalist movement. In Vietnamese Communist historiography and in the moral economy approach adopted by Geoffrey Gunn, Sam Bram is elevated to the status of patriotic hero, precursor of later, more successful nationalist movements. For Gerald Hickey and Jacques Dournes he is an early prophet of Montagnard ethno-nationalism, which would develop in due course. In this sense, the interests of present-day anthropologists converge with those of their colonial predecessors in a common concern with the construction of an ethnic identity of the Montagnards. Now, their essential cultural unity is no longer denied – in spite of considerable cultural difference among them; but politically they were undeniably divided until Sam Bram came as an anthropological *deus ex machina* to demonstrate the fundamental political unity of the Montagnards. The questionable evidence was simply too tempting to resist, even if Montagnard ethnic identity was conceived of in different terms by the anthropologists concerned.

However, if we take both the colonial records and the testimony of present-day Highlanders seriously, it is obvious that Sam Bram was not the leader of any Montagnard (proto)nationalist movement. In colonial records, Sam Bram was often depicted as a half-witted Montagnard who enjoyed high status in his village, and who as a sign of his status was emulating Viêt cultural practices in the field of clothing and architecture. More importantly, he was on good terms with the French, since he held a position in the indigenous administrative hierarchy and was slated to become *chef du canton* (district chief). According to the officers who interrogated him, he never made any statements which could be interpreted as political, anti-colonial or anti-French. In the same vein, the millenarian activities provoked by Sam Bram cannot be taken to be the expression of a Montagnard ethnic community, if only because such a community, however 'imagined', simply did not exist at the time. Even the existence of tribal communities was still largely fictitious, as the incomplete result of a process of tribalization which turned ethnographic classification into reality through administrative practice. If in some regions Sam Bram was associated with violent rebellions against French colonial rule, this was not because there was some anti-colonial 'Python God Movement' at work, but because these populations carried forth the traditions of resistance symbolized by N'Trang Lung and Kommadam, and used the protective magic provided by Sam Bram in much the same way as they had used such magic in the past.

Yet, in the accounts discussed so far, Sam Bram is accorded the status of 'national hero', albeit under the varying banners of *proto*nationalism, *ethno*-nationalism, or patriotism. If developments in Indochina after 1945 promoted the construction of a Montagnard ethnic or national community – either in opposition to or in alliance with the new nation-states of Vietnam, Laos and Cambodia – this was necessarily an imagined community, in the sense meant by Benedict Anderson. In this context, the projection of national heroes into the past was common practice, for 'if nation-states are widely conceded to be "new" and "historical", the nations to which they give political expression always loom out of an immemorial past' (Anderson 1983: 19). In the same vein, the millenarian leaders Saya San and Dipanegara have after independence acquired nationalist credentials in Burma and Indonesia respectively, although any notion of nationalism and even nation might have been alien to them. In this context, it is interesting to note that both Michael Adas in his *Prophets of Rebellion* (1979: 180) and Ben Anderson in his *Imagined Communities* (1983: 19) comment on the former Indonesian President Sukarno's transformation of prince Dipanagara into an Indonesian nationalist hero against Dutch colonial rule of Indonesia. But whereas Adas still sees him as a Javanese leader of a 'millenarian protest movement against the Dutch colonial order', caused by political and economic changes in Java (Adas 1979: 43–79), Anderson claims that 'the Prince's own memoirs show that he intended to conquer [not liberate!] *Java*, rather than expel 'the Dutch'. Indeed, he clearly had no concept of 'the Dutch' as a collectivity' (Anderson 1983: 19n).

For Gunn and for the Vietnamese anthropologists, the Central Highlanders constitute 'national minorities' in the Vietnamese and Laotian nation-states, respectively. Although different from the majority peoples, the Highlanders form an integral part of the nation, held together by the concept of *Đoàn kết dân tôc* (ethnic/national solidarity – see Chapter 8). This is symbolized by the Highlanders' contribution to the anti-colonial and anti-imperialist struggles; hence the status of patriotic hero conferred upon Sam Bram in Vietnamese and – to a lesser extent – Laotian national historiography. On the other hand, for Dournes and Hickey, both anthropologists playing a part in the foreign interventions in the Vietnamese Highlands, Sam Bram is an expression of ethno-nationalism, which is directed against the policies of the majority peoples and of their respective states in the Highlands. In their work, the Montagnards are portrayed as alternately victimized by the Vietnamese and resisting 'ethnocide'.[40] Montagnard resistance, capitalizing on their nascent ethno-nationalism, was expressed in a series of autonomy movements, like Bajaraka (the initials of the four main 'tribes': Bahnar, Jarai, Rhadé, Koho), FULRO, the Autonomy Movement linked to the communist National Liberation Front in South Vietnam, the Montagnard elite associated with South Vietnam's Ministry for Development of Ethnic Minorities, and the present, expatriate *Dega* community. Whether ethno-nationalism or a plural nationalism including national minorities, these nationalisms refer to perennial communities that are imagined in history.

Discussion

Since World War II, millenarian movements and cargo cults have been privileged topics in anthropology. After the publication of Peter Worsley's classic *The Trumpet Shall Sound* in 1957, it is almost a truism to hold a politicized view of millenarian movements as 'religions of the lower orders', having their roots in colonial oppression, and creating the 'first stirrings of Nationalism'. In various wordings, chroniclers of cargo cults and millenarian movements in Asia and Oceania, such as Michael Barkun, Kenelm Burridge, Norman Cohn, I.C. Jarvie, Sylvia Thrupp, and Bryan Wilson, stressed their political aspects. The political causation of millenarian movements was superbly put forward in Michael Adas' comparative study *Prophets of Rebellion: Millenarian Protests Movements against the European Colonial Order* (1979). There, Adas developed a theory – close to James Scott's 'moral economy' approach – that the relative deprivation experienced by colonized groups led those to resort to millenarianism when other forms of protest failed. This kind of reasoning has become so pervasive, that in a recent comparative study of *Cargo Cults and Millenarian Movements*, the editor Gary Trompf remarks that most millenarian movements and cargo cults have been pictured as a kind of anti-colonial resistance movements, and criticizes the neo-Marxist Peter Worsley for underestimating the religious implications of millenarian movements (Trompf 1990: 2–3).

As noted in the introduction to this chapter, ethnography and history converge in the study of millenarian movements. Their study has to be undertaken with historical methods because few anthropologists have actually witnessed such movements (cf. Jarvie 1963: 2). Already in 1957, Peter Worsley remarked on the dubious documentary basis for anthropological analysis of millenarian movements:

> Nearly all our material comes from sources hostile to the movements. Frequently, internal evidence reveals contradictions, but often one can only infer from comparative knowledge that certain interpretations are distortions, either through lack of understanding, or deliberate. Such distortions, of course, provide valuable insights into the attitudes of those who make the reports.
>
> (Worsley 1968[2]: 190)

Similar opinions are echoed by subsequent analysts, like Bryan Wilson (1973: 493–4) or I.C. Jarvie, who states that colonial administrators favored a kind of 'conspiracy theory', in that the prophet is either a demagogue who seeks wealth and power, or a tool for others, e.g. Communists (Jarvie 1964: 85). If the original material which forms the basis for later historical/anthropological analysis is generally biased as is argued by Worsley and Jarvie (amongst many others), then such analysis is hazardous indeed, and necessitates a clear assessment of the historical context in which the relevant colonial reports were produced.

All too often, neocolonial and post-colonial anthropologists who rely on colonial sources when dealing with millenarian activities, do not engage in a critical historical analysis of these sources. It is not simply a matter of biased reports, which depict the millenarian movements in a negative fashion, but of textual constructions of series of events as rebellions or movements caused by and directed against colonial rule. We may take it that colonial officials of all sorts were mainly preoccupied with the maintenance of the colonial order, implying an extraordinary sensitivity to anything resembling political opposition – indeed, their careers depended on their success in achieving colonial 'peace'. Roughly, colonial administrators had two strategies for dealing with 'insubordination' or 'unrest' in the form of millenarian movements. One common reaction was portraying millenarian behavior as criminal behavior (branded 'banditry' or 'piracy'), especially when such behavior entailed acts of violence or insubordination. A contrasting, but equally common reaction was to depict all sorts of events that in their eyes threatened colonial peace ('sorcery', new religious movements) as rebellions, revolts or anti-colonial movements. Often, both strategies were employed simultaneously or consecutively with respect to one and the same movement.

In their eagerness to sympathize with subaltern groups and their struggle against colonial rule and oppression, neocolonial and post-colonial anthropologists have recognized the first strategy as an attempt to downplay a political interpretation as resistance against colonial rule. On the other hand, they tended to adopt politicized, colonial constructions of such movements and cults as rebellions against the European colonial order from the colonial records, thus inflating their political content. This is reflected in the anthropological concepts used to denote millenarian activities. According to accepted social science knowledge embodied in the *International Encyclopedia of the Social Sciences* (1968), millenarian, nativist, and revivalist movements are types of social movements which are inherently political. A quick glance at the articles on 'Millenarism', 'Nativism and Revivalism' and 'Social Movements' in the *Encyclopedia* conveys the impression that such movements are more or less tightly organized, involve some degree of group consciousness, and generate concerted action aimed at a radical change. Invariably, such movements are attributed to the frustration and deprivation caused by modernization, which makes their 'religious revolutionism' comparable to 'secular revolutionism'.

Referring to the study of African religious movements, Johannes Fabian notes the 'positive bias' of anthropologists who 'view religious movements *a priori* as constructive, integrative, and functional' and who tend to 'overlook that religious movements, like other kinds of communal human action, may have little concern for utilitarian respectability' (Fabian 1981: 116–7). Indeed, he suggests that 'anthropologists found in religious movements surrogate 'tribes', that is, social entities with clear boundaries and marked internal structures' (Ibid.: 111). In sociological practice the concept of (millenarian) movement has acquired the connotation of a bounded group organized for more or less concerted, political action. Yet, a narrow focus on politicized interpretations of millenarian movements as caused by colonial penetration preempts the possibility of other motives, reducing millenarian activities to inadequate, irrational responses to Western domination, and serves to perpetuate colonial constructions of millenarianism. The comparative method, propagated by Worsley and others, is no guarantee for overcoming colonial bias; on the contrary, facile comparisons may tempt analysts to refrain from serious contextual analysis of the original sources, with the result that colonial constructions of millenarian movements carry over into post-colonial analyses.

Conclusion

Returning to the Python God movement, we see that Johannes Fabian's generalization holds true for this case. Although *Dieu Python* was initially interpreted in the light of a process of tribalization, it was conceived of as a positive, integrative and functional movement by contemporary analysts, who had their reasons for doing so. Disconcerted by what they perceived as a lack of tribal homogeneity and of tribal antagonism, missionaries and colonial officials detected a secret political agency behind the religious activities. Instead of a surrogate tribe, the construction of a Python God movement was a way to leave the tribal edifice intact in colonial times. In a changing political context which highlighted the strategic value of the Central Highlands for control of Indochina, the 'multi-ethnic' character of the 'movement' led the colonial authorities to reconsider their ethnic classification of the Highland tribes. The result was the construction and constant emphasizing of the essential ethnic unity of the Highland groups from World War II onward, epitomized in a *hausse* of ethnographies after 1945. This will be the subject matter of the next chapter. Political and military developments in the region since 1945 have created a situation in which Montagnards developed a common ethnic identity as *Dega*, who not only feel fundamentally different from the lowlanders in Indochina, but claim political and cultural control over their territory through various autonomy movements. Thus, for neocolonial anthropologists, the 'Python God Movement' was a historical contribution to the construction of a Montagnard ethnic identity out of a plurality of tribes.

If we now return to the statement by Peter Worsley on the dubious documentary basis for anthropological analysis of millenarian movements, it may be clear by now that comparative knowledge was not the cure Worsley takes it to be, at least with respect to *Dieu Python*. For the colonial ethnographers in the Highlands, the rebellions by N'Trang Lung and Kommadam, though historically connected, proved fallacious models for the interpretation of the Python God cult as it seduced observers to construe a political movement out of scattered and varying millenarian activities. For neocolonial historians and anthropologists, the apparent similarity of the 'Sam Bram movement' with millenarian movements, magical nativistic movements, prophetic movements and cargo cults as described in anthropological classics only served to corroborate a politicized interpretation, implied in a positivist conception of 'movement'. The historical sequence millenarianism-*proto*nationalism-(ethno)nationalism tempted them into construing a politicized Python God movement out of the *Dieu Python* cult, and to portray the 'prophet' Sam Bram as a national hero of sorts.

Despite the fact that similar millenarian activities took place well before the colonial era, both colonial and neocolonial ethnographies interpret the actions and beliefs of Sam Bram and his followers solely as a response to Western colonial domination, rather than a renewed manifestation of millenarianism among populations whose religious beliefs and practices have some similarity and comparability. This common tendency on the part of Western observers and nationalist historiographers alike – to conceive of any Montagnard action as a response to foreign encroachment – reduces Montagnards to the (militarily useful) puppets which they were taken to be during the consecutive Indochina wars. Thus, the Central Highlanders are denied agency, along with space for autonomous action. Seen from this perspective, the claim of my Jarai interlocutors – namely, that the cult was theirs only, and had nothing whatsoever to do with the French colonial regime – may be seen as an attempt to open up space for *their* action in history. By resisting the ethnographic classifications and interpretations forced upon them by the very outside forces which intervened in their history, they reclaim the agency which they were thought to have lost with the coming of the colonial era.[41]

Although this chapter has so far been deliberately non-comparative, it is hard to refrain from comments on the comparative efforts of others concerning millenarianism. Much of the debate in this field refers implicitly or explicitly to nationalism. Western preoccupations concerning nationalism and national communities are mirrored in the study of millenarianism. Millenarian movements have all too often been construed as essentially political, anti-colonial movements – indeed as embryonic nationalist movements. This is most evident from the attempt to see (proto/ethno)nationalist heroes in millenarian 'prophets'. One other frequent theme is the multi-ethnic character of millenarian movements, which reflects Western concern with ethnic boundaries through the analogy of national boundaries rather than the existence of such boundaries in 'reality'. A common concern of colonial states was the classification of tribal or ethnic groups who were fixed to a bounded territory, graphically conveyed in the ethnographic map (see Noyes 1994). Although in recent times central anthropological concepts like 'tribe' and 'ethnic group' have been problematized – for tribalization was not exclusive for Vietnam – students of millenarianism often take ethnic boundaries for granted. It is time to look anew at the material constituting the basis for studies of cargo cults and millenarian movements. If Sam Bram is not an historical exception, we may speculate that many similar events have been studied with preconceived ideas.

5 War and ethnography

Territorialization, ethnicization and cultural relativism[1]

Introduction

Strategic considerations were never absent from French designs with respect to the Central Highlands and other mountain areas in French Indochina. In preceding chapters we have described Colonel Galliéni's method of military pacification, combining the political measures of divide-and-rule with the military 'oil-spot' tactics (*tache d'huile*), which became an influential model for later counterinsurgency tactics. At an early stage of penetration, the captains Cupet and De Malglaive of the *Mission Pavie* stressed the strategic value of the *Hinterland Moï* in the context of territorial conflicts with Siam and of the *Cân Vuong* movement in Vietnam. During the conflict over Sabatier, Lieutenant-Colonel Ardant du Picq stressed the military value of the Montagnards in a study of the military potential of the Central Highlands in the context of French strategy in Indochina. Such military considerations became more important in the 1930s, especially after *Dieu Python*. When the mountain areas of Vietnam were subject to competing claims by French colonialists, Americans, Japanese, and various Vietnamese nationalist groups, these were seen as strategically crucial areas for the control of Indochina. According to the Communist General Vo Nguyên Giáp the Central Highlands were of crucial strategic importance for the control of Indochina. Control of the ethnic populations was seen as the key element in any political and military struggle for Indochina. In the context of guerrilla warfare, which started with World War II and lasted for the successive Indochina Wars, the support of local populations was seen as an important asset, both for the employment of guerrilla tactics and for most counterinsurgency schemes. The minorities policy of the Vietnamese Communist Party has been described as a coherent effort to appease ethnic minorities in order to attain their support. According to both Vietnamese and Western studies, the results showed in the battle of Ðiên Biên Phu, in the mountain regions of northern Vietnam. Analysts like Chesneaux, Fall and McAlister attributed the ultimate French defeat at Ðiên Biên Phu in 1954 to the qualitative difference of the Viêt Minh's ethnic policy compared to French ethnic policy, although recent testimonies also point at massive Chinese assistance as a major cause for the Viêt Minh victory.[2]

In contrast, French minorities policy in the mountain regions has been described as a colonial divide-and-rule policy characterized as *ad hoc* by most observers. The most notable example is the 'sudden' detachment of *the Pays Montagnard du Sud-Indochinois* (PMSI) from Vietnam by *Haut-Commissaire* Thierry D'Argenlieu in 1946, which was seen as an attempt to thwart an eventual agreement between France and the Viêt Minh on Vietnamese independence. This move was put in one line with the separation of the 'Cochinchinese republic' from Vietnam, and with the later (1948) establishment of the 'Tai Federation' in the north of Vietnam, which was an 'autonomous region' mainly inhabited by Tai-speaking groups, under a French-controlled feudal regime. Although in 1949 the French were forced to allow for the formal reintegration of the PMSI as the Emperor's Crown Domain in a nominally independent Vietnamese state under Bao Ðai, it continued to enjoy direct French rule under a *Statut particulier*, which was completely abolished after formal independence in 1955 by President Ngô Ðình Diêm. But whereas most historians would note the 'artificial' character of the two latter units, an exception was made for the PMSI because of the cultural difference and alleged antagonism of the Montagnards *vis-à-vis* the lowland Vietnamese, a theme which was loudly proclaimed by the French during the First Indochina War. As such, the Montagnards were conceptualized as a 'natural' obstacle for Vietnamese nationalism. This view was seemingly corroborated by the development of a Montagnard autonomy movement with definite separatist leanings during the Second and Third Indochina Wars.[3]

Despite the importance attached to minorities in official Communist doctrine, hardly any effort has been made to account for the alleged lack of success of Communist ethnic policies in the Central Highlands. Most analysts have compared Communist policies there unfavorably to the mountain areas in northern Vietnam where the Viêt Minh has been able to overcome ethnic antagonism.[4] In fact, the situation in the Central Highlands has been more ambiguous than has been contended by most Western observers – the most notable exceptions being Bernard Fall and Wilfred Burchett. First, Viêt Minh policy was not without results in the Central Highlands, as was shown in the progressive deterioration (*pourrissement*) of the French position. By 1954, French movement in the Central Highlands was restricted to two cities and a few military camps. The most tangible demonstration of French defeat was the annihilation of the elite corps *Groupe Mobile 100* on Route 19 near An Khê, in the Spring of 1954 (Fall 1963b: 195–6). Second, the establishment of the PMSI was not a sudden move capitalizing on some 'eternal' antagonism between the Montagnard and Viêt populations, but a carefully planned action which had historical antecedents in French ethnic policy in the Central Highlands before 1945. In fact, it was just one step – albeit an important one – in a longer process of *territorialization* of colonial state power. As defined by Robert Sack, territoriality is the 'attempt by an individual or group to affect, influence, or control people, phenomena, and relationships by delimiting and asserting control over a geographic area ... [It] is not an instinct or drive, but a rather complex strategy, ... [and] the device through which people construct and maintain spatial organizations' (1986: 19–20, quoted in Thongchai's *Siam Mapped*: 16). In their analysis of 'Territorialization and state power in Thailand', Peter Vandergeest and Nancy Peluso claim that '[t]erritorialization is about excluding or including people within particular geographic boundaries, and about controlling what people do ... within those boundaries' (1995: 388). Though Vandergeest and Peluso apply this concept to control over natural resources, this concept is equally useful to interpret French strategic moves with respect to the Central Highlands in the 1930s and 1940s.

As this process of strategic territorialization was aimed at the management of distinct populations by their physical separation, it was accompanied by a process of ethnographic classification which distinguished and/or merged cultural identities from a governmental perspective. In reference to the French construction of a separate 'ethnic territory', I shall argue that this policy has effectively resulted in the construction of a distinct Montagnard ethnic identity as opposed to Vietnamese lowlander identity. Whereas in the 1930s the Montagnards were conceived of as a number of mutually exclusive and antagonistic tribes, French ethnographers and administrators started to stress the essential ethnic unity of the Montagnards through World War II and the First Indochina War. Through this process of *ethnicization*, such ethnographic classifications attained a political reality, which was most tangible in the construction of tribes and their linking to territories. The culmination of this process was the PMSI, which was defined as an 'autonomous' Montagnard territory (albeit under direct French rule). The ethnographic discourse which supported an increasingly bureaucratic and hegemonic ethnic classification was fed by an ethnographic practice which – in the late 1930s and through the war years – became institutionalized and professionalized. The substantive changes in the discourse, notably the renewed cultural relativist tendency, can be seen in the light of French territorializing designs, which assigns distinct territories to different 'ethnic groups' in the context of French Indochina.

The *fait accompli* of D'Argenlieu made it indispensable for any subsequent power seeking the support of the Montagnards for strategic reasons to promise some degree of cultural and political autonomy in a clearly defined territory within the Vietnamese State. Although the history of the Montagnards and their development toward a common ethnic identity have been dealt with extensively and sympathetically by Gerald Hickey, I shall put slightly different accents. Hickey noted the 'mixed effects' of French military policy in the Highlands, that 'while it increased the awareness of a common highlander identity, many died or were wounded' (Hickey 1982a: 413). In his work, Hickey stresses the first effect, i.e. the development toward ethnonationalism as the natural historical outcome of a fundamental cultural unity. Alternatively, I would contend that it was a construction on the part of outside powers which was only viable to the extent that it was supported by these powers, and consequently stress the second effect noted by Hickey, namely death and destruction. As an illustration of the effects of French ethnographic discourse and ethnic policies ostensibly aimed at

Figure 5.1 Wooden figure of French officer carved on top of a 10 meter high pole serving for a funerary ritual.

Source: Musée de l'Homme, BF 67.1701.702. Photo: Jacques Dournes.

'protection' of minorities, I devote the last section of this chapter to the gender transformation among Montagnards brought about during the war years.

The politics of tribalization

In the context of a debate among French officials and colonists on the desirability of colonization of the Highlands during the Sabatier era, an assessment of the strategic value of the Highlands was made by Lt.-Col. Ardant du Picq in a secret report *Etude du Pays Moy au point de vue militaire* (1923 – published in the *Revue des Troupes Coloniales* in 1925/26), commissioned by the military commander of French Indochina. The object of the study was not simply to 'speak of geography, ethnography and history – elements of the military problem'; rather, its intention was to provide the military with data to influence 'the Administration and the indigenous policy which dominate the military question and give it, in the moy country, a particular aspect'.[5] Referring to the work by the *Mission Pavie*, Ardant du Picq stressed the strategic value of the Highlands in case of a foreign attack or a revolt in the Vietnamese lowlands. As mentioned in Chapter 3, Ardant du Picq chose to side with Sabatier on the conflict over the colonization of the Central Highlands, because he anticipated the possibility of a guerrilla war in which the Montagnards might act as partisans, if the colonial administration could gain their confidence. Therefore, Ardant du Picq emphasized the martial qualities of the Montagnards, which were evident in the resistance of some groups to French penetration, but which could also be a military asset for the French if Sabatier's model were followed.[6]

Despite strong military backing, the economic interests won the day in April 1926, and Sabatier's administrative model, which had been prescribed by *Résident-supérieur* Pasquier of Annam in a circular of 30 July 1923, was temporarily dropped. The ensuing colonization process, though slowed down by the world economic crisis of the 1930s, carried the politically undesirable aspects of appropriation of Montagnard lands and the migration of lowland Vietnamese coolies and settlers into the Highlands. It exacerbated relations between the French and the Montagnards, eventually erupting in armed attacks by Montagnards on rubber plantations and trucks in 1929, thus threatening the *pax gallica*. As has been described in Chapter 4, this prompted the colonial administration to mount a number of military campaigns against hitherto 'unpacified tribes' (*tribus insoumises*) during the first half of the 1930s, in an effort to root out all pockets of resistance within the borders of French Indochina. In a report of 1935 on the progress of French 'penetration' and on the causes of the 'revolt of the Mnong', the Governor of Cochinchina, Pagès, blamed the excessive use of Montagnard labor on rubber plantations with the habit of duping Montagnards into labor contracts and of forcing them to perform corvee labor in the plantations (Pagès 1935: 216). However, the military actions to subdue the revolts of the Boloven and the Mnong in the far northern and southern parts of the Central Highlands demonstrated the military value of the *Tirailleurs montagnards* composed of Rhadé (now known as Edê) and Jarai warriors. In time, the issue of Montagnard autonomy would invariably be linked to the issue of recruitment of Montagnard soldiers. By 1935, the military pacification of the Highlands seemed to be more or less completed, but further colonization was delayed as the establishment of new plantations was effectively precluded by the world economic crisis.

In a changing historical climate, characterized by the rise of Vietnamese nationalism, the issue of Montagnard autonomy and the ethnic policy pattern set by Sabatier would come in view for political reasons. Moreover, with the rise of nationalism, Fascism and Communism in other parts of Asia, the French colonial regime in Indochina felt increasingly threatened from abroad, and the French colonial government took measures to defend the colony. The growing concern with security and strategic affairs naturally channeled official attention to the Central Highlands, which were of strategic importance in any scheme for the defense of the colony. Against this background, in 1935 the possible merits of an administrative reorganization of the Central Highlands began to be debated in French administrative and military circles. In this context the possibility of autonomy for the Central Highlands was advocated by the military. In *La Lance Militaire* of 12 May 1935, General Pruneau pleaded for the 'creation of an autonomous Moï territory directly under the Governor-General', to be administrated by military officers. The Highlands would then become an administrative unity under military rule, instead of the current division in Cambodian, Cochinchinese and Annamese provinces, which did not coincide with the tribal boundaries. The main argument was the ineffectiveness of military coordination from the various Indochinese 'countries' involved in the suppression of the 'Mnong revolt' in the Central Highlands. A report of 22 May 1935 by the *Direction des Services Militaires* to the Governor-General of Indochina contained a similar proposal. In June of that year, the Governor of Cochinchina and the *Résident-supérieur* of Annam, however, pleaded in favor of a continuation of the civil administration from the different 'countries' involved, because of the expertise of the administrators. Interestingly, one of the arguments against the establishment of one administrative unit in the Central Highlands was the wide geographic and ethnic variation. In advice to the Minister of Colonies in Paris, Governor-General René Robin followed the line of his civil subordinates, adding that administrative collaboration already existed.[7]

This debate took place, as Robin had already indicated, in a climate of administrative reorganization and increasing collaboration between the colony of Cochinchina and the protectorates of Annam, Cambodia, and – to a lesser extent – Laos. Based on ethnographic studies of 'the main tribes' and on studies of the indigenous administration, Maurice Graffeuil, *Résident-supérieur* of Annam, decided in 1935 to reorient indigenous administration toward a 'Moï hierarchy' directly under the Resident, without a parallel 'Annamese mandarinate'.[8] In the same period, there was a nascent cooperation between the highland provinces belonging to different constituent 'countries' of French Indochina, punctuated by meetings of provincial administrators. The first conference took place in July 1935 in Dalat. Major themes were the codification of Montagnard customary law for reasons of policing and administration, and the transcription of Montagnard languages for educational policies, both to be undertaken under the auspices of the *Ecole Française d'Extrême-Orient*. These issues were also taken up in subsequent conferences on policy in the Highlands in January 1936 and May 1937.[9] Thus, the model set by Sabatier and prescribed by *Résident-supérieur* Pasquier of Annam in 1923, was belatedly adopted in the late 1930s, effectively resulting in the construction of tribes. Through the identification of ethnolinguistic groups and their classification as 'tribes', ethnic identities and ethnic boundaries were constantly (re)constructed and rigidified in a process baptized *tribalization* by Georges Condominas (1966: 168), and symbolized by the semi-official ethnographic map of the *Société des Études Indochinoises* of 1937.[10] Even contemporary ethnographers observed that the convergence of ethnography and administration, most notable in the conflation of linguistics and education and of costumary law and policing, resulted in a practical reduction of the number of tribes for administrative purposes through the identification of four 'major tribes' dominating the four Highland provinces of Vietnam (Guilleminet 1952a: 8, 91). This process is perhaps most visible in Paul Guilleminet's *Coutumier de la tribu Bahnar, des Sedang at des Jarai de la province de Kontum*, published in 1952 by the EFEO but based on jurisprudence of the French-installed customary law court of Kontum before 1945, when the author was Resident of Kontum province. This *tribunal coutumier* grouped together three major 'tribes' in the Highlands with major cultural and kinship differences and even belonging to different language families because they happened to find themselves living within the same administrative unit.

As the tribal classification would be pursued through three decades of colonial warfare, when the French and later the Americans sought the support of the Montagnards against the nationalist movements of the Vietnamese, this tribalization was increasingly reflected in Montagnard consciousness and self-organization. During the 1930s, however, the tribal classification realized in ethnographic and administrative practice was reflected in a French classificatory grid distinguishing tribal groups rather than in 'real' ethnic boundaries. In the next section we shall discuss how this tribalizing classificatory grid yields to a discourse which construes the Highland peoples as a separate ethnic group, distinct from the other 'nations' of French Indochina.

The administrative construction of a common ethnic identity

The tribalizing classificatory grid seemed to preclude the possibility of a 'pan-tribal' movement emerging in the Highlands. Yet, this is what happened in 1937/38 with the *Dieu Python* movement (see Chapter 4). The immediate political consequence of the movement was an acceleration of the implementation of a special ethnic policy concerning the Montagnards. This coincided with a more lenient policy of the colonial administration during the 'Popular Front' era in France (1936–37), resulting in a growing humanitarian concern with the 'social question', both in France and in the French colonies. The newly elected Popular

Figure 5.2 Scene in the life of the ethnologist Georges Condominas, carved in bamboo by a Mnong Gar artist.

Source: Musée de l'Homme, D.94.220.493. Photo: M. Delaplanche.

Front government responded to left-wing criticisms of French colonial rule by installing the *Commission d'Enquête dans les Territoires d'Outre-Mer* (shortly *Commission Guernut*) in 1937. This speeded up the process of assessing the consequences of the Python God Movement, and of formulating a 'racial policy' with respect to the Montagnard population. In his report for the Commission, M. d'Hugues pleaded against the old 'divide and rule' formula, stating that 'it appears to be redundant to maintain among the Moï populations the tribal rivalries which have kept them in a deplorable state of stagnation ... in order to be able to repress more quickly those among them who might one day rise against our authority'.[11] Instead, a *politique d'apprivoisement* (policy of domestication) was attempted, which combined seduction – medical services (campaigns against smallpox and malaria) and educational facilities in the vernacular languages – with coercion, as embodied in the French monopolization of the scarce product salt – the so-called 'salt policy'. One of the professed aims of this policy was to increase the number of Montagnard recruits for the *Bataillon des tirailleurs montagnards du Sud-Annam* (BTMSA) from 1938 onward.[12] Thus, with respect to Montagnard policies, the humanitarian concerns professed during the Popular Front era converged with the strategic preoccupations manifest after it.

In the late 1930s, the French colonial regime in Indochina felt increasingly threatened from abroad – first of all by Japan, which sought to expand its empire in East Asia, starting with China. In the west, the military government of Siam had expansionist ambitions, aspiring to incorporate all Tai-speaking nations, like Laos, and to reconquer territories which it had been forced to cede to France around the turn of the century. Since the densely populated areas (the deltas, the coastal strip and the Mekong Valley) were narrow and vulnerable in case of attack or uprising, the colonial government and army turned their attention to the strategic Central Highlands, from which most of Indochina could be controlled. In June 1938 a 'Commission charged with the Establishment of a General Action Program in the Moï country' was installed in Annam, which promoted 'the vigilant protection of the natural qualities of the Moï races' for both human and strategic reasons. This resulted in a 'Plan of penetration and organization of the Moï Regions', based on the principles of the 'evolution of the Moï in his natural environment and direct administration'. In July 1938, Governor-General Jules Brévié sent his study of the *Pays Moï* to the Minister of Colonies, arguing that the Moï – despite mutual differences – constitute one racial group, distinct from the other Indochinese races. Referring to the danger of revolt, as embodied by the recent millenarian movement, he pleaded for a direct French administration in all the area and for a central coordinating body. In October 1939, Georges Mandel, Minister of Colonies, and the French President inaugurated the *Inspection Générale des Pays Moïs*, which was largely grounded in strategic arguments (recruitment of Montagnards, construction of strategic roads), as the increasing political tension highlighted the political and military value of the area. To his subordinates, the new Governor-General Catroux defended this Inspection with reference to the *Inspection du Travail* (Labor Inspection) established during the Popular Front era in France, by stating that 'from the political and social points of view, *faire du 'Moï'* is not less interesting than *faire de 'l'ouvrier'*; it is only much more delicate'.[13]

In his first report to Governor-General Catroux (1940), the newly appointed *Haut-commissaire des pays moïs* Lieutenant Omer Sarraut emphasized the ethnic and geographic unity of the *Pays Moïs*, which should include 'the totality of autochthonous [indigenous – OS] populations' both in upland Annam and Cochinchina and in eastern Cambodia and southern Laos (p. 8). In his view, the cultural difference and the strict geographic separation of the territories inhabited by Montagnard and lowland populations would justify the territorial detachment of the Pays Moï from the constituent states of French Indochina. Sarraut found in the Moï a number of virtues '[which] differentiate him [sic!] enough from the other peoples of the peninsula, and which situate him near our mentality; the management [of the virtues] should make him into a first rate auxiliary' (p. 3). In this context, their much ridiculed credulity would be a major advantage, as it 'transforms, upon contact with us, very often in trust, a bit childlike, but total' (p. 5).[14] Sanctioned by these political developments, the theme of an 'essential cultural unity' of the Montagnards began to crop up in ethnographic writing. This is perhaps most obvious in the oeuvre of Paul Guilleminet, Resident of Kontum province and ethnographic collaborator of the *Ecole Française d'Extrême-Orient*, who in an article on the 'economy of the Moï tribes' stated that despite their ethnic diversity, the *Moï* not only share a fundamental economic unity but also a cultural unity. But French administrative practice had led to the formation of one group – 'ethnographically speaking' – which made it imperative for the French to suppress ethnic rivalries (Guilleminet 1943a: 82–6, 124). Such discursive developments took place in the dual context of a *proliferation* of ethnographic writing and of an *institutionalization* of ethnographic practice, which is the topic of the next section.

The institutionalization of ethnographic practice

As increasing political tension highlighted the political and military value of the area, the colonial administration became concerned with the effects of unfettered colonization on the attitude of the indigenous population of the Central Highlands, and began once again to encourage ethnographic work. Usually, ethnographers stressed the necessity of a special ethnic policy *vis-à-vis* the Montagnards, while the protagonists of an ethnic policy emphasized the relevance of ethnographic knowledge. Within this context both the policy and the ethnography by Sabatier were rediscovered, and his relativist image of the Montagnards eventually came to dominate ethnographic discourse with respect to Montagnards.

Practiced mostly by colonial officials, the ethnographic research concentrated on the possibilities of political management of the ethnic groups, viewed from the perspective of direct rule. There was an attempt to combine a policy of economic development with a conservative indigenous policy that played on ethnic sentiments in order to exclude Vietnamese influence. This ethnographic practice was increasingly institutionalized, notably within the framework of the *Ecole*

Française d'Extrême-Orient, France's most prestigious research institute in Indochina. The EFEO became more active in the discipline of ethnography after the founding in 1937 of an ethnographic branch headed by the respected French ethnologist Paul Lévy. For an orientalist institute with mainly historical, archaeological and philological interests, this was a major step toward the study of contemporary social issues, as the French historian Georges Boudarel observed (1976: 147). Besides the EFEO, the *Société des Etudes Indochinoises* (SEI) in Saigon was turning again to ethnography after an earlier interest around 1880, and the *Institute Indochinois de l'Etude de l'Homme* (IIEH), a joint venture of the EFEO and the medical faculty of the University of Indochina in Hanoi, was founded to cover research in the fields of ethnography and physical anthropology. All these institutions, knit closely together through personal networks, had their own scientific journals (*bulletin*) or publication series (*cahier*), and exercised editorial control over ethnographic publications. Moreover, the EFEO exercised supervision over the ethnographic practice, through its attempts at ethnographic standardization in the fields of ethnolinguistic classification, linguistic notation, and customary law (*coutumier*).

As early as 1923, the colonial administration had instructed the Residents to see to it that *coutumiers* were compiled for every ethnic group in the Central Highlands, in collaboration with the EFEO, which undertook to guide research by their members and correspondents, attempting to avoid the usual evolutionist terminology. In this atmosphere the composition of a *coutumier* was to be the test of an aspiring ethnographer's ability. Next to the *coutumiers*, ethnolinguistic research was being promoted, intended to result in transcriptions of the various Montagnard languages and, eventually, in school primers. In 1935, the EFEO established a commission to supervise and coordinate the linguistic notations. Furthermore, physical anthropology was a field of interests for physicians and military officers, often working for the IIEH. This discipline developed outspoken racist overtones during World War II, when the Decoux administration in French Indochina allied itself to the Fascist Pétain regime in France and to Japan. During World War II, the Decoux Administration – feverishly constructing strategic roads in the Highlands and promoting conferences on Highlands policy – organized again a *Palabre du serment*, attended by Decoux himself, and claimed a special relationship with the Montagnards. A positive image of the Montagnards as 'loyal warriors' was cultivated and popularized in numerous publications, notably in articles in the semi-official, Pétainist weekly *Indochine*, to which many members of the EFEO contributed.

A renewed appreciation of Montagnard culture and the revived ethnographic interest necessitated a new attempt at ethnographic classification and ethnographic mapping. In 1935 and 1936 the province chiefs of Indochina were required to turn in exact ethno-linguistic maps of their provinces for the benefit of the *Ecole Française d'Extrême-Orient* (Cf. *BEFEO* XXXVI–2, 1936: 598). On the basis of these maps, the Georges Taboulet charted a *Carte Ethnographique*, which found a place in a publication of the *Société des Études Indochinoises, Groupes Ethniques de l'Indochine Française* (1937). The semi-official character of that publication is brought out by the official sanction of the *Gouvernement général*, the *Gouvernement de la Cochinchine*, the Protectorate of Annam, and the *Direction Générale de l'Instruction Publique en Indochine*. Louis Malleret, conservator of the Museum of Saigon and member of the EFEO, wrote the texts of the album, which contained furthermore, 100 photographs. In 1949 the exercise would be repeated, this time under the auspices of the EFEO. The *Carte ethnolinguistique*, drawn by the *Service Géographique de l'Indochine*, was very detailed indeed, and was for some time considered to be *the* ethnographic map of Indochina; the considerable population movements of the years to come were obviously not anticipated.

The ethnic classification arrived at by Malleret and Taboulet (1937), however, was far less detailed than the classification by Henri Maitre (1912) or the later *Carte ethnolinguistique* of the EFEO (1949). On the one hand, this was due to the popular character of the book, which discouraged a too rigid, 'scientific' classification. On the other hand, this reflected a trend toward the identification of larger units, partly on the basis of linguistic similarities, but also motivated by administrative exigencies, as the provincial administrations were based on the largest or dominant groups within the province, which in turn would subsume the smaller 'ethnic groups' previously identified. This process was most evident in Haut-Donnai, where groups like the Sre, Çop, Cil, Lat, were increasingly identified as Koho (with the former name sometimes as affix, e.g. Koho Sre). This resulted in a situation, where the provinces were more or less identified with the main constituting group: Kontum – Bahnar; Pleiku – Jarai; Darlac – Rhadé; Haut-Donnaï – Koho. In a situation where ethnic and linguistic differences tended to be gradual and fluid, such administrative divisions tended to become ethnic boundaries, resulting in an administrative process of tribalization. The *coutumiers*, compiled for the major groups only, would be applied to the smaller groups, too, as was the case with Sabatier's *coutumier* Rhadé, which was made to apply to Darlac's Mnong population. Resident Guilleminet of Kontum province went as far as to declare his *coutumier* Bahnar valid for the Sedang and Jarai groups as well, even though Bahnar and Sedang descent is patrilineal, and Jarai descent matrilineal (Guilleminet 1952a).

The discursive changes in ethnographic writing provided the administration both with tools for cultural management and with an appropriate ideological legitimation for their direct rule policy. The ethnographic practice not only facilitated French rule in the Highlands, but also put the Montagnards and their relations with the French and the Vietnamese in a different light. Despite major cultural differences, Montagnards were increasingly seen as one group, to be opposed to the ethnic Vietnamese. Their languages, belonging to the Malayo-Polynesian (Austronesian) and Mon-Khmer (Austroasiatic) language groups, were seen as fundamentally opposed to the Vietnamese tonal language. Their *coutumiers*, although varying considerably, made them comparable to each other to the exclusion of the Vietnamese (who, of course, have their own village-based customary law). Their cultural identity was symbolized by certain cultural emblems like the *coutumiers* and the oath swearing ceremonies – actually French inventions – and rituals like the ritual buffalo sacrifice – redefined as a folkloric

Figure 5.3 Georges Condominas participating in the ritual exchange of food before a ritual buffalo sacrifice in Sar Luk (1949).

Source: Georges Condominas. Photo by a Mnong Gar informant.

spectacle to be gazed at by outsiders. Put in terms as used by Miles and Eipper (1985), Montagnard cultural identity was reified and bureaucratically prescribed by the colonial state, and the Montagnards were made to conform to this image of their culture insofar as it suited the colonial administration. The French claimed that Montagnard culture was valuable in itself, and had no need for assimilation to Vietnamese culture. However, it was the French who defined what constituted Montagnard culture, which aspects of it were to be preserved, and which aspects were to be changed. Cultural expressions which did not suit the colonial administration were not recognized as valuable or even authentic. For example, the Montagnards had to give up shifting cultivation, allegedly because it would destroy the forest, but in reality because it did not suit French economic interests. And the *Dieu-Python* movement, which could hardly be a more authentic cultural expression, was conveniently reinterpreted as organized by Vietnamese Communists, and participants in this millenarian movement were sentenced by customary law courts (see Chapter 4).

Under French auspices the Montagnard culture would be protected, meaning respected and even 'perfected' by means of an appropriate development policy, a *politique d'égards*, termed *faire du moï*.[15] In the ethnographic discourse underpinning this ethnic policy an image of the Montagnards was constructed which sought to legitimize direct French rule in the Central Highlands, officially an integral part of the protectorate of Annam. The ethnographic discourse provided the arguments to exclude the ethnic Vietnamese from the region, to counter Vietnamese nationalist claims to the Highlands, and even to separate the Highlands from Annam. The sheer fact of ethnography by the French seemed enough evidence of their concern for the local populations, as opposed to the ethnic Vietnamese who were portrayed as only concerned with cheating and landgrabbing. The usual metaphor was of a benevolent father (France) who had to be stern to the elder son (Vietnam) because he intimidates the little children (Montagnards). The Montagnards were often likened to children, labeled credulous, naïve, often violent, but very loyal if you knew how to handle them; they needed the firm but just guidance into the twentieth century from France.

This image became very persistent. It had been loudly proclaimed during World War II when the colonial administration considered the oeuvre by Sabatier as being a model to follow. Publications by Antomarchi (1941), Boudet (1942), and Ner (1943) in *Indochine* glorified Sabatier's oeuvre, after the translation (by Antomarchi) and publication (by the EFEO) in 1940 of his *coutumier rhadé* as *Recueil des coutumes rhadées du Darlac*. They and others boasted about the good relationship which the French had with the Montagnards, and their accomplishments in the development of the region. In this context, Guilleminet (1943f: 26–7) stated that nobody would then repeat the words by Lavallée, that the Montagnards would 'remain a useless force for the civilizing action' (Lavallée 1901: 291), a stark example of an earlier evolutionist representation of Montagnard culture. Governor-General Decoux himself installed commissions for policy planning and an inspection for the Central Highlands, and eventually was present himself at the *palabre du serment*. Through World War II the myth of a special relationship between the Montagnards and their French protectors was loudly proclaimed. Decoux often toured the Highlands and repeatedly presided over the *palabre du serment*, which was widely publicized in semi-official, Pétainist periodicals like *Indochine* as the culmination of France's *mission civilisatrice* (Decoux 1950: 281–3). In this view, the Montagnards needed protection from the neighboring nations, which would justify direct French administration in a secluded area, presented as Montagnard 'autonomy'.

With reference to the Montagnards' essential unity, their difference from the other Indochinese nations, their amenability and 'similarity' to the French, and their need to be protected by France – themes which were constantly echoed in French ethnographic writing – the Central Highlands were turned into a military base area during World War II under the governorship of Admiral Decoux, Marshall Pétain's confidant in Indochina since the defeat of France by Nazi Germany in Spring, 1940. The *Pays Moï* was one of Decoux' favored projects, as is evident from the fact that he even made the mountain resort of Dalat the 'summer capital' of French Indochina, and moved a number of central administrative services there. During a *Conférence des Pays Moïs*, held in 1942 in the presence of Decoux, the ethnographic and administrative oeuvre of Sabatier was rediscovered and reapplied, with this crucial difference that his most famous creations – the *coutumier*, the *palabre du serment*, the *franco-rhadé* school – which were intended for the reconstruction and defense of the Rhadé tribe only, were now oriented toward the construction of a separate Montagnard identity and territory.

In this section, I have argued that French ethnographic practice was institutionalized in the context of mounting political tension in the region before and during World War II. The resulting ethnographic discourse, which harked back to the early relativist oeuvre by Léopold Sabatier, no longer applied to a wide variety of disparate tribes, but to a separate ethnic group of *Moï* or Montagnards who were seen as having a common identity, fundamentally opposed to the other nations in French Indochina. This process of ethnicization constituted the Montagnards – culturally, if not politically – as one of the constituent 'nations' of French Indochina, to be placed in one line with the other groups. As in other colonial contexts, this resulted in an ethnographic discourse characterized by a cultural relativism which aimed to preserve a distinct Montagnard identity and tradition, governed by customary law insofar as it did not harm French interests. The logical corollary of this process of ethnicization was the increased territorialization of French rule, as evidenced in attempts at ethnographic classification, mapping, and the linking of populations to bureaucratically prescribed territories. The French preferred to call the cultural and political separation of Montagnards from Vietnam, 'autonomy' of the *Pays Moï*. In the next section, we shall see that this autonomy acquires definite contours in the light of competing claims to the Highlands.

Competing claims to sovereignty

Further French ambitions with respect to the Central Highlands were obstructed by the Japanese military presence in the southern part of Indochina from July 1941. The Japanese military command left the French administrative infrastructure more or less intact, but it thwarted the French designs in the Highlands by obstructing the complete territorial detachment of the *Pays Moï* from Annam. Moreover, the Japanese posed as protectors of Vietnamese sovereignty in an effort to appease conservative nationalists, who would be offended by further territorial dismemberment. In 1942, a first French-language study was published by the Vietnamese lawyer Trân Chánh Thành, who on the basis of historical, political and juridical considerations argued that the provinces of Kontum, Pleiku, Darlac, Haut-Donnaï and Langbian were an integral part of the protectorate of Annam, in spite of French-imposed administrative practice. But while conservative Kinh nationalists claimed Montagnard *territory* as an historical part of imperial Vietnam, they had not developed a policy with respect to what amounts to ethnic minorities within the Vietnamese State. This contrasts with the Indochinese Communist Party (ICP), which since its inception in 1930 had a well-defined minorities policy, naturally influenced by Stalin's policies in the Soviet Union through the Komintern (Rousset 1978; Thierry 1989; Tangac

1989). Moreover, the merging of the ICP with the Viêt Minh by 1941, directed against both French colonialism and Japanese Fascism, underscored the strategic need for an attractive minority policy, because the base area from which the Viêt Minh waged its guerrilla struggle was located in the northern mountain areas. Thus, the mountain areas were in theory and practice claimed as part of Vietnam by nationalists at a time when the French colonial administration under Admiral Decoux made a considerable effort to deny the Vietnamese any influence in the *Pays Moï.*

Decoux's policy was not entirely successful. On a more practical level, the myth of Montagnard antagonism toward the Viêt was shattered by the increasing agitation of Vietnamese Communists in parts of the Central Highlands. Some Montagnard groups in the northern part of the Highlands adjacent to Laos, as well as some groups on the Boloven Plateau in southern Laos remained 'unruly' after the millenarian movement mentioned above, and continued to resist French attempts at 'pacification' throughout World War II. Eventually, the 'tribal' resistance in the mountain districts of Quang Ngãi, Quang Nam and Quang Tri connected up with the activities of Vietnamese Communists from 1940 onward. Already in 1940–41, French *Sûreté* reports mention the activities of Communist cadres like Trân Miên among the *Moï Khaleu* (Bru) in upland Quang Tri.[16] In Vietnamese Communist historiography, a direct line is traced from this tribal resistance movement to the 'Revolt of Ba-To' in upland Quang Ngãi (1945). This revolt, related to the Vietnamese August Revolution which culminated in Hô Chí Minh's Declaration of Independence in September 1945, continuated a rebel tradition which carried over into the Trà Bông rising by the Cor and Hrê minorities (1959–60) – one of the events which led to the formation of the National Liberation Front of South Vietnam, also known as Viêt Công.[17]

The liberation of France from Nazi occupation in the fall of 1944 brought with it the downfall of the Fascist Pétain regime in France. This rendered the position of the Decoux administration in French Indochina awkward, for in theory and practice – albeit secretly – the colonial administration was now linked to one of the Allied nations fighting Japan. The increasing actions by the Free French of General De Gaulle against the Japanese position, and the ambiguity of the Decoux administration made the Japanese military command suspicious of French motives in Indochina. A Japanese coup on 9 March 1945 dismantled French positions in all Indochinese centres in just one day, making a farce of France's claim of being the *Nation protectrice.* French military and administrative personnel were interned by the Japanese, a move which more often than not was applauded by the local population. Meanwhile, the Japanese installed a regime of 'nationalists' which was only nominally independent. The Viêt Minh, however, attempted to acquire a place among the Allies, and continued the struggle for independence, claiming to be the only serious nationalist movement of stature which combined the anti-colonial and the anti-Fascist struggle. With the French supervision gone, the Viêt Minh was able to extend its activities considerably, building an underground infrastructure and preparing for the seizure of power after the inevitable Allied victory over Japan. The Japanese capitulation came quite unexpectedly in August 1945, after the dropping of atomic bombs on Hiroshima and Nagasaki. In a rush of events, the Viêt Minh capitalized on its political and military groundwork in what is known as the August Revolution. During a mass manifestation in Hanoi on 2 September 1945, the Communist leader Hô Chí Minh proclaimed the independent Democratic Republic of Vietnam (DRV), comprising the two protectorates of Annam and Tonkin and the colony of Cochinchina, which for the Viêt Minh were nothing more than the three Vietnamese regions making up the country of Viêt Nam.

The August Revolution had the character of a series of localized attempts to fill the power vacuum left by the Japanese capitulation and the continued internment of French *Délégués* (see Marr 1995). In the Central Highlands, the Revolution manifested itself in the revolt of Bà-To where it linked up with existing resistance patterns, and among young Montagnard intellectuals in the major centres in the Highlands. After the Japanese coup in March 1945, the opening of detention centres in Kontum, Ban Me Thuot and Lao Bao and the release of Communist Vietnamese prisoners in the Central Highlands had facilitated contacts between the Viêt Minh cadres and Montagnards living in the towns. Mostly Jarai and Rhadé youngsters – schoolteachers and medical workers like Nay Der, Nay Phin, Ksor Ni and Y Ngông Nie Kdam – were attracted by the nationalist fervor which gripped Vietnam, and by the Viêt Minh's promise of development with respect for the *national minorities'* own languages and cultures. In particular, the literacy campaigns organized both among ethnic Vietnamese and minorities were welcomed by these young intellectuals. In April 1946, a Congress of the Southern National Minorities took place in Pleiku under the auspices of the Viêt Minh, which elected representatives for the National Assembly of the Democratic Republic of Vietnam. In a letter of 19 April 1946 to this Congress, President Hô Chí Minh stressed the multinational character of the Vietnamese State, which was the country of the Kinh majority and the 'national' minorities alike. In the past the Vietnamese populations had been divided due to lack of contacts and to French policy, but this was going to change in the new Republic which had a place and a policy for the minorities. For, in the words of Ho, 'Today Viet-Nam is our common country. In the National Assembly there are deputies of all nationalities. In the Government there is a Department for National Minorities, which takes charge of all affairs concerning them' (Ho Chi Minh in Fall 1967: 156; see also Nguyên Duong Binh 1990).

The French under General De Gaulle, however, did not acquiesce in the Vietnamese assertion of independence, and tried to reassert their authority over Indochina. Already in his declaration of 24 March 1945, De Gaulle announced the future form of French rule – the *Fédération Indochinoise*, which granted some degree of autonomy under close supervision by the French, who reserved the right for themselves to make the key decisions in economic, political and military affairs. In the fall of 1945, the French regained control of Saigon with the support of the British occupation force that had taken over from the Japanese in southern Indochina. From Saigon, an expeditionary army reconquered the major towns in the Mekong Delta and the rubber plantations in Cochinchina. In November

1945, a cavalry force under Colonel Massu reached Ban Me Thuot, capital of Darlac province, and unofficial capital of the *Pays Moï*, where the reconquest was temporarily halted. In the following year, a series of negotiations and half-hearted agreements aimed at preventing an all-out war between France and the DRV alternated with armed conflicts.[18] On 11 March 1946, just before the ratification of the Agreements of 6 March 1946 between France and the DRV, the new French High Commissioner in Indochina, Admiral Thierry D'Argenlieu, received instructions from Marius Moutet, *Ministre de la France d'Outre-Mer* (Minister of Colonies), to investigate the political feasibility of an autonomous Moï territory. Just after the preparatory *Conférence Franco-Vietnamienne*, held in Dalat in April 1946, the minister stated in a telegram to D'Argenlieu that the *Pays Moï* was not discussed, but that a *Commissariat du Gouvernement Fédéral pour les Populations Montagnardes du Sud-Indochinois* (PMSI), amounting to autonomy under French tutelage, would be very advantageous, though it could offend 'Hanoi'. Although the practical elaboration was left to D'Argenlieu, it is evident that only the timing but not the decision of creating the PMSI was his own, contrary to the opinions of Chesneaux, Lê Thành Khôi and other historians. The decision was prepared and made in Paris, but executed in Saigon by D'Argenlieu who used it as a tactical move against Vietnamese nationalism.[19]

On 17 May 1946, High-Commissioner Admiral D'Argenlieu presided over a *Palabre du serment* in Ban Me Thuot, which was presented as a popular manifestation for direct French rule in the Highlands. Yet, Hickey reported that many Rhadé who participated had supported the Viêt Minh before only to rally to the French after the conquest of Darlac. In his telegram to Moutet, D'Argenlieu said that the oath ceremony was a prelude to the establishment of the PMSI, which was actually established ten days later. As the name said, it was Montagnard territory which was placed directly under the French-controlled *Fédération Indochinoise*. Contrary to earlier circumscriptions of the *Pays Moï*, the PMSI was made up of the five upland provinces of Annam (the middle part of Vietnam), excluding important Montagnard populations in other parts of Annam, in Cochinchina, in Cambodia and in Laos. Incidentally, most of the excluded Montagnard groups had been resisting French penetration in the recent past, and some still posed a threat to the *pax gallica*. Thus, the boundaries of the PMSI did not follow any 'ethnic boundaries', but followed the border of the nation-state which had to be dismembered: Vietnam. The Montagnard populations in the southern part of Vietnam, Cochinchina, were excluded from the PMSI because D'Argenlieu carried through his plan for a separate Republic of Cochinchina on 1 June 1946, only four days after the proclamation of the PMSI, which guaranteed their remaining within the French sphere of influence. On 21 June, French troops received order to attack Viêt Minh positions in Pleiku and Kontum, just before the start of the decisive Franco-Vietnamese conference at Fontainebleau. This French attempt to effectively control the remaining territory of the PMSI was only partly successful, as the French were stopped north of Kontum and east of An-Khê.[20]

Of course, the detachment of Cochinchina and the PMSI from the territory claimed by the DRV incited vehement protests from the Vietnamese government. It is interesting to take a closer look at the arguments for either detachment or integration. Devillers noted that at the preparatory Dalat conference, the Viêt Minh argued that 'Cochinchina (Nam Bô) was an integrative part of Vietnam, whose ethnic, geographic, historical, cultural and psychological unity was impossible to deny'. During the Fontainebleau Conference Hô Chí Minh asserted that 'ethnically, historically, Cochinchina is a part of Vietnam, just like Bretagne or the Basque country is a part of France' (Devillers 1952: 264, 303). In a reply dated 31 July 1946 to Hô's protests against the French occupation of the *Pays Moï*, Labrouquère of the *Comité interministériel de l'Indochine* claimed that France had a special responsibility for the minorities, and that 'neither geographically, historically nor ethnically, the High Plateaux can be considered a part of Vietnam'.[21] Thus, the arguments concerning Cochinchina and the PMSI mirror each other perfectly, betraying different conceptions of ethnic and national identity. The Viêt Minh, as the strongest vehicle of Vietnamese nationalism, claimed to embrace all 'nationalities' on Vietnamese territory as part of a 'multinational' or multi-ethnic nation-state. The ethnic relations between the groups were likened to family relations, with the Viêt or Kinh majority group as the elder brother – the adult guiding the younger siblings into a bright future of maturity and development, with *cu Hô* ('old man' Hô, or *Bôk Hô* in the Bahnar language) as a common ancestor. In a letter of 19 April 1946 to the Congress of the Southern National Minorities, held in Pleiku, President Hô Chí Minh wrote that 'compatriots of the Kinh majority or of the ... minorities are all Viet-Nam's children, are all blood brothers and sisters'. As in the best families, conflicts occurred between ethnic groups, but family solidarity was emphasized. For, in the words of 'Bôk Hô', 'rivers can dry up, mountains can wear away, but our solidarity will never decrease'.[22]

The French also resorted to a family analogy in order to legitimize their claim to direct rule in an 'autonomous' Montagnard territory, but their role was that of a father of different children in a wider family of Indochina. Ever since Sabatier, who designated himself as *Ay Prong* (grandfather in Rhadé) and who took it as his task to 'guide and chide' (*guider et gronder*) the 'big children' (*grands enfants*) that are the Rhadé, the French attitude toward the Montagnards was characterized by paternalism (Sabatier 1930: 12–13; Dorgelès 1930: 26). In the historical context of rising nationalism, France's *mission civilisatrice* was conceived of as the educational task of guiding all their 'children' (ethnic groups within Indochina) with a just but firm hand to maturity. This was clearly expressed in one propaganda speech (among many) intended for a Montagnard audience:

> Why does the Resident grumble? It is for the well-being of the Montagnards, not for himself. The Resident, that is France, has come here to bring up the Montagnards like a mother brings up her children. ... you must become equal to the Vietnamese. The Montagnards must be on the same level. It should not be, like before 1945, that the Vietnamese is up there and the Montagnard down below.[23]

Pursuing this analogy, the major nations within French Indochina might have reached the age of adolescence, but France had the special responsibility of protecting the minors/ities within the *Fédération Indochinoise*, and preserving their traditional cultures.

At the Dalat Conference of August 1946, convened by D'Argenlieu to further the development of the *Fédération* (and which had the desired side-effect of frustrating the Fontainebleau Conference between France and the Viêt Minh), the French delegation claimed a special treatment for the ethnic minorities both in northern and in southern Vietnam, who for the first time in colonial history were officially designated as civilizations – as befitting French 'offspring'. France, then, should guarantee this special treatment by endowing the minorities with autonomous territories, to be separated from Vietnam and brought under French control through the *Fédération Indochinoise* – a process which was described as liberation. While the three major nations in Indochina claimed an independent state for themselves, D'Argenlieu tried to preserve De Gaulle's idea of a French-controlled 'pentagonal federation', made up of the five 'countries' of pre-war French Indochina. The French countered any nationalist claims by claiming separate territories for often widely diverging ethnic minorities, thus placing them on an equal footing as the majority populations of the 'countries' of Indochina. Not only were new ethnic territories and geographic boundaries created in this way, but by reserving for themselves the right of arbitrage in conflicts between minority and majority groups, the French increasingly rigidified once fluid ethnic boundaries.[24]

The French claims were supported by a 'PMSI delegation' which the French had summoned up for the occasion of the Dalat Conference of August 1946. The head of the delegation was the malleable Ma Krong, president of the costumary law court of Darlac province, and the nephew of and successor to the *Khun Jonob*, once a close collaborator of Sabatier. Their first 'wish' (*voeu*) was that the Vietnamese delegation at the Fontainebleau Conference would not speak for other 'member states' of the Federation – in this case for the PMSI. Their second wish was that 'all the individuals wearing loincloths' – who in one sentence were reduced to the five provinces making up the PMSI – would be protected directly by France, and acquire independence – from Vietnam, that is. The motive given was that the Montagnards had no resemblance whatsoever with the other Indochinese races – a strange argument for Ma Krong, who derived his authority from his uncle who was of mixed Lao-Mnong descent. While two 'motions' entailed the preservation of minority education in French and of Montagnard costumary law, a third motion presented on 6 August concerned the incorporation of Montagnard soldiers in the French colonial army. The keyword here was Montagnard *loyalty* to the French, which may be contrasted with the *solidarity* propagated by the Viêt Minh. For the French and the PMSI delegation, this loyalty was symbolized by the Odyssey of a Rhadé batallion that followed their French officer through Laos to China after the Japanese takeover in Indochina. Loyalty was also the symbolic substance of the *palabres du serment* which were immediately organized in the newly 'liberated' towns in the presence of High Commissioner d'Argenlieu. The Montagnard 'chiefs' who spoke out against 'Annamese tutelage' were rewarded with medals, guns, and occasionally a *Légion d'Honneur*.[25]

In his study of Viêt Minh minorities policy in northern Indochina as a key for understanding the battle of Điên Biên Phu, John McAlister argued that the Viêt Minh's 'interests were best served by creating an organization for military participation which gave the minorities opportunities for mobility and status'. McAlister found it 'instructive to note the Viet Minh's effectiveness in using military organization to achieve [political integration] which in Southeast Asia is thought to depend on economic or social prerequisites' (McAlister 1967: 933). However, the Viêt Minh had no monopoly in this, since their adversaries attempted the same thing among the southern minorities. It was obvious that the military potential of the Montagnards against the Vietnamese was their main attraction for the French. But whereas the Viêt Minh used the army as an instrument to tie different groups together, the French had to create a national territory for the Montagnard batallions to fight for in the face of Vietnamese nationalism, apart from providing avenues for the ambitions of Montagnard warriors. The ideas of a separate territory and a separate Montagnard army reinforced each other – indeed were inseparable – and effectively created a Montagnard military elite harboring separatist aspirations. The establishment of 'autonomous zones' in North Vietnam in 1955 was a practical elaboration of the concept of the multinational state as defined in the DRV constitution (Kunstadter 1967: 682–5). But while these autonomous zones in practice served to link the minorities firmly to the Vietnamese state, the establishment of the PMSI in an early stage of the war was entangled with a foreign presence there and would produce separatist tendencies among segments of the Montagnard population groups.

In this section, I have argued that D'Argenlieu's establishment of the PMSI, grounded in military and political motives in the struggle against the Viêt-Minh, was the logical outcome of earlier developments in the area. Although based on a fictional Montagnard ethnic identity, this move in fact created a 'homeland' for a Montagnard ethnic nation, distinct and detached from a Vietnamese nation-state. In the next section, I shall describe the French attempts to gain military control of the PMSI through direct rule in the guise of Montagnard 'autonomy' (from Vietnam, that is) until the Vietnamese claims to Montagnard territory could no longer be denied.

The First Indochina War: Struggle for control

After the occupation of Pleiku, Kontum and An Khê in June 1946, the French expeditionary force encountered heavy Viêt Minh resistance in the mountain area north of the line Kontum-An Khê, inland of the provinces of Quang Tri, Quang Nam and Quang Ngãi. A coastal strip remained firmly in Viêt Minh hands, and became known as the *Rue sans joie* (Street without Joy, see Fall 1963b). A military stalemate developed, with Kontum and An Khê as French bastions on the front. Later Vietnamese historiography has glorified the resistance by Hre, Katu, Kor and other groups, continuing a tradition of anti-French revolt in alliance with the Viêt Minh. In his biography, the Bahnar 'hero Núp' is depicted as having led his own village and other Bahnar villages against the French – against all odds and virtually without Viêt support (Nguyen Ngoc 1958). But Viêt Minh cadres tried to remain in contact with minority groups, and were increasingly successful in organizing anti-French resistance behind the frontlines, leading to what is known as the *pourissement* – the 'rotting away' of territory defended by the French. French actions were increasingly restricted to the major towns and roads, to the effect that by 1950 the town of Kontum was a French pocket in enemy territory.

The French responded in various ways to the military threat posed by the Viêt Minh. First, they stepped up their efforts to recruit Montagnard youngsters into the colonial militia. The military potential of the Montagnards – especially the Rhadé – had been one of the main motives for the rapid French reconquest of the Central Highlands in 1945–46. In a 1949 assessment of French policy in the PMSI, *Inspecteur général des Colonies* Gayet noted that the Rhadé in particular, were 'excellent troops', both as Montagnard soldiers in the French forces (5000) soldiers and in the *Garde montagnarde* (2500) militias (Gayet 1949: 77). Although for many Montagnard youngsters a military career seemed attractive, the French demand for fresh recruits exceeded voluntary supply, and French-appointed village headmen were tempted or forced to provide the French authorities with young recruits. In French morale reports from 1948 onward, mention is made of low morale, difficult recruitment, and even steady desertion of Montagnard soldiers from the French colonial army. In comparison with Gayet, the local socialist leader Louis Caput was less optimistic with respect to the French presence in the PMSI:

> The mountain people of these regions … certainly did not like the more enterprising Vietnamese, but are beginning to detest singularly the French who recruit them as soldiers, subject them to exactions and impose labor upon them. As a result, there has been growing malaise, an abandonment of work and land, a retreat into the forest, and the least one can say is that the situation in the … PMSI begins to become very disquieting.[26]

A second French response to the Viêt Minh threat was in fact very classical, and was connected to another *raison d'être* for the French presence in the Highlands: the rubber, tea and coffee plantations. In November 1946 the French commander of Darlac province, Colonel Massu, submitted a plan for the military colonization of the Highlands by supporting demobilizing French soldiers to establish plantations there. Massu felt that a '*colonisation à la romaine*' was desirable, for it remained 'the mission of France in Indochina … to protect the ethnic minorities against the Annamese imperialist tendency.' The plan was adopted by D'Argenlieu who stressed the political advantages of the presence of French cadres in the Highlands, and the economic advantages of the plantations, which in turn would render the PMSI economically viable. One of these settlers, Jean Boulbet, would make the uncharacteristic career move from soldier to plantation owner (near Blao – present-day Bao Lôc – in Lâm Đông province, in Ma territory) to professional ethnologist. According to Boulbet a major aim of the colonization plan was to 'secure the bases of a sufficiently viable economy to sustain the thesis of autonomy for the ethnic minorities' (Boulbet 1967: 2). The French military had experience with a military colonization project on the Plateau of Trân Ninh in Laos in the late 1930s. Historically, similar colonization schemes had been employed by the Romans when their legions occupied Europe (hence *colonisation à la romaine*), but also by the Vietnamese themselves who established military colonies (*đôn điên*) in Cham and Khmer territory during their historical 'March to the South' (*nam tiên*). The *đôn điên* system was to be recapitulated in different form by the Diêm regime's settlement of Catholic Vietnamese refugees from the north (1956) and by the current regime's creation of 'New Economic Zones' in the Central Highlands. With respect to the *plan Massu*, the Minister of Colonies, Marius Moutet, not only found the financial burden of six colonization centres too great, but also had practical scruples concerning the political effects of either utilizing Montagnard labor or 'importing' Viêt labor to work the plantations. In the course of 1947, the colonization experiment was allowed to continue on a limited scale.[27]

By 1949, around one hundred French veterans had settled as colonists in three centres (Ban Me Thuot, Djiring, Dak Mil), partly on previously abandoned plantations. While the results of the colonization effort were hailed, the labor problems signaled by Minister Moutet in 1946 were also observed, for 'the Montagnard workers come with limited enthusiasm and for strictly regulated periods, in order not to spoil the bit of goodwill, which must be strongly encouraged' (Gayet 1949: 75). However, any goodwill which the French might have wanted to promote with the military colonization was lost by an increasing resort to forced labor on the plantations. In 1949, the British journalist Norman Lewis observed how Montagnards were forced to perform corvée labor on the plantations. Plantations often forced Montagnards to sign binding labor contracts under threat of excessive violence. French colonial officials were acquainted with such labor and recruitment practices bordering on slavery, but did not have the authority or willingness to change anything about what had become the economic rationale for the French presence in the Highlands, and maintained a 'conspiracy of silence' (Lewis 1951: 121–47). Besides, despite their attempts to segregate populations in and around their plantations, the French could not prevent the mostly ethnic Vietnamese plantation coolies from getting in touch with the Montagnards living around the plantations. Former plantation worker and Viêt Minh member Trân Tu Bình, for example, described how Vietnamese plantation workers got in touch with ethnic groups living near the Phu Riêng plantation in order to secure their support during strikes – in spite of the premiums that French plantation owners would pay Montagnards for captured plantation workers (1985: 28–31, 66). The end result was that more and more Montagnards joined the nationalist struggle, gradually resulting in a situation where the Việt Minh controlled an increasingly large part of the Central Highlands.

The economic exploitation of the Highlands was politically self-defeating, in that any possible gains won by propaganda, medical and educational programs, were nullified by such practices. In fact, the quest for economic gain led to a downward spiral as its political and military consequences caused defeatism among French plantation owners who increased their exploitation of Montagnard labor, for as long as it would last. Lewis describes how plantation owners hired armed gangs to hunt down male workers in Montagnard villages, and even tried to recruit members of the *Garde montagnarde*, apparently unconcerned about the discontent their actions caused among Montagnards (1951: 147). Added to the imposition of taxes and corvee labor and the forced recruitment of Montagnard soldiers, the plantations and the abuse of labor to which these gave rise, rendered any ethnic policy by the French ineffective in the long run, as Louis Caput noted in the citation above. Furthermore, the presence of plantations imposed an extra burden on the French military who were supposed to defend the plantations against Việt Minh attacks. Complaints by plantation managers led in the summer of 1950 to a heated exchange between the *Deuxième Bureau* (Intelligence), High Commissioner Pignon, his *Délégué* for the PMSI Cousseau, and the senior General of the French forces, Alessandri on the feasibility of the defense of plantations in the PMSI.[28]

Not only was French policy in the Highlands self-defeating, but wider developments made it imperative for France to accommodate to some form of Vietnamese nationalism in order to isolate the Việt Minh, and come to terms with the Vietnamese claims to the Highlands. While other Asian nations attained independence, and the Việt Minh position became stronger, both militarily and politically, France sought to present the colonial conflict in terms of the emerging Cold War. The Communist takeover in China, early in 1949, raised American concerns about a worldwide Communist expansion, which should be contained by all means, first of all by fighting Communist movements which were thought to be Soviet pawns. While the US financed an increasing share of the French military effort in Indochina, it exerted pressure on the French to soften its intransigence and make concessions to non-Communist Vietnamese nationalists, as a 'third force'. Since 1947, the new High Commissioner for France in Indochina, Emile Bollaert, who presided over the *Palabre du serment* of 1948, attempted to get the former emperor Bao Đai to take up position as head of an 'independent' Vietnamese state within the framework of the newly formed *Union Française*. But even this playboy monarch did not agree with a Vietnamese state from which Cochinchina, the northern Tai Federation and the PMSI were excluded.

In the agreement of 8 March 1949 between Bao Đai and the French President Auriol the territorial unity of Vietnam as an associated state within the French Union was recognized, effectively excluding a negotiated settlement with the Việt Minh as a possible solution. Nominally, France retained control of the army, the political police and international relations through the Indochinese Federation, but in actual practice continued to control 'French Indochina', certainly in the

Figure 5.4 Montagnard troops armed by the French military during the First Indochina War.

Source: Archives des Missions Étrangères de Paris.

PMSI. While France recognized the formal Vietnamese sovereignty over the Central Highlands, it demanded a *statut particulier* (special status) for the Highlands because of special French obligations toward the Montagnards. This special regime would remain France's responsibility, while the five provinces were linked to the person of Bao Đai as the Emperor's Crown Domain. The relation of the Emperor to his *Domaine de la Couronne du Pays Montagnard du Sud* (PMS – significantly, the 'I' of *Indochinois* had fallen off now it was again part of Vietnam) consisted merely of shares in rubber plantations and a hunting lodge at Dalat, but in June 1949 he presided over the *Palabre du serment* in Ban Me Thuot, along with Bollaert's successor as High Commissioner, Léon Pignon. While French sources now stated that 'these territories ... indisputably belong to the ancient Empire of Annam', the nominal transfer of sovereignty hardly affected the regime of direct French rule, which, of course, was the substance of the 'special status'.[29] For the time being, the only tangible change on the ground was a further opening of the Highlands for plantations, which now benefited from credits and tax exemptions. Still, many Montagnard soldiers were upset by the fact that their contracts with the French Army were dissolved, and replaced by contracts with the Vietnamese Army – which they had been told to hate and fight in the first place.[30] In retrospect, this move was to be resented a generation later by Y Bham Enuol, the Rhadé leader of the Montagnard autonomy movement FULRO, who in 1965 complained that the French 'arbitrarily, without consulting us, had ... reunited the PMS to the domain of the Crown of Emperor Bao Dai'.[31]

In this section, I have described how the French colonial administration attempted to preempt any Vietnamese claims over the upland parts of the protectorate of Annam and to counter any Vietnamese influence in that area, by detaching the PMSI from Vietnam. This resulted in a curious mix of *indirect* and *direct rule* with respect to the Montagnards. The French themselves called their policy 'direct rule' (*administration directe*), as opposed to the 'indirect' administrative system that had been in place in the protectorates of Annam, Tonkin, Cambodia and Laos, where the French – at least in theory – governed through intermediary strata of indigenous rulers, mandarins and other dignitaries. If compared with British forms of colonial rule in Africa and Malaya, however, the French administrative system in the PMSI might be termed *indirect*, insofar as it claimed to respect and protect local cultural forms. The French view was that in wartime conditions, this administrative system needed a heavy French presence in the area – both militarily, politically, and economically. Though that particular combination of tactics appeared to be largely self-contradictory and therefore self-defeating, it proved fertile ground for a surge in ethnographic research and writing. Even contemporary observers, like Georges Hardy of the *Bureau Scientifique de l'Armée*, noted in a review of scholarly articles on Asia that 'the prolonged drama of which the Indochinese peninsula is the theatre seems to have spurred on the ethnographic research, especially concerning the Moï populations' (Hardy 1951: 300). In the next section, I shall describe how this battleground formed a *préterrain* that proved fertile ground for a particular form of ethnographic practice, which was increasingly professionalized in the wake of the earlier process of ethnographic institutionalization before 1945.

The politics of ethnographic professionalization

When in 1946 the Central Highlands, formerly known as the *Pays moï*, was rebaptized as *Pays Montagnard du Sud-Indochinois* (PMSI), the indigenous populations underwent a few name changes:

> The administration and the ethnographers abandoned the term 'savages', which was considered vague and insulting. First, they adopted the term 'Moï' which they borrowed from the Vietnamese, while specifying it and stripping it from its pejorative connotations. More recently, the 'policy of consideration' [*politique d'égards*] was prescribed. One tried 'Indomalais', and then 'populations montagnardes du Sud-Indochinois', whose initials produced 'Pémsiens'.
>
> (Ner 1952: 45)

The term *Pémsien* was enthusiastically embraced by the ethnographer Jacques Dournes in the journal *France/Asie* (1950). Although he claimed that this label had no political connotations, he stressed that it would symbolize Montagnard unity as opposed to the Vietnamese. For Dournes, the 'Indonesian race' was as different from the 'yellow race' as from the 'white race' (Dam Bo [pseudonym for Dournes] 1950: 5–6, 19). With the abolition of the PMSI, the term *Pémsien* was soon replaced by Condominas' *Proto-indochinois* (1953), which is still being used in French scholarly circles. The most enduring ethnonym, however, would be *Montagnard*, which seemed less offensive than *Moï*, less politicized than *Pémsien*, and less 'scholarly' than *Proto-indochinois*, while being sufficiently vague to encompass a wide variety of groups or tribes and being sufficiently French to hint at that 'special relationship' between France and Montagnards. Condominas (1953: 658) reported that 'developed Moï reject this offensive label and prefer the French word 'Montagnard' which [he] often heard often in the middle of a conversation in vernacular dialect'. Ironically, the use of the gallicism 'Montagnard' would become most widespread during the era of American involvement in Vietnam.

In ethnographic discourse, the theme of a special relationship between France and the Montagnards was reiterated again and again – in ethnographic or popular publications, at conferences, in political statements, and at other occasions. While the Montagnards were effectively reduced to the status of 'ethnic minorities' with the rise of Vietnamese sovereignty, the French claimed the protection of minorities as their exclusive responsibility, as an integral part of their *mission civilisatrice*. Often, the French used Montagnards willing to give voice to this 'special relationship' in public fora. Malleable Montagnards, demanding autonomy, or a *Statut particulier* under French protection, could always be found among the French-appointed chiefs, as was evident during the Dalat Conference of 1946. This conceptualization of the upland populations as a separate ethnic group which had a special relationship with the French and which would become extinct under Vietnamese sovereignty provided the conceptual context for the ethnographic writing after 1945. This involved both amateur ethnographers working and publishing under the supervision of special ethnographic institutes, or professional ethnographers working under the auspices of mostly the same institutions: in Indochina, the EFEO and the SEI; and in the metropole, the *Institut d'Ethnologie*, the *Office de la Recherche Scientifique Coloniale* and the *Centre de Formation aux Recherches Ethnologiques*, partly financed by the colonies or 'associated states' of the French Union.

The first serious ethnographic publication after World War II was a detailed description of Rhadé funerary rituals by the medical doctor of Ban Me Thuot, Bernard Jouin, a 'veteran' of the Highlands. Jouin's monograph, claiming academic status, was published by the prestigious *Institut d'Ethnologie* at the University of Paris. Co-founded by the famous ethnologists Marcel Mauss, Lucien Lévy-Bruhl and Paul Rivet in 1926, the *Institut d'Ethnologie* published works by such renowned ethnologists as Henri Labouret, Marcel Griaule, André Leroi-Gourhan, Georges Dumézil, and Maurice Leenhardt. In his conclusion, Jouin denied any historic cultural relationship of the Rhadé with the Vietnamese:

> From these collected data on the funerary customs of the autochthonous people of Darlac, it appears clearly that the basis for these customs is the same everywhere in the province; that if certain borrowings have been made from the Laotians or the Cambodians, these are insignificant ...; in one respect, the Chams have left traces, which were clearer but which remained outside of the custom; in no respect, however, is an Annamese [ethnic Vietnamese – OS] contribution perceptible.
>
> (Jouin 1949: 207)

It was usual for French ethnographers to stress French concern for the Montagnards, and to denie any legitimacy of Vietnamese claims to the Highlands. Jouin concluded from his description of the funerary rituals, that the French had to save the Montagnards from extinction caused by economic, political, and demographic factors, even though there does not seem to be a logical connection between this political conclusion and the ethnographic narrative. In order to save the rich Montagnard culture that Jouin just had described, the French had to change it by fighting diseases, laziness, carelessness and superstitions. Only by developing to the same level as the neighboring nations, the Montagnards would be able to resist the latter's 'invasions'.

Other 'serious' publications in the context of the EFEO and the SEI by 'amateur' ethnographers who had held positions with the colonial administration or the colonial army before 1945 were a *Coutumier Stieng* by Théophile Gerber (1951–2); a *Coutumier Bahnar* (1952a) and a study of Bahnar worldview and religion (1952b) by the erstwhile Resident of Kontum province, Paul Guilleminet, all published under the auspices of the EFEO; an 'ethnopsychological' study of the 'archaïc Moï populations' in the *Revue de Psychologie des Peuples* by Marcel Ner (1952); and studies of Rhadé agricultural rituals and Rhadé society by the military officer Maurice (1947, 1951, 1956) and with Proux (1954). Captain (as he was then) Albert-Marie Maurice was an old hand in the Central Highlands. Involved in the suppression of the 'Mnong revolt' of the 1930s, he had co-published (with Paul Huard) a study on 'Les Mnong du Plateau central indochinois' in the *Travaux de l'Institut Indochinois pour l'Etude de l'Homme*.[32] After 1945, Maurice became involved in the reconquest of the Central Highlands, and again commanded Rhadé *Tirailleurs*; hence his ethnographic writing on the Rhadé. In several post-1945 publications, Maurice tended to focus on Montagnard warfare and the utilization of their warrior instinct in the *bataillons montagnards* – against the Vietnamese. Maurice became more critical of French rule in the Highlands as their position became weaker. After their retreat from Vietnam in 1955, Maurice even wrote critically of Sabatier, whom he had praised before, for distorting authentic cultural traditions in the interest of colonial administration. He gave the examples of the subsumption of the *mnam thun ian prong* (Rhadé 'New Year') celebration into the *Palabre du serment* and the modifications to the *coutumier rhadé* (Maurice 1956: 11). Marcel Ner, a former civil servant and ethnographer of the Montagnards as correspondent of the EFEO who had played a role during the 1946 negotiations with the Viêt Minh, was after World War II, appointed Professor of Ethnology of Indochina at the *Ecole Nationale de la France d'Outre-Mer* which trained future colonial administrators. His 'ethnopsychological' analysis, aiming at the instruction of aspiring colonial administrators, is depressingly chaotic, with streaks of racism, as in his 'psychological' assessment that '[t]he Moï is not entirely free from the fear that fire instills in the animal' (Ner 1952: 163). Nevertheless, Ner contended that even these 'creatures' could be led into civilization, as they were being forged into one nation by the evolution which French rule brought toward them.

One of the most prolific ethnographers after 1945 was Paul Guilleminet, the former Délégué of Kontum province, who had dealt with the Dieu Python movement in 1937, and had analysed it in detail in 1941. He published a *Coutumier de la tribu Bahnar, des Sedang et des Jarai de la province de Kontum* (1952a) which is significant in many different ways, because it was quite frank about the rationale and the method of codification:

> The customary law [*coutumier*] ... can be defined as the totality of rules that the authority now has respected, basing itself on the juridical customs of Kontum, in order to avoid that anyone trouble public order or the peaceful life of the community, harm or bring material, ritual or moral damage to others. The principles stated at each article express the state of affairs in 1941. They are the result of a slow and progressive modification of customs [*coutumes*] that adapt by themselves, or by decision of the chiefs and assessors, to the evolution of practices [*moeurs*], to the new needs of the era, to the desire that the political Administration has to reform them without shocks.
> (Guilleminet 1952a: 101)

While acknowledging that orally transmitted customary law is by its very nature flexible and adaptible – until it is codified in writing – there are many rules that refer to the colonial administration in Guilleminet's version. Obedience to (appointed) headmen and other colonial officials, punishment of resistance, corvée labor, regulation of travel and prohibition of relocation of villages may be expedient for the colonial authorities but can hardly be construed as in line with tradition. Again, while acknowledging that the establishment of statutory law requires a redefinition and circumscription of customary law, it is useful to see this as an essentially political process. Yet, the *coutumiers* that were invariably presented as the embodiment of Montagnard tradition, meticulously recorded by careful ethnographers eager to preserve that tradition, were essentially the outcome of that political process at a certain point in time.

One striking example of 'reinterpretation' of custom is discernible in those 'articles' (the format follows French legalistic traditions rather than the poetic tradition of Montagnards) that deal with land rights. Bahnar society traditionally assigned land use rights through an institution called *to'ring*:

> Les *to'ring* ... divide up all the territory. There is no soil or portion of river in Kontum province that is not affected. Their use rights are fixed; whoever does not belong to the *to'ring* can buy a plot that an inhabitant of the *to'ring* owns, but cannot occupy one. Since the arrival of the French Administration the situation has been complicated by the fact that the Administration has its rights defined in articles 35 and 71.
>
> (ibid.: 460)

> At article 71, I don't say that the *to'ring* are the proprietors of the soil, that term seems improper to me; on the contrary, at article 74 I indicate that the fields can be occupied as well as bought; finally, in the commentaries on article 71, I indicate that the village owns nothing.
>
> (ibid.: 459)

> The Administration is the outstanding proprietor of all the territories and goods that do not form the object of private individual ownership. It can therefore mark objects or carve out plots from the territory that it needs, to occupy or to give in occupation, provisionally or not, to establish services, liable to pay compensation to stakeholders in those cases where: 1) These plots are private property, are effectively used or worked by an individual or a group; 2) Crops are underway, planted trees exist on these plots.
>
> (ibid.: 463)

Thus, while all the land was communally owned or at least claimed, by disavowing all land rights that did not fit the Western category of private property (almost all the land) and proclaiming the state sole proprietor of these lands, Guilleminet could legally appropriate lands for plantations and other uses.

In the rotational shifting cultivation systems common among many highland communities, only a small portion of the land needed for its sustainable use was actually cleared and in use; the remainder was left fallow for the forest to regenerate. The appropriation of the latter plots would contribute to the degeneration of the forest and the soil, and in time rendered the indigenous agricultural systems unsustainable. By the legalistic reasoning of Guilleminet and others, Bahnar, Sedang and Jarai communities of Kontum could be legally alienated from their lands in the name of their own custom. Small wonder, then, that this part of 'their' customary law was unpopular among Montagnards themselves, as Guilleminet was well aware:

> But nothing has justified (in the eyes of the Moï, of course) the installation of French or Vietnamese colonists; the licensing of group privileges to individuals; nor the installation of fishermen or hunters under the conditions that this was done ... The Moï was in fact forced to bow, and has accepted this situation because he could not do otherwise.
>
> (ibid.: 464–5)

Obviously, such tactics of dispossession were in the interest of (aspiring) plantation owners, who of course had more means to claim land as private property. But even these tactics were presented as not only conform to the 'letter' of the customary law, but as beneficial for the Moï who would be lifted up from their 'backward, primitive and destructive' agricultural condition – combining *mission civilisatrice* with *mise en valeur*.

The influential ethnographic publications by Ner, Jouin, Maurice, and Guilleminet had explicit scientific pretensions, and were all intended to provide the French administration with a framework for action in the Central Highlands, by representing Montagnard culture as valuable enough to protect against the Vietnamese, while simultaneously in need of development for economic, social, demographic or political reasons. Already in a 1942 article in the *Cahiers de l'Ecole Française d'Extrême-Orient* entitled 'Recherches ethnologiques in pays moï', Paul Guilleminet gave a frank statement about the objectives of ethnography in the Highlands:

> The ethnographic researches in the highlands have for objective to make the tribes known that the planters, the Administration, as well as the Army employ more and more regularly; to contribute to the establishment of an inventory of the races that populate the Indochinese Peninsula, but also and mainly to give to ethnographers [ethnologists? – OS] precise information on human groupings that have, in contact with neighboring civilizations, evolved without disappearing.
>
> (1942: 21)

Guilleminet was right that the work of amateur ethnographers like himself would inform and contextualize the narratives of ethnologists and professional anthropologists. Still in 1960, the founding father of French structural anthropology, Claude Lévi-Strauss, upheld Guilleminet's work as a model to follow and as an ethnographic goldmine in a conference paper entitled 'Méthode et conditions de la recherche ethnologique en Asie' (Lévi-Strauss 1960).

Not surprisingly, then, Montagnard culture was represented in rather similar ways by a new generation of young, aspiring ethnographers, who conducted fieldwork in the Central Highlands, applying the methods of participant observation. This new generation of French ethnographers of the Montagnards either started off as professional anthropologists conducting fieldwork (Georges Condominas, Pierre-Bernard Lafont), or as amateur ethnographers who gradually moved into the profession of anthropology by applying the research methods of modern ethnographic fieldwork (Jacques Dournes, Jean Boulbet). Thus, the process of institutionalization of ethnographic practice, starting with the foundation of the EFEO and receiving a new impetus in the 1930s, was combined with a process of professionalization. The new professional anthropologists referred to anthropological theory, and followed the instructions given at the newly founded *Centre de Formation aux Recherches Ethnologiques* (1946) according to the posthumously published *Manuel d'Ethnographie* by the famous anthropologist Marcel Mauss (1947). In pre-war France, a distinction had been maintained between academic ethnologists and local ethnographers. The latter would provide the former with research data, which could then be used for scientific abstraction. There were, of course, ethnologists who did fieldwork themselves, but long-term field research based in participatory observation as a scientific method did not receive the attention it got in the Anglo-Saxon part of the world. In French Indochina, for example, the composition of a *coutumier* played a similar role as fieldwork elsewhere. As late as the 1960s, French anthropologists were still publishing *coutumiers*, often complete with the jurisprudence of the colonial court (Boulbet 1957; Lafont 1963). Since there was no tradition of fieldwork in France, the *Centre de Formation* had to cross the Channel, even the Atlantic, to find the model of participant observation, and the ideas of functionalism, structuralism and cultural relativism which permeated research praxis there. Directly or indirectly, the courses taught at this Center made aspiring French anthropologists aware of the theories attending the Anglo-Saxon view of fieldwork. The *Centre de Formation* was sponsored by different parts of the 'Union Française', the post-war name of the former 'Empire Française', and its graduates were employed in the 'associate state' (Read: colony) which needed research.

Before 1954, the most productive of these ethnographers was Jacques Dournes. Dournes was a Catholic missionary of the *Missions Etrangères de Paris* who was sent to the Central Highlands immediately after World War II, and soon found himself engaged in all kinds of ethnographic work, including, of course, the composition of a *coutumier* (1951) and ethnolinguistic research (1950). He was well aware of anthropological theory and practice, and gradually shifted away from the church into the anthropological profession, to become a professional anthropologist in the 1970s. Dournes loved the Montagnards, most of all their Tradition (with capital!) and their oral literature, and he was concerned about the eventual disappearance of their culture (significantly, he would use the singular). From this perspective, Dournes could be critical about French policies that seemed detrimental to the preservation of traditional society and culture. In several publications he wrote disapprovingly about the use of straw men as village heads who started to form a separate, corrupt class propped up by colonial rule, undermining the real, spiritual authority of the village elders. Though he underscored the need for education, he was weary about the effects in terms of Westernization and hence the cultural uprooting of Montagnard children. He saw the latter process even more strongly represented among the Montagnard soldiers fighting for the French (Dournes 1955: 72; see also Dournes 1948a; 1949). Moreover, Dournes commented that the French administration built too few schools and hospitals, while simultaneously allowing Montagnard land and labor to be appropriated by plantations:

> It is not unfounded to conclude that in the economic domain the *Pémsiens* have not gained from the change in domination, as the European wave has reduced their circulation, slowed down the streams of exchange, and diminished their ancient prosperity.
>
> (Dam Bo 1950: 47)

Nevertheless, he did not distance himself from French rule, which he saw as the best guarantee against a Vietnamese 'invasion' of the Highlands. On the contrary, he promoted direct rule, and was the one of the major protagonists of the 'one Montagnard nation' thesis.

Dournes was the inventor of the term *Pémsiens*, 'these poor relatives among the Nations, these men of another race and another time' (Dam Bo 1950: 5–6). The term *Pémsien* had to express Montagnard unity, as opposed to the Vietnamese nation. Thus, his major monograph pretended to describe all the *Pémsiens*, although it was based solely on research among the Koho Sré of the province of Haut-Donnaï. Dournes justified this *Pémsien* unity on geographical, ethnic and racial grounds, specifying that the Montagnards belonged to the 'Indonesian race', which would be as different from the 'Yellow' as from the 'White Race'. He denied that the term *Pémsien* had any political connotation, despite the contested character of the PMSI (Dam Bo 1950: 5–6, 19). Yet, in that same publication, he acknowledged the largely fictional character of this eternal antagonism between Montagnards and Viêt:

> At present there are Elders, quite old, who have known the time before the arrival of the French, and they keep a happy memory of their travels ... and of their relations with the Vietnamese in those days. The Vietnamese had developed the administrative organization begun by the Cham.
>
> (Dam Bo 1950: 25)

Despite the acknowledgments that Montagnard-Vietnamese relations have not always been antagonistic and that French rule has not always been beneficial for

Montagnard society, Dournes apparently found it expedient to reinscribe the prevailing discourse about their need for French protection against the Vietnamese onslaught. That, after all, was the rationale for his own presence in the Central Highlands. This trope in the ethnographic narratives was premised on the conception of Montagnards as one nation comparable to the other nations making up French Indochina. The cultural relativism that was the most convincing perspective to bolster such claims was expressed most forcefully by those who applied the anthropological method of ethnographic fieldwork to which Dournes also subscribed:

> [S]ince the Tradition is only oral, it is the human contact that constitutes our principal source ... Our analyses are the result of observations and personal conversations, obtained during several years of life in common with these people, thus excluding fantasy and gratuitousness
>
> (1950: 6).

The first professionally trained anthropologist after World War II to conduct modern fieldwork in the Central Highlands was Georges Condominas. His research, commissioned in 1947 by the Office of Colonial Scientific Research in France, was carried out in 1948–49. In Indochina, supervision was exercised by the director of the EFEO, the ethnologist Paul Lévy. With the agreement of colonial officials, the isolated Mnong Gar village of Sar Luk was chosen as location for the research, which was meant to be a study of acculturation:

> We think that the study of the contacts [with Western and Vietnamese civilization] and of the transformations which they produce in the autochthonous society, must be the main concern of the 'colonial' anthropologist because it allows for a practical and efficient extension of the ethnographic work.
>
> (Condominas 1952a: 305)

In other words, Condominas positioned his ethnographic work firmly in colonial governmentality, conceived as the scientifically informed management of native populations.

This opinion about the use of ethnography was typical of post-war French anthropology, which had been profoundly reformed to be able to meet the demands of the newly formed 'Union Française', successor of the former 'Empire Française'. In the two volumes of the *Ethnologie de l'Union Française* (1953), to which Condominas contributed an article on the ethnology of Indochina, a kind of applied anthropology was proposed:

> Only anthropology can form a valid basis for a policy. It would be vain to pretend to advise and direct an indigenous society without proceeding with the methodical study of its habits and mentality ... French anthropological

research, then, seems to be of national interest; formerly, colonization could not do without it, and now it is one of the vital conditions of the Union.

(Leroi-Gourhan and Poirier 1953: 897)

This anthropology, practised within the framework of new institutes like the *Office de la Recherche Scientifique Coloniale* and the *Centre de Formation aux Recherches Ethnologiques*, and financed by the colonies or associated states, could only be of value on the basis of fieldwork by professional anthropologists. Much later, Condominas would note in retrospect that 'certain ethnologists, and not the lowliest, wanted to be taken seriously by the colonial environment. Hence the creation of the 'applied antropology', a good deal of which has taken to function as an instrument of government, i.e. government of colonial oppression.' (Condominas 1980: 125, or. 1973)

The new brand of professional anthropology, encompassing both ethnographic research, writing and theory within a colonial context, stressed problems of acculturation, education, and economic development (Leroi-Gourhan and Poirier 1953: 898). The research by Condominas, however, did not produce the desired results, since he became aware early of the less positive effects of colonial rule on the local populations, notably the recruitment for the army, the plantation regime, and the exploitation by French-appointed chiefs (Condominas 1977: 459). In the context of emerging anti-colonial critique in the metropole by prominent anthropologists like Michel Leiris and Georges Balandier, he started to doubt the value of the opinion of the colonial milieu as a favorable context for ethnographic field research, for which he coined the term *préterrain* (Condominas 1972: 9–10). The use of that term in front of his students in courses he gave back in Paris prompted the French colonial administration of Madagascar to deny him permission to enter that colony for research (Condominas, personal communication). His newly acquired political sensitivity did not stop Condominas from contributing to the *Ethnologie de l'Union Française* (1953). There, however, he rejected the neologism *Pémsien*, which he found too politicized, as well as the pejorative term *Moï* and the vague term *Montagnard*. Instead, he proposed the term *tribus proto-indochinoises* (thereby confirming tribalizing classifications that he would denounce in later writing) to designate the Montagnards as the oldest, if not the aboriginal population of Indochina (Condominas 1953: 658).

When Condominas published his ethnographic monograph of the Mnong Gar in 1957, after the French military withdrawal from Indochina, it was in the form of a highly influential and innovative ethnographic experiment – an ethnographic diary, which included his own role in the society under study. Other professional ethnographers, like P.B. Lafont and Jean Boulbet, also published after the end of the First Indochina War. Though their work reinscribed the dominant French discourse, for instance by presenting the minutes of the colonial customary law court as data from indigenous society, their research results was not made available in time to be used for the counterinsurgency programs that the French military developed and applied from the late 1940s onward against the Việt Minh. These programs that combined military and political tactics will be dealt with in the next section.

Assessments about the quality of the ethnographic work by Lafont and Boulbet varied,[33] but the impact of their work after 1955 was minimal in the context of South Vietnam, at a time when French political and discursive influence in Vietnam was waning.

The same is not true for some of the ethnographic work that had preceded them, like that by Dournes. In 1950, the *Haut-Commissariat des PMS* gave Dournes a subsidy to have his *Dictionnaire Sre (Koho)-Français* published by the official *Imprimerie d'Extrême-Orient.* Just one year later, Gilbert Bochet of the *Service Géographique de l'Indochine* published *Éléments de conversation Franco-Koho: Us et coutumes des Montagnards de la province du Haut-Donnaï* (1951), mainly intended as a practical guide for the military traveler in that area. According to the reviewer Groslier (1952b), the main source must have been Dournes' publications and those of his predecessor, Mgr. Cassaigne of the Dalat diocese. The first part of the booklet was a sort of Koho phrasebook complete with cultural *dos* and *don'ts*, including paying attention to matrilinearity. The second part contained an introduction to Koho culture and social organization, including psychological warfare tips. Bochet argued for a sort of 'localized' propaganda to counter Việt Minh propaganda, but warned that 'the Montagnards have heard many discourses ... to the extent that though they may be satisfied that one addresses them, they will in the final analysis judge their interlocutor, whoever he may be, by his practical achievements' (Bochet 1951: 82). In other words, insofar as the French military needed the support of local populations, these needed to be taken seriously. It is this realization which contextualized the ethnographic practice after World War II, especially its institutionalization and professionalization.

The processes of institutionalization and professionalization of ethnographic practice did not necessarily mean that ethnography acquired a more scientific or scientistic character. Inserting themselves into a more encompassing ethnographic discourse, 'serious' ethnographers had to come to terms with more politicized or popular ethnographic statements, and often contributed to such publications. Before 1945 EFEO members had already contributed articles to the Pétainist weekly *Indochine* which had also published and propagated the anti-Jew decrees promulgated by the Decoux regime in French Indochina. After 1945, serious ethnographers, often administrators themselves, would lend their names and their writing to publications with an overt propagandistic character. The most striking example is *Revue Éducation* No. 16 (1949). The *Revue Éducation*, a semi-official 'popular scientific' journal published by the *Rectorat d'Académie* in Saigon, devoted a special ethnographic issue to the PMSI even though by then the PMSI had been officially abolished and reattached to Vietnam as the Emperor's Crown Domain. Edited by the *Inspection des Colonies* and with articles contributed by 'serious' ethnographers like Guilleminet, Dournes and Jouin as well as administrators, school teachers and missionaries, the *action civilisatrice* of France was glorified and contrasted with the barbarism which allegedly characterized the Việt Minh, falsely represented as a Japanese war ally. *Inspecteur général des*

Colonies Gayet self-complacently proclaimed the beneficial effects of French policies on the Montagnards' development, and hence France's right and responsibility in terms of protection of their traditional culture by safeguarding their 'autonomy'. The *Statut particulier* provided for a 'free evolution of these populations while respecting their traditions and their customs'. The road to development consisted of the imposition of a social and political organization by the Administration on the one hand, and on the other the establishment of plantations coupled with suppression of the shifting cultivation system (*rây*) that formed the economic basis for Montagnard society and culture (Gayet 1949: 78–9). The need for suppression of shifting cultivation was repeated by many other contributors to the *Revue Éducation*. In retrospect, it seems ironic that the 'free evolution' apparently necessitated the suppression of indigenous land rights, part and parcel of traditional custom. But perhaps 'free' referred to the freedom to establish plantations on appropriated Montagnard lands, thus illustrating the inherent ambiguity of the French economic and politico-military presence in the Central Highlands.

The volume contained a novelty, namely ethnographic articles written by Montagnard (mostly Rhadé) intellectuals. Montagnards who contributed articles, wrote how happy they were to eat French food, wear Western clothes, to have acquired qualities like obedience, loyalty and respect taught at school, in short, to enjoy the benefactions of civilization:

> This quick overview allows already the appreciation of the benefactions of France in the montagnard region. From plundering and warring tribes, without laws or beliefs, France has made them ... a race that is almost ready for modern civilization. But in many respects, the Montagnards lag behind, and their evolution remains incomplete. If the realizations continue, the Montagnards will not be destined for extinction, but on the contrary will become a strong and beautiful race, worthy of its educators.
>
> (Y-Bih Nie-Kdam 1949: 90)

Of course, such attempts at self-representation were only acceptable insofar as these narratives supported French direct rule in the PMSI. The irony of this is, that in spite of other, more relativist French narratives, Montagnards like Y Bih Nie-Kdam basically disavowed their own culture as primitive and backward, and hence in need of 'improvement'. Other – mostly French – authors in the *Revue Éducation* also stressed the blessings of French administration in the Highlands, while at the same time depicting the Montagnards as destitute, due to the shifting cultivation which many of them practised. They needed guidance and development, which only France could bring them, as protector of minorities.

The ethnographic descriptions in *Revue Éducation* had the effect of legitimizing direct French rule in the Highlands, at a time when there were competitors for power. The ethnographic narratives, written by amateur ethnographers including many of the well-known names, were intended for a popular audience and were meant to serve educational purposes, as indicated in the title of the journal. Even though the descriptions were rather superficial, they realized two goals. First, the overall message was communicated that the Montagnards were different from the Viêt people, indeed closer to the French than to the Viêt. This rendered them sufficiently valuable in French eyes to protect them against the 'imperialist' Vietnamese civilization, considered as an aberration from Chinese civilization and a 'swallowing monster' in the context of Indochina. Second, the sheer act of ethnography would be enough to demonstrate French concern with the Montagnards. The only critical notes in *Revue Éducation* (1949) could be found in Jacques Dournes' contributions, which expressed doubts about the effects of Western-style development on Montagnards, especially Montagnard youth.

The French Indochina War proved to be fertile ground for the emergence of professional ethnographic fieldwork, resulting in cumulative and mutually influencing processes of institutionalization and professionalization of ethnographic practice. Thus, despite occasional professional doubts about the legitimacy and the morality of the colonial *préterrain*, the war itself appeared as a favorable ethnographic occasion for professional ethnographic fieldwork. Concerned with funding and usefulness of the research, professional anthropologists by and large operated within the boundaries of established colonial discourse and colonial governmentality. Working locally in the framework of the very same institutions as the amateur ethnographers before, during and after them, the new professional anthropology was part and parcel of the same ethnographic tradition which shifted the locus of research from individual 'tribes' to the 'Montagnards' as an ethnic category. Focusing on subjects like ethnolinguistic research and customary law, professional anthropologists carried on an ethnographic tradition started by Léopold Sabatier thirty years before. The major conceptual innovation that professional anthropologists promised – the study of 'acculturation' – was meant to insert it more firmly into the colonial governmentality that had caused the surge in ethnographic practice in the first place.

Yet, the *methodological* ethnographic innovations implied in professional anthropology would lead to a reconceptualization of self as the subject of research and to the (temporary) adoption of a new identity by the new generation of professional researchers. This is best brought out by the late Jacques Dournes who published his major pre-1954 monograph under the pseudonym Dam Bo, which was the name given to him by the 'Koho Sré' group. In this way he tried to convince his audience of the degree of his integration in Montagnard society. This adoption of indigenous names was typical of the new generation of anthropologists after World War II, who conducted fieldwork among the Montagnards. Writing in hindsight (1977), Dournes would analyse this pose of himself (Dam Bo), Condominas (Yo Sar Luk) and Boulbet (Dam Böt) in romantic terms:

> Yo Sar Luk, Dam Böt ... and myself, Dam Bo at the time, publicized our 'savage' names as the program of our dreams: This was the integration into a people, quite different from our community of origin, knowing well that we remained the Whites in the eyes of those who, we pretended, had adopted us – although we had been imposed upon them – and for whom our

strangeness excused our marginal lives and our privileges, within a context of colonization.

(Dournes 1977: 76)

Alternatively, we could analyse this pose in the perspective of the triangular relationship between 'colonial subjects', conceived as the universalizing subject of colonialism; as the subjects of colonial rule; and as the substantive topics of colonial discourse (cf. Pels and Salemink 1999: 3). Where earlier claims to ethnographic authority would be derived from the identification of the ethnographer with the universalizing colonial subject, the professional anthropologists would try to distance themselves from that governmental identity by assuming an identity as part of the community where they did their field research – the subjects of colonial rule. Positioning themselves in a mediating role between colonial subjects in the first and second senses, anthropologists thus enhanced claims to ethnographic authority when making statements on colonial subjects in the third sense. Intended to sanction professional anthropologists' claim to expert status in cultural brokerage and cultural management, this move had a similar discursive effect as those French-sanctioned fora where Montagnards were allowed to represent themselves, like at the Dalat Conference of 1946, or in the special issue of *Revue Éducation* (1949). This effect was to emphasize the empathetic proximity of French and Montagnard mentalities and the appropriateness of direct French rule in the Central Highlands, while subverting other (read: Vietnamese) claims to ethnographic authority concerning the Montagnards.

Ethnography as martial art

In the last section, we have seen that despite the formal reattachment of the *Pays Moï* to the Vietnamese state, French ethnographic discourse continued to emphasize the essential cultural unity of the Montagnards as fundamentally opposed to Vietnamese identity – both in ethnographic writing and in military propaganda. It was implied that the French not only bore the responsibility of protecting the Montagnards from the Vietnamese, but they even saw themselves as 'closer' to the Montagnards than the Kinh. Consequently, French ethnic policy was glorified as the 'salvation' of the Montagnards, both physically and culturally, who were depicted as loyal to the French. In the course of the French Indochina War, this image of a 'natural' Franco-Montagnard alliance became increasingly marred by the political and military developments in the Highlands. The French separatist ambitions in the Highlands proved to be formally untenable, while the burdens that their demand for manpower for the army, for corvée and for the plantations imposed on Montagnard society had the effect of alienating the Montagnards from the French. But the image was not only marred because of the failure of French ethnic policy in the Highlands, but also because of an apparent *'rapprochement'* between Montagnards and Viêt Minh. The steady military advance of the Viêt Minh in the Highlands was also attributed to their accommodation to Montagnard culture. The guerrilla tactics employed by the

Viêt Minh could only be successful if they heeded Mao Zedong's adage that the guerrilla had to move among the population like a fish in the water. In this respect, the training of Communist cadres was increasingly geared to the exigencies of life among non-Viêt peoples in the jungle. The famous 'eight orders' given by Hô Chí Minh, which amounted to professing respect for the local population and their culture, were important guidelines for establishing good working relations with local populations, including Montagnards. There were also stories of Viêt Minh cadres who totally immersed in local Montagnard societies by learning the language, dressing in loincloths, marrying local women and even filing their teeth. Undoubtedly, such stories were exaggerated, but the importance of such rumors lay in the fact that they were believed, and therefore stirred the French into action. In an intelligence report on the rapid Viêt Minh advance in Darlac province in 1951, it is observed that 'The Viet-Minh has a Moï policy, too', necessitating political action by the French military.[34]

The Viêt Minh successes on the battlefield, which by 1950 could no longer be denied, prompted a reassessment of the military tactics employed by the French military. In general, this entailed a move away from conventional warfare tactics to guerrilla tactics. This was not simply a tacit acknowledgment of the Viêt Minh military successes in the Highlands, but entailed an awareness that the war between the French and the Viêt Minh was as much a political as a military struggle. In fact, the French attempted an adaptation to the Viêt Minh strategy of incorporation of the local population in the war effort by responding to local aspirations on a more basic level than promising some sort of abstract autonomy in a fictional homeland. The new tactics employed by the French were the *Action psychologique* and the *Maquis*, which were both initiated in the Highlands in 1950.

The *Action Psychologique* was set up by Jean le Pichon, who had been commanding Montagnard militia for twenty years. In 1938 he had published an account of the Katu 'blood hunters (Pichon 1938), and during World War II he was a regular contributor to the weekly *Indochine*. The psychological action unit he headed was an integral part of the military effort, and consisted of three coordinated elements: propaganda, social action, and military action. Schools that had been set up in response to literacy campaigns mounted by the Viêt Minh were transformed into 'formation centres of Montagnard propagandists'. These *propagateurs* took care of the political training of village headmen, who were informed about the dubious character of Viêt Minh promises of autonomy, and of the Viêt in general. From 1953 a propaganda journal, *Le Petit Montagnard*, was available in four languages (Rhadé/Jarai, which were close anyway, Koho, Bahnar, Sedang) and distributed among Montagnard soldiers and other Montagnard 'brothers' [sic!]. The 'social action' which was coordinated with the Catholic mission consisted of the distribution of salt (a scarce product in the Highlands) and of medical care, in an effort to win Montagnards over to the French side. For the military action the Viêt Minh concept of the 'fighting village' was adopted and changed to suit French objectives. Characteristically, the French resettled the population of a number of scattered hamlets into one big agglomeration (*regroupement des villages*), which would then be defended by armed

Figure 5.5 Medical care as part of the French psychological warfare effort during the First Indochina War.

Source: Archives des Missions Étrangères de Paris.

youths from the village, trained and led by French soldiers (*organismes d'autodéfense*). These small-scale resettlement schemes, aimed at preventing Viêt Minh guerrillas from contacting village populations, heralded later, more massive American attempts to concentrate the rural population in strategic hamlets.[35]

The *Maquis* were commandos who tried to set up counter-guerrilla groups in enemy territory, and thus went much further in adapting to local cultures than the *Action psychologique*. Colonel Trinquier, the genius behind the *Maquis* in Indochina (*Maquis* was also the name of the anti-Nazi resistance in France during World War II), stated that it would be in vain to try to interest 'half savage peoples with a limited horizon' for the complexity of the Indochina War. Therefore, the only way to reach them was to play on their immediate interests and ambitions, and to revive old antagonisms, in particular against the ethnic Vietnamese. The idea was to parachute one or more French commandos of the *Groupes de Commandos Mixtes Aeroportés* (GCMA) among such groups to set up a self-defense system and to train recruits. Most of the ten *maquis* were in the northern mountains, where most of the heavy fighting took place; in the Central Highlands the French capitalized on a revolt against the Viêt Minh by the Hrê 'tribe' in Quang Ngãi. Among the Hrê, the Viêt Minh had felt sufficiently safe to step up their exactions in terms of taxes in foodstuff and labor, and to settle thousands of Việt migrants in Hrê territory, in a way making the same political mistake as the French with their plantations. When the Hrê revolted against this regime, reportedly killing hundreds of ethnic Vietnamese in their midst, the French immediately sent Captain Hentic to try and turn the Hrê, who feared a Việt Minh retaliation, into 'partisans'. In 1955, Hentic published his experiences among the Hrê under the pseudonym René Riesen, relating how he learned the language and adopted their lifestyle in order to win their confidence; how he married a Hrê girl in order to ally himself to a Hrê leader; and how he baptized his partisans *Độc Lập Hrê* ('Hrê Independence'), for they fought only for themselves – albeit against the same enemy as France, as Trinquier aptly noted.[36]

Even when the Hrê *Maquis* was initially successful, Hentic's eight batallions were no match for the regular Việt Minh units supported by Montagnard guerrillas from 1951 onward. Although the *Action Hrê* lasted until 1954, the French military efforts were not successful, as was shown in the steady deterioration of their position in the Highlands after 1950. This culminated in the annihilation of the elite *Groupe Mobile 100* near An Khê in June 1954. By that time – during the Geneva Conference of 1954 – only Ban Me Thuot and Dalat were still in French hands. According to Bernard Fall, 'whatever tribesmen had remained loyal to the French were now in the posts and camps, and the remainder retreated with the Viets into the inaccessible hills a few miles off the paths and roads' (Fall 1963b: 195–6). This may be explained by the fact that the Việt Minh had an overall strategy combining political and military struggle without disrupting factors. The example of the revolt of the Hrê shows that the Việt Minh also paid dearly when they broke their own code. However, the combination of political and military struggle remained a tactical ploy for the French, whose strategy was compounded by a continued reliance on conventional warfare tactics and undermined by the economic interests of the plantations. But even the political struggle was waged clumsily, if we may believe the British journalist Norman when he described the arrest of around 80 inhabitants of a village who did not wish to inform on the Việt Minh; 20 'had been strung up', the others were tortured and kept in prison for at least another three months (Lewis 1951: 144).[37] It is hard to imagine what sort of propaganda could undo the effects of such action.

In this section I have briefly described two French counterinsurgency programs, the *Action psychologique* and the *Maquis*, which attempted to draw Montagnards into the French war effort by adapting to some degree to local culture and society. These programs were prompted by Việt Minh military successes in the Highlands which effectively subverted a self-complacent French ethnographic discourse on mutual Kinh-Montagnard antagonism. On the other hand, these programs could only be implemented in the context of this powerful discourse, and were conditioned by constant reference to the cumulative discursive effect of decades of ethnographic practice. But even that position became politically untenable as the nominally independent Vietnamese state under Emperor Bao Dai asserted sovereignty over the 'PMS' with its own *Plan de Développement économique pour les PMS du Domaine de la Couronne* drafted by Bao Dai's *Chef de cabinet* Nguyên Dê (1953). Like the French, Nguyên Dê wished to fix the 'primitive and nomadic' Montagnard populations to the soil by introducing modern agricultural techniques, but the main difference with French programs was that he wished to promote the migration of lowlanders into the Central Highlands (1953: 5–6). Though conceived too late to be implemented before 1954, Nguyên Dê's plans heralded later, massive internal colonization schemes by the Diêm regime and the Socialist Republic of Vietnam. In the next section, I briefly sketch some of the effects of these complex discursive and political developments on Montagnards in one of the most intimate ways how people conceive of themselves in society: their gender identity.

Ethnography and gender transformation in matrilineal societies

Until now we have practically reinscribed the process of ethnicization by using the generic term 'Montagnard' as a general label for the highland populations of Central Vietnam, thus ignoring cultural difference within and between these populations. In the same vein, we have virtually ignored gender differences and differentiation, even though French rule had marked consequences for gender relations and identities. This is especially true for the matrilineal societies of the Rhadé and Jarai, which were drawn into a war that almost exclusively engaged males, providing men with avenues to – albeit subordinate – power in the colonial hierarchy, while denying women the rights they traditionally enjoyed. Observers like Marcel Ner, Professor of the Ethnology of Indochina at the French Colonial School, argued for preservation of this gender balance. In an 'ethnopsychological' analysis, he assigned the Montagnards low evolutionary status:

> To the extent that he [sic!] is penetrated by the social, the Moï is, according to the formula of psychoanalysts, a 'familial animal,' or more exactly a 'domestic animal,' rather than a 'political animal'.
>
> (Ner 1952: 166)

Given the female domestic predominance, Montagnard males would not be bothered by an Oedipus complex, resulting in psychological resistance not against the father but against the outside world. In order to preserve harmony with nature and within the community, Ner argued that the prominent position of females better not be undermined:

> It appears serious to us to break that equilibrium while we are not capable of reestablishing it on a new level.
>
> (Ner 1952: 177)

Others however, like the aforementioned military ethnographer Albert Maurice, spoke favorably of the weakening of the position of women in matrilineal Rhadé society, which was often labeled 'matriarchal'. Maurice chose to call this process, brought about by Western colonization, 'male emancipation' (Maurice 1956: 11).

This process, which I would rather analyse in terms of gender transformation, was accelerated during the consecutive Indochina Wars. In using the concept of gender transformation, I am inspired by Carla Risseeuw's definition:

> This term implies that through macro-economic and social change, women and men find themselves in changed positions vis-à-vis each other, both in society at large and on the micro-level of family and interpersonal relationships. Secondly, their conception of themselves and their sex is similarly subject to change, which validates the use of the term gender over that of sex.
>
> (Risseeuw 1988: 14)

Risseeuw applies this concept to analyse changes affecting women in colonial Ceylon in order to better understand current resistance strategies for women in contemporary Sri Lanka. In this context, the term gender transformation appears to be particularly appropriate to trace the effects of ethnographic discourse and related ethnic policy in the Highlands, linked to changes in control and disposal of property through kinship, marriage and inheritance. In her book, Risseeuw notes an apparent lack of open conflict and a seeming female acquiescence concerning loss of control over land and resources. In one of the propositions accompanying her dissertation (1988), she asserts that '[i]n the course of history the position of women in various societies has deteriorated more often because of an intensified struggle over resources among the more powerful (males) than by a direct attempt of the latter to curb their position.' The ultimate struggle waged by males over resources is, of course, war. In Chapter 3 I have briefly analysed the consequences of gendered ethnographic occasions with respect to Sabatier's codification of Rhadé customary law. In this section, then, I shall focus on the gendered effects of war as an ethnographic occasion privileging men and excluding women from access to essential resources, by gleaning the scarce references to this largely 'invisible' process.

Among the two major matrilineal, matrilocal Austronesian language groups in the Highlands, Rhadé and Jarai, women traditionally played an important position in society because they controlled access to land and assets through the inheritance system which largely excluded in-marrying males. Village-wide periodic reallocation of land in the rotational shifting cultivation system, and continuous redistribution of food within clans or extended families (traditionally living together in longhouses) or through feasting, all combined to ensure women and their families had more or less secure livelihoods. This security was upheld by practices concerning adoption, taking domestic servants or 'slaves' (for indebtedness), and by marriage rules which proscribed marriage partners from clans belonging to the same phratry (considered incest) while prescribing preferential partners from certain other clans (real or classificatory cross cousins). While courting was initiated by the girl or her family, there were certain rules about replacement of a deceased husband by his younger brother in order to continue the alliance between the two families and in order not to upset the economic exchanges between the two families. Outsiders considered this to be to the advantage of the wife and her family (Dournes 1972; De Hautecloque-Howe 1985).

Missionaries, administrators, military officers, teachers and medical personnel would condemn and combat precisely those practices as 'savage' which provided support for women's access to assets and resources within this agricultural and kinship system. Shifting cultivation was seen as a waste of forest resources, and communal land rights, periodically ritually affirmed by a (female) guardian of the land (*pô lan*) in Rhadé society, were not recognized by the colonial administration. 'Slavery' and domestic service – often confused and misunderstood – were actively combated, depriving poor or indebted people from a secure livelihood by becoming part of the creditor's household. Also, colonial administrators discouraged the custom of substituting a deceased husbands by their younger brothers as 'tyrannical', thereby not simply reflecting their male bias, but in practice eroding the livelihoods of widows and their offspring.

In order to be able to govern the disparate and diverse Montagnard populations, the colonial administration had appointed village headmen early on, and invested these headmen with a degree of authority that village elders had never had before. In a 1937 report to the Minister of Colonies, then Governor-General Brévié linked the question of village headmen to the administrative circumscription of ethnic groups and the codification of customary law:

> It will be essential to determine the groupings that could be constituted, and that will be encompassed in distinct administrative circumscriptions. We shall re-create the ancient tribes, and we shall give each village a chief whom we will support with all our authority. We shall create chiefs where we need. ... It will therefore be all-important to codify these oral arrangements [*coutumiers* – OS] while making, with caution, the necessary modifications.[38]

References to the 're-creation' of the 'old tribes' by appointing village heads in an effort to strengthen Montagnard society against the putative onslaught by Kinh colonizers have dotted French administrative/ethnographic narratives ever since Sabatier's *Palabre du Serment* (1930; see also Guilleminet 1952a: 394). By instituting male village headmen and modifying (by codifying) customary law as part of colonial governmentality, ethnographic occasions became institutionalized as an exclusively male interaction between native chiefs and colonial administrators from which women were systematically excluded. The *Palabre du serment*, the oath-swearing ceremony of (male) Montagnard 'chiefs' to the French administration is a case in point. Thus, the space for women to represent themselves in their own societies and to protect their interests was effectively curtailed.

Other changes in the matrilineal societies occurred not because of direct administrative interventions on the village level, but because of new career opportunities for men outside the confines of village society. Many ethnographic narratives hinted at the appetite for adventure among younger Rhadé and Jarai males, as evidenced in epics (*khan*) and other forms of oral literature. Condominas, for instance, interprets the Rhadé *Chant épique de Kdam Yi* as 'revenge by the man [the hero of the epic-OS] for the grip by the clan dominated by the women: "Superman" in revolt against almighty "Mom"' (1980: 228). In his 'Observations sociologiques sur deaux chants épiques rhadés' of 1955 (reprinted in 1980), Condominas interprets the exploits and adventures of the (male) heroes of the epics as an escape from female predominance in Rhadé society, and therefore as revolt against the authority of mothers, sisters and/or wives – even though the most famous culture hero *Dam San* ultimately conforms to matrilineal custom (for Jarai *akhan*, see also Dournes 1972: 257). Writing about changing male and female identities in Jarai society, Dournes describes the male tendency to escape their customary responsibilities by resorting to adventurism – war, vagabondage, and peddling. In the context of the French colonial presence and the Indochina War, Dournes observes 'at present an alarming number of youngsters that are recruited as mercenaries in this foreign war, which interests them only as a convenient life style' (Dournes 1972: 262). Not surprisingly, then, both the French colonial army and the Viêt Minh were able to recruit the largest numbers of Montagnard youngsters among the Rhadé and Jarai groups, providing these young men with new (military) career and lifestyle options vaguely reminiscent of the adventures of their culture heroes – warriors from a mythical era. In the words of the military ethnographer Captain Maurice (1947), the French:

> presence has established peace and put an end to the political anarchy that still reigned at the beginning of the century and, undoubtedly, since millennia. Today, the warrior instincts of the [Rhadé] tribe bloom within our *bataillons montagnards.*

Perhaps Maurice was too optimistic about that peace, but he was right about the military career opportunities for Montagnards.

During French colonial rule, military careers were not the only new alternatives to the escapist series of 'warrior, vagabond and peddler', noted by Dournes. The administration created new administrative positions such as village headmen, *chefs du canton*, judges in the customary law tribunals, clerks or schoolteachers. The 'Franco-Montagnard' schools, based on the model of Sabatier's Franco-Rhadé school, were mostly male affairs. These new career opportunities were an exclusively male domain, the more so in a situation of matrilocality where males were effectively circulating and where women, guardians of the family land and assets, were traditionally tied to the (long)house from which they derived their dominant economic status. As a departure from matrilineal custom, Dournes (1972: 239–73) notes a tendency toward urbanization among Jarai, fed by male contempt for manual, agricultural labor and by their ambition to take up new, more prestigious positions: 'The man finds new occupations and attracts the woman to follow suit' (251; see also De Hautecloque 1985: 85–6). This male ambition is well brought out in a the writing of a Rhadé schoolteacher, Y Bih Nie Kdam, also quoted by Condominas (1955):

> Nominally the man is head of the house, but in reality it is the woman who has a preponderant place there. Since he is more or less bought by the woman, he comes to live with her in order to work for her family's well-being and in order to increase the heritage of his wife. The poor husband, who has slaved to enrich the house with gongs, jars, buffaloes and elephants, can only enjoy these assets while living with his spouse or when, after her death, a replacement is selected from her sisters or grand-daughters; without that he loses all his rights and has to leave the house, taking only a very small number of his [sic!] belongings with him. All the rest goes back to the family. On the other hand, if the husband dies, his family also must give a replacement to the widow, chosen from the brothers or nephews of the deceased, in order to continue to feed the family and guard the assets.
>
> (Y Bih Nie-Kdam 1949a: 31–32)

This assessment of men's status may have been a gross exaggeration since Jarai and Ede men had dominant roles in most military, political and ritual affairs as well as a key positions in economic decision-making in their own clan by virtue of their position as brother or uncle. In contrast to women, in the traditional system men could become 'big men' by manipulating these various roles and distributing accumulated goods through feasting (De Hautecloque 1985: 74–86). Yet, Y Bih Nie-Kdam's statement evokes the sentiment among 'acculturated' Ede and Jarai men that the traditional matrilineal and matrilocal system was effectively stifling their ambitions to develop their own careers and assets.

The imposition of colonial rule and the construction of a Vietnamese nation-state effectively turned the Montagnards into ethnic minorities whose cultural practices were at best at variance and at worst in conflict with statutory law, despite French 'recognition' of customary law. The male monopolization of relations with the outside powers that would become arbiters in any dispute gradually disadvantaged the position of women in the villages. The appropriation of Montagnard lands for the establishment of plantations – and later by Kinh settlers – ate away from the assets guarded by matrilineal clans, thus gradually undermining the economic underpinnings of relative gender equality. The recruitment of Montagnard males for the colonial army and for plantation labor, the taxation in terms of money and especially corvée labor led to a scarcity of male labor in the villages, rendering the position of the mostly women, children and elderly people who stayed behind, more difficult. More career opportunities for men gave them sources of income and of authority that went beyond the usual, thereby creating strains in a system of matrilocal residence where assets traditionally remained within the wife's clan. The imbalance grew out of proportion during the war which ravaged the Central Highlands. With thousands of Montagnards in the French colonial army (and thousands more fighting with the Viêt Minh); with thousands of others working on plantations, as porters or as road workers as part of the corvee system, away from their native villages; with villages being destroyed by fighting, being relocated into the jungle (to flee the fighting or as Viêt Minh 'fighting village' or being resettled as part of a Government-sponsored program), traditional residence patterns were disrupted. While the tragedy of war touched the lives of everybody in the Central Highlands, women were disproportionately affected in their social position as well as through a number of interlocking processes that took place over a longer period of time but that gained momentum during the First Indochina War.

I would like to highlight three of these processes here, two of which have to do with changes in residence patterns. The frequent relocation of villages during the war effectively sped up the process of breaking up of the longhouses, traditionally comprising of varying numbers of individual households (hearths) belonging to the same clan, into individual household units. Like the other processes of gender transformation described in this section, this process began earlier and is still going on under the influence of consecutive wars and policies of the two consecutive Vietnamese governments before and after 1975. While the first French missionaries and explorers in the Central Highlands tended to see the longhouses as dominated by the clan elder(s) or big man who happened to be representing the clan to the outside world, in fact the longhouse constituted a resource for the women who formed the backbone of the matrilineal clan and who supported each other in various ways. Even if each household within the longhouse retained some degree of autonomy, its splitting up into individual units tended to render women more dependent on their husbands – and therefore more vulnerable if their husbands were away.

A closely related development in residence patterns was the situation where wives followed their husbands in their pursuit of new careers, as soldiers, clerks, teachers, plantation workers, etc. While the breaking up of the longhouses did not necessarily mean a departure from matrilocal residence if the husband came to live in the village and in the vicinity of the wife's extended family, this definitely meant a break with tradition, even if it is not a transition to a patrilocal residence system. More often than not, the wife would follow her husband to a new location altogether, wherever he made his living; this could be a school, a town or a military camp. For the woman, the result was that she would be physically separated from her clan and from the family assets, while becoming dependent on her husband's income and on her own labor (if she continued to grow food) for a livelihood. While she would perhaps have a better income this way and derive some indirect prestige from her husband's position, she would become more vulnerable as she would no longer have easy access to the security provided by an extended family – a badly needed asset during the vagaries of war.

A third, and again related development was a gradual change in customary ownership and inheritance arrangements, reflecting the social changes taking place in these traditional matrilineal societies. With men acquiring their own sources of income through salaries or through successful commercial or agricultural enterprises (in particular small coffee or tea plantations), they would develop their own assets (e.g. individual land titles) which they would be less inclined to share with their wives' families. With the expansion of state governance over the Central Highlands and the resulting superimposition of state law on societies governed by culturally very different customary law arrangements, people have more strategic options to choose from, and customary law becomes only one of these options. In actual practice, customary law is not immutable but changes over time – despite French codification – to reflect social and cultural changes in society, and the changing terms for reconciliation between groups. De Hautecloque (1985: 255–64) reported one case from 1962 regarding the summoning back of a husband to live with his wife's family after having already spent three years with his mother. During the three day-and-night rituals and deliberations between the two families for the series of compensations required for settling this case, the husband's mother makes a remarkable statement regarding one asset, a coffee plantation that the husband had developed:

> By the way, says she, Y Suai's coffee plantation that normally should remain our property will continue to be taken care of by him. He alone has taken the pain to weed and plant. This year there will be flowers, next year there will be fruits. If he succeeds in selling them, he will divide the revenue of the sale with H'Dang [his daughter] and that will do. In two years, she continues, his parents-in-law will have fully recuperated the value of the gong in the dowry with the value of the coffee.
>
> (De Hautecloque 1985: 261–2)

The novelty in this is that the husband retains title to the plantation that he started as customary law practice adapts to changing social and economic circumstance.

In this section, we have seen how war has accelerated a process of gender transformation in the two main matrilineal societies of Vietnam, leading to a redefinition of gender roles and identities in changing circumstance. These changing gender relations have by and large been disadvantageous for women, who gradually lost access to some of their most important resources, sometimes even their traditional assets, including land. While it is impossible to determine precisely cause and effect, it is obvious that men's monopolization over the ethnographic occasions that form the basis for ethnographic discourse, and women's exclusion from representing their interests, have resulted in a situation in which men benefited from changes to the detriment of women. In a situation where ethnographic discourse claimed to protect Montagnard tradition from outside corruption, this may be an ironic observation. On the other hand, insofar as this ethnographic discourse was part and parcel of a colonial governmentality aiming at controlling the strategic Central Highlands area and its population militarily, this observation is not very surprising, for during wartime one of the main ethnographic occasions is contextualized by male camaraderie in the colonial army.

Concluding remarks

Although the French lost the First Indochina War, the effects of the War and wartime ethnographic discourse on Montagnard identity were very real. In the first sections we noted how strategic and political considerations led the French authorities to reconsider Montagnard ethnic identity. After a process of tribalization (construction of tribes with their own territories) a process of ethnicization (construction of an ethnic minority within a state) was inaugurated, which was closely connected to the territorialization of French power over the Highlands. From tribes with different languages and cultures, inhabiting bounded territories, the Montagnards were now conceived of as fundamentally one ethnic group – despite perceived linguistic and cultural differences – opposed to the major nations of Indochina, in particular the Vietnamese. This was attended by a revival of ethnographic practice, institutionalized in scientific institutes, and by an ethnographic discourse which proclaimed the value of the Montagnards for colonial rule as well as their cultural 'value' as equal to that of their neighbors. Though the imposition of this discourse was hampered by competing claims to sovereignty over the Central Highlands, the creation of the PMSI by D'Argenlieu created a political community with a fixed territory comprising four Highland provinces in Annam plus Dalat, reflecting the habitats of the four major 'tribes' (Bahnar, Jarai, Rhadé, Koho). Although the boundaries of the PMSI did not coincide with those of the ethnolinguistic map of Indochina (with many Montagnard populations living in Laos, Cambodia and other Vietnamese provinces, and with Kinh living in Highland towns), it was taken for granted that this was exclusive 'Montagnard territory'. The *Statut particulier* was the legal body for this colonial territorializing policy. Thus, for strategic purposes the French created a Montagnard political community within the Vietnamese State, implying the merging of a plurality of tribes into one Montagnard ethnic group.

The war proved to be fertile ground for the professionalization of ethnography, which partly coincided with the process of the institutionalization of ethnography. This resulted in new forms of cultural relativism, linked to the new method of ethnographic fieldwork and a redefinition of self by researchers as mediators between the subjects of colonial rule and the universalizing colonial subject. Yet, the discursive effect of the new, professional anthropology was similar to that of the 'relativist' amateur ethnography, in that it construed the Montagnards as fundamentally different from and antagonistic to the lowland Vietnamese. This hegemonic ethnographic narrative formed the discursive context for French counterinsurgency programs, which inserted themselves in this discourse, although they were more directly motivated by military and political developments on the battlefield that seemed to negate and subvert this discourse of Franco-Montagnard closeness and Montagnard-Viêt antagonism. In the last section, then, I sketched some effects of the changing colonial discourse and practice in terms of changing gender relations in two matrilieal societies. War proved a special *préterrain* as well as a special ethnographic occasion, which resulted in an ethnographic proliferation as well as in changing relations between people, e.g. in terms of gender.

6   Romancing the Montagnards

American counterinsurgency and Montagnard autonomy

'To seize and control the highlands is to solve the whole problem of South Vietnam,' General Giap once said, and most American and Vietnamese military experts agree with him.

Robert Shaplen, The Lost Revolution (1966: 173)[1]

Introduction

In July 1954 the Geneva Agreements were concluded, providing for a ceasefire, a troop partition and a temporary division of Vietnam along the 17th parallel, pending general election scheduled for 1956. The United States government, present at the Geneva Conference, did not subscribe to its outcome, fearing a Communist takeover in Vietnam, either by way of arms or through democratic elections which Hô Chí Minh was expected to win. Instead, the southern part of Vietnam was consolidated as a separate state, on the basis of the nominally independent regime under Emperor Bao Đai and of the Vietnamese troops who had fought for the French. Since 1950, French military effort had been increasingly dependent on American financial and material support, coordinated by the Military Assistance Advisory Group (MAAG Indochine). In the spring of 1954 American advisors had been detached with pro-French Vietnamese units, expanding the American military role even before Geneva. After Geneva, the staunchly anti-Communist Catholic mandarin Ngô Đình Diêm was appointed Prime Minister at US insistence. An American advisory team under Colonel Edward Lansdale succeeded in wresting control over key elements in the South Vietnamese Army from the French, and secured Diêm's position by eliminating important political rivals, including the emperor himself. By the end of 1955, Diêm had become President of an independent and anti-Communist Republic of Viet Nam (RVN), which was financed, advised and to a large extent controlled by the United States.

While the Americans succeeded the French as protectors of a nominally independent Vietnamese state, the context of American domination of South Vietnam from 1954 to 1975 was very different from French colonial rule. Although Vietnam had been recognized as an independent state within the *Union*

Française in 1949, the French continued to exert direct influence over the *Domaine de la Couronne du Pays Montagnard du Sud* through the persons of emperor Bao Ðai and his *Chef de cabinet* Nguyên Ðê. After 1954, however, direct American rule was impossible, as the Geneva Agreements obliged the US to restrict their performance to an advisory role through a numerically limited presence. As a result, the American advisors relied more on their Vietnamese counterparts in the 1950s. During that period, there was no American presence worth mentioning in the Central Highlands. This changed in the early 1960s, when American Special Forces under CIA control started to organize Montagnard warriors in the so-called Village Defense Program, later known as Citizens' Irregular Defense Groups (CIDG) and Regional and Popular Forces (RF/PF). The direct American presence changed both the political and the cultural landscape of the Central Highlands, apart from the tremendous changes brought about by the war and the various counterinsurgency and pacification programs. Before turning to the Special Forces narratives and its relation to Montagnards, we will examine earlier American plans and discourses on the Highlands and its population.

OSS plans in World War II

The model for the American experience with the Montagnards had been set in World War II by the well-known ethno-psychiatrist Georges Devereux. Devereux was born in 1908 as György Dobo in Lugoj, which passed from Hungary to Romania in the wake of World War I. In 1926 he fled from Rumanian discrimination and from his petty bourgeois milieu to Paris, where he tried several studies and trades. Only in 1931 did he start studying ethnology at the *Institut d'Ethnologie*. His teachers Lucien Lévy-Bruhl, Paul Rivet and especially Marcel Mauss were impressed by his rapid progress, and succeeded in obtaining a Rockefeller grant for him to do ethnographic fieldwork, after which he was promised an assignment with the *Musée de l'Homme*. In line with the earlier interests of both Mauss – who wrote the *carnet d'ethnographie* for the *Ecole Française d'Extrême-Orient* in 1900 – and Lévy-Bruhl – who stimulated Sabatier to publish his ethnographic notes on the Rhadé – this fieldwork was to be executed among the Sedang. The Sedang were a 'Moï tribe' that had hardly been studied because they were considered dangerous. Devereux was first sent to the United States, were he was to learn the anthropological profession at Berkeley. After a successful field study among the Mohave Indians, he was sent to Indochina, where he would stay for 18 months among the Sedang. After his Ph.D. in 1935, he published several small articles on the Sedang in *Man* and *Primitive Man*, with titles like 'Functioning Units in Ha(rh)ndea(ng) Society' (1937). Influenced by psychoanalysis after World War II, he acquired fame as ethno-psychiatrist in the United States, where he developed friendships with major anthropologists like Ralph Linton, Weston La Barre and Margaret Mead. His most influential work, partly based on his Sedang fieldnotes, is *From Anxiety to Method in the Behavioral Sciences* (1967), preceded by a foreword by Weston La Barre. In it, Devereux argues that the study of man produces psychological anxieties which should not be warded off with pseudo-methodology, but which the observer should take seriously and analyse.[2]

Right from the outbreak of World War II in 1939, Devereux tried to be admitted to the US Army, because he wished to fight Hitler's tyranny. Because of his 'suspicious' background he succeeded only in 1943. In that year he was attached as psychological warfare expert with the rank of US Navy lieutenant to the Office of Strategic Services (OSS) in China. The OSS was the American agency responsible for unconventional warfare, and is generally regarded as forerunner of the CIA. The commander of Naval Group, China, and director Far East of the OSS was Commodore Milton E. Miles, at a time when the China-Burma-India theatre was not yet split up, and Japan still had the upper hand in Burma and China. Miles was 'to prepare the China coast in any way [...] for US Navy landings in three or four years' (Tuchman 1970: 314; also Spector 1985: 24–8). This also entailed the preparation of French Indochina, which was linked to the Axis through the Fascist Vichy government in France, and which acquiesced in a strong military presence of Japanese troops on its soil. Not only was Miles interested in using the naval possibilities offered by Cam Ranh Bay, but he also set up various intelligence networks, involving Free French in China and Indochina, and Vietnamese nationalists. Apart from an important intelligence action under the French Captain Meynier, Commodore Miles set up a 'Special Military Plan for Indochina' which envisaged the utilization of the Montagnards for guerrilla warfare against the Japanese. This plan, thought out and developed by Georges Devereux, and was to be executed by a group of twenty unconventional warfare experts, to be headed by Devereux himself.

In 'A Program for Guerrilla Warfare in French Indochina', drafted by Miles and Devereux, the group should either be landed near Kontum or parachuted in the nearby region of Tea Ha, where Devereux had done fieldwork among the Sedang, in May 1943. The purpose was to hold some 10,000 square kilometres of jungle and recruit a minimum of 20,000 men in the hinterland of Annam within four to five months, in order to 'interfere with communications, tie up enemy forces, offer a rallying ground for French patriots and native opponents of the Japanese, and to operate behind enemy lines in the coming battle of Burma'. Burma was not only the major reason for the action, but also the model to follow, in particular the use of Karen warriors by the British. Devereux wanted educated, tolerant people in his team, preferably anthropologists and psychologists, who should be fluent in French. After chapters on training, equipment, conduct, 'the sex problem', and 'tactics vs. superstitions', the general strategy was outlined as 'pit the brown races (jungle-tribes, Laotian, Cambodian) against the yellow races, by asserting that the Japanese are just another kind of Annamites'. Under the caption 'the problem of command', Devereux stated that political considerations should precede military viewpoints, because 'partisans can be had only by the use of personal influence and political tact', not by 'a call to arms for freedom's sake'. He was very insistent on the issues of courtesy and 'gentle behavior' toward the Montagnard partisans and of respect for their beliefs and customs.[3]

In June 1943, however, Rear Admiral W.R. Purnell of the US Navy and Colonel W.J. Donovan of the OSS expressed doubts about Devereux' capacities as military commander of the guerrilla group, which was then being trained in Fort Benning, Georgia.[4] Devereux objected strongly to a change of command in a 'Memorandum on the proposed change in command' of 22 June to Purnell, Donovan, and Captain J.C. Metzel of the Joint Chiefs of Staff. He stated that the very success of the venture depended on it being executed by an explicitly American unit, because a group 'under French command and represent(ing) France … will be massacred by the very natives we hope to secure as allies'. The reasons were that 'the natives hate the French as bitterly as they hate the yellow races', and that the French would 'think of these natives as subjects who can be ordered to fight' instead of 'coax(ing) them into fighting'. Also, a 'French' group would be unwilling to fight a French regime, and would be technically regarded as 'rebels', even if it included Americans. Devereux clearly resented being sent on what he considered a 'suicide mission'.[5] On the other hand, his person was indispensable for the action, the more so since most of the group members were handpicked by Devereux himself from among his friends, including the anthropologist Weston La Barre.

Despite the urgency of the operation, which should have started in the middle of August if it was to help the Burma campaign, and in spite of the transport facilities promised by General Claire Chennault of the Fourteenth US Air Force (Flying Tigers), a stalemate developed. The matter was further complicated by the formation of the 'Committee for National Liberation' under the joint leadership of Generals De Gaulle and Giraud on 3 June 1943, which put up *la France combattante* as one of the allied partners and immediately sent a mission to China. Naturally, the 'Free French' were not much enamored of Devereux' plans which were based on an alleged anti-French sentiment among the Montagnards. Not content with only two French officers participating, the Free French claimed command of the action, which was to take place in their colony, and demanded coordination with the Meynier group operating in Indochina, which had their full support. Although General Joseph Stillwell, commander of the China Theatre and chief advisor to Chiang Kai-Shek, gave moral support to the Indochina plans, he was not prepared to allow the Devereux group to enter China because of the presence of a De Gaulle mission to China in early July.[6]

On July 5, Devereux requested to be relieved of his command as his authority was increasingly questioned, and he was replaced as executive officer by Major William Young. This did not end the quarrels, because his superiors in OSS training camps were reported to 'feel strongly against sending this man into the field with any command or responsibilities whatsoever', basing their conclusions upon their 'experiences with the subject in (their) own camps, plus the knowledge … obtained concerning him from his contemporaries in the academic world'. The whole plan was jeopardized further when the senior French officer in the group wrote to Captain Metzel that he would withdraw if Devereux were to be part of the group at all.[7] Whatever the personal issues, the change in personnel did not resolve the political dilemma of American action in a French colony, however, and the plan was delayed until it was finally shelved by October, 1943. Of course, other developments deprived the plan of its priority status. American strategic attention in Asia shifted from the China Theatre to the Pacific, rendering an invasion of China superfluous. Also, the growing importance of the Free French made open action against Vichy-French colonial possessions rather awkward, the more so because of the wavering attitude of President Roosevelt on (French) colonialism and self-determination for Asian nations. Soon after, health problems caused Devereux to be discharged from active duty altogether.

After the war, Devereux speculated on 'the potential contributions of the Moi to the cultural landscape of Indochina' in a small article in the *Far Eastern Quarterly*, at a time (1947) when an American audience began to be interested in Indochina as one of the hot spots of the nascent Cold War. Stressing the Moi tribes' perennial independence from the surrounding nations, he clearly chose sides against the Vietnamese claims to the Highlands and for the French, whose rule he now described as 'neither harsh nor exploitive' (1947: 392). Perceiving 'inherent potentialities for cultural development' (1947: 391) among the Montagnards, Devereux felt that the necessary guidance should 'be provided by the racially and linguistically related Cambodians', for:

> A Cambodian-Moi cultural unit, in which the somewhat effete, though delightful, Cambodian civilization would be rejuvenated by Moï vigor, could contribute a rich and leavening element to the creative and dynamic cultural balance of the Indochinese Union.
>
> (1947: 395)

In retrospect, it is possible to discern in Devereux' 'special plan' of 1943 a model for later American action toward the Montagnards. First, the Americans considered themselves as uncommitted to any French, Vietnamese or other historical claims to the Central Highlands, and regarded the area as *res nullius*, at least initially. Second, they could claim no sovereignty over the Highlands, as did the French or the Vietnamese, which posed formal restrictions on any action in the region. Third, despite this lack of immediacy, they had a strong urge for direct action in order to engage the Montagnards against their enemies, be they Japanese, French, or Vietnamese. Fourth, the problems concerning Devereux' command may seem personal, but they anticipate later conflicts between political and military views of guerrilla warfare with respect to the Montagnards, which became very much evident in the command problems over the Special Forces in the 1960s. Last, the political approach propagated by Devereux played on an assumed sense of animosity of Montagnards against any others ('yellow races', 'French'), and thus effectively promoted their political autonomy. Although organizational difficulties and political arguments with the 'Free French' caused the delay and eventual cancellation of the plan late in 1943, a model of direct contact with the Montagnards to the exclusion of anything other than American influence had already been set well before the later Indochina Wars.

Nation-building and assimilation of minorities

With the conclusion of the Geneva Agreements in 1954, the Central Highlands fell into the French-controlled zone, although by that time the French position had become almost as untenable there as in the northern mountain region. During the troop withdrawal on both sides, around 140,000 persons went north with the Viêt Minh, including around 6000 Edê warriors (Hickey 1982b: 13–16). Naturally, these Montagnards believed – as did their leaders – that they would return victoriously to their homeland within two years, after successful elections. In the mean time, they were prepared for their future leading positions in the Hanoi-based Southern Ethnic Minority Cadre School. Also, some 800,000 migrants, mostly Catholics, went southward, exhorted by their priests and by American propaganda, to escape the anticipated oppression by the Communist regime in the north. Many of the northern refugees were resettled in the Central Highlands, on lands which were considered empty by Vietnamese officials and American advisors alike, but which Montagnards considered theirs (Fall 1966; Pelzer 1961; Wickert 1959). Wolf Ladejinsky, for example, a Cold War agricultural expert who became personal advisor to Diêm after being introduced by Colonel Lansdale, approvingly described President Diêm's 'agrarian policy' of resettling 60,000 lowlanders in the High Plateau, which he described as a 'wilderness ... where three years ago virtually none but nomadic tribesmen lived', and hence 'little more than Bao Ðai's hunting preserve' (Ladejinsky 1961: 164, 306).

Diêm's Republic of Viet-Nam (RVN) received massive military, economic and political support from the United States. American development discourse during the Cold War was informed by the influential modernization school of Walt W. Rostow, which focused on economic development and nation building (Gendzier 1985).[8] From this perspective, the Montagnards were regarded as minor obstacles in the process of establishing an integral Vietnamese nation-state. Some American experts like Frederic Wickert even foresaw their imminent extinction as an ethnic group, as they 'will have to integrate themselves economically and politically into the larger, more aggressive Vietnamese culture' (Wickert 1959: 135). In his monumental *Free in the Forest* (1982b) Gerald Hickey noted the leveling tendencies of a modernization discourse shared by political leaders and social scientists, who tend to either ignore cultural and ethnic diversity or treat it as a nuisance to the nation-building project. He cites, among others, Fredric Barth (1969) who maintains that modernization, while reducing cultural difference, does not necessarily entail a decreasing importance of ethnic boundaries. In his post-war *Ethnohistory*, Hickey claims that Diêm's policy of assimilation and 'Vietnamization' has effectively contributed 'to the rise rather than the demise of ethnic identity' (1982b: 7). Yet, during the war Hickey, too, shared the feeling that Montagnard 'culture is fatal. Modernity is spreading; the old ways are being displaced by the new ways ... The Montagnard culture is gradually being destroyed'.[9]

Considered strategically unimportant during the 1950s, the Montagnards did not receive much attention from Americans, whose opinions generally reflected and rationalized South-Vietnamese practice. This is evident from the attitude of

Lt.-Gen. Samuel ('Hanging Sam') Williams, head of the Military Assistance and Advisory Group (MAAG) in Vietnam in 1954–55, when a separate Republic of Viet Nam (RVN) was being forged out of the French zone after the armistice. Gen. Williams was responsible for building the Army of the RVN, geared toward conventional rather than guerrilla warfare. In 1955, French officers offered to turn over their tribal *Maquis* in the Highlands to the Americans. This concerned the *Maquis* of the *Action Hrê, Sedang* and similar programs like the *Bataillons Montagnards*, and the *Action Psychologique* led by Jean le Pichon, because French officers involved in these programs – first of all Colonel Roger Trinquier who had set up the *Maquis d'Indochine* – were known to resent the abandonment of their tribal *protégés* to the Vietnamese, an act which they regarded as betrayal. Trinquier expressed his shame for this episode in the epilogue to *Les Maquis d'Indochine* (1976: 189–90), where he also reported that in 1964 he turned down an offer of the American Institute for Defense Analysis to direct their Special Forces program for fear that the *anciens maquisards* would be betrayed again – this time by the Americans.[10] The French-born Lucien Conein, a former liaison officer between the OSS and the French resistance during World War II who worked for the CIA in Saigon as member of the famous Lansdale Mission, transmitted the message to General Williams in Saigon and to his superiors in the Department of Defense, but he never even received a reply for lack of interest.[11] Basing himself on an interview with Lucien Conein, Alfred McCoy claims that the plan was dismissed by the Department of Defense in Washington, because 'they wanted nothing to do with any French program' (McCoy 1972: 107; see also Dassé 1976: 169–72), but in an interview in 1990 Lucien Conein told the present author that no particular reason was given.[12] Martial Dassé noted that by 1961, however, the Special Forces would resume just this French program, albeit on a much larger scale (Dassé 1976: 169–72).

On the other hand, we have Edward Lansdale's account of his pressure on Diêm to reform Vietnamese policies in tribal areas, and of their organization in 'Self-Defense Corps'. He noted that 'officers on [his] staff started sporting bracelets that denoted their adoption into tribes, although I kept the visits of the Americans brief, not wanting us to get between the tribes and the Vietnamese as the French had done – and as the US military men were to a decade later' (Lansdale 1972: 327). Lansdale, who was credited to be the American counterinsurgency expert *avant la lettre* as the one who put down the Huk Rebellion in the Philippines, perceived the political importance of combining 'improved social programs' for the Montagnards with military training, but he was reluctant to have Americans involved directly. Right at the beginning of the American intervention in Vietnam, then, we may discern the contours of two conflicting strategies for dealing with Communist subversion, and of the two related ethnographic discourses concerning the Montagnards. Warner cites an American officer (probably Lucien Conein again) who blames Gen. Williams for failing to grasp guerrilla warfare:

'Hanging Sam' was a great conventional instructor, but he didn't know anything about Communist guerrilla war. The French officer handling the intelligence organization embracing all the montagnard tribes in the High Plateau and the Annam Cordillera offered to turn it all over to Williams. He was not interested. He didn't even look through the files. When things got tough on the High Plateau, we didn't even know where to begin. We had to start all over again, right from the beginning. ... 'Hanging Sam' saw the threat as purely conventional, and coming only from the Viet Minh divisions in the North.

(Warner 1964: 129–30)

Although this may seem a personal anecdote, Gen. William's refusal to consider taking over the French *Maquis* expresses a tendency among large sections of the US Army, Navy and Air Force to conceive of the conflict in Vietnam as a conventional war. This is tantamount to refusing to see the conflict as a political conflict, for in conventional warfare military strategy has primacy over political strategy. Purely military strategy is about the control of territory and people's bodies; a political strategy aims at the control of their minds. Or, as Colonel Charles Simpson of the Special Forces put it, 'while the conventional military thinks in terms of the seizure of a piece of critical terrain, or the control or destruction of a major industrial or transportation center, the insurgent thinks first, last, and always of the population' (Simpson 1983: 51). Although in any situation of war the two are always combined, it makes a difference where the emphasis is laid. In Communist strategy the control of minds ('political struggle') was of paramount importance, because territory could hardly be held with conventional means when outnumbered and outgunned by a superior enemy army. And although the great North Vietnamese strategist, General Võ Nguyên Giáp, emphasized the importance of a 'stable rear base area' for guerrilla warfare, the outstanding qualities of guerrilla warfare are the combination of military with political (that is revolutionary) struggle (Giap 1970: 56–74). Or, as he phrased this in his famous essay *People's War, People's Army*:

> The most appropriate guiding principle for activities was *armed propaganda . . .; political activities were more important than military activities, and fighting less important than propaganda*; armed activity was to safeguard, consolidate and develop the political bases.
>
> (Giap 1962: 78–9, emphasis in original; see also pp. xxiv–xxv)

Put otherwise, a political strategy is bound to adapt to the interests of local populations in its tactical choices in order to better mobilize their resources. Guerrilla strategy considers local populations as a strategic asset, as is clear from Mao Zedong's well-known adage that the guerrilla has to move among the population as a fish in the water. Conventional military strategy on the other hand seeks to adapt local populations to the exigencies of conventional warfare, e.g. by resettlement schemes, the creation of 'free-fire zones', forced urbanization, defoliation and whatnot, in order to 'separate the fish from the water' and create an empty battlefield. In this sense, local populations are considered a strategic nuisance rather than an asset. From this it may be evident that a military strategy usually links up with an ethnographic discourse which differs from the ethnographic discourse attending a political strategy, simply because it matters whether a population is considered a strategic asset or a nuisance. It must be borne in mind, however, that the difference between political and military strategy is an analytical distinction, and that all three parties in the conflict (Vietnamese Communists, the South Vietnamese government, and the Americans) combined both strategies in varying ways and with varying degrees of success. This chapter considers the American counterinsurgency strategy rather than the Communist and South Vietnamese policies, and the ethnographic discourses that attended the American intervention.

During the 1950s, however, American policy was by and large an endorsement of the policies of their creation, the Republic of Vietnam under President Diêm. After 1954, South Vietnamese policy was directed at the construction of a strong nation-state in the South, capable of competing politically and militarily with the Democratic Republic of Vietnam (DRV) in the North. For Diêm, nation-building was tantamount to forced assimilation, or 'Vietnamization' of the Montagnards. On 11 March 1955, the *Statut particulier* governing the French-installed *Pays Montagnards du Sud* – officially Emperor Bao Dai's Crown Domain – was abolished, and the French Residents were replaced by a Vietnamese administration. Teaching in the vernacular languages, which used French as lingua franca, was replaced with primary education in Vietnamese only – if the schools continued to exist at all. The customary law courts (*tribunaux coutumiers*) were abolished, and Vietnamese statutory law applied everywhere. There were even attempts to make Montagnards dress in Vietnamese style, especially in the cities and markets (Hickey 1982b: 46; Fall 1962: 141–4; Fall 1966: 190–6; Sheehan 1967: 89–92). Montagnard land claims were not recognized, and their lands were confiscated by the state to resettle migrants from the North and the coast. President Diêm, however, retained one Montagnard 'tradition' which fitted well with his mandarin-style rule, i.e. the *palabre du serment*, the Montagnard 'oath of allegiance'. Diêm had adopted this ceremony from emperor Bao Dai, who in turn had participated in this colonial ceremony, invented by Sabatier, from 1950 onward. Earl Young describes such a ceremony in Phu Bôn province (Cheo Reo) which took place in 1962, attended by 'a thousand [Jarai] tribespeople, neatly formed into groups of fifty by age and sex, ... lined up along the path' (Young 1966a: 85–6). After rituals were conducted by the 'Kings of Fire, Water and Wind', USOM goods were distributed, as a 'symbol of the tons of materials ... distributed through the refugee centers to the montagnards.' (ibid.: 88; see also Young 1966b)

In that era, political aid and advice was mainly channeled through the Michigan State University in East Lansing. From 1955 to 1962 the Michigan State University Vietnam Advisory Group (MSUG) under the direction of Professor Wesley Fishel managed a series of advisory programs in Vietnam in the fields of research and education, administration, police, and technical policies. It is instructive to take a closer look at the curriculum taught at the National

Institute of Administration, set up by the MSUG. Here we find the case method propagated by John D. Montgomery in the bilingual training manual *Cases in Vietnamese Administration* (1959). One case deals with 'Resettling the Highland Tribes at Binh Tuy Province' (pp. 348–58). Here we find the province chief wishing to change the 'tribal customs' of the 'nomadic Highlanders' in order to develop the forest and agricultural resources in the province. Illiterate and primitive, the Montagnards were thought to know no measure, no boundaries, no property, and to destroy the valuable forests of Vietnam with their backward agricultural practices – an assumption which acquires ironical overtones in the light of later defoliation campaigns. 'Resettl(ing) the Highlanders into land development centers in the fertile valley of the La Nga ... was not a problem to which a military solution could be found' (Montgomery 1959: 350). By patiently overcoming 'superstition', 'ignorance and backwardness' (pp. 354–5), many Highlanders were persuaded to move to the resettlement centers, where they received agricultural, medical and educational support. There, they were subjected to legal restrictions on their kinship and marriage system, traditional leadership and, of course, (ritual) drinking habits 'by not permitting Highlanders to keep rice in excess of basic needs' (p. 356) – although one of the justifications for resettling them was the eradication of hunger, which allegedly would continually plague them. 'Within two more years', the province chief concluded, 'we hope to bring all the Highlanders together in a single city, with a modern market place and an airport. ... In another generation the tribal customs of the Binh Tuy mountaineers will be only a memory' (p. 358).

Given the assumption, shared by Vietnamese officials and American advisors, that Montagnards would assimilate in the course of one generation, interest in their lifestyles and cultures was predicated on considerations of political security, insofar as Montagnards posed a risk in that respect. Next to the National Institute of Administration, the establishment of the National Police Academy was the other major project of the MSUG, which until 1960 contained a CIA unit (Scigliano and Fox 1965: 11). When MSUG and the USAID Public Safety Division launched the National Identity Card Program, which encompassed 'the fingerprinting and photographing of, and issuance of identity cards to, every person 18 years or over living in Viet Nam' (Adkins 1962: 1), Montagnard name-giving practice posed a problem, necessitating *A Study of Montagnard Names in Viet Nam* (1962). Fingerprinting was not a problem. A remarkably effective offshoot of physical anthropology, it had been developed in the last century by British police officers in colonial Bengal in the course of their attempts at classification of criminal tribes and castes (Haddon 1910: 32–3; Dirks 1995: 335). Fingerprinting allowed for individual identification, just as photographing, although at the beginning of ethnographic photographing – in British India again – it was aimed at the identification of physical types (i.e. ethnic groups) rather than individuals (Pinney 1990). Elmer Adkins of the MSUG was simply able to introduce *The Science of Fingerprints* (1961) as a readily available identification technique for the Vietnamese police. In the process of identification, however, Montagnard names posed a problem because 'Montagnards customarily have only one 'given' name, and that of one syllable'; besides, lacking vernacular scripts, it was unclear how to write these names. This made it imperative to study the ethnic and linguistic differentiation of the Montagnards, and the customs surrounding naming. The existing names were tabulated in order to develop a standard spelling for names. Individual identification would then be possible by combining name, sex, village and hamlet of birth (but not ethnic affiliation, although this was recorded) and residence with the photograph and fingerprint on the identity card. Strangely, though, a number of complicating problems were overlooked. Contrary to the situation in the province where the pilot study took place (Tuyên Duc), a number of Montagnard groups (e.g. Jarai, Edê) have clan names to classify individuals; but the matrilinial descent system of these groups might have clashed with Vietnamese family law. Furthermore, it is customary among at least a number of groups to give nick names (see Condominas 1957) or to change names in the course of a lifetime (e.g. to be named after one's first child, like in Ama Thuôt: father of Thuôt).

It was decided not to add to Montagnard names without proper legislative action, ostensibly because this was considered 'arbitrary and presumptious [sic]' (Adkins 1962: 15). Changing names had no high priority, though, given the common assumption that Montagnards would have to assimilate with Vietnamese culture. In this sense, American development discourse was predicated on the same assumptions as French evolutionist discourse around the turn of the century. A 1961 study by the US Information Service (USIS) entitled *Montagnards of the South Vietnam Highlands* still described the Montagnards as 'anarchical' (USIS 1961: 3), having 'no social traditions, no tombs, no altars' (pp. 4–5). It was assumed that Montagnard culture simply could not cope with the inevitable modernization process. If Montagnards were to survive, therefore, they would have to assimilate into Vietnamese culture, thus contributing to the process of nation-building. Anything less than that was considered politically subversive. As if to underscore the inevitability of the process, American advisors like Adkins made frequent allusions to resemblance of the Montagnards to Native Americans (Indians), both in appearance and in situation (Adkins 1962: 9; Hickey 1957: 4–5; Wickert 1959: 128; Donoghue et al. 1962: 16; Warner 1963: 180; Colby 1989: 89). In a letter of 10 April 1956, to the Bureau of Indian Affairs in Washington DC, Wesley Fishel, chief advisor of the MSUG, expresses his interest in information concerning American policy concerning the Indians 'in the past half century or so'. According to Fishel:

> This request may seem surprising, but the fact is that Viet-Nam has an Indian problem of its own, resembling in certain respects that of our own.[13]

Ironically, only a few decades before, French administrators like Pasquier also referred to the fate of the American Indians in the reservations as a model which the French colonial administration should not follow.

Put in practice, Vietnamese modernization discourse meant resettlement for the Montagnards, as already noted in the 'case study' concerning the resettlement of highlanders in Binh Tuy province. The history of resettlement of populations is almost as long as the history of South Vietnam as a separate state. Respectively known as Land Development Centers, Agrovilles, Village Defense, Strategic Hamlets, Rural Development, etc., resettlement has been a constant feature in South Vietnam, and it did not stop after 1975 under the present Communist regime. The Land Development Program, initiated in 1956, aimed at regrouping lowlanders from the overcrowded coast and Catholic refugees from the North in agricultural centers in the Highlands. Ominously, the Land Development Centers were called *đinh điên* (land clearing/development), recalling the *đồn điên* (colonization centers) through which the Vietnamese settled newly conquered areas during their historical Southward March (*Nam Tiên*); Hickey (1982b) aptly notes that the colonization scheme of the 1950s (and after 1975, we might add) might be called a Westward March (*Tây Tiên*).

The Vietnamese colonization of the Highlands, however, contrasts in scope with the French colonization schemes of 1946/47, which aimed at keeping the Kinh out of the Highlands by settling French veterans among Montagnards for economic and political purposes.[14] Besides the settlement of Kinh in the Highlands, the 1957 Land Development Program and later resettlement programs aimed at regrouping Highlanders within their region so as to better 'protect' them from Communist infiltration. In fact, Highlander resettlement started as early as 1955, thus continuing the resettlement programs managed by the French in what was called the *Domaine de la Couronne du Pays Montagnard du Sud* (PMS).[15] Both resettlement schemes – the Vietnamese colonization and their own resettlement – were resented by Montagnards, who complained about land grabbing by Vietnamese, the failure to recognize colonial land titles and land claims. In a comparison of northern and southern minority policies, Bernard Fall claims that the 'highly centralizing approach' of the RVN was 'unfortunately backed by the Michigan State University team in Saigon' (Fall 1959: 138).

This is not to say that all MSUG members were unaware of the adverse effects of Diêm's policy, or backed it. One of the first 'field trips' of a MSUG team to the *Pays Montagnard du Sud* (PMS), as the Central Highlands were called then, yielded a report of 16 pages, signed by the senior MSUG members Walter Mode and Frederic Wickert, a psychology professor at MSU. Thirteen pages were quotations from interviews with Montagnards blaming 'the' Vietnamese for taking their lands, stealing cattle, cutting down fruit trees, administrative abuses, lack of medical care, lack of educational opportunities, etc.[16] This was followed in June 1957 by a 'Preliminary Research Report on the High Plateau', prepared by the Chicago anthropologist Gerald Hickey with the assistance of Frederic Wickert. The report stressed the alienating effects of RVN policy on the 'Mountaineers', claiming that they would turn against the government if their legitimate grievances go unheeded. The report started with the conclusion that '*[l]and grabbing* and *fear of land grabbing* is one of the *primary causes* of *Mountaineer discontent*' (Hickey 1957: 1; original emphasis). The only remedy, according to Hickey, was the issuance of land titles on the basis of traditional land rights, next to a score of other recommendations concerning medical services, education, administration, and markets. In order to back up his analysis, Hickey appended two lengthy translations of portions of the *coutumier Rhadé* of Darlac, by Léopold

Sabatier (1940), and of the *coutumier Bahnar, Sedang* and *Jarai* of Kontum, by Paul Guilleminet (1952a), on land rights and land use. In the same month of June, 1957, Price Gittinger of the US Operations Mission (USOM) Agricultural Division in Saigon filed a report on 'Tenure in Ban Me Thuot Land Development Projects: Situation and Recommendations'. This report, based on fieldwork undertaken with Gerald Hickey, also made a case for recognition of Rhadé land rights, extolling the 'wisdom' of 'the Rhadé agricultural system', which Gittinger would term 'extended fallow agriculture' rather than 'shifting cultivation' (p. 4). Gittinger also proposed a 'General Land Tenure Accord' on the basis of traditional land rights, lest the Rhadé would turn against the government and – worse still – turn to the Communists for support.[17]

The reports carried messages which were unwelcome at the time, and hence went unheeded. It is hardly surprising that reports which were critical about every conceivable aspect of RVN policy concerning Montagnards – indeed accused Vietnamese administrators, army and civilians of blatant discrimination – were rejected by the Vietnamese government (Scigliano and Fox 1965: 25). According to Hickey, President Diêm flew to Ban Me Thuot (present-day Buôn Ma Thuôt) to be greeted by provincial officials, including Montagnards dressed in Vietnamese clothes for the occasion, in order to be reassured that 'the highland people ... loved the Vietnamese and desired to emulate them' (Hickey 1982b: 44).[18] Another critical report came from Sir Richard O.D. Noone, an anthropologist in the British secret service MI6, who was advisor on Aborigines in the Federation of Malaya in the 1950s, and organized 'Dayak' groups against the Indonesian *Konfrontasi* in North Borneo (Petersen 1988: 167–70; McNeill 1982). In a secret study of August 1956 on the 'Highlanders' problem', Noone concluded that '(c)ontinued infringement on the territorial claims of the Montagnards ... will result in unrest which would be exploited by the Viet Minh thus presenting a most serious threat to the government'.[19] Diêm was displeased with the foreign performance in the Highlands, and one result of the incidents was that the Vietnamese government obstructed follow-up research and abandoned the MSUG Highland project. Furthermore, Diêm decreed that MSUG advisors had to receive permission from the Presidency and the relevant Vietnamese counterpart to go on field missions, which resulted in delays and even denials (Scigliano and Fox 1965: 50–1). Gerald Hickey was one of the MSUG team barred from further research in the Highlands, whereafter he did his fieldwork in the Mekong Delta, on which he based his *Village in Vietnam* (1964a).[20]

More surprising than the Vietnamese response, however, was the reaction from other American agencies in Vietnam. Hickey recounts the criticism from Wolf Ladejinsky, a personal land reform advisor to Diêm, who said that the report was 'the worst ever issued' by the MSUG. 'How do you expect the government to deal with these children?', he asked Hickey, who claims that Ladejinsky had not even read the report. But it did not matter who was right: the report by Price Gittinger was withdrawn by USOM, the recommendations of Gittinger, Hickey and Wickert were ignored, and the Land Development Program went ahead 'without regard for highlander land claims' (Hickey 1982b: 44; Emerson 1978:

283–290). In the 1950s, American agencies like USOM were simply not interested in studies of rural Vietnam. Scigliano and Fox claim that the tendency of MSUG members to conduct research in Vietnamese villages resulted in friction between the MSUG and USOM, which deemed it 'a waste of tax-payers' money'. This attitude would change only by 1961, when the Communist insurgency proved highly effective in most of the countryside, in particular the Central Highlands (Scigliano and Fox 1965: 47). John Montgomery of the MSUG claims that the great majority of the American technical advisors had misgivings about the Land Development Program, but being a Vietnamese program privileged by President Diêm and his brother Ngô Đình Nhu, it was hesitantly sponsored by the US at the instigation of its political representatives in Vietnam, like Ambassador Durbrow (Montgomery 1962: 78–82).

Once again, we find a conflict over which strategy to follow in Vietnam – after Devereux' 'Special Plan' concerning OSS-instigated insurgency among tribal groups against the French and Japanese in Indochina (1943), and after Gen. 'Hanging Sam' Williams' refusal to even look at the French counterinsurgency programs involving ethnic minorities, known as *Maquis* (1955). Whereas the Devereux plan might have appeared a personal affair in a complicated international situation, and the Conein plan could simply be dismissed as a French plan, the division within the MSUG was an American affair. In all three cases, there was an attempt to take – at least temporarily – local populations seriously, albeit for ulterior motives. Although the use of tribal warriors involves a certain amount of cynicism, the work on the ground simultaneously requires a certain degree of respect of local cultures. In all three cases, then, it is possible to discern a relativist ethnographic discourse underlying the use of minorities in colonial situations. In the days of Sabatier (see Chapter 3), 'his' relativist discourse concerning – and addressing – the Rhadé had to give way to an evolutionist ethnographic discourse which was hegemonic because it was linked to the dominant economic and political interests of the time – the rubber plantations. The growing American intervention in Indochina was attended by the modernization/nation-building discourse of the time, which for Vietnam's minorities was an evolutionist discourse in disguise.

It could be objected that the difference simply was that relativist discourse was informed by ethnographic knowledge and evolutionist or modernization discourse was not. It is generally true that there is a qualitative and quantitative difference between the bodies of ethnographic knowledge informing both discourses. Such an easy distinction seems to preclude the possibility, however, that the evolutionist and modernization discourses made sense to intelligent people. The assumption that the Montagnards were strategically irrelevant as they would die out or assimilate in the course of one generation or so also made sense to cultural relativist ethnographers like Sabatier and Hickey. They would relate this prediction to the quality of ethnic policy in the Highlands. Sabatier was quite clear about this: he would say to both the French colonial administration and the Rhadé that if they did not follow him, the Rhadé would be kicked off their land by Viêt colonists and be subjugated, or worse – die out.

Similarly, MSUG researchers like Hickey and Wickert were pessimistic about the fate of the Highlanders if their advice went unheeded. Sabatier and Hickey may have been outstanding ethnographers in their times, but it was not the quality of their ethnographic knowledge which made the difference. In the previous chapter, we saw that Sabatier's oeuvre was rehabilitated when the strategic and political interests of defending the colony became more important than the economic interests of the plantations. In the next section, we shall see that the rising insurgency in Vietnam triggered a 'Counterinsurgency Controversy' within the American civilian and military bureaucracy, which would bring in the Special Forces and – again – a relativist ethnographic discourse. The point that I wish to make here, is that individuals may produce ethnographic knowledge, but that the reception of this knowledge and its incorporation in a discourse is generally beyond the reach of such individuals, because discourses are linked up with and embedded in institutional interests. Hence, it is possible to analyse the discursive contents, context and effects of a text without necessarily attributing intentions to its author.

The complexity of the issue of competing discourses is attested to by the fact that the most voluminous report on Montagnards produced by the MSUG was not written from a relativist perspective, but from a perspective of inevitable cultural assimilation of Montagnards into Vietnamese society. The report *People in the Middle: The Rhade of South Viet Nam* (1962) by John Donoghue, Daniel Whitney and Iwao Ishino was the result of 'several weeks of field work in the hamlet of Ko-Sier, Darlac Province', and was not intended to be published, given the short research period (Donoghue et al. 1962: 4).[21] However, the authors were requested to prepare a publication 'in light of the current events and the particular significance of the highland peoples of South Viet Nam' (ibid.: Preface) – which could only mean the increased NLF activities in the Highlands, and the Special Forces deployment there from 1961 onwards. The report fits into the classical 'manners and customs' genre, with chapters on human relations, the traditional community, religion and world view, social structure and economy. However, this is interspersed with chapters on 'The Montagnard: a Problem of Integration', on 'The Changing Community' and 'Rhade Aspirations and Government Policy'. In other words, Rhadé 'traditional' culture was observed through a lens of modernization in that as it was perceived as a problem in terms of national integration. Not surprisingly, then, the problem was sought in the cultural difference between Vietnamese and Montagnards (who seem to be identical to Rhadé in this report):

> If the Montagnard [sic] are to be brought into the full scope of national life and complete identification with national aims, something must be done to reduce this cultural gap.
>
> (Donoghue et al. 1962: 70)

The report was not optimistic about the solution to this problem. While it noted some willingness to accept change among Rhadé, it mildly criticized Vietnamese assimilationist policies, especially the Land Development Centers. In other words, 'in any inter-cultural situation like this, one must understand that it takes two to tango' (ibid.: 104).

The American-backed nation-building policy by South Vietnam's Diêm regime was expressed in land grabbing, exploitation, discriminination, and repression of ethnic cultures and languages, as was noted in the MSUG reports. And as predicted, this provoked resentment among the Montagnards. In 1958, Montagnard civil servants who since 1955 had been active in a *Front de la Libération des Montagnards*, founded the Bajaraka Movement (*Ba*hnar, *Ja*rai, *Rha*dé, *Ko*ho) to protest against the Diêm regime's ethnic policy and to demand autonomy for the former PMS. President Diêm was outraged about the 'highland gang', and most of the leaders were arrested and put in jail. What is more, all the crossbows – personal items used for hunting – were confiscated from the Rhadé men, the most active group in the movement. One of the leaders, Y Bih Aleo, escaped arrest and went underground to join the Communist resistance. He would become Vice-Chairman of the National Liberation Front (NLF) after its establishment in 1960, and President of the Central Highlands Autonomy Movement. As noted in the same MSUG reports and by Bernard Fall, the Viêt Minh continued to propagate against the Diêm regime in radio transmissions in the vernacular languages, condemning land grabbing and promising autonomy (as in the ill-fated autonomous zones in the North, which would be abolished after 1975).

Simultaneously, ethnic minority cadres who had gone North in 1954, filtered back into the Highlands with a thorough political training, and often accompanied by ethnic Vietnamese who adopted the lifestyles of the population where they lived (Hickey 1982b: 47–73).[22] In 1959–60, guerrilla warfare in the Highlands was renewed with the Trà Bông rising of the Kor and Hrê minorities in the mountains of Quang Nam and Quang Ngãi.[23] Significantly, in *War by Other Means* (1989), Carlyle Thayer argues that the Highlanders acted as the catalyst for the resumption of guerrilla warfare in South Vietnam. In other words, although there already was a North-Vietnamese presence in the Central Highlands, it was the rise of violence in the Highlands that preceded and prepared the Communist Party's decision to resume armed struggle and establish the NLF. In the course of one year, the guerrilla had spread to most of the Highlands, and by 1961 many villages had come under the influence of the NLF. It became increasingly clear that the Army of the Republic of Vietnam (ARVN), which was trained for conventional warfare, was no match for the guerrillas – neither in the Highlands nor in the Mekong Delta (cf. Halberstam 1964; Schell 1988; Sheehan 1989). By then, many American observers and policymakers felt that 'Something Extra and Special' had to be done; this was to be provided by the US Army Special Forces.

The rise of counterinsurgency

The Kennedy and Johnson Administrations' involvement with Vietnam has been the subject of many scholarly publications as well as memoirs by key persons in the administration. This era was characterized by the coming to power of a new elite of American 'internationalists', controlling the various aspects of American foreign policy from the White House.[24] The key organization which coordinated policy was the National Security Council (NSC). The NSC was the focal point for the various agencies involved in military planning (Department of Defense – DOD), political planning (Central Intelligence Agency – CIA, State Department, and US Information Agency – USIA), and economic planning (Agency for International Development – AID – the successor of the International Cooperation Agency) overseas (Deitchman 1976: 2–17; Hatcher 1990: 8–16). The US administration did not simply respond to the deteriorating situation at the Vietnamese battlefield. The – what Michael Shafer (1988: 240–1) calls 'realist' – analysis of American policymakers dismissed the circumstances in Vietnam as irrelevant, for what threatened Vietnam was Communist expansion. The struggle in Vietnam was seen as a struggle between the 'Free World' and 'World Communism' (the Soviet Union and China) which had to be contained. It was necessary to 'make a stand' in 'Free Vietnam', for the loss of Vietnam would be a defeat for the United States as the champion of the Free World, and a corresponding loss of credibility and security elsewhere. If South Vietnam should fall to Communism, its neighbors would fall, too. This was known as the 'domino theory': if one domino was to fall, its neighbors would be subverted and fall, too, until the US would ultimately have to fight Communism on the shores of California.

Just before John Kennedy's inauguration as US President in January 1961, Secretary-General Khrushchev had declared Soviet support for 'Wars of National Liberation', which placed worldwide Communist subversion high on the new President's agenda. President Kennedy urged all the members of his staff to read Krushchev's speech. As a senator, Kennedy had been interested in – as he called them – 'subterranean wars', and he had read the works of Mao and Che Guevara on guerrilla warfare. Right after his inauguration, Kennedy received an alarming report on the situation in Vietnam from Gen. Edward Lansdale, just back from a secret mission commissioned by the previous administration. Considered the outstanding American counterinsurgency expert at the time, Lansdale noted the revolutionary successes in the battlefield and the failure of conventional tactics in counterinsurgency. One of Kennedy's first decisions, made against the opposition of the regular Army and Joint Chiefs of Staff, was to upgrade the US Army Special Forces which had its Special Warfare Center in Fort Bragg, NC, as an elite corps military instrument to combat insurgency with unconventional tactics. Also, he supported a process which had already been underway under the Eisenhower administration, that is the move of the CIA to couple intelligence gathering to (covert) operations in order to back up American policy abroad. Furthermore, he established a 'Special Group – Counterinsurgency' which had to formulate a 'comprehensive strategic concept for counterinsurgency', and establised a counterinsurgency course as part of the State Department's regular training program. Finally, he installed the Vietnam Task Force at the State Department, which would be responsible for coordinating the Vietnam policies of the various involved US agencies in the early 1960s (Hilsman 1967: 413–39; Prados 1986: 224; Shafer 1988: 240–75).

The people responsible for counterinsurgency in the Kennedy administration were Roger Hilsman and especially Walt W. Rostow, who became advisor on national security affairs. Rostow had been part of the influential Massachusetts Institute of Technology (MIT) Center for International Studies. In January 1960 the MIT had issued a report for the US Senate Committee on Foreign Relations, pleading for the integration of economic, political and military planning in US foreign policy in order to better intervene in unstable, newly independent countries liable to Communist subversion. The report boiled down to a 'rationalization of military intervention' in what was then known as 'internal wars'.[25] The Special Forces entered the scene as the appropriate instrument to deal with subversive activities. In an address to the graduating class of the Special Warfare School in Fort Bragg, June 1961, Walt Rostow pleaded for the merging of economic and political development policies with military action in a counterinsurgency policy. President Kennedy himself was very much interested in the Special Forces, and bestowed them the right to wear the famous green beret during a visit to Fort Bragg in the Fall of 1961, much to the dismay of the regular army and the Joint Chiefs of Staff who were not enthusiastic about irregular warfare. With the growing strength of the Communist guerrilla movement in Vietnam in the early 1960s and with the American military presence there, Vietnam was to be the test case for the use of Special Forces counterinsurgency tactics.

Special forces

In the beginning of the Cold War era, the Special Forces had been trained for guerrilla warfare behind enemy lines in case of a Soviet attack on allied nations in Europe and Asia, thus assuming the role of an insurgency rather than a counterinsurgency instrument.[26] Their job was to raise and command irregular friendly forces against the Soviet Army. In Asia, however, Special Forces units were deployed to train elite forces of allied nations. From 1957 onward, the 1st Special Forces Group which had been activated in Okinawa, was training South Vietnamese units in Nha Trang which would form the nucleus of the Vietnamese Special Forces and the Vietnamese Army Rangers. This training effort was part of the US Military Assistance Advisory Group (MAAG) in Vietnam. Under the provision of the Geneva Agreements, the US were only allowed to station a limited number of military advisors in Vietnam, but no troops capable of direct military engagement. In fact, however, American 'advisors' often played a more direct military role, effectively commanding units of the Army of the Republic of Vietnamese (ARVN) (Halberstam 1964; Schell 1988; Sheehan 1988). With the 1961 deployment in Vietnam of the 5th Special Forces Group, trained at Fort Bragg, the counterinsurgency doctrine was introduced. The Special Forces were increasingly seen as counterinsurgency rather than insurgency (behind enemy lines) instruments, given the enhanced role of economic, political and military development that the US assumed in the 'underdeveloped countries'. Thus, it was only a matter of time that the Special Forces would turn to the theatre where their talents could be developed best: to the Central Highlands where the indigenous population were coming under the influence of Communist cadres from both southern and northern Vietnam (Hilsman 1967: 421; Prados 1986: 222–6; Simpson 1983; Kelly 1973).

In October 1961, President Kennedy dispatched his chief military advisor, Gen. Maxwell Taylor, on a group mission to assess the political and military situation and possibilities. With him went some senior officials like Walt Rostow and Edward Lansdale. Although the tone of their reporting was rather optimistic, their major recommendation was a rapid expansion of the number of American advisors, and the deployment of American combat troops in Vietnam, in order to seal off the Lao-Vietnamese border – a recommendation which was not adopted by Kennedy who felt that guerrilla warfare was essentially a political rather than a military struggle. Another recommendation for a 'radical increase in numbers of Green Berets' (Prados 1986: 243) would, therefore, be realized at short notice. In a 'top secret' memorandum of 14 October 1961, from Robert Johnson, head of the Vietnam Task Force in Washington, to Walt Rostow, Johnson stated that a 'US-developed plan for assisting the Montagards [sic] has recently been submitted to the GVN' and suggested to 'examine it and determine what can be done to speed action'. In the secret 'Covert Annex' to the Taylor Mission report on Pacification in Frontier Areas, it was observed that without Montagnard support it would be impossible to close the border to Communist infiltration, but that there were serious problems in enlisting their help. For one thing, it was estimated that the NLF had recruited Montagnards since 1954, whereas 'the Vietnamese [= South Vietnamese Government – OS] have looked upon the Montagnards as something almost sub-human, and this is known to the Montagnards'. It was noted that 'Americans serving in the High Plateau and French missionaries long resident believe that the Montagnards should be armed for village self-defense and can be used far more extensively for intelligence collection'.[27] Thus, later developments in the Highlands like the 'Village Defense Program' were foreshadowed in the reports submitted by the Taylor Mission in October 1961.

The start of Special Forces' involvement with Montagnards had been rather accidental, and shows the strong hand of the CIA in it – not so strange, if one takes into account that both SF and CIA trace their origins to the OSS in World War II (Bank 1986). In 1961, the newly established NLF made great gains in the Central Highlands, to the effect that American advisors feared that the entire area would soon be controlled by the NLF, and lost for the GVN. Many Americans attributed this to the high-handedness of GVN officials and ARVN in dealing with the Montagnards. At the time, one of the senior officers in Vietnam of the CIA (or, as it was then called, the Combined Studies Division) was Colonel Gilbert Layton, an OSS veteran of World War II. He was informed about the activities of David Nuttle, a young volunteer of the International Voluntary Services, Inc. (IVS – the predecessor of Kennedy's Peace Corps) who had gained firsthand knowledge of the Rhadé group where he worked, and had gained their trust by adapting to their way of life. David Nuttle was recruited by the CIA to start the so-called Village Defense Program, together with an SF medic, Paul Campbell. The first village to be 'converted' was Buon Enao, just north of the provincial capital Ban Me Thuot, after the village had been attacked and ransacked by NLF forces. Before that, William Colby, the CIA chief of station in Saigon at the time, had to secure permission to arm the Highlanders from both the Vietnamese President Diêm, through his brother Ngô Đình Nhu who was in charge of the pacification operations, and from the American ambassador in Saigon, in the face of bureaucratic opposition from AID and MAAG. Notably, on the Vietnamese side, the Village Defense Program was handled by the Presidential Survey Office, a civilian organization, rather than the Army.[28]

The idea was to adopt the Communist concept of the 'fighting village' by training the village population to defend themselves against NLF attacks, distributing weapons, and by building a moat and fence around the village. According to a CIA report of January 1964, the concept was directly derived from the book by Giap, for 'the Viet Cong appeared to be operating exactly in accordance with Giap's principles, therefore our solution was to use these same proven principles against the Viet Cong'. The program was not simply military or even paramilitary. The Montagnards involved were not only given 'something to fight with' but also 'something to fight for' through an elaborate social and economic program, involving school building, provision of fertilizer, tree nurseries, and other economic projects, but most of all medical care, provided by the SF medic.[29] An official history of the *US Army J.F. Kennedy Special Warfare Center* (1964: 5) called the 'new dispensary – a most important resource in the counterinsurgency effort – ... but one of many facets in a program designed to sway Montagnard public opinion to resist the VC'. Because of the success of the social action, the experiment proved a military success, too, and more SF personnel under Captain Ronald Shackleton came in to organize three companies of Rhadé militia, and one strike force of better armed militia which could come to the rescue of any village under attack. According to the Special Forces' Historical Report of 1964, '[s]oon the village came to resemble an American pioneer fortress' (*US Army J.F. Kennedy Center for Special Warfare*: 3). The program rapidly spread over the Highlands, organizing and training forty villages from the center of Buon Enao by April 1962. Four other training centers were established in Darlac province in August 1962, from where another 160 villages were trained and armed in order to be able to defend themselves. By the end of 1962, Darlac province was officially declared 'secure'. The program, now rebaptized Citizens' Irregular Defense Groups (CIDG) program, spread all over the Highlands.

If we look at the map 'Buon Enao Expansion' (see the section Maps and Charts) reproduced by Col. Francis Kelly (1973: 29), the official historian of the Special Forces in Vietnam – a map which appeared in many other Special Forces-related publications – we see the 'security zone' radiating from Buon Enao and eventually the five training centers in Darlac province. In time, most of the territory of the province was covered, not through territorial defense but by applying the concept of population self-defense. In his memoir of the Vietnam War, the CIA's William Colby (1989: 91) makes a reference to the 'political tactic ... advocated a half-century earlier by Marshal Lyautey, redoubtable Resident-General of Morocco in 1912–1925 (and member of the French Academy), under the concept of the 'ink-spot' (in French, tache d'huile or 'oil-spot')'. Of course, we know this tactic from Marshal Galliéni rather than Marshal Lyautey. Both developed the tactic together when they were 'pacifying' the mountain areas in northern Vietnam in the 1890s (see Chapter 2). Galliéni, then a colonel, was the architect of the French version of classical, colonial divide-and-rule policy, capitalizing on cultural difference and other real or potential social divisions. In actual colonial practice, this meant accommodating local elites after a thorough ethnographic study of the locality. At the operational level, the Special Forces adopted the tactics developed by Colonel Trinquier of the French army for the *Maquis* which operated behind Viêt Minh lines during the First Indochina War, in which specially trained soldiers lived with the Montagnards and adopted their lifestyles, thus copying the successful methods of the Communist cadres (see Chapter 5). Further developed by the Special Forces, the *Maquis* constituted a *faire du moi*-policy par excellence, in that it adapted in some respects to local customs, in order to better use the local population for political goals which transcended their social space. This did not imply, however, that the Montagnards had much influence on ethnic policy, for this policy was motivated by interests which were beyond their control – which caused Colonel Trinquier to fear that the 'tribes' would be sacrificed again for ulterior goals (Bodard 1950; Fall 1963a: 195–6; 1963b: 117–18; Kelly 1973; Stanton 1985; Trinquier 1976: 85–8).

In the 1960s, the American CIA and Special Forces attempted to repeat this pacification pattern in South Vietnam. This implied that the Special Forces recruited mainly from ethnic minorities in Vietnam, mostly Montagnard, but also Khmer Krom (ethnic Khmer living in the Mekong Delta), Cham and Nung (a mountain minority from the North, some of whom had come south in 1955). But religious divisions were also exploited for counterinsurgency purposes, as in the so-called 'Fighting Fathers' program, 'wherein resistance to insurgent activity centered on Catholic parish priests and a number of priests under the program made the arming and training of their parishioners possible' (Kelly 1973: 33). However, the political circumstances under which the Americans operated were quite different from the colonial era, the main difference being that in contrast to the French, the Americans had to respect Vietnamese sensitivities regarding their sovereignty over the Central Highlands. Theoretically, the American Special Forces would train and advise the Vietnamese Special Forces, or *Luc Luong Ðac Biêt* (LLDB), who would control operations. But in actual practice, Americans trained, armed and commanded the participating Montagnards, and financed the whole operation. On the American side, there was a good deal of contempt, repeated over and over again in after-action reports and even official histories of the Special Forces, of the military and civil performance of the Vietnamese

Special Forces in commanding the Montagnards. In actual practice, the Vietnamese Special Forces were used by President Diêm and his brother Ngô Đình Nhu as the main politico-military tool to keep the Army under control, as became clear during the coup against Diêm in November 1963.

In 1962, the expanding Village Defense Program was rebaptized Citizens' Irregular Defense Groups (CIDG). The success of this unconventional warfare program, however, provoked jealousies on the part the South Vietnamese army and authorities. Many Vietnamese officers and officials regarded the direct American presence in the Central Highlands as an infringement on Vietnamese sovereignty, comparable to the French attempt to dissociate the PMSI from Vietnamese territory in the 1940s. Moreover, there was a serious apprehension on the part of Vietnamese authorities of the potential consequences of arming the Montagnards, who, according to Diêm regime, harbored separatist aspirations, as seemed evident from their attitude during the First Indochina War and from the Bajaraka movement in late 1958. In fact, Montagnards were considered unreliable subjects of the Vietnamese state, hardly truly Vietnamese at all. This apprehension showed in two events. From February 1962 onward, Colonel Lê Quang Trong, the Province Chief of Darlac, made repeated attempts to collect the weapons which had been distributed to the Rhadé at Buon Enao for their self-defense. This caused considerable unrest among participating Rhadé who considered the weapons as American gifts to them.[30] In a letter dated 19 January 1963 to Ngô Đình Nhu, who had personally assumed responsibility for Highland pacification in August 1962, the American Ambassador urged him to review the disarmament, but to no avail.[31]

The other event was a CIA contact with Y Bih Aleo, the Rhadé Vice-President of the South-Vietnamese National Liberation Front, and chairman of its Central Highland Autonomy Front, who was in command of an unknown number of Montagnard VC (MVC), as they were called in classified CIA documents. Through the good services of American missionaries in the Highlands, like Bob Ziemer of the Christian and Missionary Alliance,[32] and Drew Sawin whose missionary status was a cover for his CIA work, Col. Layton received word from Y Bih Aleo in late 1962 that the latter was ready to rally to the South Vietnamese side, together with 50 Montagnard NLF soldiers. His main condition was the release of Y Bham Enuol, the outstanding Rhadé leader of the Bajaraka movement and the later FULRO (*Front Unifié de Lutte des Races Oppimées*) autonomy movement, from jail, where he had been held since 1958. In late 1962 and early 1963 the surrender was meticulously prepared by Col. Layton and his collaborators (codename: Operation Linus), while the American ambassador and General Harkins, US military commander in Vietnam, were kept informed, together with the Vietnamese President Diêm and his brother Nhu. However, on the proposed day (15 March 1963), the agreed meeting place was bombed by the South-Vietnamese Air Force, at the instigation of Col. Trong, the Darlac province chief. According to Layton, Col. Trong explained his action against the meeting by stating that he saw no reason for contacting Y Bih Aleo, and that he had received no orders in this regard from the President or his brother. Apparently, there had been a change in South-Vietnamese policy concerning US-Montagnard relations. After the bombing, Y Bih Aleo broke off contact, accusing the Americans and Bajaraka officials of bad faith.[33]

Politically, this was a very confused period anyway. From the American perspective, there had been a promising change in the Highlands, due to the initial success of the Village Defense/CIDG programs in countering NLF 'insurgency'. Apparently, however, many of the former Bajaraka leaders felt encouraged by the possession of weapons and the support of American officials to re-establish the provincial Bajaraka committees and to claim autonomy for the Highlands. And, judging from the CIA/Combined Studies Division records (Special Reports on Highland Autonomy), American officials were persistently pushing their South Vietnamese counterparts to grant autonomy. Simultaneously, weekly American intelligence reports warned about the possibility of a Montagnard revolt in a situation of continuing discrimination against Montagnards. In order to more or less keep control of events, American CIA and Special Forces officers and unofficial representatives (like the cited Christian and Missionary Alliance missionaries and Summer Institute of Linguistics personnel) constantly maintained communication with the technically illegal opposition of Bajaraka, to the point that the CIA-agent-*cum*-missionary Drew Sawin visited the Bajaraka President Y Bham Enuol (a Protestant Rhadé) several times in jail.

For the Americans, the eventual surrender of Y Bih Aleo along with his NLF soldiers would have meant an enormous boost for the RVN, and an irredeemable loss to the NLF in their struggle for the allegiance of the Montagnards. According to Bui Van Luong, the RVN Minister of the Interior in 1962–63, Ngô Đình Nhu was contemplating the idea of granting autonomy to the Montagnards. The growing influence of US officials in Highland affairs, however, made the RVN increasingly wary of such a move, which would have established a Montagnard pseudo-state under strong American control. For the Americans, on the other hand, granting autonomy would be instrumental in warding off a Montagnard rebellion and enlisting them in the struggle against Communism. According to a CIA report of January 1964, the Montagnards were not 'pro-Communist any more than they were pro-Government. They were not pro-anything. They did not know anything to be pro about except themselves, their families, their crops, and their peace and security. We believed that they would fight for their own local pros and in so fighting would commit themselves against the common enemy and consequently to our side'.[34] The CIA firmly believed that the lack of state loyalty of Southeast Asian minorities was exploited by the Chinese Communists, who were believed to support the idea of a 'minorities state' in mainland Southeast Asia, stretching from northern Burma and Thailand in the West to Laos and upland Vietnam in the East. The way to counter such insurgency was to support paramilitary autonomy movements in a systematic way. In a 45-page CIA study entitled 'Permanent Tribal Requirements' (1970), Col. Gilbert Layton, the architect of American involvement with Montagnards in Vietnam, cited a number of other cases where minority groups had been mobilized and utilized for ulterior political purposes, e.g. the Kachin Detachment 101 in Burma during World War II, the Hmong or Meo in Laos, and the Rhadé in Vietnam. Layton concluded, however, that the United States lacked the (covert) instruments for a systematic, semi-permanent minorities policy in Southeast Asia, given the sensitivities of the existing states.[35] Throughout the 1960s, the official American attitude would remain wavering and opportunistic in this respect.

This complex situation was further compounded by two more or less fundamental changes in the CIDG concept. These changes were the so-called Operation Switchback and the 'turn-over' of Buon Enao. Operation Switchback (November 1962 – July 1963) entailed the transfer of operational control over the CIDG program (and of the American Special Forces involved) to the regular army structure, coordinated by the Military Assistance Command-Vietnam (MACV). Only the logistics continued to be organized by the CIA, which was more flexible with its fleet of Air America planes. The main reason for the move was the CIA responsibility for the Bay of Pigs incident in 1961, the invasion of Cuba by US-supported irregulars. After this, the CIA lost part of its prerogatives in organizing large-scale operations (Hilsman 1967: 30–2, 133–4; Colby 1989: 163; Stanton 1985: 51; Turkoly-Joczik 1986: 90). Many of the CIA personnel involved feared that the character of the program (village defense) would change with the transfer in the direction of a regular (para)military program geared toward attack instead of local defense. This is exactly what happened. Under the regular military umbrella, the CIDG units were considered soldiers rather than civilians defending their own villages. Special Forces camps were created, implying that Montagnard CIDG soldiers came to live in American military camps (often with their dependents) instead of American Special Forces living in Montagnard villages. Often, these camps were established as border surveillance camps, far away from the soldiers' home area (Hilsman 1967: 455). In his memoirs, William Colby, who would become Director of Central Intelligence and hence chief of the CIA, aptly notes that the change in strategy to offensive guerrilla operations and border interdiction against North Vietnamese infiltration was reflected in a retention of the acronym CIDG but a change in meaning, where 'Citizens" was replaced by 'Civilian' (Irregular Defense Groups). In the words of Colby, this 'apparently reflected the military belief that, not really being military, they must be civilian' (Colby 1989: 166, 214).

It is not surprising, then, that many Montagnards serving with the American Special Forces, considered themselves to be serving in the American Army – just as they had served in the French colonial army before (and had received pensions for that). After all, they received their training, their weapons, their salaries from Americans, and often were de facto commanded by American soldiers who told them to fight the Vietnamese.[36] This perception was reinforced by the so-called 'turn-over' of Buon Enao – together with other villages and CIDG camps – to the Vietnamese, taking place after the completion of Operation Switchback. Although the sites that were turned over were considered technically secure, they were still in an experimental stage, hardly ready for transfer of control. When the province authorities took responsibility for the CIDG, everything seemed to go wrong – that is, from the American point of view. Montagnard units were transferred to other places without prior notice, they did not receive their regular pay anymore, and often were forced to hand in their weapons against their will. In Buôn Enao, for instance, the day after the turn-over in April 1963, the Strike Force was transferred to Ban Me Thuot for indoctrination, and from there to other camps, leaving Buôn Enao and surrounding villages exposed to guerrilla attacks. The remaining units and village health workers did not get their pay, but mass desertion was averted in July 1963 as American Special Forces provided back pay. The heart of the program, the medical dispensary, was moved to other villages (Kelly 1973: 41–4). In time, the Buôn Enao complex was left to its own devices. Thus, when the Australian captain Barry Petersen – a veteran of the Malay Emergency – arrived in Vietnam in the Fall of 1963 to set up the CIA-sponsored Mountain Scout program in the Central Highlands, he selected as training site 'Buon Enao, a half empty Montagnard village [which] had previously been used by the CIA-sponsored American Special Forces, as a training base' (Petersen 1988: 37; see also McNeill 1982). The turnover turned out to be a complete failure, which the official historiographer of the Special Forces, Col. Francis Kelly, attributed to mutual hostility between Rhadé and Vietnamese officials, and to the generous distribution of weapons by Americans (Kelly 1973: 43–4).

Montagnard claims to autonomy

The character of the American Montagnard policy might be best demonstrated by their response to the *Front Unifié de la Lutte des Races Opprimées* (FULRO), which was considered a Montagnard autonomy movement, although it claimed to represent the Khmer and Cham minorities in Vietnam as well. The rank and file of the movement were the Montagnard CIDG units headed by the American Special Forces. The already difficult triangular relationship between Montagnards, Vietnamese and Americans was further compounded by the series of FULRO rebellions which took place in the ranks of the CIDG. The first rebellion took place in September 1964, in five CIDG camps around Ban Me Thuot. Montagnard (mostly Rhadé) militia took over the camps, killed a number of Vietnamese Special Forces and took the remaining Vietnamese and American Special Forces prisoner. Then they marched to Ban Me Thuot, where they temporarily controlled the local radio station. Although Saigon wanted to repress the rebellion severely, American anthropologists, Special Forces officers and CIA agents tried to avoid a clash, which would turn the Montagnard population against the government, and negotiated a solution between Saigon and the less radical rebel leaders (Sochurek 1965: 38–64). Thus, the rebellion was quelled due to bad coordination of the rebels and to successful American intervention, and a number of Montagnard units went to Cambodia with their leader Y Bham Enuol.

In October 1964, a conference of Montagnards and Vietnamese was held in Pleiku. Gerald Hickey, the anthropologist who had joined the US Navy think tank Rand Corporation and who had played a role in the negotiations, observed how the Montagnards saw the Americans as a protective buffer against the Vietnamese, who in turn were annoyed by American interference (Hickey 1982b: 83, 98–109). In December, 1965, another FULRO rebellion took place in a number of Special Forces camps all over the Highlands, but this rebellion was put down aggressively by the South Vietnamese Army. Some of the most important FULRO demands were restoration of the French-installed *Statut particulier* of the PMSI (1951), recognition of land claims and *coutumiers*, primary education in the vernacular languages, halting of resettlement programs, and direct American aid bypassing the GVN. After 1965, FULRO continued to be active both within and outside of the ranks of the Special Forces, and for some time there was a tacit agreement that FULRO forces could control portions of Darlac province if they would fight the NLF – which they did more aggressively than the regular South Vietnamese Army. There were various attempts at reconciliation between FULRO and the GVN, often brokered by individual Americans working for the CIA or the Special Forces or pressured by high-ranking American authorities. From 1964 onward, the GVN started to give in to some of the demands of FULRO during a series of negotiations and following massive American pressure. In 1964, with substantial American (CIA, AID) support, the GVN had established a Directorate for Highland Affairs, which in 1967 was raised to the status of Ministry for Development of Ethnic Minorities. Pressure was exerted to bring the Saigon government to accept Montagnard candidates for the 1967 elections. Some Montagnard leaders, including Paul Nur, Touneh Han Tho, Nay Luett and Touprong Ya Ba, were incorporated into government agencies, and in 1969 FULRO was persuaded to formally surrender to the Saigon government, after the latter had made some concessions concerning the recognition of Montagnard land titles, primary education in pupils' own language, and representation in parliament.

The GVN, however, remained lax in following up on promises made, and its performance in the Highlands was continuously plagued by the usual discriminatory attitude and corruption of its officials. The Saigon government, suspicious of American motives in the Highlands after the 1964 uprising, managed bring the CIDG units under formal control of the Vietnamese Special Forces, which had the effect of reducing direct American contacts with the Montagnards. Many initial Bajaraka and FULRO adherents outside the CIDG units, viewing the concessions by the Saigon government as merely cosmetic, remained in exile in Cambodia with their leader Y Bham Enuol or took sides with the NLF, like Y Bih Aleo. In 1972 FULRO was in fact re-established outside the CIDG forces, and eventually took sides against the Saigon government. In March 1975 it was the non-cooperation of the Montagnards with the Vietnamese authorities that would make the Communist surprise attack at Ban Me Thuot, capital of Dak Lak (Darlac) province, possible – an event which eventually triggered the fall of South Vietnam as a separate state (see Văn Tiên Dũng 2000: 56–70; Hickey 1982b: 266 ff.).[37]

In this context, much more could be said about FULRO, which has been one of the major exponents of Montagnard ethno-nationalism as decribed in Gerald

Hickey's *Free in the Forest: Ethnohistory of the Vietnamese Central Highlands, 1954–1976* (1982b). I refer to this book for more details, and refrain from further elaboration for want of time and space.[38] Suffice here to notice that the development of the FULRO movement further strained the relationship between the South Vietnamese and American governments and their local representatives. The GVN blamed the Americans, and mostly the Special Forces and the CIA, of at best taking a soft stand on, and at worst of actually supporting the FULRO movement, and hence of interfering with Vietnamese sovereignty. Thus, both the South Vietnamese government of the 1960s and the Socialist regime after 1975 took it for granted that FULRO, the Montagnard autonomy movement which started in the rank and file of the CIDG, was a CIA inspired and supported movement.[39] Many Americans, on the other hand, reproached the GVN for its discriminatory policies and attitudes with regard to the Montagnards, in virtually every American text on the Montagnards passages to this effect can be found.[40]

However, official American policy was to oppose FULRO and to support the GVN. In 1965, General Westmoreland issued an instruction to that effect, explicitly forbidding Special Forces to become involved in any dealings with FULRO. This instruction was circulated by 5th Special Forces commander Colonel William McKean (and taken up again in the 1966 *A Detachment Handbook*) in the form of three rules for US personnel: not to deal with FULRO or other Montagnard political representatives; to inform Vietnamese counterparts of any such contact; and to avoid interposing themselves between Vietnamese and Montagnards.[41] Sometimes, the presumed unofficial protection of Montagnard interests went too far from the official political point of view. For example, in a book intended to devise a winning strategy in Vietnam, Herman Kahn, director of the Hudson Institute on National Security and International Order, noted with some concern that 'many US military or political officials have, in effect, supported the FULRO movement among the Montagnards, which, given some of its objectives (the attainment of relative or complete independence of the mountain people), really represents a kind of subversive movement' (Kahn et al. 1968: 327). Notwithstanding official policy, many Special Forces and CIA personnel, however, continued to maintain low-profile contacts with FULRO, if only because many CIDG militia were FULRO-supporters. Moreover, many Special Forces found consolation in the idea of a special bond between Montagnards and Americans during their often bewildering experience of an atrocious, incomprehensible war during their tour of duty. This contributed to the creation of a mystique of a special bond between Montagnards and Americans which is carried over to this day through narrative and practice.

The Special Forces' myth of origin: Creating past and present

Many Special Forces veterans consider their Vietnam assignment with Montagnards as the real, operational origins of the Green Berets. The presumed bond between American Special Forces and Montagnards acquired almost mythical proportions, which have been retained until this day. This mystique of a special Montagnard–American bond was enhanced by numerous 'historical' publications, like Robin Moore's *The Green Berets* (1965), Donald Duncan's *The New Legions* (1967), Gordon Patric's *The Vietnams of the Green Berets* (1969), or Hans Halberstadt's *Green Berets: Unconventional Warriors* (1988). The latter, for example, claimed that:

> these Americans did more than just unload a bunch of antique firearms on the tribesmen, they came to stay and to lead and live with the people in the villages. They patrolled with them, lived with them, died with them. They learned to speak Jarai and Rhadé and all the other languages. They were initiated into tribal brotherhood, formally and informally. In the highlands in the '60s you could see American soldiers with half a dozen tribal bracelets on a wrist. each signifying a personal alliance and commitment to a tribe.
>
> (Halberstadt 1988: 15)

In the 1960s, collecting and wearing Montagnard gear, especially bracelets, became a sport among Special Forces (Stanton 1985: 187). At the insistence of Gen. Edward Lansdale, this collecting spirit was formalized by the establishment of US Army Special Warfare Museum at Fort Bragg, North Carolina, which looks more like a Montagnard ethnographic museum than anything else. This SF allegiance to the Montagnard tribes was also professed in war novels, like Smith Hempstone's *A Tract of Time* (1966), Jim Morris' *War Story* (1979) and *The Devil's Secret Name* (1990) and Don Bendell's *The B–52 Overture* (1992) and, of course, in films like Francis Ford Coppola's *Apocalypse Now* (1979).[42]

This special relationship is celebrated even now, with the various Special Forces veterans' chapters in Fort Bragg sponsoring the Montagnard refugee community, centered mainly in North Carolina. To this goal, SF veterans have established the General Cooperative Montagnard Association, which purposely shares the acronym GCMA with the French commandos of Colonel Trinquier's *maquis montagnard*. Twice a year, the GCMA organizes a 'Montagnard barbecue party' somewhere in North Carolina, where the special bond is reaffirmed by sharing reminiscences of the war, and by exchanging objects like Montagnard bracelets. In a sense, the Montagnard refugees, who are partly dependent on financial support from SF veterans, are appropriated by the latter in order to underscore the narrative of the mythical origins of the Special Forces by their physical presence. This act of appropriation can be very material indeed. Traditionally, Montagnard bracelets were exchanged during a ritual of alliance, and worn as a token of friendship; during these parties, however, they can be bought. An almost physical act of appropriation was performed during one such party in 1990, when a tall SF veteran slapped his arm around the shoulders of a much smaller, embarrassedly looking Montagnard, exclaiming: 'I don't care whether you're Jarai or Bahnar; you're my Yard!' [Yard being SF slang for Montagnard].

On their part, many Montagnard informants who fought for the Special Forces in the 1960s considered themselves as American soldiers rather than

South Vietnamese soldiers. Both in the United States and in present-day Vietnam, Montagnard veteran informants said they were armed, trained, commanded and paid by Americans, and told to fight against Vietnamese. Some even resented that they do not receive a US Army pension now, while others who reside in Vietnam desperately try to make contact with their former American commanders – and that is how the Montagnard expatriate community in North Carolina got there in the first place.[43] According to many observers and actors alike, the Americans were able to establish 'a warm relationship' with the Montagnards, despite 'all the enmity between the Montagnards and the South Vietnamese government'. General Westmoreland, commander of the US Armed Forces in Vietnam during the military build-up stage (1964–68), found this relationship so close, 'that many Vietnamese were quick to suspect American motives in the Highlands' (Westmoreland 1976: 78–9). In 1965, he eventually forbade the Special Forces to maintain any kind of contact with Montagnards related to the FULRO autonomy movement, in order not to jeopardize official American relations with the South Vietnamese government (see note 37).

In actual practice, the relationship between Americans and Montagnards was much less 'cosy' than was generally assumed. Although there were cases of genuine friendship and affection between Americans and Montagnards, this observation cannot easily be generalized. First, there were many Montagnards who took sides with the NLF, or remained aloof in the conflict. Second, many Montagnards who served with American Special Forces were either forced to do so, or simply fought as mercenaries paid by the United States, as Brigadier General S. Marshall observed early on (Marshall 1967: 22). Furthermore, for all the narratives about Special Forces living in Montagnard villages and adopting their lifestyles, this was a very temporary phenomenon, which effectively ended with the completion of Operation Switchback: as noted above, from 1963 onward, the CIDG were not defending their own villages anymore, but were more or less regular soldiers, following their American commanders where these led them. In a secret Pentagon-ordered counterinsurgency study by Donald Bloch (1967: 16), the spontaneity of Montagnards rallying to the Special Forces in the Buôn Enao period was already being questioned. Another classified study by Philip Worchell and Samuel Popkin – who later acquired academic fame with his book *The Rational Peasant: The Political Economy of Rural Society in Vietnam* (1979) – made the following observation:

> Almost all Montagnards desire to lead an easy life and stay home to cultivate the soil. They hated military life and being forced to carry out military obligations. For this reason, I was somewhat surprised when the Americans told me the Montagnards were good workers and good combatants. I felt it would be more correct to say they were faithful and docile.
>
> (Worchell and Popkin 1967: 173)

Moreover, after 1963, the NLF mounted three more or less successful attacks on Special Forces camps, helped by partisans inside these very camps, indicating that Montagnard 'loyalty' had been undermined by NLF propaganda. As this implied that American Special Forces could not simply rely on the Montagnards, the CIA started to contract Nung soldiers directly – i.e. without South Vietnamese interference – as security officers and bodyguards for SF personnel in the camps. These Nung people, an ethnic minority from northern Vietnam, were considered fierce soldiers who had fought with the French before, and were considered loyal if paid well.[44]

This might have shattered the image of Montagnards as loyal warriors on behalf of the Americans, but apparently it did not. The question then becomes, why this relationship continued to be considered so unproblematic, despite evidence to the contrary? On the part of the Montagnards, they were looking for a protective buffer against what they regarded as Vietnamese domination, in the new situation of South Vietnamese nation-building (Hickey 1982b: 83, 98–109). Even the Montagnard autonomy movement FULRO, which was organized in 1964 in the ranks of the Special Forces, again and again turned to American (CIA, embassy) officials for help, despite the official order issued in 1965 by General Westmoreland that Americans should avoid all contacts with FULRO. On the part of the Americans, they were parachuted as young individuals into a conflict situation where they could not make out who the enemy was, resulting in great frustration over the inability of engaging the enemy on conventional military terms; after all, all 'gooks' seemed to look alike. In that situation, a culturally and physically different population may appear as a potential ally. Thus, both Montagnards and Americans were looking for easily recognizable allies in a hostile and fundamentally unstable environment, and found each other to be 'natural allies', albeit for different reasons. Many American Special Forces felt that even their sheer physical survival depended on their rapport with Montagnards. Therefore, their affection for Montagnards went beyond what was the usual affection for mercenaries in a classical divide-and-rule policy. It also went beyond French affection for the Montagnards, despite the fact that French involvement with Montagnards had been longer and deeper.

In this situation, the constant reiteration of the originally French discourse on the longstanding antagonism and fundamental opposition between lowland Vietnamese and Montagnards – the latter conveniently taken to be one monolithic group – seemed to legitimate direct American intervention, who posed as brokers in the conflict. The official historiographer of the Special Forces in Vietnam, and in 1966–67 commander of the 5th Special Forces Group, Colonel Francis Kelly, spoke of the 'animosity between Montagnards and Vietnamese' as a result of an indifferent and even discriminatory 'attitude on the part of the Vietnamese' (Kelly 1973: 20). William Colby, CIA chief of station in Saigon at the time of the start of the Village Defense Program, found the Montagnards 'uncommonly good fighters, in part because of their anti-Vietnamese sentiments'. These sentiments were a Montagnard reaction to the 'prevailing Vietnamese attitude toward the mountain people [which] had about the same degree of compassion we Americans had displayed for our Native American population in the West' (Colby 1989: 283). In his narrative of the Special Forces, Hans Halberstadt

(1988: 14, 15) noted that Montagnards and Vietnamese 'hate each other', and 'as far as the tribes were concerned, the Vietnamese from the south were not much better than or different from those from the north. For centuries, they had been insulted and displaced and persecuted'. This is directly followed by a eulogy on the American intervention:

> Into this equation came a few Americans: giants, aliens from another world. They listened as the tribal leaders described the problems of the highlands and asked for help. The Americans made the leaders an offer: to help the tribes protect themselves
>
> (Halberstadt 1988: 15).

In the context of American intervention in the relationship between Montagnards and Vietnamese, the question then becomes: protection against whom? Many of the unsettling South Vietnamese policies in the Central Highlands, including the settling of northern refugees there and the resettlement of Highlanders in strategic hamlets, had been devised and supported by American agencies under the banner of 'nation-building'. Given the response on the part of Montagnard leaders to these policies since the late 1950s, it never seemed to occur to American experts – not even to knowledgeable anthropologists like Gerald Hickey – that the American interference might have aggravated the situation for the Montagnards. After all, any Montagnards' striving after autonomy was rendered suspect, because it was interpreted as a fifth column for foreign intervention undermining Vietnamese sovereignty. After the landing of American combat forces in 1965, the tropes of protection and affection in the standard narrative of American Special Forces intervention began to sound wry in the context of massive resttlement schemes, indiscriminate bombing, creation of free-fire zones, and defoliation campaigns, which had to prepare the terrain for conventional warfare by the US Army and Air Force. But apparently, such considerations hardly affected both wartime and post-war narratives of benevolent intervention and protection of Montagnards by American Special Forces.

The tropes of protection and affection in the standard narrative of American Special Forces intervention were often directly preceded or followed by another familiar trope in the narrative of Montagnards in Vietnam. This trope was the essential 'primitiveness' of the Montagnards. Halberstadt, for instance, describes Montagnards as 'essentially Bronze Age people – subsistence hunters, gatherers, and farmers using slash and burn methods' (1988: 14). The ethnographic fact that all groups used iron instruments, and many villages had blacksmiths, could not alter this historical verdict. Col. Kelly calls them 'primitive mountain people' whose life is 'governed by many taboos and customs' (Kelly 1973: 20, 22). William Colby, again, found the Montagnard 'cultures and economies ... truly primitive, little changed from their origins before the Vietnamese moved down from the North and pushed them from the rice-growing coastal plain into the mountains' (Colby 1989: 282–3). And then, in the words of Gordon Patric (1969:

45), 'the little people [= Montagnards] ... suddenly found themselves dragged into the 20th century and its Vietnam wars'. According to Halberstadt, 'there was no way for people with crossbows and spears to effectively resist people with firearms' (1988: 15). Much of this discourse was articulated for a large American and international audience in the popular journal *National Geographic* through Howard Sochurek's article 'Viet Nam's Montagnards Caught in the Jaws of a War', which carried headlines like 'Yesterday's People Face Today', 'Jeh Women Give Birth in Forest', and – referring to a Jeh legend on the common ancestry of monkey and man – 'Which Are Monkeys – and Which Are Men?' (Sochurek 1968: passim). But even in an official progress report to the American Congress, Deputy Ambassador Robert Komer (1966: 19, in Komer 1986) in charge of the CORDS (Civil Operations and Revolutionary Development Support) program in Vietnam, stated that the 'Revolutionary Development' training programs for Montagnards in Pleiku constituted 'a major step forward in the effort to bring these tribal people forward into the 20th century'. This tendency to equate cultural difference with temporal distance, and to regard contemporary cultural 'others' as relics of the past, has been termed 'denial of coevalness' by Johannes Fabian in his seminal *Time and the Other* (1983).

The assumption that Montagnards were primitive underscored their inherent vulnerability and innocence with respect to modernity, implying that they were victimized by the context of modern warfare. This discursive victimization of the Montagnards (by the Vietnamese, *not* by the French or Americans – despite the indiscriminate bombing, defoliation and resettlement!) moved the Americans to protect the underdog in this centuries-old antagonism, and hence provided an extra argument for American intervention, similar to the way the French before them had posed as *nation protectrice des minorités* in the Indochinese context. This denial of coevalness construed Montagnards as in need of US protection, despite the American reputation of racism and discrimination against Native Americans and Afro-Americans (who in the US context only found 'refuge' in 'Indian reservations' and 'Negro ghettos', respectively). Simultaneously, this discourse denied agency to the Montagnards: they were the victims of history, they could only react to outside developments without being capable of change themselves. The plain fact was conveniently overlooked, that many Montagnards had decided to follow the Viêt Minh in the past, and the Viêt Công in the 1960s – with Montagnard revolts being the ultimate stimulus to establish the NLF; or that many simply did not follow the Americans, and thus made a clear choice. In this narrative, Americans could not only act and think of themselves as protective heroes – good guys in an essentially corrupt cultural environment – but they could stress their essential benevolence, too, in a context which constantly seemed to question the legitimacy of their actions.

7 Moving the Montagnards

The role of anthropology

Introduction

In the course of the 1960s, increasing numbers of American advisors and agents employed by agencies like the Central Intelligence Agency (CIA), the US Agency for International Development of the State Department (AID), the International Voluntary Service (IVS), or the US Army Special Forces, started working with Montagnards or became otherwise active in the Central Highlands. From 1965 to 1973, a direct military intervention in Vietnam resulted in an important additional presence of the US Army, Air Force and Marines in the Central Highlands, sometimes in direct or indirect competition with the 'civilian' agencies like the CIA and AID and even the Special Forces. The American presence in Vietnam ended with the 1975 North Vietnamese Spring Offensive resulting in the downfall of the Southern regime. Because the Americans had no important economic interests in plantations or industry in Vietnam, there was no sharp contradiction between economic and politico-military interests, as had developed under French colonial rule. However, other contradictions developed, as the strategic options represented by different military and political institutions became vested interests: the Army and Navy wanting more – and more modern – firepower; the CIA concerned about the political allegiance of the population; USAID busy developing the countryside in order to counter peasant insurgency. The conflicting ethnographic discourses which attended these differing strategic options will form the subject matter of this chapter.

The need for anthropology

Whatever the nature of American Special Forces discourse on Montagnards, their political and military activities involving Montagnards created a need for more, and more accurate, knowledge on the Montagnards. When the Special Forces moved in by late 1961, they had only the practical knowledge of IVS 'volunteer' Dave Nuttle to guide them, together with the MSU report by Gerald Hickey (1957) and a small brochure entitled *Montagnards of the South Vietnam Highlands*, issued by the US Information Service in Saigon (1961). If this latter brochure is representative of the practical ethnographic knowledge of American agents, one can only wonder how the Special Forces met any success in organizing various Montagnard groups. The latter were called 'anarchical' (USIS 1961: 3), having 'no social traditions, no tombs, no altars' (pp. 4–5), their agriculture being 'characterized by primitive and destructive methods' (p. 9); while 'laziness is omnipresent and pillage easier than regular work'. Evidently, such knowledge would not do in the long run, and more specific ethnographic knowledge was needed. This is not to say that the Americans working in the field expressed any desire to be taught anthropology; on the contrary, 'anthropology' seemed to be a dirty word among army officers, sufficient to discredit the one accused of invoking it. Thus, Charles Simpson relates how Special Forces objected to the fact that in 1965 Rhadé CIDG were ordered to open a road near An Khê in Bahnar territory, but were told by MACV 'in no uncertain terms to stop clouding the issue with a "bunch of anthropological crap"' (1983: 168). Similarly, Gilbert Layton, the CIA architect of the Buôn Enao program, stated the following opinion on anthropologists in a letter of October 7, 1968, to his daughter Bonnie:

> As you know I've had many educated, degreed Anthropoligists [sic] working for, with, around, and against me. Those that begin to understand that they never will understand become pretty good men, some others rush across a surface, look, and then put out a series of books regarding the sexual mores of the 'Gluk Gluk' tribe which often sells because it is thinly disguised pornographic material.[1]

Although disdainful of (academic) anthropologists ('Hail the Anthropologist, may there always be anthropoids for him to hunt.'), Layton did have use for anthropological knowledge acquired through practical work, or better – ethnographic knowledge produced by others than professional anthropologists. This is attested by the importance that Layton, the unofficial CIA 'liaison officer' with the FULRO leadership in Cambodia and Vietnam, attached to a sort of quintessential piece of ethnographic information, reported in February 1963 to the CIA. This concerned the Rhadé myth of origin, which said that all Montagnards came from the Hole of Drung in Darlac province, south of Ban Me Thuôt. The CIA agents were told that Y Bham Enuol was not simply a political leader, but was regarded the most senior Montagnard leader by virtue of his descent: according to this Rhadé myth of origin, the ancestors of each clan and each group ('tribe') of all Montagnards had come from the narrow Hole of Drung – one at a time. The implication was that the order of emergence from the hole was the order of prestige in Montagnard society; Y Bham, then, was the senior member of the Enuol clan, the senior clan of the most prestigious group, the Rhadé. Although this legend undoubtedly reflects a definite Rhadé bias, which is not necessarily shared by other groups, it is still important because it was generally Rhadé who assumed leadership of Montagnard autonomy movements. For Americans, the relevance of this information was that Y Bham Enuol was not a political leader due to his leadership qualities, but because of his culturally prescribed prestige. This implied that Y Bham could not be simply replaced as leader of Bajaraka or – later – FULRO. According to the same legend, the Rhadé will be finished when the Hole of Drung closes, which many Rhadé believed to be the happening in 1962/63, according to the same CIA informants – four junior Rhadé officials in Darlac.[2]

Obviously, Gilbert Layton and other CIA agents and SF officers had good use for such ethnographic knowledge, whether produced by professional anthropologists or by others. But they realized that time was too short to rely on the 'practical men', and even where individuals acquired the kind of anthropological sensitivity needed in SF work, the tours of duty were too short to construct a systematic body of knowledge. Of course, the CIA had its own files and records which in due time developed into an archive of its own; the Army developed the so-called 'Lessons Learned' program, designed to carry over acquired experience both to the higher echelons in the military hierarchy and to successors through the systematic analysis of this experience. Still, there was a constant need for systematic ethnographic and political information on the Highlands which could not be generated in-house. The construction of a systematic body of ethnographic knowledge started in earnest. But despite the rhetoric concerning the special American–Montagnard bond, Montagnards were not really accepted as reliable informants on their own cultures and political views: Montagnards were found too primitive to acquire any ethnographic authority. This created the need for other ethnographic informants. One category of informants included 'patriotic' American missionaries working in the Central Highlands.

Crusading the Highlands

In the early 1960s, the American Protestant missionaries in the Central Highlands were an important source of ethnographic information. There were three major denominations in Vietnam, two of which concentrated on the Montagnards (Reimer 1975: 568–70). The Christian and Missionary Alliance (C&MA – also known as Worldwide Evangelization Crusade) led by Rev. Gordon Hedderly Smith and his wife Laura Irene Smith, started working in Ban Ma Thuôt in 1934, with the missionaries Rev. Herbert Jackson and Rev. Stebbin working from Dalat and Huê, respectively. The Smiths have published widely on their missionary experiences. While the Smiths spent the period of Japanese presence in French Indochina in the United States, Gordon Smith published one missionary narrative and two theoretical accounts on the use of anthropology in the missionary endeavor, *The Missionary and Anthropology* (1945) and *The Missionary and Primitive Man* (1947), in which he goes at great lengths to try to discredit and ridicule the 'credulity and superstition of the natives' (70). In *The Blood Hunters: A Narrative of Pioneer Missionary Work Among the Savages of French Indo-China* (1942), Smith characterized 'the savage [as] nothing but a big lazy child' (p. 49), just like Sabatier before him. Smith sketches a gloomy picture of utter savagery, of 'savages [who] lived as they did hundreds and maybe thousands of years ago.

They were like animals, owning no master but themselves, free to work or sleep as they themselves desired' (p. 43). But, in spite of this alleged liberty, 'These people are bound by the chains of an all-embracing system of superstition. Practically everything they do is governed by superstitious beliefs and fears' (p. 56). The most 'horrific' of the tribes lent its name to the title of the book; they 'were the Katu, the Bloodhunters we call them, for they not only sacrifice animals, but also human beings' (p. 18).

Like the French Catholic missionaries before them, the Smiths portrayed their potential converts as dangerous savages, and their missionary endeavour as potential martyrdom, in order to evoke sympathy from a devout audience and raise funds. Such titles as *The Blood Hunters* (1942), *Gongs in the Night* (1944), *Farther into the Night* (1952), and *The Ten Dangerous Years* (1975) conveyed this sense of living on the margin of civilization. Not surprisingly, the 'official organ of the Tribes of Viet-Nam Mission of the Christian and Missionary Alliance' in the 1950s and 1960s was entitled *Jungle Frontiers*. The juxtaposition of light and dark, of good and evil, called for a crusade, just as with the French Catholic missionaries in the nineteenth century. But in time, the word 'crusade' acquired an additional meaning in wartime Vietnam. In the 1960s, the old 'paganism' trope gave way to Communism as the Devil's device – a trope which found its first expression in Jannin's report which blamed the Sam Bram movement on Communist activities. As with the old French missionaries, the hardship endured by the missionaries was stressed: 'the missionaries and national workers have been able to carry on, under strain and difficulty, of course, but with tremendous success' (Smith 1975: 15). Renewed emphasis was put on martyrdom of the preachers as well as the (Christianized) tribal people, who were 'captured' by the Communists. Whereas the plight of the tribes was that Communism allegedly prevented them from hearing the Gospel, the plight of the missionaries was the physical danger they endured.

There was a small but flourishing missionary press, focusing on the martyrdom of American missionaries captured by the Việt Cộng. Books like Evangeline Blood's *Henry Florentine Blood* (1968), Carolyn Miller's *Captured!* (1977), and James and Mart Hefley's *No Time for Tombstones* (1969) purported to illustrate the heroism of American missionaries, captured in Vietnam. But the genre is epitomized by Homer Dowdy's *The Bamboo Cross: Christian Witness in the Jungles of Viet Nam* (1964 – on the flap the subtitle reads 'The Witness of Christian Martyrs in the Communist-ridden Jungles of Viet Nam'), almost as legendary and influential as Dr. Tom Dooley's exploits in Laos (1958).[3] Based on the missionary experiences of C&MA's Herbert and Lydia Jackson in Dalat, the book starts with a distorted version of the Sam Bram legend, in which the evil sorcerer was told by the spirit of the white python to kill off everything white, including white men, and their tribal allies, the Christian converts. The main character in the romanticized narrative is one such convert of the Jacksons, Sau, who learns to neatly distinguish between God-Followers and 'pagans' among his fellow-tribesmen. But he also learns about Communism, for 'the Viet Cong were thoroughly committed [to Communism]. If the Gospel stood in the way of communism, the new guerrillas, Sau knew, would oppose it bitterly' (Dowdy 1964: 151). And indeed, just like Moses led his people from Egypt to the Promised Land, Sau led his converts from atheist Communism into a resettlement area in the lowlands: 'This place is protected ... God has brought us here' (Dowdy 1964: 236). Significantly, in the missionary journal *Jungle Frontiers* the resettlement of Montagnards is seen to offer 'strategic opportunities for missionaries' in that the resettlement site constituted an 'easily reachable ... wide-open mission field' (Funé 1961: 2, 3).

The missionary effort, portrayed as a struggle against 'paganism' and 'savagery', is equated with the struggle against Communism, and conceptualized as a crusade. In his book *Doctor in Vietnam* (1968), Stuart Harverson of the Worldwide Evangelization Crusade regards the conflict as not simply 'Communism versus Capitalism':

> The real warfare is between militant atheism, an anti-God system of lawless violence, and the old, well-tried governments of just law and order which reverence the Gospel of Christ.
>
> (Harverson 1968: 13)

Somehow, bombs and bullets from one side had a political identity ('Communist bombs'), whereas American soldiers were simply and justly defending freedom. And indeed, the Protestant missionaries often stayed in the well-protected cities or in (the vicinity of) Special Forces Camps. But despite the obvious danger, there was not the slightest trace of doubt about the direction of the crusade:

> Vietnam has not taken God by surprise. He knows all about the Communists' plans for conquering S.E. Asia and the world.
>
> (Harverson 1968: 88)

From this perspective, the American intervention in Vietnam appears as a just war, sanctioned by God himself ('herself' would be inconceivable). Thus, Mrs Gordon Hedderly Smith could not understand that 'there are people in the United States and Canada who are blind as to what Communism is! ... We should hate and fear Communism...' (1975: 219). Small wonder then, that many missionaries saw it both as their religious mission and as their patriotic duty to inform American agencies (notably the CIA) on any intelligence concerning Communist activities and movements (Hostetter 1973; see above).

Writing about the other major denomination among the Montagnards, the Wycliffe Bible Translators/Summer Institute of Linguistics, Laurie Hart (1973: 21–2) notes the military terminology used by the missionaries – facilitating the association between the military and religious levels of the interventionist discourse. This is also evident from the titles featuring the C&MA journal *Jungle Frontiers*, such as 'Occupied', 'Break in the Mnong!', 'Steadfast under Threat', or 'The Call, the Command, the Conquest'. This last article by Grady Mangham (1959) explains the use of such words:

Call... Command... Conquest! Such a combination of vibrant, stirring words bring to us mental pictures of military action.... These words are no less familiar to the militant, aggressive Church of Jesus Christ.

(Mangham 1959: 2)

The C&MA militancy in the context of war transpires through such titles as 'Leave? Things Are Just Beginning!'. In a similar vein, Stuart Harverson of the Worldwide Evangelization Crusade tried to reassure the parents of American boys sent out to fight in Vietnam by stressing the militancy of the Gospel:

Jesus still held the initiative when He chose the way of the Cross. He said, 'I come not to send peace but a sword.' Shame on those who cry 'Peace at any price!'

(Harverson 1968: 87)

In her analysis of the Wycliffe Bible Translators/Summer Institute of Linguistics (WBT/SIL), Laurie Hart interprets their publications in a similar way:

The continual alternation ... between two planes, practical (the Viet-Nam War) and mythical (the War of Souls) and their corresponding protagonists and antagonists (the United States vs. communists; God vs. Satan) and the borrowing of terminology between planes ... results in the association of the two levels as: Viet-Nam War = War of Souls.

(Hart 1973: 22)

WBT/SIL's founder, William Cameron Townsend, saw it as the mission of his organization to save all 'pagan', illiterate ethnic groups in the world for Christianity by translating the Bible into the local languages. Obviously, linguistic research would be needed, then, for those languages without script. Overseas, the organization called (and still calls) itself Summer Institute of Linguistics, and poses as a neutral, scientific institution. In the US, on the other hand, the same organization is known as the Wycliffe Bible Translators, a missionary society waging an 'onslaught against ignorance and superstition' (Wallis and Bennett 1960: viii; see also Brend and Pike 1977), and most successful in raising funds (Hvalkov and Aaby 1981: 9–15; Stoll 1982: 1–17).

Entering Vietnam in 1957 through an introduction by President Magsaysay of the Philippines to President Diêm, the SIL obtained a contract from the Vietnamese Ministry of Education to provide school primers in the minority languages. From 1966 onward, USAID provided extensive funding for bilingual education programs in the context of Montagnard claims to cultural autonomy.[4] Although the SIL claimed to be non-political, it tended to see the American war effort in Vietnam as part of an anti-Communist missionary crusade. Often working in Special Forces camps or provincial capitals for security reasons, its researchers were part of the information network that surrounded the American counterinsurgency efforts in the Central Highlands (Stoll 1982: 86–92). In addition to school primers and bible texts, they published ethno-linguistic articles in their series *Mon-Khmer Studies*, as well as ethnographic studies focusing on folklore items (Gregerson 1972; Gregerson and Thomas 1980). While these ethnographic reports seemed harmless and a-political, the very superficiality of the non-analytical, descriptive narrative and the exotic topics (Katu blood hunters again!) served to reify Montagnard cultural identity as 'traditional' and hence antithetical to Communist doctrine.

To keep in line with the military/missionary idiom: the sword of the Gospel can be sharpened by anthropology. In *The Missionary and Anthropology*, Gordon Hedderly Smith, the senior Protestant missionary in the Central Highlands, was already claiming in the 1940s that 'anthropology can become a sharp tool, cutting through superstition and ignorance, and rendering the veils that hide poor lost humanity from our all too clumsy efforts to reach them with the Gospel' (1945: 17). Ethnographic knowledge and sensitivity were seen as prerequisites for efficacious ethnic and missionary policies. Robert Shaplen cites Gordon Smith as commenting on Vietnamese highhandedness regarding the Montagnards, by claiming that 'the Vietnamese don't know how to handle them. They have no anthropology to guide them' (Shaplen 1965: 184). For the missionaries of C&MA and WBT/SIL (as for the French Catholic missionaries in the nineteenth century), ethnographic knowledge was instrumental in converting Montagnards and changing their cultures. The missionary ethnographic discourse was not relativist, because Montagnard cultures were described as systems of 'savage', 'pagan' practices and beliefs, necessitating missionary intervention. Indeed, there was a tendency to focus on certain aspects (blood hunting, shamanism and sorcery) which were despicable – even sub-human – from a Christian fundamentalist perspective. Nevertheless, Montagnard cultures were conceived of as integrated social systems, albeit governed by evil principles. In describing the various cultural phenomena as parts of a social system – a system of 'savagery', a system of 'heathenism' – American missionary ethnographies can be labeled functionalist, although this theoretical perspective is never spelled out. Writing of a different era, George Stocking in his 'definitive' *Victorian Anthropology* has called this 'a functionalism of the abhorrent' (Stocking 1987: 104–05) – a functionalism which resembles the proto-functionalism which we discerned earlier in the ethnographic writing of French Catholic missionaries.

Not surprisingly, anthropology was associated with the very 'primitivity' which it was supposed to study. Anthropology was a discipline which was considered helpful in dealing with 'primitives', but which would be rendered obsolete as something of the past as soon as development took place. In the words of Robert Shaplen again:

> The American Special Forces and some Vietnamese cadres were doing their best to skip anthropology and leap all the way up to the present. They were teaching groups of volunteer Sedang and Katu tribesmen how to shoot guns, lay explosive chains of fire for ambush, and use walkie-talkie radios.
>
> (Shaplen 1965: 184)

For the time being, anthropology was seen as necessary knowledge that should guide action as long as the tribes were there. Contrary to the missionaries, however, Special Forces seemed much more eager to delve into Montagnard cultures. Their narratives spoke of adapting to tribal custom and being accepted by the tribe (usually by marrying the village leader's daughter), of assuming tribal leadership – one author, Jim Morris, a former SF officer, even calls himself 'brigadier general of FULRO' in his *War Story* (1979) – and benevolently protecting the tribe against malevolent Vietnamese and Americans. In the context of the Vietnam War, Special Forces' perception of Montagnards was often more relativistic than the missionary narrative which emphasized the need for (religious and political) change, but Special Forces simply lacked ethnographic information. The need for more, and better, ethnographic knowledge resulted in huge research efforts, known as Project Agile, CINFAC, and Project Camelot, as part of the counterinsurgency effort under the Kennedy and Johnson Administrations.

In the foregoing chapters we have spoken of the process of tribalization in response to the exigencies of colonial administration and enhanced by ethnographic classifications. In the context of French colonial rule, we noted that Catholic missionary ethnographers were much less interested in ethnographic classification, because of their interest in conversion as a process inducing cultural change. In that sense, conversion was meant to 'detribalize'. The opposite is true, however, for the WBT/SIL people, who concentrated on ethno-linguistic research and Bible translation into vernacular languages. This implied that they wanted to have a clear conception of what precisely constituted a separate language in the Vietnamese context. In other words: their initial effort was oriented to identifying linguistic groups and thus establishing a linguistic classification in Vietnam. And, as in colonial times, the adjective 'linguistic' was prefixed by 'ethno', implying an ethnic classification as well. Not surprisingly, then, the SIL-branch in Vietnam produced a map under the heading 'Tribes of South Vietnam' which was revised annually, based on new or better information; from 1970 onward, the term 'tribes' was replaced with 'ethnic minorities'. The map neatly showed the 'tribal boundaries' and the 'tribal names' printed on the territory of the 'tribes'. With the map went a list of 'Vietnam Minority Languages' which provided additional information on 'subgroups', population estimates, location, and linguistic affiliation (i.e. to a sub-branch of the Austroasiatic or Austronesian language families).[5]

This tribal map, the first version of which appeared in 1961, quickly became the basis for the American ethnic classification of Vietnamese 'tribes' and for further ethnographic research. The first SIL-map was further reproduced in the USIS publication *Montagnards of the South Vietnam Highlands* (1961), and in many subsequent American studies of Montagnards, including prestigious scholarly publications like Frank LeBar et al.'s *Ethnic Groups of Mainland Southeast Asia* (1964: vii, x) for the Human Relations Area Files, and Peter Kunstadter's *Southeast Asian Tribes, Minorities and Nations* (1967: 701). Since the SIL studies and later American ethnographies were for a large part based on French ethnographic sources, it is hardly surprising that this tribal classification is to a large extent based on the French ethno-linguistic classification, e.g. by Maitre (1912a), Malleret and Taboulet (1937), and especially the official *Carte ethnolinguistique de l'Indochine* of the *Ecole Française d'Extrême-Orient* (1949). This implies that American studies tended to follow the French tribalized model, although this model was sometimes contradicted by their own data. If their classification would have been based on their own field research, the outcome might have been different. For instance, in the context of a 'Mountain People Study' for the MSU in 1956, Robert Gilkey had interviewed various Montagnards, like K'Greng in the village of Tchrong Trambor, asking for their 'tribal affiliation'. In his research notes, Gilkey commented that 'they don't know; supposed to be Riong Sre, but they say not' (p. 11).[6]

Although American ethnographers generally followed the French tribalized model, they did not necessarily follow the same ethnographic classification. Americans often identified other groups and drew the boundaries differently. For instance, the SIL grouped the Lat, Chil, Sre and Ma together as Koho, where the French had made a distinction. On the other hand, the SIL (and later Army studies) distinguished various groups in northern Kontum and Western Quang Ngãi, Quang Tin, Quang Nam, Thùa Thiên and Quang Tri provinces, like Pacoh, Phuong, Takua, Cua, Duan, Katua, Kayong, Todra and Monom – groups which were rarely mentioned in French ethnographic sources. This ethnic differentiation may be partly explained by American interest in the northern portion of the Central Highlands and the Annam Cordillera, because of the location close to the 17th parallel and the Laotian border. The American Special Forces had a major presence there (termed 'border surveillance') to try to cut off the supply of goods and troops flowing down the Ho Chi Minh-trail. But there is something else at stake here, too. For it can be observed that with every change in political regime in Vietnam or Indochina, a new ethnographic classification was adopted, officially or unofficially. Of course, the French colonial classifications had been very different from the (often crude) pre-colonial Vietnamese distinctions. During the First Indochina War, the French felt the need to regroup the various 'tribes' into a few, larger 'ethnic' Montagnard territories. After 1954, the South-Vietnamese regime made the official distinction between '*nguòi thuong*' (highlanders) and '*kinh*' (thus effectively translating the term 'Montagnard' into Vietnamese), while Americans adopted a new 'tribal' classification. After Vietnam's reunification (1976), the government of the Socialist Republic would make a renewed effort at ethnic classification based on extensive scientific research, eventually producing an official list of 54 ethnic groups, indicated on an ethnographic map (which became soon outdated because of the massive population movements after 1975). These official ethnic identities would be applied in censuses and identity cards. Apparently, every new political regime needs to redefine the identities and locations of the various population groups on its territory. From the foregoing, it is obvious that these classifications related to the various needs and interests of a particular regime in terms of military conquest or pacification, administration, economic exploitation and conversion. This amounts to a process of appropriation of the indigenous communities, which increasingly have to fit into the current classificatory grid and its attending ethnographic discourse in order to be seen, heard, or receive any minority-related benefits.

Army research and ethnography

After World War II, American ruling elites were convinced that society could be managed and steered into the desired direction, as is evident from such frequently used terms as 'progress', 'development', 'modernization' and 'nation-building'. During the Kennedy era, a new generation of technocrats, often with academic credentials, rose to power, among whom Robert McNamara, Secretary of Defense under Presidents Kennedy and Johnson, became enigmatic (Gendzier 1985; Halberstam 1969; Hatcher 1990; Shafer 1988). Paradoxically, it was McNamara, famed for his reliance on statistical data, who would not heed to evidence contradicting his idea of how to fight guerrilla wars; and it was the same McNamara, advocate of the hard line in Vietnam, who in his recent account of the Vietnam War acknowledged that this elite, nicknamed 'the best and the brightest', had been 'wrong, terribly wrong' (McNamara 1995: xvi). With respect to Vietnamese society, American officials were generally in agreement that it could be controlled if the right tools were used – specifically, those of applied social science and social engineering, including anthropology. In contrast to French ethnography before 1954, American anthropology was already thoroughly institutionalized and professionalized, and in the context of the Vietnam War, research for the military was oriented toward the needs of counterinsurgency, a new field in which careers could be made in a discipline where jobs were – and still are – scarce.[7]

The interest of Department of Defense (DOD) in social science research was stimulated by the 'Ad Hoc Advisory Group on Psychology and Social Sciences', which on 19 December 1957 issued a report for the Defense Science Board of the Office of the Assistant Secretary of Defense, Research and Engineering, advocating the use of social science in military affairs. As a result of this report, the Smithsonian Institution established in 1959 the 'Research Group in Psychology and the Social Sciences' under Dr. Charles Bray, comprising 65 psychologists and social scientists, and financed by the Office of the Director of Defense Research and Engineering, to advise on long-term research planning. After the inauguration of the Kennedy administration with its emphasis on counterinsurgency, the Research Group changed its focus from internal DOD management of personnel to the questions pertaining to DOD operations abroad, in other cultures through a series of studies. For instance, in a report on 'limited wars' for the Joint Chiefs of Staff (1961), it was noted that:

> the greatest single deficiency which we perceive in the capability of the United States to cope with limited wars in remote areas is the lack of readily available knoweldge [sic] about the political antecedents and aspects of these

wars and of agreed doctrine based upon such knowledge... It is the function of research, especially social science research, to supply – along with intelligence – the materials for the formulation of the policy, and to aid in its formulation.[8]

The series of studies culminated in *Social Science and National Security* (1963), a lengthy study edited by Ithiel de Sola Pool, a leading political scientist at the Massachusetts Institute of Technology. The report stressed the relevance of social science research for an understanding of revolutionary processes going on in the Third World, especially in Vietnam. Science, it stated, could make a substantial contribution to the American counterinsurgency effort, since it would stimulate the use of political methods where military methods did not succeed. The report resulted in an increased recruitment of scholars by the military research institutions for applied social science research in support of the counter-insurgency effort.[9]

In *The Best-Laid Schemes: A Tales of Social Research and Bureaucracy* (1976), Seymour Deitchman, himself an advocate of applied social science research, and engaged in its coordination within the Defense Department, has provided a revealing sketch of many of the institutions engaged in social science research for the Pentagon. Deitchman was Special Assistant (Counterinsurgency), Office of the Director of Defense Research and Engineering (DDRE) of DOD from 1964 to 1966, and Director Overseas Defense Research of Advanced Research Projects Agency (ARPA) from 1966 to 1969. Briefly, counterinsurgency research was sponsored by the Navy (Office of Naval Research), the Air Force (Air Force Office of Scientific Research), the Army (Special Operations Research Office – SORO), the Advanced Research Projects Agency (ARPA), and the Office of the Assistant Secretary of Defense for International Security Affairs (ISA). The research was either performed in-house, or under contract by outside organizations such as the Rand Corporation and the Simulmatics Corporation, by academic institutions like the Michigan State University, the Stanford Research Institute, the Massachusetts Institute of Technology, or by individual scientists on a freelance basis. Ideally, all research activities for defense purposes were supervised by the Director of Defense Research and Engineering. His staff, however, dealt primarily with budgetary issues, and was unable to handle the large quantity of research activities itself.

Already in 1961, ARPA established a counterinsurgency research program, called Project Agile 'to signify the project's ability to respond rapidly to urgent requests for research' (Deitchman 1976: 68). These urgent requests sprang from the American military activities in Southeast Asia in the field of counter-insurgency, but initially concentrated on the technical and hardware aspects of guerrilla warfare. Only around 1964, did the emphasis shift to the social sciences, partly under the influence of an evaluation by a Defense Science Board (DSB) study group of existing scientific research programs initiated by the Defense Department. The DSB study group tried to formulate new research directions. A Behavioral Sciences Panel that, again, included Ithiel de Sola Pool, was asked to 'conduct a study and evaluation of research and development programs and findings related to ethnic and other motivational factors involved in the causation and conduct of small wars among the peoples of Southeast Asia' (ibid.: 95). While the Behavioral Sciences Panel report was rather critical of research performance of DOD, it regarded the 'exploratory research' within Project Agile as promising:

> ... studies have been made of ... the anthropology of the Montagnards, tribal groups in Vietnam. They have yielded much useful information and opened up promising areas for investigation, but, with regard to the solution of these important, complex problems, they have barely scratched the surface.
>
> (ibid.: 117–18)

The DSB report concluded that the counterinsurgency programs in Vietnam had been ineffective since they were based on insufficient knowledge of Vietnamese society and especially of the population the programs were aimed at. A large-scale research program was proposed which could help launch a successful counterinsurgency strategy.[10]

Research was increasingly channeled along the lines laid down in the DSB report. The three main counterinsurgency research projects were Project Agile, CINFAC and Project Camelot. Project Agile was a coordinated research effort directly serving the counterinsurgency effort in Southeast Asia. It was initiated by ARPA which tried to improve American counterinsurgency methods, such as the Strategic Hamlets program forcing the rural population into 'protected' villages in order to 'separate the fish from the water'. It also studied the impact of the American Special Forces on the attitude of the local population. In 1964, SORO established a Counterinsurgency Information and Analysis Center (CINFAC) at the Center for Research in Social Systems (CRESS) of the American University, Washington D.C., which drew upon available studies about tribal groups and social systems in developing societies in general for the benefit of any government agency that needed information on counterinsurgency. The scope of the research effort broadened: the locus of research was extended from Southeast Asia (Vietnam) to worldwide, while the focus of research was also extended, starting from the evaluation of counterinsurgency programs to include finally the causation of insurgency. This culminated in the fateful Project Camelot, also initiated by SORO, which was to be a worldwide research effort, intended to generate valid models for predicting the occurrence of 'internal wars'. In these research programs one can distinguish a shift from the social aspects of counterinsurgency (Project Agile) via political, cultural, and development-oriented dimensions (CINFAC) to social and economic issues dealing with the causes of insurgency (Project Camelot).

The disclosure of Project Camelot in 1966 caused many virulent debates in the academic anthropological community. In 1968, a lesser dispute was triggered by the advertisement in the *American Anthropologist* (70: 852) for a 'Research Anthropologist for Vietnam', to be positioned with the 'Psychological Operations Directorate Headquarters' of MACV. Then, in 1969, the heated debates flared up again over the so-called 'Thailand Controversy'. Although this is not the place to dwell on these debates and their consequences in academe, it should be noted that the publicity surrounding the debates had serious consequences for research sponsored by the military. With the deployment of regular US troops in Vietnam in 1965, opposition to the Vietnam War was mounting. Thus, the War was not simply a conflict between the NLF/North Vietnam and South Vietnam/US, but increasingly a conflict between protagonists and opponents of the war in the US and South Vietnam, too. In an atmosphere of mounting domestic crisis over the war in Vietnam, the Defense Department had to cancel Project Camelot in order not to endanger counterinsurgency research which was already being carried out in Vietnam. Eventually all social science research for defense purposes came under attack. In particular, the Congressional Hearings over this subject, prompted by Senators William Fulbright, Mike Mansfield and Eugene McCarthy at various occasions, critiqued the commissioning of secret or confidential research for military purposes. As counterinsurgency research in Vietnam by the military was becoming more and more embarrassing, the responsibility and the means for the sponsorship were partly transferred to civil agencies such as USAID and to its more 'academic' research branch SEADAG (Southeast Asian Development Advisory Group), established in 1965. Around 1970 it was evident that the US government faced a severe legitimacy crisis, which had its repercussion on research carried out for military purposes.[11] In the context of the Vietnamese Highlands, only research conducted in the context of Project Agile and the CINFAC program are relevant for this book, because it pertained to the Montagnards in Vietnam (as well as to both minority and majority groups in other Southeast Asian states).

Ethnographic sources

There were three sources of information regarding the Montagnards: past research by anthropologists or other (military, administrative) ethnographers, mostly French; American representatives in the field, who acquired practical knowledge of the ethnic groups; and sponsored research on specific topics deemed vitally important. Regarding the first avenue, American counter-insurgency practice often drew upon French experience in their dealings with the Montagnards and the Vietnamese in general (as well as from the British experience in Malaya and previous American experience in Greece and the Philippines), trying to transform this experience into applicable concepts.[12] Some French experts like Bernard Fall and Marcel Vigneras worked directly in the service of the Americans, either in Vietnam or in the United States, and Colonel Trinquier who set up the *Maquis montagnard* in Vietnam, claimed that he was asked to be involved in Special Forces training but that he declined for ethical reasons (Trinquier 1976: 85–8). Yet, his *La Guerre Moderne* (1961) was published in English in 1964.

A number of key ethnographic documents were translated into English through the Joint Publications Research Service (JPRS), like *The Montagnards of*

South Vietnam [*Les traits caractéristiques dans les moeurs et coutumes des tribus montagnardes au Sud du Vietnam*] (13 April 1962, JPRS 13443), a study by the *Direction de l'Action Sociale pour les Pays Montagnards* (n.d.); or *We Have Eaten the Forest – South Vietnam* [*Nous avons mangé la forêt*] by Georges Condominas (4 September 1962 [or. 1957], JPRS 15108 – For Government Use Only). But other institutes also commissioned translations. In 1967, USAID had Bernard Bourotte's 'Essai d'histoire des populations montagnardes' (1955) translated.[13] Just like Trinquier did not want to contribute his expertise to the American Special Forces, the original (French) authors sometimes did not agree with the uses to which their ethnographic writing was put. As mentioned in Chapter 1, in Condominas' 1972 'Distinguished Lecture' for the American Anthropological Association, he commented critically on the pirated translation of his 1957 monograph and on its uses by the Green Berets, 'the technicians of death' (Condominas 1973: 4; see also Condominas 1965: 442–70; and 1976: xi–xv). Another way in which French expertise was made available for the American counterinsurgency effort was the processing and analysis of French material by American experts working in American universities, research institutions, government agencies or the US Army. Sometimes translation was combined with processing, as in the case of Gerald Hickey's 'Preliminary Research Report on the PMS' (1957), which was partly based on French sources, and portions of the *coutumiers* by Sabatier and Guilleminet (dealing with land rights) as annexes (pp. 33–55). Most of the ethnographic studies conducted for the DOD were for a major part based on French sources.

The second source was American 'practical men' (rather than women) working in the Highlands. The first such example, of course, was Dave Nuttle, the IVS volunteer who made his practical knowledge and his networks available for the CIA and for the Special Forces. After that, many others received requests to make their practical knowledge available in a more systematic way, thus contributing to the creation of what could be termed an ethnographic archive. For the CIA, creating such an archive in the course of intelligence gathering and reporting was their *raison d'être*. From the quality and quantity of information in the previously cited CIA report 'Highlanders of South Vietnam 1954–1965' (1966), it is evident that this job was taken seriously.[14] In line with general US Army guidelines, the Special Forces produced their archive in the form of Intelligence, After Action Reports, Operational (or Lessons Learned) Reports, and Senior Officer Debriefing Reports at the end of the tour of duty.[15] With regard to the Montagnards, many 'returnees' were requested to complete a 'Questionnaire on the Montagnard Tribal Study', which were collected at the Special Warfare School (later rebaptized J.F. Kennedy Special Warfare School) in Fort Bragg, NC. In time, the 'Returnee Responses to Questionnaire on the Montagnard Tribal Study' would form an ethnographic archive in itself, which was used, for instance, as source material for the Special Forces study *Montagnard Tribal Groups of the Republic of South Viet-Nam* (1964) or the *Minority Groups in the Republic of Vietnam* volume (1966), prepared by CINFAC, American University. Some Special Forces officers indulged in more in-depth studies, like Col. Francis

Kelly's *The United States Army Special Forces in the Republic of Vietnam*, Lt. Col. Thomas McGuire's anthropological term paper 'The Montagnards of the Republic of Vietnam, the RHADE Tribe' (1964), the 'Historical Resume of Montagnard Uprising, September 1964', prepared by the Headquarters of the 5th Special Forces Group (Airborne), 1st Special Forces, or the evaluation report 'Employment of a Special Forces Group' (U).[16] Eventually, such information would be processed, along with the research reports by professional scientists, and be transformed into course material for the Special Warfare School in Fort Bragg (e.g. *Program of Instruction for 33-G-F6 Counter-Guerrilla Operations Course* (1961), or into numerous (revised or new) Field Manuals, following the systematic program laid down in the *US Army Combat Developments Command's Program for Analysis and Development of US Counterinsurgency Doctrine and Organization* (1964).[17]

However, the Special Forces and CIA agents were not the only 'practical men' around. There were also civilian organizations interested in ethnographic detail for a variety of reasons. Above, the role of missionaries has been outlined in some detail. Here might be mentioned the 'serious' ethnographic publications of the linguists of the Summer Institute, aiming at academic credibility (Gregerson 1972; Gregerson and Thomas 1980), as well as the fact that missionaries such as Charles Long and Donald Voth gave interviews at Fort Bragg or attended development seminars.[18] Also, the US Operations Mission (from 1965 the Agency for International Development), the Civil Operations and Revolutionary Development Support (CORDS – the civilian 'pacification' program of MACV) and voluntary organizations like IVS were involved in building an ethnographic archive. Though all these organizations were in one way or another involved in development activities, these were without exception geared toward the overriding goal of 'counterinsurgency' and 'pacification' of the countryside.[19] The underlying idea was that a population which shares in growing economic wealth would have no cause to support the Revolution. In their attempt to 'win the hearts and minds' of the Vietnamese – not by military force, but by economic support – they developed more interest in the local population, that is, those who would have to be developed. Not surprisingly, development workers in the Highlands started to collect and share ethnographic information.

Occasions to systematically write up ethnographic observations and sharing them, were typically provided by development seminars, like the 'IVS Ethnic Minorities Seminar' of May 1969, and the 'Conference on Economic Development among Montagnards at the Village Level' of November 1970. Such meetings were usually attended by people from IVS, SIL, voluntary organizations and, of course, Dr. Gerald Hickey, who by then was an old hand in Vietnam, and considered the main American expert on Montagnards. Significantly, there were only Americans but no Vietnamese attending these seminars, which is not surprising given the low opinion of Vietnamese development projects in the Highlands, as voiced by Tracy Atwood:

A [US] development worker who closely follows Vietnamese programs to help the Montagnards may also unknowingly pick up some of the cultural

Figure 7.1 Bishop Paul Seitz drinking rice wine during a tour of Catholic Montagnard villages after his release from NLF captivity in 1973.

Source: Archives des Missions Étrangères de Paris.

biases that the Vietnamese have towards Montagnards. The development worker is then working to defeat his own good intentions because, while he helps the Montagnards with one hand, his other hand is working to destroy them. By trying to change the Montagnard into a Vietnamese you are actually destroying his self esteem, identity, and belief in his own value and ability.[20]

The stress laid by American 'practical men' on an alleged Montagnard 'inferiority complex' *vis-à-vis* the Vietnamese was anathema in their writing on Montagnards, and legitimized their presence in the Highlands while delegitimizing Vietnamese presence there. In this respect, while the IVS seminars resembled the regular meetings of French colonial administrators in the Highlands in the 1930s, the (ethnographic) rhetoric in the documents produced bore similarities with French allegations concerning a Montagnard inferiority complex in the context of strong Vietnamese claims to sovereignty over the Highlands.

Often, the expertise and ethnographic knowledge of voluntary organizations carried over in official organizations like USAID. USAID, which in Vietnam collaborated closely with the CIA, made it a point to recruit former Special Forces (like Edmond Sprague, AID representative in Phu Bôn province) or IVS personnel. Some of this ethnographic and developmental expertise came together in *Some Recommendations Affecting the Prospective Role of Vietnamese Highlanders in Economic Development* (1971), officially authored by Gerald Hickey and published by the Rand Corporation. In the preface, IVS volunteers Lynn Cabbage and Tracy Atwood were thanked for their assistance, along with 'staff members of the Summer Institute of Linguistics, while the author mentions the interaction with MACV, CORDS, and USAID. In the report, four major recommendations were made: (1) to devise development programs in the Highlands tailored to the needs and capabilities of the Highlanders, e.g. in the field of commerce and cash cropping; (2) to resolve the issue of Montagnard land claims; (3) to study the effects of the resettlement of Kinh people in the Highlands; (4) and to suspend resettlement of Highlanders themselves. The recommendations were backed up by case materials on traditional and innovative economic activities by Montagnards, and by appendices on Highlanders' land claims, Vietnamese migration into the Highlands, and on Highlander resettlement schemes. In short, the report was a plea to take Montagnards seriously, both politically and economically.[21]

Another example of this continuity between ethnographic expertise in voluntary organizations and 'official' development practice is the 322-page 'Five Year Plan for Highland Agriculture Development' composed by the same Lynn Cabbage and G. Tracy Atwood (November 1972), two IVS volunteers with a keen interest in ethnography, for AID and for the South-Vietnamese Ministry for Development of Ethnic Minorities (MDEM). The Five Year Plan contained scattered ethnographic information in a series of more or less coherent programs, project proposals, and case studies concerning Montagnards. Like the French before them and the Communist regime after them, the idea was to devise 'methods of breaking the slash-and-burn farming pattern', thought to be untenable in a situation of rapidly decreasing per capita agricultural land area, and to introduce market 'incentives'.[22] This plan eventually resulted in the 'Five Year Plan for Agricultural Development for Montagnards, 1974–1978' of the MDEM, to be financed for the greater part by USAID and NGOs.[23] If useful, USAID enlisted the organized expertise of other organizations by subcontracting the implementation of projects to universities or research institutes. The Summer Institute of Linguistics, for instance, had, from 1967 onward, been contracted by USAID to compose textbook materials in Montagnard languages.[24] In the late 1960s and early 1970s, AID would become closely associated with Montagnard policy, with AID officials effectively running some of the most important programs of the MDEM. But the role of AID and other civilian organizations in feeding a particular ethnographic discourse and ethnic policy will be dealt with in a next section.

Regarding the third avenue to the construction of an ethnographic archive (sponsored research on specific topics or groups deemed vitally important), Michael Klare, in his study of American research for 'defense' purposes, observed that 'the Department of Defense could obtain most of the information it required on minority groups from literature of scholarly anthropological research' through the Cultural Information Analysis Center (CINFAC) and the Defense Documentation Center. Therefore, it was 'only when vital gaps exist[ed] in academia's knowledge of strategically located minority peoples [that] the

Pentagon found it necessary to sponsor original research in this field' (Klare 1972: 111; see also Deitchman 1976: 133–9). If research was needed for the Army, Navy or Air Force, it was either performed in-house, or on a contractual basis by defence-related research institutes like the Rand Corporation or the Simulmatics Corporation, or by special research institutes attached to universities, like the Massachusetts Institute of Technology (MIT) or the Special Operations Research Office (SORO – later rebaptized Center for Research in Social Systems [CRESS]) at the American University (Washington, DC) which was responsible for CINFAC. To reduce the risk of bias, the research was spread out over a number of research institutes (Deitchman 1976). With regard to the three sources of information (French experience, American 'practical men', and actual sponsored research), they were usually used simultaneously, as is reflected in the composition of the *Montagnard Tribal Groups* volume (1964), prepared by the Special Warfare School at Fort Bragg; and of the *Minority Groups in the Republic of Vietnam* volume (Schrock et al. 1966), prepared by CINFAC of the Center for Research in Social Systems (CRESS) of the American University.

Ethnographic research and CINFAC

Apparently, the gaps in the body of knowledge were numerous, for Project Agile and the CINFAC program were pouring out a veritable avalanche of studies directly or indirectly related to Vietnam's Montagnards from 1964 to 1967. The CINFAC program aimed to provide cultural information on relevant ethnic groups, and therefore commissioned ethnographic research *tout court*, if necessary. Project Agile, on the other hand, initiated problem-oriented research, which related directly to the American counterinsurgency effort; hence, it focused on specific phenomena which might involve Montagnards, like intercultural communication, the effectiveness of Special Forces performance, or refugee movements. This was the case, for example, for the study on Montagnard leadership, commissioned from ARPA in 1965. The research was based on the assumption that 'if pacification programs in the highlands are to be effective, account will have to be given to prepring [sic] the emerging leadership of the minority groups for an increased role in economic and social development'. This assumption was similar to the assumption of French military explorers around the turn of the century, who formulated a *politique des chefs* because they did not know how to connect their colonial order to an indigenous order (see Chapter 3). This search for tribal leaders – whether traditional or 'modern' – was predicated on the assumption that such tribal leaders exist, and that they are male. One effect of this search was that such leaders came to exist, and that they were male. On this issue, the need for information was met by the research done by Gerald Hickey (1967), who was employed by the Rand Corporation, as well as by the secret CIA study 'Highlanders of South Vietnam 1954–1965' (1966), on political developments among the Montagnards, which included biographical sketches of over one hundred Montagnard leaders – but we shall turn to the large ethnographic oeuvre of Gerald Hickey below.[25]

Given the sheer number, it will not even be possible to name all the relevant reports put out under Project Agile and CINFAC. The CINFAC studies were mostly no more than ethnographic sketches of tribes. Typically, these reports had titles such as *Brief Notes on the Tahoi, Pacoh, and Phuong of the Republic of Vietnam* (Fromme 1966), *Customs and Taboos of Selected Tribes Residing along the Western Border of the Republic of Vietnam* (Fallah 1967), *A Brief History of Ethnically Oriented Schools within Vietnam's Educational System* (Fallah and Stowell 1965), and CINFAC's *Bibliography of Materials on Selected Groups in the Republic of Vietnam* (1966). Most of these studies were pre-studies of individual groups, based on bibliographic research and interviews, of specific groups in preparation for the magnum opus of CINFAC, *Minority Groups in the Republic of Vietnam*, composed by Joann Schrock et al. (1966); or, as in the case of *Brief Notes on the Tahoi, Pacoh, and Phuong* (Fromme 1966), they were additions to the latter volume. Eventually, the newly acquired ethnographic insights were incorporated in the revised *Area Handbook for South Vietnam* (1967) composed by Harvey Smith for the American University's Foreign Area Studies, under contract of the Department of Defense.[26]

The most curious study from CINFAC certainly is *Customs and Taboos of Selected Tribes Residing along the Western Border of the Republic of Vietnam*, by Skaidrite Maliks Fallah (1967). This study covers nine 'tribes', with for each group only three sections: on psychological characteristics, on religious beliefs, and on customs and taboos. This last section consists of two columns, the left column listed as 'folk beliefs', the right column as 'commentary'. One example from Fallah (1967: 25) on Jarai customs and taboos:

Folk Beliefs	*Commentary*
The Jarai fear dying away from their home village.	This fear has a tendency to inhibit Jarai to travel away from the village.

Knowledge of such 'folk beliefs' was thought to be useful for American officers commanding Jarai soldiers or irregulars (CIDG); in this case, an officer would better not order his Jarai troops away from their home area. This study is the result of a letter of 3 September 1965 from the Commanding General, 173rd Airborne Brigade, requesting 'sociological research into native superstitions that can be exploited in our favor to bolster the friendly natives; put fear into enemy natives; and convert those on the fence'.[27] It was believed that such ethnographic knowledge, especially with reference to their religious beliefs and practices ('customs and taboos'), could be used to force Montagnards into political and military compliance. The intimidating nature of these intended uses of ethnographic knowledge is reminiscent of the accounts of French Catholic missionaries in the last century, who presented themselves as mightier sorcerers than the local ones.

The volume *Montagnard Tribal Groups in the Republic of South Viet-Nam*, was prepared by the US Army Special Warfare School at Fort Bragg (1964) with the advice and support of the Special Operations Research Office (SORO, the predecessor of CRESS at the American University). Less 'academic', this volume intended to assist the Special Forces in their undertakings in Vietnam, and hence was characterized by a certain urgency to publish the available ethnographic information as soon as possible. It is interesting to take a closer look at the argument for this type of research:

> Perhaps a ... word of explanation is needed as to why a research project of this type, normally in the domain of cultural anthropologists, has been conducted by the Special Warfare School. The School has always stressed that ultimate victory consists of winning over, not fighting against, people; that the strategic struggle is for men's minds; and that the first step in such struggle is one of understanding.
>
> (US Army Special Warfare School 1964: iv)

This statement testifies to the degree of professionalization of the discipline, in that ethnographic representation had become the 'domain of cultural anthropologists'.

Conversely, it should not surprise us that the Special Warfare School sought professional help in constructing ethnographic knowledge, naturally from those institutes especially set up by the DOD to produce such knowledge for military purposes. The ethnographic research and its representation adopted the format of the usual professional categories of the time. Typically, the defence-related ethnographies were molded into prefab categories, neatly fitting into the 'manners and customs' genre. Although, the section headings and ethnic categories displayed slight variation, the overall format of the ethnographies was remarkably similar. The major CINFAC volume had, for each ethnic group, the following sections: 1. Introduction; 2. Tribal Background; 3. Individual Characteristics; 4. Social Structure; 5. Customs and Taboos; 6. Religion; 7. Economic Organization; 8. Political Organization; 9. Communication Techniques; 10. Civic Action Conderations; 11. Paramilitary Capabilities; 12. Suggestions for Personnel Working with the xxx (one of the 18 highland groups represented in this volume, along with other minorities in Vietnam, cf. Schrock et al. 1966). Other ethnographic volumes were remarkably similar in outline.[28]

The natural academic reference for such ethnographic surveys was the prestigious Human Relations Area Files, established at Yale University by George Murdock. While Asian studies in America had been regarded as a rather exotic and esoteric pastime between the two World Wars, this gradually changed in the course of the Cold War. In the 1960s there was a rapid expansion of Asian studies in the US, due to 'a major infusion of federal government funding under the terms of the National Defense Education Act of 1958, which favored especially the teaching of modern languages and the Social Sciences' (Wyatt 1994: 53). As the title of the law indicated, the new educational and scientific policies were perceived as enhancing American national interest in military matters. Not surprisingly, then, in 1960 George Murdock's Human Relations Area Files received a grant from the National Science Foundation in order to prepare a book on Southeast Asia, one of the hot areas of the Cold War. This resulted in the volume on *Ethnic Groups of Southeast Asia*, compiled by Frank LeBar, Gerald Hickey and John Musgrave (1964). This volume had the following divisions: Orientation (= introduction, background); settlement pattern and housing; economy; kin groups; marriage and family; socio-political organization; religion; bibliography. The notes and bibliographies of the various volumes reveal that the volumes not only referred to the same sources, but to each other as well, indicating a cross-fertilization of academic and military ethnographies. The similarity and exchangeability of the military and academic ethnographic discourse was epitomized in the person of Gerald Hickey, to whom we return later.[29]

The main difference between military and professional ethnographies was, that the military ethnographies had, apart from purely 'ethnographic' sections, sections containing 'practical guidelines' under the headings 'Political Subversion', 'Psyops [psychological operations] Considerations', 'Civic Action Considerations', 'Paramilitary Capabilities' (US Army Special Warfare School, Montagnard Tribal Groups, 1964), or 'Communications Techniques', 'Civic Action Considerations', and 'Suggestions for Personnel Working with the Montagnards' (Schrock et al., Minority Groups in the Republic of Vietnam, 1966). But even this distinction between academic and military ethnography is none too subtly subverted by John O'Donnell's article on the 'strategic hamlet progress' in Peter Kunstadter's *Southeast Asian Tribes, Minorities and Nations* volumes, published in 1967 by Princeton University Press. In a book with obvious academic pretensions, O'Donnell reports on the counterinsurgency successes of the strategic hamlet program in one Vietnamese province in a not overly impartial way – even the style betrays his partiality (and involvement, as provincial AID representative). His contribution ends with a number of suggestions for 'improvement'. The same volume also contains a contribution by Hickey on Vietnam's Montagnards, partly based on his Rand report of 1964, but adding historical narrative, mainly on FULRO and on Montagnard-government relations. Incidentally, the volume is partly the outcome of ARPA programming, as the editor, Peter Kunstadter, had been using ARPA funds to organize a conference at Princeton University on 'Minority and Tribal Peoples of Southeast Asia and Relations with Central Governments'. Kunstadter cut off relations with the DOD after criticism from colleagues in the wake of the disclosure of Project Camelot.[30]

With or without practical guidelines, both military and academic ethnographies clearly conform to the 'manners and customs' genre in anthropology. This genre in ethnographic writing has been the object of radical critique before. One of the main themes in the 'literary turn' in anthropology in the 1980s has been the preoccupation with the textual construction of ethnographic authority (cf. Fabian 1983; Clifford and Marcus 1986; Marcus and Fischer 1986; Said 1978 and 1989a; Nencel and Pels 1991). In the Introduction, I have outlined the trajectory of the genre as the outcome of a process of systematization knowledge based on travel since the Renaissance. The companion method of the 'manners and customs', the ethnographic questionnaire, only became redundant with the emergence of extended anthropological fieldwork, but by then ethnographic knowledge had been textually construed as taxonomic knowledge. Robert Thornton (1988) has shown how the idea of 'social wholes', to be known by an ethnographer adhering to the ideal of ethnographic holism, is a rhetorical construction which derives its force from the structure of the text rather than its conformity to reality:

> [T]he ethnographic text is made up of parts or 'chapters' that are compilations of many disparate observations of behavior, language, ritual, ... and so on. These small fragments of patterned, usually formalized behavior and thoughts are the elements of the fieldwork record, that is, they are 'real' ... Chapters and divisions of books reflect an idea of society as a 'sum of parts'.
>
> (Thornton 1988: 291)

Following Fabian (1983; 1991), Thomas (1989) and Pels and Nencel (1991), we can see how this rhetorical construction of indigenous cultures as 'social wholes' effectively distances the author from both her/his ethnographic 'objects' and her/his audience. The ethnographer assumes ethnographic authority, claiming an almost panoptical view of a local culture, 'understood' in its totality, and neatly divided in parts. For both academic anthropologists and military ethnographers, their superior, systematized ethnographic knowledge of indigenous society enabled them to know better than others, whether these others are Vietnamese, Montagnard, or French. Thus, the 'understanding' sought in the Special Warfare School ethnography (see citation above) was a cognitive rather than hermeneutic effort, despite all rhetoric concerning the mutual sympathy between Americans and Montagnards.

Still, the dominance of one ethnographic genre contributed to the similarity of ethnographic images and to the exchangeability of these images, couched in the same idiom. In this context, it is important to note that the creation of an ethnographic archive tended to coincide with a process termed 'bureaucratic reproduction' by Henk Schulte Nordholt. Writing of 'the making of traditional Bali', Schulte Nordholt showed how the powerful ethnographic images created by early colonial officials and scholars were constantly reproduced in bureaucratic reports. In time, these images would influence not only academic anthropologists working in Bali, but also Indonesian officials and Balinese people who adapted to the 'fixed and authoritative models' which had been imposed by colonial bureaucrats, and which now abound in the tourist brochures on Bali (Schulte Nordholt 1994: 120; for a similar analysis, see Said 1989a: 218). A similar process took place in Vietnam, with respect to the Montagnards, in that a limited number of ideas, which often originated in French, colonial times, were used over and over again in narratives concerning the Montagnards. The most important of these ideas was that the Montagnards, despite considerable cultural variation, constituted essentially one ethnic group which uniformly hated (and were themselves despised by) the ethnic Vietnamese. In the Vietnamese context, bureaucratic reproduction of ethnographic representations would merge with a process of 'academic reproduction', in that bureaucratically produced images of Montagnards would be reproduced in academic ethnographic discourse. What follow in the next paragraphs are just a few examples of this.

The chapter on Bahnar culture in *Minority Groups in the Republic of Vietnam* (Schrock et al. 1966) was for the major part based on the ethnographic oeuvre by Guilleminet and on Hickey's 1957 report for the MSUG (which again incorporated portions of Guilleminet's *Coutumier Bahnar*); Guilleminet himself had been influenced by the work of Mgr. Kemlin and his predecessor Father Guerlach. Thus, it is noted that the Bahnar universe is divided into three worlds (Schrock et al. 1966: 29), an observation attributed to Guilleminet (1952b), but which was first described by Kemlin (1917). More interesting is the notion of the *toring*, described as an 'arrangement under which the territory within several villages is collectively administered by these villages' (Schrock et. al. 1966: 34). This definition is culled from a report by Gerald Hickey (1965) who does not refer to Guilleminet's *Coutumier* (1952a) but repeats that much land is not claimed by Montagnards, and therefore *res nullius*.[31] Elsewhere, I have argued that Guilleminet, missing among the Bahnar the formal, oral *coutumier* which Sabatier had described for the Rhadé, had modelled his *coutumier bahnar* on the *coutumier rhadé* by Sabatier and Antomarchi (1940) and the *coutumier stieng* by another colonial administrator, Gerber (1951), as well as on the exigencies of colonial rule (Salemink 1987: 140–1). With respect to the *toring*, Guilleminet explicitly stated that the *toring* defined usufruct rights to the land only, not property rights, because 'the Administration is the eminent owner of all the territories and goods which are not the object of individual private property' (Guilleminet 1952a: 463). This attempt, disguised as ethnography, to deny Bahnar land rights and appropriate the lands as state property for the benefit of plantation concessions (cf. Salemink 1987: 140–1), carried over into subsequent ethnographies of Hickey and others, including the Army studies.

In the same vein, the *pô lan*, Sabatier's female guardian of the land, hardly existed anymore when he described her (and by the same token defined Rhadé land rights, cf. De Hauteque-Howe 1985: 67–8). In fact, Sabatier tried to revive the tradition, in order to keep out colonial settlers from the Darlac Plateau (see Chapter 3). Yet, the notion was repeated over and over again in the context of continual violation of Rhadé land rights. Schrock et al. (1966: 695) note that Hickey's MSUG report (1957: 14) signals a decline of the *pô lan* system, but this is seen as a recent phenomenon. What is remarkable in this – inevitably gendered – discourse, is that a high status of women, and their control of land and goods, is equated with tradition and therefore situated in the past. In other words, American ethnographers like Hickey found it expedient to refer to 'traditional' female roles in their defense of 'traditional' land rights. However, any plea for bringing the fruits of modernity (education, health care, modern agriculture, economic innovation) to Montagnards implied the male sex only.

In this light, it seems cynical that ethnographers like Hickey paid so little attention to the gender effects of war on highland populations. It was men who could go to schools, get jobs and wages, enlist in the army, become 'chief' (either 'traditional' or 'modern'), not women – in spite of the relatively high status that Rhadé and Jarai women in particular, used to have. While men were enlisted by French, American and Vietnamese armies, women tended to follow, upsetting the matrilocal residence patterns in their societies, and thus undermining their own positions. However, the alternative was being left behind to take care of the children and the elderly, while doing all the subsistence activities on their own. It is ironical to read, then, in *Minority Groups in the Republic of Vietnam* (Schrock et. al. 1966), that the Rhadé division of labour is such that men do the 'heavy work' (like hunting) while women do the 'lighter' jobs associated with the household, while in reality the men were being drawn out of this domestic orbit to do military, political and economic jobs elsewhere. Simultaneously, there was (and still is) a policy of breaking up the longhouse, which gradually reduced the extended families to series of nuclear families. Resettlement areas had no use for longhouses and tore extended families apart. These developments increasingly deprived women (rather than men) of the comfort and support provided by family networks (e.g. mothers, sisters and cousins in matrilineal societies). None of the American ethnographies paid attention to such processes, although these could already be observed in the early 1960s, when Anne de Hautecloque did her field research among the Rhadé (De Hautecloque-Howe 1985: 195–7).

Applied research under Project Agile

Contrary to CINFAC, Project Agile did not provide basic information on ethnic groups, but coordinated applied research on specific problems. The majority of the studies conducted under Project Agile did not relate to the Montagnards, but a number of them did. Apart from the work by Gerald Hickey for the Rand Corporation, which will be discussed in the next section, these were mainly unpublished, often secret studies on the (potential and actual) role of ethnic minorities in counterinsurgency programs, like Joyce and Wing (1967), Bloch (1967) and Worchell and Popkin (1967); studies on the performance of American Special Forces in the cultural landscape of Indochina, like Stires (1964) and Ello et al. (1969); and studies on cultural and social factors affecting the American war effort, like Havron et al. (1968), Sternin et al. (1968), and Hickey (1965).[32]

The first serious study of American-Montagnard relations, then, was Frederick Stires' *The US Special Forces CIDG Mission in Viet-Nam: A preliminary case study in counterpart and civil-military relationships* (U) for SORO (1964). A large portion of the report is devoted to the 'Montagnard problem', explaining it in terms of former French policy of segregation and Diêm's policy of assimilation (1964: 10; in fact using the same distinction between segregation, assimilation and cultural pluralism as Donoghue et al. [1962: 105–7]). Stires points out that both Operation Switchback (transfer of operational control over the Special Forces from the CIA to MACV in 1963) and the 'turn-over' of the CIDG program to the Vietnamese authorities (1964) were detrimental for the original strategic concept, which had been sound and effective. The author maintains that the American military tended to employ the CIDG in offensive operations and to neglect the 'civic action' and 'psychological operations' which had made up a major part of the Buôn Enao program. The Vietnamese authorities were suspicious of the program as an American interference with Vietnamese sovereignty over the Highlands, and were not prepared to continue the program as originally devised. Significantly, where the author explains that the CIDG was essentially a defensive concept (but was now used for offensive operations, contrary to the idea of local militia defending their home area), the copy at the National Archives carries the hand-written comment of a military officer: 'The best defense is the offensive' (Stires 1964: xii).

In a discussion of the 'position of the Montagnard' (1964: 84–6), the author signals a tendency in 'descriptive studies of the Montagnard' to 'treat the Montagnard tribes as a homogeneous group' (where the Rhade political leadership claims to speak for all the 'tribes'), whereas it would be useful to 'identify any differences in tribal political attitudes and motivations'. Frederick Stires opposes the oft-heard 'suggestion that the Montagnard tribes be granted an autonomous status within the national community', because of the actual tribal diversity; because of the resistance of the successive Vietnamese governments; and because of the uncertainty whether Montagnards, once granted autonomy, would automatically rally to the Government side. For Stires, the answer should start from 'the current *partial assimilation* policy' of the GVN (1964: 83), although he admits that the 'task of accommodating the Montagnard minority within the Vietnamese national community ... is a complex politico-military one' (p. 85). Given the 'historical conditions which kept these people backward and apart' (i.e. the 'traditional hostility' between Montagnards and Vietnamese), Stires pleads for further research into the 'motivation and conditions which might gain the cooperation of the Montagnard' (p. 85). All in all, Stires claims that '[t]he recruitment and arming of members of these [minority] groups has been described as 'a calculated political risk', thus presenting 'a possible source of friction' (p. 94). One concrete proposal by Stires is 'to assign one Civil Affairs officer at Sector Headquarters' and of 'specialists in the fields of civic action and psychological operations' to the Special Forces A-detachments (p. 96).

In 1967, two classified reports on the use of Montagnards for counter-insurgency purposes were issued almost simultaneously. Richard Joyce and Roswell Wing wrote *The Mobilization and Utilization of Minority Groups for Counterinsurgency* (Confidential) for the Research Analysis Corporation, in which the strategic importance of such groups was assessed because of hostility with the dominant ethnic groups, lack of contact with the national government, and the strategic importance of the terrain they occupy. The authors argue that conditions for success are a careful preparation of the local population, sound cultural knowledge, 'civic action' activities (like medical aid), and implementation 'through the existing tribal or minority-group leadership structure' (p. 9). The report argues that the Village Defense Program conformed to these criteria, but the CIDG program much less so, partly because of American haste, partly because of the 'turn-over' to the Vietnamese Special Forces. The report signals that some of the requirements for success of the CIDG program had been known by the Special Forces, but they could not do anything about it 'because they lie within the purview of the Vietnamese government' (p. 14) The key to successful 'mobilization and effective utilization of each group' is 'more basic information on the attitudes, customs, aspirations and other characteristics' (p. 15). In a sense, the authors invented the wheel anew, in that their conclusions came close to the observations by Col. Galliéni at the end of the 19th century (see Chapter 2).

The other secret study of 1967, *A Review of United States Military Counterinsurgency Activities with Selected Minority Groups in South Viet-Nam: Some Policy and Doctrinal Considerations*, composed by Donald Bloch (with Marshall Andrews) for the Center for Research in Social Systems of the American University, focused on the responsibility of the US Army advisors in the triangular relationship with the minority groups and the 'host government' in programs 'designed to gain the support of minority groups for the host government' (Bloch 1967: iii). One of the problems was motivation: to many observers, it seemed that NLF fighters were generally much better motivated than soldiers or militia fighting on the RVN side. Regarding the loyalty of minorities, the study 'suggests that motivation is not a function merely of local attitudes but of the manner in which these attitudes are manipulated or cultivated' (p. 7). Regarding the so-called 'humanitarian approach' – 'you can't fight ideas with guns', the author concluded that military and 'humanitarian' action are interdependent:

> To maintain control of an area, a force must be armed, able, and willing to fight for control. All of these attributes are mutually dependent: an armed force is worthless if untrained and consequently not able; if armed and able, it is still worthless if unwilling. It is this last attribute with which US Army effort has become concerned and indications that it has not been fully developed have provided the impetus for this and many other studies.
>
> (Bloch 1967: 8)

In the sizable chapter on the Montagnards, the author repeats the tropes of 'strong feelings of mutual distrust and suspicion' between Montagnards and Kinh and of 'the immutability of Montagnard customs and thought' (p. 10). In a historical narrative of the Montagnard autonomy movement FULRO, the author asks himself why 'these long-standing conditions did not lead to ancient, continuous and sometimes violent attempts at independence'. He suggests an answer in 'the tribal fragmentation, the absence of a concept of ethnic unity under an adequate leader, and perhaps the habits of lifelong acceptance by the hillmen' (p. 12). Resuming the trope of the Special Forces' 'natural sympathy with [Montagnard] aspirations', p. 19), the study concludes that US military assistance to the Montagnards has resulted in some tensions between the tribesmen and the Vietnamese and consequently between the Vietnamese and US governments' (p. 22). Donald Bloch further notes that among Vietnamese 'it was widely believed that US arms and training made possible the Rhade uprising of September 1964, and indeed, that the revolt was either US inspired or supported' (p. 23). Simultaneously, the Vietnamese were thought to resent 'their lack of control over the CIDG program' (p. 23). Thus, contrary to the self-image of many Americans as 'cultural brokers' in the 'perennial conflict' between Montagnards and Vietnamese, the author felt that American presence exacerbated the tensions. Still, the author's main conclusions were that the 'principles underlying US Army Special Forces operations among minorities ... are sound', and that '[u]ndesirable side effects from USASF activities with minorities will be inevitable in any politically and economically unstable society' and had to be solved at policy levels within the US government (p. 37). Bloch warned, on the other hand, that effective counterinsurgency had to protect minority populations from the guerrilla as well as from the 'pacification' effort, by which he meant forced relocations, creating resentment among Montagnards. It is this issue of forced resettlement and consequent land grabbing which crop up time and again in the Highlands, and which is the subject of a next section.

Contradicting the trope of the 'natural sympathy and understanding' between Americans and Montagnards was the *Socio-Psychological Study of the Regional/Popular Forces in Vietnam* (1967), conducted by Philip Worchel, Samuel Popkin et al. (1967) for the Simulmatics Corporation. The Regional and Popular Forces (RF/PF in US Army jargon) were to a major extent the successor units of the CIDG, in the sense that many former CIDG were converted into RF/PF, the local militia in the Vietnamese military hierarchy. As the American military were generally very disdainful of the RF/PF ('Ruff-puff', was the slang designation), a study into the reasons of their 'ineffectiveness' was conducted. Worchell and Popkin gave the following 'factors':

> (a) poor national identification and commitment to mission due to the feelings ... that there is little official concern over their personal and family needs and welfare ..., (b) leadership problems ..., (c) violation of expectations and official commitments in regard to rewards, allowances, pay and promotions, (d) lack of recognition of importance and accomplishments, (e) relative inferiority of status compared with other branches ..., (f) poor relationships between villagers and troops.
>
> (Worchell, Popkin et al. 1967: iv)

Although this study is only partially on Montagnards serving in the RF/PF, it is interesting to see that Worchell and Popkin attribute poor judgement to Americans portraying Montagnards as loyal, valiant warriors, for they hated to be away from home for military duties (ibid.: 173; see also citation in Chapter 6).

Increasingly, the research effort became cumulative. For instance, as a number of studies pointed at poor counterpart relationships between Americans and Vietnamese, a series of studies were undertaken by the Human Sciences Research Inc. in 1968 to deal with the problems rising from differing cultural values encountered by Americans in Vietnam.[33] Similarly, the 'refugee problem' was felt to be a growing problem, especially since the deployment of American combat troops in 1965. This inaugurated a series of studies on refugees in Vietnam.[34] In a similar vein, both the CRESS and the RAC were building up an archive on counterinsurgency, drawing both on Vietnamese and other experiences. Thus, SORO/CRESS augmented the studies by Frederick Stires and Donald Bloch with Adrian Jones and Andrew Molnar's study *Internal Defense against Insurgency: Six Cases* (1966), which took together the Malaya Emergency, the Huk Rebellion in the Philippines, the Cuban and Algerian Revolutions, the guerrilla in Venezuela, and, of course, the Revolution in Vietnam. The discussion of Vietnam reiterated the trope of 'longstanding animosity between Vietnamese and montagnard' and US advisors' 'good working relationship with the montagnards', with the 'possibility that the distrust between the two ethnic groups may affect the relationship between United States advisors and Vietnamese Armed Forces personnel' (Jones and Molnar 1966: 113).

The Research Analysis Corporation augmented its studies by Vigneras (1966) and Joyce and Wing (1967) with the study *US Army Special Forces and Similar Internal Defense Operations in Mainland Southeast Asia, 1962–1967* by Paul Ello (et al., 1969), which took together American counterinsurgency experiences in Laos (1959–62), Thailand (1960–67) and Vietnam (1964–67). This study noted the impact of the growing US Army presence in Vietnam since 1965 on Special Forces operations, making 'CIDG operations ... subordinate and complementary to those of US divisions and separate brigades' (Ello et al. 1969: 219). In this situation of American build-up, the Special Forces specialized in intelligence for the simple reason that it worked closely with 'native auxiliaries' (Ello et al. 1967: 3, 221). Ello c.s. also noted the 'counterpart problems' of the SF, blamed on 'graft' on the part of the Vietnamese military, and related to the 'clash of US and oriental value systems' (ibid.: 6). Under the heading 'The Montagnard Problem', the authors noted, again, that 'Montagnards distrusted the lowlanders; the Vietnamese regarded the highlanders as savages [while] the Americans sympathized with the Montagnards and resented the Vietnamese attitude toward them' (ibid.: 53). For Ello c.s., the 'lesson was clear':

> [A]dvisors in developing countries must not compromise themselves by becoming unduly attached to an ethnic minority group that might challenge the authority of the government that is host to the advisors.
>
> (ibid. 53)

With a view to the Montagnard revolt in 1964 and the resulting diminished effectiveness of the CIDG, Ello et al. stated that 'the Montagnard camps were the most striking examples of the danger and counterproductiveness of expanding the advisory role beyond its proper limits to the point of arrogating the command function' (ibid.: 54). But despite the degree of involvement of Special Forces with their 'native auxiliaries', the report is critical of what Special Forces effectively brought about in the one field in which they were supposed to be strong, i.e. civic action and psychological operations:

CA/PSYOP has clearly been unsuccessful in Vietnam in winning hearts and minds. US Army PSYOP officers and NCOs [non-commissioned officers – OS] are insufficiently trained for the task in Vietnam. Their basic training and background are *deficient in anthropology*, knowledge of Vietnamese culture, and ability to speak the language. It is difficult, to put it mildly, to conduct PSYOP among people with whom you cannot communicate. The effort has been shallow and pro forma. The first image that comes to mind when PSYOP is mentioned is of a chap dropping leaflets from a small aircraft. The general criticism is applicable to the US effort as a whole.

(ibid.: 158 – emphasis added)

From this, it becomes evident that the studies become more and more critical as the years of American intervention in Vietnam go by: Americans take command, but don't know the language and culture; Americans try to fight a political struggle, but they are unable to; Americans do not respect the indigenous hierarchical structures, and tend to sympathize with the 'underdog' – the Montagnards – thereby alienating the host Government and aggravating tensions between minority groups and the Kinh majority.

In the previous chapter, we deconstructed the Special Forces narrative regarding their attachment to Montagnards. What the Army-sponsored studies show us, is that this narrative is simplistic in the sense that Special Forces performance was much less effective than they themselves claimed (and still maintain). They not only antagonized their Vietnamese counterparts by assuming operational command, but they contributed to the antagonism between Vietnamese and Montagnards by their sympathetic pose toward the Montagnard underdog. If we may lend any credence to the study by Paul Ello, discussed above, this sympathy was superficial and hardly based on knowledge of Montagnard cultures. Still, the tropes in the ethnographic discourse on Montagnards remain more or less the same in the Army studies. The premises still are the fundamental and perennial antagonism between Montagnards and Vietnamese – a gap which Americans try to bridge, with adverse effects. The first studies signal a lack of ethnographic knowledge and political and cultural sophistication on the part of Americans working with Montagnards, but convey the idea that this can be mended by providing more, and more accurate, cultural information. The last studies, however, point to the inability to even communicate, rendering the whole effort of trying to 'win hearts and minds' futile – a verdict that is cast upon the American intervention as a whole. Small wonder, then, that Special Forces were gradually phased out of Vietnam between 1969 and 1971, even before President Nixon's 'Vietnamization' policy got off the ground.

The counterinsurgency research effort under Project Agile was by no means monolithic. Still, the variables were limited, and seemed firmly linked to the strategic perspective adopted. With the deployment of American ground troops to Vietnam, the nature of the war altered considerably. In a context of mutual contempt between Special Forces and regular Army,[35] a situation of conflict and mutual hostility developed in which differing – and contradictory – perspectives on the war were adhered to and practiced next to one another. This ambiguity was evident in the inconsistency of the US war effort, especially in the US Army counterinsurgency policy. Various strategic options competed for primacy, as did the institutional interests they represented. The method used by Special Forces of trying to gain confidence through adaptation to local customs clashed with the nation-building approach of the regular army, epitomized by the forced urbanization scheme, the establishment of free-strike zones and the use of defoliants. One bombardment or defoliation raid could destroy not only the population's habitat, but also months of careful work by Special Forces or other 'civic action' agents (e.g., of CORDS – the 'Civil Operations and Revolutionary Development Support' under MACV) trying to win the confidence of the population. One forced relocation or resettlement would alienate people whose hearts and minds could not easily be won anymore. This structural inconsistency resulted in a failure to achieve pacification. It led to an ongoing search for new and better programs, as exemplified by the rapid succession of pacification programs. As far as the research effort under Project Agile was concerned, the possible outcomes varied according to the perspective adopted in a conflictive context. And even if the research or advice was clear, it was often not heeded, as will be evident from the career of Gerald Cannon Hickey.

Gerald Hickey, 'action anthropologist'[36]

The outstanding American expert regarding the Montagnards was – and still is – the anthropologist Gerald C. Hickey. Together with Bernard Fall he would become one of the links between the French and the American discourses regarding the Montagnards, and one of the links between academic and the 'practical' ethnographic discourse on Montagnards. A student from Chicago, Hickey's career began in 1953 with a fellowship to study the ethnology of Indochina in Paris, where he was impressed by the wide range of ethnographic material on the Montagnards (Hickey 1988: xxvii). After travelling to Saigon in 1956 as a member of the Michigan State University Vietnam Advisory Group, he wrote a report encouraging the South Vietnamese government to accommodate to the 'highland people's desire to preserve their ethnic identity'. Barred from further travel in that region by high-ranking Vietnamese officials who reacted negatively, he carried out his first research in the lowlands. But between 1964 and 1973, with funding from the Rand Corporation, one of the major 'Federal Non-Profit Research Centers', he did extensive research in the Highlands. Even with Rand Corporation, his position was in a sense anomalous, in that he was not hired for a short period of time to study specific problems, but employed more or less on a personal title, as the expert on Montagnards.

In the 1960s, he was already considered an 'old hand' in Vietnam – one of the few who had been there in the 1950s, one of the few who had a working knowledge of the Vietnamese language and who had conducted an in-depth study of Vietnamese culture and society.[37] Moreover, despite his employment by

Figure 7.2 Ritual reception by the P'tau Apui ('King of Fire') in Bon Ama Jong, September 1967. At the end of the ceremony the P'tau collects his sweat in a bowl, which may serve as magic water.

Source: Musée de l'Homme, D73-181-702. Photo: Jacques Dournes.

Rand Corporation, he was considered a very independent thinker, as witnessed by his conflicts with President Diêm and Wolf Ladejinsky over his 1957 report on the Highlands (see Chapter 6). Similarly, the confidential Rand study of 'strategic hamlets' which he wrote together with John Donnell (1962) was not well received by the American and Vietnamese political and military establishments because it was deemed too 'negative' – for the simple reason that the authors aimed to convey the opinions and complaints of participating (or better: targeted) farmers. Despite his reputation as a rather critical researcher he was employed *qualitate qua* by the Rand Corporation to conduct research and advise on Montagnard affairs and publish on other issues that crossed his way (such as his *The American Military Advisor and his Foreign Counterpart* [1965], his 'Problems of Social Change in Viet-Nam' [1958], and his *Accommodation and Coalition in South Vietnam* [1970]). His frankness won him a certain reputation, allowing him to express opinions which were not always well received, but on the other hand he was appreciated for that. In 1987, Dr. Donald Marshall, an anthropologist and military officer who during the 1960s and 1970s had been working for ARPA, lauded Hickey as 'the only full-fledged anthropologist doing serious research in Vietnam', as 'a social scientist of high ethics and principles' and 'a totally independent thinker and reporter.'[38]

During the Second Indochina War, Hickey was regarded the major expert of the Montagnards, and being sympathetic to their cause as he perceived it, developed into their major spokesman *vis-à-vis* American agencies. As such, he became increasingly critical of conventional warfare tactics advocated by the regular Army and the Air Force that proved detrimental to the Montagnards and their way of life. Hickey sided instead with those segments within the American camp that stressed the political aspects rather than the military aspects of the struggle – organizations like the Special Forces, the CIA, and USAID, which were inclined to achieve pacification through a more balanced counter-insurgency program, taking account of the social, economic and political situation of the population to be pacified. He tried to influence American advisors in the Central Highlands to refrain from the use of indiscriminate firepower and herbicides, and opposed the forced relocation programs which resettled thousands of Montagnards into guarded camps in order to create 'free fire zones' (Hickey 1988: 196–207). His commitment to the Montagnards led him to 'act' on their behalf – in fact, he considered himself an 'action anthropologist' in the Chicago tradition of Sol Tax. Yet, though he often opposed the tactics used by the Vietnamese and American military, he never spoke out against the war effort as such, on the grounds that he was 'a scholar, not an activist' (Emerson 1978: 287). His critique of the way the Americans fought the war brought him even to the US Senate Foreign Relations Committee on 13 May 1971. He made a statement to the effect that the war should not be fought by American troops at all, but that the conflict should be solved in a traditional, Vietnamese way – through political accommodation between the various groups in Vietnam, including the NLF.[39] Yet, he was a staunch anti-Communist, and firmly believed that a Communist victory would mean the end for the Montagnards' way of life, as is also attested by his post-war publications.

Hickey was a central figure in the American network covering the Highlands. He is thanked and referred to in Special Warfare School publications. He was negotiating during the FULRO rebellion in 1964. He was the central figure in IVS and AID conferences on Highland development. He was participating in SIL workshops, and supervised their ethnographic publications. He was the only member of CORDS' Ethnic Minorities Council who was not a government official. From 1965 onward, he started to put out large numbers of short 'memoranda for the record' under Rand cover, but he soon learned that the memoranda had to be very short if they were to be read by those in power:

> I had to really use politics. So when I wrote one-page memos, which was the only thing they would read about relocation projects, I always had to couch the thing in terms of security. That's the only thing that cuts any ice with the Americans. Your lead line had to be a shocker. You'd say 'Security is going to tumble in Pleiku province unless ...' Then I'd say 'Because of the following reasons ...' And then you'd show you did your homework. ... You double-spaced the whole thing. One-page memo. We sent them to the military and they hand-carry them, to give to Bunker and to the science advisor, who

would get them directly to Westmoreland or Abrams and not through channels. That's how I'd get things done, it was the only way to do it. And then you had to grab people at a cocktail party or somewhere and put the bee in their bonnet.

(Emerson 1978: 287)

From 1965 till 1971, Hickey put out no less than 27 memoranda, albeit on a limited number of topics.[40] Some concerned FULRO and the question of Highlander leadership;[41] some papers focused on refugee problems;[42] on customary law;[43] on the putative arrest of Siu Choi, nephew of Siu Anhot, King of Fire;[44] on Montagnard land tenure, land rights, and forced relocation;[45] and mixed accounts of specific provinces or of the situation after the Têt Offensive.[46] As Hickey explained in the quotation above, most of the memoranda or reports were really comments on specific events, like new GVN legislation or a FULRO rising, or protests against certain actions, like relocations. The latter was maybe the most quintessential issue discussed by Hickey. Already in his June 1957 'Preliminary Research Report on the High Plateau', prepared for the Michigan State University Group, the violation of land rights is mentioned as one of the main causes of 'Mountaineer discontent' (see Hickey 1957: 1). As noted in the previous chapter, Hickey saw the issuance of land titles on the basis of traditional land rights as the only remedy, whereby these traditional land rights were to be established according to former French accounts, like those of Sabatier and Guilleminet. Hickey's repeated reference to their *coutumiers* effectively reinscribed the French colonial discourse on Montagnard land rights contra Vietnamese colonization schemes.

As we have seen earlier, the statements on Montagnard agriculture and land tenure were important in the light of what Hickey labelled 'land grabbing' in his MSUG report. As we have seen earlier, colonization of the Highlands was predicated on assumptions regarding 'slash-and-burn' agriculture, namely that it was a crude, primitive and therefore backward method which caused deforestation to the land and starvation to the 'nomads' (cf. Dournes 1980: 12–16). Like the French cultural relativist ethnographers before him (see Chapter 4), Hickey countered such ideas in his ethnographic writings, his reports and his memoranda, starting with his 1957 MSUG report. For instance, in his 'Memorandum for Record: Montagnard Agriculture and Land Tenure' of 2 April 1965, Hickey describes the 'swidden technique employed by montagnards' as follows:

Among most (if not all) groups it is a system of rotating agriculture wherein a plot is farmed for a given period – usually between one and three years – and then is left to lay fallow while the cultivators move to a series of other fields, returning to the overgrown plot in due time. ... It often is assumed that swidden agriculture is destructive. ... Using the swidden method has the advantage of leaving tree roots in the soil which helps to retain the structure. If a plow were used in these circumstances there would be grave danger of having the top soil wash away. (pp. 1–2)

After having stated that swidden agriculture as practised by most Montagnards is well adapted to the natural environment and not 'destructive', Hickey refers to the land tenure systems of the Rhadé (*pô lan*) and the Bahnar (*toring*), claiming that 'most of the other montagnard groups have village territories in which the residents farm' (p. 2). According to Hickey, the land rights are well defined, and generally acknowledged by other families, clans, villages and highland groups. But, '[t]he land tenure systems noted above embrace only a portion of the area. The remainder is land *res nullius*, unclaimed by anyone' (p. 4). In several other memoranda and reports referred to above, Hickey makes similar statements, most extensively in *The Highland People of South Vietnam: Social and Economic Development* (Hickey 1967b: 76–102). The traditional land rights were not recognized by the Vietnamese State, which regarded all the untilled land as *res nullius*. The resulting appropriation of lands by Vietnamese settlers was one of the main grievances of dissident Montagnards, including FULRO (see also Hickey 1967b, and 'The Highlander and FULRO Context', May 1969). On the basis of his more relativist ethnographic analysis of Montagnard swidden agriculture as a rational farming method, he pleaded for recognition of land rights and issuance of land titles (albeit individual land titles, which would have the effect to greatly reduce the stake of women in land in most matrilineal societies), while promoting commerce and cash cropping among Montagnards.

Time and again, Gerald Hickey would actually campaign for what he regarded as an equitable distribution of land in the Highlands, together with those civilian American agencies in the Highlands which were involved in the economic and political rather than purely military aspects of pacification (and saw it as their mission to 'win hearts and minds'), like USAID and CORDS. The combined American and Montagnard pressure on the Vietnamese leadership achieved partial success in August, 1967, when President Nguyên Văn Thiêu signed Decree No. 003/67, which gave 'special rights' to minorities, including titles to lands 'farmed in rotation' (Hickey 1982b: 163). In a memorandum dated 12 December 1968 on 'Land Titles for the Highlanders', Hickey argued that the decree only acknowledged permanent fields. It excluded swidden fields as eligible for land titles, while 'villages [were not] grant[ed] corporate title to a given territory, as Hickey had advocated in *The Highland People of South Vietnam: Social and Economic Development* (Hickey 1967b: 91). Moreover, the decree was hardly implemented. In 1969, the Ministry of Land Reform, established after considerable American pressure and with massive AID support, decreed that land titles should be issued by Land Identification Teams in each village, specifying an acreage of ten hectares for each highlander family. However, the MDEM followed Hickey in proposing legislation giving hamlets communal title to a delineated land area (called Main Living Area), which was finally enacted on 9 November 1970 (Hickey 1982b: 203–4).[47]

As before, the issuance of land titles was slow, much to the frustration of AID officials who performed an 'advisory and operational' role in the implementation; and as before, South-Vietnamese Government officials were blamed for the lack of progress because of the 'longstanding cultural gap between the Vietnamese and

Montagnards'.⁴⁸ In his 'End of Tour Report: The Montagnard Land Program' (June 1973), Will Muller of AID gave – with reference to the work by Gerald Hickey – as the political rationale for the program 'to help win the goodwill and support of the Montagnard people for the GVN'. Muller sketches a picture of hard-working and benevolent American advisors 'who work and travel extensively in the highlands', but against the grain, because of the 'reluctant attitude of too many [GVN] officials toward the program'. The first reason Muller gave for the slow and defective implementation was that '[t]he GVN doesn't really support the program'.⁴⁹ In other words, prompted by a relativistic ethnographic discourse on Montagnards and by a gloomy analysis of the 'cultural gap' between Montagnards and Kinh, AID assumed almost sole responsibility for the program, devised to win the Montagnards for the South Vietnamese Government. In what was almost a colonial intervention except for an overt claim to sovereignty over the Highlands, this American ethnographic discourse resembled more and more the French discourse attending the latter's efforts to win Montagnards over to the side of the colonial forces. This 'relativist' ethnographic discourse was directed against a modernization discourse, which saw resettlement of Montagnards as a solution for their 'nomadic' existence. Not surprisingly, the issue of 'relocation' of Montagnards became a constant source of conflict between two strategic options, embodied by different civil and military organizations. Thus, the conflict pitted not only Americans and Vietnamese against one another, but also various American organizations. Since this conflict is most instructive in this context, it will be dealt with in more detail in the next section.

As is evident from the above, once in a while critical reports appeared on the American and South Vietnamese war effort, which sometimes even admitted that the policy of the National Liberation Front proved far more effective and attractive for a large part of the rural population. Many of Hickey's reports belong to this category, as we have seen. But although his reports often reached top-level policymakers and sparked debates in the ranks of CORDS, the American Embassy and even MACV, these critical reports were mostly ignored by those in charge. Thus many researchers saw their advice either being ignored or failing, which had a disciplining effect on their work. In his recent book on the Vietnam War, Robert McNamara, Secretary of Defense under Presidents Kennedy and Johnson, gives an example of the mechanism of this creation of ignorance, where he tells how a 'negative report' by an informal Navy Vietnam Appraisal Group (1967) was blocked by top Navy officers, who attempted to prevent distribution by blocking careers (McNamara 1995: 274–277). This neglect of available bodies of knowledge and insight could have disastrous effects when military interests overshadowed political considerations. This was the case with the Army fixation on acquiring new technologies, advanced weapon systems and more firepower, a fixation that led to the ignoring of the effects of indiscriminate American bombing on the political attitude of rural populations. The war was perceived as a military struggle rather than a political one, as Hickey told the Senate in 1971, due to American reluctance to see the revolution as a home-grown one rather than an imported and imposed affair.

Such a realization could raise doubts as to the legitimacy of US involvement in Vietnam. Communism was straightforwardly equated with evil, aggression and terror. It had to be fought against with every conceivable means, preferably scientifically sanctioned. The conviction that the conflict in Vietnam could be won with military means formed part and parcel of the discourse which shaped American policy in Vietnam, and was shared by the majority of the scientists who conducted counterinsurgency research in Vietnam.[50] This discourse prevented most concerned American researchers from gaining insight into the motivations and attitudes of 'the' Vietnamese population, which thus appeared as 'mysterious'. And if researchers diverged from the dominant discourse, their advice was not heeded.[51] In his book *The Best-Laid Schemes*, Seymour Deitchman had already shown at great length that the outcomes of research were only accepted if they 'generally fit the pattern of operations and philosophy for prosecution of the war that were common among the military and civil authorities, both in Washington and Saigon, at the time' (1976: 342).

This is evident throughout Deitchman's book, but also from an instructive response to Murray Wax' review of his book in *Human Organization* (1978), where Deitchman had this to say on the effects of Hickey's advice:

> Even in cases where the official is well educated and has all the necessary understanding, he may not be able to act as his outside advisors think he should. Secretary McNamara, for example, was fully apprised of Hickey's work on the tribes of the Vietnamese Highlands. Later, the implication of his work were brought to the attention of Henry Kissinger when he chaired the National Security Council. (In both cases I shared the responsibility for forwarding these results.) But the need to insist that a duly constituted government in South Vietnam must assume its borders overrode the knowledge that the ethnic Vietnamese couldn't effectively govern the Montagnard. Therein lay one of the keys to the final panic in the Central Highlands and the fall of Saigon. What could the responsible official do when the potential was brought to his attention? He could be grateful; he could accept the knowledge; he could weigh it; he could weigh the pressures from the President, the press, his military advisors, the Congress, and others; and then he could do what he concluded he must and take his (and the country's) chances.
>
> (Deitchman 1978: 410)

While his memoranda and recommendations were gracefully ignored by those in power, Hickey's research reports for Rand and his later publications stressed the difference between the lowland Vietnamese and the Highlanders – who, 'although divided into many ethnic groups,' shared 'many sociocultural characteristics that historically have set them apart from the more advanced Cham, Khmer, and Vietnamese' (Hickey 1982b: xiv). While his research reports mainly dealt with the 'Highlanders' in general, his *Ethnohistory* (1982a, b) described the attainment of a common ethnic identity and the rise of ethno-nationalism among the Montagnards. His strong sympathy for the Montagnards was expressed in an ethnographic discourse which borrowed heavily from cultural relativism, stressing the value of the original Montagnard culture, and seemingly avoiding overtly political statements. Yet, Hickey considered FULRO and the Montagnards working in the South Vietnamese Ministry for Development of Ethnic Minorities as the genuine expression and culmination of Montagnard ethno-nationalism, where French anthropologists like Dournes and Condominas, as well as critical American scholars, saw FULRO as a movement of tribal mercenaries organized and supported by the CIA. Many observers remarked that the distinction between FULRO and the CIDG, organized by the US Special Forces, was slight; even Brigadier General S. Marshall remarked that the Montagnards were mercenaries paid by the United States (Marshall 1967: 22).

In hindsight, Hickey's personal tragedy lay in his constantly betting on the wrong horse, from a historical perspective. While his criticism of the high-handed behavior of the American and South-Vietnamese military went largely unheeded, he effectively endorsed the war effort by his involvement in it, covering the war effort with a veneer of morality – as the prophet or the clown, who once in a while speaks the truth, but who is not taken seriously by those who make politics. His actual involvement cost him the respect of part of the academic anthropological community and a job at the University of Chicago. His research involvement in the American war effort made him the symbol of the 'evil professor' working for the military in the eyes of the opponents of the war in the US. When after the war Hickey was offered a job at the University of Chicago, faculty members there successfully opposed his appointment. While there is no doubt about his commitment to Montagnards, he definitely gave insight into Montagnard culture and politics, insight which was used as intelligence to draw the Montagnards into the war, and made many of them choose sides with the Americans (rather than with either Vietnamese side). Insofar as this effort was successful, it turned out to be counterproductive for the many Montagnards who were prosecuted by the Communist regime after the 'liberation' (or 'fall', depending on one's perspective) of Ban Me Thuôt (March 1975) and Saigon (April 1975). Or, to put it differently, whereas his commitment was to improve the lot of the Montagnards, the net effect of his effort was to improve American access to Montagnards and use them for ulterior purposes.

After 1975, many Montagnards chose to continue to fight the Communist regime under the FULRO banner for a variety of reasons. One was the expectation of American support after a visit of Montagnard leaders in the MDEM to the American Embassy on 4 April 1975, to offer to wage an anti-Communist guerrilla after the impending takeover. During the conversation, Deputy Ambassador George Jacobson smiled and nodded at each suggestion, according to a Montagnard and an American witness.[52] Another reason was the Vietnamese policy of 're-education', which came in waves and which many former Montagnard leaders tried to escape by going underground or taking to the jungle. A third reason was the Vietnamese policy of 'sedentarization' of Montagnards and the massive in-migration of lowlanders to New Economic

Zones in the Highlands (see next chapter). Thus it was that by 1982 there was a full-fledged guerrilla against the Communist regime going on in the Highlands, waged by Montagnards belonging to FULRO.[53] In that year, Hickey's magnum opus, the *Ethnohistory of the Vietnamese Central Highlands* came out (1982a, b), complete with names of FULRO leaders and genealogical charts of an emerging 'pan-Highlander' leadership. As told in the Introduction (Chapter 1), the volumes found their way to Vietnam, where they were carefully studied by the security forces, who started to arrest people mentioned in the book. The prisoners were interrogated but eventually released, due to interventions on their behalf from Vietnamese anthropologists. Thus, Hickey's work seemed even useful to a Communist regime which he has fought and which he abhors – just like Condominas' Mnong Gar ethnography was used for ends that Condominas did not endorse.

Strategic options and ethnographic discourses

This section deals with the issue of discord among various American agencies speaking of and dealing with the Montagnards. Some American institutions working with the Montagnards developed a perspective which resembled that of the French before – playing on ethnic differences between Montagnards and ethnic Vietnamese in an effort to discredit the Viêt Công, and posing themselves as the trustworthy protectors. The influence of this ethnographic perspective, however, was limited, because of the build-up of a conventional US military presence in Vietnam, and because of official American policy to back up the South Vietnamese government. With the deployment of American combat troops in Vietnam, American counterinsurgency doctrine was increasingly geared to the demands of conventional strategy, which coupled a reliance on abundant firepower and on the actions of the Air Force to the belief that guerrilla warfare was supported from outside, if not imported outright by the North Vietnamese People's Army. The Special Forces, the main American instrument for direct contact with the Montagnards, were increasingly curtailed, not only by Vietnamese suspicion of American motives in the Highlands, but also by their progressive incorporation into the conventional Army which was equally suspicious of the strategy of irregular warfare developed by the CIA for the Special Forces (Kelly 1973: 151–75; Blaufarb 1977: 243–95; Cable 1986: 141–57; Clarke 1988: 195–207).[54]

As before, we shall try to get a clear picture of the oppositions by focusing on a specific event, in this paragraph a conflict among American agencies over forced relocation of Montagnards. While the issue of 'Montagnards' had been a CIA and Special Forces interest since the late 1950s and early 1960s, AID became involved in a Montagnard Affairs Project in Vietnam since USOM been transformed into AID in 1965, and, of course, since the Montagnards had become a touchy political problem after two aborted rebellions. The first American Project Manager for Montagnard Affairs, Lamar Prosser, wrote in his End of Tour Report (1966: 2) that when he 'became Project Manager for

Montagnard Affairs in January, 1965, neither the Government of Vietnam nor USAID had a coordinated program for Montagnard development'. Among the bottlenecks noted by Prosser was not only the existence of FULRO and the bad relationship between Montagnards and Vietnamese, but also the lack of coordination among American agencies dealing with Montagnards, such as the Special Forces and the Office of the Special Assistant (OSA) in the American Embassy. From the records, it appears that USAID was not only involved in 'Montagnard affairs', but had effectively been designing and implementing the various Montagnard policies in Vietnam, in particular from the MDEM.[55]

Lamar Prosser was not the only one to note the lack of American coordination, which became worse with the numerical growth of the American combat presence in Vietnam, eventually attaining 549,500 in 1968 (Clarke 1988: 524). With the deployment of American combat troops, it became clear that military force alone could not win this war. In other words, it was assumed that successful 'pacification' comprised both military and political–economic aspects. On the other hand, the early 1960s had known a succession of failed pacification schemes, with such beautiful names as Rural Construction, Rural Reconstruction, Revolutionary Development [!] and New Life Development. It was agreed upon that the loose array of 'civilian' support activities had to be linked to the military action, but throughout 1966 there had been debates how this should be done. Finally, in April 1967 President Lyndon B. Johnson decided that the American Embassy's Office of Civil Operations would become part of MACV, and thus fall under military command. The inevitable compromise, however, was that the new organization, named Civil Operations and Revolutionary Development Support (CORDS), would be headed by a high-ranking civilian. The first to be appointed director of CORDS was Robert Komer, a former CIA analyst who had been special assistant in national security affairs to President Johnson. In November 1968, Komer was succeeded by his deputy William Colby, also a senior CIA official, who was honored with the title of Deputy Ambassador to Vietnam (Clarke 1988: 171–81, 209–12; Colby 1989: 225–90; Prados 1986: 308–10).

In the provinces, CORDS' representatives advised and assisted local projects under the heading New Life Development. One geographical area where CORDS was working was, of course, the Central Highlands. Within CORDS, an Ethnic Minorities Affairs Program was set up, with the purpose ...

> to assist the Government of Vietnam, especially the Ministry for Development of Ethnic Minorities, in devising and carrying out projects which will benefit the minority peoples of Vietnam and hence win their loyalty to the central government.[56]

One of the areas of concern was – with reference to the demands made by FULRO and to the work by Gerald Hickey – the issuance of land titles to Highlanders. In the same year that President Nguyên Văn Thiêu signed his decree giving Montagnards the right to own land (1967), large-scale forced resettlement of Montagnards was taking place again with the inauguration of the Edap Enang project in Pleiku province. The resettlement of Jarai villagers was a complete failure, because most of them, receiving hardly any support and left without subsistence, tried to make it to their former home areas, sometimes repeatedly. In the wake of the Têt Offensive of February 1968, General William Peers, commander of the US I Field Force in the Central Highlands, and the CORDS staff of the II Corps Region (Central Highlands – but not the Ethnic Minorities Affairs personnel) decided to clear a populated area completely of its inhabitants for military reasons, and move them to the new Plei Ring De settlement. The results were equally disastrous for the Jarai involved, many of whom tried to go back to their former living areas, now labelled 'free-strike zones'.[57]

The renewed forced resettlements of Montagnards – with hardly any prior notice and with inadequate assistance – angered the Montagnard leadership which had chosen sides with the GVN (even FULRO formally surrendered to the South Vietnamese authorities on 1 February 1969). But it also angered American officials directly working with Montagnards. On 28 January 1969, a first meeting took place of the 'Montagnard Committee' of the American Mission Council, the 'political section' of the US Embassy in Saigon, and therefore the political pendant of CORDS' Ethnic Minorities Affairs. Its name notwithstanding, this 'Montagnard Committee' consisted entirely of US nationals, from the American Embassy, the Office of Special Affairs, CORDS, MACV, Special Forces, and, of course, Gerald Hickey of the Rand Corporation, as the only non-Government member. The issue of the meeting being 'US participation in resettlement of Montagnards', L.M. Guess of CORDS' Ethnic Minorities Affairs prepared a memorandum dated 24 January 1969, arguing against relocation, unless absolutely necessary and well-prepared. Guess referred to the problem of land alienation and other, psychological and cultural problems as a result of resettlement. Gerald Hickey prepared two similar memoranda, both dated 11 January 1969 – one called 'Perpetuation of Error' and a more prudently voiced 'Myths Concerning the Highlanders'. In both memoranda, Hickey argued that Montagnards are not nomadic, as shifting cultivation does not mean here that villages are moved; that their land claims are real; and that consequently, relocation is a disrupting affair for them.

The Montagnard Committee drafted a 'Statement Concerning Resettlement of Highland Villages' dated 20 February 1969, pleading that 'no US civilian agency or military command shall initiate or support any population within or into the Central Highlands of South Vietnam until the project for such relocation has been thoroughly examined by the interested US agencies and until final approval has been received by the Mission Council' (cf. Hickey 1982b: 194). This proposal would take effective control over these 'pacification' measures out of the hands of the military (MACV/CORDS) and into the hands of the political US authorities in Vietnam. The statement was forwarded to General Creighton Abrams, commander of MACV, and to Ambassadors Ellsworth Bunker and William Colby, the head of CORDS. Not surprisingly, the statement was received badly by Abrams, while General Peers (who had initiated the resettlements in the first place) saw it as an attack on his policy. As Hickey noted, the statement highlighted 'a conflict between CORDS and the Political Section of the US Embassy' (ibid.: 195). The Montagnard Committee then decided to propose a 'draft policy ... concerning US participation in resettlements of Montagnards', which was further discussed on 4 March 1969.[58] The urgency of this meeting was enhanced by an anonymous memorandum dated March 2 by one of the members of the committee, stating that the Plei Ring De settlement was a 'dust bowl', where the resettled Montagnards were forced to pay most of their resettlement allowance to a contractor providing building materials of inferior quality. In spite of the danger, 117 out of 817 residents left the site in one month.

The conflict between both sides was exacerbated by a memorandum by Gerald Hickey, entitled 'Population Relocation in the Highlands' (20 March 1969). In a history of resettlement policies in Vietnam, Hickey stressed the negative consequences both for populations involved and for 'security', including Edap Enang and Plei Ring De. Hickey coupled his critique of resettlement to an analysis of Montagnard agricultural practices and their land claims. Moreover, Hickey proceeded to give military arguments why resettlement would not work, claiming that resettlement would not only disrupt their communities, but alienate them from the South Vietnamese Government. The person to decide was the person occupying the institutional middle ground, i.e. William Colby, as the civilian head of CORDS which was technically under the ultimate command of MACV. In his memoirs, Colby saw the issue as a conflict between '[s]ympathizers with the mountain people [who] condemned this uprooting of the Montagnards from their homes' versus 'the practical area commanders [who] contended that this was the only solution in view of the impossibility of protecting each distant collection of one or two long houses [sic!]'. Colby further noted that 'the most passionate on both sides of the argument being their American friends and advisers' (Colby 1989: 284); indeed, it seemed to be an all-American conflict. In his book, Colby claimed that he 'devised ... a reasonable compromise' by giving the political authorities the last say, more or less as proposed by the 'Montagnard Committee'. This was hardly a solution, however, for the coordination would take place at the highest echelon, and not at the practical executive levels.[59]

The military clearly had their way in this conflict, for there would be no prohibition of forced resettlements. In an interview, Colby conceded that the compromise did not work, since a number of civilian officials working with Montagnards Committee were disappointed and did not wish to participate anymore.[60] Hickey noted that 'the Montagnard Committee was never to meet again' (Hickey 1982b: 196), symbolically signifying the demise of American Montagnard policy in an era of an overwhelming American armed presence in Vietnam. While MACV had no use for criticism of the way it produced 'pacification' or for civilian meddling with military affairs, it could do with a directive how to go about resettlement. Therefore, its next move was the drafting of a 'MACV directive which would provide COMUS [Commander, USMACV, i.e. Gen. Abrams] policy guidance on forced resettlement of population groups'.[61] Following a suggestion by William Colby, the directive should refer to South Vietnamese policies in the matter, in particular the directive on 'Pacification and Development in the Highlands' of the Central Pacification and Development Council headed by Gen. Tran Thien Khiem. Whereas this shifts the issue of resettlement back to the Vietnamese side, the ensuing correspondence bogs down in bureaucratic procedure, in an attempt to regulate and standardize resettlement procedures. Thus, the conflict faded away in the Spring of 1969, leaving the responsibility for resettlement with the military.[62]

For Gerald Hickey, however, the issue did not fade away. In his writing, he consistently focused on the issues of resettlement and land ownership, which he now related to the issue of 'Highlander dissidence'. In his memorandum 'The Highlander and FULRO Context' of May 1969, Hickey incorporated his piece on 'Population Relocation in the Highlands' of 20 March, appending it to a discussion of FULRO and its struggle for a *statut particulier*, the special status granted by Bao Đai (and before that by the French Admiral Thierry d'Argenlieu) during the First Indochina War (see Chapter 5). In a Memorandum for Record on 'Montagnard Land Ownership and Area Defense' (20 July 1970), Hickey presents the issuance of land titles to Montagnards as an alternative strategy to resettlement. In the words of Hickey, '[g]ranting titles for Montagnard hamlet land would have some very definite political, military, and economic advantages for the GVN' (p. 3). Such a move would contain the fear for land grabbing and create a bond between GVN and Montagnards, who could then be induced 'to defend their communally owned land, an important element in a well-motivated Hamlet Self Defense Force' (p. 4). In a published Rand report, *Some Recommendations Affecting the Prospective Role of Vietnamese Highlanders in Economic Development* (September 1971), Hickey substantiates his argument of grounding economic innovation in traditional patterns with appendices on the legitimacy of Highlander land claims, on the influx of Kinh settlers in the Highlands, and on the disruptive effects of resettlements.

This same issue of forced resettlement would surface again in 1970, at a time when the number of American troops was steadily decreasing as a result of President Nixon's policy of 'Vietnamization' of the war effort, inaugurated in the Spring of 1969. General Ngo Dzu, the Vietnamese commander of the II Corps region covering the Central Highlands (as well as the coastal provinces in the central part of South Vietnam), produced some 52,000 Montagnard refugees in 1970–71 through resettlement schemes (Clarke 1988: 464).[63] This prompted Hickey to draft a memorandum for the record, entitled 'Unlearned Lessons of History: Relocation of Montagnards' (13 February 1971), which again told the story of Montagnards losing everything they could not carry and being robbed of their most valuable belongings by the soldiers who came to resettle them; the story of burning the houses left behind; the story of being settled on a barren windy hill with hardly any provisions. Hickey claimed that the relocations effectively marginalized the Montagnards, and that the social and economic disruptions outweighed the gains in population control. He recommended that forcible relocations be avoided, and that resettled Montagnards be given the choice to go back to their former locations.[64]

In March, the matter was picked up by Edward Kennedy, chairman of the Senate Judiciary Subcommittee on Refugees, when Colby appeared before the Subcommittee, but the latter defended the resettlements as necessary for security reasons. While admitting that 'some relocations were handled badly', he claimed that 'most of them were handled effectively' (Clarke 1988: 464–5). In April, the resettlement issue was publicized in the *New York Times* and the *Washington Post*, which both presented Hickey's views. The *Post*, on the other hand, also recorded the opinion of Lt. Col. Wayne Smith, at the time Senior Adviser in Darlac province, as saying that Montagnards 'are going to have to be assimilated into society, be modernized, go to school. A lot of them are basically lazy'.[65] Often, such ethnographic assumptions underlay the modernization discourse which is an evolutionist discourse, similar to the French evolutionist discourse which attended the establishment of plantations in the Highlands. Such evolutionist discourses facilitated and legitimized the alienation and appropriation of lands and residences claimed by Montagnards, although the reasons were different. In that same month of April 1971, Hickey raised the resettlement issue again with William Colby in the presence of John Paul Vann, who was to be appointed Senior Adviser in the II Corps region. This time, and with Vann's support, Hickey seemed to be more successful than in 1969, as the relocations stopped in May under pressure of both the American Embassy and MACV. In the words of General Dzu, who started the relocations, 'American sensitivity prevented it' (Hickey 1982b: 223). One can only wonder at the change of attitude which apparently took place in the MACV high command between 1969 and 1971. In 1971, the war was to a large extent fought by the South Vietnamese Army, which perhaps was not allowed to create the 'free-strike zones' which the US Army had claimed for itself.

In his book *Kingdom in the Morning Mist* on Mayréna, Hickey mentions John Paul Vann as the last in a series of outsiders who tried to take control of events in the Highlands (the other ones being Mayréna, Sabatier, and – surprisingly – Bao Đai). Vann, who had acquired fame for his critique of US strategy in the Mekong Delta in the early 1960s, promised Hickey that 'he would do what he could for the highlanders', and '[u]pon assuming this position [of Senior Adviser in II Corps] immediately organized an Office for Highland Affairs' (Hickey 1982b: 223). Having no obstacles for his power ambitions anymore, Vann soon started to act as the virtual Viceroy of the Highlands, much to the dismay of the Vietnamese military who resented his dictatorial manner. Simultaneously, his strategic thinking changed in that he increasingly relied on firepower, including aerial bombardments by B-52 strategic bombers, which created a flow of refugees during the 1972 North Vietnamese Easter Offensive against Huê and Kontum. Shortly after the offensive, Vann was killed in a helicopter crash. In the words of Hickey, Vann 'ultimately subscribed to a military strategy he had hitherto criticized. This strategy led to Vann's death and the failure of the Americans to realize victory in Vietnam' (Hickey 1988: 207; 1982b: 231–50).

This statement by Hickey points at two different and conflicting American strategies in Vietnam, i.e. conventional warfare and the political struggle to 'win hearts and minds'. The career of John Paul Vann seems to symbolize how the political struggle was time and again subordinated to the military strategy of using indiscriminate firepower and bombardments for which free-strike zones had to be created by resettlement and defoliation. While Hickey represents Vann's death as symbolic of the failure of the conventional American strategy, the site of his crash is even more ominous. Neil Sheehan, author of the best-selling biography of Vann, went to see the site, a Montagnard graveyard, not far from the road between Kontum and Pleiku. The graveyard, a sacred forest, was the only place in the immediate environs where high trees had been left standing, so in a sense it was lack of ethnographic knowledge and sensitivity that ultimately did him in:

> The grove was the hamlet graveyard. The tribal people had left the trees in their natural state to guard the graves and to provide shade for their burial rites. Now I also knew what had happened on that night. John Vann had come skylarking up the road again, unaware that these figures of death were waiting for him in this grove.
>
> (Sheehan 1988: 789)

The use of abundant firepower, the defoliation, the forced urbanization, and the resettlement schemes provoked an adverse response among Montagnards, which lead to the reconstitution of FULRO in 1973. This time, various FULRO groups started to cooperate with the NLF and the North Vietnamese Army, directly leading to the unexpected assault of Ban Me Thuot in March 1975. The liberation of Ban Me Thuot precipitated the rapid takeover of the Central Highlands and the collapse of the South Vietnamese regime in what is alternatively known as the Spring Offensive or the Ho Chi Minh Campaign. This led to the reunification of Vietnam under the Hanoi government.

Given the interest of the South Vietnamese government in asserting control in the Highlands, the relativist discourse had political as well as strategic implications. Insofar as the Americans pictured the Montagnards as loyal warriors and victims of warfare among the ethnic Vietnamese, this led to friction between Americans – posing as protectors of minorities – and ethnic Vietnamese in the Highlands. Simultaneously, this led to conflicts between various American agencies, which had different interests and proposed different strategies. Naturally, the modern US Army relied on its firepower, while the US Air Force was eager to prepare the ground for aerial attacks. But as the use of abundant firepower, the defoliation, the forced urbanization, the resettlement schemes provoked an adverse response among the Montagnards, the NLF and the North Vietnamese were able to reap the profit.

Hickey's statement concerning the failure of American strategy implies that Americans could have won the war in Vietnam, if they would have adopted a different strategy – a strategy predicated on a different ethnographic discourse.

This assumption was wrong: this war could not be won by Americans, only by Vietnamese (although they paid dearly).[66] In this respect, Hickey – and with him the other protagonists of a relativist ethnographic discourse on Montagnards – remained firmly within the parameters of American thinking, namely that the intervention was justified and could be successful, no matter at what cost. Given the ultimate inevitability of the American withdrawal, the relativist discourse and the related practices initiated by the institutions that supported it (Special Forces, CIA, USAID), while sympathetic to Montagnards, did them immense and irreparable harm. Whether they like it or not, Montagnards live in Vietnam, and have to live with that; the American intervention made that very difficult to accept. The attempt in April 1975 of a group of pro-American Montagnards to enlist American support for continued fighting after the communist take over was ill-fated. The anti-Vietnamese guerrilla of FULRO, counting 7000 warriors around 1980, had no chance and soured ethnic relations in 'post-war' Vietnam.

Conclusion

In general, American ethnographic research with respect to the Montagnards was relativist insofar as it insisted on the value of Montagnard culture and stressed the need to protect traditional land rights. But inasmuch as the questions being asked were designed to render the ethnic groups amenable to counter-insurgency, they fitted one of the alternative strategic options in Vietnam. Social scientists were free to write critical reports with respect to alternative strategies, as Hickey demonstrated when he criticized the conventional warfare strategy of the US Army in Vietnam. However, such critical opinions had limited force. Only opinions which remained within the boundaries of the established discourse about the origins and nature of communist insurgency and the preferred course of counterinsurgency had any chance of influencing policy. Dissenting opinions outside the accepted discourse were either dismissed as immaterial or simply not read, and once the commitment to conventional warfare was no longer open to question, relativist discourse became irrelevant.

Still, the relativist ethnographic discourse and the practices which it facilitated had very tangible results in the make-up of the Highlands around 1975. For one, the process of ethnicization, started under French auspices, had become more real, as is demonstrated by the emergence of a Montagnard autonomy movement and an elite which assumed a common ethnic identity. The formation of a 'pan-highlander leadership' is one of the main themes of Hickey's two-volume *Ethnohistory* (1982a, b). Simultaneously, we should not forget that this common ethnic identity was an elite affair in the first place, starting with the Rhade or Ede 'tribe' which claimed a foremost position because of its colonial credentials. We have seen that even in the 1950s, some village heads could not even name the tribe to which they were supposed to belong. This new elite which, according to Hickey, intermarried, was very much a male affair. Membership of this new elite was predicated on one's educational or military career. The traditional patterns and structures quite literally fell apart, undercutting the – at least in the matrilineal societies – often respected status of women: with male activities dictating the residence of families in often matrilocal societies; with women losing their influence and comfortable position which came from living among kinsfolk because of the destruction of longhouses; with women losing clan title to land to men holding individual titles. The drawn-out warfare situation removed the traditional checks on male domination, and resulted in a tilting of the balance in favour of men – perhaps a sign of the 'male emancipation' advocated by the French colonial officer Maurice (1956).

While Hickey views the leadership developments in the Highlands in wartime with sympathy, there are clear parallels with of the situation at the end of the last century. That was the era of the 'big men' who did not control 'tribes' – the boundaries were fluid – but had a preponderant position in one or more villages due to their control of the long-distance trade. This trade included the slave trade which was stimulated from Siam, Laos and Cambodia, and which led to an unstable situation of raiding, inter-village warfare and hunting for humans to be sold as slaves. Similarly, in the 1960s new 'big men' emerged, who owed their influential position to their ability to manage contacts with outsiders (Americans, for instance). The modern 'big men' were again no tribal leaders, but attempted to command fluid populations – refugees, for example. There is one major difference between the two types of 'big men'. The pre-modern 'big men' spent their economic gains on feasting, thereby enhancing their political, ritual and religious status. The modern 'big men', on the other hand, used their political and religious (many of the Highland leaders were christianized) contacts to reap economic gain. The sheer fluidity of the situation in the 1960s and 1970s (the majority of Montagnards had one time or another been resettled by 1971) made the tribal distinctions increasingly irrelevant, and the search for a common name for all Montagnards more and more urgent. In this context of the emergence of a 'detribalized' but 'ethnicized' Montagnard elite, it is politically significant that the present regime does not have a common name for the Montagnards. Instead, it suppressed the new 'pan-highlander' elite while inaugurating a process of tribal identification instead, and taking over many of the programs of the *ancien régime,* including resettlement schemes and the denial of land rights.

8 The Dying God revisited

The King of Fire and Vietnamese ethnic policies[1]

> But it is with the death of the god-man – the divine king or priest – that we are here especially concerned. The mystic kings of Fire and Water in Cambodia are not allowed a natural death. Hence when one of them is seriously ill and the elders think he cannot recover, they stab him to death.
>
> (Sir James Frazer, *The Golden Bough*, Part III: *The Dying God*. London 1923: 14)

Introduction

When doing research in the Vietnamese Central Highlands (Tây Nguyên) in 1991 in order to study the effects of Vietnamese ethnic policies since 1975, I had the chance to visit Plei B'rong (also called Plei *P'tau* or Plei Oi), the village of the legendary 'King of Fire' (*p'tau apui* or *p'tau pui*). Partly because of the title of 'King' – a misnomer, as we shall see – the *p'tau pui*, and to a lesser extent his colleagues, the *p'tau ia* ('King of Water') and the *p'tau angin* ('King of Wind'), have come to symbolize Montagnard sovereignty over the Central Highlands in the eyes of neighbouring and invading nations. During my stay, there was a debate going on within the Government bureaucracy whether the Jarai could be allowed to perform the rituals for the succession of the deceased *p'tau pui*.

After fifteen years of Communist rule in southern Vietnam the last 'kings' of water and wind had died without designating successors. Also, the old *p'tau pui*, Siu Nhot or Oi Tu, had died in 1987, but a successor had already been designated in the person of his grand-nephew Siu Aluân. When I visited the village of Plei P'tau in Chu Prông district in May, 1991, Siu Aluân still had not succeeded to the office of 'King of Fire'. This was mainly due to direct and indirect interventions by the Vietnamese authorities objecting to the succession and the concomitant feasting. The delay in the ceremony caused fear among many Jarai that a catastrophe might happen during the 'absence' of a new *p'tau pui*, who was supposed to guarantee the harvest by performing elaborate rituals. However, during my stay in Gialai province, it became clear that there was a debate going on among officials and Party cadres at various levels of the bureaucracy. Cadres of Jarai descent in particular, pleaded with the higher authorities to grant permission for the performance of the rituals, in part because some of them were awed by the prospect of impending catastrophe. According to my informants, the idea was also discussed at a central level within the Ministry of Culture, and plans were being made to organize various events around the succession. These plans, however, were not carried out, and according to my latest information Siu Aluân is still waiting for permission to succeed his (maternal) grand-uncle.

In this chapter I present this case of non-succession, which is at the intersection of a number of related, sometimes conflicting discourses and policies concerning Vietnam's Montagnards. It is about 'New Economic Zones' and traditional land rights. It is about sedentarization of 'semi-nomadic' people. It is about feasting and wasting valuable resources. It is about religious freedom and eradication of superstition. It is about culture and folklorization of culture. It is about 'ethnic solidarity' (*Đoàn kết dân tộc*) and state paternalism. I shall develop my analysis in sections on the historical significance and the cultural representations of the 'King of Fire'; on the Third Indochina War and FULRO, as a backdrop for understanding some of the policies; on the field research that forms the basis for this chapter; on the policies of sedentarization and selective preservation and Montagnard responses; and on my meeting with the 'King'.

In this chapter, I shall use the 'official' ethnic labels used by the present government. This does not mean that I take these – or any – ethnic labels for granted. In the preceding chapters I have used the terms tribalization and ethnicization to denote the processes by which culturally and linguistically heterogeneous, indigenous populations were identified and made to identify themselves as tribes and ethnic groups. Nor do I take the 'perennial antagonism' for granted that mostly French and American anthropologists have assumed to exist between Kinh (ethnic Vietnamese) and Montagnards. In the previous chapters I have argued that this was a (neo)colonial fiction which was partly realized through decades of foreign intervention. In other words, my definition of ethnicity would be situationalist rather than primordialist, to borrow the terms used by David Brown (1994: xi–xxi).

Official Vietnamese ethnic classification, however, is definitely primordialist; and because it is in a position to impose its ethnic categories on the Highland population (e.g. in identity cards), it is sufficiently relevant to take into account. Like the political regimes that preceded it, the present regime embarked on a new ethnic classification, claimed to be more 'scientific' than previous ones. Significantly, the present regime has no generic name for the mountain minorities in the Tây Nguyên (Western Highlands) region (like *Moï*, Montagnard, 'Yard', or *Đồng bào thuong*). Traditionally, the various groups in the Highlands had no common name for themselves, although they employed generic terms to denote the Kinh (*Yuon*), Khmer and Lao. Recently, (former) activists of the FULRO autonomy movement have begun to use the term 'Dega' to refer to themselves. In this chapter, I shall use the generic term Montagnard or Highlander without difference.

The 'King of Fire' in history

Ever since he was mentioned in James Frazer's *The Golden Bough* (1923a: 3–6; 1923b: 14), the King of Fire gained notoriety in Western scholarly circles as a living example of primitive, divine kingship – and this image was enhanced by the mistaken assumption that he was not allowed a natural death. In earlier French accounts, the 'King of Fire', together with his companion 'King of Water' (*p'tau ia*) and the lesser known 'King of Wind' (*p'tau angin*), had come to symbolize Jarai – and by extension Montagnard – sovereignty over the Central Highlands of what is now Vietnam. Around the turn of the century, their political importance had been enhanced by the fluidity of the colonial border, which allowed for competing claims by the French and the Siamese to the hinterland east of the Mekong River. In 1893, France – *nation protectrice* of Cambodia and Annam (Vietnam) – and Siam – suzerain over Laos – clashed over control of the tribal area (see Chapter 2). France backed up its claims to the strategically important area by referring to the ritual tributary relationships that existed between the Jarai 'Kings' and both the Cambodian and Annamese courts in pre-colonial times.

However, the significance of the *p'tau*, both in the Highlands and in relation to the neighboring states, had been misconstrued as a consequence of the tendency to conceive of the tributary relations between these 'Kings' and the courts of Cambodia and Vietnam in terms of Western, diplomatic relations, which are essentially political. In fact, the title of 'King of Fire' (in Vietnamese: *Hoa xá*) is a misnomer, because the person in that office wields hardly any worldly (political) power, but derives his authority from his ritual and religious status. Apart from all his speculation about succession procedures, this aspect was correctly seen by Sir James Frazer:

> Their royal functions are of a purely mystic or spiritual order; they have no political authority; they are simple peasants, living by the sweat of their brow and the offerings of the faithful.
>
> (Frazer 1923a: 3)[2]

In the Malay and Cham languages, close to the Jarai language, the word *patao/patau* means prince or 'king'. In Cambodia and Laos the *p'tau* were known under the title of *samdech* and *sadet* respectively (meaning 'prince'), and in Vietnam the *hoa xá* and *thuy xá* were recognized as mandarins of second degree by the Vietnamese court in Hue. The French simply took over such names, and around the turn of the century the *p'tau* were generally known by the French as the *sadet d'eau* and *sadet du feu*.

The relations between the Highlands and the states of Annam, Cambodia and Laos contained important political, military and economic aspects. The political and military aspects were embedded by the strategic location of Jarai territory which controlled the routes from Annam to Cambodia within this triangular relation. The Jarai were in a position to prevent or hinder incursions from one state onto the other, also because local belief would have it that infringement could have disastrous climatic consequences. The economic aspect can be brought out by the fact that in pre-colonial times the bulk of the international trade in Cambodia and in Vietnam consisted of forest products from the highlands, as can be gleaned from Vietnamese and Cambodian annals and documents, as well as travel accounts by Chinese and European authors (see Chapter 1). Yet, the tributary relations and the exchange of gifts were foremost religious in nature. Thus, every three years the Cambodian King would receive grains of upland rice from the Jarai delegation coming down to the Buddhist monastery of Sambor at the Mekong, and use these in elaborate rituals in Phnom Penh to ensure sufficient rainfall and a good harvest in his realm. The p'tau guarded an old sword (signifying fire) and a bamboo sheath which remained green forever (signifying water). These sacred objects could only be touched and handled by the *p'tau* in a ritually prescribed way. The Jarai and the neighbouring peoples, both highlanders and lowlanders, believed that if these objects were not paid proper tribute or if they were shown to outsiders (like French explorers), the world would be burned or flooded, respectively. Legend would have it that these objects belonged to the last princes of Champa, the Hindu/Muslim kingdom on the east coast of Indochina which was progressively conquered and destroyed by the Vietnamese in the course of three centuries prior to 1800. Cham and Jarai are linguistically closely related, and the many Cham vestiges in the presentday Central Highlands of Vietnam attest to an important Cham presence there before Champa was conquered by the Vietnamese (Dournes 1970).

The confusion with regard to the status of the *p'tau* may have been partly due to the fact that both the *p'tau pui* and the *p'tau ia* were guardians of sacred objects, which, according to legend, would have been regalia of the princes of Champa. The *p'tau* were perceived as the heirs of Champa's spiritual and political leaders. The title of 'king' created a lot of misunderstanding about the religious status of the *p'tau*. In 1893, however, the French had no use for things religious and preferred to conceive of the Highlands as Jarai princedoms under formal jurisdiction of the Vietnamese emperor. After a short blockade of Bangkok, Siamese influence was ousted from the east bank of the Mekong, and Laos was placed under French protection as well, making the Central Highlands a *res nullius* territory within the confines of French Indochina. In the beginning of this century the French moved to curb any political influence of the *p'tau* over the Highlands by suppressing overt Jarai resistance against their military penetration. In that context French ethnographers started to show much interest in the secret/sacred attributes of the Jarai 'kings' but this was resisted by the Jarai. The conflict came to a head with the murder in 1904 of the military and ethnographic explorer Prosper Odend'hal who had committed the sacrilege of desiring to see the 'regalia' of the King of Water while simultaneously refusing to drink the rice wine that was offered.

When Jarai resistance to French penetration was suppressed in the following years, the French simply assumed that the prestige of the *p'tau* would wane with the establishment of colonial rule. Apart from a legendary clash in 1922 between the *p'tau apui* and the administrator Léopold Sabatier, whose column was reportedly chased away by a thunderstorm commanded by the former, the *p'tau* were more or less left alone by the French (Dournes 1977: 75). Considered shamans or sorcerers without political power, they were conveniently left out of the political discourse on the Montagnards and were consequently considered a survival of an almost forgotten past, to be studied by historians rather than ethnographers. During the First Indochina War (1946–54), the records made hardly any mention of the three *p'tau*, despite the competition for the allegiance of the Montagnard population by both parties. The Second Indochina War saw a competition for the allegiance of the Montagnards between three parties, the Vietnamese communist movement, the Americans, and – rather clumsily and unsuccessfully – the South Vietnamese regime. The then *p'tau pui*, Oi Nhot, now considered a potentially important 'traditional leader' (cf. Hickey 1957: 19), was wooed from different sides, but refused to let himself be used in the political conflict. Still, he willingly received foreign guests and entertained cordial relationships with the last (and late) South Vietnamese minister of Development of Ethnic Minorities, the Jarai Nay Luett, who gave him a wheelchair when he could not walk anymore. But he refused to have contact with representatives of the Liberation Front, resulting in a deteriorating relation with the Communists even before 1975.[3] After the reunification of the country in 1975, the *p'tau* were considered survivals of a sort of primitive feudalism. The Vietnamese anthropologist Mac Đuòng, for example, speaks of the 'primitive states within societies in the process of forming classes (for example the states of Hoa Xá and Thuy Xá among the peoples of the Central Highlands)' (Mac Đuòng 1993: 5).

Before presenting the case of non-succession at the intersection of a number of related, sometimes conflicting discourses and policies concerning Vietnam's Montagnards, the political and military contexts of these discourses and policies have to be addressed in the next section.

The Third Indochina War and FULRO

This chapter is about a cultural conflict in an area which has been ravaged by the three Indochina Wars and which knew armed resistance against the communist regime until 1992. The Third Indochina War, as it is often called, refers to the series of conflicts from 1975 till 1989, involving Vietnam, Cambodia and China as main actors. The Khmer Rouge, holding Democratic Kampuchea in an iron grip, wished to restore its control over the Mekong Delta and portions of the Central Highlands. Historically, some of these areas had once belonged to the Khmer Empire. After numerous cruel Khmer Rouge attacks on towns and villages on Vietnamese soil, Vietnam's People's Army struck back in late 1978, and effectively occupied most of Cambodia by early 1979 while installing a 'friendly' regime in Phnom Penh. China, as Cambodia's main ally and Vietnam's erstwhile benefactor, decided (in the words of Deng Xiaoping) 'to teach Vietnam a lesson' – a lesson that proved costly to both sides (for details see Chanda 1986;

and Evans and Rowley 1984). From 1979 the genocidal Khmer Rouge along with two other Khmer resistance groups were kept afloat with massive foreign aid from China, Thailand and Western countries, until the Vietnamese military withdrawal from Cambodia in 1989.

Other actors in the conflict included Thailand, the US and other nations, but also a number of smaller guerrilla groups operating in various countries. One guerrilla group that was active in Vietnam's Central Highlands after 1975 was the *Front Unifié de la Lutte des Races Opprimées*, or FULRO. During the Second Indochina War FULRO forces played a minor but decisive role in the final collapse of the Southern regime in 1975. After the Communist takeover, FULRO ranks soon swelled because of Montagnard dissatisfaction over the issues of autonomy, sedentarization, New Economic Zones and re-education. Around 1980, FULRO forces counted some 7000 guerrillas, and a full-scale war was being fought out in the Highlands, which included aerial bombardments. From 1982 on, the Communist regime adopted a more conciliatory position, which bore fruit on the battlefield. That year, one group of around 200 FULRO warriors made it through Cambodia to the Thai border, where they were held prisoner in a Khmer Rouge guerrilla camp. Since 1975 FULRO had received support from the Khmer Rouge, just as it had received support from the successive Cambodian regimes before 1975. What they did not know was that in April 1975 when entering Pnomh Penh the Khmer Rouge had summarily executed FULRO's leadership, including Y Bham Enuol. In 1986, the FULRO prisoners managed to escape to Bangkok, and were admitted as refugees to the US. In August 1992, the last remnants of FULRO surrendered to the forces of the UN Transitional Authority in Cambodia, to be shipped to the US (Thayer 1992).

Whereas the analysis offered below is critical of certain aspects of Vietnamese policy in the Central Highlands, I do not claim that it differs much from ethnic policies in other countries of Asia, Africa, the Americas or Europe. This in itself is remarkable, given the history of violence and foreign intervention in Vietnam and the Central Highlands in particular. In this sense, Vietnam's record may not be better, but is hardly worse than any country in, for example, Europe or Asia.

Entering the field

In late 1990 I arrived in Vietnam to do ethnographic fieldwork after many years of mainly historical research. According to my information, the moment would be right because the absolute prohibition for foreigners to enter the Central Highlands had just been eased. In the years past, the Highlands region, bordering on Laos and Cambodia, had been a strategic base area for the Vietnamese occupation forces in Cambodia, but with the withdrawal of the Vietnamese army from Cambodia, the base area lost its strategic significance. Also, the fierce guerrilla fought out by FULRO forces in the Vietnam-Cambodia border zone was slowly petering out after a high point in the early 1980s. After 1975, the Vietnamese authorities isolated the FULRO movement from foreign

Figure 8.1 Siu Aluân, the designated new 'King of Fire', chanting to appease the spirits when receiving visitors, Plei Patao 1991.

Source: Oscar Salemink.

contacts by simply fencing off the Highlands region. Just before my arrival, there had been an armed assault by an unidentified group on a biological expedition comprising both Vietnamese and British citizens. This effectively closed off the province of my first choice, Đak Lak.

After some waiting and negotiating in Hanoi, mostly with the various departments within the Ministry of the Interior and with provincial authorities, I received permission from the vice-minister of the Interior to conduct research in Gialai-Kontum and Lâm Đông provinces.[4] In the provincial capital of Plây Cu (Pleiku), the negotiating began anew in early 1991, and never really stopped for the duration of my stay. This left me sufficient time to visit various provincial Departments (of Education, Culture and Information, Agriculture and Forestry) to collect material on policies in these fields and on the 'Fixed Cultivation and Settlement' program (*Đinh canh Đinh cu*) carried out among the ethnic minorities. I held formal interviews with high-ranking provincial cadres within the state, the Party and the Mass Organizations under the Communist Party. This way I soon found out that most decisions were taken by Kinh people from the northern Nghê Tĩnh province, who formed an informal network which controlled the Highlands.[5]

During the first week, I also had interviews with private persons, mainly of Jarai descent. In these interviews, my interlocutors brought up the subject of the King of Fire, who was the last of the Jarai kings. Rmah Hanh, an anthropologist of Jarai descent who had retired early, mentioned the gradual disappearance of the traditional practices and beliefs among the minorities. One such instance was the waning of the spiritual authority of the *p'tau*, because they were not allowed to move around the villages anymore to perform the required rituals, and because the necessary sacrifices were too burdensome to bear for the villages. Hanh told that when the former King of Fire, Oi Nhot, died in 1987, the authorities refused to give permission for the succession rituals, which require sacrifices in terms of the slaughter of a number of buffaloes. However, at that very moment, according to Hanh, the authorities were preparing for the succession to take place.[6]

This was a surprising piece of information. From published sources and other interviews, I had gathered that everything concerning the *p'tau* was catalogued under the heading of superstition. Officially, Vietnam guarantees freedom of religion – although one may harbor legitimate doubts about that – but superstition is forbidden. Fortunately, Vietnamese officials can draw a clear line between religion and superstition. Take Kpa Eng for instance, the Vice-President of the People's Committee of Gialai-Kontum (provincial authorities) and President of the Fatherland Front, the Mass Organization dealing with issues of 'ethnic solidarity' (*Đoàn kết dân tộc*) in the province. According to Kpa Eng, himself Jarai, ethnic solidarity was not a real problem anymore, since slavery did not exist anymore and superstition was forbidden. When religion would intervene in social life, e.g. by requiring large sacrifices, or by promoting 'unscientific' medical practices, it was considered superstition.[7] The 'King of Fire' performs both evils.

Still, I perceived ambivalence. One of the ways of attaining ethnic solidarity is the organization of competitive music and dance festivals for minorities. During such festivals, music and art is decontextualized: it is separated from the cultural context of ritual and feasting – which is largely forbidden as wasteful, superstitious activity nowadays – and turned from a participative event into a performing art for an audience which generally is not aware of the 'traditional' cultural context. This is what I call the folklorization of culture, which creates an image of culture as an aesthetic survival from the past, detached from the present cultural context. In terms of politics of tradition, it is imperative to forge an organic link between presentday ethnic solidarity, and an imagined common culture in the past. The competition serves to underscore the unnerving of cultural difference. In April 1991, I watched videos recorded at two such festivals in Pleiku in 1988 and 1990. Interestingly, the *Hội cồng chiêng* minorities' music festival of 1988 celebrated the presence of the legendary hero Núp, a Bahnar who had played a much publicized role in the resistance against the French (1946–54) and later the Americans, together with Siu Aluân, who had been elected but not yet succeeded as King of Fire. Thus, the film conveys the present regime's desire to extend its genealogy of resistance against foreign rule in the Highlands by incorporating the much older genealogy of the *p'tau*. The present-day *p'tau*, then, is seen as a relic from a mythical past, who is not allowed to function in modern society. A more radical decontextualization is hardly possible.

A few days later I interviewed the person responsible for the official interest in the King of Fire. This was Nay Quách, the Vice-Director of the provincial Department of Culture and Information, who told me his life story.[8] He is a Jarai who originated from the district of Cheo Reo (or Ayun Pa, as it is called now). He attended French schools until 1945, then participated in the struggle against the French. Like many Rhadé and Jarai youngsters, he went North with the Viêt Minh in 1954, after the Geneva Agreements. In the North, he had been educated at the special Ethnic Minority School (*Trường Dân tộc*) for minority cadres. In 1961 he went South to organize the anti-Diêm and anti-American resistance in Pleiku province. Later, he went to various places in South Vietnam until he went North again in 1969, and even visited the Soviet Union and Bulgaria in 1971. Although he had married a Kinh woman in the North, he requested in 1971 to be assigned to the South again, where he remained active until 1975. After the liberation, he took up a high position in the provincial administration, as did many of the former youngsters who had gone north in 1954. In actual practice, it is such 'Vietnamized' Jarai who constituted the 'ethnic minority' element within the higher echelons of the provincial administration.

Since 1977, Nay Quách had been organizing cultural classes in music and oral literature for ethnic minorities, as part of the effort to preserve 'valuable' customs in an otherwise prohibitive context of suppression of 'bad' habits, like witchcraft, long funeral rituals and wasteful feasting, which were all deemed 'superstition'. However, he was also critical of the authorities which failed to perceive the interests of the Jarai, as in the case of Viêt immigrants who confiscate lands which are considered by the Jarai to be theirs. Another instance of the authorities' incapacity to understand the Jarai cultural context was their long-time refusal to meet with the *p'tau pui*. According to Nay Quách, the *p'tau*'s authority is neither political nor economic (which would render him suspect as a political rival of the Party), but purely religious – which was sufficient to brand his role as superstitious (*mê tín*). After the death of Oi Tu, who had received foreign visitors but had avoided contacts with the Communists for a long time, Nay Quách pleaded for a reconciliation, but was only allowed to meet the new *p'tau* in 1988. At the time of the interview, he was conducting a research project on the *p'tau*, who was to be installed shortly with permission of the authorities in a ceremony which he would film – 'if the Gods will allow it' (Nay Quách in interview, 28 April 1991). The last was a serious exclamation, as – according to Nay Quách – all Jarai are in awe of the spiritual power of the *P'tau*. He himself increasingly feared this magic power, since the health of both his family and himself had deteriorated since his first visit to the *P'tau* in 1988.

Nay Quách's account made me all the more curious about the present condition of the 'King of Fire'. My first experience with a field trip Vietnamese style in the Kontum area did not make me optimistic about the prospects of my doing research in the region. Not only was the field trip far too short to yield any reliable data, but the visits to the various Bahnar and Rongao villages around Kontum were attended by an escort consisting of representatives of every administrative level (central, provincial, district, commune and hamlet). This presence of mostly Kinh (ethnic Vietnamese) people intimidated my interlocutors both indirectly and directly. Still, one old villager made my entourage very nervous by complaining about the worsening conditions in his village since 1975, and asking for foreign assistance in the reconstruction of the traditional, high-roofed communal men's house (*nhà rông*). In another village, one person whispered in French, when out of earshot of my escort: 'Nous Montagnards sont en grande peine [We Montagnards are in great trouble].'[9]

When I was criticized during an interview for not asking the 'correct' questions, I had enough of it, and threatened to break off my research. The conflict that threatened to erupt was resolved through a new round of negotiations with local authorities. This resulted in permission to conduct research for a prolonged period of time in a number of Jarai villages in the district of Ayun Pa – the ancient Jarai heartland and the home area of the King of Fire. But before recounting the story of my visit to the latter, I shall describe in more detail two of the key aspects of Vietnam's ethnic policy in the Highlands, i.e. the sedentarization policy and the policy of selective preservation.

The official discourse on sedentarization

Most of the post-1975 foreign literature on the Central Highlands deals with the issues of sedentarization and immigration. In his 1980 rewriting of the *Minority Rights Group report no. 18* on Vietnam's Montagnards, Jacques Dournes underscored the continuity of preconceived ideas concerning the Montagnards (as 'savages', 'nomads', 'starving', 'superstitious', 'illiterate' and 'backward') from colonial times up to the present. He argued that these crude notions were used to justify sedentarization and colonization policies by the various successive powers in southern Vietnam (Dournes 1980: 12–16). In his 'Primitives to Peasants' (1985), Ron Hill made a similar observation, namely that the sedentarization of 'nomadic tribes' 'is seen as an altruistic measure of social progress' (Hill 1985: 449). He added that the results of the 'sedentarization' policy were not clear from the figures provided by Vietnamese sources, partly because the figures concerning 'sedentarization' of minorities were not kept apart from the figures of Kinh immigrants turning to wet-rice cultivation in the Highlands (ibid.: 454). In his assessment of Vietnamese population policy from 1975 to 1985, Nguyên Duc Nhuân linked the sedentarization issue to the massive migration of Kinh from the plains to the so-called New Economic Zones (NEZ) in the Highlands and to the ongoing deforestation of Vietnam. Thus, the population of Gialai-Kontum province rose from 432,000 in 1976 to 596,000 in 1979, a rise of 38 per cent which is mostly due to the immigration of Kinh settlers (Nguyên Duc Nhuân 1987: 22–30, 200–08).

Writing in 1992, Grant Evans attaches the label of 'internal colonialism' to Vietnamese policy in the Central Highlands, basing himself on official statistical data and accounts published by Vietnamese anthropologists, whom he accuses of having 'supported and approved of the government's policies in the Central Highlands' (Evans 1992: 288). He further notices a 'profound schizophrenia' among these ethnographers who sympathetically document the indigenous peoples' way of life but have to filter this documentation through a theoretical framework which rationalizes Party policy which is detrimental toward the minorities (ibid.: 289–90). On the other hand, Evans sees a more promising tendency reflected in Đang Nghiêm Van's critical attitude toward the sedentarization policy so far (Ibid.: 294–6; see also Đang Nghiêm Van 1989: 67–151). Incidentally, Evans concludes his article by referring to the non-debate over the 'King of Water' and 'King of Fire' in the Highlands, whose unclear political status in the past is used to either back up claims for Montagnard political autonomy or to assert that no supra-local identification exists apart from that imposed from outside. For Evans, 'it is clear that many traditional institutions among the highlanders, including that of the 'king of fire' [whose eventual succession is briefly discussed – OS] operate parallel to the Vietnamese-imposed administration' (Evans 1992: 300).

One problem, noted by Evans and other non-Vietnamese scholars, was the scarcity of trustworthy data on the Central Highlands. Until recently, foreign researchers were not allowed to do any substantial research in the Highlands, whereas both the official statistical data and the accounts by Vietnamese researchers are considered unreliable. This is not the place to rectify the statistics concerning Vietnamese policy in the Highlands; rather, this chapter is an attempt to go beyond such figures and observe the effects of the policy (or better: policies) in terms of human experience. Still, it is useful to note that the figures given to me on virtually every topic conflict with figures given by other institutions on central or local levels. Many statistical data characteristically bear the stamp of planning objectives rather than actual results of government policy.[10] Also, there is a lot of confusion in defining the policy terms themselves. Let me give one telling example of this.

In Vietnamese, the sedentarization program is called *Đinh canh đinh cu* [fixed cultivation and settlement], implying that among minorities both cultivation and settlement are not fixed (*du canh du cu*). As far as cultivation is concerned, the implication is partly correct, as a good deal of the highland population practised shifting cultivation. In the Central Highlands, traditional shifting cultivation was by no means at random, but was perfectly adapted to the natural conditions, in that the fields rotated within a delineated territory following an extended agricultural cycle of varying length. Erosion was prevented by the traditional use of a dibble stick instead of a plough – thus leaving the structure of the soil intact – while the soil fertility was enhanced by the manure of cattle grazing on the fields which are left to fallow (Boulbet 1966; Condominas 1972; Lafont 1967; Matras-Troubetzkoy 1983).[11] While seemingly 'primitive', these agricultural and livestock breeding techniques allowed for the regeneration of the forest cover and of the fertility of the soil, given a sufficiently long fallowing period. The indigenous populations of the Central Highlands have practiced their shifting cultivation systems for centuries, maybe even millennia, without serious damage to the forests.

As in so many other countries, however, the indigenous peoples of Vietnam are blamed for the deforestation occurring in their environment. In colloquial

Vietnamese, the word for dry rice farming/swiddening (*làm rẫy*) is often preceded by the words *phá rừng*, 'clearing', but literally meaning 'destroying the forest'.[12] This term is also used to denote the process of deforestation. Thus, shifting cultivation is etymologically and analytically linked to deforestation. During my interviews with both central and local agriculture and forestry officials, most of them conceded after some probing that it was not really the indigenous peoples who were to blame. The deforestation after 1975 was rather a result of unfettered logging by state forest enterprises and cooperatives, of slash-and-burn practice by newly migrated Kinh settlers from the lowlands who mostly had no agricultural experience in mountainous areas, and of the steep increase in population density which led to land scarcity, conflicts over land and shortening fallowing cycles.[13]

The incrimination of minorities for their alleged part in the deforestation process may be seen as an instance of blaming the victims, because their natural environment is deteriorating rapidly due to processes beyond their control. Combined with the rapidly increasing land scarcity, this results in diminishing agricultural yields. Sometimes, the effects of present conditions in the Highlands are quite unexpected. For example, since 1985 malaria has been on the rise again in Gialai province, as elsewhere in the Highlands. This may be explicable for the Kinh population, which now makes up over half of the provincial population and which had not built up immunity for the local malaria varieties. However, the new (imported or mutant, but resistant) strains of malaria do not respect the immunity of local Jarai people; not only children and elderly, but even adult Jarai are being seriously affected again, leading to increasing numbers of casualties that are hardly reflected in medical statistics for want of an effective local health system. Since 1989, many villagers in Ayun Pa district have not dared to enter the forested mountains anymore to cut firewood or construction wood, collect non-timber products or dig for gold, or even to work and stay at their dry rice fields, because they said that they were sure to contract the feared fever.[14] Thus, their resources were increasingly limited to the irrigated rice fields in the valleys, which they share with Kinh immigrants. The yield of these fields did not suffice to feed the population, rendering hunger and malnutrition endemic. Whereas the authorities legitimate the sedentarization program by referring to the hunger which they associate with 'backward' (*lạc hậu*) shifting cultivation, the net result of this policy is that indigenous populations are cut off from forest resources which formerly kept hunger at bay.

The second term in the 'Fixed Cultivation and Settlement Program' defines minority populations as 'nomadic' (*du cư*). This term is often employed in official documents to describe local settlement patterns, implying that villages are abandoned when the soil is exhausted. This concords perfectly with the official view of shifting cultivation as an irrational, backward agricultural technology. However, the norm among most groups in the Central Highlands is that villages stay at one place, because the villagers claim a definite territory as their land, which is used for rotating the rice fields. Historically, villages only moved because of natural calamities, war, violence, and forced resettlement, conditions of which the Central Highlands have had more than their share in the past decades.

Figure 8.2 Siu Aluân receiving the author on ethnographic fieldwork, Plei Patao 1991.

Source: Oscar Salemink.

During the Second Indochina War (1960–75) alone, the number of Montagnard casualties is estimated at 200,000, while more than 85 per cent of the population was forced to flee or resettle at one time (Hickey 1982b: 290). Other causes for moving villages traditionally included splitting up of existing villages and the belief that a locality was haunted by evil spirits, often following natural disasters and epidemics. In peaceful times, then, settlement patterns would be fairly stable.

In more recent ethnographic work, notably by Đang Nghiêm Van, it is acknowledged that the Montagnards are not nomads, but – as Grant Evans noted (1992: 290) – the attitude of anthropologists is often not representative of the official view. Some of the Jarai province officials in Gialai-Kontum whom I interviewed, adamantly denied that the Jarai were nomads, a view which apparently did not qualify the necessity of the sedentarization program. In interviews with officials of both central and provincial agencies, two other definitions for nomadism came up. One was, that villages may remain located at the same spot, but that the population lived half of the year on the fields, far away from the village, in order to work the fields, weed, tend the cattle, protect the fields from intruding wild animals, etc. During that season, they are barred from the amenities of normal, 'civilized' life, like schools, health care, and any of the other services and control mechanisms of the state. The second definition of nomadism or semi-nomadism developed the latter point: every village where the state is not present in whatever form is considered as not fixed. As with ethnic minorities all over the world, the real issue is the subjection of all populations within the territory of the state to the control of the state. A state which is so preoccupied by questions of sovereignty, security and territorial integrity as Vietnam is, cannot but conceive of its subjects through the prism of governmentality (cf. Foucault 1979b), while simultaneously aiming at the wellbeing and the 'improvement' of its population by making its subjects into proper citizens of the state through a variety of disciplining tactics. The Montagnards, too, must be made into civilized citizens of Vietnam, which necessitates their subjection to state surveillance and discipline. The Vietnamese program for that is Fixed Cultivation and Settlement, which permits the governmentalization of the Montagnard way of life. From the perspective of governmentality, then, the 'truth' of official discourse concerning their 'nomadic' way of life and their 'backward' agricultural practices is irrelevant.

According to Michel Foucault, in eighteenth century Europe a shift took place from the art of government to a science of government, which gave rise to the formation of a whole series of state apparatuses and to the development of a whole body of governmental knowledge, related to the various disciplines. In Vietnam, we see that such knowledge is embodied in the various institutions related to the State and Party both on central and local levels, and phrased in Marxist idiom. During wartime, Hô Chí Minh launched the idea of 'ethnic solidarity' by using a family metaphor which competed with the family metaphor employed by the French: the various ethnic groups were Vietnam's children, and within that family the elder brother (Kinh majority) had the duty to simultaneously respect and develop the minorities (see Chapter 5). With the establishment of a regular government, this idea was increasingly compounded by different, economic and political, considerations, necessitating a further refinement of this crude basis. The difficult security situation in the Central Highlands and the economic prospects offered by the region's natural resources gave rise to what was called the Tây Nguyên Research Program (I: 48-09 and II: 48C), comprising scientists of various disciplines as well as government officials. The results were presented at three major seminars in 1983, 1985 and 1988, the proceedings of which were published, along with special studies of the 'ethnic problem' in all the provinces concerned.[15]

When Grant Evans (1992) noted the 'acceptable' criticism voiced by Đang Nghiêm Van (1989), this criticism was the outcome of the huge government-sponsored research program, and was already becoming the basis for policy in the Highlands. In November, 1989, the Politbureau issued Resolution no. 22, which criticizes past mistakes concerning the establishment of New Economic Zones, state farms and cooperatives in the mountain areas. Instead, it pleads for a concerted development effort on the basis of respect for local cultures and of the 'family economy'. However, nothing was said about the sedentarization program. This Party decision was followed up in March 1990, by Decree no. 72 of the Council of Ministers, which specified that land had to be allocated to families of minority origin and to Kinh settlers, who all should have the right to profit from their own production. The Fixed Cultivation and Settlement program, which already was implemented by the Ministry of Forestry, had to be combined with forest protection. In September of the same year, the Council of Ministers installed the Committee of Ethnic Minorities and Mountainous Areas (CEMMA) in order to carry through the policy transformation, aided by UNDP. Finally, in July 1993, a new Law on the Nationalities was passed by the Vietnamese National Assembly, instituting the Nationalities Council as a standing body of the National Assembly, which controls and prepares minorities policy in Vietnam (Bô Chính tri 1989; Hôi Dông Bô truong 1990; Gammelgaard 1990; Quôc Hôi 1993).[16]

Sedentarization in practice: Gialai-Kontum and Lâm Dông

Despite the impressive legislative activity in the political center, locally few actual changes took place. Contrary to its image of Communist centralized decision-making, Vietnam is very much a decentralized state, where much decision-making is concentrated in the provinces which are virtually autonomous and self-financing. Many of the province and district officials I interviewed in 1991, let alone local cadres, were not aware of the changes in policy which had emanated from the centre – or better: the North. Those officials who were aware of the changes, had the power to interpret the new measures at will. Their viewpoint still was that they knew what was good for minority peoples, who simply had to give up backward and harmful practices and would be induced to do so by the living example of Kinh cadres and settlers who selflessly came to live among the minorities in order to help spread civilization. This ideal was maintained, despite a contrarious reality which had it that Kinh migrants might settle in the same commune (*xa*) but hardly ever in the same hamlet (*thôn, plei, buôn*); that few Kinh cadres (teachers, health workers, agricultural extension workers, even ethno-graphers!) were prepared to literally risk their lives in malaria-ridden areas for an insufficient salary; that a recent wave of Kinh migrants looking for gold, precious stones, and easy profits in profitable crops like coffee and pepper, had resulted in violent Wild West scenes, land grabbing and inter-ethnic conflict beyond the control of local authorities in one of the last frontier areas in Vietnam.[17]

Still, the results of the sedentarization program varied widely. In some places, notably on the fertile red soil plateaux in the provinces of Dak Lak, Lâm Dông and around Pleiku (the capital of Gialai province), the program worked out more or less according to the plan. In such areas, many villages grew rich through the cultivation of industrial crops (coffee, tea, rubber, pepper) or due to sericulture. Seedlings, credit, and technical assistance were provided by the cooperatives, but the plantation plots were family-owned and worked. Many families also planted such crops in the home gardens surrounding the new houses, and gradually stopped cultivating mountain rice, because they could afford to buy food on the market. Successful families showed their wealth by building Vietnamese-style, concrete houses on the ground – often next to the traditional wooden (stilted) house – filled with the insignia of modernity: shiny furniture, videos, and motorcycles. Rich hamlets financed their own schools and primary health care stations. This wealth, however, is dependent on the caprice of the world market price for their crops, and recently, families were forced to turn to dry rice and tuber farming again because the price of coffee or pepper was not sufficient to feed them – or even had to sell off their land.

In other places, like Kontum and Ayun Pa, many local Bahnar and Jarai already practised wet rice cultivation in the river valleys, often combined with dry rice cultivation on swiddens or permanent, rain-fed fields. For them, the sedentarization program meant that their land was taken over by cooperatives, in which the newly arrived Kinh settlers participated, as well. This implied that an already limited area, suitable for wet rice cultivation, now had to nourish a far greater population. Portions of land that had not been confiscated, had been leased out to Kinh settlers for want of cash money, but the rent was not enough to compensate for the loss in subsistence. In Ayun Pa district, the government tried to improve the situation through a major irrigation project, called Ayun Ha. In 1991, the only visible result of the project was the shiny headquarters along the road; at the time, the project was planned to reach Ayun Pa by 2003. According to the estimates of commune authorities, the projected increase in production would be scarcely sufficient to keep up with the natural population increase. Besides, elsewhere in Vietnam it had been observed that irrigation projects in tribal areas (often funded by international development agencies) tended to attract newcomers from the plains, who took over the irrigated land while the local minority population – the designated target group – moved further up the mountains. In the Kontum area, land scarcity may be aggravated by a series of no less than nine hydropower dams planned as part of the Yali Falls/Upper Sesane project of the Mekong Committee. If fully executed, a large surface of the fertile valley bottoms will be inundated, further limiting the wet rice acreage and necessitating the resettlement of at least thirteen villages (Electrowatt Engineering Services 1993; Lang 1994). The effects of this hydropower complex would be disastrous for both the local population and the environment.

Whatever the outcome of these major projects, already the produce of wet rice cultivation is not sufficient to feed the local populations, while no additional income can be generated from industrial crops in these locations. Additional swiddening, cattle breeding, the collection of timber and non-timber products and handicrafts provide a necessary supplementary income, but meet with a number of problems. Swiddening, for one, is not only strongly discouraged by the authorities, but traditional land rights are not recognized by the authorities, who consider all the land to be state property. Thus, many tracts of land which were left to fallow and regenerate according to the traditional *rây* (swidden) system, were portioned out to Kinh settlers. One Bahnar village near Kontum thus lost 30 hectares of valuable agricultural land between 1975 and 1985. From 1987 on, the authorities began to acknowledge the traditional land rights of the Bahnar, but there was no compensation for the land lost in the previous period. Simultaneously, the transition to cash crop production requires, besides extension of new agricultural techniques, investments without returns for a number of years.

As hardly anybody is able to make such an investment, Bahnar families turn to the cultivation of tubers, which they consider a step backward – and therefore a failure of government policy – because upland rice is appreciated for its taste, nutritional value and for its ritual qualities. For the authorities that implemented agricultural extension projects, the failure of their programs simply demonstrates the 'backwardness' of the minorities.

Cattle breeding has become difficult, too. Traditionally, Bahnar and Jarai farmers let all livestock roam in the village, under the houses, on the fields, and in the nearby woods. This has changed with the arrival of Kinh farmers who do not allow cattle belonging to others on their fields. On several occasions, cattle belonging to Bahnar families was confiscated or simply shot by Kinh settlers, with tacit consent of the authorities. One Bahnar informant expressed it as follows:

> The authorities do nothing, they put the Kinh in the right. The Kinh are never punished for their conflicts with the Bahnar, only the Bahnar are punished. We are very often punished, since 1975 every family in our village has been fined at least once.[18]

One of the results is an acute shortage of cattle and buffaloes, both among the Bahnar and Jarai, which again has negative effects on agriculture (lack of manure and draught animals), nutrition and social life (feasting, animal sacrifices during rituals).

Logging – officially the monopoly of the state at the time – is increasingly difficult because of the rapid deforestation since 1975. Traditionally, the forest was an invaluable source of wood and bamboo, of wild foodstuff and game, of grazing ground, and in general of fertility restoration. One informant stated that the indigenous people had a traditional method of preserving the forest, which was linked to the agricultural cycle of shifting cultivation. Each village had rights to the produce of certain portions of forest, and made sure that the forest was more or less kept intact. These traditional rights were not acknowledged by the authorities nor by Kinh settlers who highhandedly started to cut trees for their own use or for sale. In response, many Bahnar also started to cut the tall trees, in order not to be left empty-handed. The result is a quickened pace of deforestation, affecting the fertility and humidity of the soil and the natural resources associated with it. The present scarcity of wood is exemplified by one Bahnar village which wished to reconstruct its traditional communal men's house (*nhà rông*), but lacked the means to do so. Formerly, it had been a matter of collecting the necessary materials, organizing the labor needed for its construction, and performing the appropriate rituals; nowadays, the tall tree stems needed for construction were no longer available nearby, and had to be bought for big money from far away.

The net result of these developments has been a deterioration of the economic situation since 1975. Local authorities in Kontum and Ayun Pa mentioned that 90 per cent of the indigenous population suffers from hunger or severe malnutrition. The restrictive policy on swiddening seriously curtailed the nutrional diversity while it simultaneously diminished the consumption of dry upland rice, which, according to the French anthropologist P.B. Lafont, would contain ingredients that have an immunizing effect against malaria (Lafont, personal communication). In Ayun Pa, the famous rice alcohol, common to all local, indigenous groups and traditionally made of upland rice, was now made of corn instead of rice, giving it a sour flavor. Besides agriculture, the region offers little opportunity for earning extra incomes. Ironically, the end of the Second Indochina War in 1975 had also ended the opportunities to bring in extra incomes through an army career. In fact, many of the elderly men whom I interviewed had served in the former South Vietnamese army or with the American Special Forces. Although most of them had only recently been released from the notorious 'Re-education Camps' and were despised by the authorities, local (village and commune) Communist cadres – mostly younger Jarai and Bahnar – still respected these elder men. The latter formed an informal, traditional hierarchy alongside the formal hierarchy of party and state cadres within the village, and youngsters with positions in the formal hierarchy generally sought the consent and cooperation of the elderly in the execution of power.

The Fixed Cultivation and Settlement program aimed at amelioration of the worsening economic situation while simultaneously making an eluding population more accessible for the various disciplining strategies of state power. The official slogan of the program was *Đường – vườn – rừng* [roads – gardens – forests], indicating the three basic elements of the program: accessibility, economic viability and exploitation of the natural resources. Concerning the latter, only in the late 1980s did the idea of sustainable development took root among the central authorities, partly due to foreign influence. At the village level, sedentarization implied that the old village structure was abandoned, and a new site was selected for habitation (resettlement). Generally, the new village had a rectangular lay-out, with yards of 2000 square meters. The idea was to have home gardens around the house, where fruit trees and vegetables could be planted and small livestock could be held for immediate use, so that people would not need to fetch these on the faraway swiddens. On the fertile high plateaux, such gardens were often used to cultivate industrial crops, but elsewhere the soil was not always suitable for permanent cultivation.

Contrary to the traditional village layout, the plots were fenced, and the houses far apart. Ideally, each house would have a well or fresh water source, but in actual practice a village was lucky to have one such source; many households adopted the Kinh practice of catching rainwater from the roofs in huge jars, which form exquisite breeding ground for malaria and dengue mosquitoes. In theory, the authorities would aid the construction of the new village by providing building materials and services in the fields of agricultural extension, education and primary health care, but the means for implementing that policy were generally lacking. If the commune or village had no means of its own, schools were ramshackle, teachers were absent or away earning extra incomes, and medical workers had no medicines. One commune in Ayun Pa was in 1977

Figure 8.3 The wife of Siu Aluân, the designated new 'King of Fire', at the back of the long house, Plei Patao 1991.

Source: Oscar Salemink.

provided with a brand new primary health care centre, donated by UNICEF; after one year it ran out of medicine, became useless and was abandoned. By 1991, it was completely in ruins.

For the villagers concerned, the resettlement implied a completely new lifestyle. One of the aims – and results – of the program is the breaking up of the longhouses. Traditionally, most Montagnards lived in longhouses. In pre-colonial days, longhouses of fifty to one hundred meters could be found, containing many households belonging to one lineage and their dependents. A long longhouse was a token of wealth. Under colonial rule, the length of the longhouses diminished. This process was speeded up under the former South Vietnamese regime, which waged an assimilation policy forcing nuclear families to live separately from each other. The present regime also has a policy of breaking up the longhouses, considered a survival of 'the familial communes ... of the primitive society' (Mac Đuòng 1993: 7). Thus, breaking up the longhouses is conceived of as a necessary and progressive step toward socialist development. According to one ethnographer, the construction of a new culture and new socialist man in the Central Highlands depended on the construction of a new type of family, which 'is the splitting of families from the longhouse, with each family possessing its own house, its own garden, its own means of production, its own labor power' (Hô Lê 1984: 64). Thus, the policy of breaking up the longhouses, justified as a precondition for economic development, is simultaneously a deliberate attempt to change the minorities' lifestyle. It also had an impact on gender relations as well. The multi-generational extended families living in longhouses provided a social safety net and mutual support system for women. The imposed change in the residence patterns thus deprived women of such support systems, and made them more vulnerable and more dependent on their husbands.

Although all the longhouses I visited were not inhabited by entire lineages anymore – at most by an extended family spanning three generations – informants reported that many Montagnards resent being forced to give up their houses, let alone being forced to build Vietnamese-style houses on the ground. Coupled to the practice of storing rainwater in large jars along the house, the initial prescription but presentday fashion of building Vietnamese-style houses on the ground aggravated the occurrence of malaria and dengue epidemics, because mosquitoes tend to avoid the smoky atmosphere and the height of houses on stilts. But what is resented even more, is the new village layout. This implies a great distance between the houses, now surrounded by fenced gardens. Many informants complained about the decline in sociability and communality in the new village, and professed to regard the sedentarization program as an attempt to make them live like the Kinh. Consequently, these informants don't make much of the official policy line of 'ethnic/national solidarity' which they tend to see as a cosmetic slogan obscuring the fact that most cadres above hamlet level are Kinh. In reality, many fear and distrust their Kinh compatriots.

Recently, this has been acknowledged by Vietnamese anthropologists like Đang Nghiêm Van, Lò Giang Páo and Mac Đuòng. The latter, for example, spoke of 'inappropriate economic policies of our government [which] have led to new difficulties for ethnic minorities', and a 'contradiction … between other ethnic minorities and the Kinh'; this was due to 'impatience' in policy implementation, 'negating specific ethnic traits' and 'wishing for a rapid agglomeration into the Kinh society' (Mac Đuòng 1993: 9). This criticism, however, applied to the implementation of sedentarization through large-scale agricultural cooperatives and state-farms, rather than to the sedentarization process as such, which would now enable the minorities to 'develop a peasant individual household economy' (ibid.: 10).

'Selective preservation' of traditional culture

Many publications by Vietnamese anthropologists and policy makers extol the multi-ethnic character of Vietnamese culture, and the – mostly aesthetic – value of minority cultures. The late vice-minister in charge of minority culture in Vietnam, Nông Quôc Chân, compared a plural Vietnamese culture to a garden of scenting, colorful flowers (Nông Quôc Chân 1977). However, Mr. Chân might not have realized to what ends his metaphor might be used. For, though beautiful flowers are a gift of nature, beautiful gardens seldom grow by themselves. In gardens, flowers are sown or planted, cultivated, manured, weeded, tended, arranged and presented in a careful manner; some people – among them many

British, Japanese and Vietnamese – would even say that gardening is not a skill, but an art. Thus, the idea of Vietnamese culture as a garden of flowers presupposes a subject cultivating, arranging and presenting the flowers in the desired fashion. And this is exactly what happens in Vietnam, where the party and state assume the authority to decide which aspects of minority cultures are valuable enough to retain, which aspects should disappear, and which aspects should be transformed.[19]

Culture (*văn hóa*) in Vietnam is taken to mean the immaterial aspects of life, like language, religion, education, and manners and customs. In the socialist transformation of society, not all of that can be retained. After all, the cultural 'level' of Vietnam's minorities is seen as 'lower' than that of the Kinh, and, according to the guiding principle of mutual assistance, the latter should help the former in 'catching up' with the latter to assimilate into a new Vietnamese culture (see Nông Quôc Chân 1978a, and Pham Nhu Cuòng et al. 1987). Fortunately, the party cadres know exactly what is to be preserved as valuable, and what should be abandoned. Valuable are folklore, dances, music, handicrafts, and these are renovated for presentation for the 'masses'. Grant Evans described this policy of 'selective preservation' as a 'peculiar process of dissolution/ preservation of traditional cultural forms' (1985: 142).

Today, selective preservation is still an integral part of Vietnamese ethnic policy, as was clear from a number of Vietnamese contributions (e.g., the address by Nông Quôc Chân) to a UNESCO-sponsored international conference on the safeguarding of Vietnam's minorities' cultural heritage, held in Hanoi in 1994 (see UNESCO 1994: 5). While Vietnam's cultural diversity was celebrated by all participating researchers and politicians, the rapid cultural transformation among Vietnam's minority groups was deplored. With 'international tourism' and the 'mass media' singled out as scapegoats for the alleged cultural disintegration among the minorities, hardly any effort was made to contextualize the process of cultural change by linking it to the pervasive policies concerning migration and sedentarization.[20] Most of the projects which came out of the conference would concern the recording or collection of handicraft, music, choreography, literature, and other aesthetic cultural expressions, for the purpose of conservation and display. Thus, UNESCO may salvage for the world a sterile cultural diversity which seems no longer feasible in the reality of Vietnam today and tomorrow.

In the process of selective preservation, various cultural expressions are transformed to fit the new socialist ethic; the Department of Culture and Information of Gialai-Kontum province, for example, saw it as their task to change the lyrics of traditional folksongs, and teach these at schools.[21] On the other hand, there are 'outmoded habits' and 'obsolete and backward practices' (Nông Quôc Chân 1978a: 53) which are to be 'wiped out' and 'eradicated'. Usually, such 'bad habits' refer to religious practices – superstition, 'groundless taboos', (accusations of) sorcery, which are considered to be contrary to modern science – and feasts and sacrifices accompanying lifecycle rituals – such as burials and marriages, deemed unhygienic or wasteful. In the words of Nông Quôc

Chân, 'priests' are 'unmasked' and made to sign an agreement to the effect that they will subject themselves to disciplinary punishment if they relapse to 'backward' practices; the quantity of wedding gifts is fixed by cadres who 'advise' the families involved, etc. This attempt to discipline the population goes hand in hand with a folklorization of culture, by stressing the expressive and aesthetic aspects of culture while denying the related cognitive and ethical aspects. This amounts to what Miles and Eipper have termed a state-imposed reification of minority culture, which is celebrated as an artifact symbolized by the display of certain distinctive insignia – a process which is by no means exclusive for Vietnam under Communist rule (Miles and Eipper 1985: 1–2).[22] One significant characteristic of the process of folklorization is the decontextualization of cultural phenomena, which are considered and valuated separately and detached from each other. Thus, while dancing and music are appreciated and promoted by the authorities, the ritual occasions for performing are being suppressed, causing the valued cultural traditions to disappear. One of the standard solutions of the authorities, then, is to establish (semi)professional groups which perform music and dances in a different context, for a different audience of 'socialist workers, collective farmers and socialist intellectuals' (Nông Quôc Chân 1978b: 59, 61), and – so we may add – increasingly of Vietnamese and foreign tourists.

The Montagnards in the Central Highlands find themselves in the paradoxical situation that they are made to perform certain valuable, expressive aspects of their culture for a national and international audience, while the basis for these cultural expressions is eroding. Thus, while they are not allowed to perform rituals entailing the sacrifice of buffaloes – that is, if they would have any cattle left – the dances and music which used to accompany such rituals are performed for tourists. While traditional sociability is rendered difficult in the new, 'resettled' villages, the disappearing oral literature is being collected by ethnographers and cultural cadres and published in Vietnamese. And while the characteristic, high-roofed communal men's houses of the Bahnar and Jarai (*nhà rông*) are falling apart for want of repair or are demolished in the process of resettlement, Kinh peddlers in the towns sell small-scale *nhà rông*, produced by Kinh craftsmen, to tourists as signs of the province's highland identity as visualized by its special architecture.

Even the one domain where Vietnam boasts of its success, minority education, is much less successful than is generally claimed. Official policy has it that 'each ethnic group has the right to ... use its own speech and script' (from the Constitution of 1960, quoted in Nông Quôc Chân 1978b: 59). However, in 1991 education in the vernacular language was the exception rather than the rule in the Central Highlands. Since the pre-1975 school primers were politically suspect, these were not used in school. In 1990, the first primers were produced, and experimentally used in a limited number of schools, but the project had no high priority. As a number of officials pointed out to me in interviews, the aim of the new primers was not to teach the vernacular languages and scripts; rather, the primers in vernacular were seen as a vehicle to better learn Vietnamese, the national language. Other officials, however, maintained that it was necessary to learn read and write Vietnamese first, before turning to learning vernacular scripts. Indeed, it was policy that the rate of minority school teachers should never be more than 50 percent. In short, teaching in vernacular languages was seen as a luxury, a viewpoint which accorded with the observation of officials in the Ministry of Education in Hanoi, that only language communities of over 500,000 had a chance of survival, and were hence entitled to education in the vernacular script.

Montagnard responses

Of course, there was non-conformity and even resistance among Montagnards against their subjection to state surveillance and discipline. The overt political and military resistance by FULRO never had a chance, and slowly petered out in the late 1980s until the surrender of the last armed group in 1992 (Thayer 1992; see also Salemink 1995a: 293). Another way of escaping state control is by moving villages to remote areas, out of reach of the cadres. At a more covert level, many Montagnards try to maintain some degree of autonomy within their villages. Although mixed marriages and mixed habitation in villages became more and more common among several Montagnard groups, this did not apply to the Kinh. A commune may consist of Montagnard and Kinh villages, but one rarely finds the two groups mixing in the same hamlet, and the same goes for marriages between Kinh and Montagnards – although I have been privy to sexual phantasies by Kinh males about the alleged libertinism and libidinous nature of Edê (Rhadé) girls in Buôn Ma Thuôt. Such popular fantasies qualify semi-official discourse on the status of women in the 'feudal' societies of Vietnam's minorities, such as pronounced by the influential Women's Union, for instance. Contrary to the common assumption among many Kinh, women in Montagnard societies may lead wretched lives but are often able to maintain a degree of autonomy that many Kinh women can only dream of. This is all the more true for the matrilineal societies of Jarai and Edê, where women wield considerable power as keepers of the family heritage – despite decades of 'male emancipation', as one French colonial officer described it (Maurice 1956; De Hautecloque-Howe 1985). Indeed, one of the aims of the policy of breaking up the longhouses is to combat the so-called 'matriarchy' in the matrilineal Edê and Jarai societies, with detrimental consequences for the social position and (family) resources of women.

One domain which has hardly been touched by the present regime is Montagnard customary law, essentially a system of reconciliation between families and between this world and the world inhabited by spirits, rather than a system of punishment. Of course, customary law has changed considerably during a century of foreign intervention in Montagnards' lives (see Dournes 1988; and Salemink 1991: 248–55). While the French codified and modified the customs, and respected a reified version thereof, the South Vietnamese regime tried to suppress customary law altogether, thus inspiring a nostalgia for 'benevolent' colonial rule among many Montagnards. In their words, they like to stick to the old customs, even if the prescribed punishments are harsher than Vietnam's statutory law. The present-day Communist authorities tolerate the customs insofar as these are not considered economically wasteful. According to common opinion, the 'fines' (reconciliation sacrifices) are not so burdensome anymore, and thus more in line with Vietnamese discourse on law, superstition, and waste of valuable resources. Although the lavish sacrifices and feasts of the old days are gone now, the traditional customs are maintained by a council of respected village elders. Generally, villagers – including younger cadres – abide by their verdicts, even if these are contrary to Vietnamese law. Thus, they are able to maintain some degree of autonomy within their own villages.[23]

Nowadays, the most conspicuous act of covert resistance is in the field of religion. With their traditional religious practices branded as superstition and practically outlawed, many Montagnards turn to Christianity as an act of protest. Before 1975, many Bahnar around Kontum had been converted to Catholicism by French missionaries, while American Protestants of the Christian and Missionary Alliance (C&MA), the Seventh-Day Adventists and the Worldwide Evangelical Mission had had some success among the Edê, Jarai, Churu, Koho and Lat. Often, the converts were to be found among Montagnard soldiers recruited by American Special Forces, among residents of strategic hamlets and other resettlement schemes, and also among FULRO adherents. After 1975, Protestantism has become a success story of religious conversion. Oskar Weggel claims that its numbers rose from 200,000 in 1975 to 400,000 in 1987, despite suppression by the Communist authorities (Weggel 1993: 466–7).[24] American missionaries, fluent in the vernacular languages, continued to broadcast from the Philippines, and reached a particularly receptive audience, made up of FULRO guerrilla fighters and other discontents. When, for example, the last guerrilla group of FULRO arrived in the United States late in 1992, they were welcomed in the Special Forces camp of Fort Bragg, North Carolina, and celebrated a Christmas mass led by a former C&MA pastor in the presence of then Vice-President Dan Quayle.[25]

In the current era of increased religious freedom, religious revival, attempts at seeking religious legitimacy by the state, and religious dissent, religion can be an avenue for political protest where other forms of political protest have been rendered impossible. Elsewhere, I have described this process in greater detail with reference to political Buddhism in Vietnam (Salemink 1995b). Thus, although Protestantism may have been embraced by most of the Montagnard community in the US, as I found out during my stay in North Carolina in 1990, it is by no means confined to this politicized expatriate community. Many of the Montagnards I interviewed during my visits to Vietnam, foremost Jarai and Edê, told me that they had turned to Protestantism after 1975, despite official harassment and confiscation of churches and church property. Among these minorities, Protestantism has a reputation of fierce anti-Communism since American missionaries tended to conceive of their mission in Vietnam as a crusade – not simply against paganism, but against Communist atheism (see Chapter 6). In the eyes of the Vietnamese authorities, then, Protestantism is ideologically feeding the

Figure 8.4 Vietnamese and international social scientists on a fieldtrip among the Edê in the village of Buon Tring, Krong Buk, Dak Lak, during a workshop on customary law and rural development (1999).

Source: Oscar Salemink.

FULRO movement, and hence a fifth column of American imperialism among Vietnam's minorities (see, for instance, Nguyên Xuân Nghĩa 1989).

But although the reputation of Protestantism both among minorities and Kinh seems to corroborate a politicized interpretation, I have not come across any Montagnard counter-discourse relating Protestantism to political opposition. What Protestantism does provide, however, is an organizational and ideological autonomy which allows space for a separate Montagnard (Jarai, Edê) ethnic identity in a context of increasing discipline, surveillance and governmentalization. This ethnic identity is not maintained because Protestantism has much in common with the traditional Jarai and Edê religions and cultures – in fact, missionary activity attempted to transform Montagnard lifestyles to conform to modernity as much as any foreign interference, as Dournes (1980) complained. In line with the observation that the essence of ethnicity does not lie in its cultural substance, Protestantism reconstructs a sense of a distinct Montagnard ethnicity by redrawing ethnic boundaries along religious lines. By resurrecting the boundary between the *Yuon* (Kinh) and themselves (*Dega*, Montagnards) in the one field where the current regime leaves some space in the form of a theoretical freedom of religion, Montagnards reclaim agency after their political defeat in the construction of a Montagnard homeland with a fixed territory and *Statut particulier*. Against the disciplining strategies and institutions of the State, Montagnard agency can be described as 'indiscipline'.[26]

Meeting with the King

It was in an atmosphere of constant surveillance that I visited Plei P'tau, the village of the *p'tau pui*, on a very hot day in May 1991. The village, part of Chu Prông district, was just off the main road which links the provincial capital Pleiku to the coastal town of Tuy Hòa through the district of Ayun Pa. Ayun Pa used to be known as Cheo Reo, capital of Phú Bôn province before 1975, and is considered the heartland of Jarai culture. The village had not yet been 'resettled', and consisted of two rows of longhouses arranged in north-south direction, with much space in between the houses. Most houses looked old and run-down, and any architectural ornaments seemed ancient. Some of the households had fenced gardens around or beside the house, but most had not. The village seemed almost completely deserted, save for a few elder people; the entire village population was working in their far away *rây* (swiddens). The house of the 'King' stood a bit off the rest, in the north row of the village. In appearance, there was nothing special to it; it even seemed shorter than most of the other longhouses. Next to the house was a relatively new, well-tended grave, surrounded by a fence of poles, showing traces of recent sacrifices: small jars, bowls with rice, fruit. A photograph of the last King of Fire, Oi Nhot, was fastened to the grave. The closeness of the grave was an anomaly for the Jarai, who normally bury their dead outside of the village.[27]

After some time, a man appeared who was introduced as Siu Aluân, the designated successor of the last King of Fire, who had died in 1987. He came in the company of his assistant, J'lang Heo. Siu Aluân is a middle-aged man of small stature, lean, with ugly sores on his calves. Yet, what made his appearance impressive were his piercing eyes, which seemed to look right through you. He was clad in simple loincloth and Vietnamese-style blouse, and wore a black turban around his head. For the occasion, he quickly changed to more formal clothing, consisting of a black embroidered loincloth and a beautifully woven, black, red and white shirt. Before he could receive his guests, he would have to ask permission from Oi Nhot, whose spirit was still present as he had not yet abandoned the grave, and who therefore was still the real *p'tau pui*. For the ceremonial sacrifice of a chicken and a small jar of alcohol, he first had to catch a chicken below the house, a fate which the chicken cleverly – but in vain – tried to escape. Then the research group, including an anthropologist from Hanoi, three local officials, a driver and myself, was allowed to climb up the ladder to the veranda and admitted into the house, which was filled with objects indicating the status of the household: huge drums, two sets of gongs, ancient jars – large and small. Some objects reminded of the former King, in particular a formal portrait and a wheelchair which he had received from the former South Vietnamese Minister for the Development of Ethnic Minorities, Nay Luett (who had died in 1986).

While the chicken was cooked and the alcohol prepared at the back of the house, the company was seated in the middle of the house. Slowly, the house filled up with villagers and curious children and with smoke from the hearth and from tobacco, while Siu Aluân told his story. He started by chanting the names of his predecessors: Oi Tu, Siu Nhon, Siu Khon, Siu Pao, Siu Chi, Siu At. He also mentioned the other *p'tau*, the *p'tau ia* (master of water) and *p'tau angin* (master of wind). The last *p'tau angin* had died in the 1960s, without successor. Oi Po, the last *p'tau ia*, had died, too, and a new master of water should be elected. He himself was not from Plei B'rong, but from another village, and had followed his wife who lived in Plei P'tau. I was surprised that she did not join the ceremony. In other Jarai houses, women performed the role of host as much as did the men in the house, for Jarai women have a position which is hardly inferior to that of men, Jarai kinship being matrilineal and Jarai marriage matrilocal (the French even called their society 'matriarchal'). It turned out that she was lamenting her fate of being the wife of the designated *p'tau pui*. According to Jarai custom, the *p'tau pui* must be picked from the Siu clan, and his wife must belong to the Rmah clan. As his present wife, however, belonged to the Rcom clan, Siu Aluân would have to divorce her by the time of the succession rituals, and remarry a woman from the Rmah clan.

When the chicken was done, it was meticulously cut in precise portions for all those present. A small jar of rice wine had been prepared (filled to the brim with water, which quickly attains an alcoholic quality), and Siu Aluân plunged two long, hollow reeds into the jar, Before the food and wine was consumed, Siu Aluân chanted his prayers for some time, addressing all the relevant spirits (Yang), in particular the spirit of Oi Nhot, to beg for their consent with the present event. He also asked for good health and good fortune for all those present, whose names were mentioned individually. Meanwhile, he filled two glasses with the wine and started to drink one, after which I drank the second glass – contrary to my earlier, more 'traditional' experience of sucking a measured amount of wine through a reed. Then the company began to drink from the wine in 'hierarchical' order of presumed importance, and ate the portions of chicken that had been dealt out individually together with some cooked rice and vegetables. In a more relaxed atmosphere now, the conversation continued, primarily focusing on the scheduled succession ceremony. First, Siu Aluân told his story:

He could not yet be called *p'tau* yet, because the ritual ceremonies had not yet been performed. For that, three buffaloes had to be sacrificed: One for the succession proper in the house; one for Oi Nhot, to allow him to abandon his grave; and one for the sacred sabers, which were still kept in a secret hiding place under a nearby hillock. In addition, every year at least one buffalo had to be slaughtered in order to perform the appropriate rituals concerning the sabres. Each year, the *p'tau pui* must envelope the sabres anew with fresh sheaths, without looking at them, as this would cause the earth to burn. If the succession would not take place this year, he feared that a number of catastrophes would take place, resulting from neglect of the sabers and failure to perform the necessary rituals to please the spirits Yang Oi [spirit of heaven], Yang lan [spirit of the earth], Yang h'ri [spirit of the paddy] and Yang brin ta [spirit bestowing health]. In the past, every year in March or April the *p'tau pui* would tour the villages in the region without ever entering one – his force being too powerful. He was received by the village elders, who sacrificed one buffalo and one pig, which would be consumed by the entire village, while the *p'tau pui* chanted his prayers and performed the necessary rituals to ensure good health and abundant rainfall. In 1950 Oi Nhot changed the rule to the effect that he could now stay inside the villages; he continued to tour the villages until 1959, when he could not walk anymore. Until 1976, his power still was sufficient to keep the Jarai from using the plough, which, he feared, would cause catastrophes to happen in the form of terrible thunderstorms. After that, the authorities induced the Jarai to irrigate their fields and use ploughs.

Siu Aluân was glad now that he was permitted to succeed Oi Nhot. It would mean that he would tour the villages again, for now the relations with other villages were almost non-existent. Plei P'tau was kept isolated by the authorities, as became clear during research in nearby villages, which had applied to the authorities to allow them to organize the succession ceremony. These villages were perfectly willing to contribute to the sacrifices, but were barred from donating the required buffaloes, or simply were not aware of the debate surrounding the succession. The authorities had always had trouble in accepting buffalo sacrifices. The Kinh consider buffaloes as draught animals, necessary for ploughing. Therefore, the sacrifice of buffaloes equals destruction of capital in a land where capital is short. The Montagnards, on the other hand, traditionally did not plough the land, and consequently had no economic objections to buffalo sacrifice.

This time, however, Siu Aluân had been told that the authorities had adopted a plan to donate three buffaloes for the ceremony. This entailed a shift in policy, for at the 1988 Tây Nguyên Conference in Dalat Đang Nghiêm Van still spoke of customs which had to be changed:

> In 1987, the King of Fire in Ayun Pa died and the people there applied to the authorities to promote a new king. Meanwhile, the proposed successor managed operations in the region. The problem is how, with study, to slowly change their manners and customs in order to adapt these to current conditions without provoking unnecessary confusion.
>
> (Đang Nghiêm Van 1989: 145;
> see also the translation in Evans 1992: 301)

Although the decision to give permission for the ceremony was not yet definitively decided upon, the company in the longhouse was quite confident that it would take place soon. The permission was discussed on various state levels, most notably by the district and province authorities ('People's Committees'), and the Ministry of Culture and Information in Hanoi. Both in Hanoi, Pleiku and Ayun Pa, I had already been told that a positive decision was expected soon.

The conversation in the longhouse then moved to the modalities of the ceremony, and it became clear that the plans were more far-reaching than I thought. There were serious plans to film the rituals. According to local officials present in the longhouse, a Japanese film company had requested permission from the Vietnamese Ministry of Culture and Information to shoot a film of the ceremony. The Ministry of Culture had denied permission, because it wished to do the filming itself. There were also plans to build a stone temple for the sacred sabers, and move them there. The argument was, that the sabres would then be safe and sound; Nay Quách had told me earlier that the *p'tau pui* originally guarded one 'male' sword and four 'female' swords, but that one of the latter had been stolen in the recent past. Although stone temples are alien to traditional Jarai culture, Siu Aluân agreed with the proposed transfer of the sabres, on condition that one additional buffalo be sacrificed in order to please the spirits. Another argument for the transfer was, that the swords could be displayed without fear of catastrophe, and this fitted into a further plan to transform the village of Plei P'tau into a museum village, for the benefit of both Vietnamese and foreign tourists. Of course, the sedentarization program would not touch this village, then, which would be conserved as it was – as a specimen of traditional Jarai culture.

According to the procedure of 'selective preservation', these plans implied that the beliefs and practices surrounding the *p'tau pui* had been promoted on the scale of customs to be preserved rather than eradicated. The *p'tau pui* would be officially branded a valuable part of traditional Jarai custom, while Jarai society moved forward on the shiny path toward socialism, or – nowadays – the market. Detached from the developments taking place around them, the inhabitants of the village would act out a living past, with their village standing as a monument of this very past, conforming to the official version of Jarai traditional life. Their very lives would be turned into a permanent folkloric show, for the benefit of a national and international audience. The folklorization of their lives would simultaneously mean a commodification of their culture, reduced to artifacts on display and standardized shows for tourists. In making Jarai culture a thing of the past, the Jarai would be inserted into the 'family of Vietnamese nationalities', which sees the lowland civilization of the Kinh as the telos to which the other ethnic groups must strive, guided by the Kinh who abide to Hô Chí Minh's dictum of 'mutual assistance'. On the basis of certain linguistic and archaeological clues, Vietnamese historians and anthropologists have suggested that the Bronze Age *Đông Son* culture, considered the origin of the Vietnamese nation, would resemble the cultures of present-day minority cultures in Vietnam. Thus, all cultural diversity is interpreted to conform an evolutionary timescale, making Vietnam's minorities the Kinh's living ancestors. The cultural politics of *Đoàn kêt dân tôc* [ethnic solidarity] thus boils down to paying due homage to the mummified tokens of Vietnam's cultural past in museums, books and folklore shows.

But how does Siu Aluân feel about the plans concerning himself and his village? Like his predecessor, Siu Aluân attaches much value to his contacts with both foreigners and Vietnamese authorities. He did not object to the plans to film the ceremony, and, like his predecessor Oi Nhot, he actually enjoys sitting for his photograph in official attire. A posed picture decorated both Oi Nhot's grave and the interior of the longhouse. Siu Aluân showed me all the name cards of 'official' visitors, and told me that he expected to receive a medal from the Vietnamese authorities, like the ones Oi Nhot had received from the French, the Americans and the South-Vietnamese authorities. His consent to become a museum character, on display for a varied audience, may at first sight seem a travesty of Jarai culture, a commodification of Jarai cultural concepts for the benefit of Vietnamese and foreign consumers. However, through his subordination to Vietnamese cultural politics, his religious status is implicitly recognized. This is all the more important in a time when many Jarai feel that their very world is threatened because the necessary rituals are not performed. As to the *p'tau pui*, an intermediary between this world and the spirit world within the traditional Jarai worldview, his ritual status is eroding as increasing numbers of Jarai are turning to Protestantism as a vehicle to express their distinct identity. Official recognition would bolster his religious status.

When I left the longhouse of Siu Aluân and the village of Plei *P'tau*, there was a general atmosphere of optimism that the ceremony would take place within a few months, and that the *P'tau Pui*'s status would be officially recognized by the authorities, to the profit of both Jarai and Kinh. The ceremony, however, never took place. Apparently, the plans were dropped in the course of undoubtedly long and arduous discussions among various administrative levels (district, province, center) and several administrative departments and agencies. Of course, nobody bothered to explain why a negative decision had been taken – or maybe simply no decision had been taken. We can only guess that the Vietnamese State has no need for competing political claims in a strategic region which has been the object of territorial dispute since the 1940s, and which has witnessed the activities of a series more or less vigorous autonomy movements since 1958. However distorted the title of 'King' may be, however 'feudal' and 'primitive' the kingship may seem in the eyes of former evolutionist ethnologists and present-day Marxists, the simple existence of three 'kings' on Jarai territory has in the past shored up claims to territorial, political and cultural autonomy for the Montagnards. And although the activities of the FULRO movement have waned since the late 1980s, the very reference to autonomy would threaten the carefully maintained edifice of 'ethnic solidarity' which is the keyword for legitimizing Vietnamese policy in the Central Highlands. The 'mystic King of Fire', one of Sir James Frazer's Dying Gods, is for once allowed no natural death. This time, however, it is not the village elders but the State itself stabbing the institution to death.

Conclusion

Elaborating on the case of non-succession of the King of Fire, I have traced Vietnamese ethnic policy in the Central Highlands, and its effects on the Montagnard populations living there. In particular, I have analysed the discourses on sedentarization and selective preservation, and their effects on Montagnard lifestyles in the provinces of Gialai-Kontum and Lâm Đông. Based on erroneous and often contradictory notions of Montagnard agricultural and residential practices, sedentarization policy is both precondition and result of Kinh immigration to the Highlands, rendering traditional agricultural practices inadequate due to growing pressure on the land. In the various research locations, the sedentarization program has mixed effects, economically speaking. On the fertile high plateaux, sedentarization is feasible and partially successful, depending on the harvests and the prices of industrial crops on the world market. In other places, sedentarization and Kinh immigration has resulted in a growing land and resource scarcity and degradation.

The cultural policy of the Vietnamese State is dominated by the concept of selective preservation, which implies that the State is entitled and able to decide which aspects of a culture are sufficiently valuable to retain. Following an essentialized notion of culture, certain cultural practices are singled out for preservation and presentation, resulting in a folklorization of culture while simultaneously eroding the ritual and economic basis for these practices. Both sedentarization and selective preservation are cornerstones of a policy of subjecting Vietnam's minorities to the disciplining and surveying gaze of the Vietnamese State. The resulting governmentalization of Montagnards' lives is legitimized with reference to the central concept of 'ethnic solidarity'. On their part, many Montagnards have resisted this policy overtly, by joining the FULRO movement or by 'voting with their feet', and covertly, by maintaining their system of customary law or by converting to Protestantism, in an attempt to reclaim agency.

The debate surrounding the non-succession by Siu Aluân and its outcome is just one example of state intervention in Highlanders' lifestyles, characterized by Kinh paternalism. In assessing Vietnam's ethnic policy, however, it is good to bear in mind that despite decades of extremely violent warfare in Indochina, the level of state violence is comparatively low in presentday Vietnam. Vietnam's minorities are considered an integral part of its population – the various 'nationalities' being Vietnam's 'children'. This might help explain the policy of (discriminatory but inclusive) governmentalization rather than outright repression, as in neighboring countries dealing with national movements like China (Tibet), Indonesia (Aceh) and Myanmar (Karen) – or even ethnic cleansing, as in Europe and Africa. Still, as many minority interlocutors maintained, the ethnic solidarity propagated by Uncle Hô still has a long way to go.

9   Conclusion

French, American and Vietnamese ethnographies in comparative perspective

I conclude the book with a few general observations on French, American and Vietnamese ethnographic practices and discourses, and the ways in which those discursive practices were contextualized by historical circumstance as well as the ways in which they contextualized each other. As outlined in the Introduction (Chapter 1), the subject matter of this study is the multiple relations between the ethnographic representations of the 'Montagnard' ethnic groups in the Central Highlands of Vietnam, and the changing historical contexts in and for which the ethnographies were produced, and in which they were received and 'consumed'. Such a perspective does not exclude recognition of the remarkable achievements by outstanding individual ethnographers like Maitre, Sabatier, Condominas, Dournes, Hickey, Nguyên Huu Thâú, Đang Nghiêm Van and others, but interprets the emergence, reception and uses of their ideas in a context of competing interests. So far, I have shown how changing economic, political and military interests within the specific historical context of the Central Highlands of Vietnam conditioned ethnographic practice and ethnographic discourse with respect to the Central Highlanders. I have also shown how the ensuing ethnographic discourses in turn influenced the historical context by suggesting and facilitating ethnic policies, and by contributing to the formation and change of ethnic and gender identities. When revisiting the first theoretical assumption in the Introduction (Chapter 1), it can be argued that ethnographic practices and discourses directly contributed to the construction of colonial and neocolonial society in the Vietnamese Central Highlands.

The second assumption holds that in order to understand the historical relationship between anthropology and colonialism, it is better to regard academic anthropology as a specific instance of ethnographic practice than the other way around. This is brought out well by the continuities and discontinuities between missionary, military, administrative and other ethnographic practices and those of professional anthropologists in the Central Highlands. The modern history of the Central Highlanders can be interpreted as the outcome of a constant struggle for hegemony between two major ethnographic discourses associated with the evolutionist and the relativist theoretical perspective. Those discourses are linked with categories of ethnographers and/or certain institutions representing different, often conflicting, political, economic and military interests. In other words, the ethnographic discourses described in this book are articulated by ethnographers affiliated with different institutions sponsoring and/ or guiding ethnographic research. The forms and contents of these ethnographic discourses are closely tied to the historical context of their articulation and reception, which determines which discourse is dominant during a particular period of time.

During the French exploration and conquest ('pacification') of the Central Highlands, Catholic missionaries and military explorers inserted themselves into an ethnographic tradition that can be characterized as evolutionist, and eventually Social-Darwinist. The missionary narratives and ethnographic descriptions, destined for public consumption in metropolitan France, depicted the Central Highlanders as 'savages' and 'pagans', in need of a true religion. This contrasted with the perspectives of the military explorers who tended to credit the Central Highlanders with a rudimentary political organization which earned them the designation 'barbarian' by some of the explorers. Yet, the Social-Darwinist version of evolutionary thinking presumed that the 'primitive' tribes of Indochina would eventually disappear because they were considered a 'vanishing race', incapable of evolution, and an obstacle for the development ('evolution') which would inevitably take place under French domination. Although the Central Highlanders were assigned a low status – either savagery or barbarism – in the evolutionist classification of mankind, they were paradoxically held incapable of evolution themselves. In this respect, evolutionist theory was fundamentally ahistorical. The spread of civilization inevitably would entail the arrival of ethnic Vietnamese in the Highlands, according to the narratives of both the Catholic missionaries and the military explorers.

It would be Léopold Sabatier who broke out of this paradox and claimed that the Central Highlanders and their culture were valuable in themselves, and were perfectly capable of development. In a comparatively stable administrative context, Sabatier developed an effective administrative model of direct French rule predicated on a cultural relativist ethnographic discourse. Even when Sabatier had to give way to the economic forces of the day, in the course of the 1930s his ethnographic model (much more so than his administrative model) was emulated and became dominant. Yet, the emergence of a competing, relativist perspective on the Central Highlanders did not eliminate the evolutionist perspective, which at later times, in different contexts, would re-surface, justifying various claims to resources in the Central Highlands. The first instance would arise in the 1920s, when the fertile soils of the Plateaux were claimed for the establishment of rubber plantations. The military campaigns from 1933 to 1935 to subdue the refractory Mnong Biat and Stieng groups had certain evolutionist tinges, but eventually gave way to the cultural relativist mood of the 1940s. After the formal independence of the two Vietnams in 1954, the evolutionist discourse re-emerged as an important ingredient of South Vietnamese attempts at 'nation-building' and modernization, accompanied by forced integration of minorities. During the American intervention in Vietnam, an evolutionist discourse concerning the Central Highlanders in Vietnam would be adhered to by those factions within the US civilian and military bureaucracy that favored the use of conventional warfare tactics and the forced 'modernization' of Vietnam. Thus, the protagonists of warfare through depletion of the countryside, population resettlement in strategic hamlets, defoliation and forced urbanization, came to face more relativist factions favoring counterinsurgency strategy and tactics.

Cultural relativism, on the other hand, became the hallmark of those who wished to enlist Montagnard support – or recruit Montagnard partisans – against political and/or military rivals. Under the French, it was embraced by the protagonists of direct rule of the Central Highlands when competing Vietnamese nationalist claims for sovereignty over the Highlands emerged. In their support for an at least nominally independent Vietnamese state, Americans could not claim undisputed sovereignty over the Central Highlands. For those agencies and individuals that sought political solutions to an armed conflict and sought allies in a hostile situation, cultural relativism created the discursive conditions for working with Central Highlanders. In such a context, relativism implied critique of a putatively high-handed attitude toward minorities of the South Vietnamese regime, as well as of those US political and military authorities that implemented a purely military solution to the conflict. For Vietnamese Communists waging a guerrilla war against a powerful, better-armed enemy – French or American – a practical cultural relativism became part and parcel of a revolutionary ethos of working with and among Highland populations in their own country. President Hô Chí Minh brought that out well in the slogan of the *Ba cùng*: 'Eat together, live together, work together' (with the local people). After the reunification of their country, however, the Socialist Republic of Vietnam was in a position to more rigorously impose Marxist ideology, of which evolutionism is a constituent component.

To a major extent, cultural relativism remained a rhetorical act rather than a practical one. Despite often genuinely felt sympathies that endured the passing of time, relativist narratives were instrumental because they were subsumed under political strategies or tactics. Ethnography was often explicitly practiced for political purposes. Sabatier could not write ethnographic narratives if it did not suit the administration – *his* administration. Colonel Trinquier did not want to sacrifice Montagnard populations once more for purposes ulterior to theirs, in a war that was not theirs or his. Hickey's scholarly ethnographic work was subordinated to his Cold War anti-Communism. Senior US officials like George Jacobson cynically duped befriended Montagnards into the post-war FULRO rebellion against the future Communist regime during the 4 April 1975 meeting at the US Embassy in Saigon. Vietnamese Communist leaders changed their rhetoric almost overnight when they succeeded in reuniting the nation, and adopted a Soviet-inspired, Communist evolutionist rhetoric after 1975. Looking at the political uses of the rhetoric of cultural relativism, one can discern a discursive hierarchy which subsumes cultural relativism and subordinates it to a political equation. If evolutionism simply dismisses Central Highlanders as belonging to a past era, cultural relativism becomes an act of appropriation, as with the Special Forces veteran who tells his Montagnard interlocutor at a party in North Carolina: 'I don't care whether you're Jarai or Bahnar; you're *my* Yard!' (see Chapter 6).

In the 140 years covered in this book, ethnographic practice was increasingly institutionalized and professionalized. The institutionalization of ethnography married increased resources and publication channels with subordination to certain rules for conducting and writing ethnography, thus creating a rhetorical framework for ethnography. Increasingly, fields of study like (ethno)linguistic classification, mapping and customary law became prescribed and standardized, sometimes through administrative circulars. The 1902 ethnographic questionnaire by Mauss for the EFEO; the 30 July 1923 *Arrêté* by *Résident-supérieur* Pierre Pasquier of Annam; the EFEO guidelines for (ethno)linguistic notation; the 'senior officer debriefing reports' of the Special Forces; or the post-1975 censuses that inquire after one's ethnic identity – all these efforts introduced standards and 'disciplined' the field of ethnographic inquiry. Professionalization, while creating the gap between professional and 'amateur' ethnography, brought further unity to the 'discipline'. Yet, institutionalization and professionalization are trends, not absolute differences; there was abundant cross-referencing and cross-fertilization, and there were 'forerunners'. Ethnographic holism and cultural relativism are usually associated with professional anthropological field research, but missionary ethnographers like Father Guerlach made 'holistic' statements, while administrative ethnographers such as Sabatier were cultural relativists *avant la lettre*. In other words, ethnographic holism and cultural relativism were as much products of colonial practice as they are theoretical innovations of academic anthropology, as assumed in the Introduction (cf. the third theoretical assumption, Chapter 1).

Many ethnographic narratives, but also disciplinary 'guidelines' were devoted to ethnic classification. While early missionary narratives sometimes gave ethnonyms accompanying their descriptions of manners and customs, they did not engage in systematic ethno-linguistic classification. This work began in earnest with the military explorers who stood in contact with the ethnological and philological communities of the times. The explorers attempted to identify groups and their leaders and to link them to geographic locations. The vocabulary and the ethnographic map were the privileged genres pursued. Colonial administrators, then, started to use the ethnographic and linguistic ('ethno-linguistic') boundaries as the basis for policies, for example, in the application of customary law in colonial tribunals, or in vernacular languages taught in bilingual schools. Each change of political regime started a new process of ethnic classification with varying results, until we now officially have 54 (domestic) ethnic groups recognized by the Socialist Republic of Vietnam (see Vietnam's official ethnographic map, in Maps and charts). The ensuing tribalization not only reflected European categories of the nation-state, but increasingly the identities of the indigenous population. Through the incorporation into the nation-state of Vietnam, the governmentalization of their administration and the territorialization of their ethnicity, Montagnards became an ethnic minority in Vietnam through a process of ethnicization. At least until 1975 the Montagnards were increasingly considered as one distinct, albeit rather diffuse ethnic minority group consisting of many different tribes in the context of the Vietnamese nation and state.

The ethnographic classifications initiated a process of tribalization and eventually ethnicization. Ethnic identities and ethnic boundaries were constantly (re)constructed through French ethnographic and administrative practices – a process termed 'bureaucratic reproduction'. A concomitant of such classification is the generalization of certain local 'traits' (practices), projected on an entire 'tribe' or 'ethnic group'. Such traits tend to harden into essentialized notions of cultural practices. It is very well possible to create, as I have done in the Introduction (Chapter 1), a series of small vignettes that are recognizably Montagnard in the public and scholarly imagination, but which may be only loosely grounded in Highlander experiences. One cultural emblem that came to represent first Rhadé, and later Montagnard culture, was the *droit coutumier*, the customary law code. The composition of a *coutumier* after the model set by Sabatier became both a standard administrative and a standard ethnographic practice since its composition and utilization in tribal law courts had been prescribed by the colonial authorities. The colonial administrators and ethnographers who engaged in the composition of a tribal *coutumier* considered it to be the reflection of tribal society. Thus, the *coutumier* became the synecdoche for understanding Montagnards, and in French Indochina its composition acquired a status similar to the ethnographic monograph based on fieldwork in the Anglo-Saxon world. As I have shown, its administrative usage greatly enhanced the process of tribalization, and eventually became an icon of Highlander culture.

Where tribalization and ethnicization mirror Western categories of the nation-state, the Python God movement forms an instructive case of Highlander *negation* of those categories. While French colonial administrators initially interpreted *Dieu Python* in the light of a process of tribalization, they were puzzled by the movement's disregard of tribal boundaries. Instead, the *Dieu Python* cult was interpreted by contemporary analysts as a politico-religious millenarian movement that was positive, integrative and functional. Neo- and post-colonial historians and anthropologists subscribed to a politicized interpretation, implied in a positivist conception of 'movement'. Instead of a prophet, Sam Bram came to be seen as a political hero leading not simply a millenarian but a *proto*-nationalist movement, foreshadowing the (*ethno*)nationalism to come. The positivist interpretation of the cult as a bounded, integrative, functional movement, mirrored Western preoccupations with the nation-state and its enemies. This common tendency on the part of Western observers and nationalist historians alike – to conceive of any Montagnard action as a response to foreign encroachment – reduces Central Highlanders to the (militarily useful) puppets that they were taken to be during the three Indochina Wars. By resisting the ethnographic classifications and interpretations forced upon them by the very outside forces which intervened in their history, Central Highlanders reclaimed the agency which they were thought to have lost with the coming of the colonial era.

While the *Dieu Python* cult can be seen as an act of 'indiscipline' in the sense of negation of the categories imposed on them, historically those categories were too powerful for Central Highlanders to ignore. With the governmentalization of the modern state, ethnic classification became scientifically systematized, and consequently as rigid as a zoological taxonomy. The rigidification of the ethnic label – the 'signifier' – went hand in hand with the reification of the 'signified' – their cultures. The construction of ethnic identities articulated in censuses, identity cards and ethnographic maps implied the existence of ethnic boundaries that had to be justified by cultural difference. Cultural difference, either tribal or pan-tribal/ethnic, was expressed in certain cultural emblems through a process which can be called the folklorization of culture, focusing on certain performative expressions or aesthetic aspects. The Central Highlands conjure up images – fit for the tourist industry – of buffalo sacrifices, elephant taming, gong music and feasting on rice wine, epics and customary laws, matrilineal families living in longhouses and high-roofed communal houses, loincloths and bare breasts. But despite the fact that the tribal/ethnic categories are usually projected on an ethnographic map, thus linking ethnic identities to (geographic) localities, the land that supports their diverse cultural heritage has been and is being taken away from the Highland people.

Where putative 'matriarchy' is seen as a defining moment in assessing their society as primitive and backward, women are being disenfranchised through a process of gender transformation, sometimes deliberately imposed as 'male emancipation'. Formal education and military careers provided opportunities for men to escape constraints imposed by matrilineal kinship and/or extended family requirements. The monopolization of land by the State ignored land guardianship vested in women, or dispossessed women outright by subsequently allocating land rights to male household heads. The commercialization of agriculture values (male) labor investment into the land at the expense of more traditional uses – often embodied and performed by women. The break-up of longhouses deprives women of their extended social safety nets by making the more vulnerable nuclear family the residential unit of preference. While tickling the fantasy of outsiders, women's proactive role in courting and marriage is restrained by statutory civil law, which regards this position of women as a curious survival of ancient times. Though not uncontested, the process of gender transformation is ongoing in a context where matrilineal kinship is seen as antithetical to State law, modernity and development.

The war proved to be fertile ground for the professionalization of ethnography, which partly coincided with the process of the institutionalization of ethnography. This resulted in new forms of cultural relativism, linked to the method of ethnographic fieldwork and a redefinition of self by researchers as mediators between the subjects of colonial rule and the universalizing (neo)colonial subject. Yet, the discursive effect of the new, professional anthropology was similar to that of the 'relativist' amateur ethnography, in that it construed the Montagnards as fundamentally different from and antagonistic to the lowland Vietnamese. The paladins of professional anthropological fieldwork – Condominas, Dournes and

Hickey – show that despite ethnographic innovations engendered by their search for a different type of ethnographic occasion (immersion) and a greater distance from the (neo-)colonial *préterrain*, they are part and parcel of ethnographic traditions that are institutionally linked to those local and global historical contexts. If an ethnographer – whether amateur or professional – seeks to escape historical 'determination' (e.g. by being 'indisciplined', or by not assuming ethnographic authority when eschewing the rules of ethnographic rhetoric) there seems to be little space beyond colonial complicity and ethnographic naiveté. This illustrates the relevance of the fourth theoretical assumption in the Introduction, that a historical study of the production and consumption of ethnography must imply an analysis of the ways in which these were materially mediated.

There are relations of continuity between (neo-)colonial discourse and post-colonial ethnographic discourses on the Central Highlanders – even when some outside analysts choose to label presentday Vietnam's policies in the *Tây Nguyên* region as 'internal colonialism', characterized by frontier colonization and dispossession of Montagnards from their traditional land rights. The ethnographic discourses supporting the policies of 'sedentarization' and 'selective preservation' are articulations of the evolutionist ethnographic discourse which also attended the French penetration and conquest of the Central Highlands. This presentday evolutionist discourse is in direct contrast with earlier, cultural relativist tendencies in guerrilla doctrine – as well as with the relativist tendencies which started with Sabatier; were taken up by the French when they established the *Pays Montagnard du Sud-Indochinois*; and sided with those forces in the American intervention that sought to politically appropriate the Montagnards. It should be noted that since 1975 the Central Highlands have not been free from conflict. In fact, it was one of the few regions with armed resistance against the new Communist regime in Vietnam. Yet, Vietnamese sovereignty over the area is now less disputed than ever before, creating a more relaxed climate after an initial tense attempt to forcefully integrate the Highlands and the Central Highlanders into the reunified Vietnamese nation-state.

In Chapter 8 on the King of Fire, I have sought to analyse the discourses and policies of sedentarization and selective preservation, and their effects on Central Highlander lifestyles in the provinces of Gialai-Kontum and Lâm Đông. Based on erroneous and often contradictory notions of Montagnard agricultural and residential practices, sedentarization policy is both precondition and result of Kinh in-migration to the Highlands, rendering traditional agricultural practices inadequate due to growing pressure on the land. The concept of 'selective preservation' implies that the Vietnamese State is entitled and able to decide which aspects of a culture are sufficiently valuable to retain. Following an essentialized notion of culture, certain cultural practices are singled out for preservation and presentation, resulting in a folklorization of culture while simultaneously eroding the ritual and economic basis for these practices. Both sedentarization and selective preservation are cornerstones of a policy of subjecting Vietnam's minorities to the surveying and disciplining gaze of the

Vietnamese State. The resulting governmentalization of Highlanders' lives is legitimized with reference to the central concept of 'ethnic solidarity'. On their part, many Central Highlanders have resisted this overtly, by joining the FULRO movement or by 'voting with their feet'; and covertly, by maintaining their system of customary law or by converting to Protestantism, in an attempt to reclaim agency and maintain ethnic boundaries.

So where does this leave the Central Highlanders, the heroes of this story? Do *they* need ethnography? The only people who can answer this question are, of course, Highlanders themselves. The real eagerness that many of my informants showed to tell their story to a complete stranger, often imploring the researcher to get their stories out to the world, is an indication that many Highlanders did see a need for ethnography. This may seem paradoxical in a situation where ethnography has been practiced in the context of outside interventions in their lives, in their living areas, more often than not to their detriment – frequently despite good intentions. But now that Montagnards are firmly integrated into the Vietnamese State they know that their story needs to be told and heard, one way or another. In this sense, many Central Highlander informants seem to agree with the fifth theoretical assumption, aware that ethnography is relevant to their lives as an act of representation as such, not simply in terms of its 'truth' or 'falsity' (see Chapter 1). In all the upland provinces that they once populated almost exclusively, Central Highlanders are now a numerical minority. The autonomy aspirations embodied in FULRO were doomed to failure; embracing Protestantism or 'voting with their feet' may be acts of indiscipline but these acts become increasingly irrelevant in a situation of increasing state hegemony. But even when the debate surrounding the non-succession of the King of Fire is just one example of State intervention in Montagnards' lifestyles, it is important to keep in mind that this form of Kinh paternalism is 'benevolent' in that it seeks to include the various national minorities – as 'children' of the great Vietnamese nation – into the state system as citizens.

After decades of foreign intervention and violent warfare, Vietnam's minority policies tend to be aiming at the governmentalization of national minorities rather than outright repression, as you find in many other countries in all six continents. While many Central Highlander interlocutors claimed that the ethnic solidarity propagated by Uncle Hô still has a long way to go, one does not find the type of hate discourses supporting ethnic cleansing that one finds in Europe or Africa. Better still, in recent years there have been encouraging signs that debate about ethnic identity is opening up, now that Vietnam's sovereignty over the Central Highlands is no longer disputed. Simultaneously, Vietnam is reintegrating into the region and the world, resulting in anxiety about social and cultural change among lowlanders, and a new discourse about cultural identity. There seems to be more recognition of and respect for cultural diversity, and more willingness to listen to the voices from those communities themselves to articulate their hopes, aspirations, fears, interests, opinions – in short, to represent themselves. Those voices will find allies among (Vietnamese) anthropologists with a sympathetic understanding of minority groups; who are willing to act as advocates for the diverse groups in minority communities, but in a non-threatening manner that is respectful of the edifice of the Vietnamese State. Where this new generation of anthropologists begins to emerge, one can already note that they start to debunk some of the ethnographic vignettes described in Chapter 1. Though this is not the place to substitute one ethnographic generalization for another, I am convinced that many of the ethnographic assumptions ventured in Chapter 1 are progressively being endorsed and embraced by this new cohort of Vietnamese anthropologists – either of Kinh or of minority descent – who are critiquing ethnocentric qualifications such as 'backward', 'primitive', 'superstitious', 'nomadic', or 'isolated'.

What, if any, is the lesson for ethnography and anthropology to be gleaned from this exercise in historiography of anthropology? One important lesson is that a historiography which respects the disciplinary boundaries will remain within the realm of what is imaginable according to the prevailing discourse. An exclusive focus on the 'big men' of anthropology will confirm the anthropological canons without explaining why these canons came into existence, what role they played in society and why they became canons in the first place (cf. the first theoretical assumption, Chapter 1). A history that is insufficiently irreverent of ethnographic authority fails to see the historical relations between ethnographic authority and the changing power relations in any particular society and particular discursive field. More specifically, such a history will fail to see the multiple relations between ethnography, anthropology, and state formation; it is bound to reinscribe the hegemonic ethnographic discourse – or at best be a whiggish history in support of one ethnographic interpretation. It is time for critical anthropology to break the shackles of introspective textual analysis, and look at itself with the conceptual tools it developed to analyse other social phenomena. A contextual historiography of anthropology will be a source of support for an anthropology that likes to see itself as a source of social and cultural critique.

Epilogue

This book – in particular Chapter 8 – is partly based on field research conducted in 1991. Since then, much has happened which changed the overall situation in the Central Highlands. First of all, the strategic importance of the Central Highlands has lessened, due to the normalization of relations with Cambodia (collapse of Khmer Rouge), China, and the United States. In general, Vietnam has pursued a policy of peaceful integration into the region and the world community, as evidenced by its current membership of the Association of South-East Asian Nations (ASEAN – which was initially conceived as an anti-Communist alliance of nations).

Second, Vietnam has considerably changed its economic policies during the *Đổi Mới* period. The introduction of the household economy and the land allocation (of both agricultural and forest land) has created more space for households to benefit from market opportunities. However, many minority households have not benefited, lacking experience with a household-based economy. The official land allocation does not recognize common property regimes that traditionally governed access to natural resources among many Tây Nguyên minorities. In the traditionally matrilineal societies the allocation of land to male heads of households deprives women of their ownership over and access to land.[1] Twenty years of Fixed Cultivation and Settlement have had rather limited positive results, except on those soils where cash crops like coffee and rubber can be grown profitably.

Third, the continuing in-migration – organized or spontaneous – has dramatically changed the demography of the Central Highlands in terms of population composition and population density. After an initial period of State-sponsored and -organized in-migration of lowlanders (mostly from the North) into 'New Economic Zones', the recent commercial success of coffee plantations in the fertile plateau areas has sparked a process of 'spontaneous' migration that includes large numbers of northern ethnic minorities: Nùng, Tày, H'Mông (Mèo), Dao (Yao). This has caused an intensified competition for scarce (natural) resources. In most areas this means that the fallowing period in the shifting cultivation systems of indigenous groups has been shortened, leading to the degradation of the land and forests and rendering their agricultural practices unsustainable. In many places newcomers have also resorted to pioneer 'slash-

and-burn' methods, which – according to the study by De Koninck (1996) – is much more detrimental for forest cover and land and water quality than the indigenous shifting cultivation practices. There are many instances of indigenous villages that have moved further into the forest, clearing forest land at higher elevations.

Fourth, a new phenomenon, generated by the introduction of the market economy and the concept of private and/or household ownership of land, is the fact that indigenous households – unfamiliar as many are with the concept of private ownership of land – frequently sell off their officially allocated (fallow) land to members of other communities. This means that they lose access altogether to the little portion of their ancestral lands that was allocated to them, reducing them to landless peasants and wage laborers for those who now hold title to the land that once was theirs – and reducing them to a permanent state of poverty and marginality. When men go out to find wage labor, women are hit hardest by the sell-off because they have a heavy stake in the land. Women are are hit disproportionately because land is part of the local social safety net; besides, they become more dependent on the incomes earned by husbands and other male family members, and hence become more vulnerable. This sell-off of land is worrying policy makers both in the provinces and at the central level, but has not yet led to concrete action at the time of writing.

Fifth, there has been a marked deterioration of the environment, most dramatically visible in the rapid deforestation, and in the lowering of the ground water tables in the Central Highlands, increasing the risks of both desertification and of flash floods. An alarming recent report by Neil Jamieson, Lê Trong Cúc and Terry Rambo speaks in this regard of *The Development Crisis in Vietnam's Mountains* (1998). Until 1996, indigenous minorities were often blamed for the deforestation, because of their 'backward' agricultural practices. Since the visit by former Prime Minister Võ Văn Kiêt to Tây Nguyên in Spring, 1997, however, migration has been singled out as the most important factor in the deforestation and the degradation of the environment, prompting authorities now to attempt to halt spontaneous migration.

On the brighter side of this equation, the last few years have seen the emergence of a counter-discourse in Vietnam, that cautiously questions some of the assumptions underlying ethnic policies and upland development policies in Vietnam. Though not unrelated to the current influx of foreign aid with its rhetoric of 'participatory', 'bottom-up' development, it is encouraging to see that more and more Vietnamese social scientists, representatives of ethnic minority communities, artists, journalists and officials are creating or using more space for debate, allowing for a diversity of perspectives. Though the effect on policy, and hence on the plight of Vietnam's Montagnards, has so far been negligible, this greater space for debate is inspiring many to explore new lines of research and different types of knowledge.

Let me give some examples with which I am familiar. A group of researchers affiliated with the Vietnam Forest Science Institute led by Dr. Hoàng Xuân Tỷ has conducted research on the indigenous knowledge and practices of upland minorities in various parts of the country, including the Central Highlands. Their aim was to find out why many of their agricultural practices are much more successful than the 'scientific' solutions that were imposed on them from outside. This line of research constitutes a radical departure from the still prevailing notion that (minority) communities in the localities are 'backward' and should follow what comes to them from the 'Center'. Initial research results have been very encouraging, and have been hailed at a recent conference organized by the International Center for Research in Agro-Forestry (ICRAF) in Bogor.[2] More recently, the Communist Party newspaper *Nhân Dân* (August 26, 1999) featured an article on the value of indigenous knowledge, written by a younger researcher of the Institute of Ethnology.

Many 'ethnologists' in Vietnam have professed their desire to transform their profession into social or cultural anthropology, subscribing to the international ethos of long-term, emphatic 'field' research within the community under study. As part of a cooperation with Chiang Mai University, Gothenburg University and the University of Washington, the Hanoi-based Institute of Ethnology encouraged twenty young anthropologists to do this type of research as part of their capacity-building program. Interestingly, in this context the use of words like 'backward' and 'primitive' to denote minority cultures is progressively critiqued and banned from the professional vocabulary. In 2000, a series of seminars of Vietnamese ethnologists were held with as main topic the need for reform in the discipline. Part of the discussion was between those who like to retain the (more evolutionist) concept of 'ethnology' and those who propagated the adoption of the concept of 'anthropology' which has a more contemporary and relativist connotation.

In another project, two teams of researchers of the Institute of Folk Culture Studies under Prof. Phan Đang Nhât and Prof. Ngô Đúc Thinh conducted customary law research in the Central Highlands – a topic that not so long ago was still seen as a left-over from colonial divide-and-rule policies. The innovation for Vietnam is that the aim was not simply to record, document and publish customary law codes, but to look at their uses in practice in terms of natural resource management, of access to and ownership of resources, of community life, and of the relation with statutory law. Interestingly, one team member was a female Edê researcher affiliated with Tây Nguyên University who wrote her Ph.D. thesis on gender relations in matrilineal Edê society. The project attracted so much interest that Đak Lak province in the Central Highlands co-hosted an international workshop associated with this project, and has resulted in the publication of proceedings of over 1000 pages, published by the National Political Publishing House.[3]

In the context of the ongoing struggle for hegemony between evolutionist and relativist perspectives, the examples above definitely belong to the latter. Both personally and professionally, I endorse these developments, as evidenced by my involvement in them in my previous capacity. While it is not unreasonable to assume that the recent changes in the ethnographic discourse regarding these ethnic minorities – this time articulated by Vietnamese people themselves instead of foreigners intervening in the region – might make a positive impact in a not too distant future, the changes in Vietnam's scholarly climate still fall short of making a positive impact on the lives and livelihoods of the indigenous communities in the Central Highlands.

Then, in February 2001 – right at the time of sending this manuscript to production and just before the Ninth Party Congress of the Communist Part of Vietnam – groups of Jarai and Ede people protested in various parts of the Central Highlands, reportedly against the loss of their ancestral land and against a lack of religious freedom triggered by the destruction of new Protestant churches and the harassment of Evangelical converts. With protesters reportedly clamoring for an autonomous region, the authorities were quick to blame foreign instigators, evangelical missionaries, the Montagnard/Dega diaspora in North Carolina, and remnants of FULRO. Deep-rooted concerns about national unity and ethnic solidarity in the Vietnamese regime and allegations of human rights violations from overseas are causing tension and concern. While the political card was played by both sides, the space for debating other causes like land rights and religion diminished, again closing the window of opportunity which seemed to have been opening for some time. It is too early to know the ramifications and implications of these events – those are for future researchers to study.

Notes

1 Introduction

1 This introduction incorporates parts of Peter Pels and Oscar Salemink, 'Introduction: Five Theses on Ethnography as Colonial Practice', in Pels and Salemink (eds), 'Colonial Ethnographies', thematic issue of *History and Anthropology* 8(1–4): 1–34. An earlier draft of that paper served as a pilot study for a seminar on 'Colonial Ethnographies: Writing, Cultures and Historical Contexts', held at the Amsterdam School for Social Research, University of Amsterdam, June 1993. I thank John Kleinen, Toon van Meijl, Peter van der Veer and Han Vermeulen for their critical comments on earlier drafts of that paper. Above all, I thank my friend and colleague Peter Pels, who undertook the 'Colonial Ethnographies' and 'Colonial Subjects' projects with me, for allowing me to base this introduction on our jointly written essay.

2 I received this information verbally from two sources whose identity I will not disclose.

3 The theme recurs in the discussion: see Diamond (1974), Gluckman (1974), Leach (1974), Scholte (1974).

4 See Diamond 1974: 37; Firth 1977: 145; Gluckman 1974: 43; Leach 1974: 33, 34; Loizos 1977: 141; Scholte 1974: 41.

5 See 'Part 2: Case Studies' of Asad (1973). Some responses to it, in a special issue of *Anthropological Forum*, also paid attention to historical detail, be it in a more 'personal' form (Loizos 1977).

6 See Evans-Pritchard (1981); Harris (1968); Hoebel (1960); Leaf (1979); see the critique of Kuper's mythification of Malinowski (1983: 13) below.

7 Before 1973: Leiris (1950), Maquet (1960), Leclerc (1972), Lewis (1973), Stocking (1968). After: Copans (1975), Copans and Jamin (1978), Diamond (1980), Fardon (1990) and Said (1978, 1989a).

8 Wilhelm Schmidt is ignored by Evans-Pritchard (1981) and Leaf (1979); his missionary background is ignored by Honigmann (1976), Kuper (1983), Lowie (1937: 193), and Voget (1975). Harris (1968: 389) is an exception, but he is an adherent of a rival religion.

9 The use of the word 'anthropography' seems to have been rather idiosyncratic: the *Oxford English Dictionary* gives as its original meaning a medical one (description of the human body) and its 'ethnographic' meaning is restricted to the same source that mentioned the German origin of 'ethnography'.

10 See also Copans and Jamin (1978), Moore (1969) and Stocking (1964).

11 The debate between monogenists and polygenists was essentially a debate whether the various human 'races' belonged to the same species of man, or not (see Bitterli 1976; Stocking 1987).

12 The examples of Richards and Hurston also suggest that sexism was important in the selection of monographs that were deemed important at the academy (cf. Gordon 1990).
13 And not only in the 'anthropological' form which Urry (1992: 22) distinguishes from 'romantic', 'spectatorial' and 'environmental' forms of the tourist gaze.
14 Parts of Chapter 3 are loosely based on sections of my (1991) essay '*Mois* and *Maquis*: The Invention and Appropriation of Vietnam's Montagnards from Sabatier to the CIA', in: George W. Stocking, Jr. (ed.), *Colonial Situations: Essays on the Contextualization of Ethnographic Knowledge* (History of Anthropology, volume 7). Madison: University of Wisconsin Press, pp. 243–84.
15 Chapter 4 is based on Oscar Salemink (1994), 'The Return of the Python God: Multiple interpretations of a millenarian movement in colonial Vietnam', *History and Anthropology* 8(1–4): 129–64.
16 Chapter 5 is partly based on Oscar Salemink (1995a), 'Primitive Partisans: French Ethnic Policy and the Construction of a Montagnard Ethnic Identity in Indochina', in: Hans Antlöv and Stein Tønnesson (eds), *Imperial Policy and Southeast Asian Nationalism 1930–1957*. London: Curzon Press, pp. 261–93; and on Oscar Salemink (1999), 'Ethnography as Martial Art: Ethnicizing Vietnam's Montagnards, 1930–1954', in: Peter Pels and Oscar Salemink (eds), *Colonial Subjects: Essays on the Practical History of Anthroplogy*. Ann Arbor: University of Michigan Press, pp. 282–325.
17 Chapter 8 is partly based on Oscar Salemink (1997), 'The King of Fire and Vietnamese Ethnic Policy in the Central Highlands', in: Don McCaskill and Ken Kampe (eds), *Development or Domestication? Indigenous Peoples of Southeast Asia*. Chiang Mai: Silkworm Books, pp. 488–535; and on Oscar Salemink (2000a), 'Sedentarization and Selective Preservation among the Montagnards in the Vietnamese Central Highlands', in: Jean Michaud (ed.), *Turbulent Times and Enduring Peoples: Mountain Minorities in the South-East Asian Massif*. London: Curzon Press, pp. 124–48.

2 Missionaries, explorers, and savages

1 The official chronicler of the *Société des Missions Étrangères*, Adrien Launay, mentions an attempt by P. Vachet to baptize Montagnards inland of Faifo (present-day Hoi An), but fever forced him to go back to the plains (Launay 1894–I: 199). Lajoux (1977: 124) mentions an unpublished manuscript by the Portuguese Jesuit priest João Loureira, *De nigris Moï et Champanensibus* (1790), which is preserved in Lisbon. No published accounts, however, exist of these ventures.
2 Van Wuysthoff probably refers here to the *Pnong*, as the Montagnards were generically known by the Khmer, bearing connotations of 'slave' and 'savage'. Possibly, but not necessarily, the Mnong groups are meant.
3 The standard work and official history of the *Société des Missions Étrangères* remains the three-volume *Histoire Générale* ... (1894) by Adrien Launay. Three scholarly works deal specifically with the role of the Société in the relations between France and Vietnam: E. Vo Duc Hanh's *La place du Catholicisme dans les relations entre la France et le Viet-Nam de 1851 à 1870* (3 vols: 1969); N.-D. Lê's *Les Missions Étrangères et la pénétration française au Vietnam* (1975); and Patrick Tuck's useful documentary survey *French Catholic Missionaries and the Politics of Imperialism in Vietnam, 1857–1914* (1987). Christian Simonnet's *Les Tigres auront plus pitié* (1977) relates the history of the Kontum mission, partly based on the books by Dourisboure (1873) and Guerlach (1906). Raymond Le Jariel devoted an article in the *BAVH* 29 (1942) on how the Catholic mission in the Central Highlands has served French policy and interests.
4 Three other early ethnographic accounts are the ones by Abbé Bouillevaux, Henri Mouhot, and by P. Azémar. Bouillevaux, who first mentioned the ruins of Angkor in his *Voyage dans l'Indochine, 1848–1856* (1858), visited the Kontum area in 1851, one year after the settlement of the missionaries. His rival with regard to the 'discovery' of

Angkor, Henri Mouhot, also enjoyed the hospitality of the Kontum mission (1872). Both drew upon the missionaries for their ethnographic descriptions, so I will turn my attention to the latter instead. Père Azémar was one of three missionaries who in 1861 founded a mission station at Brelam among the Stieng, who live to the north of Saigon, in the border area between Cochinchina and Cambodia. Civil war in Cambodia ravaged the region, forcing the last surviving missionary out by 1866. His ethnographic account and Stieng dictionary were published in the colonial journal *Excursions et Reconnaissances* in 1886, at a time when interest in the Highlands was growing. (Azémar 1935).

5 Officially, Annam and Tonkin (as well as Cambodia and later Laos) were French protectorates, but in actual practice these lands were considered and ruled as French colonies.

6 For the Mayréna Affair and for the reports by Cupet and De Malglaive, see the next section.

7 Although *Cân Vuong* literally means 'Save the King', the movement is also referred to as the 'Revolt of the Literati', as it was led by mandarins.

8 Also in 1888, Auguste Pavie had been sent to Laos in order to secure the mountain area between Tonkin and Laos for France. Simultaneously, Captain Luce searched in the Vietnamese Imperial archives in Hue for evidence of Vietnamese overlordship of Laos and the Highlands, which could back up French territorial claims on the east bank of the Mekong. Luce's 'evidence', produced in May 1889, was published in L. de Reinach's *Le Laos* (1901: 30–1).

9 Governor-General Richaud, 14 December 1888 [ANSOM Indochina AF 19/ A30(77)]. The English translations of the French documents concerning the Mayréna Affair are by Patrick Tuck (1987: 236–47).

10 Rheinart [AOM Indochine, Amiraux 11.894].

11 M. Guiomar, Vice-Résident at Qui-Nhon, to M. Hector, Résident-supérieur of Annam, 6 May 1889 [AOM Indochine, Amiraux 11.896].

12 The story of the Mayréna adventure is too complex to be told here *in extenso*, and would merit a separate case study. I refer to Hickey's book in particular for a more detailed description (1988).

13 [RSA 4048, 4049 (1913); RSA 1912 (1926); RSA 3041 (1933)].

14 D'Hugues (1937), [AOM Gougal 53.647: 26].

15 I will not go into the debate on the hierarchy of motivations for French colonial expansion by such scholars as J.-F. Cady (1954), Jean Chesnaux (1955), Joseph Buttinger (1958), John Laffey (1969) and Jacques Valette (1969). Suffice it to mention here economic motivations, national pride – both military and cultural – and missionary preoccupations.

16 It is often noted that the condition of slaves in Asia was much better than the condition of the slaves in Africa and in the American plantations, where they were completely commoditized and dehumanized. However, it should also be noted that the condition of slaves who were traded for the provision of the markets of Siam and Cambodia was qualitatively different from slavery as it existed within Montagnard communities. Slavery was known there as a consequence of indebtedness, serious crimes, or could even be voluntary. Their condition resembled that of domestics or of adoptive children, and would more or less be the same as that of other members in the household. The enslaved condition was not hereditary, and slaves could buy themselves free. The history of the Central Highlands abounds with testimonies of former slaves who rose to high positions (Cf. Condominas 1965, but also Gautier 1882: 48–50; Condominas 1998; Leger 1998).

17 The person concerned here is not related to the three *patao/p'tau* of the Jarai, who entertained tributary relations with the courts of Cambodia and Vietnam. The word *patao* is of Cham origin, employed to designate politically and/or religiously superior persons, like kings, princes, local leaders, but also influential priests or *shamans*. The

Patao referred to here used this 'title' with the connotation of 'king' in order to impress both his patronage and interested outsiders.

18 Maitre's indebtedness to Cabaton is significant for the extent to which Maitre relied on the ethnographic and linguistic descriptions provided by others before him. Cabaton (1905) is an analysis of ten vocabularies of different groups, collected by Prosper Odend'hal before he was killed by partisans of the *p'tau apui*, the Master of Fire, because of his insistence on seeing the sacred saber meticulously guarded by the Jarai. Odend'hal was considered an expert of the Montagnards, having participated in the 'Mission Pavie' and being commissioned by the *École Française d'Extrême-Orient* to do archaeological, ethnographic and linguistic research in the Highlands, conform the *Carnet d'instruction pour les collaborateurs de l'EFEO* (1900), composed by Bonifacy and Marcel Mauss. In the next chapter, I shall deal with the role of Marcel Mauss in the orientation of ethnographic research in Indochina.

19 In later eras, the correct terms would be Malayo-Polynesian and Mon-Khmer, respectively Austronesian and Austroasiatic language families, terms which would acquire political substance in due course.

3 Léopold Sabatier

1 Parts of this chapter are loosely based on sections of my essay '*Mois* and *Maquis*: The Invention and Appropriation of Vietnam's Montagnards from Sabatier to the CIA', in: George W. Stocking, Jr. (ed.), *Colonial Situations: Essays on the Contextualization of Ethnographic Knowledge* (History of Anthropology, Volume 7). Madison: University of Wisconsin Press, pp. 243–84.

2 Although I am not interested in precise, and therefore restricting rather than illuminating, conceptual definitions, I followed Melville Herskovits' influential definition of cultural relativism as the principle which, 'recognizing the values set up by every society to guide its own life, lays stress on the dignity inherent in every body of custom' (Herskovits 1973: 76–7). It has been argued by others that there is a direct connection between cultural relativism and an established colonial rule, and that cultural relativists tended to be conservative in their protection of indigenous values and traditions, thereby accepting existing inequalities and legitimizing colonial rule (Lemaire 1976: 174–81). With reference to the ethnographic and administrative oeuvre of Sabatier, I shall argue that specific colonial situations are propitious for the adoption of the concept of cultural relativism, which is not confined to professional, Anglo-Saxon anthropology.

3 These territories by and large coincide with the current mountain districts of these provinces. Most of the territories which are now make up the highland provinces proper of central Vietnam, were from 1898 until 1905 an administrative part of Laos.

4 Durand 1899 [EFEO Mss. Europ. 367]; Durand 1907: 1055–68; 1158–71; Lê Tiêu Phu Su 1905: passim.

5 De Goy 1903 [AOM Gougal 22.316].

6 Both the status and the boundaries of the Central Highlands territories were in a constant flux during the first three decades of this century: now a district depending from Laos, then a province of this state; subsequently reduced to a district of an Annamese province, to be elevated to the status of province in the same state again. The precise administrative moves, limits, decrees and dates are not as interesting as the status of the Central Highlands, which was not settled until 1954, when it definitively became an integral part of the state of Vietnam, only to become a battle ground between North and South again.

7 Outrey 1900 [AOM Gougal 22.316].

8 In the provinces, four administrative levels were distinguished: the province, the district (*secteur*), the *canton*, and the village (*commune*). While the province chief was invariably a French *Resident*, the district chief could either be French or Kinh, according to the local

conditions. The *chef du canton* and *chef du village* were Montagnards, appointed by the colonial administration. The French accepted the existence of an indigenous council of elders besides the designated village chief, comparable to the 'council of notables' in Vietnamese villages. In general, the council of elders took care of the village affairs, while the village chief represented the village *vis-à-vis* the colonial administration, notably in matters concerning taxes and corvée labor.

9 Only the French anthropologist Georges Condominas revealed his indebtedness to Marcel Mauss, among other French anthropologists, in his partly autobiographical book *L'exotique est quotidien* (1965: 87–9, 242).

10 By far the best source on Léopold Sabatier is a 228-page biography by Pierre Dubois, *Notes sur L. Sabatier, résident du Darlac 1913–1926* (1950). This unpublished manuscript was written as a *mémoire* (thesis) for the *Ecole Coloniale* in Paris, and is now kept in Colonial Archives in Aix-en-Provence [ANSOM D 3201]. Its author had the opportunity to consult a number of relevant records, which are now missing. The small biographical note by the archivist Paul Boudet, 'Léopold Sabatier, apôtre des Rhadés', *Indochine* 3(113), 1942: I-VII, is more suspect. During World War II, *Indochine* was the mouthpiece of the French colonial government of Indochina, which was associated with the Pétain régime in France. While this régime was collaborating with the Nazis who occupied a major part of France, the colonial Decoux régime in Indochina was allied to the Japanese from 1940 onward, and both régimes were leaning toward Fascism, as is clear from their treatment of Jews. The article by Boudet was an attempt at rehabilitation of the person of Sabatier, whose oeuvre had by then become the model for French policy in the Central Highlands, which were of crucial strategic importance in a time when French domination of Indochina was contested. Also in 1942, Boudet published a booklet with the same title in Hanoi, but I have not been able to locate a copy in France or Vietnam.

11 For a discussion of the politics of customary law (*adat*) codification in colonial Indonesia and its effects on indigenous society, see Benda (1958: 66–81), Ellen (1976) and Schulte Nordholt (1994).

12 Brévié, 'Inspection Générale des Pays Mois en Indochine' [ANSOM 137.1240]. 'Programme de travaux et projet d'organisation administrative de l'Hinterland moi', 1918 [AOM Gougal 19.188].

13 'Programme de travaux et projet d'organisation administrative de l'Hinterland moi', 1918 [AOM Gougal 19.188].

14 It is not necessary here to dwell on the etymology of the word 'coolie' which has been studied by others. Suffice here to say that the word coolie was widely used in a wide variety of colonial contexts to denote either indigenous labor, or imported labor – but always in sharp distinction with the white, colonial rulers. The use of the derogatory word coolie had the effect of dehumanizing the people denoted in that way, and thus legitimizing the often inhuman treatment that these people suffered. I chose to use the word coolie in the text, not to continue a practice of colonial abuse but in order to paint a clearer picture of the discourse of colonial abuse in its own terms.

15 Ardant du Picq, 'Etude du pays Moy au point de vue militaire', 1923: 110–11 [AOM Gougal 49.506]. Although Ardant du Picq's report judged Sabatier's oeuvre positively, Sabatier himself did not at all agree with its contents, ridiculing the qualifications 'courageous warriors' conferred upon the Montagnards in a report to the Governor-General (Cf. Dubois 1950). In general, Sabatier was not very adept at maintaining good relations with those who showed a favorable attitude toward his policy. In a letter of 22 December 1923 to *Résident-supérieur* Pasquier, Sabatier ridiculed Professor Jean Brunhès of the *Collège de France*, who had visited Darlac in 1923 (Brunhès 1923; Sabatier 1923, [RSA 1392]). A similar story goes for his relation with the novelist Roland Dorgelès, who published enthusiastically about his visit to Darlac in *Sur la route mandarine* (1925), but was criticized by Sabatier for illegally copying parts of the *coutumier* Rhadé.

16 [RSA 1501]; see also Dubois 1950.
17 There had been instances in 1925 when Sabatier objected to the arrival of geographic missions and colonists to Darlac, either because of the conditions of the roads during the rainy season, or because of the attitude of rebellious groups [RSA 1501]. In 1926, after the resignation of Sabatier, an extensive exploration of of the *terres rouges* of Darlac was undertaken by the *Service Géographique de l'Indochine* (Lt.-Col. Edel, Chef du Service Géographique, au Résident-Supérieur en Annam, 5–10–1926, [RSA 1647]).
18 'Correspondance 9/8/1926 to 21/6/1927' [RSA 1640].
19 'Sabatier to Lochard, 1/5/27' [RSA 1640].
20 'Gouverneur-général Pasquier to Sabatier, 11 June 1930' [GG 7243].
21 [ANSOM Gougal 268.2342; ANSOM 271.2397; AOM Gougal 53.659].
22 Marcel Ner, 'Rôle des Pô lan. Régime foncier des habitants du Darlac' (n.d.) [EFEO Mss. Europ. 163].
23 Brévié 1938 [ANSOM 137.1240]; [RSA 1747]; *L'Impartial,* June 1927; Brenier 1929: 184; Monfleur 1931: 47; Robequain 1944: 66–7, 237; Thompson 1937: 150–1; Murray 1980: 270–1; Trân Tu Bình 1985. To this day, there is a hamlet called *Javakul* in Chau Doc province, made up of Austronesian-speaking Muslims who are different from surrounding Cham; it would be interesting to find out whether this group are descendants of the Javanese laborers at the rubber plantations.

4 The return of the Python God

1 This chapter is a revised version of an essay with the same title, which appeared in *History and Anthropology* 8(1–4), 1994: 129–64. I have benefited from critical comments on papers read at the Centre of Asian Studies Amsterdam, University of Amsterdam (March 1992), at the Centre for Pacific Studies, University of Nijmegen (April 1992), and from comments on an earlier draft of this chapter made by the participants of the 'Colonial Ethnographies' seminar held in Amsterdam, 14–16 June 1993. Furthermore, critical comments by Talal Asad, the late Peter Kloos, Peter Pels, Jan Pluvier, Christopher Pinney, and Nicholas Thomas were helpful in rewriting the original paper.
2 Interviews with Ksor Ktong, Ksor Xe and R'com Hin in Bôn Chu Ma (7 May 1991), and with Rmah Dok, Ksor Nim, Rcom Anit in Bôn Tong Xe (8 May 1991).
3 The Boloven Revolt has been described by Bernard Bourotte (1955), E. Daufès (1934), J.-J. Dauplay (1929); Geoffrey Gunn (1985; 1990), Henri Maitre (1912a), and François Moppert (1978; 1980). Kommadam was one of the leaders of the so-called 'Holy Man's Rebellion' which took place in the border area of southern Laos and northeastern Siam around the turn of the century. The events on the Siamese side of the border have, amongst others, been analysed by Walter Skrobanek (1972), Yoneo Ishii (1975), Tej Bunnag (1977), Charles Keyes (1977), Stanley Tambiah (1976), and Chatthip Nartsupha (1984). Published accounts of the suppression of the Stieng/Mnong Biat resistance led by N'Trang Lung are found in P. Pagès (1935), Paul Huard (1937), Cdt. Nyo (1937), Gerald Hickey (1982a), and Albert Maurice (1993). Unpublished pacification reports are by Cdt. Nyo ('Étude sur la partie sud-occidentale du Pays Moï et sur l'action qui s'est déroulée en 1934', October 1934 [PPM]), and by Cap. Boucher de Crèvecoeur (Division Cochinchine Cambodge, Information No. 34(1), 3–2–1938 [QM]; Boucher de Crèvecoeur 1939 [EFEO Mss. Europ. 480].
4 For the universal role of 'magic water' in Theravada Buddhism, see Marlière (1978).
5 [ANSOM 271.2397] Mouvement insurrectionnel Moï; [ANSOM 268.2342] Incidents de Kontum; [ANSOM 271.2398–1] Mort du chef rebelle Kommadam à Boloven, 1936; Daufès 1933–4: 179–91; Moppert 1978; Moppert 1981: 47–62; Gunn 1990: 122–6.
6 'La pénétration française en pays moï 1931–1935' [ANSOM 137.1240].
7 Cdt. Nyo, Etude sur la partie sus-occidentale du Pays Moï et sur l'action qui s'est déroulée en 1934, October 1934 [PPM]; Pagès 1935; Nyo 1937; Maurice n.d.

8 In the above section I am using the word 'sorcerer' as it was used by French colonial officials, to denote any Montagnard associated with religion, or having mystical or healing power. Montagnards themselves made a clear distinction between several kinds of sorcery (based on alliances with spirits) and witchcraft (see Hickey 1982a: 23–7). I shall deal with the confusion surrounding this concept in a later section.

9 Division Cochinchine-Cambodge, Information No. 34(1), 3–2–1938 [QM]; Boucher de Crèvecoeur n.d.: 25–30 [EFEO Mss. Europ. 480].

10 [AOM Gougal F 03.79] Rapport politique de l'Annam, September 1937.

11 Rapport Jardin, 15 June 1937, in 'Rapport politique de l'Annam', September 1937 [AOM Gougal F 03.79].

12 'Rapport politique de l'Annam', September 1937 [AOM Gougal F 03.79].

13 'Dieu nouveau, religion nouvelle: Supplément au compte-rendu de la Mission de Kontum, Annexe du rapport politique de l'Annam', September 1937 [AOM Gougal F 03.79].

14 'Rapport politique de l'Annam', September 1937 [AOM Gougal F 03.79].

15 'Rapport Mensuel de la Direction de la Sûreté de l'Annam', September 1937 [AOM Gougal 7F 17]; 'Affaire du sorcier Sam-Bram, dit Sam-Bam, Mang-Lo, Ma-Cham, et Dam-Bam' [AOM Annam F03.78].

16 'Rapport politique de l'Annam', October 1937 [AOM Gougal F 03.79].

17 Gén. Deslaurens, Brigade d'Annam, CR-sécret-1053/BA-SR, 8 November 1937 [QM].

18 'Rapport politique, Annam', November 1937 [AOM Gougal F6+03.79].

19 Inspecteur Jardin, 'Note au sujet de l'affaire dite du sorcier Sam-Bram', 16 December 1937, 3092/API [QM].

20 'Rapport politique, December 1937' [AOM Gougal F03.97].

21 'Rapport politique, February 1938' [AOM Gougal F03.97].

22 'Rapport politique de l'Annam', December 1937 [AOM Gougal F03.79]; Sûreté d'Annam, 'Rapports mensuels', 1938; Rapport mensuel, October 1940; August 1941 [AOM Gougal 7F17].

23 Général Martin, Division Cochinchine-Cambodge, Information no. 34(1), 3–2–1938 [QM].

24 Boucher de Crèvecoeur established a link between N'Trang Lung and Sam Bram through the sorcerer N'Iong and his brother Bedak NgIong. N'Iong had assured the party of N'Trang Lung before a final attack on the French post Gatille in April 1935, that the French bullets would not leave the guns. N'Iong was to be killed first during the attack, but his spirit urged Bedak NgIong to take revenge for his brother. Bedak NgIong was one of the main inspirators of the millenarian activities of 1937 and 1938 in Haut-Chhlong, cf. Boucher de Crèvecoeur 1939: 25–30 [EFEO Mss. Europ. 480].

25 'Rapport politique d'Annam', December 1937 [AOM Gougal F03.79].

26 'Rapport politique d'Annam', December 1937 [AOM F03.79]; Sûreté D'Annam, 'Rapport mensuel', December 1938 [AOM gougal 7F17]; [RSA 3934].

27 In an article on 'The Ideology of Holy Men Revolts in North East Thailand', Chatthip Nartsupha examines a number of peasant revolts against Siamese rule from 1699 to 1959, primarily on the basis of oral history and of archival material of the Ministry of the Interior of Siam (National Archives of Thailand, Bangkok). Interestingly, in three of these revolts (Chiang Kaeo Revolt of 1791; Sakiatngong Revolt of 1820; 'Holy Men' Revolt of 1901–2) non-Tai 'ethnic minorities' participated which now inhabit the border area between Laos, Cambodia and Vietnam (or the 'greater' Central Highlands including portions of the Annam Cordillera and eastern Conchinchina) – including Jarai and Rhadé. Chatthip's account of the Sakiatgnong Revolt differs considerably from Maitre's account of the revolt led by Ia Pu, which actually was the same revolt.

28 This is a reference to the 'Phu Mi Bun' movement or 'Holy Men's Rebellion', which marked the beginning of the Boloven Revolt led by Kommadam (see further on, this section).

29 This is evident from a report dated 15 April 1937, concerning witchcraft and ordeals in the area inhabited by Sam Bram (Inspecteur Elie Cabanes de la Garde Indigène à Pleiku au Résident-supérieur d'Annam, 15 April 1937 [RSA 4011]).

30 As Resident of Kontum, he was known for his ethnographic interest; in 1938 he was elected secretary of the Institut Indochinois pour l'Etude de l'Homme, and affiliated with the ethnographic branch of the *Ecole Française d'Extrême-Orient* (EFEO), engaging in ethnographic work on the Bahnar, and eventually publishing a *coutumier* and a dictionary.

31 'Procès-verbal de la commission', 2/3–6–1938 [ANSOM 137.1240].

32 The participants were convicted for violation of article 21, paragraph 1, which reads as follows: 'It is forbidden ... to provoke or try to provoke troubles or an uprising; to participate in a rising (aggravating circumstances are applied in the case of an armed rising or the use of pretended miraculous powers); to illegally exert or try to exert authority, to use to this effect true or false administrative pieces' (Guilleminet 1952a: 195). This reads like French judicial prose rather than Bahnar reconciliation chants.

33 Résident-supérieur en Annam à Gouverneur de la Cochinchine, confidential note no. 1125SE, 8 Novembre 1937 [QM].

34 Maurice Graffeuil, 'Rapport politique de l'Annam', November 1937 [AOM Gougal F03.79].

35 The process of *ethnicization* (i.e. the social construction of a common ethnicity) in the context of conflicting strategic interests in the Central Highlands will be described in the next chapter. The attainment of a common Highlander identity is also the main theme of Hickey's two-volume *Ethnohistory of the Vietnamese Central Highlands* (1982a, b).

36 FULRO stands for *Front Unifié de la Lutte des Races Opprimées*, a Montagnard autonomy movement that was established in the ranks of US Army Special Forces-led paramilitary units in 1963. In its political and cultural program FULRO harked back to French concepts of autonomy, in particular the *Statut particulier* granted to the Central Highlands in 1946. FULRO played a key political role in the Central Highlands from 1963 until the mid-1980s when its force had dwindled under Vietnamese pressure.

37 The 27 January and 20 February 1938 issues of the conservative newspaper *Tiêng Dân* (People's Voice) reported attacks by bands of *Moi* on Vietnamese villages, while Viêt gangs contributed to the turmoil by trafficking *sou* for rice. A bit later in 1938, the left-wing Vietnamese newspaper *Le Peuple* gave a critical account of the events, despite a grave warning issued by the Governor of Cochinchina to newspaper editors concerning reporting on the *pays moï* (*Le Peuple*, 1 and 8 March 1938; [QM] Circulaire Gouverneur de la Cochinchine, 7 February 1938).

38 Cf. La Van Lô 1973: 103; Pham Kiêt 1976; Cao Van Luong et al. 1981: 122–212.

39 There are several versions of what happened to Sam Bram. The part about joining the Viêt Minh excepted, Hickey's version is similar to Van's (Hickey 1982a: 357). According to Bernard Bourotte, who published a more or less sanctioned history of the Montagnards in 1955, Sam Bram was acquitted (Bourotte 1955: 100–1). But Dournes' Jarai interlocutors told him that Sam Bram died after having been tortured by the French (Dournes 1977: 95).

40 The term 'ethnocide' was effectively coined by the anthropologist Georges Condominas to designate South-Vietnamese policy regarding the Montagnards (Condominas 1965: 469).

41 Writing this section only became possible by the contributions of Vicente Rafael, Smadar Lavie and Achille Mbembe at the Colonial Ethnographies seminar. In particular, the concept of 'indiscipline' as elaborated in Mbembe's paper served as an eye-opener for me.

5 War and ethnography

1 This chapter is partly based on my 'Primitive Partisans: French Strategy and the Construction of a Montagnard Ethnic Identity in Indochina', in Hans Antlov and Stein Tønnesson, (eds), *Imperial Policy and South East Asian Nationalism*. London 1995: Curzon Press, pp. 261–93; and partly on my 'Ethnography as Martial Art: Ethnicizing Vietnam's Montagnards, 1930–1954', in Peter Pels and Oscar Salemink (eds), *Colonial Subjects: Essays on the Practical History of Anthropology*. Ann Arbor 1999: University of Michigan Press, pp. 282–325.

2 See, for example, Bernard Fall (1962: 129–52; 1963: 195–6); Peter Kunstadter (1967: 677–92); John T. McAlister (1967: 771–844); Viet Chung (1967: 3–24). For the role of Chinese assistance during the First Indochina War, see Chen Jian (1993) and Quang Zhai (2000).

3 See, for example, Jean Chesneaux (1955: 252–3); Philippe Devillers (1952: 273–4); Jacques Dournes (1975: 1552–82); Bernard Fall (1962: 140–1); Ellen Hammer (1955: 203–91); Gerald C. Hickey (1982a: 393–401); John T. McAlister (1967: 789, 837); and Paul Mus (1952: 75).

4 Such explanations usually refer to the French 'protection' of minorities – a circular argument, as this presupposes ethnic antagonism. Other explanations have an evolutionist tinge in that they refer to the 'primitive' character of the Montagnards which would distance them from the more 'evolved' Vietnamese (and Tai, one could add) – a feature which would distance them even more from the 'truly civilized' French. Yet, Montagnard-French mutual likability and similarity was stressed in such accounts.

5 Ardant du Picq, 'Monographie du Pays Moy', 1923, p. 4 [AOM Gougal 53.659].

6 Ardant du Picq, 'Monographie du Pays Moy', 1923, p. 110–1 [AOM Gougal 53.659].

7 'Création d'un territoire Moï autonome', 1935 [ANSOM 137.1239].

8 Maurice Graffeuil, 'Décret confidentiel 91-S/E, 1er Février 1936' [RSA 3656].

9 'Procès-verbal de la Commission chargée de fixer la transcription alphabétique des dialectes moï', 30 July 1935 [QM].

10 For the often arbitrary nature of ethnolinguistic and ethnographic classification, see Hickey (1982a: 4–19). The ethnographic map was published in a semi-official photographic/cartographic album by Louis Malleret (text) and Georges Taboulet (map), *Groupes ethniques de l'Indochine française* (1937).

11 Commission d'Enquête, Cochinchine, 'Questions Sociales/Minorités ethniques', 1937 [AOM Gougal 53.647]; also [ANSOM Commission Guernut Be-Bf].

12 'Programme de recrutement en pays moï', 1937–8 [RSA 3996].

13 'Pays Moï 1938–1940: Procès-verbal de la commission', 2/3–6–1938; Brévié, 'Lignes générales du plan de pénétration', 21–7–1938; 'Réplique du Gougal à Résuper', April 1940 [ANSOM 370.1240].

14 'Rapport du lieutenant Omer Sarraut', 1940 [ANSOM 137.1240].

15 'Gouverneur-général à Résident-supérieur d'Annam', 1940 [370.1240].

16 'Rapport politique de l'Annam', December 1937 [AOM Gougal F03.79]; Sûreté d'Annam, 'Rapports mensuels', 1938; 'Rapport mensuel', October 1940; August 1941 [AOM Gougal 7F17].

17 La Van Lô (1973: 103); Pham Kiêt (1976); Cao Van Luong, Pham Quang Toàn, Quynh Cu (1981: 122–212). See also Ta Xuan Linh (1974a, b); Chaffard (1969) and Thayer (1989).

18 This is not the place to discuss this complicated history in detail. For the interested reader, I refer to the work by Devillers (1952); Hammer (1955); and Buttinger (1967).

19 'Projet de territoire Moï autonome', 1946 [ANSOM 137.1241]; see also Chesneaux (1955: 252–3); Lê Thành Khôi (1969: 433). For the policy line advocated by Marius Moutet, see Stein Tønnesson (1987: 129 ff).

20 'Visite de D'Argenlieu en pays moï, projet de territoire moï autonome', 1946
   [ANSOM 137.1241]; *Indochine Française* 24, 1946; Devillers (1952: 264–74); Hickey
   (1982a: 388).
21 'Labrouquère à Ho Chi Minh', 31 July 1946 [ANSOM 137.1241].
22 Hô Chí Minh in Bernard Fall (ed.) (1967: 156). Later, President Ho Chi Minh would
   be called – more affectionately – *bác Hô*, or 'uncle Hô'.
23 Bureau de la Guerre Psychologique, no. 185/EMIFT/GP/SC, 26 August 1953
   (secret/confidentiel), 'Thème des Cinq Palabres destinées à la population civile et aux
   militaires des Plateaux Montagnards' (2.2) [SHAT 10H437].
24 'Visite de D'Argenlieu en Pays Moï', 14–8–1946 [ANSOM 137.1241]; Conférence de
   Dalat, August 1946: 'Notes sur les Minorités Ethniques' [ANSOM 56 PA 6].
25 'Visite de D'Argenlieu en Pays Moï, serment Ban Me Thuot' (17 May 1946, 11 August
   1946), Kontum (12 August), Pleiku (13 August) [ANSOM 137.1241]; Conférence
   franco-vietnamienne de Dalat, 'notes sur les minorités ethniques', août 1946
   [ANSOM 56PA6]. On the *Khun Jonob* and Ma Krong, see Botreau-Roussel and
   Jouin (1943: 377).
26 'Rapport sur le moral, Forces terrestres Plateaux Montagnards', FTCVP/4.439/3.s,
   third quarter 1949 [SHAT 10H351]; see also the morale reports of 1948/3, 1949/1,
   1949/2; Louis Caput (1949), quoted in Hammer (1955: 219–20).
27 'Projet de création de centres de colonisation militaires en Cochinchine', 1946–47
   [ANSOM 386.3167]; see also An., 'Un centre de colonisation militaire en Indochine',
   Revue des Troupes Coloniales 256 (1938: 1020–25); Massu (1974: 278, 288–9); for an
   account of one of the settlers, see Boulbet (1967: 2).
28 'Délégué du Haut Commissaire pour les PMSI Cousseau à Haut Commissaire', no. 31
   Del/D/S, 21 May 1950 (sécret); 'Général de Division Alessandri à Haut
   Commissaire', no. FAEO/3 S, juin 1950 (très secret); 'Haut Commissaire de France
   en Indochine Pignon à Commandant en Chef des Forces Armées en Extrême-Orient',
   no. 9476/CAB, 29 July 1950 (secret) [SHAT 10H917]; see also Y-Bih-Nie-
   Kdam,'Évolution culturelle des Populations montagnardes du Sud-Indochinois',
   Éducation 16 (1949), p. 89.
29 For the extent of French control over the 'Crown Domain', see 'Haut Commissaire et
   Commandant en Chef Gén. J. de Lattre, Décision no. 1779/CAB/MIL', 14 March
   1951 [SHAT 10H5936].
30 'Rapport sur le moral, no. 895/FTCVP/3.S', 23 April 1950 [SHAT 10H351]; FTPM
   and 4e DVN, Etat-major, 1er Bureau, 'Note de service no. 210', 23 January 1953
   (secret) [SHAT 10H3676].
31 Y Bham Enuol in Kunstadter (1967: 683).
32 In 1993, Albert-Marie Maurice would rework his and Paul Huard's work on the
   Mnong in a two-volume study on the Mnong, enouraged by Georges Condominas.
   For a critique of this work, see my review in *Anthropos* (1996: 278–9).
33 Colleagues like Jacques Dournes did not think highly of the work by Lafont which was
   not based on long-term field research and not grounded in in-depth knowledge of Jarai
   language and culture (cf. Dournes 1988: 12–13). Boulbet's work, on the other hand,
   was highly regarded by his French colleagues, but hardly known beyond that circle.
34 Deuxième Bureau, 'Fiche critique a/s d'une Etude sur la Situation Militaire des
   Plateaux', 13 March 1951 [SHAT 10H917]; Chesneaux (1955: 285); Viet Chung (1967).
35 Direction de l'Action Psychologique, Cap. Caniot, 'Stage de Guerre Psychologique';
   Chef de Bataillon Fossey-François, 'Historique de l'Action Psychologique en
   Indochine de 1945 au 20 juillet 1954', both in [SHAT 10H346]; Action
   Psychologique, Plateau du Centre, '"tracts", comptes-rendus des activités de
   propaganda, 1953–54' [SHAT 10H433]; see also Bochet (1951: 64); Nguyên Dê
   (1953: 5–22); Pagniez (1954: 135–42); Hickey (1982a: 409–13).
36 'Plan de stationnement des troupes', no. 341/FTPM/3S, December 1951; 'Plan de
   stationnement des troupes', no. 341/FTPM/3S, 10 August 1953, both in [SHAT

10H3734]; '2me Bureau, télégrammes officiels (1951–1953)' [SHAT 10H3677]; see also Bodard (1950: 16–33), Riesen (1955); Trinquier (1976).

37 In his book, Norman Lewis also speaks of Viêt Minh cruelty against (Bahnar) villagers – including the execution of 12 village leaders – for reporting to the French on Viêt Minh movements, but he found that 'even severer punishment awaited those who offended the French from fear of the Viet-Minh' (Lewis 1951: 142).

38 Brévié, 'Inspection Générale des Pays Moïs en Indochine' [ANSOM 137.1240].

6 Romancing the Montagnards

1 This quotation of General Giap also serves as motto for an influential, 123-page CIA study 'The Highlanders of Vietnam' [NSA]. I have not been able to trace the original source for this quotation.

2 See George Devereux (1937: 1–7) and (1967). The biographical information is provided by Ulrike Bokelman, 'Georges Devereux', in: Hans Peter Duerr (1967), pp. 9–31; and in 'Application for employment and personal history statement' by George Devereux, APR 12 1943, Admiral Miles papers #47824–9 [National Archives (Washington DC), Records Group 38, NHC–75, box 36]. Hereafter referred to as MILES papers.

3 'A Program for Guerrilla Warfare in French Indochina', Captain Miles and Lt. Devereux (n.d.) [MILES #47849–47878].

4 From Purnell and Donovan COMINCH to Miles ALUSNOB Chungking, June 8, 1943 [MILES #48235–6].

5 'Memorandum on the proposed change of command', Lt. Devereux to Rear Admiral W. Purnell, Brigadier General W. Donovan, Captain J. Metzel, 22 June 1943 [MILES #47919–28]; Memorandum from Lt. Devereux to Captain Miles, 26 June 1943 [MILES #47929–32].

6 Cable to Donovan from Buxton and Purnell on Indochina Projects, 1 July 1943 [MILES #47969].

7 Memorandum from Lt. Devereux to Captain Mentzel, 5 July 1943 [MILES #47969]; Special Project Order Number 1–43, 5 July 1943 [MILES # 47970]; Lt. Commander R. Davis Halliwell (OSS) to captain J.C. Mentzel, 19 July 1943 [MILES #47987]; Captain G. de Poncins, Fort Benning, to Captain Mentzel, 22 July 1943 [MILES #47989–90]; Captain Metzel, Headquarters Commander in Chief, Navy Department, Washington, DC, to Captain G. de Poncins, French Army, Fort Benning, Georgia, 27 July 1943 [MILES #47992].

8 In *Managing Political Change: Social Scientists and the Third World* (1985), Irene Gendzier provides a lucid analysis of the emergence of a powerful discourse on modernization and development in the US within the context of the Cold War. She stresses the importance of such figures as Walt Rostow, Samuel Huntington and Lucien Pye, as well as of institutions like the MIT Center for International Relations, Harvard University and Syracuse University, for the formulation of political theories of modernization and development.

9 Hickey in Hugh Manke (ed.), 'I.V.S. Ethnic Minorities Seminar', 20–21 May 1969, Nha Trang [WASON].

10 For more information on the *maquis*, see Chapter 5. In an interview with Alfred McCoy (1972: 107), Trinquier suggested that he refused because he feared that as a Frenchman he would not have 'sufficient authority to accomplish anything'.

11 Interview with Lucien Conein, 10 May 1990; see also Warner 1963: 129–30; McCoy 1972: 107; Dassé 1976: 169–72; Hickey 1982b: 65.

12 Interview with Lucien Conein, 10 May 1990.

13 Wesley R. Fishel to Bureau of Indian Affairs, 10 April 1956 [Michigan State University Archives, UA 2.9.5.5 Vietnam Project (MSUG Archives), box 676, folder 60].

14 See Chapter 5.

15 See Montgomery 1962: 78–82; Zasloff 1961; Scigliano 1964: 142–4.

16 Report of Field Trip to PMS, 18 May 1956, to Wesley Fishel through Walter Mode and Frederic Wickert. [MSU Box 676, Folder 64].

17 Price Gittinger, Tenure in Ban Me Thuot Land Development Projects: Situation and Recommendations. Saigon: USOM Agricultural Division, 18 June 1957 (mimeographed) [WASON].

18 This must be a *palabre du serment* ceremony, as described by Earl Young (1966a, b).

19 The Noone report is cited in a recently declassified CIA study, 'The Highlanders of South Vietnam 1954–1965', of 15 June 1966. This 123-page CIA study is extremely well-informed on the events in the early 1960s, and contained an annex with biographical sketches of 117 Montagnard leaders.

20 Hickey in an interview, Chicago, 6 April 1990; See also Emerson 1978: 283–90.

21 An abstract of this collective MSUG report was published in *Current Anthropology*, authored by John Donoghue (1963).

22 Interviews and conversations of the author with a number of Vietnamese living in northern Vietnam confirm the picture that as early as 1957 Vietnamese soldiers and political cadres were sent to the South in order to prepare for the Revolution. See also Karnow 1983: 237.

23 The Trà Bông rising reactivated an existing rebel tradition in this area, dating back to the 1945 Ba To rising (cf. Pham Kiêt 1976; Ta Xuan Linh 1974a, b) and even further back to the *Dieu Python* movement (see Chapters 4 and 5).

24 Scholarly analyses of the rise of the concept and practice of counterinsurgency in American foreign policy are provided by Blaufarb (1977); Cable (1986); Gendzier (1985); Halberstam (1967); Hatcher (1990); Prados (1986); Shafer (1988) – to name but a few. Relevant memoirs have been written by a great number of more or less senior officials in the Kennedy and Johnson administrations, like Arthur Schlesinger (1965); Roger Hilsman (1967); Chester Cooper (1970); Seymour Deitchman (1976); William Colby (1978; 1989), and most recently, Robert McNamara (1995). These short lists are, of course, by no means exhaustive.

25 'Economic, Social, and Political Change in the Underdeveloped Countries and Its Implication for United States Policy', report prepared at the MIT Center for International Studies, for the Committee on Foreign Relations, US Senate, 31 January 1960; see also Gendzier 1985, pp. 22–48.

26 Many historical accounts have been written of the Special Forces presence in Vietnam. Most of these have been written by military officers themselves, as official or unofficial military historiographies, as memoirs, and as novels. Public interest in the Special Forces activities in Vietnam started with the romanticized semi-fictional account by Robin Moore, *The Green Berets* (1965), which became the source for John Wayne's movie *The Green Berets* (1968) extolling Special Forces virtues – even today, John Wayne is celebrated by SF veterans, who called one of the veteran chapters after him. Later films dealing with the relation between Special Forces and Montagnards are Francis Ford Coppola's *Apocalypse Now* (1979); and Jerry London's *Vestige of Honor*, which related the escape of a group of over 200 FULRO warriors to Thailand and, eventually, the United States, from the perspective of Special Forces veterans. General accounts are to be found in Banks (1987); Buschmann (1978) and Simpson (1983). Relevant books on SF activities in Southeast Asia are Kelly (1985); Stanton (1985); Turkoly-Joczic (1986). Semi-fictional accounts are to be found in great numbers; the most relevant are Bendell (1992) and Morris (1979). Apart from the published or otherwise easily accessible studies, there is a wealth of material in the Washington National Records Center in Suitland, MD, of the US National Archives, and in Marquat Memorial Library in the J.F. Kennedy Special Warfare Center at Fort Bragg, NC.

27 Memorandum on 'Subjects for Exploration in Viet Nam' for Mr. Rostow, from R. Johnson, head of the Vietnam Task Force, State Department, October 14, 1961;

Taylor Mission, Counterinsurgency – Intelligence: Covert Annex: Frontier Force, Vietnam, October 1961 [Cornell University, Department of Manuscripts and University Archives, 'Kahin Papers']; 'Taylor-Rostow Report', in: *The Pentagon Papers* (edited by Neil Sheehan/New York Times), 1971, pp. 141–6.

28 Colby 1989: 88–92; CIA 1966: 39–45; interviews with William Colby, 20 April 1990, and Gilbert Layton, 7 April 1990.

29 Col. Gilbert Layton, CSD Report on Montagnard problem, January 1964 [Layton Papers]; Interviews with Col. Gilbert Layton, 7 and 14 May 1990; Paul Campbell, 12 May 1990; William Colby, 20 April 1990.

30 In a mid-1963 petition to Colonel Layton of the CIA, two Rhadé representatives from Buon Enao phrased the question of ownership as follows:

> Mr. Dave [Nuttle] explained to all the people as follows: 'Do you know whose are these weapons?' Everyone replied: 'These arms are American officers' possessions; we are receiving them to protect our property and lives.' 'O.K.', Mr. Dave said, 'But these weapons become yours now; you have not contributed your blood for nothing; now you may receive and keep them for your descendants. Nobody will pick them up from you.' ('What becomes of Buon Enao', n.d., CIA files [Layton Papers].

31 'Buon Enao and Withdrawal of Weapons from the Rhade', Attachment E to CIA Special Autonomy Report, 29 January 1963 [Layton Papers]; CIA, The Highlanders of South Vietnam 1954–1965, pp. 46–52 [NSA]; Kelly 1973: 41–4.

32 Rev. Robert Ziemer was killed during the fierce North Vietnamese/NLF attack on Ban Me Thuot of Têt, 1968, together with four other American missionaries. Ziemer had been warned several times by FULRO connections (even by FULRO leader Y Bham Enuol from Cambodia) about the build-up around the town. He informed the US Army intelligence personnel in Ban Me Thuot, who dismissed the information, claiming that missionaries did not understand military intelligence. This shows a marked difference from the CIA attitude on intelligence provided by missionaries, as well as the hand of General Westmoreland, who in 1965 had forbidden accepting any messages from FULRO (Letter of Drew Sawin to Mr. and Mrs. Layton, March 6 1968 [Layton Papers]).

33 Col. Gilbert Layton in interviews, 7 and 14 May 1990; CSD–549, 5 March 1963: Memorandum to Chief, Combined Studies Division, on Operation LINUS Progress Report; CSD–610, 22 March 1963, from Chief, Combined Studies Division to Special Assistant to the Ambassador, on Stalemate in Autonomy Movement Effort [Layton Papers]; CIA, The Highlanders of South Vietnam 1954–1965: 53–58 [NSA]; Hickey 1982b: 86.

34 Gilbert Layton, CSD, Report on Montagnard Problem, January 1964, pp. 13–14 [Layton Papers].

35 Col. Gilbert Layton (CIA), Permanent Tribal Requirements, 5 March 1970 [Layton Papers].

36 This theme of a special relationship between Montagnards and Special Forces came up during numerous interviews held with many Montagnard veterans who served with the Special Forces, both during my field research in the Central Highlands (1991) and during my research among Montagnard refugees in North Carolina (April/May 1990). For reasons of the protection of informants, I choose not to reveal their identities.

37 About the controversy surrounding the Generals Văn Tiên Dũng's and Trân Văn Trà's books, see Bùi Tin (1995: 73–87).

38 A more detailed analysis of the FULRO movement would necessitate at least another chapter, for which I do not have space in this book. However, I am planning a separate publication on the FULRO movement, which stresses its connections to the various other actors in the field. For other (published) sources than Hickey (1982b), see Meyer

(1966), Sochurek (1965); Brigadier General Vinh-Loc (1965); Jaspan (1969); Po Dharma (1993); Christie (1996); and the many Vietnamese-language publications on FULRO, like Nguyên Trac Dĩ (1969); Ngôn Vĩnh (1982); and Thành Tín (1983). For unpublished documents, see the various FULRO statements, e.g. the FULRO Historique (1965) and Y Bham Enuol's 'Extraits de l'Histoire des Hauts-Plateaux du Centre-Vietnam' (1965) [FULRO Papers], the 'Historical Resume of Montagnard Uprising, September 1964', Headquarters, 5th Special Forces Group (Airborne), 1st Special Forces, San Francisco (Confidential: declassified 19 April, 1990, by order NND 903607), 472 Records of the US Army, 5th Special Forces Group [NNRR]; the CIA study 'The Highlanders of South Vietnam 1954–1965' (quoted extensively before), and – above all – Norman Labrie's well-documented MA thesis on FULRO (1971).

39 In translation, the title of a Vietnamese publication of 1983 on FULRO reads 'Smashing the CIA's Postwar Instrument: FULRO' (Thành Tín 1983). In my view, this is a gross simplification, given the variety of international connections that FULRO entertained, including with both Vietnamese regimes, Cambodia, America, Australia, England, France, Malaysia, China and the Soviet Union. Bùi Tin (1995: 77; 173), the defected Deputy Editor of *Nhân Dân*, claims that Thành Tín was his pen name.

40 See, for example, Captain Vernon W. Gillespie's 'After Action report, CIDG Revolt at Camp Buon Brieng', Detachment A–312, US Army Special Forces, Vietnam, 30 September 1964; annexed in 'Historical Resume of Montagnard Uprising, September 1964', Headquarters, 5th Special Forces Group (Airborne), 1st Special Forces, San Francisco (Confidential: declassified 19 April, 1990, by order NND 903607), 472 Records of the US Army, 5th Special Forces Group [NNRR]; see also the suspicions voiced by South Vietnam's Prime Minister Gen. Nguyen Khanh to US Ambassador Maxwell Taylor 'that US Special Forces advisors may have encouraged the uprising, or at least did not try to stop it' (Director of Intelligence, CIA, 'The Situation in South Vietnam, 17–23 September, 1964', p. 2; Lyndon Baines Johnson Library, also in *DDRS* 1979: 23 A/B). This prompted Ambassador Taylor and commander General Westmoreland to authorize Bigadier General Depuy 'to convey to the leaders of the rebellious Rhadé camps the strong displeasure of the United States government with their rebellious conduct'. In a paternalistic attempt to discipline their disobedient mercenaries, Gen. Depuy would 'add that the United States will not continue to pay or support in any way Rhade CIDG who do not submit to proper GVN authority and conduct themsleves henceforth as loyal military units' (Telegram from American Embassy Saigon to Department of State [CINCPAC for POLAD], 25 September 1964; declassified 13 March 1978 by National Archives and Records Service, Kahin Papers, Cornell University Archives, Department of Manuscripts). Later on, 'General Westmoreland and ARVN Chief of Staff General Vien [were to meet] to work out new ground rules governing the often uncomfortable relationships in CIDG between the Vietnamese military, the US Special Forces, and tribal CIDG units' (Director of Intelligence, CIA, 'The Situation in South Vietnam, 24–30 September, 1964', p. 1; Lyndon Baines Johnson Library, also in *DDRS* 1979: 23 A/B). In a set of proposals [secret] by the CIA's William Colby forwarded on 12 April 1965 to President Lyndon Johnson, proposal no. 8 contains the recommendation to resume the original CIDG concept on the premise that 'GVN is willing to hold out some kind of autonomy within national structure. Consequences of failure to offer some degree of autonomy will almost certainly be serious dissidence and loss of highlands' (*DDRS* 1986: 40–4). Just before the landing of American combat troops at Cam Ranh Bay on 29 July 1965 – two months after the formal beginning of the Second Indochina War marked by the landing of US Marines in Danang – the CIA Chief of Station in Saigon, Gordon Jorgensen, went one step further, and endorsed a GVN proposal 'that US Forces assume primary responsibility for the highlands area (specifically Kontum-Pleiku – Pleiku Darlac) ... with ARVN Forces taking responsibility for the coastal plains and the delta' on the grounds that 'the population

there i.e. Montagnards, will rally to US presence and leadership' (Gordon Jorgensen, 'Memorandum [secret] to mr. Chester Cooper: Comments on Vietnamese Highlands Concept, 20 July 1965; declassified 16 October 1978. *DDRS* 1979: 366 A).

41 Col. William McKean, 'FULRO Policy Letter: Remarks Made by Commanding Officer, 5th Special Forces Group, to All Incoming Personnel'; Inclosure 8 to Section II to Operational Report on lessons Learned (RC8 CSGPO–28 (R1)), 30 April 1966; attached to: 'Employment of a Special Forces Group (U), Final Report', Army Concept Team in Vietnam, JRATA Project No. (1B–154.0), 20 April 1966 (Confidential), [DDRS (R), 204 B]. See also Col. Francis Kelly, 'A Detachment Handbook', 1966. 5th Special Forces Group (Airborne), 1st Special Forces, pp. 12–13 [MHI USARV SSFG ADH–1966].

42 Smith Hempstone's novel resumes themes from René Riesen's adventurous account of the latter's work with Trinquier's *maquis* among the minorities, albeit in a different setting. Indeed, Hempstone's novel borders on plagiarism, where his main character, Harry Coltart, marries the daughter of a Montagnard leader while he lives with and gradually takes over the tribe; even the names of the girls are similar (Ilouhi and Ilouha). Even Coppola's celebrated *Apocalypse Now* (1979), acknowledgedly based on Joseph Conrad's *Heart of Darkness*, resumes themes and contexts from the Mayréna affair and from André Malraux' novels which refer to Mayréna: *La voie royale* and *Antimémoires*. Morris' novels give fictionalized and romanticized accounts of his encounters with FULRO as a Special Forces soldier. In Morris' *The Devil's Secret Name* (1990) the author – senior editor at Dell Publishing – is introduced on the cover as 'Former Green Beret (Maj.) and Brig. General, FULRO'.

43 The first contingent of over 200 Dega (as they call themselves now) was one group of FULRO, the Montagnard guerrilla movement which continued to fight the Vietnamese authorities after 1975. In 1982, this group escaped the mounting military pressure in the Central Highlands and made it for the Thai-Cambodian border, which was then the scene of a guerrilla war between the Khmer Rouge and the Vietnamese occupation forces in Cambodia. There, they were technically considered Khmer Rouge soldiers, and forced to fight for Pol Pot. In 1986, they escaped from the Khmer Rouge camp where they were detained, made it for Thailand, and managed to contact some of their former Special Forces supervisors in the States. With their support the machine of immigration was put in motion, with the various Special Forces veteran chapters sponsoring their residence in the States.

44 Kelly 1973: 49–57; Marchetti and Marks 1974: 132–4; Stanton 1985: 72–6; Turkoly-Joczik 1986: 357–83; Stires, Frederick H., 'The US Special Forces CIDG Mission in Viet-Nam: A Preliminary Case-Study in Counterpart and Civil-Military Relationships' (Secret). Washington DC, November 1964: The American University/Special Operations Research Office (SORO) [NNRS, declassified April 19 1990]; Warren Pochinsky in interview, 28 May 1990.

7 Moving the Montagnards

1 Gilbert Layton, 'Letter to Bonnie on Anthropologists', 7 October 1968 [Layton Papers].

2 Attachment 5 (Central Highland Superstitions Regarding Origins of the Montagnards, 7 February 1963), Combined Studies Division (CIA South Vietnam) Memorandum 'Meeting with General Khanh Re Autonomy Problem', 8 February 1963 [Layton Papers]; see also CIA, 'The Highlanders of South Vietnam 1954–1965', 15 June 1966, pp. 53–4 [NSA].

3 In 1979, during a Catholic sainthood investigation, it was alleged that the famous Dr. Tom Dooley had had close ties with the CIA in the 1950s (McGehee 1983: 132, 208). For a balanced but unflattering biography, see James Fisher's *Dr. America. The Lives of Thomas A. Dooley 1927–1961* (1997).

4 USAID, *Program and Project Data, Presentation to the Congress, 1966–1975. Republic of Vietnam, Field Operations: Progress in the Highlander Affairs Program in FY 1966*, p. 185. Summaries of Activity, End of Fiscal Year 1966. Saigon, 14 July 1966 [AID]; see also Sarah Gudschinsky (1970), Bilingual Education for South Vietnam's Highlanders: An introduction to the dynamic new curriculum and materials for the ethnic minorities of South Vietnam. Summer Institute of Linguistics, n.p. [AID VS 495.922 G923]; and Debrief of an AID Education Advisor, Region II, Vietnam 1967–1968, No. 116710, Honolulu: Asia Training Center [MML].

5 See the publication series *Mon-Khmer Studies* (Nos. 1–4, published by SIL in Saigon), e.g. David Thomas and Nguyen Dinh-Hoa (eds) *Mon-Khmer Studies IV* (1973); David Thomas (ed.), *Papers on Four Vietnamese Languages*. Auckland 1966: Linguistic Society of New Zealand; Summer Institute of Linguistics, 'Tribes of South Vietnam (map); Vietnam Minority Languages'. Saigon: SIL (revised May 1968) [WASON Pamphlet PL Vietnam 50+].

6 Robert Gilkey, Mountain People Study, Field Trip 26, 27, 28 March 1956, accompanied by Nguyen-Tien-Hoanh, research assistant and interpreter [MSU, Box 676, folder 64]. Recently, in the context of the 1999 population census in Vietnam, 'Associate Doctor' Hà Quôc Thach in an article entitled 'Ethnonyms and the General Census' in the newspaper *Nhân Dân* of 18 March 1999, expressed his dismay at the fact that many respondents to questionnaires do not fill in their ethnonyms, or do not fill in the correct ones – and that the numbers of 'incorrect answers' are even growing.

7 This is not to say that there were no American scholars and journalists who were critical of American intervention and opposed the war. In this chapter, however, I do not pay attention to this radical tradition of American scholarship for a number of reasons. One reason is that while there was an abundant literature on Vietnamese society as a whole, there was little specific attention to minorities' issues in Vietnam from that perspective – perhaps because the alleged closeness of Americans and Montagnards did not fit the discourse on national liberation as a legitimate expression of Vietnamese nationalism. Notable exceptions may be John McAlister (whose work on northern mountain minorities is discussed in Chapter 5), Alfred McCoy (whose superb *The Politics of Heroin in Southeast Asia* [1972] deals with minorities in northern Indochina, Thailand and Burma, bot not with Montagnards), and the Australian Communist journalist Wilfred Burchett (whose accounts of life in the NLF-controlled portions of the Central Highlands was often referred to by anti-war activists). For an overview of American scholars opposed to the war – partly organized in the Committee of Concerned Asian Scholars – I refer to the special issue of the *Bulletin of Concerned Asian Scholars* vol. 21(2–4), 1989, on this topic – especially the contributions by George Vickers, Douglas Allen and Marvin Gettleman. Of course, this radical tradition in American scholarship, while certainly not flawless, contributed greatly to the American withdrawal and eventually to the end of the Second Indochina War. Similarly, there was a tradition of critical scholarship and journalism outside the US, located mainly in Europe (France) and Asia (India, Japan; see for example the report on 'The Montagnards' by Katsuichi Honda [1972]).

8 Introduction, Joint Chiefs of Staff Idea Program Limited War (1961), p. 2 [SIA, Record Unit 179, Research Group in Psychology and the Social Sciences, 1957–1963, box 4].

9 Ithiel de Sola Pool et al. (1963), *Social Science Research and the National Security*. Washington DC: Smithsonian Institution (under Office of Naval Research, Contract No. 135418), extensively quoted by Deitchman 1976: 28–35.

10 The conclusion of the DSB Report reads as follows:

> There is an important need for quantitative data on the anthropological, sociological, political and psychological aspects of societies in which insurgency is

a threat. In Vietnam, we now appear to be in a difficult situation because our decision to commit ourselves to a certain kind of counterinsurgency action was based on insufficient knowledge of the sort of people we were dealing with and the way they might react to our efforts and those of their own internal groups. (Deitchman 1976: 113).

11 Since the debates on 'Project Camelot' and other forms of army-sponsored research have been widely publicized, I do not dwell on them, but refer to others who have discussed them (Chomsky 1967, 1969; Horowitz 1969; Wolf and Jorgensen 1970; Klare 1972; Hymes 1973; Deitchman 1976; Huizer and Mannheim 1979). Relatively recent publications on the so-called Thailand Controversy in the American Anthropological Association include Davenport (1985), Berreman (1991), Fluehr-Lobban (1991), and Wakin (1992). On the issue of congressional interest in DOD-related social science research and the shift of control over research from DOD to the State Department (including AID, the Asia Society, and SEADAG), see Klare (1972: 99–101; 344–6); Deitchman (1976: 209–54; 413–34), and the *US Senate's Department of Defense Appropriations*, Hearings for 1965, 1966, 1968, 1969, and 1970 (resp. 1964; 1965; 1967; 1968; 1969).

12 See Shafer (1988).

13 Other translations of French studies of Montagnards include ones by Georges Coedès (JPRS/CSO 6757, 1950); Condominas' contribution on the ethnology of Indochina to Leroi-Gourhan and Poirier's *Ethnologie de l'Union Française* (JPRS 13652, CSO 6727-D, 1962); and Louis Malleret's 1937 *Ethnic Groups of French Indochina* (JPRS 12359/CSO 6481-D, 1962).

14 This 123-page CIA report was extremely well-informed about political developments in the Central Highlands, and contained 123 biographical sketches of Montagnard leaders. In an undated Rand Memorandum entitled 'Comments on the Highlanders of South Vietnam, June, 1965', the anthropologist Gerald Hickey – apparently unaware of the origin of the report – finds that '[i]n general, the report is quite well done'. But as he finds some inaccuracies and 'curious deletions', he proceeds to give specific comments and additional information [Hickey Papers].

15 See, for instance, Col. Francis Kelly, Senior Officer Debriefing Report, 5th Special Forces Group (Airborne), 1st Special Forces, 13 June 1966–12 June 1967, Republic of Vietnam. San Francisco: Headquarters, 5th Special Forces Groups (Airborne), 1st Special Forces [NSA]; Col. Jonathan Ladd, Senior Officer Debriefing Report, 5th Special Forces Group (Airborne), 1st Special Forces, 4 June 1967–4 June 1968, Republic of Vietnam. Washington: Office of the Adjutant General, Dept. of the Army [MHI]; Col. Harold Aaron, Senior Officer Debriefing Report, 5th Special Forces Group (Airborne), 1st Special Forces, 4 June 1968–29 May 1969, Republic of Vietnam. Washington: Office of the Adjutant General, Dept. of the Army [MHI]; or the various 'Operational Reports for quarterly period', released by the *DDRS* (R 204 c; R 208 b; R 231 b).

16 Col. Francis Kelly, The United States Army Special Forces in the Republic of Vietnam, 5th Special Forces Group (Airborne), 1st Special Forces, 1971 [NSA] (in 1973, a revised version of this Special Forces history was published); Lt. Col. Thomas McGuire, *The Montagnards of the Republic of Vietnam, the RHADE Tribe* (18 March 1964). Fort Bragg, NC: US Army Special Warfare Center [MML]; Historical Resume of Montagnard Uprising, September 1964, prepared by the Headquarters of the 5th Special Forces Group (Airborne), 1st Special Forces, San Francisco [NNRR NND 881531, declassified 19/4/1990]; Employment of a Special Forces Group (U): Final Report. Army Concept Team in Vietnam, JRATA Project No. 1B–154.0, 20 April 1966 [DDRS (R) 204 B].

17 Special Warfare School, *Counter-Guerrilla Operations: Program of Instruction for 33-G-F6 Counter-Guerrilla Operations Course, May 1961*. Fort Bragg, NC: US Army Special

Warfare School. According to this course material, 'planning for counterinsurgency operations requires that a detailed study be made of the area and the population where the counterinsurgency force will be operating', which implied the study of 'sociological factors' like 'customs and traditions', 'attitudes and living patterns', 'ethnic groups', 'race relations', 'language', 'social structure' (including 'social standing or position of racial groups' and 'social opportunities and restrictions between and among racial groups'), and 'family structure' (Appendix III); the course on 'culture' was based on the anthropological classics of Benedict, Kroeber, and Linton. The field manuals include *Guerrilla Warfare and Special Forces Operations*. Washington. DC: Dept. of the Army, *Field Manual FM 31–32* (1961) [LC U408.3.A13]; and Col. Kelly's A Detachment Handbook. San Francisco: 5th Special Forces Group (Abn), 1st Special Forces (1966) [MHI USARV SSFG ADH–1966]. The program for revision of the field manuals is to be found in USArmy Combat Developments Command's Program for Analysis and Development of US Counterinsurgency Doctrine and Organization (U). 23 November 1964, Fort Belvoir, VA [NNRR, Records Group 472, declassified 19/4/90].

18 The interviews are mentioned as sources in Schrock et al. (1966: 315; 806).

19 This will become obvious from a brief look at the stated 'objectives' in specific projects supported by the United Stated Operations Mission to Vietnam (USOM, as USAID Vietnam was called prior to 1965), as cited in USOM, Office for Rural Affairs, *Provincial Representative's Guide*. Saigon, January 1963, p. 128; and the objectives of USAID, as cited in USAID, *Program and Project Data, Presentation to the Congress, 1966–1975*. Republic of Vietnam, Field Operations: *Progress in the Highlander Affairs Program in FY 1966*. Summaries of Activity, End of Fiscal Year 1966. Saigon, 14 July 1966 [AID].

20 G. Tracy Atwood, Problems of Montagnard Development within the Vietnamese Society. Paper presented at: Conference on Economic Development among Montagnards at the Village Level of November 1970, p. 66 [Hickey Papers]; IVS Ethnic Minorities Seminar, May 20, May 21, 1969, Nha Trang [Wason Pamphlet DS Vietnam 651+]; see also Tracy Atwood, Some Views of Jarai Customs and Personality [WASON Pamphlet DS Vietnam 649+].

21 The role of the anthropologist Gerald Hickey and the issues of land titles and resettlement will be dealt with more extensively further on in this chapter.

22 G. Tracy Atwood and Lynn Cabbage, Five Year Plan for Highland Agriculture Development. AID, November 1972 [AID VS 630.9597 A 887]. In an interview, Edmond Sprague, former Special Forces and AID offical in various Highland provinces of Vietnam, professed to have been 'deep, deep undercover for the CIA' (Interview 17 May 1990). Sprague is nicely portrayed in James Fenton's 'The Fall of Saigon' (1985).

23 See 'Briefing Paper for Draft Five Year Agriculture Development Plan for Montagnards 1974 – 1978', Ministry for Development of Ethnic Minorities, Saigon, December 1973 [AID VM 630.9597 V666h].

24 USAID, *Program and Project Data, Presentation to the Congress, 1966–1975*. Republic of Vietnam, Field Operations: 'Progress in the Highlander Affairs Program in FY 1966', p. 185. 'Summaries of Activity, End of Fiscal Year 1966'. Saigon, 14 July 1966 [AID]; see also Sarah Gudschinsky (1970), 'Bilingual Education for South Vietnam's Highlanders: An introduction to the dynamic new curriculum and materials for the ethnic minorities of South Vietnam'. Summer Institute of Linguistics, n.p. [AID VS 495.922 G923]; and 'Debrief of an AID Education Advisor, Region II, Vietnam 1967–1968', No. 116710, Honolulu: Asia Training Center [MML].

25 'Ethnic Minorities in the South Vietnamese Highlands', Research and Development Field Unit, Vietnam. Semi-Annual Report, 16 May 1965 – 15 November 1965. Washington: DoD, OSD/ARPA, p. 21 [NNRR AD 369 224]. In the same report, a research on 'Psychological Warfare Employment of Belief Systems in Vietnam'

(pp. 21–22) is proposed by the Commanding General, 173rd Airborne Brigade, in a letter of 3 September 1965 which would refer to 'native superstitions that can be exploited'.

26 The sections on Montagnards in the 1967 *Area Handbook* (Smith et al. 1967: 72–87; 244–7; and passim) were greatly expanded in comparison to the 1962 edition, composed by George Harris (Harris 1962: 54–7; 65–6; 207).

27 'Psychological Warfare Employment of Belief Systems in Vietnam'. Research and Development Field Unit, Vietnam. Semi-Annual Report, 16 May 1965 – 15 November 1965. Washington: DoD, OSD/ARPA, pp. 21–22 [NNRR AD 369 224].

28 *The Montagnard Tribal Groups of the Republic of South Viet-Nam* (US Army Special Warfare School 1964) had the following sections: I. Introduction; II. Geography; III. Ethnology; IV. History; V. Social Structure; VI. Individual Characteristics; VII. Customs and Taboos; VIII. Health and Medical; IX. Religion; X. Economy; XI. Political; XII. Subversion; XIII. Psyops Considerations; XIV. Civic Action Considerations; XV. Paramilitary Capabilities; for each of 13 groups surveyed. Robert Mole (1970) uses the following headings: Individual and group characteristics, village (and its buildings), social structures, economics, religion, (social customs and behavior patterns), guidelines for rapport.

29 Hickey's *The Major Ethnic Groups of the South Vietnamese Highlands* (1964) had the following outline: settlements, sociopolitical organization, religion (cultural origins and traits). Ironically, his recent *Shattered World* (1993) has a similar lay-out: pre-1960 situation, religion, settlements and houses, family-kinship-marriage, economic activities-subsistence-livelihood, village leadership, war. The main difference is now the attention paid to the consequences of war from an ethnographic perspective.

30 See O'Donnell (1967); Hickey (1967); and Kunstadter (1967a, b). It is ironical to see O'Donnell's overly optimistic account of the Strategic Hamlet program in Kien Hoa, where Hickey had issued a very critical report on Strategic Hamlets with John Donnell – not the same person – in 1962, partly based on data from the same province. For the implication of Kunstadter in ARPA programming, see the following AAA documents: 'Miscellaneous notes from the Washington meetings (18 January 1966); Letter from ARPA to Dr. Stephen T. Boggs, executive secretary, AAA, 4 April 1966; 'Minutes, 54th Meeting of the Executive Board', Pittsburgh, 20–21 May 1966. Stephen Boggs maintained close contacts with both civilian (AID) and military (ARPA) government agencies, in order to match demand and supply of anthropologists, so to say [NAA, Thailand Controversy].

31 Gerald Hickey, 'Memorandum for the Record: Montagnard Agriculture and Land Tenure'. San Francisco: Rand Corporation, OSD/ARPA R and D Field Unit, 2 April 1965.

32 Of course, there are many more relevant studies than the ones mentioned here. It is, however, my aim to give insight in the discourse on Montagnards, not an overview of all the studies conducted under Program Agile.

33 See Havron et al. (1968), and Sternin et. al. (1968). In March, 1965, Gerald Hickey had already made a study of 'The American Military Advisor and his Foreign Counterpart in the framework of Special Forces action among the Montagnards', with one section entitled 'Bridging the Cultural Gap' (pp. 22–7); on the long list of conclusions and suggestions, Hickey proposes to set up 'language and cultural training centers, similar to those that some missionary societies have found useful' (Hickey 1965: xv).

34 See, for instance, Lenoir (1966) and both reports by the Human Sciences Research Inc. (1969a, b).

35 The Special Forces felt themselves to be an elite corps, and prided themselves to be airborne; amongst themselves, they call regular Army men 'legs'. On their part, the regular Army is often equally contemptuous of Special Forces, because of their use of unconventional (hence 'unmilitary') tactics; an officer choosing a career with Special

Forces jeopardized his chances of promotion to the rank of general. The conflict drew wide publicity during the so-called Rheault affair in 1969. Colonel Rheault, commanding officer of the 5th Special Forces Group in Nha Trang, was arrested for the murder of a Vietnamese double agent. During the interrogation, it was revealed that Special Forces acted under orders of the CIA when 'they got rid of' the double agent. Eventually, Col. Rheault and his immediate subordinates were released and the charges were dropped, on the grounds that the CIA was not willing to let personnel appear as witnesses (cf. Col. Francis Kelly, The United States Army Special Forces in the Republic of Vietnam, 5th Special Forces Group (Airborne), 1st Special Forces, 1971, pp. 210–16 [NSA] – in 1973, a revised and 'sanitized' version of this Special Forces history was published; see also L. Fletcher Prouty 1969; An. 1969).

36 Apart from the literature cited, this section is based on a series of interviews with Dr. Hickey on 4, 5, 6 April, 1990.

37 See Hickey's *Village in Vietnam* (1964a). A lively portrait of Hickey is sketched by journalist Gloria Emerson in *Winners and Losers* (1978).

38 Letter from Dr. Donald S. Marshall to Dr. Peter Kloos, 22 February 1987.

39 Statement by Gerald C. Hickey before the Senate Foreign Relations Committee, May 13, 1971 [Hickey Papers]. Hickey's statement on the Senate floor resumes the main themes from his influential but disputed essays, *Accommodation in South Vietnam: The Key to Sociopolitical Solidarity* (1967c), and *Accommodation and Coalition in South Vietnam* (1970), both published by the Rand Corporation. The first essay provoked both consenting and critical response, mostly from political scientists like Samuel Huntington (1968) and Allan Goodman (1968).

40 These are the unpublished memoranda which I found in Gerald Hickey's personal papers; it is possible that he wrote more memoranda and reports. The items cited in this paragraph are from the Hickey Papers.

41 Memorandum for General Boles: Comments on Y Bham's Address to the Indochinese People's Conference as Reported in the Agence Khmer de Press [sic], 15 March 1965, 24 March 1965; Notes on a Meeting with Mr. Bui Diem, Special Assistant to the Prime Minister, 6 December 1965; Memorandum for Record: Buon Ea Shift from CIDG to Regional Forces, 21 June 1966; Memorandum to General William C. Westmoreland, General Creighton W. Abrams: 'Comments on the Current Situation in the Highlands', 3 May 1968; 'Comments on CIDG-Conversion to RF', 2 January 1969; FULRO Events of December 1968–January 1969', 8 January 1969; 'The Highlander and FULRO Context', May 1969; Memorandum for the Record from Gerald C. Hickey, Brian Jenkins: Potential Katu Chieu Hoi in Quang Nam Province, 10 November 1969; The View from Phnom Penh, D–20224-ARPA, 1 May 1970 [Hickey papers].

42 Memorandum for Record: 'Montagnard Refugee Problems: The Bru and Hre of the Central Vietnamese Highlands', 4 May 1965; Memorandum for Record: 'Refugee and Montagnard Situation in Pleiku Province', 25 August 1965; Memo for Record: 'The Uncertain Future of Montagnard Refugees in Cam Lam District, Khanh Hoa Province', 9 September 1970.

43 Memorandum for Record: 'Comments on Recent GVN Legislation Concerning Montagnard Common Law Courts in the Central Vietnamese Highlands', 8 June 1965.

44 Memorandum for the Record: 'The Arrest of Siu Choi', 13 July 1970 (but see Hickey 1982b: 261–2, for the context of the disappearance of Siu Choi, at a time when Nay Luett, the Jarai who later became Minister for Development of Ethnic Minorities, tried to upgrade the status of the King of Fire throughout the Highlands in an attempt 'to preserve the ethnic identity of the Jarai and other highlands groups' [ibid.: 225]). On the King of Fire, see Chapters 1 and 9.

45 Memorandum for Record: 'Montagnard Agriculture and Land Tenure', 2 April 1965; Memorandum for Record: 'Kontum Province Montagnard Aspirations and the Land

Tenure Question in Kontum, Pleiku and Tuyen Duc Provinces', 28 October 1965; Memorandum for Record: 'Land Titles for the Highlanders' 12 December 1968; Memorandum for Record: 'Perpetuation of Error', 11 January 1969; Memorandum for Record, 24 January 1969; 'Population Relocation in the Highlands', 20 March 1969; Memorandum for Record: 'Montagnard Land Ownership and Area Defense', 20 July 1970; Memorandum for Record: 'The GVN Work Plan for Montagnard Land Reform', 2 February 1971.

46 'Material on Kontum Province', 17 March 1965; Memorandum for Record: 'Current Montagnard Situation in Darlac and Kontum Provinces', 22 July 1965; Memorandum for Record: 'The VC/NVA Offensive: Effects on Highlanders' Attitudes. Relations between the GVN and FULRO, and on Social and Economic Programs for the Highlanders', 5 March 1968.

47 An example of the extent of Hickey's influence on debates, is the report 'Montagnard Attitudes toward Government Land Program' (10 Nov70), prepared by Major Gordon K. Young of CORDS with Mr. Nguyen Xuan Duyen and Mr. Dao Van Giam of the Pacification Studies Group [Hickey Papers]. The report was prompted by Hickey's memorandum of 20 July 1970 on 'Montagnard Land Ownership and Area Defense', and aimed at an evaluation of GVN programming among Montagnards. On the basis of interviews with Rhadé and Mnong villagers in Darlac and Quang Duc province, evaluators concluded that more attention should be paid to the Montagnard land question, if further interethnic conflicts were to be avoided and if Montagnards were to actively support the South Vietnamese government.

48 United States Accounting Office (1973: 17, 21).

49 Willard C. Muller, 'End of Tour Report: The Montagnard Land Program' (June 1973). Saigon: AID, pp. 3, 5, 4 [AID VS 301.35 M 958a].

50 For a formulation of this discourse see Laird (1972) on the Nixon Doctrine and Rostow (1960) on the relation between economics and political development, who became very influential once he changed his university chair for a prominent position within the State Department.

51 Examples of the disciplining force of this anti-Communist discourse can be found in Deitchman, 1976: 325–59, 385–412; Emerson, 1976: 278–90; Kolko, 1985: 145, 170, 194–6.

52 Interviews with Pierre K'Briuh, 15 April 1990; with Michael Benge, 9 and 15 May 1990; with Edmond Sprague, 17 May 1990; letter from Jean Pierre Marie K'Briuh and Touneh Han Tho to Mr. Richard English, Deputy Assistant Secretary of State for Refugee Admissions, Dept. of State, 7 June 1985, and 'Memorandum of Conversation: Montagnard Political Attitude During National Crisis; Request for Political Asylum in Event of Fall of Saigon', US Embassy Conference Room, 4 April 1975 (participants: Nay Luett (Minister of Ethnic Minorities), Senator Ksor Rot, Senator Y-Ba [sic], Pierre Marie K'Briuh (MDEM), Touneh Han Tho (Ethnic Minorities Council), Nay Alep (Commander, National Training Center, Pleiku), G.D. Jacobson (SAAFO), L.M. Prosser (SAAFO), E. Sprague (SAAFO) [Benge Papers]; Meeting with Mr. Jacobson, 4 April 75 (handwritten report) [Sprague Papers]. In 1982, a FULRO group of over 200 Montagnards escaped the suppression of their resistance movement in Vietnam and the war in Cambodia and made it to the Thai border, where they were held against their will in a Khmer Rouge 'refugee camp'. In 1986, the group managed to contact former Special Forces acquaintances in the US, who succeeded in bringing them out of Thailand and into North Carolina, despite active obstruction from the American Embassy in Bangkok. Their Odyssey, and especially their putative 'loyalty' to American Special Forces was romanticized by Jerry London in his 1990 film *Vestige of Honor*; needless to say, the film was told from the perspective of American veterans who tried to get the Montagnards to America, thus recapturing some of their honor lost during the Vietnam War. In this film, there is talk of an official document of the US Embassy in Saigon, promising help and arms for the anti-Communist struggle,

and which was confiscated by American officials in Thailand in 1986. Although I have heard similar rumors in North Carolina, I have not seen direct evidence of the existence of such a document. The minutes of the meeting on 4 April 1975, however, indicate that the subject was positively discussed.

53 FULRO Papers; interviews with Y Djuh Mlo, Y Yok Ayun, and Rmah Dock, 15 April 1990; with Y Tiak Buon Ya, 20 May 1990; with Thomas Y Tlur Eban and Nay Rong, 27 May, 1990.

54 This conflict between Special Forces and regular US Army came to a head in the Rheault affair, or the 'case of the Green Berets', which was precisely on the issue of command and control (see note 32).

55 Lamar M. Prosser, 'Montagnard Affairs Project in Vietnam. End of Tour Reports' [classified]. Saigon: USAID Vietnam, Project no. 730–11–995–335 [AID VS 301.4519592]. USAID, Program and Project Data: Presentation to the Congress, 1966–1975. *Republic of Vietnam Operations. Program Progress – FY 1966: Summaries of Activity, End of Fiscal Year 1966.* Saigon, 14 July 1966 [AID].

56 'Overview of the CORDS Ethnic Minorities Affairs Program', 1968, p. 1 [MHI MACV/CORDS files 2024].

57 Gerald C. Hickey, 'Population Relocation in the Highlands', 20 March 1969 [MHI MACV files 2028]; unless otherwise stated, the documents on this conflict are from these MACV files in the Military History Institute of the Army War College, Carlisle Barracks, PA. See also Hickey 1982b: 192–6.

58 LTC William E. Thomas, Special Forces Staff Officer, 'Memorandum for Record: Montagnard Committee Meeting', 5 March 1969, MACJ3-032.

59 Daniel S. Ely, 5017, 'Significant Issues: Forcible Relocation of Montagnards', n.d.

60 Interview with William Colby, 20 April 1990.

61 Memo, MG Elias Townsend, Chief of Staff, to ACofS, CORDS, 'MACV Directive on Resettlement Population Groups', n.d.; BG John Wheelock III, Acting ACofS, J3, 'Proposed Mission Council Policy Statement on Relocation of Montagnards', 28 March 1969.

62 W.E. Colby, DEPCORDS/MACV, Memorandum for Mr. Jacobson, ACofS, CORDS, subject: 'Pacification and Development in the Highlands', 19 April 1969; MACV directive (n.d.),'Relocation of Civilian Population Groups'; Outline Draft CPDC Directive 'Pacification and Development in the Highlands'; Gen. Tran Thien Khiem, vice-minister in charge of Pacification and Development, to All Regional/ Provincial/Municipal Pacification and Development Councils, 17 April 1969, No. 408-TTh.T-BDXD; Gen. Cao Van Vien, Chief of the Joint General Staff/RVNAF, Instructions, ref. 969 Pacification and Development Plan, 24 April 1969; Norman P. Firnstahl, Deputy Director, CORDS/REF, 7 May 1969, subject: 'Relief Assistance to Temporary Evacuees'.

63 This paragraph is based on the accounts by Hickey (1982b: 221–3) and Jeffrey Clarke, the official US Army historian (1988: 464–5). The records to which Clarke refers are in the Center for Military History, Southeast Asia Branch, in Washington, DC. At the time of my research in Washington (1990), the Center for Military History was not accessible because of a fire emergency. Therefore, I have not been able to see the primary sources on this second conflict over resettlement in 1971.

64 Research of 1970, sponsored by USAID, had established that most of the resettled Montagnards wished to go back to their home area (Bush 1970).

65 Gloria Emerson, 'Anthropologist in Vietnam Seeks Montagnard Gain', *New York Times*, 25 April 1971; Peter Osnos, 'Security a Disaster for Montagnards', *Washington Post*, 25 April 1971; both in Hickey 1982b: 223.

66 This is more or less acknowledged by Charles Joiner, in a chapter on 'Administration and Political Warfare in the Highlands', where he advocates a policy of accommodation similar to Hickey. Following on a paragraph on US policies in the Highlands, he adds that '[u]ltimately, of course, political success in the highlands is

contingent not upon what American military and civilian personnel do, but upon what the government of South Vietnam does' (Joiner 1974: 210).

8 The Dying God revisited

1 This chapter is an adaptation from my 'The King of Fire and Vietnamese Ethnic Policy in the Central Highlands', in: Don McCaskill and Ken Kampe (eds), *Development or Domestication? Indigenous Peoples of Southeast Asia.* Chiang Mai 1997: Silkworm Books, pp. 488–535; parts are based on my 'Sedentarization and Selective Preservation among the Montagnards in the Vietnamese Central Highlands', in: Jean Michaud (ed.), *Turbulent Times and Enduring Peoples: Mountain Minorities in the South-East Asian Massif.* London 2000: Curzon Press, pp. 124–48.

2 For a thorough analysis of the political and religious status of the three *p'tau*, see Jacques Dournes, *Pötao: Une théorie du pouvoir chez les Indochinois Jörai*, Paris 1977: Flammarion.

3 Information provided by Siu Aluân; interviews with Nay Rong, Nay Luett's brother, in North Carolina, April/May, 1990; Dournes 1977: 195–206; Hickey 1982b: 146–53, 224–5, 261–2.

4 In 1991 the province of Gialai-Kontum was split in two provinces – Gialai and Kontum – much like it was in colonial times. After decades of in-migration and relocation, the Kinh (or Viêt, the lowland majority group of Vietnam) make up more than half of the population of these highland provinces. The most important minority group in Gialai are the Jarai (Giarai in Vietnamese). In Kontum province the most important minorities are the Bahnar (Bana) and Sedang (XoĐăng).

5 All over the Central Highlands people from Nghê An and Hà Tĩnh seemed to have the key positions in party and state. These provinces, just south from the Red River delta, are reputedly poor provinces with a long scholarly tradition; in fact, the mandarinate was the royal way to escape poverty. Under colonial rule, the poverty and the scholarly tradition blended in a revolutionary tradition, epitomized by the fact that Hô Chí Minh was born there, and even more by the famous Nghê Tĩnh Soviets of 1930/31. These days, a bureaucratic career is the royal way for people from Nghê An and Hà Tĩnh provinces, who recognize each other by their dialect and form networks when outside their home province. In the Central Highlands, such networks attain a mafia-like character because of the degree of control which is exerted over the administration and its resources through informal channels.

6 Interview with Rmah Hanh, 24 April 1991.

7 Interview with Kpa Eng, 24 April 1991. For the question of religious freedom in Vietnam, see Salemink 1995b.

8 Interview with Nay Quách, 28 April 1991.

9 There have been ways of circumventing official scrutiny, about which I cannot be more specific without possibly hurting the courageous informants who came forward. The information provided by them is interwoven through this chapter.

10 See, for example, the report by Hoàng Lê (1990), which attributes failures in meeting the planning objectives to the propaganda by FULRO.

11 What follows is a gross generalization about traditional farming systems in the Central Highlands, simply because there is no space to do justice to the wide variety of agricultural techniques. Suffice here to mention that traditional systems include wet rice cultivation and dry rice cultivation on permanent fields, while more recent innovations include gardening and plantation farming.

12 More recently, the word '*nuong rây*' is used frequently, meaning 'upland field'.

13 A recent study by Rodolphe de Koninck with a team of Vietnamese researchers using Geographical Information Systems (GIS) mapping techniques pointed at the role of migration in as main factor in the deforestation process in two highland provinces (De Koninck 1996). A visit by then Prime Minister Võ Văn Kiêt to Tây Nguyên in the

summer of 1997 prompted him to forbid further migration into the Central Highlands.

14 In many regions in Asia and Africa malaria is on the rise again, Vietnam not excepted. For the Central Highlands the statistics show a sharp upward curve since 1985, although many more casualties are not reported and remain out of the statistics. The official statistics of Gialai-Kontum province as a whole counted eight malaria victims for Ayun Pa district in 1990, whereas the district figures counted 13. Within that district, the commune authorities of Ia Trôk mentioned two dead for 1990, while in three hamlets respectively 3, 6 and 20 (!) dead from malaria were counted in 1990. In a report on malaria in Gialai-Kontum I identified a number of probable causes (Salemink 1991 n.p.). The parasite is increasingly resistant to prophylactic and curative medication. The mosquitos do not have to fear DDT from the Soviet Union anymore since the shipments stopped, but there is hardly any money to buy other insecticides. The massive immigration of lowlanders without specific immunity must have increased the occurrence of malaria in the Highlands. Other human-inspired changes might have played a role, like deforestation, the cultivation of and semi-permanent residence on distant fields for want of nearby fields, and the construction of houses on the ground. Changes in the diet might have decreased immunity, while the rundown health care system is not in a position to alleviate the situation.

15 The proceedings of these conferences are published in a special issue of the journal *Nghiên cuú Kinh tê* [Economic Studies], 1(137), 1984; in a special issue of *Tap chí Dân Tôc Hoc* [Ethnographic Magazine], no. 1 (1984); in a number of agronomical publications edited by Nguyên Van Chiên; and in the volumes *Môt sô vân Đê kinh tê-xã hôi Tây Nguyên* [Some socio-economic problems of Tây Nguyên] (1986) and *Tây Nguyên trên Đuòng phát triên* [Tây Nguyên on the road to development] (1989). Other results of the research programs were published separately in various journals and volumes.

16 The new ethnic policy lines were discussed in special issues of *Tap chí Dân Tôc Hoc* [Ethnographic Magazine]: no. 1 (1990); no. 3 (1990); and no. 3/79 (1993).

17 In 1991 rumor had it that almost one hundred gold diggers had died in the course of mutual conflict while panning for gold in Kontum province. Although the numbers are probably exaggerated, it is significant that such rumors went round anyway.

18 For reasons of protection, the name of this informant cannot be made public. Elsewhere in this chapter, I have been deliberately vague about localities and names.

19 After writing this text in 1994, I found that Terry Rambo had made a similar observation on this metaphor: 'The Vietnamese national community may constitute, as one Kinh ethnologist has written, a garden in which a hundred flowers of different colors and perfume bloom, but the overall plan for the garden is exclusively determined by the head gardener (i.e. the state).' (Rambo 1995: XVII) Although Rambo did not reference this observation, it presumably refers to the same book by Nông Quôc Chân – not a Kinh ethnologist, but a Tây minority poet, and former Vice-Minister of Culture and Information.

20 Out of 60 participants, only three – Lò Giang Páo, Grant Evans and this author – mentioned the far-reaching cultural consequences of sedentarization and migration policies in their presentations. Incomplete collections of contributions have been published in Vietnam but without permission from the authors; see Nông Quôc Chân, Vĩ Hông Nhân and Hoàng Tuân Cu (1996) and Mai Ly Quang (1994).

21 One special way of adapting old songs to new uses was embodied in the Edê troubadour Y Dol, who toured the villages with songs calling for reconciliation under the present regime. While the authorities considered this to be effective propaganda against FULRO, the latter organization left the troubadour alone because of his popularity (Đăng Nghiêm Van, personal communication). Changing the lyrics of existing songs for political reasons had already been tried by the French and the South Vietnamese regimes.

22 I have described a similar process of folklorization and reification of Montagnard culture during the last decades of French rule over the Vietnamese Highlands (Salemink 1987: 119–23; see also Salemink 1991a).

23 At the time of editing this manuscript, the author was involved in the funding of customary law research by researchers attached to the Institute of Folk Studies, as a part of the Ford Foundation's support for social sciences and upland development based on local knowledge and practices in Vietnam. See Ngô Đúc Thinh, Chu Thái Son and Nguyên Hũu Thâú (1996) and Ngô Đúc Thinh (1998).

24 These figures are contested by Nguyên Xuân Nghĩa (1989: 62), who claims that the 1979 census counted 45,059 Protestants in the Central Highlands.

25 This information is to be found in the newsletter ('After action report' no. 8, 1993) of the General Cooperative Montagnard Association (GCMA), a Montagnard-Special Forces friendship association based in Tampa, Florida.

26 I owe this insight to Achille Mbembe, during the 'Colonial Ethnographies' seminar in Amsterdam, June 1993 (see Chapters 1 and 4).

27 Jarai (and Edê) burial rituals are a matter of much debate. The elaborate rituals, and especially the *abandon de la tombe* [leaving the grave] after one to three years, have been described in great detail by Bernard Jouin (1949). The present regime has tried to suppress the funerary rituals which are considered wasteful and contrary to hygienic prescriptions ('obsolete and backward, expensive and time-consuming practices connected with funerals ... are discouraged', cf. Nông Quôc Chân 1978b: 60).

Epilogue

1 See Salemink (2000b and 2000c).
2 See also Hoàng Xuân Tý and Lê Trong Cúc (1998).
3 See Ngô Đúc Thinh and Phan Đăng Nhât (2000).

Bibliography

Manuscript sources

AID   US Agency for International Development library, Rosslyn, VA.

AOM   Centre des Archives d'Outre-Mer, Fonds des Amiraux et du Gouvernement Général de l'Indochine; Aix-en-Provence.

ANSOM   Centre des Archives d'Outre-Mer, Fonds du Ministère des Colonies; Aix-en-Provence (formerly Paris, Ministère des Colonies/d'Outre-Mer).

BJL   Professor M.A. Jaspan Collections, Brynmor Jones Library, University of Hull.

BPTST   Bô Phát-triên Sác-tôc [Ministry for Development of Ethnic Minorities], Trung Tâm Luu Tru Quôc Gia 2; Ho Chi Minh City.

DDRS   Declassified Documents Reference System (published microfilm collection, until VII–2, June 1981: Washington, DC: Carrollton Press; after that: Washington, DC: Research Publications, Inc.) [In: Library of Congress, Washington, DC].

EFEO   Ecole Française d'Extrême-Orient, Collection manuscrits en langues européennes (MSS Europ.); Paris.

GG   Gouvernement Général d'Indochine, Trung tâm Luu tru Quôc gia 1 (Vietnamese National Records Center No. 1); Hanoi.

HDCST   Hôi-dông các Sác-tôc [Ethnic Minorities Council – South Vietnam], Trung Tâm Luu Tru Quôc Gia 2, Ho Chi Minh-City.

LCTR   Library of Congress, Technical Reports (declassified, microfilmed), Science Reading Room, Washington, DC.

MACCORDS   Military Assistance Command/Civil Operations and Revolutionary Support files, US Military History Insitute, Carlisle Barracks, PA.

MEP   Missions Etrangères de Paris, Archives, Paris.

MHI   US Military History Insitute, Carlisle Barracks, PA.

MILES   Admiral Miles Papers, National Archives, Records Group 38, NHC-75, box 36, Washington, DC.

MML   Marquat Memorial Library, J.F. Kennedy Special Warfare Center, Fort Bragg, NC.

MSU   Michigan State University Archives, UA 2.9.5.5 Vietnam Project (MSUG Archives), East Lansing, MI.

NA   National Archives, Washington, DC.

NAA   National Anthropological Archives, American Anthropological Association, Smithsonian Institution, Washington, DC.

NNRR   National Archives, Suitland Reference Branch, Records of the United States Army, Suitland, MD.
NSA   National Security Archive, Washington, DC.
PPM   Pénétration du Pays Moï, 1931–35. Cochinchine, Cabinet du Gouverneur records; Cornell University Library, Dept. of Manuscripts and University Archives, #3482.
QM   Questions Moï, 1937–38. Cochinchine, Cabinet du Gouverneur; Cornell University Library, Department of Manuscripts and University Archives, #3482.
RSA   Résidence Supérieure d'Annam, Trung tâm Luu tru Quoc gia 2 (Vietnamese National Records Centre No. 2); Hô Chi Minh City.
SHAT   Service Historique de l'Armée de Terre, Vincennes, France.
SIA   Smithsonian Institution Archives, Washington, DC.
TTTLLT1   Trung Tâm Tài Liêu Luu Tru 1, Hanoi.
TTTLLT2   Trung Tâm Tài Liêu Luu Tru 2, Hô Chi Minh City.
WASON   Cornell University, Olin Library, Ecolls Collection (Wason), Ithaca, NY.

Private collections

Benge Papers   Papers in possession of Michael Benge, Washington, DC.
FULRO Papers   Papers in possession of the Montagnard refugee community in Greensboro, NC.
Hickey Papers   Papers in possession of Gerald C. Hickey, Chicago, IL.
Layton Papers   Papers in possession of Col. Gilbert Layton, Vienna, VA.
Sprague Papers   Papers in possession of Edmund Sprague, Antrim, NH.

Official documents

Argenlieu, T. d' (1946), Ordonnance fédérale du 27 Mai 1946 portant création d'un Commissariat du Gouvernement Fédéral pour les Montagnards du Sud-Indochinois, *Journal Officiel de la Federation Indochinoise* 23, 6 June 1946.

Bô Chính tri Trung uong Đang (1989) Nghi Quyêt sô 22-NQ-TW ngày 27/11/1989 vê chu truong, chính sách lón phát triên kinh tê – xã hôi miên núi [Politbureau of the Party, Resolution no. 22-NQ-TW on the major guidelines and policy on the socio-economic development of the mountain regions], in: *Tap chí Dân Tôc Hoc* 1–1990: 2–12.

Direction Fédérale de l'Information (1946), *Conférence Franco-Vietnamienne, Dalat, 8–5–1946, Commission Politique no. 7, Notes sur les minorites ethniques.* Saigon: Direction Fédérale de l'Information.

Gouvernement de la Cochinchine (1935), *Variétés sur les Pays Moïs.* Saigon: Gouvernement de la Cochinchine.

Hôi Đông Bô Truong (1990) Quyêt Đinh sô 72-HDBT ngày 13/3/1990 vê môt sô chu truong, chính sách cu thê phát triên kinh tê – xã hôi miên núi [Council of Ministers, Decree no. 72-HĐBT on socio-economic development policy for the mountain region].

Inspection des Colonies (1949), *Revue Éducation* 16, numéro spécial consacrée aux populations montagnardes du Sud-Indochinois. Saigon: Rectorat d'Académie.

Nguyên Đê (1952), *Plan de développement économique pour les pays Montagnards du Sud du Domaine de la Couronne.* Saigon: Editions de la Délégation impériale du Domaine de la Couronne.

Nguyên Đê (1953), *Plan d'Action Sociale pour les Pays Montagnard du Sud du Domaine de la Couronne*. Saigon: Editions de la Délégation Impériale de la Domaine de la Couronne.

Nguyên Văn Tài (1984), *Ban Đô các Dân tôc*. Hanoi.

Quôc Hôi, khóa IX, ky hp thú 3 (1993) Quy chê Hot Đông cua Hôi Đông Dân tôc [National Assembly, Regulation of the activities of the Nationalities Council], 7/7/1993. *Tap chí Dân Tôc hoc* 3/79: 3–9.

US Accounting Office (1973), *Progress and Problems of US Assistance for Land Reform in Vietnam: Agency for International Development, Department of State (B–159451)*. Report to the Congress by the Comptroller General of the United States. Washington, DC.

US Army Combat Development Command (1964), *Program for Analysis and Development of US Counterinsurgency Doctrine and Organization*. Washington, DC: Department of the Army.

US Senate, Subcommittee of the Committee on Appropriations (1964), *Department of Defense Appropriations for 1965, Hearings* (part 5), 88th Congress, 2nd session. Washington, DC: US Government Printing Office.

US Senate, Subcommittee of the Committee on Appropriations (1965), *Department of Defense Appropriations for 1966, Hearings* (part 5), 89th Congress, 1st session. Washington, DC: US Government Printing Office.

US Senate, Subcommittee of the Committee on Appropriations (1967), *Department of Defense Appropriations for 1968, Hearings* (part 3), 90th Congress, 1st session. Washington, DC: US Government Printing Office.

US Senate, Subcommittee of the Committee on Appropriations (1968), *Department of Defense Appropriations for 1969, Hearings* (part 2), 90th Congress, 2nd session. Washington, DC: US Government Printing Office.

US Senate, Subcommittee of the Committee on Appropriations (1969), *Department of Defense Appropriations for 1970, Hearings* (part 1), 91st Congress, 1st session. Washington, DC: US Government Printing Office.

US Senate, Subcommittee of the Committee on Appropriations (1969), *Department of Defense Appropriations for 1970, Hearings* (part 5), 91st Congress, 1st session. Washington, DC: US Government Printing Office.

Unpublished sources

Anonymous (1962), *The Montagnard Tribes of South Vietnam* [Les traits caractéristiques dans les moeurs et coutumes des tribus montagnardes au Sud du Vietnam], Direction de l'Action Sociale pour les Pays Montagnards (n.d.). Washington D.C.: JPRS 13443, 13 April 1962.

Ambler, John and Oscar Salemink (1997), *Media and Minorities: The Communication of Upland Development in Vietnam*. Amsterdam: Paper presented at the Euro-Viet III Conference, 2–4 July 1997.

Bloch, Donald (May 1967), *A Review of US Military Counterinsurgency Activities with Selected Minority Groups in South-Vietnam: Some Policy and Doctrinal Considerations* – Secret (with Marshall Andrews). Washington DC: American University, CRESS DA-49-092-ARO-7 [NNRC AD 381 804].

Bourotte, Bernard (1967), *History of the Mountain People of Southern Indochina up to 1945* [Essai d'histoire des populations montagnardes du Sud Indochinois jusqu'à 1945]. Washington DC: USAID, Division of Language Services no. 54787 [or. 1955].

Bush, Henry C. (1970), *Montagnard Desire to Return to Original Hamlet Sites and Vietnamese Farming within Montagnard Hamlets*. Saigon: Control Data Corporation, AID contract no. AID–730–3249 [WASON Pamphlet DS Vietnam 947+].

Condominas, Georges (1962), *We Have Eaten the Forest – South Vietnam* [Nous avons mangé la forêt, by Georges Condominas; for government use only]. Washington DC: JPRS 15108, 4 September 1962 [or. 1957].

CINFAC (1966), *Bibliography of Materials on Selected Groups in the Republic of Vietnam*. Washington, DC: American University, CRESS/CINFAC [LC Z3228 V5A74 1966].

Donnell, John C. and Gerald C. Hickey (1962), *The Vietnamese 'Strategic Hamlets': A Preliminary Report (U)* (confidential). Santa Monica: RAND Corporation, Memorandum RM-3208-ARPA, August 1962 [NNRC Declassified 903607, 18/4/90].

Dubois, Pierre (1950), *Notes sur L. Sabatier, résident du Darlac 1913–1926*. Mémoire, Ecole Coloniale [ANSOM D 3201].

Electrowatt Engineering Services (1993), Final Report: Environmental and Financing Studies on the Yali Falls Hydropower Project (Basin Wide). Bangkok: Mekong Secretariat/Hanoi: Ministry of Energy, SR Vietnam.

Ello, Paul, Richard Joyce, Robert Williams, and William Woodworth (1969), *US Army Special Forces and Similar Internal Defense Operations in Mainland Southeast Asia, 1962–1967 (U)*. McLean, VA: Research Analysis Corporation, RAC-TP-354 [NSA].

Fallah, Skaidrite Maliks (1967), *Customs and Taboos of Selected Tribes Residing along the Western Border of the Republic of Vietnam*. Washington, DC: American University, CRESS/CINFAC report R-0426 [NNRC AD 649 981/WASON Pamphlet DS Vietnam 1038].

Fallah, Skaidrite Maliks and John Stowell (1965), *A Brief History of Ethnically Oriented Schools within Vietnam's Educational System*. Washington, DC: American University, SORO/CINFAC R-0198 [MHI].

Fromme, Marilou (1966), *Brief Notes on the Tahoi, Pacoh, and Phuong of the Republic of Vietnam*. Washington, DC: American University, CRESS [LC GN 635.V5 F76].

FULRO (1965), *Historique: Front Unifié de Lutte de la Race Opprimée (FULRO)*. Phnom Penh: Diffusé lors de la Conférence des Peuples Indochinois à Phnom Penh, 25 February 1965.

Gammelgaard, Jørgen (1990), *Ethnic Minorities in Vietnam. Report on a mission to Vietnam, 12 November–14 December*. Hanoi: UNDP.

Havron, M. Dean, Martin Sternin and Robert Teare (1968), *The Use of Cultural Data in Psychological Operations Programs in Vietnam*. McLean, VA: Human Sciences Corporation, ARPA TIO 72–4, February 1968 [NNRR AD 813 853].

Hickey, Gerald (1957), *Preliminary Research Report on the PMS*. Saigon: MSUG (mimeographed).

Human Sciences Research Inc. (1969a), *A Study of Mass Population Displacement in the Republic of Vietnam*. McLean, VA: Human Sciences Research Inc., July 1969 [AID VS 36.53 H918e].

Human Sciences Research Inc. (1969b), *Refugee Movement in Revolutionary War: A Study of the Causes and Characteristics of Civilian Displacement in Viet-Nam*. McLean, VA: Human Sciences Research Inc., HSR-RR-68/4-Te, July 1969 [NNRR AD 747 259].

Jones, Adrian H. and Andrew R. Molnar (1966), *Internal Defense against Insurgency: Six Cases*. Washington, DC: American University, Center for Research in Social Systems, December 1966.

Jonsson, Hjorleifur (1990), *Fooled by the Name? Millenarian Movement and Ethnicity in Mainland Southeast Asia*. Reykjavik: Paper for the 14th Conference of Nordic Anthropologists, 9–11 June 1990.

Jonsson, Hjorleifur (1992), *Health Issues among Uplanders in Ratanakhiri Province, Cambodia: Final report*. London and Phnom Penh: Health Unlimited.

Joyce, Richard P., and Roswell B. Wing (1967), *The Mobilization and Utilization of Minority Groups for Counterinsurgency* (Confidential). McLean, VA: Research Analysis Corporation, RAC-TP–241, February 1967 [NNRR AD 380 100].

LaBrie, Norman C. (1971), *FULRO: The History of Political Tension in the South Vietnamese Highlands*. University of Massachusetts, unpublished M.A. thesis.

Lang, Chris (1994), *Vietnam: The Yali Falls Dam Project in Social and Environmental Context*. Oxford: Earth Action Resource Centre, unpublished paper.

Langton, Patricia (1974), *Aspects of Religion among the Hill People of South Vietnam*. University of London, M.Ph. thesis.

Legay, Roger (1965), *La réimplantation des montagnards sur le plateau du Lang Bian*. thesis.

Legay, Roger (1971), *Srae ou la Rizière. Chez les Lac du Lang Biang, minorité ethnique des Hauts Plateaux du Sud-Vietnam*. [EFEO].

Lenoir, John D. (1966), *Notes on the Refugee Situation in Darlac Province, Republic of Vietnam*. McLean, VA: Human Sciences Research Inc., June 1966 [AID VS 361:53 H 918d].

Lockhart, Bruce (1985), *Looking down from a Tightrope: Ethnology in Vietnam*. Ithaca NY: Cornell University, unpublished paper.

Maran, Jacques (1892), *Marie I, Roi des Sédang*. Anvers [EFEO MSS Europ].

Maurice, Albert-Marie (1956), *La Société Rhadé*. Algers: Centre des Hautes Etudes d'Administration musulmane.

Mole, Cdr. Robert L., Navy Personal Response Officer (1968), *The Tribes of I Corps, South Vietnam. Volume I of the Peoples of Tribes of South Vietnam*. Saigon: COMNAVSUPPACT Saigon, Summer 1968.

Pierson, Harry H. (1965), *The Asia Foundation's Programming with Respect to Tribal and Minority Peoples in Southeast Asia*. Princeton, NJ: conference paper.

Salemink, Oscar (1987), *Ethnografie en kolonialisme. Minderheden in Vietnam, 1850–1954*, Amsterdam: University of Amsterdam, Instituut voor Moderne Aziatische Geschiedenis, M.A. thesis.

Salemink, Oscar (1991), *Malaria in Gialai-Kontum (Vietnam)*. Amsterdam: Report for the Medical Committee Netherlands-Vietnam.

Salemink, Oscar (1998), *Moral versus Political Economy and the Vietnam War*. London: paper presented at EIDOS Conference, SOAS.

Salemink, Oscar/UNESCO (1994), *Final Report: International Expert meeting for the Safeguarding and Promotion of the Intangible Cultural Heritage of Minority Groups in Viet Nam* (held in Hanoi, 15–18 March 1994). Paris: UNESCO CLT/ACL/94/IH/02.

Schaeffer, Joerg (1979), *Traditionnelle Gesellschaft und Geschichte der Rhadé im suedvietnamesischen Hochland*. Freiburg: inaugural dissertation, Albert Ludwigs Universitaet.

Sternin, Martin, Robert Teare, and Peter Nordlie (1968), *A Study of Values, Communication Patterns and Demography of Rural South Vietnam*. McLean, VA: Human Sciences Corporation, ARPA order 930, DAHC-19-67c-0014 [NNRC AD 893 854].

Stires, Frederick H. (1964), *The US Special Forces CIDG Mission in Viet-Nam: A preliminary case study in counterpart and civil-military relationships (U)*. Washington, DC: American University, SORO [NNRC, declassified 18/4/90].

Thomas, David (1961), *Classification of Southern Vietnamese Malayo-Polynesian Languages*. Saigon: Summer Institute of Linguistics (mimeographed).

Thomas, David (1962), *Mon-Khmer Subgroupings in Vietnam*. University of North Dakota: Summer Institute of Linguistics (mimeographed).

Turkoly-Joczic, Robert L. (1986), *The Military Role of Asian Ethnic Minorities in the Second Indochina War, 1959–1975*. Aberystwyth: University College of Wales, Ph.D. thesis.

Vigneras, Marcel et al. (1966), *US Army Special Forces Operations under the Civilian Irregular Defense Groups Program in Vietnam, 1961–1964 (U)*. McLean, VA: Research Analysis Corporation, RAC-T-477, April 1966.

Volk, Nancy Dorcas (1979), *A Temporary Community in a Temporary World: A Montagnard Resettlement Area in Southern Vietnam*. Seattle, University of Washington, Ph.D. thesis.

Worchell, Philip, Samuel Popkin et al. (September 1967), *A Socio-Psychological Study of the Regional/Popular Forces in Vietnam* – for official use only. Washington, DC: Simulmatics Corporation, ARPA contract DA 49-092-ARO-152 [NNRC AD 816 407].

Y-Bham-Enuol (1965), *Extraits de l'Histoire des Hauts-Plateaux du Centre-Vietnam (Pays Montagnard du Sud-Indochinois)*. Phnom Penh (mimeographed).

Published sources

Anonymous (1874), *Notes and Queries on Anthropology*. London: Royal Anthropological Institute of Great Britain and Ireland.

Anonymous (1903), Les transactions des Annamites et des Chinois avec les Moïs et les Khas-lu en Annam, *Bulletin Economique d'Indochine* VI(22): 725.

Anonymous (1921), L'Ecole Française d'Extrême-Orient depuis son origine jusqu'en 1920: ethnographie indochinoise, *BEFEO* XXI: 166–96.

Anonymous (1931), *Indochine Francaise. Section des services d'intérêt social: la pénétration scolaire dans les minorités ethniques*. Hanoi: Imprimerie d'Extrême-Orient.

Anonymous (1934), La pénétration en pays Mnong et Stieng insoumis (1931–1933), *Revue des Troupes Coloniales* 28/221: 601–18.

Anonymous (1938), Un centre de colonisation militaire en Indochine, *Revue des Troupes Coloniales* 256: 1020–5.

Anonymous (1946), D'un mois à l'autre, pays Moï, *Indochine Francaise* 24.

Anonymous (1969), The War in Vietnam: The Case of the Green Berets, *Newsweek*, August 25, 1969: 35–8.

Anonymous (1974), *The Montagnards of South Vietnam*. London: Minority Rights Group, Report No. 18.

Adas, Michael (1979), *Prophets of Rebellion: Millenarian Protest Movements against the European Colonial Order*. Cambridge.: Cambridge University Press.

Adkins, E.H., Jr. (1961), *The Science of Fingerprints*. Saigon: Michigan State University Vietnam Advisory Group.

Adkins, E.H., Jr. (1962), *A Study of Montagnard Names in Viet Nam*. Saigon: Michigan State University Vietnam Advisory Group.

Allen, Douglas (1989), Anti-war Asian Scholars and the Vietnam/Indochina War, *Bulletin of Concerned Asian Scholars* 21(2–4): 112–34.

Alvarez Roldán, Arturo (1995), Malinowski and the origins of the ethnographic method. In: Han Vermeulen and Arturo Alvarez Roldán (eds), *Fieldwork and Footnotes: Studies in the History of European Anthropology*. London: Routledge. pp. 143–155.

Anderson, Benedict (1983), *Imagined Communities. Reflections on the Origin and Spread of Nationalism*. London/New York: Verso.

Antoine, F. (1954), L'école montagnarde, *Indochine/Sud-Est Asiatique* 29: 33–7.

Antoine, F. and Y Blul Nie Blo (1952), Le sacrifice du buffle, *Sud-Est Asiatique* 11: 36–43.

Antomarchi, Dominique (1941a), Le fête du serment, *Indochine* I(20): xi–xv.

Antomarchi, Dominique (1941b), Le 'Bi-Duê', recueil des coutumes rhadées, *Indochine* II(25): 5–10.

Antomarchi, Dominique (1946), *Premier Livre de lecture Rhadée. 1ʳᵉ année: Cours enfantin*. Ban Me Thuôt.

Antomarchi, Dominique (1955), Klei Khan Kdam Yi, *BEFEO* XLVII: 569–615.

Ardant du Picq (1925/6), Monographie des pays Moï (Indochine, provinces de Kontum et de Ban Mê Thuot), *Revue des Troupes Coloniales* XIX, XX: passim.

Asad, Talal (ed.) (1973), *Anthropology and the Colonial Encounter*. London: Ithaca Press.

Aubert, Officiers de l'Etat-major du Général de Division (1930), *Histoire militaire de l'Indochine Francaise des débuts à nos jours* (2 vols). Hanoi/Haiphong: Imprimerie d'Extrême-Orient.

Aurillac, H. (1870), *Cochinchine. Annamites, Moïs, Cambodgiens*. Paris: Challamel.

Ayard, A. (1935), *L'Union Indochinoise Française ou Indochine orientale. Régions naturelles et géographie économique*. Hanoi: IDEO.

Aymonier, Étienne (1885), Notes sur l'Annam, *Excursions et Reconnaissances* 24: 199–340; 26: 179–218; 27: 5–29.

Aymonier, Étienne (1892), Une mission en Indo-Chine (relation sommaire), *Bulletin de la Société de Géographie de Paris* XIII: 216–49; 339–74.

Azémar, P. (1935, or. 1886), Les Stiengs de Bro'lam. In: Gouvernement de la Cochinchine, *Variétés sur les Pays Moïs*. Saigon: Gouvernement de la Cochinchine.

Balandier, Georges (1962), Les mythes politiques de colonisation et de decolonisation en Afrique, *Cahiers internationaux de sociologie* XXXIII: 85–96.

Ban nghiên cuu lich su Đang (1983), *Lich su Đang bô tinh Đak Lak, tap 1*, Buôn Ma Thuôt: Ban châp hành Đang bô tinh Đak Lak.

Bank, Colonel Aaron (1986), *From OSS to Green Berets: The Birth of the Special Forces*. Novato CA Presidio Press.

Barkun, M. (1974), *Disaster and the Millennium*. New Haven, CT: Yale University Press.

Barth, Fredrik (ed.) (1969), *Ethnic Groups and Boundaries: The Social Organization of Cultural Difference*. Boston: Little, Brown.

Barthélemy, Cte. de (1899), Au pays des Moïs, *Bulletin de la Société de Géographie de Paris* XX: 330–43.

Barthélemy, Cte. de (1901), Un voyage chez les Moïs-Stiengs vivant au pied de la Chaîne de Djambara, *Bulletin de la Société de Géographie Commerciale de Paris*: 28–37.

Barthélemy, Cte. de (1903), *Au pays Moï*. Paris: Plon-Nourrit.

Bastian, Adolf (1873), *Geographische und Ethnographische Bilder*. Jena: Hermann Costenoble.

Bastide, Roger (1971), *Anthropologie appliquée*. Paris: Payot.

Bateson, Gregory and Margaret Mead (1942), *Balinese Character. A Photographic Analysis*. New York: New York Academy of Sciences Press.

Baudenne (1913), Les Kha d'Attopeu, *Revue Indochinoise* XIX (1): 260–74.

Baudesson, Capt. H. (1919), *Indochina and its primitive people*. London: Hutchinson and Co.

Baudesson, Capt. H. (1932), *Au pays des superstitions et des rites. Chez les Moïs et les Chams*. Paris: Plon.

Benda, Harry (1958), *The Crescent and the Rising Sun: Indonesian Islam under Japanese Occupation 1942–1945*. The Hague/Bandung: W. van Hoeve.

Bendell, Don (1992), *The B–52 Overture: The North Vietnamese Assault on Special Forces Camp A–242, Dak Pek*. New York: Dell.

Berreman, Gerald D. (1991), Ethics versus 'Realism' in Anthropology. In: Carolyn Fluehr-Lobban (ed.), *Ethics and the Profession of Anthropology: Dialogue for a New Era*. Philadelphia: University of Pennsylvania Press, pp. 38–71.

Bertrand, G. (1952), *Le peuple de la jungle. Hommes, bêtes et legendes du pays Moï.* Paris: Editions Je Sers.

Besnard, H. (1907), Les populations Moï du Darlac, *BEFEO* VII: 61–86.

Bezacier, L. (1951), Interprétation du tatouage des Moï Ka-Tu. *BSEI* XXVI: 39–52.

Birou, A. (1961), Les sociétés primitives ou coutumières face à leur développement: les montagnards du Viêt-Nam Sud, *Revue Développement et Civilisation* 16: 52–64.

Bitard, P. (1951), Chasse magique chez les Khas, *Sud-Est Asiatique* 26: 25–32.

Bitard, P. (1952), Rites agraires des Kha Braou, *BSEI* XXVII: 9–17.

Bitterli, Urs (1976), *Die 'Wilden' und die 'Zivilisierten': Die europaeisch-ueberseeische Begegnung.* Munich: C.H. Beck.

Blaufarb, Douglas S. (1977), *The counterinsurgency Era: US Doctrine and Performance, 1950 to the Present.* New York: Free Press.

Blok, Anton (1977), *Antropologische perspectieven.* Muiderberg: Coutinho.

Blood, Evangeline (1968), *Henry Florentine Blood.* Santa Ana: Summer Institute of Linguistics.

Bochet, Gilbert (1951), *Eléments de conversation Franco-Koho. Us et coutumes des Montagnards de la Province du Haut-Donnaï,* Dalat: Service Géographique de l'Indochine.

Bodard, Lucien (1950), La révolte des Rhés, *Sud-Est Asiatique* 17: 16–33.

Bokelman, Ulrike (1976), Georges Devereux. In: Hans Peter Duerr (ed.), *Die wilde Seele: Zur Ethnopsychoanalyse von Georges Devereux.* Frankfurt 1987: Suhrkamp.

Bonifacy, Lt.-Col. (1919), *Cours d'Ethnographie Indochinoise, professé aux élèves de l'Ecole Supérieure d'Agriculture et de Sylviculture.* Hanoi/Haiphong: Impr. d'Extrême-Orient.

Bonifacy, Lt.-Col. (1925), *Roland Dorgelès et l'Indochine.* Hanoi: Ed. de la Revue Indochinoise.

Boon, James A. (1989), Lévi-Strauss, Wagner, Romanticism: A Reading-Back.... In: G.W. Stocking (ed.), *Romantic Motives. Essays on Anthropological Sensibility.* History of Anthropology vol. 6. Madison: University of Wisconsin Press.

Borri, Christoforo (1811, or. 1631), Cochin-China in Two Parts. In: John Pinkerton (ed.), *A General Collection of the Best and Most Interesting Voyages and Travels in All Parts of the World, Vol. IX.* London: Longman, Hurst et al.

Botreau-Roussel, Y. and B. Jouin (1943a), Un sacrifice au génie des éléphants à Bandon chez l'héritière de Kundjonob, *TIIEH* VII: 375–86.

Botreau-Roussel, Y. and B. Jouin (1943b), Les potières Bih de Buon Tur H'ma, *TIIEH* VII: 387–90.

Boucher de Crèvecoeur, Cap. Jean (1938), Au Pays Mnong: Les Biat du Haut-Chlong, *Revue des Troupes Coloniales* 249: 320–34.

Boudarel, Georges (1976), Sciences sociales et contre-insurrection au Vietnam. In: H. Moniot (ed.), *Le mal du voir.* Paris: Cahiers Jussieu, pp. 136–97.

Boudet, Paul (1942), Léopold Sabatier, apôtre des Rhadés, *Indochine* III (113): I–VII.

Bouillevaux, Abbé C.E. (1858), *Voyage dans l'Indochine, 1848–1856.* Paris: Victor Palmé.

Boulbet, Jean (1957), Quelques aspects du coutumier (N'dri) des Cau Maa, *BSEI* XXXII: 110–78.

Boulbet, Jean (1966) Le Miir, culture itinérante avec jachère forestière en pays Maa, *Bulletin de l'Ecole Française d'Extrême-Orient* LIII(1): 77–98.

Boulbet, Jean (1967), *Pays de Maa', domaine des génies (Nggar Maa', nggar yaang). Essai d'ethno-histoire d'une population proto-indochinoise du Viêt Nam central.* Paris: EFEO.

Bourotte, B. (1955), Essai d'histoire des populations montagnardes du Sud Indochinois jusqu'à 1945, *Bulletin de la Société des Etudes Indochinoises* XXX: 17–116.

Boyarin, Daniel, and Jonathan Boyarin (1989), Toward a Dialogue with Edward Said, *Critical Inquiry* 15: 626–33.

Brandewie, Ernest (1990), *When Giants Walked the Earth. The Life and Times of Wilhelm Schmidt SVD.* St. Augustin: Anthropos-Institut/Universitätsverlag Freiburg.

Breman, Jan (1987), *The Shattered Image: Construction and Deconstruction of the Village in Colonial Asia.* Amsterdam: Centre for Asian Studies Amsterdam.

Breman, Jan, Peter Kloos and Ahwani Saith, (eds) (1997), *The Village in Asia Revisited.* New Delhi: Oxford University Press.

Brend, Ruth M. and Kenneth L. Pike (eds) (1977), *The Summer Institute of Linguistics: Its Works and Contributions.* The Hague/Paris: Mouton.

Brenier, H. (1929), L'Indochine économique. In: Georges Maspéro (ed.), *L'Indochine, un empire colonial francais.* Paris/Brusells: Van Oest.

Brière, M. (1890), Notice sur les Moï du Binh Thuan et du Khanh Hoa, *Excursions et Reconnaissances* XIV (32): 235–54.

Brière, M. (1904), Culture et commerce de la cannelle, *Bulletin Economique d'Indochine* 6(33): 935–50.

Boeke, J.H. (1955), *Oosterse Economie: Een Inleiding.* Haarlem: Tjeenk Willink.

Brown, David (1994), *The State and Ethnic Politics in Southeast Asia.* London/New York: Routledge.

Brown, Richard (1973), Anthropology and Colonial Rule: The case of Godfrey Wilson and the Rhodes-Livingstone Institute, Northern Rhodesia. In: Talal Asad (ed.), *Anthropology and the Colonial Encounter.* London: Ithaca Press.

Brown, Richard (1979), Passages in the Life of a White Anthropologist: Max Gluckman in Northern Rhodesia, *Journal of African History* 20: 525–41.

Brunhès, Jean (1923), Chez les primitifs de l'Indochine central, *Journal de la Marine Marchande* 210–11.

Brunhès, Jean (1925), Observations sur les tribus à structure social de type matriarcale de l'Indochine, *L'Anthropologie* XXXV: 347–9.

Bùi Tin (1995), *From Cadre to Exile: The Memoirs of a North Vietnamese Journalist.* Chiang Mai: Silkworm Books (Or. *Following Ho Chi Minh* published by C. Hurst in London in the same year).

Burchett, Wilfred (1957), *Mekong Upstream*, Hanoi: Foreign Languages Publishing House.

Burchett, Wilfred (1963), *The Furtive War: The United States in Vietnam and Laos.* New York: International Publishers.

Burchett, Wilfred (1965), *Vietnam: Inside Story of the Guerrilla War.* New York: International Publishers.

Burchett, Wilfred (1966), *My Visit to the Liberated Zones of South Vietnam.* Hanoi: Foreign Languages Publishing House.

Burridge, Kenelm (1969), *New Heaven, New Earth: A Study of Millenarian Activities.* New York: Schrocken Books.

Buschmann, Klaus (1978), *United States Army Special Forces 1952–1974: Untersuchung im Licht der verfügbaren Literatur und Quellen.* Frankfurt/Main: Peter Lang.

Buttinger, Joseph (1958), *The Smaller Dragon: a Political History of Vietnam.* New York: Praeger.

Buttinger, Joseph (1961), The Ethnic Minorities in the Republic of Vietnam. In: W.R. Fishel (ed.), *Problems of Freedom: South Vietnam Since Independence.* Chicago: Free Press of Glencoe.

Buttinger, Joseph (1967), *Vietnam: A Dragon Embattled* (2 vols), London: Pall Mall Press.

Byrnes, Giselle M. (1994), 'The Imperfect Authority of the Eye': Shortland's southern journey and the calligraphy of colonization, *History and Anthropology* 8: 207–36.

Cabaton, Antoine (1905), Dix dialectes indochinois recueillis par Prosper Odend'hal, *Journal Asiatique* V: 265–344.

Cable, Larry E. (1986), *Conflict of Myths: The Development of American Counterinsurgency Doctrine and the Vietnam War*. New York/London: New York University Press.

Cadière, Léopold (1931), L'Annam, Partie II: Les Habitants, *BAVH* 18(1–2): 87–91.

Cadeire, Léopold (1940), Note sur les Moï du Quang-Tri, *TIIEH* III: 101–08.

Cady, J.F. (1954), *The Roots of French Imperialism in Eastern Asia*. Ithaca, NY: Cornell University Press.

Canivey, Jules (1913), Notice sur les moeurs et coutumes des Moïs de la région de Dalat, Plateau de Lang-Biang, province de Phan-Rang, *Revue d'Ethnographie et de Sociologie* IV (1–2): 1–30.

Cao Van Luong (1966), The Struggle of the National Minorities of Tay Nguyen, *Vietnamese Studies* No. 8 (South Vietnam 1954–65). Hanoi: Xunhasaba.

Cao Văn Luong, Phm Quang Toàn, Quynh Cú (1981), *Tìm hiêu phong tráo Đông khoi miên nam Viêt Nam*. Hanoi: NXB Khoa hoc xa hôi.

Carrau, P. (1935, or. 1884), Du commerce et de l'agriculture chez les Moïs. In: Gouvernement de la Cochinchine, *Variétés sur les Pays Moïs*. Saigon: Gouvernement de la Cochinchine.

Carte Ethnolinguistique (1951), Carte ethnolinguistique de l'EFEO. *BSEI* XXVI: 4.

Cassaigne, Mgr. J. (1930), *Petit manuel de conversation courante en langue moï (Koho et Chau Sore)*. Tândinh-Saigon: Imp. de la Mission.

Cassaigne, Mgr. J. (1952), Les montagnards de la région de Djiring, *France-Asie* 74/75: 352–9, 504–12.

Cell, John W. (1989), Lord Hailey and the Making of the African Survey, *African Affairs* 88: 481–505.

Céloron de Blainville, M. (1903), Les Moïs de la Région du Song Ba et du Darlac, *Revue de Géographie* LIII: 128–47; 229–53.

Chaffard, Georges (1969), *Les Deux Guerres du Vietnam. De Valluy à Westmoreland*. Paris: Ed. de la Table Ronde.

Chanda, Nayan (1986), *Brother Enemy. The War after the War: A History of Indochina since the Fall of Saigon*. San Diego/New York: Harcourt Brace Jovanovich.

Chatthip Nartsupha (1984), The Ideology of 'Holy Men' Revolts in North East Thailand. In: Andrew Turton and Shigeharu Tanabe (eds), *History and Peasant Consciousness in South East Asia*. Osaka: National Museum of Ethnology, Senri Ethnological Studies No. 13, pp. 111–134.

Chen Jian (1993), China and the First Indo-China War, 1950–1954, *China Quarterly* 133: 85–110.

Chen Jian (1995), China's Involvement in the Vietnam War, 1964–1969, *China Quarterly* 142: 357–87.

Chesneaux, Jean (1955), *Contribution à l'histoire de la nation vietnamienne*. Paris: Editions Sociales.

Chomsky, Noam (1967), *American Power and the New Mandarins*. New York: Random House.

Chomsky, Noam (1969), *At War with Asia: Essays on Indochina*. New York: Random House.

Chomsky, Noam (1973), *The Backroom Boys*. Bungay: Fontana.

Chomsky, Noam, and E. Herman (1979), *After the cataclysm: Postwar Indochina and the Reconstruction of Imperial Ideology*. Montreal: Black Rose Books.

Christie, Clive J. (1996), *A Modern History of Southeast Asia: Decolonization, nationalism and separatism*. London/New York: Tauris Academic Studies.

Claeys, J. (1939), A propos des Moï chasseurs de sang, *Cahiers de l'Ecole Française d'Extrême-Orient* 18: 10–19.

Clammer, John (1973), Colonialism and the Perception of Tradition. In: T. Asad (ed.), *Anthropology and the Colonial Encounter*. London: Ithaca Press.

Clarke, Jeffrey J. (1988), *Advice and Support: The Final Years, 1965–1973*. Washington, DC: Center of Military History.

Clifford, Sir Hugh (1926), *In Days that Are Dead*. London: John Murray.

Clifford, James (1982), *Person and Myth. Maurice Leenhardt in the Melanesian World*. Berkeley: University of California Press.

Clifford, James (1983a), On Ethnographic Authority, *Representations* 2: 118–46.

Clifford, James (1983b), Power and Dialogue in Ethnography: Marcel Griaule's Initiation. In: G. Stocking (ed.), *Observers Observed. Essays on Ethnographic Fieldwork.* (History of Anthropology Vol. 1). Madison: University of Wisconsin Press, pp. 121–156.

Clifford, James (1985), On Ethnographic Self-Fashioning: Conrad and Malinowski. In: T. Heller, D. Wellburg, M. Sosna (eds), *Reconstructing Individualism*. Stanford, CA: Stanford University Press, pp. 140–162.

Clifford, James (1986), Introduction: Partial Truths. In: J. Clifford and G. Marcus (eds) *Writing Culture. The Poetics and Politics of Ethnography*. Berkeley: University of California Press.

Clifford, James, and George Marcus (eds) (1986), *Writing Culture: The Poetics and Politics of Ethnography*. Berkeley: University of California Press.

Coedès, George (1948), *Les Etats Hindouisés d'Indochine et d'Indonésie*. Paris: E. de Boccard.

Coedès, George (1966), *The Making of South-East Asia*. London: Routledge and Kegan Paul.

Cohn, Norman (1970, or. 1957), *The Pursuit of the Millennium*. London: Granada.

Colby, William (1978), *Honorable Men: My Life in the CIA* (with Peter Forbath). New York: Simon and Schuster.

Colby, William (1989), *Lost Victory: A Firsthand Account of America's Sixteen-Year Involvement in Vietnam* (with James McCargar). Chicago/New York: Contemporary Books.

Combes, P. (1855), Missions du Laos, *Annales* 27: 405–37.

Commandant, Le (1940), Les tirailleurs du Sud-Annam, *Indochine* I: 12.

Condominas, Georges (1951), Aspects of a minority problem in Indochina, *Pacific Affairs* 24.

Condominas, Georges (1952a), Rapport d'une mission ethnologique en pays Mnong Gar (PMSI), *Bulletin de l'Ecole Française d'Extrême-Orient* XLVI: 303–13.

Condominas, Georges (1952b), Enquête linguistique parmi les populations montagnardes du Sud-Indochinois, *Bulletin de l'Ecole Française d'Extrême-Orient* XLVI: 573–98.

Condominas, Georges (1953), Ethnologie de l'Indochine et bibliographie ethnographique. In: André Leroi-Gourhan and Jean Poirier (eds), *Ethnologie de l'Union Française* (2 vols). Paris: Presses Universitaires de France.

Condominas, Georges (1955), Observations sociologiques sur deux chants épiques Rhadés, *Bulletin de l'Ecole Française d'Extrême-Orient* XLVII: 555–68.

Condominas, Georges (1957), *Nous avons mangé la forêt de la Pierre-Génie Gôo (Hii saa Brii Mau-Yaang Gôo). Chronique de Sar Luk, village mnong gar (tribu proto-indochinoise, des Hauts-Plateaux du Vietnam central)*. Paris: Mercure de France.

Condominas, Georges (1965), *L'exotique est quotidien*. Paris: Plon.

Condominas, Georges (1966), Classes sociales et groupes tribaux au Sud-Viêtnam, *Cahiers Internationaux de Sociologie* XL: 161–70.

Condominas, Georges (1972), De la Rizière au Miir. In: J.M.C. Thomas and Lucien Bernot (eds), *Langues et techniques, nature et société*, vol. 2. Paris: Klincksieck.

Condominas, Georges (1973), Ethics and Comfort: An Ethnographer's View of His Profession (Distinguished Lecture, 1972). *Annual Report, American Anthropological Association*. Washington, DC: American Anthropological Association.

Condominas, Georges (1974), L'entre-aide agricole chez les Mnong Gar (Proto-Indochinois du Vietnam central), *Études Rurales* 53–6: 407–20.

Condominas, Georges (1977), Preface to the English-Language Edition. In: *We Have Eaten to the Forest: The Story of a Montagnard Village in the Highlands of Vietnam*. New York: Hill and Wang.

Condominas, Georges (1979), Notes on the present state of anthropology in the Third World. In: G. Huizer and B. Mannheim (eds), *The Politics of Anthropology*. Paris: Mouton.

Condominas, Georges (1980), *L'espace social à propos de l'Asie du Sud-Est*. Paris: Flammarion.

Condominas, Georges, ed. (1998), *Formes Extrêmes de Dépendance: Contributions à l'étude de l'esclavage en Asie du Sud-Est*. Paris: Éditions EHESS.

Condominas, L. (1951), Notes sur les Moïs du haut Sông Tranh (1934–'47), *BSEI* XXVI: 101–06.

Cooper, Chester (1970), *The Lost Crusade: America in Vietnam*. New York: Dodd, Mead and Co.

Copans, Jean (1975), *Anthropologie et impérialisme*. Paris: Maspéro.

Copans, Jean and Jean Jamin (1978), *Aux origines de l'anthropologie française: Les Mémoires de la Société des Observateurs de l'Homme en l'an VIII*. Paris: Ed. du Sycomore.

Cosserat, H. (1926), La route de Hué à Tourane dite 'route des montagnes' et le tracé Debay, *BAVH* 13: 308–11.

Costello, Nancy (1972), Socially approved homicide among the Katu, *Southeast Asia* 2–1: 77–81.

Cottes, Capt. A. (1905), Moïs ou Khas de la partie méridionale de la Chaîne d'Annam. *Revue Coloniale* 22: 193–204.

Crapanzano, Vincent (1986), Hermes' Dilemma: The Masking of Subversion in Ethnographic Description. In: J. Clifford and G. Marcus (eds) *Writing Culture. The Poetics and Politics of Ethnography*. Berkeley: University of California Press.

Crawfurd, John (1967, or. 1823), *Journal of an Embassy to the Courts of Siam and Cochin China*. With an introduction by David K. Wyatt. Kuala Lumpur: Oxford University Press.

Cuénot, Mgr. (1841), Lettre, *Annales* 13: 139–45.

Cuisinier, Jeanne (1927), Au Darlac: Institutions et état social, *Bulletin de l'Association française des Amis de l'Orient* 10 (NS): 1–10.

Cupet, Capt. P. (1893), Chez les populations sauvages du Sud de l'Annam, *Tour du Monde* 12–16: 177–256.

Currey, Cecil B. (1988), *Edward Lansdale: The Unquiet American*. Boston: Houghton Mifflin.

Curtin, Philip D. (1964), *The Image of Africa. British Ideas and Action, 1780–1850*. (2 vols) Madison: University of Wisconsin Press.

Cuu-Long-Giang and Toàn Ánh (1974), *Miên thuong Cao nguyên*. Saigon: Viêt Nam Chí Luoc.

Dam Bo [Ps. Jacques Dournes] (1950), Les Populations Montagnardes du Sud-Indochinois, *France-Asie* 49–50. (special issue).

Đang Nghiêm Van (1989) *Tây Nguyên trên duòng phát triên* [The Western Highlands on the road of development]. Hanoi: NXB Khoa hoc Xa hôi.

Đang Nghiêm Van (1993), *Quan hê giua các tôc nguòi trong môt quôc gia dân tôc* [The relations between ethnic groups in one nation state]. Hanoi: NXB Chính tri quôc gia.

Đang Nghiêm Van (1998), *Ethnological and Religious Problems in Vietnam*. Hanoi: Social Sciences Publishing House.

Đang Nghiêm Van, Chu Thái Son, Luu Hùng (1993), *Ethnic Minorities in Vietnam*. Hanoi: Gioi Publishers.

Đang Nghiêm Van et. al. (1981), *Các dân tôc tinh Gia Lai-Công Tum* [Ethnic groups of Gialai-Kontum province]. Hanoi: NXB Khoa hoc xa hôi.

Darnell, Regna (1971), The professionalization of American anthropology: A case study in the sociology of knowledge, *Social Science Information* 10/2: 83–103.

Darnell, Regna (1982), The Role of History of Anthropology in the Anthropology Curriculum, *Journal of the History of the Behavioral Sciences* 18: 265–70.

Dassé, Martial (1976), *Montagnards, Révoltes et Guerres Révolutionnaires en Asie du Sud-Est Continentale*. Bangkok: DK Bookhouse.

Daufès, E. (1933–34), *La garde indigène de l'Indochine, de sa création à nos jours, t. II: Annam*. Avignon.

Dauplay, J.-J. (1929), *Les terres rouges du plateau des Boloven*, Saigon: Impr. Commerciale C. Ardin.

Davenport, William (1985), The Thailand Controversy in Retrospect. In: June Helm (ed.), *The Social Contexts of American Ethnology, 1840–1984*. Washington, DC: American Ethnological Society, pp. 65–72.

De Bekalowicz, I. (1906), Notes sur les deux peuples de Darlac (Laos) les Radés et les Khas Pi, *Revue Coloniale* XII: 129–41, 225–45.

De Grandmaison, Capt. L. (1898), *L'Expansion Française au Tonkin. En territoire militaire*. Paris: Plon Nourrit.

De Hautecloque-Howe, Anne (1985), *Les Rhadés: une société de droit maternel*. Paris: Editions du CNRS.

De Koninck, Rodolphe (1996), *Le Défi Forestier au Vietnam: L'articulation des impéritifs et des contingences*. Sainte-Foy (Québec): Université Laval.

De Lanessan, J. L. (1895), *La colonisation française en Indochine*. Paris: Alcan.

De Lanessan, J. L. (1897), *Principes de colonisation*. Paris: Alcan.

De Lanessan, J. L. (1907), *Les missions et leur protectorat*. Paris: Alcan.

De Malglaive, Capt. M. de (1893), Six mois au pays des Kha (sauvages de l'Indochine Centrale), *Tour du Monde* 25: 385–400.

De Montaigut, F. (1929), *La colonisation française dans l'Est de la Cochinchine*. Limoges: Perrette.

De Reinach, L. (1901), *Le Laos* (2 vols). Paris: A. Charles.

De Sola Pool, Ithiel (1963), *Social Science Research and National Security*. Washington, DC: Smithsonian Institution, under Office of Naval Research contract 1354(18).

Decoux, Amiral (1950), *A la barre de l'Indochine*. Paris: Plon.

Deitchman, Seymour J. (1976), *The Best-Laid Schemes: A Tale of Social Research and Bureaucracy*. Cambridge, MA: MIT Press.

Deitchman, Seymour J. (1978), Another Step Toward Nirvana [Response to Murray Wax' Review of *The Best-Laid Schemes*], *Human Organization* 37(4): 408–11.

Descours-Gatin, Ch. and H. Villiers (1983). *Guide de recherches sur le Vietnam. Bibliographies, archives et bibliothèques de France*. Paris: L'Harmattan.

Devalle, S. (1985), Clandestine culture of protest in colonial situations, *Canberra Anthropology* 8 (1/2): 32–57.

Devereux, Georges (1937), Functioning Units in Ha(rh)ndea(ng) Society, *Primitive Man* X (1): 1–7.

Devereux, Georges (1947), Potential Contribution of the Moï to the Cultural Landscape of Indochina, *Far Eastern Quarterly* 6(4): 390–5.

Devereux, Georges (1967), *From Anxiety to Method in the Behavioral Sciences*, The Hague/Paris: Mouton.

Devillers, Philippe (1952), *Histoire du Viêt-Nam de 1940 à 1952*. Paris: Ed. du Seuil.

Diamond, Stanley (1974), End Games of Empire? Reply to Leach, *New York Review of Books* 17–10–1974: 37–8.

Diamond, Stanley (ed.) (1980), *Anthropology: Ancestors and Heirs*. The Hague: Mouton.

Dirks, Nicholas (1992), Castes of Mind, *Representations* 37: 56–78.

Dirks, Nicholas (1995), Reading Culture: Anthropology and the Textualization of India. In: E. Valentine Daniel (ed.), *Culture/Contexture: Explorations in Anthropology and Literary Studies*. Berkeley: University of California Press.

Donoghue, John (1963), The Rhade of South Vietnam: A preliminary report, *Current Anthropology* 4(4): 382–4.

Donoghue, John, Daniel Whitney and Iawo Ishino (1962), *People in the Middle: The Rhade of South Viet Nam*. East Lansing: Michigan State University.

Donzelot, J. (1979, or. 1977), *The Policing of Families*. New York: Pantheon Books.

Dooley, Thomas A. (1958), *The Edge of Tomorrow*. New York: Farrar, Straus and Cudahy.

Dorgelès, Roland (1925), *Sur la route mandarine*. Paris: Albin Michel.

Dorgelès, Roland (1930), *Chez les beautés aux dents limées*. Paris: Martinet.

Dorgelès, Roland (1933), 'Twentieth Century Savages.' The Moïs of Indochina suddenly assaulted by white man's civilization, *Extrême-Asie* 78: 317–25.

Dorgelès, Roland (1944), *Routes des Tropiques*. Paris: Albin Michel.

Dourisboure, Abbé P. (1873), *Les sauvages Ba-Hnars (Cochinchine Orientale). Souvenirs d'un missionnaire*. Paris: Tequi/Les Missions Etrangères.

Dourisboure, P. and C. Simmonet (1961), *La mission des Grands Plateaux*. Paris: Editions France-Empire.

Dournes, Jacques (1948a), Structure sociale des montagnards du Haut-Donnai. Tribu des riziculteurs, *BSEI* XXIV–2: 101–6.

Dournes, Jacques (1948b), Chants antiques de la montagne, *BSEI* XXIV–3: 9–111.

Dournes, Jacques (1949), L'âme et les songes. Etude Moï pour servir à la philosophie des primitifs, *France-Asie*, 55: 1107–23.

Dournes, Jacques (1950), *Dictionnaire Sre (Koho)-Francais*. Saigon: Imprimerie d'Extrême-Orient.

Dournes, Jacques (1951), Nri (Coutumier Srê; extraits), *France-Asie* 60: 1232–41.

Dournes, Jacques (1952), Le chant et l'écriture, *France-Asie* 73: 229–34.

Dournes, Jacques (1954), Fêtes saisonnières des Srê, *BEFEO* XLVI: 599–609.

Dournes, Jacques (1955), *En suivant la piste des hommes sur les Hauts-Plateaux du Viêt-Nam*. Paris: Julliard.

Dournes, Jacques (1962), Les racines d'un art missionnaire, *Art Sacré* 1–2 (Sept.–Oct.).

Dournes, Jacques (1963), *Dieu aime les paiens. Une mission de l'église sur les plateaux du Viet-Nam*. Paris: Ed. Montaigne.

Dournes, Jacques (1965), *Le Père m'a envoyé. Réflexions à partir d'une situation missionnaire*. Paris: Les Editions du Cerf.

Dournes, Jacques (1967), *L'Offrande des Peuples. Recherches et remarques sur le binome activité – action liturgique*. Paris: Les Editions du Cerf.

Dournes, Jacques (1969), *Au plus près du loin. Projet pour la Mission*. Paris: Ed. Montaigne.

Dournes, Jacques (1970), Recherches sur le Haut-Champa, *France-Asie* 24 (2): 143–62.

Dournes, Jacques (1972), *Coordonnées: Structures Jörai familiales et sociales*. Paris: Institut d'Ethnologie.

Dournes, Jacques (1975), Les marches sauvages: Chez les minorités ethniques du Sud-Indochinois, *Les Temps Modernes*: 1552–82.

Dournes, Jacques (1977) *Pötao: Une théorie du pouvoir chez les Indochinois Jörai*. Paris: Flammarion.

Dournes, Jacques (1978a), Sam Bam, le Mage et le Blanc dans l'Indochine centrale des années trente, *L'Ethnographie* 76/1: 85–108.

Dournes, Jacques (1978b), The history of the natives of central Vietnam. In: G. Michaud (ed.), *Identités collectives et relations interculturelles*. Brussels: Editions Complexe.

Dournes, Jacques (1980), *Minorities of Central Vietnam: Autochthonous Indochinese Peoples*. London: Minority Rights Group, Report No. 18 (revised edition).

Dournes, Jacques (1988), The Spirit of Laws: A first presentation of data on the 'customary laws' of the Indochinese Jorai people, *Contributions to Southeast Asian Ethnography* 7: 7–25.

Dowdy, Homer E. (1964), *The Bamboo Cross: Christian Witness in the Jungles of Viet Nam*. New York, Evanston, London: Harper and Row.

Dô-Xuân-Hop (1943), Nouvelle étude des crânes moï, *TIIEH* VI: 31–2.

Dubourg, M. (1950), Une tentative de colonisation en pays Moï: la mission A. Gautier, 1881–1883, *Revue d'Histoire des Colonies* XXXVII: 101–38.

Duclos and M.P. Miche (1844), Lettres de MM. Duclos (et Miche) à Mgr. Cuenot, datées des prisons de Hué les 29 et 23 mai 1842, *Annales* 16: 89–105.

Duerr, Hans Peter, ed. (1987), *Die wilde Seele: Zur Ethnopsychoanalyse von Georges Devereux*, Frankfurt: Suhrkamp.

Duncan, Donald (1967), *The New Legions*. London: Victor Gollancz.

Durand, E. (1907), Les moy du Son-Phong, *Revue Indochinoise* VI: 1055–68; 1158–71.

École Française d'Extrême-Orient (1949), *Carte ethnolinguistique de l'Indochine*. Hanoi: Service Géographique de l'Indochine.

Ellen, Roy F. (1976), The Development of Anthropology and Colonial Policy in the Netherlands, *Journal of the History of the Behavioral Sciences* 12(4): 303–24.

Emerson, Gloria (1978), *Winners and Losers: Battles, Retreats, Gains, Losses and Ruins from the Vietnam War*. New York/London: Harcourt Brace Jovanovich.

Engels, Friedrich (1972, or. 1894), *The Origin of the Family, Private Property and the State*. New York: International Publishers.

Enjolras, F. (1932). Reconnaissance de la région de Moï Xe et du tracé de la route coloniale 14 entre Tân-an et Dac Main, *BAVH* 19: 411–41.

Enjoy, Paul d' (1895), Une incursion chez les Moï, *Bulletin de la Societe de Geographie de Paris* XVI: 267–76.

Enloe, Cynthia H. (1980), *Ethnic Soldiers: State Security in Divided Societies*. Harmondsworth: Penguin Books.

Evans, Grant (1985), Vietnamese Communist Anthropology, *Canberra Anthropology* 8(1–2), 116–47.

Evans, Grant (1992), Internal Colonialism in the Central Highlands of Vietnam, *Sojourn* 7(2): 274–304.

Evans, Grant (1999), Apprentice Ethnographers: Vietnam and the Study of Lao Minorities. In: Grant Evans (ed.), *Laos: Culture and Society*. Chiang Mai: Silkworm Books, pp. 161–90.

Evans, Grant and Kelvin Rowley (1984), *Red Brotherhood at War: Indochina since the Fall of Saigon*. London: Verso.

Evans-Pritchard, Edward E. (1981), *A History of Anthropological Thought*. London: Faber and Faber.

Ezzaoui, J. (1940), Une version de la légende des deux Sadets (le roi de l'eau et le roi du feu), *TIIEH* III: 169–74.

Fabian, Johannes (1981), Six Theses Regarding the Anthropology of African Religious Movements, *Religion* 11: 109–26.

Fabian, Johannes (1983), *Time and the Other: How Anthropology Makes Its Object*. New York: Columbia University Press.

Fabian, Johannes (1990), Presence and Representation: the Other and Anthropological Writing, *Critical Inquiry* 16: 753–72.

Fabian, Johannes (1991), Dilemmas of Critical Anthropology. In: Lorraine Nencel and
Peter Pels (eds), *Constructing Knowledge: Authority and Critique in Social Science*. London: Sage.

Fall, Bernard (1959), Commentary on Wickert. In: Richard Lindholm (ed.), *Viet-Nam: The
First Five Years*. East Lansing: Michigan State University Press, pp. 135–40.

Fall, Bernard (1962), Problèmes politiques des états poly-ethniques en Indochine, *France-
Asie* 172: 129–52.

Fall, Bernard (1963a), *The Two Viet-Nams: A Political and Military Analysis*. New York:
Praeger.

Fall, Bernard (1963b), *Street Without Joy: Insurgency in Indochina, 1946–1963*, London: Pall
Mall Press.

Fall, Bernard (1966), *Viet-Nam Witness 1953–1966*. New York: Praeger.

Fall, Bernard, (ed.) (1967), *Ho Chi Minh on Revolutions: Selected Writings 1920–1966*, New
York: New American Library.

Fardon, Richard, (ed.) (1990), *Localizing Strategies. Regional Traditions of Ethnographic Writing*.
Edinburgh: Scottish Academic Press.

Fasseur, Cees (1993), *De Indologen. Ambtenaren voor de Oost 1825–1950*. [The Indologists. Civil
Servants for the Orient 1825–1950]. Amsterdam: Bert Bakker.

Fenton, James (1985), The Fall of Saigon, *Granta* 15: 27–116.

Fernandez, Caporal-chef (1949), L'odyssée d'un caporal-chef dans la jungle montagneuse
du Centre Viêt-Nam, après le 9 mars 1945, *Sud-Est* 2: 45–7.

Finot, L. (1928), A propos des Moï à queue, *BAVH* 15–4: 217–21.

Firth, Raymond (1977), Whose Frame of Reference? One Anthropologist's Experience,
Anthropological Forum 4: 145–67.

Fischer, Hans (1970), 'Völkerkunde', 'Ethnographie', 'Ethnologie'. Kritische Kontrolle der
frühesten Belege, *Zeitschrift für Ethnologie* 65/2: 169–82.

Fishel, Wesley E. (ed.) (1961), *Problems of Freedom: South Vietnam since Independence*. New York:
Free Press of Glencoe.

Fisher, James T. (1997), *Dr. America: The Lives of Thomas A. Dooley, 1927–1961*. Amherst:
University of Massachusetts Press.

Fluehr-Lobban, Carolyn (1991, 1991a), Ethics and Professionalism: A Review of Issues
and Principles within Anthropology. In: Carolyn Fluehr-Lobban (ed.), *Ethics and the
Profession of Anthropology: Dialogue for a New Era*. Philadelphia: University of Pennsylvania
Press, pp. 13–35.

Fluehr-Lobban, Carolyn (ed.) (1991, 1991b), *Ethics and the Profession of Anthropology: Dialogue
for a New Era*. Philadelphia: University of Pennsylvania Press.

Forest, Alain (1980), *Le Cambodge et la colonisation française: Histoire d'une colonisation sans heurts
(1898–1920)*. Paris: L'Harmattan.

Forest, Alain (1981), Les manifestations de 1916 au Cambodge. In Pierre Brocheux (ed.),
Histoire de l'Asie du Sud-Est. Révolte, Réformes, Révolution. Lille: Presses Universitaire de
Lille.

Forster, Peter G. (1973), A Review of the New Left Critique of Social Anthropology, in
T. Asad (ed.) *Anthropology and the Colonial Encounter*. London: Ithaca Press.

Forster, Peter G. (1989), *T. Cullen Young: Missionary and Anthropologist*. Hull: Hull University
Press.

Forster, Peter G. (1991), Cullen Young, Yesaya Chibambo and the Ngoni, *Society of Malawi
Journal* 4/1: 34–61.

Forster, Peter G. (1994), Politics, Ethnography and the 'Invention of Tradition': The case
of T. Cullen Young of Givingstonia mission, Malawi, *History and Anthropology* 8 (1–4):
299–320.

Fortes, Meyer (1974), Social Anthropology at Cambridge since 1900. In: R. Darnell (ed.) *Readings in the History of Anthropology*. New York: Harper and Row (first published 1953).

Fortes, Meyer, and Edward Evans-Pritchard (1940), Introduction. In: M. Fortes and E. Evans-Pritchard (eds), *African Political Systems*. London: Oxford University Press.

Foucault, Michel (1969), *L'Archéologie du Savoir*. Paris: Gallimard.

Foucault, Michel (1970), *The Order of Things. An Archeology of the Human Sciences*. New York: Vintage Books (orig. French 1966).

Foucault, Michel (1972), In: M. Foucault, *The Archeology of Knowledge and The Discourse on Language*. New York: Harper and Row (orig. French 'L'ordre du discours', 1971).

Foucault, Michel (1979a), *Discipline and Punish. The Birth of the Prison*. New York: Vintage Books (orig. French, 1975).

Foucault, Michel (1979b) Governmentality, *Ideology and Consciousness* no. 6: 5–21.

Fournier, C. (1949), *Prok, fils du prisonnier moï. Récit documentaire sur les sauvages d'Indochine*. Lausanne: Ed. Novos.

Fox, Robin (1967), *Kinship and marriage*. Harmondsworth: Penguin Books.

Fraisse, A. (1951), Les villages du Plateau des Boloven, *BSEI* XXVI: 53–72.

Frazer, Sir James (1913), *The Golden Bough*, Part I: *The Magic Art and the Evolution of Kings*, vol. 2. London: Macmillan and Co.

Frazer, Sir James (1923) *The Golden Bough*, Part III: *The Dying God*. London: MacMillan and Co.

Funé, Jean (1961), Resettlement – Opportunities and Problems, *Jungle Frontiers* 13: 2–3.

Furuta, Motoo (1991) *Revolution and Ethnicity: The Historical Process of the Vietnamese Communist Search for a New Vietnamese Identity in Connection with Other Ethnic Groups in Indo-China*. Tokyo (abstract of Japanese publication).

Gagelin, M. (1832), Mission de Conchinchine. Lettre de M. Gagelin, missionnaire apostolique, à M. (12 mars 1829), *Annales de la Propagation de la Foi* XXVII: 356–86.

Gaide, Dr. L. (1928), Les hommes à queue, *BAVH* 15–2: 102–24.

Galliéni, J. (1941, or. 1913), *Galliéni au Tonkin (1892–1896), par lui-meme*. Paris: Berger-Levrault.

Galtung, Johan (1967), Scientific Colonialism: The lessons of Project Camelot, *Transition* 6/30: 11–15.

Garnier, Francis (1873), *Voyage d'Exploration en Indochine effectué pendant les années 1866, 1867 et 1868, par une Commission Française présidée par M. Le Capitaine de Frégate Doudart de Lagrée ... et publié par les Ordres du Ministre de la Marine sous la Direction de M. Le Lieutenant de Vaisseau Francis Garnier. Avec le Concours de M. Delaporte, Lieutenant de Vaisseau, et de MM. Joubert et Thorel, Médecins de la Marine, Membres de la Commission*. Paris: Hachette (2 vols.)

Gautier, Amédée (1882), Exploration de M.A. Gautier au Nord de la Cochinchine. Extraits de des lettres, *Bulletin de la Société Académique Indochinoise* II: 411–25.

Gautier, Amédée (1884), Les Moï, *Bulletin de la Société de Géographie de Rochefort* VI(2): 139–49.

Gautier, Amédée (1902–03), Etude sur les Moïs, *Bulletin de la Société de Géographie Commerciale du Havre* 1902–03: 95–109; 95–109; 172–82; 234–48; 305–17; 371–79; 428–40.

Gautier, Amédée (1935, or. 1882), Voyage au Pays des Moïs accompli par A. Gautier, Lieutenant de l'Infanterie de Marine. In: Gouvernement de la Cochinchine, *Variétés sur les Pays Moïs*. Saigon: Gouvernement de la Cochinchine.

Gayet, Georges (1949), Evolution récente des P.M.S.I., *Revue Éducation* 16: 69–82.

Gayet, Georges (ed.) (1949), *Revue Éducation* 16 (Numéro spécial consacré aux Populations Montagnardes de Sud-Indochinois). Saigon: Rectorat d'Académie.

Gendzier, Irene (1985), *Managing Political Change: Social Scientists and the Third World*. Boulder, CO/London: Westview Press.

Gerber, Théophile (1951), Coutumier stieng, *Bulletin de l'Ecole Française d'Extrême-Orient* XLV/1: 227–71.

Gerber, Théophile and Louis Malleret (1946), Quelques légendes des Moï de Cochinchine, *BSEI* XXI: 61–5.

Gettleman, Marvin E. (1989), Against Cartesianism: Preliminary Notes on Three Generations of English-Language Political Discourse on Vietnam. *Bulletin of Concerned Asian Scholars* 21(2–4): 136–43.

Giap, General Vo Nguyen (1962), *People's War, People's Army: The Viet Công's Insurrection Manual for Underdeveloped Countries* (Foreword by Roger Hilsman; Profile of Giap by Bernard Fall). New York et: Praeger.

Giap, General Vo Nguyen (1970), *Banner of People's War, the Party's Military Line* (Preface by Jean Lacouture; Introduction by Georges Boudarel). London: Pall Mall Press.

Gluckman, Max (1974), Report from the Field. Letter to the Editors, *New York Review of Books* 28 November 1974: 43–4.

Goddard, David (1972), Anthropology: The Limits of Functionalism. In: R. Blackburn (ed.), *Ideology in Social Science: Readings in Critical Social Theory*. London: Fontana Books.

Gomane, Jean-Pierre (1976), Les minorités ethniques en Asie du Sud-Est continentale, vues par quelques voyageurs occidentaux, *ASEMI* VII–4: 113–24.

Goodman, Allan E. (1968), *Government and the Countryside: Political Accommodation and South Vietnam's Communal Groups*. Santa Monica, CA: RAND Corporation, P-3924 (September 1968).

Gordon, Deborah (1990), The Politics of Ethnographic Authority: Race and writing in the ethnography of Margaret Mead and Zora Neal Hurston. In: M. Manganaro (ed.), *Modernist Anthropology. From Fieldwork to Text*. Princeton, NJ: Princeton University Press.

Goscha, Christopher (1996), Annam and Vietnam in the New Indochinese Space, 1887–1945. In: Hans Antlöv and Stein Tønnesson (eds), *Asian Forms of the Nation*. London: Curzon Press, pp. 93–130.

Gregerson, Marilyn (1972), Ethnic Minorities of Vietnam, *Southeast Asia* II(1): 11–17.

Gregerson, Marilyn (ed.) (1972), *Southeast Asia* II(1), special issue on ethnic minorities in Vietnam.

Gregerson, Marilyn and Dorothy Thomas (eds) (1980), *Notes from Indochina on Ethnic Minority Cultures*. Dallas, TX: SIL Museum of Anthropology.

Griffin, Robert J. (1989), Ideology and Misrepresentation: A Response to Edward Said, *Critical Inquiry* 15: 611–25.

Groslier, B.P. (1952a), La carte ethnolinguistique de P. Bitard, *BSEI* XXII: 4–7.

Groslier, B.P. (1952b), Commentaire de Gilbert Bochet, Eléments de conversation Franco-Koho, *BSEI* XXVII: 234–5.

Groslier, B.P. (1952c), Histoire et ethnologie en Indochine, *BSEI* XXVII: 333–42.

Grossheim, Martin (1995), Village Laws (huong uoc) as a source for Vietnamese studies. In: Philippe le Failler and Jean Marie Mancini (eds), *Việt Nam: Sources et Approches*. Aix-en-Provence: Publications de l'Université de Provence.

Grossheim, Martin (1997), *Nordvietnamesische Dorfgemeinschaften: Kontinuität und Wandel*. Hamburg: Institut fuer Asienkunde.

Guénot, M. et Mme. Jules (1917), Aux confins de l'Indochine: Chez les Moï, *Bulletin de la Société de Géographie de Toulouse*: 95–132.

Guerlach, Jean (1884), Chez les sauvages Bahnars. Journal de voyage de M. Guerlach, *Les Missions Catholiques* 16: 22–466, passim.

Guerlach, Jean (1887a), Moeurs et superstitions Bahnars, *Les Missions Catholiques* 19: 441–527.

Guerlach, Jean (1887b), Deux ans de captivité chez les Bah-nars, *Les Missions Catholiques* 19: 538–89.

Guerlach, Jean (1905), Quelques notes sur les Sadet, *Revue Indochinoise* IV (15 February): 184–8.

Guerlach, Jean (1906), *L'oeuvre néfaste*. Saigon: Imprimerie Commerciale.

Guignard, Th. (1911), Note sur une peuplade des montagnes du Quang-binh, les Tac-cui, *BEFEO* XI: 201–05.

Guilleminet, Paul (1940), *Lexique francais-bahnar et bahnar-francais*. Hanoi: Taupin.

Guilleminet, Paul (1941a), Recherches sur les croyances des tribus du Haut-Pays d'Annam, les Bahnar du Kontum et leur voisins, les magiciens, *TIIEH* IV: 9–36.

Guilleminet, Paul (1941b), La fête moï chez les Bahnar, *CEFEO* 29: 9–10.

Guilleminet, Paul (1941c), La notion de beauté du corps humain chez les Bahnars du Kontum, *TIIEH* IV: 251–6.

Guilleminet, Paul (1942a), La chasse chez les Bahnar, *CEFEO* 33: 16.

Guilleminet, Paul (1942b), Recherches ethnologiques in pays moï: But, résultats, difficultés, *CEFEO* 33: 21.

Guilleminet, Paul (1942c), Le sacrifice du buffle chez les Bahnar de la province de Kontum, la fête, *BAVH* 29: 214–18.

Guilleminet, Paul (1943a), L'économie des tribus moï de l'Indochine (contribution à la connaissance de l'économie des peuples attardés), *Revue Indochinoise Juridique et Économique* 31/1: 69–124.

Guilleminet, Paul (1943b), Genres de vie chez les Moï, *CEFEO* 35: 30–1.

Guilleminet, Paul (1943c), La mort et l'enterrement chez les Bahnar du Kontum, *CEFEO* 37: 17–18.

Guilleminet, Paul (1943d), Note sur les amas d'objets à sens religieux dans le Haut-Pays moï, *TIIEH* VI: 261–4.

Guilleminet, Paul (1943e), Note sur le culte du chien et des animaux chez les Moï de Kontum, *TIIEH* VI: 369–72.

Guilleminet, Paul (1943f), Ebauche d'une classification des Moïs au point de vue de culture, *Indochine* 169: 21–5.

Guilleminet, Paul (1951a), Remarques suggérées par des rapprochements entre l'article du Capitaine Maurice relatif à trois fêtes agraires rhadé et celui du R. P. Kemlin sur les rites agraires des Reungao, *BEFEO* XLV: 209–12.

Guilleminet, Paul (1951b), L'aspect du temps et les météores dans une tribu du Kontum, *BEFEO* XLV: 213–21.

Guilleminet, Paul (1952a), *Coutumier de la Tribu Bahnar, des Sedang at des Jarai de la Province de Kontum*. Hanoi: Ecole Française d'Extrême-Orient.

Guilleminet, Paul (1952b), La tribu Bahnar du Kontum. Contribution à l'étude de la société montagnarde du Sud-Indochinois, *Bulletin de l'Ecole Française d'Extrême-Orient* XLV: 393–561.

Gunn, Geoffrey (1985), A Scandal in Colonial Laos: The Death of Bac My and the Wounding of Kommadan Revisited, *Journal of the Siam Society* 73: 42–59.

Gunn, Geoffrey (1987), Minority Manipulation in Colonial Indochina: Lessons and Legacies, *Bulletin of Concerned Asian Scholars* 19(3): 20–8.

Gunn, Geoffrey (1988a), *Political Struggles in Laos (1930–1954): Vietnamese Communist Power and the Lao Struggle for National Independence*, Bangkok: Editions Duang Kamol.

Gunn, Geoffrey (1988b), Sambran (The White Python): The Kha (Lao Theung) Revolt of 1936–39, *Sojourn* 3/2: 207–16.

Gunn, Geoffrey (1990), *Rebellion in Laos: Peasant and Politics in a Colonial Backwater*. Boulder, CO/San Francisco/Oxford: Westview Press.

Haddon, Alfred C. (1910), *History of Anthropology* (The Thinker's Library, No. 42). London: Watts and Co.

Haguet, H. (1905), Notice ethnique sur les moïs de la région de Quang-Ngaï *Revue Indochinoise* 4(2): 1419–26.

Halberstadt, Hans (1988), *Green Berets: Unconventional Warriors*. Novato: Presidio Press.

Halberstam, David (1964), *The Making of a Quagmire: America and Vietnam During the Kennedy Era*. New York: Random House.

Halberstam, David (1969), *The Best and the Brightest*. New York: Random House.

Hammer, Ellen (1955), *The Struggle for Indochina 1940–1955: Viet Nam and the French Experience*. Stanford, CA: Stanford University Press.

Hammersley, Martyn, and Paul Atkinson (1983), *Ethnography: Principles in Practice*. London and New York: Tavistock.

Hanson, Allan (1989), The Making of the Maori: Culture invention and its logic, *American Anthropologist* 91: 890–902.

Hardy, Georges (1925), Histoire coloniale et psychologie ethnique, *Revue de l'Histoire des Colonies Francaises* 50–2: 161–72.

Hardy, Georges (1951), A travers les revues qui nous parlent de l'Asie, *Revue de Psychologie des Peuples* 3: 289–303.

Harmand, Jules (1876), Voyage au Cambodge, *Bulletin de la Société de Géographie* XII: 337–67.

Harmand, Jules (1877a), Les îles de Poulo-Condor, le Haut Don-Nai et ses habitants, *Bulletin de la Societé de Géographie* XIII: 523–34.

Harmand, Jules (1877b), Notes sur les provinces du bassin méridional du Se Moun (Laos et Cambodge siamois). Excursion de Bassac à Attopeu, *Bulletin de la Societé de Géographie* XIV: 225–47.

Harmand, Jules (1879a), De Bassac à Hué (avril-août 1877), *Bulletin de la Societé de Géographie* XVII(1): 75–104.

Harmand, Jules (1879b), Le Laos et les populations sauvages de l'Indochine, *Le Tour du Monde* XXXVIII: 1–48.

Harmand, Jules (1879c), Rapport sur une mission en Indo-Chine, de Bassac à Hué (16 avril – 14 août 1877), *Archives des Missions Scientifiques et Littéraires* 5: 247–81.

Harmand, Jules (1882), Les races de Indo-Chinoises, par le docteur Harmand, *Mémoires de la Société d'Anthropologie*: 314–68.

Harmand, Jules (1912), De l'état de l'ethnographie indochinoise, *Revue d'Ethnographie et de Sociologie* 1–2: 60–72.

Harris, George et al. (1962), *US Army Area Handbook for Vietnam*. Washington, DC: Department of the Army, Pamphlet No. 550–40.

Harris, Marvin (1968), *The Rise of Anthropological Theory. A History of Theories of Culture*. New York: Random House, Vintage Books.

Hart, Laurie (1973), Story of the Wycliffe Translators: Pacifying the Last Frontiers, *NACLA's Latin America and Empire Report* VII(10): 15–31.

Harverson, Stuart (1968), *Doctor in Vietnam*. London: Lutterworth Press.

Hatcher, Patrick Lloyd (1990), *The Suicide of an Elite: American Internationalists and Vietnam*. Stanford, CA: Stanford University Press.

Heberle, Rudolf and Joseph Gusfield (1968), Social Movements: Types and Functions. In: David Sills (ed.), *International Encyclopedia of the Social Sciences*, Vol. 14, pp. 438–52. London/New York: MacMillan and Free Press.

Hefley, James and Marti (1969), *No Time for Tombstones: Life and Death in the Vietnamese Jungle*. Wheaton, IL: Tyndale House.

Hempstone, Smith (1966), *A Tract of Time*. Greenwich, CT: Fawcett Crest.

Herskovits, Melville J., (ed.) (1973), *Cultural Relativism: Perspectives in Cultural Pluralism*. New York: Random House, Vintage Books.

Hickey, Gerald C. (1957), *Preliminary Research Report on the High Plateau (PMS)*. Saigon: Michigan State University Vietnam Advisory Group.

Hickey, Gerald C. (1958), Problems of Social Change in Viet-Nam, *BSEI* XXXIII(4): 407–18.

Hickey, Gerald C. (1964a), *Village in Vietnam*. New Haven, CT: Yale University Press.

Hickey, Gerald C. (1964b), *The Major Ethnic Groups of the South Vietnamese Highlands*. Santa Monica, CA: Rand Corporation, Memorandum RM-4041-ARPA.

Hickey, Gerald C. (1965), *The American Military Advisor and his Foreign Counterpart: The Case of Vietnam* (with the assistance of W.P. Davison). Santa Monica, CA: RAND Corporation, Memorandum RM-4482-ARPA, March 1965.

Hickey, Gerald C. (1967a), Some Aspects of Hill Tribe Life in South Vietnam. In: Peter Kunstadter (ed.), *Southeast Asian Tribes, Minorities and Nations*, 2 vols Princeton, NJ: Princeton University Press, pp. 745–70.

Hickey, Gerald C. (1967b), *The Highland People of South Vietnam: Social and Economic Development*. Santa Monica, CA: RAND Corporation, Memorandum RM-5281/1.

Hickey, Gerald C. (1967c), *Accommodation in South Vietnam: The Key to Sociopolitical Solidarity*. Santa Monica, CA: RAND Corporation, P-3707, October 1967.

Hickey, Gerald C. (1970), *Accommodation and Coalition in South Vietnam*. Santa Monica: RAND Corporation, P-4213, January 1970.

Hickey, Gerald C. (1971), *Some Recommendations Affecting the Prospective Role of Vietnamese Highlanders in Economic Development*. Santa Monica, CA: RAND Corporation, September 1971.

Hickey, Gerald C. (1982a), *Sons of the Mountains: Ethnohistory of the Vietnamese Central Highlands to 1954*. New Haven, CT/London: Yale University Press.

Hickey, Gerald C. (1982b), *Free in the Forest: Ethnohistory of the Vietnamese Central Highlands, 1954–1976*. New Haven, CT/London: Yale University Press.

Hickey, Gerald C. (1988), *Kingdom in the Morning Mist: Mayréna in the Highlands of Vietnam*. Philadelphia: University of Pennsylvania Press.

Hickey, Gerald C. (1993), *Shattered World: Adaptation and Survival among Vietnam's Highland People during the Vietnam War*. Philadelphia: University of Pennsylvania Press.

Hill, Ron (1985) 'Primitives' to 'Peasants': The 'sedentarisation of the nomads' in Vietnam, *Pacific Viewpoint* 26(2): 448–59.

Hilsman, Roger (1967), *To Move a Nation: The Politics of Foreign Policy in the Administration of John F. Kennedy*. Garden City, NY: Doubleday.

Hirschkind, Charles (1991), 'Egypt at the Exhibition': Reflections on the Optics of Colonialism, *Critique of Anthropology* 11: 279–98.

Hô Lê (1984), Môt sô y kiên vê nên văn hóa mói và con nguòi Tây Nguyên trong chăng duòng Đâù tiên cua thòi kỳ quá đô [Some ideas on the new culture and personality in the Central Highlands in the first stage of the transitional period], *Tap Chí Dân Tôc Hoc* 4–1984: 61–5.

Hoàng Lê (1990), Đê thuc hiên Đinh canh Đinh cu Đông bào dân tôc và tiêp nhân lao Đông dân cu mói o Gia Lai – Kon Tum [To realize the fixed cultivation and settlement among the ethnic groups and receive a new worker population in Gialai-Kontum], in: *Chính sách dân tôc: Nhung vân Đê Lý luân và thuc tiên* [Ethnic policy: Theoretical and practical problems]. Hanoi: NXB Su Thât, pp. 145–53.

Hoang Van Thai, General (1996), *How South Vietnam Was Liberated (Memoirs)*. Hanoi: Thê Giói Publishers (2nd edition).

Hoàng Xuân Tý and Lê Trong Cúc (eds) (1998), *Kiến thúc Ban Địa cua Đồng bào Vùng cao trong Nông nghiêp và Quan lý Tài nguyên Thiên Niên* [Indigenous knowledge of highland compatriots in agriculture and natural resource management]. Hanoi: NXB Nông Nghiêp.

Hobsbawm, Eric and Terence Ranger (eds) (1983), *The Invention of Tradition*. Cambridge: Cambridge University Press.

Hoebel, E. Adamson (1960), William Robertson: An 18th Century Anthropologist-Historian, *American Anthropologist* 62: 648–55.

Hoffet, J. (1933), Les Moïs de la Chaîne annamitique entre Tourane et les Boloven, *Terre, Air, Mer, la Géographie* LIX: 1–43.

Honda, Katsuichi (1972), *Vietnam War: A Report through Asian Eyes*. Tokyo: Mirai-Sha.

Honigmann, J.J. (1976), *The Development of Anthropological Ideas*. Homewood, IL.: Dorsey Press.

Horowitz, Irving L. (ed.) (1967), *The Rise and Fall of Project Camelot: Studies in the Relationship between Social Science and Practical Politics*. Cambridge, MA.: MIT Press.

Horowitz, Irving L. (ed.) (1971), *The Use and Abuse of Social Science*. New Brunswick: Transaction Books.

Hostetter, Doug (1973), Religious Agencies in Viet-Nam: An insider's story, *NACLA's Latin America and Empire Report* VII(10): 3–14, 31.

Huard, Cap. Paul (1937), Les croyances des Mnôngs du plateau central indochinois, *Revue des Troupes Coloniales* XXXI: 242–85.

Huard, Cap. Paul (1947), Raciologie de l'Indochine Française, *BSEI* XXII: 123–32.

Huard, Paul and Albert-Marie Maurice (1939), Les Mnong du Plateau central indochinois, *Travaux de l'Institut Indochinoise de l'Etude de l'Homme* II: 27–148.

Huizer. Gerrit (1975), The a-social role of social scientists in underdeveloped countries. In: P. Kloos and H. Claessen (eds), *Current Anthropology in the Netherlands*. The Hague: NSAV/Ministerie van Onderwijs en Wetenschappen.

Huizer, Gerrit and Bruce Mannheim (eds) (1979), *The Politics of Anthropology*. Paris: Mouton.

Humann, R. (1935, or. 1884), Excursion chez les Moïs indépendants. In: *Variétés sur les Pays Moï.* Saigon: Gouvernement de la Cochinchine.

Humann, R. (1892), Exploration chez les Moïs (Indo-Chine) (1888–1889), *Bulletin de la Société de Géographie de Paris* XIII: 496–514.

Huntington, Samuel P. (1968), The Bases of Accomodation, *Foreign Affairs* 46 (July 1968): 642–56.

Hvalkov, Søren and Peter Aaby (eds) (1981), *Is God an American? An Anthropological Perspective on the Missionary Work of the Summer Institute of Linguistics*. Copenhagen/London: IGWIA/SI.

Hymes, Dell (1972), *Reinventing Anthropology*. New York: Random House.

Iliffe, John (1979), *A Modern History of Tanganyika*. Cambridge: Cambridge University Press.

Iouleff, G. and G. Bornet (1956), *Sous les cases moïs*. Paris: Plon.

Izikowitz, Karl G. (1951), *Lamet: hill peasants in French Indochina*. Goteborg: Etnografiska Museet, Etnografiska Studier 17.

Jackson, Larry (1969), The Vietnamese Revolution and the Montagnards, *Asian Survey* 9(3): 313–30.

Jamieson, Neil, Le Trong Cuc and A. Terry Rambo (1998), *The Development Crisis in Vietnam's Mountains*. Honolulu: East-West Center Special Reports No. 6.

Jarvie, I.C. (1964), *The Revolution in Anthropology*. London: Routledge and Kegan Paul.

Jaspan, Mervyn A. (1969), *Recent Developments among the Cham of Indochina: The Revival of Champa*. Hull: Publications of the Centre for South-East Asian Studies, University of Hull.

Johnson, Douglas H. (1979), Colonial Policy and Prophets. The 'Nuer Settlement', 1920–1930, *Journal of the Anthropological Society of Oxford* 10: 1–20.

Johnson, Douglas H. (1982), Evans-Pritchard, the Nuer, and the Sudan Political Service, *African Affairs* 81: 231–46.

Joiner, Charles (1965), Administration and Political Warfare in the Highlands, *Vietnam Perspectives* 1(2): 19–37.

Joiner, Charles (1974), *The Politics of Massacre: Political Processes in South Vietnam*. Philadelphia, PA: Temple University Press.

Jouin, Bernard (1949) *La mort et la tombe, l'abandon de la tombe*. Paris: Institut d'Ethnologie.

Jouin, Bernard (1950a), Les traditions des Rhadés. *BSEI* XXV–3: 365–374.

Jouin, Bernard (1950b), Enquête démographique au Darlac, 1943–44. *BSEI* XXV–3.

Jouin, Bernard (1951), (1) Légende du Sadet du Feu. (2) Rituel prophylactique des Rhadés K'drao. (3) Deux contes Rhadé, *BSEI* XXVI: 73–109.

Kahn, Herman et al. (1968), *Can We Win in Vietnam? The American Dilemma*. London: Pall Mall Press.

Karnow, Stanley (1983), *Vietnam: A History*. New York: Viking Press.

Kelly, Col. Francis (1973), *US Army Special Forces, 1961–1971*. Washington, DC: Dept. of the Army.

Kemlin, J. (1909a, b), Rites agraires des Reungao, *Bulletin de l'Ecole Française d'Extrême-Orient* IX: 493–522; X: 131–58.

Kemlin, J. (1910), Les songes et leur interprétation chez les Reungao *Bulletin de l'Ecole Française d'Extrême-Orient* X: 507–538.

Kemlin, J. (1917), Alliances chez les Reungao, *Bulletin de l'Ecole Française d'Extrême-Orient* XVII: 1–119.

Kemlin, J. (1922), *L'immigration annamite en pays moy, en particulier dans la province de Kontum*. Quinhon: Impr. de Quinhon.

Kemp, Jeremy (1987), *Seductive Mirage: The Search for the Village Community in Southeast Asia*. Amsterdam: Centre for Asian Studies Amsterdam.

Keyes, Charles (1976), Towards a New Formulation of the Concept of Ethnic Group, *Ethnicity* 3: 202–213.

Keyes, Charles (1977), Millennialism, Thervada Buddhism and Thai Society, *Journal of Asian Studies* 36/2: 283–302.

Keyes, Charles (1997), Cultural Diversity and National Identity in Thailand. In: Michael Brown and Sumit Ganguky (eds), *Government Policies and Ethnic Relations in Asia and the Pacific*. Cambridge, MA: The MIT Press.

Kirk-Greene, H.M. Anthony (ed.) (1965), *The Principles of Native Administration in Nigeria. Selected Documents, 1900–1947*. London: Oxford University Press.

Kirsch, A. Thomas (1973), *Feasting and Social Oscillation: Religion and Society in Upland Southeast Asia*. Ithaca, NY: Cornell University Southeast Asia Program.

Klare, Michael (1972), *War Without End: American Planning for the Next Vietnams*. New York: Vintage Books.

Kleinen, John (1996), Ethnographic Praxis and the Colonial State in Vietnam. In: Philippe Le Failler and Jean Marie Mancini (eds), *Viêt Nam, Sources et Approches: Actes du colloque international EUROVIET, Aix-en-Provence 3–5 mai 1995*. Aix-en-Provence: Publications de l'Université de Provence, pp. 15–48.

Kleinen, John (1997), The Village as Pretext: Ethnographic Praxis and the Colonial State in Vietnam. In: Jan Breman, Peter Kloos and Ashwani Saith (eds), *The Village in Asia Revisited*. New Delhi: Oxford University Press, pp. 353–93.

Kloos, Peter (1984a), De crisis in de westerse antropologie, *Antropologische Verkenningen* 3–1: 1–31.

Kloos, Peter (1989), The sociology of Non-Western Societies: The Origins of a Discipline, *The Netherlands Journal of Social Sciences* 25(1): 40–50.

Kloos, Peter (ed.) (1983), *De rol van onderzoekers in situaties van open conflict in de Derde Wereld*. Leiden: Institute of Cultural and Social Studies, Working Paper 41.

Kloos, Peter (ed.) (1984b), *Onderzoekers onderzocht. Ethische dilemma's in antropologisch veldwerk*. Leiden: SAS/DSWO Press.

Kolko, Gabriel (1985), *Anatomy of a War: Vietnam, the United States and the Modern Historical Experience*. New York: Pantheon Books.

Komer, Robert W. (1986), *Bureaucracy at War: US Performance in the Vietnam Conflict*. Boulder, CO: Westview Press.

Kuhn, Thomas (1970), *The Structure of Scientific Revolutions*. Chicago: University of Chicago Press, 2nd edn (first published 1962).

Kunstadter, Peter (1967), Vietnam: Introduction. In: Kunstadter, Peter (ed.), *Southeast Asian Tribes, Minorities and Nations*, 2 vols Princeton, NJ: Princeton University Press, pp. 677–702.

Kunstadter, Peter (ed.) (1967), *Southeast Asian Tribes, Minorities and Nations*, 2 vols Princeton, NJ: Princeton University Press.

Kuper, Adam (1983), *Anthropology and Anthropologists: The Modern British School*. London: Routledge and Kegan Paul.

La Văn Lô (1973), *Buóc Đâu tìm hiêu các dân tôc thiêu sô Viêt-Nam trong su nghiêp dung nuóc và giũ nuóc*, Hanoi: NXB Khoa hoc xã hôi.

Laborde, A. (1929), La province du Phu-Yên, *BAVH* 16: 199–254.

Lackner, Helen (1973), Colonial Administration and Social Anthropology: Eastern Nigeria 1920–40. In: T. Asad (ed.), *Anthropology and the Colonial Encounter*. London: Ithaca Press, pp. 123–51.

Ladejinsky, Wolf (1961), Agrarian Reform in the Republic of Vietnam, 1961. In: Wesley E. Fishel (ed.), *Problems of Freedom: South Vietnam since Independence*. New York: Free Press of Glencoe, pp. 153–75.

Ladejinsky, Wolf (1977), *Agrarian Reform as Unfinished Business: The selected papers of Wolf Ladejinsky* (edited by Louis J. Walinsky). Oxford: Oxford University Press.

Laffey, J. (1969), Les racines de l'impérialisme français en Extrême-Orient, *Revue d'Histoire Moderne et Contemporaine* 16: 282–99.

Lafont, Pierre-Bernard (1959), The 'slash-and-burn' (Ray) agriculture system of the mountain populations of Central Vietnam, *Proceedings of the Ninth Pacific Science Congress of the Pacific Science Association*. Bangkok.

Lafont, Pierre-Bernard (1960), *Les recherches ethnologiques au Centre Vietnam*. Paris: Fondation Singer-Polignac.

Lafont, Pierre-Bernard (1963), *Toloi Djuat: Coutumier de la tribu Jarai*, Paris: Publications de l'EFEO.

Lafont, Pierre-Bernard (1967) L'agriculture sur brûlis chez les Proto-Indochinois des hauts-plateaux du Centre Viet-Nam, *Cahiers d'Outre-Mer* XX: 37–48.

Lamarche, J. (1950), Croquis Montagnards, *Sud-Est* III: 29–30.

Laird, Melvin R. (1972), *The Nixon-Doctrine. A Town-Hall Meeting on National Security Policy*. Washington, DC: American Enterprise Institute for Public Policy Research.

Lajoux, Jean-Dominique (1977). *Le tambour du déluge. Villages des montagnes d'Indochine*. Paris: Ed. du Seuil.

Lamb, Helen (1972), *Vietnam's Will to Live: Resistance to Foreign Aggression from Early Times through the Nineteenth Century*. New York/London: Monthly Review Press.

Landes, A. (1904), Légende djarai sur l'origine du sabre sacré par le Roi du Feu, *Revue Indochinoise* III: 345–52.

Lansdale, Edward (1972), *In the Midst of Wars: An American's Mission to Southeast Asia*. New York: Harper and Row.

Laubie, Y. (1939), Tablettes divinitoires d'une peuplade Kha, *TIIEH* II: 221–30.

Launay, Adrien (1894), *Histoire Générale de la Société des Missions-Etrangères* (3 vols). Paris: Téqui.

Laurent, Cdt. (1928), Une reconnaissance de la route des montagnes entre Sông-Cu-Đê et Rivière de Hué, *BAVH* 15: 265–81.

Lavallée, A. (1901), Notes ethnographiques sur diverses tribus du Sud-Est de l'Indochine (Boloven, Naheun, Alak, Lave, Kaseng, Halang), *BEFEO* I: 291–311.

Lê, Nicole-Dominique (1975), *Les Missions Etrangerès et la pénétration française au Viêt-Nam*. Paris/La Haye: Mouton.

Le Jariel, Raymond (1942), Comment la mission catholique a servi la France à pays Moï, *BAVH* 29: 37–53.

Le Pichon, J. (1938), Les chasseurs de sang, *BAVH* 25: 357–404.

Lê Thành Khôi (1969[2], or. 1955), *3000 Jahre Vietnam: Schicksal und Kultur eines Landes*, München: Kindler. (Or. In French: *Le Vietnam, histoire et civilisation*).

Lê Thành Khôi (1981), *Histoire du Viet Nam des origines à 1858*. Paris: Sudestasie.

Lê-Tiêu-Phu-Su' (1905, or. 1871), Phu mán tap luc, la pacification de la région des Moï, *Revue Indochinoise* II: 455–796, passim.

Leach, Edmund (1925a), Les Moïs du Centre Indochinois. L'Indochine seconde, *Revue Indochinoise* XLII–XLIII: 37–58.

Leach, Edmund (1925b), Roland Dorgelès chez les Moïs, *Revue Indochinoise* XXVIII (7–8): 61–72.

Leach, Edmund (1954), *Political Systems of Highland Burma: A study of Kachin social structure*. Cambridge, MA: Harvard University Press.

Leach, Edmund (1974), Anthropology Upside Down. Review of Hymes 1974, *New York Review of Books* 4 April 1974: 33–5.

Leaf, Murray J. (1979), *Man, Mind and Science. A History of Anthropology*. New York: Columbia University Press.

LeBar, Frank, Gerald Hickey and John Musgrave (1964), *Ethnic Groups of Southeast Asia*. New Haven, CT: Human Relations Area Files Press.

Lechesne, Paul (1924), *L'Indochine seconde, régions moïs*. Quinhon: Imprimerie de Quinhon.

Leclerc, Gérard (1972), *Anthropologie et colonialisme. Essai sur l'histoire de l'Africanisme*. Paris: Fayard.

Leclerc, Gérard (1989), *L'Observation de l'Homme: Une histoire des enquêtes sociales*. Paris: Ed. du Seuil.

Leclère, A. (1904), Légende Djaray sur l'origine du sabre sacré par le roi du feu, *Revue Indochinoise* II: 366–9.

Leger, Daniel (1977), De quelques considérations d'un bahnarisant sur les minorités ethniques de la péninsule indochinoise. *ASEMI* VIII–1: 59–76.

Leger, Daniel (1978), A propos des missionnaires de Kontum, 'dupes et complices' dans l'affaire Mayréna en 1888, *ASEMI* IX–1/2: 231–47.

Leger, Daniel (1998), L'esclavage en pays bahnar-lao (Centre Vietnam). In: Condominas, Georges (ed.) (1998), *Formes Extrêmes de Dépendance: Contributions à l'étude de l'esclavage en Asie du Sud-Est*. Paris: Éditions EHESS, pp. 101–63.

Leiris, Michel (1950), L'Ethnographe devant le colonialisme, *Les Temps Modernes* 6/58: 357–74.

Lemaire, Anton (1976), *Over de waarde van kulturen*. Baarn: Ambo.

Lerat, Mary-Paule (1987), Jacques Dournes: ethnologue, missionnaire, colonisateur? *Sudestasie* 48–49: 67–71.

Leroi-Gourhan, André and Jean Poirier (eds) (1953), *Ethnologie de l'Union Française* (2 vols). Paris: Presses Universitaires de France.

Lester, Robert F. (ed.) (1982), *CIA Research Reports: Vietnam and Southeast Asia 1946–1976*. Frederick, MD: University Publications of America Microfilm Project.

Lester, Robert F. (ed.) (1987), *CIA Research Reports: Vietnam and Southeast Asia, Supplements*. Frederick MD: University Publications of America Microfilm Project.

Lévi-Strauss, C. (1958), *Anthropologie Structurale*. Paris: Plon.

Lévi-Strauss, Claude (1960), Méthode et conditions de la recherche ethnologique en Asie, In: *Actes du VIe Congrès Internationales des Sciences anthropologiques et ethnologiques*. Paris: Lahure.

Lévy-Bruhl, Lucien (1910), *Les fonctions mentales dans les sociétés inférieures*. Paris: Felix Alcan.

Lévy-Bruhl, Lucien (1922), *La mentalité primitive*. Paris: Felix Alcan.

Lewis, Diane (1973), Anthropology and Colonialism, *Current Anthropology* 14: 581–91.

Lewis, Martin D. (1962), One Hundred Million Frenchmen: The assimilation theory in French colonial policy, *Comparative Studies in Society and History* IV(2): 129–53.

Lewis, Norman (1951), *A Dragon Apparent: Travels in Indo-China*, London: Jonathan Cape.

Lieurade, L. (1941), Trois campagnes d'assistance mobile dans les pays Moïs du Centre Annam (province de Kontum) (1935–1938), *Médicine Tropicale*-1: 77–91.

Lieurade, L. (1945), Un des aspects peu connus de l'Indochine: les pays Moïs, *Revue d'Alger* II–8: 273–90.

Lieurade, L. (1952), Généralités sur les P.M.S.I., *BSEI* XXVI: 5–12.

Lindholm, Richard (ed.) (1959), *Viet-Nam, The First Five Years: An International Symposium*. East Lansing: Michigan State University.

Lin Hua (1994), *Chiang Kai-Shek, De Gaulle contre Hô Chi Minh: Viêt-nam 1945–1946*. Paris: L'Harmattan.

Lin Hua (1995), The Chinese Occupation of Northern Vietnam, 1945–1946: A Reappraisal. In: Hans Antlöv and Stein Tønnesson (eds), *Imperial Policy and Southeast Asian Nationalism 1930–1957*. London: Curzon Press.

Loizos, Peter (1977), Personal Evidence: Comments on an Acrimonious Debate, *Anthropological Forum* 4: 137–44.

Loureira, João (1790), *De nigris Moi et Champanensibus*. Lisbon.

Lowie, Robert H. (1937), *The History of Ethnological Theory*. London: George G. Harrap and Co.

M.C. (1923), Pénétration et organisation de l'Hinterland Moï, *La Revue du Pacifique* 5: 548–64.

Mac Đuòng (1977), Chu nghĩa thuc dân mói cua My đôi vói vân đê dân tôc ít nguòi o Miên Nam nuóc ta [American neocolonialism with regards to the ethnic minorities problem in the South of our country], *Tap chí Dân tôc hoc* 2: 50–71.

Mac Đuòng (1978), Chu nghĩa thuc dân mói cua My và các dân tôc thiêu sô o Miên Nam nuóc ta [American neocolonialism and the ethnic minorities problem in the South of our country], *Công san* 2, 1978: 89–96.

Mac Đuòng (1993) The Issue of Nationalities in Southern Vietnam in the Process of Socialist Revolution, *Vietnam Social Sciences* 3(37): 3–10.

Mac Đuòng (ed.) (1983), *Vân Đề dân tôc o Lâm Đông* [The ethnic problem in Lam Dong]. Đà Lat: So Văn Hóa Tinh.

Macey, Paul (1907), Études ethnographiques sur les Khas, *Revue Indochinoise* V: 240–1424, passim.

Mai Ly Quang (ed.) (1994), The Intangible Cultural Heritage of Minority Ethnic Groups in Southeast Asia, *Vietnamese Studies* 112 (1994).

Maitre, Henri (1909), *Les Régions Moï du Sud-Indochinois: Le Plateau du Darlac*. Paris: Plon-Nourrit.

Maitre, Henri (1912a), *Les Jungles Moï: Mission Henri Maitre (1909–1911), Indochine Sud-Centrale*. Paris: Larose.

Maitre, Henri (1912b), Les populations de l'Indochine (Conférence Broca), *Mémoires de la Société d'Anthropologie de Paris* 6-III: 107–15.

Malinowski, Bronislaw (1922), *Argonauts of the Western Pacific. An Account of Native Enterprise and Adventure in the Archipelagoes of Melanesian New Guinea*. London: George Routledge and Sons.

Malinowski, Bronislaw (1929), Practical Anthropology, *Africa* 2: 22–38.

Malleret, Louis and Georges Taboulet (1937), *Groupes ethniques de l'Indochine française*. Saigon: Société des Etudes Indochinoises.

Malraux, André (1930), *La voie royale*. Paris: Grasset.

Malraux, André (1947), *Antimémoires*. Paris: Gallimard.

Mangham, Grady (1959), The Call, the Command, the Conquest. *Jungle Frontiers* 9: 1.

Maquet, J.-J. (1962), Le conditionnement de l'anthropologie culturelle. In: *VIᵉ Congrès International des Sciences Anthropologiques et Ethnologiques*, vol. 2. Paris: Musée de l'Homme.

Marchand, Géneral Jean (1951a), *Dans le jungle 'Moï'*. Paris: Peyronnet.

Marchand, Géneral Jean (1951b), Combats sur la chaîne annamitique, *Revue des Troupes Coloniales* 329: 4–7.

Marchetti, Victor and John D. Marks (1974), *The CIA and the Cult of Intelligence*. New York: Alfred Knopf.

Marcus, George and Michael Fischer (1986), *Anthropology as Cultural Critique: An Experimental Moment in the Human Sciences*. Chicago: University of Chicago Press.

Marlière, Michel (1978), L'eau lustrale dans les cérémonies propriatoires du Bouddhisme theravadin, *L'Ethnographie* 76/1: 77–84.

Marquet, Jean (1927), Un aventurier du XIXᵉ siècle: Marie Iᵉʳ, Roi des Sédangs (1888–1890), *BAVH* XIV (1–2): 9–130.

Marr, David (1971), *Vietnamese Anticolonialism, 1885–1925*. Berkeley/London: University of California Press.

Marr, David (1981), *Vietnamese Tradition on Trial, 1920–1945*. Berkeley/London: University of California Press.

Marr, David (1995), *Vietnam 1945: The Quest for Power*. Berkeley: University of California Press.

Marshall, Brig. Gen. S.L.A. (1967), *Battles in the Monsoon: Campaigning in the Central Highlands, South Vietnam, Summer 1966*. New York: William Morrow and Co.

Maspéro, Georges (1914), *Le Royaume de Champa*. Leiden: Brill.

Maspéro, Henri (1929), Moeurs et coutumes des populations sauvages. In: Georges Maspéro (ed.), *L'Indochine, un empire colonial français*. Paris/Brussels: G. van Oest.

Massu, Jacques (1974), *7 ans avec Lecerc*. Paris: Plon.

Massu, Jacques and J.J. Fronde (1980), *L'aventure Viêt-Minh*. Paris: Plon.

Matgioi ([prend. Albert de Pouvourville] (1897), *L'Affaire de Siam, 1886–1896 (études coloniales)*. Paris: Chamuel.

Matras-Troubetzkoy, Jacqueline (1983) *Un village en forêt. L'essartage chez les Brou du Cambodge*. Paris: SELAF.

Maurice, Albert-Marie (1941a), A propos des mutilations dentaires chez les Moï, *TIIEH* IV: 135–40.

Maurice, Albert-Marie (1941b), Rudiments de l'anthropologie des Mnongs du Lac (Mnong Rlam), *TIIEH* IV: 225–6.

Maurice, Albert-Marie (1947), Croquis rhadé, *Revue de Troupes Coloniales* 292.

Maurice, Albert-Marie (1951), Trois fêtes agraires rhadé, *Bulletin de l'Ecole Française d'Extrême-Orient* XLV: 158–207.

Maurice, Albert-Marie (1956), *La société rhadé*. Algiers: Centre des Hautes Etudes d'Administration Musulmane.

Maurice, Albert-Marie (1993), *Les Mnong des Hauts-Plateaux (Centre-Vietnam)*. Paris: L'Harmattan (2 vols).

Maurice, Albert-Marie and Georges Proux (1954), L'âme du riz, *Bulletin de la Société des Etudes Indochinoises* XXIX: 129–258.

Mauss, Marcel (1900), *Carnet 'Instruction pour les collaborateurs de l'Ecole Française d'Extrême-Orient'*. Saigon: Imprimerie Ménard et Legros.

Mauss, Marcel (1902), Essai d'une instruction pour l'étude sociologique des sociétés indochinoises. In: *Premier Congrès International des Etudes sur l'Extrême-Orient*. Hanoi: Schneider.

Mauss, Marcel (1967, or. 1947), *Manuel d'Ethnographie*. Paris: Payot.

Mauss, Marcel and Col. Bonifacy (1903), *Questionnaire de l'Ecole Franaise d'Extrême-Orient*. (Composé par M. Mauss et expliqué par le Colonel Bonifacy). Hanoi: Imprimerie d'Extrême-Orient.

Mazrui, Ali (1972), *Cultural engineering and nation-building in East Africa*. Evanston, (IL): NorthWestern University Press.

McAlister, John T. (1967), Mountain Minorities and the Viet Minh: A Key to the Indochina War. In: Peter Kunstadter (ed.), *Southeast Asian Tribes, Minorities and Nations*, 2 vols Princeton, NJ: Princeton U.P., pp. 771–844.

McCoy, Alfred W. (1972), *The Politics of Heroin in Southeast Asia* (with Cathleen B. Read and Leonard P. Adams II). New York: Harper and Row.

McGehee, Ralph (1983), *Deadly Deceits: My 25 Years in the CIA*. New York: Sheridan Square Press.

McLeod, Mark W. (1999), Indigenous Peoples and the Vietnamese Revolution, 1930–1975, *Journal of World History* 10(2): 353–89.

McNamara, Robert S. (1995), *In Retrospect: The Tragedy and Lessons of Vietnam*. New York: Times Books.

McNeill, Ian (1982), Petersen and the Montagnards: An Episode in the Vietnam War. *Journal of the Australian War Memorial*, October 1982: 33–46.

Mensbrugghe, A. van der (1949), *De Moï's: het natuurvolk van den Opper-Donnaï in Vietnam*. Leuven/Brugge: Bibliotheca Alfonsiana/De Kinkhoren.

Meyer, Charles (1965), Les mystérieuses relations entre le Roi du Cambodge et les Pötao des Jarai, *Etudes Cambodgiennes* 4: 14–26.

Meyer, Charles (1966), Kambuja et Kirata. *Etudes cambodgiennes* 5: 17–33.

Meijl, Toon van (1990), *Political Paradoxes and Timeless Traditions. Ideology and Development among the Tainui Maori, New Zealand*. Nijmegen: Centre for Pacific Studies.

Michel, Pierre (1951), Les Djarais et la Tradition, *France-Asie* 59: 1097–102.

Michel, Pierre (1952), Commentaire de Nri, coutumier Srê, de Jacques Dournes, *France-Asie* 68: 765–6.

Miles, D. and C. Eipper (1985) Introduction, *Canberra Anthropology* [special issue 'Minorities and the State] 8(1–2): 1–3.

Miller, Carolyn (1977), *Captured!* Cappaqua, NY: Christian Herald Books.

Mitchell, Timothy (1988), *Colonizing Egypt*. Cairo: American University in Cairo Press.

Mogenet, Luc (1980), Les impôts coloniaux et les incidents au Sud-Laos en 1937, *Péninsule* 1: 73–93.

Mole, Robert L. (1970), *The Montagnards of South Vietnam: A Study of Nine Tribes*. Rutland and Tokyo: Charles Tuttle Co.

Monfleur, A. (1931), *Monographie de la province du Darlac (1930)*. Hanoi: IDEO.

Montandon, G. (1934), *Traité d'ethnologie cyclo-culturelle*. Paris: Payot.

Montgomery, John D. (1959), *Cases in Vietnamese Administration – Trường hợp hành chánh Việt Nam*. Saigon: Michigan State University Vietnam Advisory Group.

Montgomery, John D. (1962), *The Politics of Foreign Aid: American Experience in Southeast Asia*. New York: Praeger.

Moore, F.T.C. (1969), *The Observation of Savage People (by J.-M. De Gérando)*. (With preface by E.E. Evans-Pritchard). Berkeley: University of California Press.

Moore, Robin (1965), *The Green Berets*. New York: Crown Publishers.

Moppert, François (1978), *Mouvement de résistance au pouvoir colonial français de la minorité proto-indochinois du Plateau des Bolovens dans le Sud Laos: 1901–1936*, Paris: Université de Paris VII, thesis.

Moppert, François (1981), La révolte des Bolovens (1901–1936). In: Pierre Brocheux (ed.), *Histoire de l'Asie du Sud-Est. Révolte, Réformes, Révolutions*. Lille: Presses Universitaire de Lille.

Morgan, Lewis H. (1985, or. 1877), *Ancient Society: Researches in the lines of human progress from savagery through barbarism to civilization*. Tucson: University of Arizona Press.

Morris, Jim (1979), *War Story*. New York: Dell.

Morris, Jim (1990), *The Devil's Secret Name*. New York: Dell.

Mougeot, Dr. (1887), Un rapide voyage chez les Moïs, *BSEI* 5: 29–44.

Mouhot, H. (1872), *Voyage dans les royaumes de Siam, de Cambodge, de Laos et autres parties centrales de l'Indochine*. Paris: Hachette.

Mudimbe, Valentin (1988), *The Invention of Africa. Gnosis, Philosophy and the Order of Knowledge*. Bloomington/London: Indiana University Press/James Currey.

Muller, Hendrik (1917), *De Oost-Indische Compagnie in Cambodja en Laos: Verzameling van bescheiden van 1636 tot 1670*. 's-Gravenhage: Linschoten Vereeniging.

Murdock, John (1974), The 1901–1902 'Holy Man's' Rebellion, *Journal of the Siam Society* 62/1: 47–65.

Murray, Martin (1980), *The Development of Capitalism in Colonial Indochina (1870–1940)*. Berkeley/London: University of California Press.

Mus, Paul (1936), Un aspect des problèmes Moï, les plateaux de Djiring et de Dalat, *L'Anthropologie* 46: 750–1.

Mus, Paul (1952), *Viêt-Nam, sociologie d'une guerre*. Paris: Ed. du Seuil.

Navelle, E. (1887), Etude sur la langue bahnar, *Excursions et Reconnaissances* XIII: 309–15.

Neill, Stephen (1986), *A History of Christian Missions* (Or. 1964: revised for the second edition by Owen Chadwick). Harmondsworth: Pelican.

Néis, Dr. Paul (1880), Rapport sur une excursion scientifique faite chez les Moïs de l'Arrondissement de Baria, du 15 mai au 15 juin 1880, *Excursions et Reconnaissances* 6: 405–35.

Néis, Dr. Paul (1881–2), Excursions en Cochinchine en 1880 et 1881, *Bulletin de la Société de Géographie Commerciale de Paris*: 289–93.

Néis, Dr. Paul (1935, or. 1880), Rapport sur une excursion scientifique faite chez les Moïs de l'Arrondissement de Baria, du 15 mai au 15 juin 1880. In: Gouvernement de la Cochinchine, *Variétés sur les Pays Moïs*. Saigon: Gouvernement de la Cochinchine.

Nencel, Lorraine, and Peter Pels (eds) (1991), *Constructing Knowledge: Authority and Critique in Social Science*. London: Sage.

Ner, Marcel (1927a), Compte-rendu sur Marie 1er, roi des Sedangs, *BEFEO* XXVII: 308–50.

Ner, Marcel (1927b), Compte-rendu des missions, *BEFEO* XXVII: 483–5.

Ner, Marcel (1928), L'organisation familiale en pays moï, *Cahiers de la Société de Géographie* (Hanoi) 15: 1–27.

Ner, Marcel (1930), Compte-rendu des missions, *BEFEO* XXX: 533–76.

Ner, Marcel (1940a), Rapport sur les Coutumiers, *CEFEO* 22: 4.

Ner, Marcel (1940b), Rapport sur les Coutumiers, *CEFEO* 23: 3.

Ner, Marcel (1940c), 'Moï de la mer', Chronique d'Annam, *CEFEO* 24: 5–6.

Ner, Marcel (1940d), Moï de la mer, *BEFEO* XL: 476–7.

Ner, Marcel (1942a), Les coutumiers moïs, *CEFEO* 30: 14–15.

Ner, Marcel (1942b), Les coutumiers Moï du Haut-Donnai, *Indochine* III (101): 7–8.

Ner, Marcel (1943a), La France en Pays Moï: Humbles constructeurs de l'Empire, *Indochine* IV (143): 7–9; (144): I–VII.

Ner, Marcel (1943b), L'habitation rhadée, *CEFEO* 35: 25–6.

Ner, Marcel (1943c), Les jeux moï, *CEFEO* 35: 31–2.

Ner, Marcel (1952), Psychologie des populations archaiques (Moï) du Sud de l' Indochine, *Revue de Psychologie des Peuples* I: 44–61: 157–77.

Nghiêm Thâm (1961), Towards Understanding the Aborigines of Vietnam, *Asian Culture* 3: 91–9.

Nghiêm Thâm and Donald Voth (1972), Seeking to Understand the Highland People: The two tribal kingdoms of the Vietnamese court in the past, the King of Fire and the King of Water, *Southeast Asia* 1: 335.

Ngô Đúc Thinh (ed.) (1998), *Luât Tuc M'nông (tap quán pháp)* [M'nong Customary Law (legal customs)]. Hanoi: NXB Chính tri Quôc gia.

Ngô Đúc Thinh, Chu Thái Son and Nguyên Hũu Thâú (1996), *Luât Tuc Edê (tap quán pháp)* [Edê Customary Law (legal customs)]. Hanoi: NXB Chính tri Quôc gia.

Ngô Đúc Thinh and Phan Đăng Nhât (eds) (2000), *Luât tuc và Phát triên Nông thôn hiên nay o Viêt Nam: Kŷ yêú hôi thao khoa hoc*. [Customary Law and Present-day Rural Development in Vietnam: Conference Proceedings]. Hanoi: NXB Chính Tri Quôc gia.

Ngôn Vĩnh (1982), *FULRO?* Hanoi: NXB Công an Nhân dân.

Nguyên Chu Hoàng (1985), *Nhũng con lôc cao nguyên* [The whirlwinds of the highlands]. Hanoi: NXB Công an Nhân dân.

Nguyên Đúc Nhuân et al. (1987) *Le Viet Nam post-révolutionnaire: Population. Économie. Société, 1975–1985*. Paris: L, Harmattan.

Nguyên Duong Binh (ed.) (1990), *Chu tich Hô Chí Minh và vân đê dân tôc* [President Ho Chi Minh and the National Problem]. Hanoi: NXB Khoa hoc Xa hôi.

Nguyên Hũu Thâú (1964), Phong trào N'Trang Lung (1912–1935) [The N'Trang Lung Movement], *Nghiên cúu lich su* 69: 55–62.

Nguyên Ngoc (1958), *The Village that Wouldn't Die: A story of Vietnam's Resistance War*, Hanoi: Foreign Languages Publishing House (Or. 1956: Đât nuóc Đúng lên).

Nguyên Trăc Dĩ (1969), *Tìm hiêu phong-trào tranh-đâu F.U.L.R.O. (1958–1969)* [Seeking to understand the struggle movement FULRO]. Saigon: Bô Phát-triên Sác-tôc.

Nguyên Văn Chính (1999), Truòng nghiên cúu viên đông vói nghành dân tôc hoc Viêt Nam [The École d'Extrême-Orient and the discipline of ethnology in Vietnam], *Dân tôc & Thòi Đai* 5: 24–25.

Nguyên Xuan Linh (1973), Monarchie Vietnamienne et minorités ethniques, *ASEMI* IV–2: 149–70.

Nguyên Xuan Linh (1975b), Note sur les rapports des minorités et autorités politiques au Sud Viêtnam, *Pluriel* 6: 27–46.

Nguyên Xuan Linh (1976a), Documents sur quelques groupes ethniques du Viêt-Nam au XVIIIe siècle, *ASEMI* 7(4): 101–12.

Nguyên Xuân Nghĩa (1989) Thiên chúa giáo và Đao Tin lành o các dân tôc thiêu sô Tây Nguyên [Catholicism and Protestantism among the ethnic minorities of the Central Highlands], *Tap chí Dân Tôc Hoc* 4(64): 59–68.

Nông Quôc Chân (1977) *Môt vuòn hóa nhiêu huong sác* [A flower garden with many scents and colours]. Hanoi: NXB Văn hóa Dân tôc.

Nông Quôc Chân (1978a) Thirty Years of Cultural Work among Ethnic Minorities, *Vietnamese Studies* No. 52 (special issue: Cultural Problems): 50–6.

Nông Quôc Chân (1978b) Selective Preservation of Ethnic Minorities' Cultural Traditions, *Vietnamese Studies* No. 52 (special issue: Cultural Problems): 57–63.

Nông Quôc Chân, Vi Hông Nhân, Hoàng Tuân Cu (eds) (1996), *Giũ gìn và bao vê ban sác văn hóa các dân tôc thiêu sô Viêt Nam* [Preserving and Protecting the Cultural Identity of Vietnam's Ethnic Minorities]. Hanoi: NXB Văn hóa Dân tôc.

Nouet, L. (1935, or. 1882), Excursion chez les Moïs de la frontière Nord-Est. In: Gouvernement de la Cochinchine, *Variétés sur les Pays Moï.* Saigon: Gouvernement de la Cochinchine.

Noyes, John K. (1992), *Colonial Space: Spatiality in the Discourse of German South-West Africa 1884–1915.* Chur etc.: Harwood Academic Publishers.

Noyes, John K. (1994), The Natives in their Places: 'Ethnographic cartography' and the representation of autonomous spaces in Ovamboland, German South West Africa, *History and Anthropology* 8: 237–64.

Nyo, Commandant (1937), La pénétration française en pays Moï, *BSEI* XI(2) (n.s.): 45–67.

Oddéra, H. (1900), Un tueur d'éléphants, *BSEI* 38: 11–16.

Odend'hal, Prosper (1894), Les routes de l'Annam au Mekong (de Hué à Saravane et à Attopeu), *Revue Indochinoise Illustrée* IV, July 1894: 131–61; August: 1–50.

O'Donnell, John (1967), The Strategic Hamlet Progress in Kien Hoa Province, South Vietnam: A Case Study of Counter-Insurgency. In: Peter Kunstadter (ed.), *Southeast Asian Tribes, Minorities and Nations,* 2 vols Princeton, NJ: Princeton University Press.

Olivier, Dr. G. (1951), Documents anthropologiques sur les Moïs d'Indochine (Montagnards de type indonésien), *Bulletin de la Société d'Anthropologie* X: 189–200.

Orléans, Prince H. d' (1901), De Kratié à Nhatrang à travers la province du Darlac, *La Geographie* IV: 153–60.

Ortner, Sherry (1984), Theory in Anthropology since the Sixties, *Comparative Studies in Society and History* 26: 126–65.

Osborne, Milton (1978), Peasant Politics in Cambodia: The 1916 Affair, *Modern Asian Studies* 12/2: 217–43.

Owen, Roger (1973), Imperial Policy and Theories of Social Change: Sir Alfred Lyall in India. In: T. Asad (ed.) *Anthropology and the Colonial Encounter.* London: Ithaca Press.

Pagès, P. (1935), Rapport sur la pénétration en pays Moï au cours des cinq dernières années. In: Gouvernement de la Cochinchine, *Variétés sur les pays moïs.* Saigon: Gouvernement de la Cochinchine.

Pagniez, F.P. (1954), Sur les Plateaux d'Indochine, guerre psychologique, *Revue des Deux Mondes* janvier 1954: 135–42.

Pagniez, Y. (1954), *Le Viet Minh et la Guerre Psychologique*. Paris: La Colombe.

Pâris, Camille and Alfred Barsanti (1905), *Missionaires d'Asie. Oeuvre néfaste des Congrégations. Protectorat des Chrétiens*. Paris: 'Le Papier'.

Parkin, David (1990), Eastern Africa: The View from the Office and the View from the Field. In: R. Fardon (ed.), *Localizing Strategies. Regional Traditions of Ethnographic Writing*. Edinburgh: Scottish Academic Press.

Parmentier, H. (1951), La maison commune du village bahnar de Kombraih près de Kontum, sur la route de Konplong, *BEFEO* XLV: 223–25.

Parsons, Talcott (1968), Professions. In: D. Sills (ed.), *International Encyclopedia of the Social Sciences* vol. 12. London: Macmillan Co.

Pasquier, P. (1935, or. 1923), Les principes directeurs de l'administration des régions moïs. In: Gouvernement de la Cochinchine, *Variétés sur les Pays Moïs*. Saigon: Gouvernement de la Cochinchine.

Patté, Paul (1906), *Hinterland Moï*. Paris: Plon.

Patric, Gordon (1969), *The Vietnams of the Green Berets*. Chesterton: Indiana University Northwest.

Pavie, Auguste (1900), *Mission Pavie, Géographie et Voyages, t. 3: Voyages au Laos et chez les sauvages du Sud-Est de l'Indochine par le Cap. Cupet*, Paris: Ernest Leroux.

Pavie, Auguste (1902), *Mission Pavie, Géographie et Voyages, t. 4: Voyages au centre de l'Annam et du Laos et dans les régions sauvages de l'Est de l'Indochine par le Cap. De Malglaive et par le Cap. Rivière*, Paris: Ernest Leroux.

Pels, Peter (1986), Positivisme en historicisme in de geschiedenis van de antropologie, *Skript* 8–4: 272–83.

Pels, Peter (1990), Anthropology and Mission: Towards a Historical Analysis of Professional Identity. In: R. Bonsen, H. Marks and J. Miedema (eds), *The Ambiguity of Rapprochement. Reflections of Anthropologists on their Controversial Relationship with Missionaries*. Nijmegen: Focaal.

Pels, Peter (1993), *Critical Matters: Interactions between Missionaries and Waluguru in Colonial Tanganyika, 1930–1961*, Ph.D. University of Amsterdam, thesis.

Pels, Peter (1994), The Construction of Ethnographic Occasions in Late Colonial Uluguru. *History and Anthropology* 8(1–4): 321–51.

Pels, Peter (1996), The Pidginization of Luguru Politics. Administrative Ethnography and the Paradoxes of Indirect Rule, *American Ethnologist* 26: 163–83.

Pels, Peter (1997), The Anthropology of Colonialism: Culture, History and the Emergence of Western Governmentality, *Annual Review of Anthropology* 26: 163–183.

Pels, Peter (1999), *A Politics of Presence: Contacts between Missionaries and Waluguru in Late Colonial Tanganyika*. Chur: Harwood Academic Publishers.

Pels, Peter and Lorraine Nencel (1991), Introduction: Critique and the Deconstruction of Anthropological Authority. In: Lorraine Nencel and Peter Pels (eds), *Constructing Knowledge: Authority and Critique in Social Science*. London: Sage, pp. 1–21.

Pels, Peter and Oscar Salemink (1994), Introduction: Five theses on Ethnography as Colonial Practice. *History and Anthropology* 8(1–4): 1–34.

Pels, Peter and Oscar Salemink (1999), Introduction: Locating the Subjects of Anthropology. In: Peter Pels and Oscar Salemink (eds), *Colonial Subjects: Essays on the Practical History of Anthropology*. Ann Arbor: University of Michigan Press, pp. 1–52.

Pels, Peter, and Oscar Salemink (eds) (1994), 'Colonial Ethnographies', thematic issue of *History and Anthropology* 8(1–4).

Pels, Peter, and Oscar Salemink (eds), *Colonial Subjects: Essays on the Practical History of Anthropology*. Ann Arbor: University of Michigan Press.

Pelzer, Karl (1961), Mass Migrations and Resettlement Projects in Southeast Asia since 1945. In: *Proceedings of the Ninth Pacific Science Congress*, vol. 3, *Anthropology and Social Sciences*. Bangkok.

Perham, Margery (1934), A Re-Statement of Indirect Rule, *Africa* 7: 321–34.

Petersen, Barry (1988), *Tiger Men: An Australian Soldier's Secret War in Vietnam* (with John Cribbin). Melbourne: Macmillan.

Pham Kiêt (1976), *Tù núi rùng Ba To. Hôi ký* [From the mountains and forests of Ba To. Reminiscences]. Hanoi: NXB Quân Đôi Nhân dân.

Pham Nhu Cuòng et al. (1987) *Môt sô vân đê phát triên văn hóa các dân tôc thiêu sô* [Some problems concerning the cultural development of ethnic minorities]. Hanoi: NXB Văn hóa Dân tôc.

Pike, Douglas (1966), *Viet Cong: The Organization and Techniques of the National Liberation Front of South Vietnam*. Cambridge, MA: MIT Press.

Pinney, Christopher (1990), Colonial Anthropology in the 'Laboratory of Mankind'. In: C.A. Bayly (ed.), *The Raj: India and the British 1600–1947*. London: National Portrait Gallery Publications.

Pluvier, Jan (1983, or. 1975), *Vietnam, Laos, Cambodia. Om de bevrijding van Indochina. Een geschiedenis vanaf 1850*. Nijmegen: SUN.

Po Dharma (1993), Le FULRO: Moment de l'histoire ou tradition de lutte des peuples du sud de Champa. In: P.V. Pozner and O.V. Ribina (eds), *Deuxième Symposium Franco-Soviétique sur l'Asie du Sud-Est*. Moscow: Présentation Sonat.

Popkin, Samuel (1979), *The Rational Peasant: The Political Economy of Rural Society in Vietnam. Berkeley, CA: University of California Press*.

Prados, John (1986), *Presidents' Secret Wars: CIA and Pentagon Covert Operations since World War II*. New York: Morrow.

Pratt, Mary Louise (1985), Scratches on the Face of the Country, or: What Mr. Barrow Saw in the Land of the Bushmen, *Critical Inquiry* 12: 119–43.

Pratt, Mary Louise (1986), Fieldwork in Common Places. In: J. Clifford and G. Marcus (eds), *Writing Culture. The Poetics and Politics of Ethnography*. Berkeley: University of California Press, pp. 27–50.

Pratt, Mary Louise (1992), *Imperial Eyes. Travel Writing and Transculturation*. London/New York: Routledge.

Prouty, L. Fletcher (1969), Green Berets and the CIA: General Abrams Strikes Back. *New Republic* 30 August 30, 1969: 9–10.

Pruneau, Gén. (1935), Création d'un territoire Moï autonome, *La Lance Militaire* 12 May 1935.

Quéguiner (1943), Note sur une peuplade moï de la Chaîne annamitique du sud: les Cau S're, *TIIEH* VI: 395–402.

Qiang Zhai (2000), *China and the Vietnam Wars 1950–1975*. Chapel Hill/London: University of North Carolina Press.

Rabinow, Paul (1986), Representations are Social Facts: Modernity and Post-Modernity in Anthropology. In: J. Clifford and G. Marcus (eds) *Writing Culture. The Poetics and Politics of Ethnography*. Berkeley: University of California Press, pp. 234–61.

Rambo, A. Terry (1995), Defining Highland Development Challenges in Vietnam: Some Themes and Issues Emerging from the Conference. In: A. Terry Rambo, Robert Reed, Le trong Cuc and Michael DiGregorio (eds), *The Challenges of Highland Development in Vietnam*. Honolulu: East-West Center, pp. xi–xxvii.

Ranger, Terence O. (1983), The Invention of Tradition in Colonial Africa. In: E. Hobsbawm and T.O. Ranger (eds), *The Invention of Tradition*. Cambridge: Cambridge University Press.

Raulin, Henri (1946), L'évolution des Stieng de la délégation de Hon-quan, *BSEI* XXI: 67–71.

Raulin, Henri (1947), Les techniques de la percussion et de la production du feu chez les Stieng, *BSEI* XXII: 111–21.

Reimer, Reginald (1975), South Vietnam, in: Donald Hoke (ed.), *The Church in Asia*. Chicago: Moody Press.

Reining, Conrad (1962), A Lost Period of Applied Anthropology, *American Anthropologist* 64: 593–600.

Richard (1811, or. 1778), History of Tonquin. In: John Pinkerton (ed.), *A General Collection of the Best and Most Interesting Voyages and Travels in All Parts of the World*, Vol. IX. London: Longman, Hurst et al.

Richards, Audrey I. (1954), *Chisungu. A girl's initiation ceremony among the Bemba of Zambia*. London and New York: Routledge (rev. reprint, 1982).

Richards, Audrey I. (ed.) (1959), *East African Chiefs*. London: Faber & Faber.

Riesen, René (1955), *Mission spéciale en forêt moï*, Paris: France-Empire.

Riesen, René (1957), *Jungle Mission*. London: Hutchinson.

Risseeuw, Carla (1988), *The Fish Don't Talk About the Water. Gender Transformation, Power and Resistance among Women in Sri Lanka*. Leiden: Brill.

Robequain, Charles (1944, or. 1939), *The economic development of French Indo-China*. London: Oxford University Press.

Robequain, Charles (1947), *Les races montagnardes de l'Indochine*. Paris: Collège Libre des Sciences Sociales et Economiques, Section d'Outre-Mer.

Rochet, J. (1941), Le problème scolaire en pays Moï, *Indochine* 20: 12–15.

Rosaldo, Renato (1986), From the Door of his Tent: The Fieldworker and the Inquisitor. In: J. Clifford and G. Marcus (eds) *Writing Culture. The Poetics and Politics of Ethnography*. Berkeley: University of California Press, pp. 77–97.

Rostow, Walt W. (1960), *The Stages of Economic Growth: A Non-Communist Manifesto*. London: Cambridge University Press.

Rousset, Pierre (1978), *Communisme et nationalisme vietnamien: Le Vietnam entre les deux guerres mondiales*. Paris: Editions Galilée.

Roux, Cdt. H. (1929), Les tombeaux chez les Moï Jarai, *BEFEO* XXIX: 346–8.

Sabatier, Léopold (1921), *Dak Lak: Hdrôm hra bah, blu bi k'bin kdrech brey ko phung h'deh hriam hra to Dak Lak* [Recueil de mots rangés d'après le sens à l'usage des élèvs de lécole franco-rhadé du Darlac]. Hanoi: Imprimerie d'Extrême-Orient.

Sabatier, Léopold (1927), *La chanson de Damsan*. Paris: Leblanc et Trautmann.

Sabatier, Léopold (1927), *Hdruôm hra klei duê klei bhian du'm* [Bidué: Code des tribus du Darlac]. Hanoi: Imprimerie d'Extrême-Orient (all copies were 'purchased' meaning confiscated by the Deuxième Bureau).

Sabatier, Léopold (1930), *Palabre du serment au Darlac*. Hanoi: Imprimerie d'Extrême-Orient.

Sabatier, Léopold and Dominique Antomarchi (1940), *Recueil des coutumes rhadées du Darlac*. Hanoi: Imprimerie d'Extrême-Orient.

Said, Edward (1978), *Orientalism*. London: Routledge and Kegan Paul.

Said, Edward (1989a), Representing the Colonized: Anthropology's Interlocutors, *Critical Inquiry* 15: 205–25.

Said, Edward (1989b), Response, *Critical Inquiry* 15: 634–46.

Salemink, Oscar (1991), *Mois* and *Maquis*: The Invention and Appropriation of Vietnam's Montagnards from Sabatier to the CIA, in: George W. Stocking, Jr. (ed.), *Colonial Situations: Essays on the Contextualization of Ethnographic Knowledge* (History of Anthropology, Vol. 7). Madison: University of Wisconsin Press.

Salemink, Oscar (1994), The Return of the Python God: Multiple interpretations of a millenarian movement in colonial Vietnam. *History and Anthropology* 8(1–4): 129–64.

Salemink, Oscar (1995a), Primitive Partisans: French Ethnic Policy and the Construction of a Montagnard Ethnic Identity in Indochina, in: Hans Antlöv and Stein Tønnesson (eds), *Imperial Policy and Southeast Asian Nationalism 1930–1957*. London: Curzon Press, pp. 261–93.

Salemink, Oscar (1995b), Buddhism on Fire: Religious protests against authoritarian regimes in Vietnam, in: Paul E. Baak (ed.), *CASA Nova: Aspects of Asian Societies*, vol. 1. Amsterdam: Centre for Asian Studies Amsterdam/Thesis Publishers, pp. 35–54.

Salemink, Oscar (1996), Review of Maurice, Albert-Marie, *Les Mnong des Hauts-Plateaux* (Paris, 1993), *Anthropos* 91: 278–9.

Salemink, Oscar (1997), The King of Fire and Vietnamese Ethnic Policy in the Central Highlands. In: Don McCaskill and Ken Kampe (eds), *Development or Domestication? Indigenous Peoples of Southeast Asia*. Chiang Mai: Silkworm Books, pp. 488–535.

Salemink, Oscar (1999), Ethnography as Martial Art: Ethnicizing Vietnam's Montagnards, 1930–1954. In: Peter Pels and Oscar Salemink (eds), *Colonial Subjects: Essays on the Practical History of Anthropology*. Ann Arbor: University of Michigan Press, pp. 282–325.

Salemink, Oscar (2000a), Sedentarization and Selective Preservation among the Montagnards in the Vietnamese Central Highlands. In: Jean Michaud (ed.), *Turbulent Times and Enduring Peoples: Mountain Minorities in the South-East Asian Massif*. London: Curzon Press, pp. 124–48.

Salemink, Oscar (2000b), Luât tuc, Quyên so hũu đât vá vân đê di cu [Customary law, land rights and internal migration]. In: Ngô Đúc Thinh and Phan Đăng Nhât (eds), *Luât tuc và Phát triên Nông thôn hiên nay o Viêt Nam: Ký yêú hôi thao khoa hoc*. [Customary Law and Present-day Rural Development in Vietnam: Conference Proceedings]. Hanoi: NXB Chính Tri Quôc gia, pp. 814–62.

Salemink, Oscar (2000c), Customary Law, Land Rights and Internal Migration, *Vietnam Social Sciences* 2(76): 65–79.

Sarraut, Albert (1923), *Mise en valeur des colonies françaises*. Paris: Payot.

Schell, Jonathan (1988), *The Real War: The Classic Reporting on the Vietnam War with a New Essay*. New York: Pantheon Books.

Schlesinger, Arthur F., Jr. (1965), *A Thousand Days: John F. Kennedy in the White House*. Greenwich, CT.: Fawcett Books.

Schmidt, Wilhelm (1907–08), Les peuples Mon-Khmèr, trait d'union entre les peuples de l'Asie centrale et de l'Austronésie, *BEFEO* VII: 213–64; VII: 1–36.

Scholte, Bob (1966), Epistemic Paradigms: Some Problems in Cross-Cultural Research on Social Anthropological History and Theory, *American Anthropologist* 68: 1192–201.

Scholte, Bob (1974), Insult and Injury. Letter to the Editors, *New York Review of Books* 18 July 1974: 41–2.

Scholte, Bob (1975), Reply. Letter to the Editors, *New York Review of Books* 23 January 1975: 45.

Scholte, Bob (1978), Critical Anthropology since its Reinvention: On the Convergence between the Concept of Paradigm, the Rationality of Debate and Critical Anthropology, *Anthropology and Humanism Quarterly* 3 (1and2): 4–17.

Scholte, Bob (1983), Cultural Anthropology and the Paradigm-Concept: A Brief History of their Recent Convergence. In: L. Graham, W. Lepenies and P. Weingart (eds), *Functions and Uses of Disciplinary Histories*. Dordrecht: Reidel.

Schrock, Joann, William Stockton, Elaine Murphy and Marilou Fromme (1966), *Minority Groups in the Republic of Vietnam*. Washington, DC: Dept. of the Army, Ethnographic Study Series.

Schulte Nordholt, Henk (1994), The Making of Traditional Bali: Colonial ethnography and bureaucratic reproduction, *History and Anthropology* 8(1–4): 89–128.

Scigliano, Robert (1964), *South Vietnam: Nation under Stress*. Boston: Houghton Mifflin.

Scigliano, Robert and Guy Fox (1965), *Technical Assistance in Vietnam: The Michigan State University Experience*. New York: Praeger.

Scott, James C. (1976), *The Moral Economy of the Peasant: Rebellion and Subsistence in Southeast Asia*. New Haven, CT and London: Yale University Press.

Scott, James C. (1995), *State Simplifications: Some Applications to Southeast Asia*. Amsterdam: Centre for Asian Studies Amsterdam, Wertheim Lecture 5.

Scott, James C. (1998), *Seeing like a State: How Certain Schemes to Improve the Human Condition Have Failed*. New Haven, CT and London: Yale University Press.

Seitz, Paul (1975), *Men of Dignity: the Montagnards of South Vietnam*. (realised by Jacques Barthélemy). Cambridge: J. Jackson.

Seitz, Paul (1977), *Les hommes debout. Les Montagnards du Sud-Vietnam*. Paris: Ed. Saint-Paul.

Shackleton, Ronald (1975), *Village Defense: Initial Special Forces Operations in Vietnam*. Arvada, CO: Phoenix Publishing.

Shafer, D. Michael (1988), *Deadly Paradigms: The Failure of US Counterinsurgency Policy*. Princeton, NJ: Princeton University Press.

Shaplen, Robert (1966), *The Lost Revolution: The US in Vietnam, 1946–1966*. New York: Harper and Row.

Sharpe, Barrie (1986), Ethnography as a Regional System. Mental maps and the myth of states and tribes in Northern Nigeria, *Critique of Anthropology* 6: 33–65.

Sheehan, Neil (1971), *The Pentagon Papers: The Complete and Unabridged Series as Published by the New York Times*. London, New York, Toronto: Bantam Books.

Sheehan, Neil (1988), *A Bright Shining Lie: John Paul Vann and America in Vietnam*. London: Jonathan Cape.

Sheehan, Susan (1967), *Ten Vietnamese*. New York: Alfred Knopf.

Shokeid, Moshe (1992), Commitment and Contextual Study in Anthropology, *Cultural Anthropology* 7: 464–77.

Simonnet, Christian (1977), *Les Tigres auront plus pitié: La mission des Grands Plateaux*, Paris: Ed. France-Empire.

Simpson, Colonel Charles M. III (1983), *Inside the Green Berets: The First Thirty Years. A History of the US Army Special Forces*. San Francisco: Presidio Press.

Skrobanek, Walter (1972), *Buddhistische Politik in Thailand*, Heidelberg: Universität Heidelberg, Beiträge zur Süd-Ost Asienforschung, 23.

Smith, Gordon Hedderly (1942), *The Blood Hunters: A Narrative of Pioneer Missionary Work among the Savages of French Indo-China*. Chicago: World Wide Prayer and Missionary Union.

Smith, Gordon Hedderly (1945), *The Missionary and Anthropology*. Chicago: Moody Press.

Smith, Gordon Hedderly (1947), *The Missionary and Primitive Man: An Introduction to the Study of his Mental Characteristics and his Religion*. Chicago: Van Kampen Press.

Smith, Mrs. Gordon Hedderly [= Laura Irene Smith] (1944), *Gongs in the Night: Reaching the Tribes of French Indo-China*. Grand Rapids: Zondervan Publishing House.

Smith, Harvey et. al. (1967), *Area Handbook for South Vietnam*. Washington, DC: American University, Foreign Area Studies, April.

Smith, Laura Irene (1955), *Farther into the Night: Missionary Adventure in Indo-China*. Grand Rapids: Zondervan Publishing House.

Smith, Laura Irene (1965), *Victory in Viet Nam*. Grand Rapids: Zondervan Publishing House.

Smith, Laura Irene (1975), *The Ten Dangerous Years*. Chicago: Moody Press.

Smith, R.B. (1983), *An International History of the Vietnam War* (2 vols). London: Macmillan.

Sochurek, Howard (1965), American Special Forces in Action in Viet Nam: how coolness and character averted a bloodbath when mountain tribes rose in revolt, *National Geographic* 127(1): 38–65.

Sochurek, Howard (1968), Viet Nam's Montagnards Caught in the Jaws of a War, *National Geographic* 133(4): 443–87.

Soulié, M. (1927), *Marie I, Roi des Sedangs (1888–1890)*. Paris: Marpon et Cie.

Spector, Ronald (1983), *Advice and Support: The Early Years 1941–1960. The US Army in Vietnam*. Washington DC: US Army Center of Military History.

Stagl, Justin (1974), August Ludwig Schlözers Entwurf einer 'Völkerkunde' oder 'Ethnographie' seit 1772, *Ethnologische Zeitschrift Zürich* II, 1974: 73–91.

Stagl, Justin (1980), Der wohl unterwiesene Passagier. Reisekunst und Gesellschaftsbeschreibung vom 16. bis zum 18. Jahrhundert. In: B.I. Krasnoaev, Gert Nobel Herbert Zimmermann (eds), *Reisen und Reisebeschreibungen im 18. und 19. Jahrhundert als Quellen der Kulturbeziehungsforschung*. Berlin: U. Camen.

Stagl, Justin (1990), The Methodizing of Travel in the 16th Century. A Tale of Three Cities, *History and Anthropology* 4: 303–38.

Stagl, Justin (1995), *A History of Curiosity: The Theory of Travel 1550–1800*. Chur: Harwood Academic Publishers.

Stanton, Shelby L. (1985), *Green Berets at War: US Army Special Forces in Southeast Asia 1956–1975*. Arms and Armour Press.

Stocking, George W., Jr (1964), French Anthropology in 1800, *Isis LV*: 134–150.

Stocking, George W., Jr. (1968), *Race, Culture and Evolution. Essays in the History of Anthropology*. New York: Free Press.

Stocking, George W. Jr. (1971), What's in a name? The origins of the Royal Anthropological Institute: 1837–1871. *Mom* 6: 369–390.

Stocking, George W., Jr. (1983a), The Ethnographer's Magic: Fieldwork in British Anthropology from Tylor to Malinowski. In: G.W. Stocking, Jr. (ed.), *Observers Observed. Essays on Ethnographic Fieldwork*. History of Anthropology vol. 1. Madison: University of Wisconsin Press.

Stocking, George W., Jr. (1985), Philanthropoids and Vanishing Cultures: Rockefeller Funding and the End of the Museum Era in Anglo-American Anthropology. In: G. W. Stocking, Jr. (ed.), *Objects and Others. Essays on Museums and Material Culture*. History of Anthropology vol. 3. Madison: University of Wisconsin Press.

Stocking, George W., Jr. (1987), *Victorian Anthropology*. New York: Free Press/London: Collier Macmillan.

Stocking, George W., Jr. (1991a), Maclay, Kubari, Malinowski: Archetypes from the Dreamtime of Anthropology. In: G.W. Stocking, Jr. (ed.), *Colonial Situations. Essays on the Contextualization of Ethnographic Knowledge*. (History of Anthropology vol. 7). Madison: University of Wisconsin Press.

Stocking, George W., Jr. (ed.) (1974), *The Shaping of American Anthropology, 1883–1911. A Franz Boas Reader*. New York: Basic Books.

Stocking, George W., Jr. (ed.) (1983b), *Observers Observed. Essays on Ethnographic Fieldwork.* History of Anthropology vol. 1. Madison: University of Wisconsin Press.

Stocking, George W., Jr. (ed.) (1991b), *Colonial Situations. Essays on the Contextualization of Ethnographic Knowledge* History of Anthropology vol. 7. Madison: University of Wisconsin Press.

Stoll (1982), *Fishers of Men or Founders of Empire? The Wycliffe Bible Translators in Latin America.* London: Zed Press.

Swedenburg, Ted (1992), Occupational Hazards Revisited: a reply to Moshe Shokeid, *Cultural Anthropology* 7: 478–89.

Sylvestre, M. (1880), Rapport sur l'esclavage, *Excursions et Reconnaissances* 14: 95–144.

Ta Xuan Linh (1974a), How Armed Struggle Began in South Vietnam, *Vietnam Courier* March 1974: 19–24.

Ta Xuan Linh (1974b), Armed Uprisings by Ethnic Minorities along the Truong Son, *Vietnam Courier* September 1974: 15–20; October 1974: 18–21.

Taboulet, Georges (1955), *La geste française en Indochine*. Paris: Maisonneuve.

Taboulet, Georges (1970), Le voyage d'exploration du Mékong (1866–1868): Doudart de Lagrée et Francis Garnier, *Revue Française d'Histoire d'Outre-Mer* 57: 5–90.

Talmon, Yonina (1968), 'Millenarism', In David Sills (ed.), *International Encyclopedia of the Social Sciences*, Vol. 10. London/New York: MacMillan and Free Press.

Tambiah, Stanley (1976), *World Conqueror and World Renouncer: A Study of Buddhism and Polity in Thailand against a Historical Background*, Cambridge: Cambridge University Press.

Tangac, René (1989), The Soviet response to the Minority Problem. In: Gérard Chaliand (ed.), *Minority Peoples in the Age of Nation-States*. London: Pluto Press.

Taupin, J. (1888), Huit jours au pays des Braous, *BSEI* 6: 49–64.

Taylor, H.R. (1939), *Jungle Trader*. Leipzig/Paris/Bologna: Albatross.

Tedlock, Dennis (1987), Questions Concerning Dialogical Anthropology, *Journal of Anthropological Research* 43/4: 325–47.

Tej Bunnag (1977), *The Provincial Admninistration of Siam 1892–1915: The Ministry of the Interior under Prince Damrong Rajanubhab*, Kuala Lumpur: Oxford University Press.

Thành Tín (1983), *Đập nát công cu hâu chiên CIA: FULRO* [Smashing the CIA's Post-War Instrument: FULRO]. Ho Chi Minh City: NXB TP Hô Chí Minh.

Thayer, Carlyle (1989), *War by Other Means: National Liberation and Revolution in Viet-Nam, 1954–1960.* Sydney: Allen and Unwin.

Thayer, Nate (1992), The Forgotten Army: The rebels time forgot, *Far Eastern Economic Review* 10 September: 16–22.

Thibault, Lt. (1941), Aperçu sur la question Moï, *Indochine* II (221): 3–5.

Thierry, François (1989), Empire and Minority in China. In: Gérard Chaliand (ed.), *Minority Peoples in the Age of Nation-States*. London: Pluto Press.

Thion, Serge (1988), Remodeling Broken Images: Manipulation of Identities Towards and Beyond the Nation, an Asian Perspective, in: Remo Guidieri, F. Pellizzi and S. Tambiah (eds), *Ethnicities and Nations: Processes of Interethnic Relations in Latin-America, Southeast Asia and the Pacific*. Austin: University of Texas Press/Rothko Capel Book.

Thomas, David D. (1973), A Note on the Braches of Mon-Khmer. In: David D. Thomas, and Nguyen Dinh-Hoa, (eds) (1973), *Mon-Khmer Studies IV*. Saigon: Center for Vietnamese Studies and Summer Institute of Linguistics.

Thomas, David D. (ed.) (1964), *Mon-Khmer Studies I*. Saigon: Linguistic Circle of Saigon.

Thomas, David D. (ed.) (1966), *Papers on Four Vietnamese Languages*. Auckland: Linguistic Society of New Zealand.

Thomas, David D. (ed.) (1968), *Tribes of South Vietnam (map): Vietnam Minority Languages.* Saigon: Summer Institute of Linguistics (revised May 1968; first edition 1961).

Thomas, David and R.K. Headley (1970), More on Mon-Khmer Sub-Groupings, *Lingua* 25(4): 398–418.

Thomas, David D. and Nguyen Dinh-Hoa (eds) (1973), *Mon-Khmer Studies IV.* Saigon: Center for Vietnamese Studies and Summer Institute of Linguistics.

Thomas, David D., Nguyen Dinh-Hoa and David Blood (eds) (1966), *Mon-Khmer Studies II.* Saigon: Linguistic Circle of Saigon.

Thomas, David D., Nguyen Dinh-Hoa and David Blood (eds) (1969), *Mon-Khmer Studies III.* Saigon: Linguistic Circle of Saigon.

Thomas, Nicholas (1989), *Out of Time: History and Evolution in Anthropology.* Cambridge: Cambridge University Press.

Thomas, Nicholas (1991a), Against Ethnography, *Cultural Anthropology* 6: 306–22.

Thomas, Nicholas (1991b), *Entangled Objects. Exchange, Material Culture and Colonialism in the Pacific.* Cambridge, MA: Harvard University Press.

Thomas, Nicholas (1992), The Inversion of Tradition, *American Ethnologist* 19: 213–32.

Thompson, Virginia (1968, or. 1937), *French Indochina.* New York: Octagon Books.

Thompson, V. and R. Adloff (1955), *Minority problems in South-East Asia.* Stanford, CA: Stanford University Press.

Thongchai Winichakul (1994), *Siam Mapped: A History of the Geo-Body of a Nation.* Honolulu: University of Hawaii Press.

Thongchai Winichakul (1996), Maps and the Formation of the Geo-Body of Siam. In: Stein Tønnesson and Hans Antlöv (eds), *Asian Forms of the Nation.* London: Curzon Press.

Thornton, Robert J. (1985), 'Imagine yourself set down. . .' Mach, Frazer, Conrad and the role of imagination in ethnography, *Anthropology Today* 1/5: 7–14.

Thornton, Robert J. (1988), The Rhetoric of Ethnographic Holism. *Cultural Anthropology* 3(3): 285–303.

Thrupp, Sylvia (ed.) (1972), *Millennial dreams in action.* New York: Schrocken Books.

Tønnesson, Stein (1987), *1946: Déclenchement de la Guerre d'Indochine.* Paris: L'Harmattan.

Tønnesson, Stein and Hans Antlöv (eds) (1996), *Asian Forms of the Nation.* Richmond: Curzon Press.

Trân Chánh Thành (1942), Statut politique et juridique des plateaux Moïs du Sud-Annam, *Revue Indochinoise Juridique et Economique* I: 118–32.

Trân Tu Bình (1985), *The Red Earth: A Vietnamese Memoir of Life on a Colonial Rubber Plantation.* Athens: Ohio University, Center for International Studies/Southeast Asian Studies.

Trinquet, Ch. (1906), Notes sur la tribu des Djarai, *Revue Indochinoise* V, December: 1903–31.

Trinquet, Ch. (1908), Le poste administratif de Lang-Ri, *Revue Indochinoise* VII–2: 346–82.

Trinquier, Col. (1976, or. 1952), *Les maquis d'Indochine. Les missions spéciales de service action,* Paris: Ed. Albatros.

Trinquier, Col. (1964), *Modern Warfare: A French View of Insurgency.* New York: Praeger.

Trompf, G.W. (ed.) (1990), *Cargo Cults and Millenarian Movements,* Berlin/New York: Mouton De Gruyter.

Trumelet-Faber, Cdt. (1897), Le Mekong et la région des Moïs, *Bulletin de la Société de Géographie de Toulouse*: 115–23.

Tuchman, Barbara (1970), *Sand against the Wind: Stillwell and the American Experience in China 1911–1945.* London: MacMillan.

Tuck, Patrick (1987), *French Catholic Missionaries and the Politics of Imperialism in Vietnam, 1857–1914: A documentary survey.* Liverpool: Liverpool University Press.

Tyler, Stephen (1987), On 'Writing Up/Off' as 'Speaking For', *Journal of Anthropological Research* 43/4: 343–4.

Tylor, E.B. (1993, or. 1871), *Primitive Culture: Researches into the Development of Mythology, Philosophy, Religion, Language, Art and Custom*. London: J. Murray.

US Army Combat Development Command (1964), *Program for Analysis and Development of US Counterinsurgency Doctrine and Organization*. Washington, DC: Department of the Army.

US Army J.F. Kennedy Special Warfare Center (1964), *Annual Report 1964*. Fort Bragg, NC: US Army J.F. Kennedy Special Warfare Center.

US Army Special Warfare Center (1964), *Montagnard Tribal Groups in the Republic of South Viet-Nam*. Fort Bragg: US Army Special Warfare Center.

US Army Special Warfare School, *Counter-Guerrilla Operations: Program of Instruction for 33-G-F6 Counter-Guerrilla Operations Course, May 1961*. Fort Bragg, NC: US Army Special Warfare School.

US Information Service (1962), *Montagnards of the South Vietnam Highlands*. Saigon: USIS.

Urry, John (1992), The Tourist gaze and the 'Environment', *Theory, Culture and Society* 9: 1–26.

Valette, Jacques (1969), L'expédition de Francis Garnier au Tonkin à travers quelques journaux contemporains, *Revue d'Histoire Moderne et Contemporaine* 16: 189–220.

Van Camelbeke, Mgr. (1887), Détails sur le délivrance de trois missionnaires chez les Bahnars, *Les Missions Catholiques*: 217–8, 313–5, 517–9.

Văn Tiên Dũng, General (2000), *Our Great Spring Victory: An Account of the Liberation of South Vietnam by General Văn Tiên Dũng*. Hanoi: Thê Giói Publishers (or. 1976).

Van Wuysthoff, G (1987), *Le journal de Voyage de G. van Wuythoff et de ses assistants au Laos (1641–1642)*. Présentation, traduction, commentaire notes et index pasr Jean-Claude Lejosne. Paris: Cercle de Culture de Recherches laotiennes.

Vandergeest, Peter and Nancy Peluso (1995), Territorialization and State Power in Thailand. *Theory and Society* 24: 385–426.

Vannel, R. (1942), La conférence des Pays Moï, *Indochine* I (79): 1–3.

Vermeulen, H.F. (1992), The Emergence of 'Ethnography' ca. 1770 in Gottingen, *History of Anthropology Newsletter* 19(2): 6–9.

Vermeulen, H.F. (1995), Origins and institutionalization of ethnography and ethnology in Europe and the USA, 1771–1845. In: Han Vermeulen and Arturo Alvarez Roldán (eds) *Fieldwork and Footnotes: Studies in the History of European Anthropology*. London: Routledge.

Vermeulen, H.F. (1996), *Taal-, Land- en Volkenkunde in de Achttiende Eeuw*. Leiden: Oosters Genootschap in Nederland.

Vermeulen, Han, and Arturo Alvarez Roldán, eds (1995), *Fieldwork and Footnotes: Studies in the History of European Anthropology*. London: Routledge.

Vickers, George R. (1989), The Vietnam Antiwar Movement in Perspective. *Bulletin of Concerned Asian Scholars* 21(2–4): 100–10.

Viet Chung (1967), Minorités nationales et politique des nationalités en R.D. du Vietnam, *Etudes Vietnamiennes* 15 (Régions montagneuses et minorités nationales en R.D. du Vietnam): 3–24.

Villarem (1900), Excursion à Djiring (province du Haut-Donnai), *BSEI* 38: 39–56.

Villemereuil (1883), *Explorations et Missions de Doudart de Lagrée*. Paris: Bouchard-Huzard.

Vinh-Loc, Brigadier-General (1965), *The So-Called Movement for Autonomy FULRO*. Pleiku – Banmethuot.

Voget, Fred W. (1975), *A History of Ethnology*. New York: Holt, Rinehart and Winston.

Volkman, Toby (1990), Visions and Revisions: Toraja culture and the tourist gaze, *American Ethnologist* 17/1: 91–110.

Wakin, Eric (1992), *Anthropology Goes to War: Professional Ethics and Counterinsurgency in Thailand*. Madison: University of Wisconsin, Center for Southeast Asian Studies.

Wallace, Anthony (1968), Nativism and Revivalism. In: David Sills (ed.), *International Encyclopedia of the Social Sciences*, vol. 11, pp. 75–80. London/New York: Macmillan and Free Press.

Wallis, Ethel E. and Mary A. Bennett (1960), *Two Thousand Tongues to Go: The Story of the Wycliffe Bible Translators*. London: Hodder and Stoughton.

Warner, Denis (1964), *The Last Confucian: Vietnam, South-East Asia, and the West*. Harmondsworth: Penguin Books.

Washabaugh, William (1979), Linguistic Anti-Structure, *Journal of Anthropological Research* 35: 30–46.

Wax, Murray (1978), Review of *The Best-Laid Schemes*. S. J. Deitchman, 1976. *Human Organization* 37(4): 400–408.

Weggel, Oskar (1993) Die Religionspolitik der SR Vietnam, *Südostasien Aktuell* November 1993: 461–68.

Weiner, Annette B. (1976), *Women of Value, Men of Renown: New Perspectives in Trobriand Exchange*. Austin: University of Texas Press.

Wekkin, Gary (1975), Tribal Politics in Indochina: The Role of the Highland Tribes in the Internationalization of Internal Wars. In: Mark Zacher and R.S. Milne (eds), *Conflict and Stability in Southeast Asia*. New York: Anchor Press.

Wertheim, Willem (1972), Counter-insurgency Research at the Turn of the Century – Snouck Hurgronje and the Achech War, *Sociologische Gids* 19–5/6: 320–28.

Westmoreland, General William (1976), *A Soldier Reports*. New York: Doubleday.

Wickert, Frederic (1959), The Tribesmen. In: Richard Lindholm (ed.), *Vietnam: The First Five Years*. East Lansing: Michigan State University Press, pp. 126–35.

Wiesner, Louis (1988), *Victims and Survivors: Displaced Persons and Other Victims in Viet-Nam, 1954–1975*. New York: Greenwood Press.

Willenberg, Ursula (1972), *Interethnisch-Oekonomische Beziehungen in Sued-Vietnam. Ihre Bedeutung fuer den Ethnogeneseprozess*. Berlin: Akademieverlag.

Wilson, Bryan (1973), *Magic and the Millennium*, London: Heinemann.

Wolf, Eric and Joseph Jorgensen (1970), Anthropology on the Warpath in Thailand, *New York Review of Books* 15, 19 November: 26–35.

Worsley, Peter (1968[2], or. 1957), *The Trumpet Shall Sound: A Study of 'Cargo' Cults in Melanesia*. London: MacGibbon and Kee.

Wyatt, David K. (1994), Asian Studies in the United States (speech given during the official opening of the International Institute for Asian Studies, October 13, 1993, Leiden). *IIAS Newsletter* 2: 53–54.

Y Bih Nie-Kdam (1949a), Notice sommaire sur le Darlac. *Éducation* 16: 31–2.

Y Bih Nie-Kdam (1949b), Evolution culturelle des P.M.S.I., *Éducation* 16: 83–90.

Yersin, A. (1893), Les Moïs de la Cochinchine et du Sud-Annam, *Revue Indochinoise Illustrée* II–2: 52–81.

Yersin, A. (1894), Les Moïs de Tra-My (Région de la cannelle), *Revue Indochinoise Illustrée* IV–2: 82–113.

Yersin, A. (1935, or. 1893a), Sept mois chez les Moï. In: Gouvernement de la Cochinchine, *Variétés sur les Pays Moïs*. Saigon: Gouvernement de la Cochinchine.

Yersin, A. (1942a), Premiers contacts avec les pays Moï de l'Annam, *Indochine* III (99): 1–3.

Yersin, A. (1942b), Rencontre vaec les pirates sur les Plateaux Moï, *Indochine* IV (100): 9–10.

Yersin, A. (1942c), Voyage de Nhatrang à Stung Treng par les plateaux Moï, *Indochine* III (103): 4–7; (104): 3–7; (109): 3–8.

Yersin, A. (1942d), Un mois chez M'siao (juillet-août 1893), *Indochine* III (117): 3–8.

Yersin, A. (1942e), De Nhatrang à Tourane par les plateaux Moï, *Indochine* IV (137): 3–9; (146): 4–6; (150): 4–8.

Yoneo Ishii (1975), A Note on Buddhistic Millenarian Revolts in Northeastern Siam, *Journal of Southeast Asian Studies* 6/2: 121–6.

Young, Earl J. (1966a), Phu Bon Province. In: George Tanham (ed.), *War without Guns: American Civilians in Rural Vietnam*. New York: Praeger, pp. 59–92.

Young, Earl J. (1966b), Provincial Representative in Phu Bon. *Army*, July 1966: 35–51.

Zasloff, Joseph (1961), *Rural Resettlement in Vietnam: An Agroville in Development*. Saigon: Michigan State University Vietnam Advisory Group.

Zasloff, Joseph (1963), Rural Resettlement in South Vietnam: The Agroville Program. *Pacific Affairs* XXXV(4).

Index

Said, Edward 9, 19, 22
Saigon 61, 93, 104, 145, 185, 203–4, 240,
    246–7, 290, 303 n.4
salt 35, 36, 89, 137, 168
    Salt policy 137
Sam Bram 100, 107–28, 214, 307 n.24,
    308 n.39
Sambor (Buddhist monastery) 40, 260
Sar Luk 162
Saravane 104
Sarraut, Albert (Governor-general) 67, 90
Sarraut, Omer 138
Sau 214–15
Sawin, Drew 200–1
Saya San 123
Schafer, Michael 195
Schlözer, August Ludwig 11
Schmidt, Wilhelm 8, 301 n.8
school *see* education
Schrock, Joanne 229, 233
Schulte Nordholt, Henk 97, 232
Scigliano, Robert 192
Scott, James 23, 121, 124
Sedang (ethnic group) 31, 32, 45, 49, 50, 51,
    52, 104, 114, 118, 135, 140, 157, 159,
    168, 180–1, 185, 191, 217, 323 n.4
Sedentarization 247, 258, 262, 266–76,
    285–7, 294 (*see also* Fixed cultivation
    and settlement; and Resettlement)
Sée, Colonel 93
Seitz, Mgr. Paul 58
Selective Cultural Preservation policy 38,
    258, 266, 276–7, 285–7, 294
Septans, Lieutenant 59, 60
Service Géographique de l'Indochine 140
Servière, Colonel 63
Sesane River 272
sexuality 33, 181, 212, 279
Shackleton, Ronald 198
Shaman/shamanism 34–5, 217, 261, 303
    n.17
Shaplen, Robert 217
Sheehan, Neil 254
Shifting cultivation 25, 32–3, 60, 62, 88–9,
    95, 105, 141, 159, 165, 172–3, 209,
    227, 243–4, 250, 267–8, 272–4,
    297–8, 323 n.12
Siam (Thailand) 35, 50, 51, 54, 62, 65, 82,
    102–4, 129, 137, 201, 238, 256, 259,
    262
Sikhs 90
Simonnet, Christian 56, 58
Simpson, Charles 186, 212
Simulmatics Corporation 221, 228, 237

Singapore 52
Sithon 105
Siu Aluân 257–8, 264, 282–6 (*see also P'tau*)
Siu Anhot 243, 257, 264, 282–6 (*see also
    P'tau*)
Siu Choi 243, 320 n.44 (*see also P'tau*)
slash and burn *see* Shifting cultivation
slave/slavery 12, 28, 35, 55, 59, 61, 62, 67,
    81, 95, 105, 118, 151, 173, 256, 264,
    302 n.2, 303 n.16
Smith, Rev. Gordon Hedderly 213–14, 217
Smith, Harvey 229
Smith, Laura Irene 213–14
Smith, Lt.-Col. Wayne 253
Smithsonian Institution 220
Sochurek, Howard 210
Social Darwinism/Social-Darwinist 41, 60,
    70–1, 73, 289
Socialist Republic of Viet Nam (SRV) 171,
    219, 290–1
Société d'Anthropologie (Paris) 69, 79
Société des Etudes Indochinoises 135, 156
*Société des Missions Etrangères see Missions
    Etrangères de Paris*
Société ethnologique (Paris) 12
Sogny 110
Son Phòng 36, 76–8, 82
Sông Ba (river) 27
Sông Bé (river) 59
sorcerer/sorcery 47, 48, 55, 57, 103, 106,
    108, 111–12, 114–18, 121, 214, 217,
    261. 307 n.8
Soulié, Marcel 53
South Vietnam *see* Republic of Viet Nam
Southeast Asian Development Advisory
    Group (SEADAG) 223
sovereignty 61, 143, 154–6, 183, 205, 209,
    225, 235, 257, 259, 270, 290, 294–5
Soviet-Union 143, 152, 195–6, 265, 290
Spanish 41
Special Forces (US Army Special Forces) 4,
    38, 180, 183, 185–6, 193–213,
    215–19, 224–6, 228, 230, 234,
    236–40, 242, 247–8, 250, 255, 274,
    280, 290–1, 312 n.26, 319–20 n.53
Special Group Counterinsurgency 195
Special Operations Research Office
    (SORO) 221–2, 228–9, 234, 238
Special status (of Central Highlands) *see*
    Statut particulier
Special Warfare Center/Special Warfare
    School (Fort Bragg, N.C.) 195, 198,
    206, 224–5, 229–30, 232, 242, 280,
    317–18 n.17